The Early Hellenistic Peloponnese

Using all available evidence – literary, epigraphic, numismatic, and archaeological – this study offers a new analysis of the early Hellenistic Peloponnese. The conventional picture of the Macedonian kings as oppressors, and of the Peloponnese as ruined by warfare and tyranny, must be revised. The kings did not suppress freedom or exploit the peninsula economically, but generally presented themselves as patrons of Greek identity. Most of the regimes characterized as 'tyrannies' were probably, in reality, civic governorships, and the Macedonians did not seek to overturn tradition or build a new imperial order. Contrary to previous analyses, the evidence of field survey and architectural remains points to an active, even thriving civic culture and a healthy trading economy under elite patronage. Despite the rise of federalism, particularly in the form of the Achaean league, regional identity was never as strong as loyalty to one's city-state (*polis*).

D. GRAHAM J. SHIPLEY is Professor of Ancient History at the University of Leicester and a leading Greek historian who has published extensively on Classical and Hellenistic Greece. His publications include *A History of Samos* (1987), major contributions to the British School at Athens *Laconia Survey* volumes (1996–2002), and the lead editorship of the *Cambridge Dictionary of Classical Civilization* (Cambridge 2006). His *Pseudo-Skylax's Periplous* (2011) offered the first fully revised text since the nineteenth century of an important work of Greek geography, and the first commentary and translation in English. He is best known, however, for his monograph *The Greek World after Alexander* (2000), which has become the standard one-volume survey of the Hellenistic period in English and was shortlisted for the Runciman Prize. He is a Fellow of a number of learned societies, including the Royal Historical Society and the Society of Antiquaries of London, as well as a Senior Fellow of the Higher Education Academy.

The Early Hellenistic Peloponnese

Politics, Economies, and Networks 338–197 BC

D. GRAHAM J. SHIPLEY

University of Leicester

CAMBRIDGE
UNIVERSITY PRESS

CAMBRIDGE
UNIVERSITY PRESS

University Printing House, Cambridge CB2 8BS, United Kingdom

One Liberty Plaza, 20th Floor, New York, NY 10006, USA

477 Williamstown Road, Port Melbourne, VIC 3207, Australia

314–321, 3rd Floor, Plot 3, Splendor Forum, Jasola District Centre, New Delhi – 110025, India

79 Anson Road, #06-04/06, Singapore 079906

Cambridge University Press is part of the University of Cambridge.

It furthers the University's mission by disseminating knowledge in the pursuit of education, learning, and research at the highest international levels of excellence.

www.cambridge.org
Information on this title: www.cambridge.org/9780521873697
DOI: 10.1017/9781139034012

© D. Graham J. Shipley 2018

First published 2018

Printed in the United Kingdom by Clays, St Ives plc

A catalogue record for this publication is available from the British Library.

Library of Congress Cataloging-in-Publication Data
Names: Shipley, D. Graham J., author.
Title: The early Hellenistic Peloponnese : politics, economies, and networks 338–197 BC / D. Graham J. Shipley, University of Leicester.
Description: Cambridge; New York, NY: Cambridge University Press, [2018] | Includes index.
Identifiers: LCCN 2018003784 | ISBN 9780521873697 (hardback)
Subjects: LCSH: Peloponnesus (Greece : Peninsula) – History – To 1500. | Greece – History – Macedonian Expansion, 359–323 B.C.
Classification: LCC DF235.3.S55 2018 | DDC 938/.608–dc23
LC record available at https://lccn.loc.gov/2018003784

ISBN 978-0-521-87369-7 Hardback

for
my wife, Anne
and my children, Joseph and Dorothea

Contents

Figure, Tables and Maps

Figure

Tables

Maps

Maps

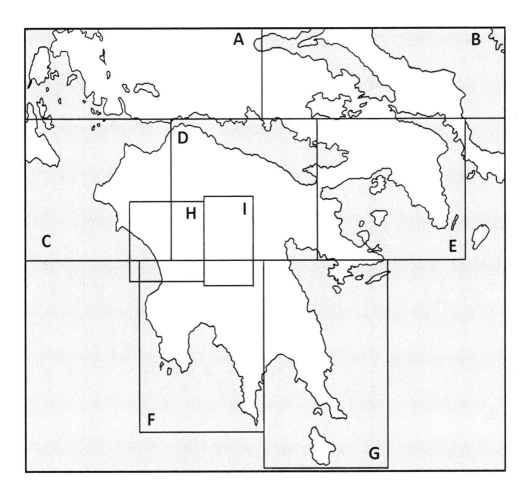

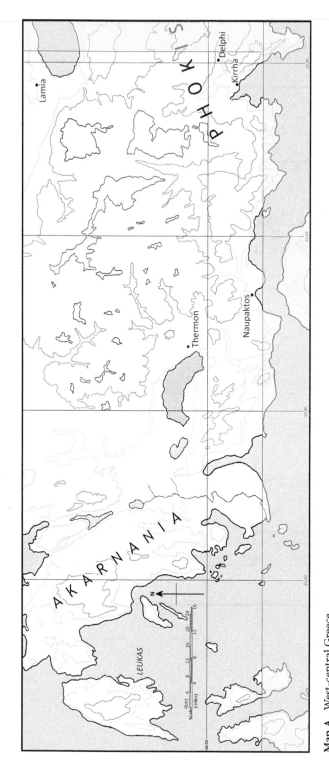

Map A. West-central Greece

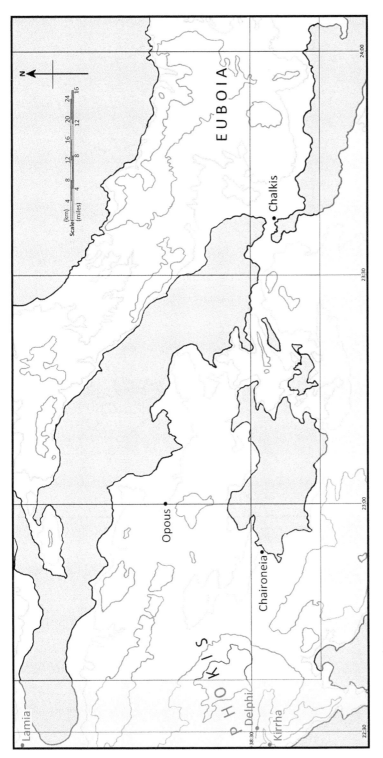

Map B. East-central Greece

xiii

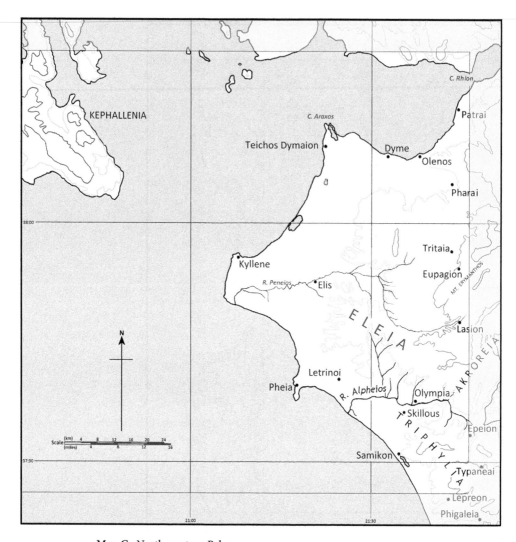

Map C. North-western Peloponnese

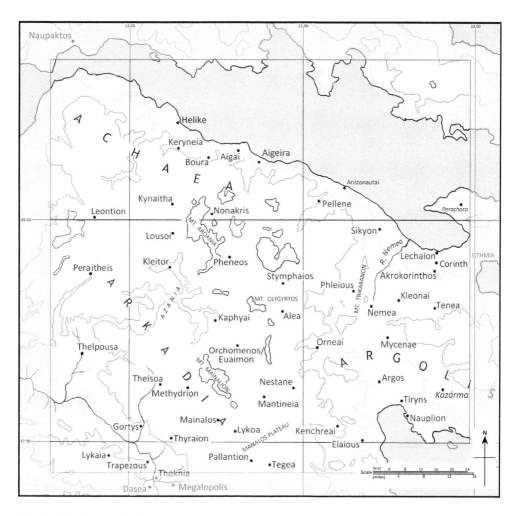

Map D. North-central Peloponnese

Map E. North-eastern Peloponnese to Boiotia and Attica

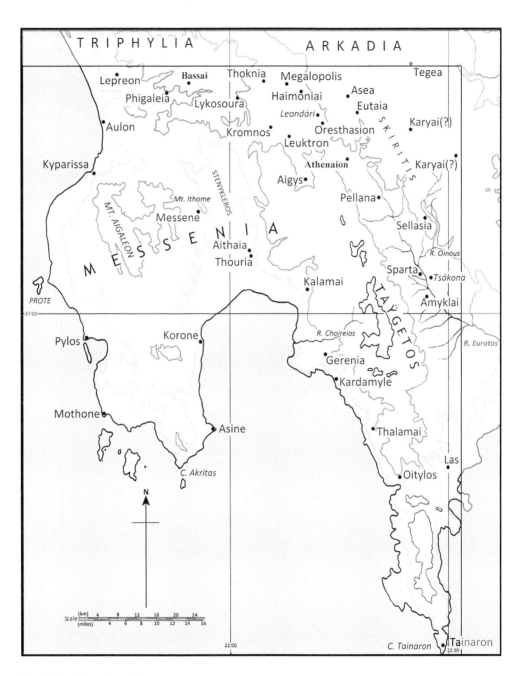

Map F. South-western Peloponnese

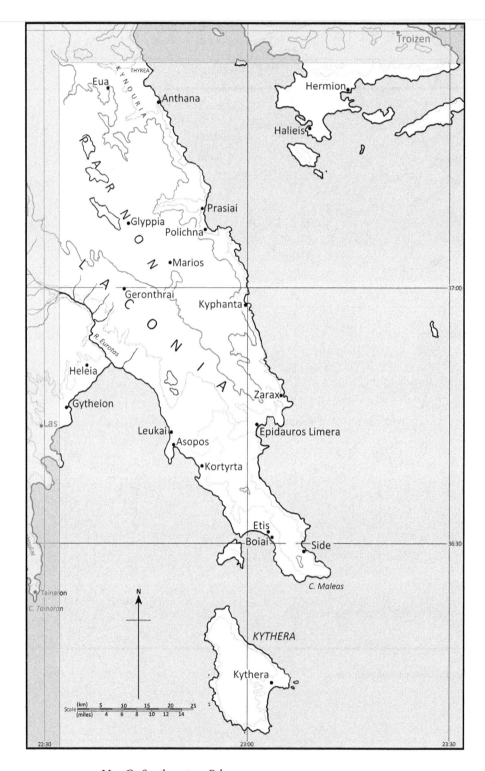

Map G. South-eastern Peloponnese

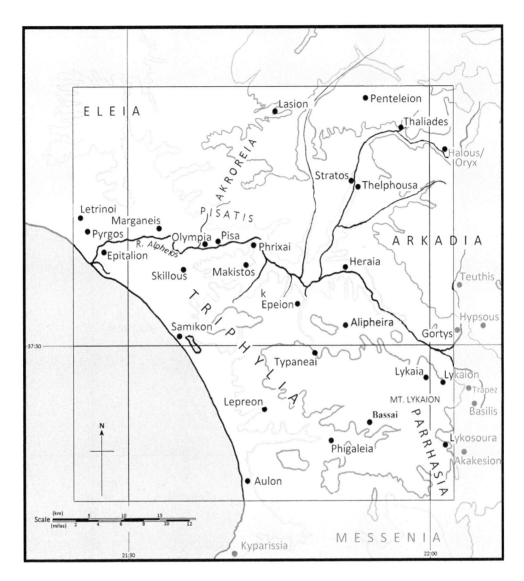

Map H. Detail of west-central Peloponnese

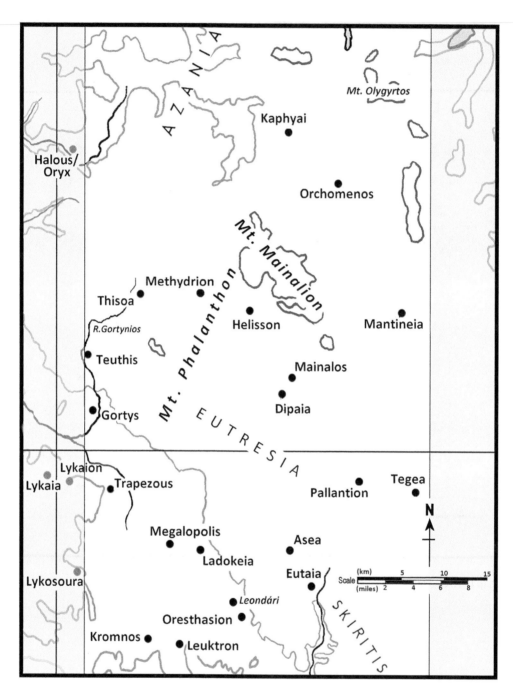

Map I. Detail of central Arkadia

Preface and Acknowledgements

Writing this book has been engrossing yet also (as Charlie says of looking after Lola) a Hard Job. The early hellenistic Peloponnese, despite its relative neglect as an entity in scholarship, is the subject of a vast and varied body of primary data; hence the predominance of studies of particular sites, states, events, and regions. An attempt to integrate them into a convincing account of, and explanation for, historical development requires the researcher to clarify a number of explanatory frameworks even before beginning an analysis, and readers may have reasons to question those; while the interpretation of particular or general sets of evidence will itself prompt questions or doubts in readers more expert than I in the particular domain of evidence.

The project began as a study of Macedonian power and its impact, but now has broader aims (see I.1.a below). It has its distant origins in 1982, in an invitation from the late Dr Hector Catling, CBE, to take part in the Laconia Survey (1983–9). That experience led me in 1985 to the notion of a 'survey of surveys' bringing together the new hellenistic landscape data for Greece. Other responsibilities supervened, notably co-writing and co-editing the Laconia Survey (Cavanagh *et al.* 2002; 1996); but active progress resumed in 1999 with the aid of a grant from the Arts & Humanities Research Board (now the Arts & Humanities Research Council) under its Research Leave Scheme, augmented by the award of a Visiting Fellowship at the British School at Athens and generous funding from the Copenhagen Polis Centre. Among the outcomes were a study of Spartan territory in the hellenistic period (Shipley 2000a), an overview of the Laconia Survey results (Shipley 2002c), a brief synthesis of hellenistic survey data for the Peloponnese (Shipley 2002a), and a study of the Laconian and Messenian *poleis* (Shipley 2004a). It is a pleasure to acknowledge the generosity of the British Academy and the Leverhulme Trust in awarding me a Senior Research Fellowship for 2004–5, when the main phase of data-gathering took place; of the University of Leicester in granting me additional leave to enable me to use the above awards, as well as a semester's research leave in 2013; and of successive heads of the School of Archaeology and Ancient History in allowing me some relief from administrative duties thereafter.

Accordingly, I must also thank those colleagues in the School of Archaeology and Ancient History who shouldered extra burdens as a result.

I am grateful above all to those who commented, at various levels of detail, on drafts of the present book and related writings; especially CUP's anonymous readers of the original book proposal and subsequent drafts; David Mattingly for frequent wise advice and sustained encouragement; Colin Haselgrove for perceptive comments on structure; and above all John Salmon, who read an entire draft closely and saved me from many errors and infelicities, and John Davies, who made important suggestions about Chapter 4. Additional comments on plans, outlines, and drafts were gratefully received from Colin Adams, Jane Ainsworth, Patricia Baker, Duncan Campbell, Neil Christie, Michael Dixon, Richard J. G. Evans, Louise Füchs, Myles Harman, Pauline Hire, Mark McLeod, Anne Sackett, Sarah Scott, Dan Stewart, John Tully, and Charlotte Van Regenmortel. I have benefited from technical advice given by Ralph Hancock, Christopher Pelling, Michael Tully, and especially John Waś.

Mogens Hansen and Thomas Nielsen generously allowed me advance access to data collected for what became the *Inventory of Archaic and Classical Poleis* (Hansen and Nielsen 2004b). The editors of *Leidschrift* (Leiden) gave permission to reuse material from Shipley 2006b. All translations are mine.

Thanks are due to a number of editors and conference organizers. Early thoughts were presented in my inaugural lecture at Leicester in 2003, revised for publication as Shipley 2005b and given a wider landscape focus in Shipley 2006b. They were taken further at the 2005 Tours conference organized by Catherine Grandjean and Camille Prieux (Shipley 2008a), at the Classical Association conference in Newcastle upon Tyne in 2006, and at a Royal Irish Academy Colloquium on ancient imperialism in Dublin in the same year. Ideas about the Spartan kings were presented at the 2005 APA–AIA meeting in Boston (Shipley 2005a; see now Shipley 2017a); I am grateful to my department for financial support on that and other occasions, and to my panel co-organizer, Ellen Millender; our co-panellists, Paul Cartledge, Joost Crouwel, Liz Langridge-Noti, Olga Palagia, and Mieke Prent; and our respondent, Thomas Figueira, for their perceptive comments. I returned to the topic of hellenistic Laconia in a paper for a meeting organized by the Alexander S. Onassis Public Benefit Foundation (USA) at New York in 2007 (Shipley 2009); I thank Professor Nikolaos Kaltsas and HE Loucas Tsilas for the invitation to participate.

Important advice, guidance, or information was received from the participants in the 2005 Tours conference (Grandjean 2008b), the 2011 Hellenistic Networks conference at Cologne and Bonn (Fenn and

Römer-Strehl 2013), and the 2012 Scientific Meeting on Hellenistic Pottery at Thessaloniki (*9th Hellenistic Pottery Meeting* 2018); and from many other colleagues. Besides many of those already mentioned, they include Elizabeth Bollen, Graeme Bourke, Kostas Buraselis, Charles Crowther, †Peter Derow, John Ellis Jones (especially with reference to the Peneios Valley Survey), Lin Foxhall, John Goodwin, Erich Gruen, Meg Harris Williams, Noreen Humble, Lars Karlsson, Sandra Karlsson, John Lund, Jane Masséglia, Robert Morstein-Marx, Maria Pretzler, Gillian Ramsey, Peter Rhodes, Susan Rotroff, Christopher Smith, Maria Stamatopoulou, and Marijke van der Veen. Discussions with present and former postgraduates at Leicester, including (besides those already named) Crysta Kaczmarek, Manolis Pagkalos, Andrea Scarpato, Dorothea Stavrou, Alexander Thomas, and Mark van der Enden, have helped me understand hellenistic history better. I apologize sincerely for any omissions, which will be made good in future reprints once I am aware of them.

At a late stage I was alerted to the important studies of Bresson 2016, Cartledge 2016, and Kralli 2017; the last arrived as the text was being finalized. It has not been possible to engage with them beyond adding a number of citations and brief remarks. In Kralli's book the reader will find a nuanced study of political relations between the Peloponnesian states from 371 to 146 BC, including detailed treatments of certain episodes treated briefly in Chapter II below. It is my confident hope that the appearance of her work and the present study at almost the same time will encourage further analysis of the Peloponnese in this period.

Numerous colleagues generously gave copies of published work relevant to this project, or allowed me to read unpublished work; their contribution cannot be overstated, even if not all the works are cited in the text. In addition to many already named, they include Susan Alcock, John Bintliff, David Blackman, Olympia Bobou, Sebastiaan Bommeljé, Duncan Campbell, Christy Constantakopoulou, Stella Drougou, Daniela Dueck, Andrew Erskine, Evangelia Eleftheriou (with Nektarios Skagkos), Pernille Flensted-Jensen, Björn Forsén, Jeanette Forsén, Klaus Freitag, Peter Funke, Masato Furuyama, Vincent Gabrielsen, Hans-Joachim Gehrke, Olivier Gengler, Henrik Gerding, Stephen Hodkinson, Kerstin Höghammar, Alan Johnston, Madeleine Jost, Nigel Kennell, Zoï Kotitsa, Eleni Kourinou-Pikoula, Ioanna Kralli, Christos Kremmydas, Ergün Laflı, Robin Lane Fox, Franziska Lang, Nino Luraghi, John Ma, Will Mack, Marie-Christine Marcellesi, Angelos Matthaiou, Ben Millis, Henrique Modanez de Sant'Anna, Silke Müth, Graham Oliver, Kostas Papagiannopoulos, Yanis Pikoulas, Jeroen Poblome, Anton Powell,

Jonathan Prag, Mieke Prent, Selene Psoma, Gary Reger, Ellen Rice, John Rich, Nicolas Richer, Joseph Rife, Athanasios Rizakis, Jim Roy, Andrea Scarpato, Lucijana Šešelj, Peter Stone, Kathryn Tempest, Nassos Themos, Peter Thonemann, Ioannis Touratsoglou, Conor Trainor, Hans van Wees, Kostas Vlassopoulos, Joanita Vroom, Malcolm Wagstaff, †Jennifer Warren (Cargill-Thompson), David Whitehead, Hans-Ulrich Wiemer, Josef Wiesehöfer, Elena Zavvou; many other contributors to Fenn and Römer-Strehl 2013; and the editors of *Journal of Roman Archaeology*.

Besides several people already named, Andrew Burnett, Basil C. Demetriadi, Amedeo Giampaglia, Emily Mackil, Katerina Panagopoulou, Phaidon Theodorou, and Alan Walker generously helped me locate numismatic publications.

None of those named is responsible for any view expressed in the book (not least because I have not always taken their advice).

Particular thanks are due to the administrative staff of the School of Archaeology and Ancient History, University of Leicester, and the staff of the Research Support Office, University of Leicester, particularly Juliet Bailey; and to the library staffs of the University of Leicester (especially Evelyn Cornell and her successor Jackie Hanes), the British School at Athens (especially Penny Wilson-Zarganis and Sandra Pepelasi), and the Institute of Classical Studies (especially Sue Willetts and, in 2004–5, Charlotte Swire). A great classical resource not often acknowledged is Andromeda Books (Athens); I am happy to do so here. I also thank Holly Morton of the School of Law, University of Leicester, for facilitating my use of the Harry Peach Library, a haven for quiet reflection.

A profound debt is owed to Michael Sharp of the Press, for his endless patience and wise advice.

The inspiration of AKUS, HCC, JRRT, and AP is acknowledged, as well as the support of individuals unnamed.

Special thanks are due to Duncan Campbell for the maps; Jane Robson for her expert copy-editing; Carla Brain for assistance with the indexes; and Amanda Kay for her eagle-eyed proofreading.

My greatest debt is to my family and above all to Anne, whose love and support have sustained me throughout the long evolution of this book.

Note on Dates

Centuries are abbreviated according to Copenhagen Polis Project conventions: e.g. C5 = fifth century BC; C4f/s = first/second half of fourth century BC; C3e/m/l = early/mid-/late third century BC; C2a/b/c/d = quarters of second century BC.

Dates are BC unless AD is specified. I intend no Western presumption if I persist in using BC and AD, even though they are derived from a Christian era (and an inaccurate one at that). The usual alternatives in anglophone scholarship, BCE and CE, are easily confused with one another and are by no means as 'common' as they pretend to be, being based on the same Western, Christian era which is not the default in other major cultures (cf. Holford-Strevens 2005, [xiii]).

Note on Spellings

Spellings in quotations are unchanged. Otherwise, for ancient Greek names I retain some familiar anglicizations (e.g. Antipater not Antipatros, Athens, Cassander not Kassandros, Corinth, Delphi, Peloponnese, Piraeus, Thucydides). I use Alexander for kings, Alexandros for other men; Achaea for the region, Achaean league for the *koinon*, Achaia only for the Roman province. Other names are made Greeklike if easily recognized (e.g. Aigion, Aitolia, Aratos, Argolis, Boiotia, Kleomenes, Lakedaimonians, Polybios, Sikyon). Note that 'Areus' (Ἀρεύς) is correct and Greeklike (with two syllables, not three); 'Areos' is a false form (despite e.g. Hoover 2011, 138–43 *passim*).

Greek terms are transliterated if familiar in anglophone scholarship (e.g. *polis, epiteichismos*); some long vowels are marked (e.g. *dēmos, chōra*). Terms less likely to be encountered in transliteration elsewhere are left in Greek (e.g. κατέφθαρτο) but translated.

The Modern Greek distinction between polytonic and monotonic is maintained, e.g. in the list of Works Cited. Placenames follow the Laconia Survey spelling rules (Cavanagh *et al.* 2002, xxiv) but are italicized with the stress marked (e.g. *Áno Mazaráki, Geráki*).

In the list of Works Cited, authors' names and initials are generally standardized on one form; this is important to note where a deuteronymous (D. G. J. Shipley), tritonymous (J. N. D. Hibler, or even tetartonymous (J. P. V. D. Balsdon) author may have been cited elsewhere with varying initials. Greek authors' names follow the same transliteration system as Modern Greek place-names, unless they have published regularly under another form (so Buraselis not Bourazelis; Steinhauer not Staïnchaouer).

Like N. G. L. Hammond, I write 'Macedonia' rather than 'Macedon'. Consistently with the treatment of other seas (e.g. 'Aegean sea'), I follow Royal Navy 1969 in writing 'Black sea' unless the context requires capitalization.

Special Abbreviations

Abbreviations normally follow the *Oxford Classical Dictionary*. Others:

1st Arkadian Congress	Πρακτικὰ τοῦ Α΄ συνεδρίου ἀρκαδικῶν σπουδῶν (Τρίπολις 14–15 Δεκεμβρίου 1974) (Πελοποννησιακά, 12 (1976–7), παράρτημα = Πελοποννησιακά, παραρτήματα, 3). Athens: Etaireia Peloponnisiakon Spoudon, 1976–7
1st Argolic Congress	Πρακτικὰ τοῦ Α΄ συνεδρίου ἀργολικῶν σπουδῶν (Ναύπλιον 4–6 Δεκεμβρίου 1976) (Πελοποννησιακά, 13 (1978–9), παράρτημα = Πελοποννησιακά, παραρτήματα, 4). Athens: Etaireia Peloponnisiakon Spoudon, 1978
1st Hellenistic Pottery Meeting	Α΄ συνάντηση για την ελληνιστική κεραμεική [*sic*] ([Ιωάννινα], Δεκέμβρης 1986). 1st edn, Ioannina: Panepistimio Ioanninon, Tomeas Archaiologias, 1989; 2nd edition, titled *Α΄ συνάντηση για την ελληνιστική κεραμική* [*sic*]*(Ιωάννινα, 6 Δεκεμβρίου* [*sic*] *1986)*, Rhodes: Archaiologiko Institouto Dodekanisou, 2000
1st Laconian Treatises Congress	Πρακτικὰ τοῦ Α΄ τοπικοῦ συνεδρίου λακωνικῶν μελετῶν (Μολάοι 5–7 Ἰουνίου 1982) (Πελοποννησιακά, παραρτήματα, 9). Athens: Etaireia Peloponnisiakon Spoudon, 1982–3 [distinct from *1st Laconian Studies Congress = Πρακτικὰ τοῦ Α΄ συνεδρίου λακωνικῶν σπουδῶν. Σπάρτη–Γύθειον 7– 11 Ὀκτωβρίου 1977.* (Λακωνικαὶ σπουδαί, 4–5). Athens: Etaireia Peloponnisiakon Spoudon, 1979]
2nd Hellenistic Pottery Meeting	Β΄ επιστημονική συνάντηση για την ελληνιστική κεραμεική: χρονολογικά προβλήματα της ελληνιστικής κεραμεικής (Ρόδος 22–25 Μαρτίου 1989). Πρακτικά. Athens: ΚΒ΄ Ephoreia Proïstorikon kai Klassikon Archaiotiton, Rodos/

	Tameio Archaiologikon Poron kai Apallotrioseon/ Nomarchia Dodekanisou, Dimos Rodou, 1990
3rd Hellenistic Pottery Meeting	*Γ΄ επιστημονική συνάντηση για την ελληνιστική κεραμική: χρονολογημένα σύνολα – εργαστήρια (24–27 Σεπτεμβρίου 1991 Θεσσαλονίκη). Πρακτικά.* (Βιβλιοθήκη τῆς ἐν Ἀθήναις Ἀρχαιολογικῆς Ἑταιρείας, 137.) 2 vols. Athens: Archaiologiki Etaireia, 1994
4th Hellenistic Pottery Meeting	*Δ΄ επιστημονική συνάντηση για την ελληνιστική κεραμική: χρονολογικά προβλήματα – κλειστά σύνολα – εργαστήρια (Μυτιλήνη, Μάρτιος 1994). Πρακτικά.* 2 vols. Athens: Ypourgeio Politismou, Κ΄ Ephoreia Proïstorikon kai Klasikon Archaiotiton, 1997
4th Peloponnesian Congress	*Πρακτικὰ τοῦ Δ΄ διεθνοῦς συνεδρίου πελοποννησιακῶν σπουδῶν (Κόρινθος, 9–16 Σεπτεμβρίου 1990)* (Πελοποννησιακά, παραρτήματα, 19). Athens: Etaireia Peloponnisiakon Spoudon, 1992
5th Hellenistic Pottery Meeting	*Ε΄ επιστημονική συνάντηση για την ελληνιστική κεραμική: χρονολογικά προβλήματα – κλειστά σύνολα – εργαστήρια [Χανιά, 1997]. Πρακτικά.* 2 vols. Athens: Ypourgeio Politismou, ΚΕ΄ Ephoreia Proïstorikon kai Klasikon Archaiotiton/Tameio Archaiologikon Poron kai Apallotrioseon, 2000
5th Peloponnesian Congress	*Πρακτικὰ τοῦ Ε΄ διεθνοῦς συνεδρίου πελοποννησιακῶν σπουδῶν (Ἄργος–Ναύπλιον, 6–10 Σεπτεμβρίου 1995)* (Πελοποννησιακά, παραρτήματα, 22). Athens: Etaireia Peloponnisiakon Spoudon, 1996–7
6th Hellenistic Pottery Meeting	*ΣΤ΄ επιστημονική συνάντηση για την ελληνιστική κεραμική: προβλήματα χρονολόγησης – κλειστά σύνολα – εργαστήρια (Βόλος, 17–23 Απριλίου 2000). Πρακτικά.* Athens: Ypourgeio Politismou, IΓ΄ Ephoreia Proïstorikon kai Klasikon Archaiotiton/Tameio Archaiologikon Poron kai Apallotrioseon, 2004
6th Peloponnesian Congress	*Πρακτικὰ ΣΤ΄ διεθνοῦς συνεδρίου πελοποννησιακῶν σπουδῶν (Τρίπολις 24–29 Σεπτεμβρίου 2000)* (Πελοποννησιακά, παραρτήματα, 24). Athens: Etaireia Peloponnisiakon Spoudon, 2001–2

7th Hellenistic Pottery Meeting	*Ζ΄ επιστημονική συνάντηση για την ελληνιστική κεραμική: χρονολογικά προβλήματα – κλειστά σύνολα – εργαστήρια (Αίγιο, 4–9 Απριλίου 2005). Πρακτικά.* Athens: Ypourgeio Politismou kai Tourismou/ Tameio Archaiologikon Poron kai Apallotrioseon/ST΄ Ephoreia Proïstorikon kai Klasikon Archaiotiton, 2011
7th Peloponnesian Congress	*Πρακτικὰ τοῦ Ζ΄ διεθνοῦς συνεδρίου πελοποννησιακῶν σπουδῶν (Πύργος– Γαστούνη–Ἀμαλιάδα 11–17 Σεπτεμβρίου 2005).* (Πελοποννησιακά, παραρτήματα, 27.) Athens: Etaireia Peloponnisiakon Spoudon, 2006–7
8th Hellenistic Pottery Meeting	*Η΄ επιστημονική συνάντηση για την ελληνιστική κεραμική (Ιωάννινα, 5–9 Μαΐου 2009). Πρακτικά.* Athens: Ypourgeio Politismou, IB' Ephoreia Proïstorikon kai Klasikon Archaiotiton/Archaiologiko Institouto Ipeirotikon Spoudon/Tameio Archaiologikon Poron kai Apallotrioseon, 2014
9th Hellenistic Pottery Meeting	*Θ΄ επιστημονική συνάντηση για την ελληνιστική κεραμική (Θεσσαλονίκη, 5–9 Δεκεμβρίου 2012). Πρακτικά.* Athens: Ypourgeio Politismou kai Athlitismou/ Aristoteleio Panepistimio Thessalonikis/ Tameio Archaiologikon Poron kai Apallotrioseon, 2018
12th Classical Archaeology Congress	*Πρακτικὰ τοῦ XII διεθνοῦς συνεδρίου κλασικῆς ἀρχαιολογίας (Ἀθήνα, 4–10 Σεπτεμβρίου 1983).* Athens: Ypourgeio Politismou, Tameio Archaiologikon Poron kai Apallotrioseon, 1988
AE	bronze
Ag.–Kl. (but *AK* in Chapter II)	(Plutarch), *Agis and Kleomenes*, here numbered continuously; for the second part, on Kleomenes, which some editions number separately, the alternative chapter no. may be found by subtracting 21
AGOnline	*Archaeology in Greece Online* (www. chronique.efa.fr)
AK	see *Ag.–Kl.*

Ar	archaic (period)
AR	silver
Austin²	M. M. Austin, *The Hellenistic World from Alexander to the Roman Conquest: A Selection of Ancient Sources in Translation* (Cambridge University Press), 2nd edn 2006
C4, C3, C2, etc.	fourth, third, second (etc.) century BC (see 'Note on Dates')
Chr.	Χρονικά section of *Αρχαιολογικόν δελτίον* (when not part of German abbreviation v.Chr.
Cl	classical (period)
EHl	early hellenistic
EImp	early Imperial
f.	father of; formerly
G	Geometric (period)
Hl	hellenistic
ID#	entry in *Archaeology in Greece Online* (www.chronique.efa.fr)
Imp	Imperial (period)
Inv. #	(with no. in italic) entry in M. H. Hansen and T. H. Nielsen, *An Inventory of Archaic and Classical Poleis.* Oxford University Press, 2004
IPArk #	G. Thür and H. Taeuber, *Prozeßrechtliche Inschriften der griechischen Poleis: Arkadien.* Vienna: Kommission für antike Rechtsgeschichte, 1994
ISE #	L. Moretti, *Iscrizioni storiche ellenistiche,* i: *Attica, Peloponneso, Beozia.* Florence: Nuova Italia, 1967
KP	W. Ziegler and W. Sontheimer (eds), *Der kleine Pauly: Lexikon der Antike.* 5 vols, Munich: Druckenmüller/Artemis, 1964–75; repr. Munich: Deutsche Taschenbuch Verlag, 1979
L. (in Chapter II)	Livy
LCl	late classical
LHl	late hellenistic
lit.	literally
LN	D. Leekley and R. Noyes, *Archaeological Excavations in Southern Greece.* Park Ridge, NJ: Noyes Press, 1976
LR	late Roman
Mel.	Μελέτες section of *Αρχαιολογικόν δελτίον*
OS	Ordnance Survey
P. (in Chapter II)	Polybios (otherwise Polyb.)
R	Roman (period)

I | The Acropolis of Greece

This is a wild area which is so mysterious, and of course the very birthplace of all the gods and myths and legends, and everything seemed to happen down here.

Lumley 2011, episode 1

I.1 The Task

I.1.a The Topic

The present study examines an under-researched topic, Peloponnesian history in the round, and a neglected period of that history. It aims to clarify how the peninsula developed during the 'long third century' of Macedonian domination, from the battle of Chaironeia in 338 BC to the end of Macedonian involvement in the peninsula in 197. After a methodological introduction (I.1) and a geographical overview (I.2), it seeks to discover (in Chapter II) how the peninsula fared in wars and under the influence of powers attempting to exert control; next (in Chapter III), the politics of the city-state or *polis*; and finally (in Chapter IV) economic conditions. As a clearly bounded space, the Peloponnese offers great potential for analysis in the light of recent approaches to geographical history; the work therefore ends with an assessment (in Chapter V) of the relative impact of factors operating at different spatial scales – peninsula, region, *polis*, and locality – as well as the interaction between societies within the Peloponnese and the world outside.

I.1.b Previous Work

The present study begins from a neutral position on the question whether – as is implied or asserted in many studies, both older and more recent – the Peloponnese in the late classical and hellenistic periods, and more broadly Old Greece, was a backwater of little interest. Given the military manpower brought to bear upon the peninsula, and the responses it evoked, one might expect its history to have attracted close attention. Yet, while individual sequences of events have been examined repeatedly, notably the histories of Sparta and of the Achaean 'league' (*koinon*), it remains the case that since the inspired synthesis of geography and history by Ernst Curtius in the mid-nineteenth century[1] there has been a lack of scholarly focus on the peninsula in a holistic sense.[2] 'Peloponnese' and 'Peloponnesian', for example, are not listed in the indexes to three recent volumes on hellenistic economies,[3] and of the major sites only Corinth, Epidauros, and Olympia appear in one of the three.[4] An influential overview of the period discusses individual states but does not index 'Peloponnese'.[5] Historians seem loath to treat this period of Peloponnesian history head-on rather than from the perspective of individual states or regions; still less from the standpoint of those who were dominated as opposed to that of commanders and kings.

Yet there are many studies of the Peloponnese and its communities in the archaic and classical periods; and Roman Greece has been a lively area of research for several decades. For the intervening hellenistic age, the peninsula and its settlements rarely feature in studies of social and economic change.[6] Historians examine the evolution of democracy, diplomacy, and federalism in Old Greece as a whole; and rarely take a synoptic view of socio-economic change or of the operation and effects of Macedonian power, despite the growing number of comparable analyses of the Seleukid and Ptolemaic empires. This relative indifference may partly reflect the huge expansion of the Greek world, in which scores of cities were founded and the Greeks lived alongside large numbers of people from a multiplicity of ethnic groups to an unprecedented extent. In view of the huge quantities and geographical spread of archaeological, epigraphic, and numismatic evidence from the eastern Mediterranean and western Asia, it is perhaps

---

[1] Curtius 1851–2. His account owes much to the data provided by Leake and by the Expédition Française de Morée, but goes far beyond them in analysis.

[2] This is not the case for prehistory, or for the Imp and LR periods (see e.g. Baladié 1980; Avraméa 1997). Sheedy 1994 brings together important studies (partly Hl) but does not aspire to a synoptic view.

[3] Archibald *et al.* 2001; Archibald *et al.* 2005; Archibald *et al.* 2011.

[4] Archibald *et al.* 2005, 364–8 ('Korinth').

[5] Shipley 2000b; surprisingly, since S. had written on Laconian landscapes.

[6] To the best of my knowledge, no study of the Hl period has centred upon the Peloponnese as a unitary landscape. A step forwards is represented by papers in Grandjean 2008a, though they form a minority of the volume. See also Grandjean n.d. [2008]. Kralli 2017, published as the present work went to press, is an excellent study focused on Peloponnesian inter-state relations in this period, offering new insight into many episodes and patterns in the narrative covered in Chapter II below, as well as diplomatic networks.

understandable that historians of this period have rarely turned their gaze upon the Peloponnese. One exception is Baladié's inspiring study of Strabo's portrayal of the peninsula, written in the reigns of Augustus and Tiberius,[7] which though inevitably focused on the late hellenistic period (roughly the first century BC) has important implications for the early hellenistic period because of the manner of Strabo's information-gathering.

This general neglect is, of course, due in part to the sparse and mostly later historical sources. The inadequate literary sources for the two generations after 301, and the dominant voice of Polybios at the end of the third century, tend to make the early hellenistic period seem a relatively obscure and unhappy interlude between classical grandeur and regrettable, but grudgingly admired, Roman rule. Still more influential have been the claims by Polybios and some later authors that the Peloponnese, and Greece as a whole, were in decline as a result of the actions of Philip II and Alexander III, and of oppression on the part of their successors.[8] But a region that may have been the victim of imperial domination surely deserves our attention no less than any other. The Macedonian takeover was the most important military–political event in Greek history up to that date, and may have marked a watershed for the Greek city-states system, even if few today would see it as bringing about 'the end of the city-state'.[9] It also gained retrospective importance, for with hindsight it could be seen as the prelude to the Roman takeover, which would last far longer than Macedonian hegemony. The 'long third century' could almost be termed an *Achsenzeit*. Furthermore, the Peloponnese had been earlier, and remained, central to the construction of Greek identity.

The view that the Peloponnese, or Old Greece more generally, was in a somnolent or depressed condition needs careful examination. In his classic 1941 study, for example, Rostovtzeff declares that there was little change in the third century and that Macedonian rule had little impact:

> Old Greece, in its hundreds of cities, remained outwardly unaltered. ... No extensive rebuilding was carried out ... Nor did the daily routine change ... Political and religious duties were regularly discharged by the body of citizens, lively discussions took place in the popular assemblies ... war interrupted from time to the peaceful flow of events ... internal conflicts arose within the cities ... The young frequented the schools and received there their mental, artistic, religious, and physical training.

[7] Baladié 1980.
[8] The idea first surfaced in the LHl period: Pretzler 2005, 144.
[9] Gomme 1937, 233–4, 247, etc., identifies 'decadence' in the Greek states from C3m.

> Business and social pursuits followed their normal course … It is unneces-
> sary to describe in detail the daily life of the Greek cities … It would show
> much the same aspect as in the fifth and fourth centuries BC.[10]

Rostovtzeff's insight that elites remained dominant agrees with recent studies. He is also right to point out that in social and political life much will have remained unaltered; historians have been too ready to assume that periods – essentially arbitrary constructs – have distinct social and cultural characteristics. Immediately after the passage quoted, however, he mentions striking innovations: a national Hellenic consciousness, the increasing frequency of diplomatic agreements and recognition of inviolability, grants of citizenship and proxeny, international arbitration, public protests against war crimes, and acts of public and private charity.[11] Contemporary philosophers began to question the cleavages in identities and entitlements between different status-groups: slave and free, barbarian and Greek, male and female.[12] Recent research confirms that relations between the sexes, and between free and slave, became more open,[13] though perhaps only within certain educated groups, just as Rostovtzeff claims. On the other hand, he minimizes such changes, dismissing them as 'partial, the outcome of special circumstances, palliatives to counteract the dominant characteristic of Greek institutions, the city particularism'.[14] It may be true that such unification of the wider Greek community as occurred took place chiefly among the elite or, in Rostovtzeff's now dated terminology, the 'bourgeoisie'.[15] 'Palliatives', however, implies a degree of deceitful manipulation by the dominant groups that would be surprising in the politically open societies characteristic of Old Greece.

Rostovtzeff seems to be working with a hard and fast divide between daily life and other aspects of society; this, too, is unhelpful. Public life and wider processes have an impact on social and personal life. Diplomatic and ceremonial networks, grants of citizenship, arbitration, and so on must have had practical and often beneficial consequences for all classes. As for rebuilding, archaeology since Rostovtzeff's day has revealed the grid-planned layouts of a number of towns, as well as extensive building or replanning of older ones. His unbalanced viewpoint presumably reflects a wish to present nascent capitalism as the motor of change, a process he situates chiefly outside Old Greece.

[10] Rostovtzeff 1941, 1109 (ellipses mine).
[11] Rostovtzeff 1941, 1109–12.
[12] Some scholars see parallels between the Hl age and our own: e.g. J. Ferguson 1973.
[13] e.g. Houby-Nielsen 1997, esp. 243–7; cf. earlier Schneider 1967–9, i. 78–117.
[14] Rostovtzeff 1941, 1114.
[15] Rostovtzeff 1941, 1115.

Strabo (8. 1. 3) describes the Peloponnese as the acropolis of Greece, as the more famous of its two mainland divisions, and as deserving the role of leadership among the Greeks for the splendour of its inhabitants and of its topography.[16] While he could be reiterating a rhetorical trope from the classical period, the assertion conveys the esteem in which the Peloponnese was held despite the, by now, deeply embedded hegemony of Rome and the recent creation of the province of Achaia under Augustus.[17]

The peninsula was rightly seen as one of the chief arenas, perhaps even the heartland, of the world of Greek states,[18] and as the setting for key legends: it was the home of Nestor, Agamemnon, Orestes, Menelaos, and Helen; the scene of Telemachos' journey; the location of some of Herakles' labours. Sparta, the *polis* with the greatest military reputation in Greece, had dominated the Peloponnese down to 371, while other venerable and populous centres included Argos and the international port of Corinth. The peninsula was home to three of the four Panhellenic religious festivals, at Olympia, Nemea, and Isthmia. It contained many of the best-known cities and sanctuaries, which carried huge ideological weight in the construction of Hellenic identity, as they did later for hellenistic benefactors, philhellene Romans, and indeed modern archaeologists. As I have written elsewhere, 'Certainly it was densely inscribed with history and (real or fictive) memory; and, as Tuan puts it, habitual routes acquire "density of meaning".'[19] Given the importance of the Peloponnese in both earlier and later periods, its hellenistic history is surely a worthy focus of our attention.

All in all, we can observe that the lack of previous focus on the hellenistic Peloponnese as an entity is partly a legacy of outdated views about the 'end' of the *polis* and about Greek social relations, and ignores the central importance of the Peloponnese to Greek culture and identity even after the classical period.

I.1.c The Sources in Brief

The shortcomings of the sources have perhaps deterred scholars from attempting to reconstruct the socio-economic make-up and political complexion of the communities of 'Old Greece', outside Athens and Sparta, in the early hellenistic period.

---

[16] There may, however, be a problem with the text, as Jones notes in the Loeb: it is possible that a phrase such as 'and Greece is the *acropolis* of the world' has fallen out. (Baladié 1980, 283–5, does not discuss this possibility, perhaps regarding it as unfounded; neither does he mention it in Baladié 1978.)

[17] Baladié 1980, 283–5.

[18] For the notion of a city-states system, see e.g. Hansen 2000a with Hansen 2002.

[19] Shipley 2006b, 34; Tuan 1977, 182.

As already noted, for the military–political narrative of a large part of
the period the literary evidence is poor in comparison with the preceding
period: either derivative or fragmentary. Down to 301 we rely chiefly on
Diodoros (books 18–20), writing in the first century BC but using fourth-
century authors; for these episodes, probably the excellent Hieronymos of
Kardia above all.[20] One might speculate whether the non-survival of the
third-century portions of Diodoros and other authors is due to conscious
deselection (on whatever basis) or to chance,[21] or reflects some real historical change at 301; but the Peloponnese was hotly contested by Alexander's
successors until the 260s, and wars continued to occur with distressing frequency in the second half of the century.

The importance and inherent interest of the period 301–229 is proved by
the partial preservation of Latin history of Trogus Pompeius, written in the
late Republic, in the form of tables of contents and Justin's later summary
of the work. Occasional mentions by Pausanias, writing in the second century AD, fill some gaps. Happily, surviving writers sometimes draw upon
third-century sources. This is true, for example, of Plutarch's *Lives* of seven
men whose actions had a heavy impact: the Macedonian king Demetrios I;
Pyrrhos; the Achaean leader Aratos of Sikyon, partly based on the subject's
own memoirs (and, unusually among Plutarch's *Lives*, not paired with a
Roman);[22] the Spartan kings Agis IV and Kleomenes III (in a single *Life*),
preserving material from the sympathetic eyewitness Phylarchos; the later
Achaean leader Philopoimen; and the Roman general Flamininus. From
229 onwards we have, first, Polybios' mid-second-century account of events;
broadly anti-Spartan, as one might expect from an Arkadian, a citizen of both
Megalopolis and the Achaean league. Strabo's portrayal of the Peloponnese,
composed under Tiberius, has been mentioned, but does not offer what we
might expect from a geographical handbook today; rather, he presents a
historical tableau based on a mixture of classical literature (notably Homer
and the Attic tragedians) and hellenistic geographers such as Artemidoros
whose interests do not extend to economic or demographic questions.[23]

---

[20] On Hieronymos, see J. Hornblower 1981; he is the best Hl source after Polyb. in the view
of Bosworth 2012b. Only books 1–5 and 11–20 of Diod. are preserved intact, the rest in
fragments (i.e. later quotations). Green 1998, criticizes Stylianou 1998 for adhering excessively
to the view that D. slavishly follows one source at time. The latter is the current orthodoxy, but
G. points out the consistency of D.'s style throughout his work (see Palm 1955).

[21] On reasons why the great C3 historians did not survive 'epitomization' in the R period, see
Shipley 2000b, 5.

[22] On the limits of accuracy afforded by these memoirs, see Meadows 2013.

[23] Baladié 1980 is fundamental. Lack of 'geographical' sources in a modern sense: Shipley
2006b, 34–5.

Despite the patchy nature of the epigraphic record, the incomplete coverage of *Inscriptiones Graecae* (*IG*) – only Laconia, Messenia, and parts of the Argolid were ever completed – has been gradually rectified since 1923 by the updates in *Supplementum epigraphicum Graecum* (*SEG*) and by publication of corpora from excavated sites such as Olympia and Corinth, complemented more recently by the massive haul of documents from Messene (particularly from later hellenistic phases) showing the continued pursuit of politics by the civic elite. There remains plenty of scope for new syntheses. As for epigraphy away from cities and sanctuaries, archaeological field surveys have yielded occasional finds, which in some cases have been used to generalize about the extreme non-rural bias of the epigraphic habit.[24]

The interpretation of numismatic data has recently taken several steps forward. Studies of Spartan coins,[25] Messenian issues,[26] and Achaean bronzes[27] have put money, rather than coinage, in the front of historians' minds; while the publication since the early 2000s (through auction catalogues) of the comprehensive haul of bronzes and small silver denominations by the collector known as BCD[28] has begun to have a profound influence upon the economic history of late classical and hellenistic Greece (some of the implications are examined in Section IV.7).[29]

The Peloponnese may not yet have produced hellenistic material culture on the scale of, for example, Alexandria with its tens of thousands of stamped amphora handles; but in aggregate there is a growing body of data that deserve to be brought together. Yet despite field survey publications and several series of excavation volumes (notably for sites in the northeast such as Corinth, Isthmia, and Kenchreai), little has been done to provide the study of settlement archaeology or of the social uses of material culture with adequate theoretical underpinnings[30] – though it is only fair to acknowledge the difficulty of distinguishing certain classes of hellenistic pottery clearly from late classical and early Roman, let alone dating it closely. There are, however, important new data from published field surveys including those carried out in Methana, the southern Argolid, Nemea, western Achaea, Messenian Pylos, and Laconia (discussed in

---

[24] Landuyt and Shipley 2003 (Laconia).
[25] Grunauer-von Hoerschelmann 1978.
[26] Grandjean 2003.
[27] J. A. W. Warren 2007.
[28] Now revealed as Basil C. Demetriadi; see e.g. his *Festschrift*, Wartenberg and Amandry 2015.
[29] See esp. Walker 2006 and the new catalogues of types by Hoover 2011 (Peloponnese except Korinthia); Hoover 2014 (Korinthia and central Greece).
[30] On this point see Shipley 2013b.

more detail at Section IV.3). These gain particular value when archaeological fieldwork is integrated with a close restudy of written and epigraphic sources.[31] Problems of interpreting survey data abound, however, and have been brought into focus by recent studies.[32] The signals are not uniform or always clear. The 'reading' of site size and duration is a vexed issue, while estimates of population at a given epoch have purely heuristic value; at best suggesting orders of magnitude which themselves rest on very problematic assumptions about the nature of rural occupation and use of the landscape. Different survey projects operate with different chronological boundaries: the classical period may be supposed to end at a 'round' date such as 350 or 300, or the date of a specific event such as Chaironeia (338), the death of Alexander (323), the end of the Lamian war (321), the battle of Ipsos (301), or even later.[33] Some surveys posit a combined 'late classical–early hellenistic' or 'late classical–hellenistic' phase. In the present study the simple conventions of the Laconia Survey are generally adopted: 'early hellenistic' denoting approximately the third century (sometimes including the late fourth), 'middle hellenistic' the second, and 'late hellenistic' the first.[34]

Despite inadequate literary sources (especially for 301–229), we now have enough epigraphic, numismatic, and archaeological evidence to justify a new construction of the early hellenistic Peloponnese. The present study cannot resolve all the problems of the archaeological evidence, but offers some initial interpretative patterns. It attempts to synthesize and generalize from archaeology in the context of written evidence (literary and epigraphic) for the Peloponnese, having in mind particularly questions of regional and other 'scales'. In ancient history it is often necessary to use inference and extrapolation to bridge gaps in the written record. Like other humanities subjects, both archaeology and ancient history rarely if ever have the luxury of dealing with complete data sets. But the undertaking is vital in order to understand the forces promoting and limiting change in the landscapes and societies of the Peloponnese, so that we may do justice to a group of Greek societies that deserve attention, not only in their own right but also because of their place in the earlier construction and later reception of Greece.

---

[31]   As excellent set of studies is Dalongeville *et al.* 1992; Rizakis 1995b; Rizakis 1998; Rizakis 2000.
[32]   Notably Stewart 2013.
[33]   Dreyer 1999 sees the Cl period at Athens as continuing well into C3.
[34]   Visscher 1996, 91 n. 1.

I.1.d Outline of the Work

Despite the shortcomings of the literary evidence that was the primary foundation of earlier work, the copious epigraphic evidence and especially the increasing quantity of numismatic and archaeological evidence justify a completely new look at the Peloponnese in the early hellenistic period.

As already outlined, the investigation begins in Chapter II, a narrative of political–military events which attempts to draw out recurrent features and trends. Like other parts of this book, the chapter also looks at the period immediately before the one on which we are focusing, particularly the generation between Sparta's loss of hegemony after the battle of Leuktra (371) and Philip II of Macedonia's victory over the southern Greeks at the battle of Chaironeia (338). Such a move is necessary because many details of the narrative are uncertain; and while the Peloponnese as an entity has not been the subject of detailed scrutiny in recent decades, the study of certain individual communities (both city-states and larger entities) has moved on. Here and elsewhere, one aim of the 'backward look' is to facilitate reasonable extrapolation from better- to less well-documented periods.

The argument depends partly on the principle that, as Rostovtzeff claims, we should assume broad social and economic continuity in the medium term unless we have evidence to suggest otherwise. If we can broadly characterize the social and economic structures of fourth-century *poleis*, we can address the succeeding period, for which we have fewer sources, with a general presumption of continuity. Likewise, since there is a compelling case that in the fourth century members of elites in a range of Peloponnesian city-states were in contact with major cultural centres such as Athens – as, for example, the military writer known as Aineias Taktikos (probably Aineias of Stymphalos, an Arkadian league general) may have been with Xenophon after he returned to Athens from exile – then it is hard to imagine that such contacts were any less frequent after Alexander's death. Warfare between states that happened to be dominated by rival dynasts need not have interrupted normal travel or communication.[35] Our watchword might be, 'We Arkadians, too, have televisions.'

Thus, in Chapter III, an outline of politics before Chaironeia permits a clearer assessment of the subsequent condition of Peloponnesian communities. The chapter compares the occurrence of non-democratic regimes, garrisons, and *stasis* (civil conflict) in the fourth century and later. It uses

---

[35] For a similar point about travel by intellectuals between Hl kingdoms hostile to another, see Shipley 2012; also Shipley 2017b.

a 'backward glance' to explore those conflicts that are presented as being between groups with different political ideologies, which leads on to the investigation of the democracy–oligarchy polarity.

Chapter IV makes a similar move in order to show that despite the prevailing orthodoxy (or, as it may be, prejudice) the Peloponnese as whole cannot reasonably be judged to have been in decline or economic depression before 338; from there, the investigation moves into the long third century.

Partly as a result of the problems of chronology and fragmentary evidence, too little attention has been paid to the question of whether the Peloponnese displays historical unity. Even in books or chapters whose titles refer to it, little or no thought has been given to the relationships and interactions between its regions, which tend to be treated separately and juxtaposed like a row of postage stamps. At times this book itself contains discussions arranged by region, but in Chapter V and elsewhere it attempts to synthesize and integrate them into a bigger picture. This chapter explores possible different 'scales' at which change and continuity can be identified: locality; region; collection of regions; and the outside world. Having considered the geographical and other constraints upon change that an external hegemon may have tried to impose, it examines the degree to which the Peloponnese behaved as a 'bloc' (giving a sceptical answer), and then moves on to consider in turn the 'region', the *polis*, and local structures within the *chōra* (rural territory) of a *polis* as possible cradles of disruptive pressures. Finally, it identifies the importance of networking between *poleis*, rather than between other spatial entities, and asks *cui bono?* The importance of internal political dynamics within Greek communities is shown to be paramount.

I.2 Historical Geography

I.2.a General Observations

The overall geography of the Peloponnese is described surprisingly rarely in current English-language scholarship. Since the present study concerns itself chiefly with political landscapes, it is appropriate to postpone the narrative sections briefly, in order to present readers who may be less well acquainted with the Peloponnese with a selection of key characteristics of each region. The reader wishing to focus on the narrative may skip to Chapter II.

With an area of some 8,000 square miles (21,000 sq km),[36] the Peloponnese is about the size of Wales or Massachusetts, with scarcely more level ground than the former. The climate is typical of southern Greece, with limited precipitation in summer and greater precipitation in the west and in the mountains; though the upland plain of eastern Arkadia, where there were three important city-states, suffers from reduced rainfall only partially offset by plentiful groundwater.[37] While climatic evidence has been adduced of a short-lived cooler phase lasting from *c.* 500 BC to the fourth century, followed by several warmer centuries,[38] it is not yet possible to specify its possible economic effects, still less any regionally specific implications.

Both during and after the period of Spartan hegemony, there was a great number of separate city-states (*poleis*) in the Peloponnese; many of them formally independent even when allied to Sparta (before *c.* 370). In the Copenhagen *Inventory*, the Peloponnesian sections contain 132 certain, probable, or possible *poleis* from the archaic and classical periods – one-eighth of all those in the Hellenic world; one-quarter of those in mainland Greece; and they include some of the largest.[39] Not all existed simultaneously, and some ceased to exist before the third century; but their large number reflects the character of the Peloponnese as a dense patchwork of *polis* territories.

These *poleis* are grouped into larger units by ancient writers. These culture regions were normally eight in number, sometimes nine. Anti-clockwise from the Isthmus, they were: Korinthia, Sikyonia (these two single-*polis* territories shared one coastal plain), Achaea, Eleia (with Triphylia to its south a separate entity at times), Messenia, Laconia, and Argolis, with Arkadia in the centre. Such a scheme is adopted, for example, in the prose *Periplous* (*Circumnavigation*) known as Pseudo-Skylax,[40] written at or near Athens in the 330s;[41] though it puts Arkadia after Eleia (because at that time Arkadia as a political entity extended to the sea via Lepreon). Since

---

[36] Ethniki Statistiki Ypiresia 1986? gives 21,379 sq km; Admiralty 1944–5, iii. 157, gives 8,356 sq mi (21,632 sq km).

[37] Gehrke 1986, 109.

[38] Bresson 2014; Bresson 2016, 40, speculates as to possible economic effects.

[39] Hansen and Nielsen 2004a (indexes to *Inv.*), nos. *227–357* and *360* (Kalaureia on its island). Mainland Greece from Akarnania to Thessaly (including the three Saronic islands but not those of the Aegean) covers 515 *poleis* (*112–626*); the whole catalogue has 1,035 entries (including four unlocated *poleis*). Only those places are numbered for which there is firm or suggestive evidence (textual or material) that *polis* status was attributed to them at some date before *c.* 300 BC. *Polis* status is a logical possibility for many further places, listed separately.

[40] Named thus in scholarship because the text is misattributed in the medieval MS to the genuine traveller Skylax of Karyanda (C6l).

[41] Shipley 2012.

the author begins his anti-clockwise Peloponnesian 'circuit' at the Isthmus, he places Argolis last and divides it into Argos and five other *polis* territories (see Section I.2.b), no doubt reflecting the narrow limits of Argive hegemony in his own time. When we evaluate material by region, however, while proceeding anti-clockwise[42] we shall usually begin with Argolis so that the communities of the north-east are discussed together.

The cultural importance of these regions cannot be overestimated. Alongside their component city-states (*poleis*), they were key markers of identity, gaining added importance in the late classical period as Sparta's domination of (most of) the Peloponnese began to be challenged.[43] Less clear, however, is whether they were the main structuring factor in areas such as the productive economy and trade (see further Chapter V).

Regional boundaries did not always follow natural features and were not necessarily fixed. (See further Section V.2.c.) To some extent these divisions, in whichever exact form they occur, are topographical, though the closeness of fit to geographical relief and political organization varies. Laconia is clearly defined by relief. A mountain wall separates it from Messenia; an upland zone divides it from eastern Arkadia. Less spectacular but still obvious is the border between Messenia and southern Eleia (or Triphylia): the mountains approaching the west coast create a defile at Aulon (possibly a perioikic *polis* of the Lakedaimonians until the mid-fourth century).[44] The expansive crests of northern Arkadia overlook the north-facing shelf of Achaea; the divisions between western Arkadia and Eleia, and between eastern Arkadia and Argolis, essentially correspond to upland–lowland transitions. Other traditional regions centre around a coherent landscape unit, such as the wide Eleian lowlands and the narrow coastal shelf of Achaea, while extending beyond their limits. Other regions are less strongly demarcated by relief. Korinthia, Sikyonia, Achaea, and Eleia can be viewed as the parts of one long coastal zone with wider and narrower sections and no obvious physical demarcation.

Other regions are not 'naturally' united; there can be strongly marked internal geographical divisions. Argolis comprises two or more major topographical zones, the Argive plain to the west and the mountainous Akte to the east (Section I.2.b). Inherently dissected, it was normally divided between several *poleis*; no prominent natural feature separates Korinthia from Sikyonia (they share a coastal shelf backed by the Argive mountains).

---

[42] This would normally mean starting from the Isthmus (like Ps.-Skylax and the Copenhagen *Inventory*: Hansen and Nielsen 2004b).

[43] Funke 2009.

[44] Shipley 2004b, 559–60 (*Inv. 314*).

Triphylia was a political creation. Arkadia clearly falls into two or three main parts (the western and eastern plains, and the mass of mountains to the north, plus Triphylia for a time after the 360s). Laconia, too, does not form a wholly unified entity: consider the Taÿgetos complex, the Eurotas valley, or the sprawling and dissected Parnon massif with its plurality of sub-ranges, upland valleys, and plains both inland and coastal.[45]

Given the limits of the 'fit' between culture region and relief, we should ask whether some economic activities were not structured with little or no reference to culture regions, whose boundaries they might cross. An unbiased observer, knowing no history, might divide the peninsula quite differently on the basis of topography, perhaps arriving at the tripartite scheme of the British Admiralty's *Greece* handbook from the second world war: (*a*) the northern and eastern highlands, (*b*) the central corridor and the low-lying north-west, and (*c*) the south-western highlands and the plains of Messenia.[46] This avoids the trap of unreflectively dividing according to ancient culture regions; but while the first and third areas are useful to think with, the second is not obviously so. The 'central corridor' is not so much a distinct zone as a group of relatively low-lying areas that seem to form a major furrow but really comprise two discrete segments: (1) the floor of the Eurotas valley in the south-east, framed by the extended massifs of Parnon (1,940 m; 6,365 ft) and Taÿgetos (2,407 m; 7,897 ft); (2) the valley of the Alpheios in the north-west, winding through quite different terrain in Arkadia and Eleia, together with its important tributaries. The two parts are separated by the hills in which each river has its headwaters, as noted by Strabo (2. 3. 12);[47] and the 'corridor' crosses boundaries between geological regions with different economic characters and cultural histories. It does not create a unity, and cannot be regarded as a region in its own right. Another scheme is needed if we are to see clearly the relationship between landscape and culture regions.

The dominant physical feature of the Peloponnese is surely the upland massif in the north, yet it is also the one least talked about in ancient sources and modern studies. While Strabo, for example, describes the Arkadians as 'mountain people' (ὀρεινοί, 8. 1. 2) and characterizes the region as mostly mountainous (8. 8. 1), he does not describe the uplands except to mention a few specific mountains (8. 3. 10, 22, and 32; 8. 4. 5; 8. 8. 3). The character of the area is worth emphasizing. Arkadia ascends to Mts Aroania

---

[45] On the sub-regions of Laconia, see Shipley 1992, 216–21.

[46] See e.g. Admiralty 1944–5, i. 27–30, cf. iii. 157–9.

[47] Strabo even asserts that the two rivers rise from springs near to one another, diving underground to reappear further downhill in either direction.

(*Chelmós*) and Kyllene in the north-east, with a north-western outlier in Mt Erymanthos – all three rise above 2,000 m (6,600 ft) – with a very slightly lower southern peak of Mainalos in the east-central part of the region. These heights are surrounded by a mass of spurs, with a plethora of small towns occupying high valleys and small upland plains. Purcell has noted this massif as the salient feature of the Peloponnese: from it project mountain ranges, like the thumb and fingers of a hand, to form the principal capes of the Peloponnese: in the north-east the dissected Argolic Akte; in the south-east Malea, the southern extension of Parnon;[48] in the centre Tainaron, the prolongation of Taÿgetos; and in the south-west Akritas,[49] which is not the extension of a single range since the uplands of south-western Arkadia and Messenia (culminating in Mt Aigaleion, *c.* 1,200 m; 3,900 ft) are fragmented clumps of high ground.

To develop this notion of the upland structure, it may be useful to think of three zones – different from those of the Admiralty handbook – each containing an upland core and shaping the topographical space within which societies move. Within each of these, and defined by them, are three lower-lying parts. (*a*) The largest upland zone, and the peninsula's core, comprises the northern massif, already defined, together with Parnon and Taÿgetos. Within this lie the elevated plains of Arkadia and the major lowland valleys such as that of the Eurotas, enclosed by mountains, while along its northern fringe is the narrow coastal shelf of Achaea. (*b*) A separate mountain zone in the north-east forms the Argolic peninsula (Akte), connected to Achaea and Arkadia by a lowland trough (running roughly from Argos to Corinth) containing a skein of easy land routes passing through the vicinity of Mycenae. (*c*) The final upland zone is formed by the broken uplands of Taÿgetos' Arkadian extension and the clumps of the Messenian mountains (no real bar to movement, for they can be bypassed on all sides). Within this zone we may situate (somewhat arbitrarily) the extensive coastal lowlands of the north-west and the Messenian plains.

Despite these *a priori* considerations of relief, the consistent grouping of communities by culture region in the written sources shows that they were deeply ingrained in people's consciousness, as well as increasingly politicized during the classical period. This, together with the tendency, at times, of *poleis* within them to cluster into regional associations, makes it legitimate to analyse the evidence in the first instance by region; but the cross-cutting relief divisions require us to be critical and not to assume

[48] Μαλέα, feminine; but masculine in Modern Greek: *Kávo Maliás*, cf. Pikoulas 1988a.
[49] Purcell 2012.

that regional organizations were the primary structuring factors in society or economy. (In Chapter V, we identify the limits of regional influence on Peloponnesian history.)

I.2.b Regional Descriptions

Argolis

The terms 'Argolis' and 'the Argolid' are commonly applied to the north-east Peloponnese as a whole, the smallest modern *nomós* but a much wider entity than just the *polis* of Argos and its city *chōra*.[50] Geographically it is divided between a lowland zone to the west and a linked mountainous region to the east, the Akte ('Headland'), which has the most indented coastline of any part of the Peloponnese. As already noted, Pseudo-Skylax in the 330s identifies a set of distinct *polis* territories (50–2, 54): first Argos with its *chōra* the Argeia, under which he subsumes Nauplia, Kleonai (one or both as dependent *poleis* of Argos), Mycenae, and Tiryns (both former *poleis* now absorbed by Argos; perhaps still villages); then separately five more *poleis*: Halieis and Hermion on the south coast, Troizen and Kalaureia on the east coast, and Epidauros with coasts on both sides of the Akte.[51] Additionally, Methana has probably dropped out of the text.[52] We might wish to add the important inland town of Phleious at the seaward end of the valley of the river Asopos; dominated by its cavalry class, the *polis* was usually loyal to Sparta and hostile to Sikyon (possible reasons for this are examined in Section V.3.d).

In a political sense, therefore, Argolis was not a single region, since it contained a plurality of states not all of which would have called themselves Argive. Its inherently fragmented face seems part of a curious feature of Peloponnesian historical geography, namely that single-*polis* regions cluster in the north-east, towards the Isthmus. (Furthermore, Megaris, the region east of the Isthmus, either had only one *polis*, Megara, down to the fourth century, or was very strongly dominated by that central place.[53])

Argos, once it had absorbed the minor lowland *poleis*, was without doubt the dominant power in Argolis, but it does not appear to have taken over the

[50] Briefly, Tomlinson 1972; more detailed description, Curtius 1851–2, ii. 335–482. *Poleis*: Piérart 2004 (*Inv. 347–57*).
[51] Shipley 2011. On these non-*poleis* and *poleis*, see Piérart 2004.
[52] Because at 46. 2 *Anthana* was corrupted to *Methana*, a copyist evidently deleted the latter from 52. 1; see Shipley 2011, 130, 215.
[53] As well as Megara, Ps.-Skylax 39 includes Aigosthena and Pagai in a list of *poleis*. See Legon 2004, 462–5 (*Inv. 224–6*).

Akte, though at an early date it forced the evacuation of the *polis* of Asine on the east side of the Argolic gulf; its people reportedly relocating to Messenia and founding a new Asine, a perioikic *polis* of the Lakedaimonians. As with many stories of the destruction of *poleis*, one must be cautious: we are told, for example, that Tiryns was destroyed by the Argives in the fifth century[54] and that the surviving population emigrated to Halieis; but in the third century votives were still being offered to the Furies at Tiryns (*SEG* 25. 372–3), and there is evidence for early hellenistic family names there (*SEG* 32. 381, *c.* 200?). Argolic Asine was supposedly refounded in the hellenistic period; had it, in fact, existed as a settlement (not a *polis*) without interruption? That would not be surprising in the light of *polis* histories elsewhere, and of the interest the Argives presumably had in exploiting the maritime links of their sub-region, not cutting them. Mycenae, too, survived throughout the classical period after being 'destroyed' by Argos, becoming a *kōmē* (civic subdivision) of Argos in the hellenistic;[55] in the early third century it gained a new temple.[56]

Argos' extensive coastal plain, partly marshy in ancient times, was complemented by the raised, cultivable Neogene hills slightly inland and by the territories of its dependencies. Proverbially dry as it was, the Argives compensated with deep wells; but Argos is only a 'middling' agricultural economy in Gehrke's classification. We shall see evidence of innovative pottery enterprises in the hellenistic period. The independent *poleis* of the Akte had small territories (TABLE I.1) and, with high marble mountains overlooking them, adapted to mixed economies. Hermion produced grain and shared grazing land with Epidauros, also drawing significant income from olive oil exports.[57] The name Halieis means 'Fishermen'; tuna-fishing is attested there,[58] and also at Methana and Troizen along with salt production.[59] Halieis and Hermion were known for the harvesting of murex from which purple dye was made (cf. Section IV.1.b).[60] Phleious enjoyed a larger territory, though only part of it consisted of cultivable valley slopes favouring the wine production noted by ancient writers. Like its Achaean neighbours, it relied on a varied economy as well as a mix of local and regional

---

[54] *c.* 470 according to Dickinson 2012; after the Persian wars, Paus. 5. 23. 3.
[55] *IG* iv. 498 (C3/C2). At Argos the *kōmē* was a political division of the citizen body; elsewhere it usually meant simply 'small town'. See e.g. Hansen 1995.
[56] Klein 1997; 2002.
[57] Bresson 2016, 361, with refs.
[58] Bresson 2016, 178, citing Antigonos of Karystos (C3) ap. Ath. 7. 50. 297e for the dedication at Halieis of the year's first tuna to Poseidon.
[59] *IG* iv² 1. 76 ~ Ager 1996, no. 138 (C2); cf. Bresson 2016, 183.
[60] See e.g. Bresson 2016, 357, 361–3, with refs.

Table I.1. *Selected* poleis *in descending size of territory, by region*

Region	Polis	Inv. Category	sq km (var.)	sq km (Beloch 1886)
Argolis	Argos	5	1,400	with Kleonai 1,405
	Epidauros	4	473	545
	Troizen	4	354	with Kalaureia 340
	Hermion	4	276	with Halieis 375
	Kleonai	3	135	*see* Argos
	Phleious	3	135	180
	Halieis	2	62	*see* Hermion
	Kalaureia		23	*see* Troizen
Korinthia–Sikyonia	Corinth	5	900	880
	Sikyon	4	380	360
Achaia	Dyme	4?	[250–500?]	My estimate; cf. Gehrke 1986, 147
	Aigion	3–4	[100–500]	
	Boura	3–4	[100–500]	
	Pellene	3–4	[100–500]	
	Aigai	1–2	[< 100]	
	Aigeira	1–2	[< 100]	
	Keryneia	1–2	[< 100]	
Eleia	**Pisatis (sub-region)**	(Pisa 4)	–	*555*
	Triphylia (as sub-region)		–	*540*
	Akroreia (sub-region)		–	*405*
	Elis	5	> 1,000	Koile Elis 1,186
	Kyllene	1–2	[< 100]	
	Pylos (Eleian)	1–2	[< 100]	
Triphylia	Lepreon	3?	[100–250]	
	Makiston	3?	[100–250]	
Arkadia	Megalopolis	4–5	1,486	1,520
	Kleitor	5	625	545
	Tegea	4	370	370
	Pheneos	4	345	325
	Mantinea	4	295	275
	Psophis	4	280	270
	Thelphousa	4	275	310

(*continued*)

Table I.1. (*Cont.*)

Region	Polis	Inv. Category	sq km (var.)	sq km (Beloch 1886)
	Heraia	4	265	250
	Kaphyai	4	220	135
	Stymphalos	3	180	with Alea 295
	Orchomenos	3	145	190
	Kynaitha	3	125	125
	Phigaleia	3	125	90
	Alea	3	110	*see* Stymphalos
	Alipheira	2–3	100	–
	Asea	2	60	–
	Pallantion	2	55	–
Messenia	Messene (independent)	4–5	[> 250]	
Laconia	Sparta	5	500	–
	Kythera	4	267	
	Boia	2?	[25–100]	
	Epidauros Limera	2?	[25–100]	
	Geronthrai	2?	[25–100]	
	Gytheion	2?	[25–100]	
	Prasiai	2?	[25–100]	
	Anthana	1	[< 25]	
	Thyrea	1?	[< 25]	
	perioikic Lakedaimon (sub-region)		*c.* 3,400	

'sq km (var.)' combines data or estimates from Gehrke 1986; E. Meyer, articles in *KP*; Nielsen 2004a; R. W. V. Catling 2002; Moggi 1974; Admiralty 1945. Where a figure or range in this column is in square brackets [ ], it is the datum implied by the *Inv.* category.

Inv. categories: (1) <25 sq km; (2) 25–100 sq km; (3) 100–250 sq km; (4) 250–500 sq km; (5) >500 sq km.

For other *poleis*, including Lakedaimonian *perioikoi*, approximate indications may be found in Hansen and Nielsen 2004b, 1320–1.

Figures in italics are uncertain.

trade and contacts outside the Peloponnese; these included the exportation of highly regarded vegetables (*holus* in Latin: Apul. *Apol.* 24, drawing on a classical source).[61]

Korinthia and Sikyonia

These large, single-*polis* territories can usefully be treated together since they share a fertile coastal shelf of alluvial fields and raised Neogene terraces.[62] Corinth possessed harbours on the Saronic gulf (an arm of the Aegean) as well as on the gulf of Corinth, and cultivable land in valleys in the directions of Argos and Epidauros. Sikyon, though hemmed in by Corinth on the east and Phleious on the west, had a plentiful water supply on its original acropolis (Diod. 20. 102. 4) and became sufficiently rich in the archaic period to build an elaborate treasury at Delphi.

Corinth possessed a restricted but fertile *chōra*, and as the controller of passage through and across the Isthmus could exercise considerable control of trade by sea and land. It became the figurehead of a network of colonies extending to the Adriatic and Sicily and had a powerful fleet, allowing it to exert pressure on Sparta as its strongest ally; but apparently never sought hegemony in the Peloponnese. Its geographical situation, and the presence of a strongly fortified acropolis, Mt Acrocorinth (1,890 ft; 575 m), made it the linchpin of others' ambitions. In the third century it became the southernmost of the four 'Fetters of Greece', the line of Macedonian strongpoints along the east coast of Greece (Section II.3.c). The details of its constitutional structures are veiled from us, though we know it had eight civic divisions and a council of 80; after the end of its archaic tyranny it seems to have been almost always a moderate oligarchy.[63] Despite its wealth and naval power, it shared its coastal plain with a much less powerful *polis* without ever, it appears, seeking to take it over even though Sikyon commanded some of the best land in the area.

Nevertheless Sikyon, though a second- rather than third-rank *polis*, saw its development inhibited because of the narrowness of the coastal shelf at the western end. An area of good land that in other circumstances it might have possessed belonged instead to Phleious, some 10 miles (16 km) to the

---

[61] Bresson 2016, 130.
[62] *Corinth and Korinthia*: see generally Gehrke 1986, 128–33; Legon 2004, 465–8. More detail, including internal routes: Salmon 1984, 19–37; Wiseman 1978; Curtius 1851–2, ii. 514–56. *Sikyon and Sikyonia*: Gehrke 1986, 138–40; Legon 2004, 468–70; Lolos 2011; more detail in Curtius 1851–2, ii. 482–505.
[63] Salmon 1984, 231–9.

south-west; but Sikyon had enough space to quarter Antigonos II's horses (Plut. *Arat.* 6. 2) and was generally known for the production and exportation of luxury footwear (Ath. 4. 42. 155c; 8. 41. 349e–f; Hsch. s.v. *sikyoniai*).[64] Prosperous in the archaic period, when it was ruled a well-known tyrant dynasty (replaced by an oligarchy), Sikyon must have benefited from the coastal trade over which its larger neighbour exercised such a magnetic attraction.

Achaea

Achaea occupies the north fringe of the Peloponnese, the south shore of the gulf of Corinth.[65] Settlement was mainly on the narrow coastal plain, rarely more than 2½ miles (4 km) wide and punctuated by coastal torrents and headlands. It is open to onshore winds and had no significant sheltered anchorage (in contrast to the Phokian shore opposite), except at Aigion, until the construction of an artificial harbour at Patrai under Augustus. In the west, Achaea includes the coastal shelf outside the narrows of the gulf.

From Sikyon westwards, the narrow coastal shelf and the mountains behind were home to old *poleis*, traditionally numbering twelve. Upland towns such as Pharai, Tritaia, and Leontion, and closer to the shore Pellene – probably the most significant Achaean *polis* – and Aigeira, will have depended on communications with those near-neighbours along the coast that tended to have larger territories, such as Patrai and Dyme in the west and, in the east, Aigai, Boura (until its disappearance in the 370s), Keryneia, and Aigion, well placed for crossings to Delphi and central Greece. Of particular importance were the harbours at Aigai, Aigion, Dyme, and Patrai. If these cities were of interest to outside powers, it was surely not because of any great wealth to be seized there, but because they had the potential to interfere with traffic along the gulf of Corinth and, in some cases, offered access to the passes of the northern Peloponnese and Arkadia.

Behind this shelf are terraces with rapidly erosible Neogene geology, separated by hills and plateaux. Behind these in turn are extensive mountains (surpassing 6,500 ft or 2,000 m in places), which provide the plentiful run-off that has created the valleys and keeps the coastal plain fertile. The arable economies of the lowlands were complemented by the upland

---

[64] Cf. Bresson 2016, 358.
[65] Gehrke 1986, 144–5; more detail in Curtius 1851–2, i. 403–95. *Poleis*: Morgan and Hall 2004 (*Inv. 229–44*).

ecologies; different *poleis* may have had different combinations of economic activities. With little scope for large estates (except in the far west) or
for regular wheeled traffic along the coast, with the lack of good harbours
limiting seaborne trade, and with a necessarily varied range of productive
activities, the *poleis* – with mostly small territories, though some were of
similar size to Sikyon's – may have tended to specialize economically, and
surely depended closely upon one another for the exchange of commodities.

Eleia and Triphylia

Strictly speaking, 'Eleia' refers to the *chōra* (rural territory) of the *polis* of
Elis, synoikized in 472, but it is also the name of the modern *nomós* (province) and may be used for the region to distinguish it from the *polis*.[66] 'Elis'
(in local dialect Walis, Ϝᾱλις, cognate with Latin *vallis*, 'valley'), was originally the geographical name of the region, referring to its wide landscape.
The only predominantly lowland area of the Peloponnese, it is a combination of inland hills and a wide coastal plain formed through alluviation,
mostly by the rivers Alpheios and Peneios.

   The *polis* of Elis was created on an inland site adjoining the Peneios, far
to the north-west of Olympia, near the point where the river valley, here
framed by low hills, enters its flatter coastal plain.[67] In the south-east of
Eleia lay Olympia, one of the most sacred sites in the Greek world, at the
confluence of the rivers Kladeos and Alpheios, in a locality known as Pisatis.

   Owing to the low coastline, there were no substantial harbours, Kyllene
in the far north-west being more of a beach anchorage; the Eleians,
accordingly, were not great sea-traders, though doubtless maritime links
existed: Strabo (8. 2. 2) describes both Eleia and Messenia as washed by
the 'Sicilian sea' and Pausanias (6. 26. 4) regards Kyllene as facing Sicily.
The extensive, open landscape seems to have facilitated the establishment
of a stable and wide elite. Polybios (4. 73. 5–9)[68] describes a rural aristocracy whose involvement in the urban centre was limited; fair or not, his
portrayal conforms to the scattered settlement pattern, with strikingly few
major centres for such a large area. Conversely, the region's agricultural and
pastoral resources made it a tempting target for those bent on plunder, as
Polybios observes (2. 5. 1). This became a major factor in the politics of the
third century.

---

[66] Eleia and Triphylia: Gehrke 1986, 103–4; Meyer 1967; more detail in Curtius 1851–2, ii. 1–118.
     Poleis of Eleia, Roy 2004 (*Inv. 245–64*); of Triphylia, Nielsen 2004b (*Inv. 304–11*).
[67] Kastler 1997, 21, though over-emphasizing geographical divisions within Eleia.
[68] Austin² 103.

Outlying communities of Eleia were designated *perioikoi*, 'circumhabitants', but less free than the Spartans' *perioikoi*.[69] The perioikic *chōra* extended to the western outliers of the great mountain massif of the north Peloponnese. The hill-land of Triphylia, across the Alpheios from Olympia, was part of Eleia for seventy years after the creation of the *polis* of Elis; but early in the fourth century, after Elis' defeat by Sparta, the Triphylians were separated off and cultivated a distinct regional identity. In the 360s they joined the newly formed Arkadian league,[70] giving Arkadia its only access to the sea (see next section). They reverted to Elis during *c.* 245–217 and again from 146, but they (or at least their leading *polis*, Lepreon) retained an Arkadian identity into the Roman imperial period.[71]

Arkadia

Ancient sources (e.g. Strabo 8. 8. 1) rightly emphasize Arkadia's mountainous character;[72] the single most important relief feature of the Peloponnese is the high mountain massif in northern Arkadia, overlooking Achaea and the north coast. Arkadia's status as the second largest region after Laconia,[73] and its essentially landlocked nature,[74] justify the attribution to it of special value as a cultural counter in the construction and maintenance of 'Hellenicity'.[75] Thucydides claims, for example, that it is not subject to frequent movements of population, unlike the rest of the Peloponnese (1. 2. 3). Xenophon, reporting a speech by Lykomedes of Mantinea,[76] says the Arkadians are the only aboriginal inhabitants of the Peloponnese, are the most numerous people in Greece, and are highly regarded as mercenaries (*Hell.* 7. 1. 25). Polybios, from an Arkadian *polis*, stresses the unavoidability of physical labour in Arkadian life (though presumably not for members of

---

[69]   Roy 1997; Roy 2009b; Roy 2009c.

[70]   Nielsen 2004b.

[71]   Nielsen 1997; Ruggeri 2009.

[72]   Detailed description: Curtius 1851–2, i. 153–400. Excellent sketch: Roy 1999, 320–1.
       Poleis: Nielsen 2004a (*Inv. 265–303*). Gehrke 1986 describes separately (*a*) the landscape in
       general and the larger *poleis* of Mantinea, Tegea, Megalopolis, and implicitly Orchomenos
       (109–13), (*b*) the smaller (151–4).

[73]   The largest modern *nomós* in the Peloponnese, it now extends to the E coast but no
       longer the W.

[74]   There was ancient speculation as to whether Arkadia had access to the sea. It did so from
       when the Triphylian *poleis* joined the Arkadian league. See Ps.-Skylax 43, with Cic. *ad Att.* 6. 2.
       3 = Dikaiarchos, fr. 79 Mirhady; Shipley 2012, 130–1.

[75]   The term adopted by Hall 2002. The use of Arkadia in the construction of Hellenic identity is
       explored by Beard and Henderson 2000.

[76]   Mantinea is the Arkadian name, Mantineia the Attic: Nielsen 2004a, 217–20 (*Inv. 281*), at 217.

the elite), the resulting toughness of character, and – an unusual comment for an ancient writer – the bad weather (4. 21. 1). In hellenistic and Roman times Arkadia became a byword for a simple, pastoral life in a bountiful landscape, to be viewed nostalgically; an image only partly consonant with reality.

It is true that Arkadia had a large percentage of population dwelling at relatively high altitude;[77] yet most of the larger settlements were located in plains rather than in mountain environments, and the dominant economy of the region was agricultural rather than pastoral (Gehrke). Of the two major plains, the eastern (more accurately south-eastern) lies *c.* 2,100 ft (*c.* 650 m) above sea level; though suited to cereals, it is too high for figs and olives, while a lack of good drainage, notably in the south, created pastures but also marshes and necessitated careful water management. This plain hosted the three main *poleis* before the mid-fourth century: Orchomenos in the north, with more limited territory, and its two larger peers Mantinea and Tegea, the Arkadian *polis* closest to Sparta.

The western (or south-western) plain, lying at a lower elevation and having greater accessibility and agricultural potential, hosted no major *polis* until the creation of Megalopolis (more accurately Megale Polis or Megalepolis, 'Great City'),[78] around 368 by *oikistai* ('founders') from Mantinea, Tegea, Kleitor, the Mainalians, and the Parrhasians.[79] Given its name, it was probably designed to be the leading Arkadian *polis*, and perhaps overshadowed the older *poleis* for a time;[80] though Mantinea is said by Polybios to have been the richest and most populous Arkadian *polis* in the late third century (2. 62. 11), while Megalopolis itself was partially deserted, or at least not fully occupied (2. 55. 2).[81]

Given that the Arkadian league broke into two after a few years, in 363,[82] it might seem valid to portray Arkadia's subsequent history as a confrontation between the two plains, home to four of the largest *poleis*. To do so, however, would be to miss the importance of the mountain environments,

---

[77] Roy 1999, 326; Frangakis-Syrett and Wagstaff 1992.

[78] On the name, see Nielsen 2004a, 520–2 (*Inv. 282*), at 520: Μεγαλόπολις is first in Strabo, 8. 4. 5, though the *ethnikon* Μεγαλοπολίτας is in *CID* ii. 4. iii. 50 (360 BC), at a time when the *polis* was still known as (He) Megale (Megala in Arkadian dialect) Polis.

[79] Nielsen 2004a, 520 (*Inv. 282*). The *ethnikon* took the form *Megalopolitēs* already by 360: Μεγαλοπολῖται ἐξ Ἀρκαδίας, *CID* ii. 4, l. 50; sing. Μεγαλοπολίτας, l. 56.

[80] There is no positive evidence that Megalopolis was the 'capital' of the Arkadian league: Nielsen 2015, 264–5.

[81] Walbank ad loc. (i. 258) cites Bury 1898 for the excessively large area within the walls; Bury's figures equate to 1.32 sq mi (3.42 sq km, or 342 ha). (B. is mistaken, however, in considering the N half the self-standing *polis*, the S half the federal capital.)

[82] For date, see Nielsen 2002, 490–9; more briefly Nielsen 2015, 267–8.

which contained the majority of the forty-odd Arkadian city-states. Most Arkadians probably lived in this constellation of widely distributed *poleis*. It is perhaps helpful to conceive of one distinct part of southern Arkadia as a circle of towns around the Mainalos range (which separates the two plains) – the circle being completed in the south by Megalopolis – with the broad western plateau of Mt Mainalos forming the centre of the circle and carrying a group of smaller west-facing towns (Gortys, Teuthis, Thisoa, Methydrion). Nor must we forget the important historical role played by *poleis* in the mountainous regions, notably Kleitor in the north, Stymphalos in the north-east, and Phigaleia and Heraia in the far west.

The hellenistic and Roman image of a pastoral Arkadia is right in some respects. It captures the importance to local identity of rural cult places, and of cult places in small *poleis*, exemplified by the excavated sanctuaries at Lousoi, Lykosoura, and Tegea (Athena Alea) and by the well-preserved Classical temple at Bassai. In economic terms, however, the reputation of Arkadia was as much built upon other animals as upon sheep and goats: the plains supported various species of domesticates, especially in wet pasture areas, as is partly confirmed by plentiful bones of large cattle at excavated sanctuaries. Ownership of large flocks need not be linked to high status,[83] so animal pastoralists at quite modest wealth levels could be seen as typical citizens; and there were wealthy landowners.[84] There was certainly trade between *poleis*, accentuated by the varying resources in which they could specialize (as in Achaea); Pheneos and Stymphalos even had upland lakes to exploit. Given Arkadia's lack of metal ores and the need for weapons, there was bound to be trade with outside regions.[85] Timber was exported (Thphr. *HP* 4. 1. 2), but we may doubt whether the region in general was heavily forested.[86] Perhaps most characteristically, livestock itself was traded with other regions.[87] Recent work has also emphasized Arkadia's interaction with maritime trade.[88]

---

[83]   Roy 1999, 345–6.

[84]   Roy 1999, 343–4, 352–3.

[85]   Roy 1999, 321.

[86]   Gehrke 1986, 151, assumes so; but the idea that ancient landscapes as a whole were once densely afforested, and only cleared as human settlement expanded, is false: see e.g. Rackham 2002 on Laconia; more generally, Rackham 1996.

[87]   *IG* v. 2. 3 shows active trade in livestock with other regions by *c*. 400; cf. Okada 2003 (seen in abstract only).

[88]   Roy 2015a.

Messenia

This region[89] comprises a lowland band joining the Taÿgetos range on its east to the shapeless cluster of lower summits in the south-western Peloponnese (the highest being Mt Aigaleion, 4,009 ft; 1,222 m).[90] These heights run out into the south-western cape, distant from the centres of cultivation but endowed with at least three good natural harbours. Often said, nowadays, to have been 'liberated from the Spartans' after Leuktra, Messenia in fact remained partly under their control until after the battle of Chaironeia (338). The two main harbours of the south coasts (not the west), Mothone and Asine, and by extension perhaps the south in general, were removed from Spartan control by Philip II after Chaironeia. The part of Messenia actually freed after 371 was centred upon the agricultural heartland: the inland Stenyklaros plain and the western coastal plain of Makaria. The hill-land of the south-western Peloponnese, too, has been described as the best in the peninsula,[91] on account of the predominance of other rocks over the ubiquitous limestone, as well as the plentiful groundwater and streams (the Pamisos being the largest perennial river in the Peloponnese).[92] The fertility of the region is repeatedly emphasized.[93]

A new Messenian capital was built after 369 at inland Ithome, which before long came to be known as Messene. It was located so as to control both the inland plains.[94] The dozen or so former Spartan perioikic *poleis* survived as settlements and as *poleis*, perhaps dependent upon Ithome–Messene or members of a federal association (see further Section III.3.b).

Laconia

The geopolitics of Laconia[95] have often been discussed, and only the basics need be noted.[96] The Spartan conquest of Messenia, conventionally dated

---

[89] Messenia, when not a feminine adjective (e.g. with γῆ, 'land'), means the territory of the new *polis* of Ithome, later Messene; only later denoting the region as a whole.

[90] Detailed description: Curtius 1851–2, ii. 121–200. See also Meyer 1969b. *Poleis*: Shipley 2004b (*Inv. 312–22*).

[91] Admiralty 1944–5, iii. 159.

[92] Pamisos: Curtius 1851–2, ii. 121.

[93] e.g. Curtius 1851–2, iii. 122 ('so zeigt sich … keine Landschaft Griechenlands in gleichem Maasse bevorzugt'); Admiralty 1944–5, iii. 196 (the SW peninsula has 'wine … among the strongest and sweetest in Greece' and 'perhaps the most luxuriant fruit orchards … on the coast of the Pelopónnisos'), 198 (the inland plains 'a sun-bitten paradise [with] "hot-house" conditions, as nowhere else in the Pelopónnisos'), 199 (densest rural population in Greece).

[94] Admiralty 1944–5, iii. 199.

[95] Lakonia, Englished as Laconia, is a post-Cl name. There is no Cl adjective *Λακώνιος (*Lakōnios*); Laconia in Pliny, *HN* 4. 5. 16, is probably a MS error for *Laconica* (i.e. Λακωνική, *Lakōnikē*). See e.g. Shipley 2004a, 570 n. 12.

[96] Detailed description: Curtius 1851–2, ii. 203–332. *Poleis*: Shipley 2004a (*Inv. 323–46*).

to the eighth and seventh centuries, brought a supply of agricultural tribute but also raised problems of control. Sparta itself, closely hemmed in on the west by the wall-like range of Mt Taÿgetos and on the east by the more complex obstacle of Mt Parnon, and situated some 25 miles (40 km) from the sea, might be thought well protected but topographically disadvantaged. Lying near the head of the wide, well-watered Eurotas valley, it had an extended *polis* territory including both pasture and cultivable hills; but control of the more distant parts of Laconia was a potential problem, since movement in and over the Parnon massif was laborious. The Spartans were obliged, by considerations of both numbers and distance, to maintain collaborative relationships with several score small towns, whose free citizens, known as the *perioikoi* or 'circumhabitants' (like those of Eleia), lived in dependent (i.e. subordinate) *poleis*, but in a relationship as fraternal as it was paternalistic.[97] Equally, a lack of metals, other than some iron ore deposits that were perhaps worked in antiquity,[98] necessitated trade with the wider world; in particular, Sparta seems to have been dependent on Attic imports of lead.[99] One benefit of delegating control to the *perioikoi* was presumably that Sparta gained access to a port on the gulf of Laconia, at Gytheion, as well as minor ports along the Malea and southern Tainaron peninsulas, though none of these developed into very active centres before the Roman period. Collaboration and delegation, nevertheless, enabled the Spartans to maintain the upper hand.

If Sparta was not particularly well placed to control all of Laconia, how much less well placed was it to control Messenia across the mountains – the other half of 'Lakonike' (the totality of Spartan-dominated territory in the classical period, both east and west of the mountains). Direct military intervention may have depended upon sailing round the dangerous Cape Tainaron; struggling across Taÿgetos by the direct route, which early modern travellers regarded as 'slow and dangerous';[100] or undertaking the quicker but still lengthy march round the north end of Taÿgetos past the south-western Arkadian *poleis* (to control some of which the Spartans expended considerable effort in the classical period). By delegating control, however, to the perioikic towns of Messenia, in some of which they had

[97]   Shipley 1992 (part reprinted as Shipley 2002b); partly superseded by Shipley 1997 and Shipley 2004a, esp. 569–71. The contrary view of Mertens 2002 is refuted by Hansen 2004d. See also Ducat 2008, emphasizing the separateness of the perioikic *poleis* while rightly limiting the degree to which we should view them as subjects.

[98]   Treister 1996, 21, 29, 144.

[99]   Gill and Vickers 2001.

[100] In the words of Sanders and Whitbread 1990, 340.

allowed incomers from other parts of Greece to settle, the Spartans succeeded in exploiting the Messenians as 'helots', a kind of state serfs. They behaved likewise towards certain subject groups within Laconia whose ethnicity is uncertain – Lakedaimonians? pre-Spartan Achaeans? relocated Messenians?

The Lakedaimonian *perioikoi*, whose number was reduced first in the 360s, continued by stages to be detached by Sparta's enemies and placed under neighbouring central places (in 338/7 and 222). Not only did the Spartans repeatedly try to reconquer Messenia and south-western Arkadia from the mid-fourth century on, but they made many efforts in the third century to recapture former perioikic territory in Laconia, particularly under Kleomenes III and Nabis. Presumably *perioikoi* removed from Spartan domination experienced changes in their internal politics; but in most cases (with the exception of some component settlements of Megalopolis in the mid-fourth century) we have no evidence of loss of *polis* status or site abandonment. In or after 195, the remaining *perioikoi*, brought by the Romans into a Lakedaimonian league or *koinon* under the protection of the Achaeans, appear to have conceived a desire to be fully independent – which means, as always, that certain leaders emerged or were identified as willing to push this agenda, others being marginalized; perhaps with popular approval. During the next half-century these *poleis* acquired the epigraphic habit, suggesting that the removal of Spartan control gave members of an elite more freedom to compete both within their city and against other cities. Despite their 'liberation', however, they still had close social and economic ties with Sparta in the Roman period. Although they eventually lost their remaining holdings in Messenia soon after 338, the Spartans continued to run Laconia partly on helot labour until at least the early or mid-second century.[101]

I.2.c Geographical Issues

The foregoing geographical outline is no mere formality; it is the underpinning of many discussions of narrative, politics, economy, and scale (including movement) in the next four chapters. While a detailed economic analysis is not attainable from the available evidence, a certain degree of specialization is already apparent, implying an equally vital feature, economic complementarity. Geographical and regional characteristics will

---

[101] Perhaps until the Roman domination: Kennell 2003. Helots in C3l Laconia: Plut. *Ag.–Kl.* 44. 1 with Shipley 2002d, 322.

also be important explanatory factors at many junctures in the following pages, though it will be important to be open-minded about whether regional groupings of communities played a primary or secondary role in developments, as compared with the role of individual city-states (*poleis*) or political grouping of cities.

> *I hear new news every day, and those ordinary rumours of war … of towns*
> *taken, cities besieged … daily musters and preparations, … battles fought,*
> *so many men slain, monomachies, shipwrecks, piracies and sea-fights;*
> *peace, leagues, stratagems, and fresh alarms.*
>
> Robert Burton, *The Anatomy of Melancholy* (1621), preface (from Powell
> 1975, 271–2)

II.1 A Narrative in Context

Our first area of investigation is how the Peloponnese was affected by wars
and the actions of external power in the early hellenistic period.[1] When
seeking evidence of change and continuity, or about the conditions under
which people lived, the narrative of events is an obvious place to start.
The present chapter first reviews the catalogue of organized violence, and
the threat of it, under which they laboured for much of the period. A discussion in a later section (IV.2) will consider whether the effects of warfare on societies and landscapes were as far-reaching and enduring as one
might suppose; or limited, and short-term, and mitigated by countervailing
factors. In the present chapter, the focus is chiefly on Macedonian military involvement and on the Achaean 'league' or *koinon*. It may be that
Macedonia's negative impact has been exaggerated. This prepares the
ground for an examination of the limits of political change (Chapter III).

Previous scholarship has made few attempts to assess systematically the
impact of the actions of Macedonian military power upon the Peloponnese
either as a unit or as a set of regions. Although the narrative remains unclear
in many details, both as regards the course of events and where Macedonian
policy is concerned,[2] it has the merit of introducing important themes for

---

[1] For ease of reading, in this chapter and elsewhere, I sometimes credit a *polis* (e.g. 'Stymphalos')
with taking an action or decision when it would be more truthful to make its people (e.g. 'the
Stymphalians') the agent.

[2] The reconstruction by Tarn (building on predecessors such as Niese and Beloch) still looms
large; but he pushes the evidence too hard (for helpful remarks, see Reger 1998). Walbank's

later detailed consideration, such as 'the problem of Sparta', the threat from
the north-west, the nature of civil conflict (*stasis*), the democracy–oligarchy
opposition, the ubiquity or otherwise of Macedonian garrisons, and the
nature of the so-called tyrannies.

To understand the history and politics of the Peloponnese in this
period, we need first to look back briefly to the sixth and fifth centuries,
when Sparta became more than a regional power and for a time exercised
supremacy over most of Greece (II.2.a). In the early and mid-fourth
century, the collapse of Sparta's Panhellenic ambition, and then of its
Peloponnesian hegemony, is followed by a period of turmoil as (in the
words of one scholar) *la marmite saute*,[3] 'the pot boils over' (II.2.b); the
legacy of this calamity continues to be influential for at least two centuries.
The early phase of Macedonian hegemony under Philip and Alexander sees
initial compliance on the part of most Greeks, which gives way to armed
insurrection provoking mildly repressive measures (II.2.c). Under the
early Successors (II.3), as the structure of governance in mainland Greece
is fractured, the Peloponnese becomes a hotly contested landscape: at first
sight surprisingly, considering its remoteness from Macedonia and relative lack of portable wealth; less so, if one sees it as a platform where those
contemplating an assault on the north can attempt to amass power. The
long era of Antigonid domination (II.4), which never extends over the
whole peninsula, is characterized by alternating phases of insurrection
and repression: the latter gradually gaining intensity until, around 250,
Gonatas' power in the Peloponnese begins to be eroded. (The participants
in insurrection are not always the same, local concerns playing a part in
their decisions.) As a possible first indication of the relative importance
of Peloponnesian affairs in the thinking of Macedonian rulers, it is worth
noting in advance that the homeland security of Macedonia often draws
its ruler's gaze to the north (see Section II.6).

Many details in what follows have been treated by other scholars, but
their accounts have not consistently focused on the Peloponnese as such.
A linking thread through this confusing and sometimes repetitious
narrative is the motives of different states, and what means they employ in
the search for power or security.[4]

modified reconstruction is largely followed here: see Walbank 1984a on the reign of Gonatas;
Walbank 1984b on 239–217 BC; Walbank 1933 on Aratos; Walbank 1940 on Philip V. Also
Walbank 1988 = chs 9–16 (pp. 199–364) of Hammond and Walbank 1988.

[3] Professor O. Picard, commenting on the present author's paper at the Tours conference in 2005
(published as Shipley 2008a).

[4] As noted in the Preface, the reader will find new insights into the political relationships
between Peloponnesian states in this period in Kralli 2017, which appeared as the present work

II.2 A Question of Upbringing: Hegemony and Anarchy down to Chaironeia (338)

This section will offer an account of how the Peloponnesian geopolitical landscape took the form in which the Macedonians found it when they became the masters of southern Greece. One reason why it is valuable to look back at the late classical period before considering the early hellenistic is that the literary sources (principally Xenophon and Diodoros) provide more detail of the internal workings and mutual interactions of states than do their now fragmentary successors or the piecemeal epigraphic evidence for the third century. With their help, we can build up a picture of Peloponnesian societies that can be regarded as broadly indicative of their complexion in the succeeding period, when recent events will have loomed large in the memories of those living under Macedonian rule. The end of the fifth century and the early fourth had also seen many changes of constitution in Peloponnesian *poleis*, which will help us understand what kind of societies the Macedonians encountered.

II.2.a Earlier Spartan Domination

The greatest geopolitical change in the Peloponnese between the fifth and the fourth century was the replacement of an almost unipolar landscape by one that was increasingly multipolar, as well as increasingly unstable until the beginning of the second century. Even if we grant that Sparta was one of the largest *poleis*, its near-total domination of the peninsula for such a long period would seem to require explanation; not least because the ambition of reviving that hegemony, once it had collapsed, was a dynamic element in Peloponnesian affairs for at least half a dozen generations and, at times, came close to being fulfilled.

Since roughly the mid-sixth century, the Spartans had dominated most of the Peloponnese through what modern scholarship has unhelpfully dubbed 'the Peloponnesian league'. This was not a collective alliance, let alone a federal union, but a plurality of one-to-one alliances made individually between Sparta and other states.[5] Known from contemporary texts as 'the Lakedaimonians and their allies', the association embraced almost all the city-states of the Peloponnese, the most notable exception being Argos.

---

went to press. A number of citations below will point the reader to detailed studies of specific episodes.

[5] Wickert 1972 was one of the first to observe its loose structure (cf. Wickert 1961). See also de Sainte Croix 1972a, appendixes 17–19 (pp. 333–41); Birgalias 2003; Bolmarcich 2005.

The alliances were probably asymmetrical in the sense that, while the ally was obliged to send forces to aid Sparta or attack a third party, the obligation was not normally reciprocal.[6] It was inevitable, given the shape of this association, that Sparta, a land-based power unlike Athens, exercised its power somewhat informally and with definite limits on its freedom of action. In a sense the 'league' existed only when called upon to act; it was not a Spartan empire.[7]

Through its nature as an relatively open entity, this plurality of relationships arguably gave greater unity to the Peloponnese than the fifth-century 'Delian league' or Athenian empire gave to Athens' allies and subjects; a *pax Laconica*, indeed. Behind the network, of course, lay the military power of a huge army, comprising three groups. First, the *Spartiatai* (in English 'Spartiates'), the citizens of Sparta proper. Second, the *perioikoi* (I.2.b), mainly in Laconia with others in Messenia; in total population about equal to the *Spartiatai*. 'Lakedaimonians' includes both Spartans and *perioikoi*. The latter were an almost equally important part of the whole community and had the same two kings as the Spartiates (officially 'kings of the Lakedaimonians', not of the Spartans) but probably no formal role in decisions about peace and war.[8] Third, a considerably larger number of serfs or 'helots' (*heilōtai*), mainly in Messenia but also in parts of Laconia.[9]

The heart of the 'league' was Lakonike, the territory dominated by Sparta and containing several dozen perioikic *poleis*.[10] Despite the Lakedaimonians' overwhelming numerical and tactical superiority in the field of warfare, political unity within the Peloponnese rested largely upon collaborative relationships between members of *polis* elites. The Spartans also seem to have promoted oligarchies, led by sympathetic members of the elite (a fellow-feeling perhaps expressed through ties of *xenia*, 'guest-friendship'),[11] as a more reliable guarantee of *polis* loyalty than could be expected from either democracy or tyranny (cf. Thuc. 1. 18–19). To this extent Peloponnesian hegemony was based on

[6] See e.g. the terms offered to Athens, Xen. *Hell.* 2. 2. 20; treaty of Olynthos and Sparta, Xen. *Hell.* 5. 3. 26; and esp. the inscribed treaty with the Erxadieis of Aitolia (C5l or C4e); recent work includes Pikoulas 2000–3; Matthaiou 2006; Antonetti 2012. On Sparta's early treaties, see Yates 2005.

[7] Rhodes 2009, 206.

[8] When I use the familiar terms 'Sparta' and 'Spartans', the reader should generally understand 'Lakedaimon' and 'Lakedaimonians'.

[9] On the helots see esp. Ducat 1990; Hodkinson 2000, 113–49; Luraghi and Alcock 2003; Luraghi 2009a. For helots in Hl Laconia, see Kennell 2003.

[10] On the *poleis*, see e.g. Shipley 2004a; Shipley 2004b.

[11] For an example of how effective such ties could be, see Cartledge 1982.

relatively 'soft' power and was deeply conservative: delegating economic and political organization, and the maintenance of the status quo, to leaders within each community. It could be characterized as 'delegated power from a distance'. In contrast, the Athenian empire – to the extent that, as Diodotos of Athens is made to say by Thucydides, 'the *dēmos* in all the *poleis* is well-disposed towards you' (3. 47) – embodied exploitation at the international level, the exploitation of tribute-paying states by the imperial hegemon; a dynamic rather than conservative formula, whether for good or ill, applied flexibly according to circumstances, and harshly only when security required (as argued by Euphemos of Athens at Kamarina, 6. 82–7).

As we shall see in Chapter V, however, regional identities had already begun to be asserted in the fifth century, in opposition to the pan-Peloponnesian ideology that the Spartans promoted at certain times – an interesting point of comparison with the era of Macedonian domination in the long third century.

II.2.b Spartan Over-reach and Collapse (404–362)

In the generation after the Peloponnesians' victory in what might be called, from their point of view, the 'Athenian war' of 431–404,[12] the leading Spartans, finding themselves in a position of unprecedented power within Greece, nurtured competing visions of how to use that power. One view came to dominate; but it proved to be over-ambitious.

Victory over Athens left the Lakedaimonians, led by the Spartans, pre-eminent in mainland Greek affairs. They were now one of a small number of major players on the southern Greek stage, the others being Athens (since the Spartans did not destroy it), Boiotian Thebes, Argos, and Corinth. The main geopolitical force within the Peloponnese was still the network of Spartan alliances. Apart from the city-states of Lakonike, the main centres of the 'league' were Corinth and Sikyon in their respective territories; the rest of the association of states comprising a plurality of middle-sized and small *poleis* in Arkadia, Achaea, and parts of Argolis. Separate from the 'league' in 404 were Argos with its local dependencies, and Elis with its own perioikic *chōra*; the Eleians were at odds with the Spartans, whom they had excluded from the Olympic festival since 420.

Within a few years of Sparta's victory over Athens, the Lakedaimonian-led structure began to show cracks. The Spartans made efforts to capitalize

[12] So designated by Cartledge 2002b, 192–227.

on their dominant position, coercing the Eleians back into the fold in a war of *c.* 402–*c.* 400 and detaching part of their southern perioikic *chōra*, where a new Triphylian confederacy was formed from about eight *poleis*.[13] Sparta's behaviour under its dynamic leading general Lysander, however, and then under the controversial Eurypontid king Agesilaos II (r. *c.* 400–*c.* 360), provoked tacit opposition from the Corinthians, traditionally their most powerful allies. Having subsequently over-reached themselves by threatening those allies and drawing heavily upon their resources for a war against the Persians in Asia Minor, but without adequately rewarding them, the Spartans in 395 found themselves opposed by a coalition of Athens, Boiotia, Argos, and – almost unprecedentedly – Corinth.[14] The ensuing 'Corinthian war', in the course of which a short-lived political union between Corinth and Argos was effected, put an end to Sparta's Aegean hegemony, thanks to a naval defeat off Knidos in south-western Asia Minor in 394. A sign of internal disagreement, as so often, is seen in the career of King Pausanias, who appears to have undermined Lysander's harsh policies and who, after his second exile in 385, published a critique of current policy.

The Spartans' generally heavy-handed approach, which was at odds with their milder behaviour in the Peloponnese during most of the fifth century, would prove unsustainable, evoking as it did the first stirrings of regional independence; for the moment, however, they maintained their position by a controversial deal with Persia. By the King's Peace of 387/6, they abandoned the Greeks of Asia to Persian rule, knowing they could not sustain war both at home and abroad. Instead they concentrated their efforts on the Peloponnese, breaking up the city of Mantinea into four smaller settlements in 385 (Xen. *Hell.* 5. 2. 7; cf. Section III.3.a) and forcing the Phleiasians, after a lengthy siege – itself a sign of Sparta's limited power – to reorganize their constitution affairs to Sparta's advantage (5. 3. 10–17, 21–5; cf. 5. 2. 8–10). But strategy was inconsistent, or perhaps limited by lack of power. They chose not to disown the unplanned seizure of Thebes in 382 by the Spartan commander Phoibidas (5. 2. 32–5). On the contrary, he and another Spartan, Sphodrias, who attempted to seize the Piraeus in 379 (5. 4. 20–4), had their deeds in effect adopted retroactively as acts of state. This resulted in the so-called Boiotian war, during which, at Boiotian Leuktra in 371, Epameinondas of Thebes inflicted on Sparta its heaviest military defeat in memory.[15] One of the chief factors in Sparta's setback was the ongoing

[13] Nielsen 1997; Nielsen 2004b; Roy 2015b, 269–71, 282, etc.

[14] Though Corinth had opposed Sparta after the peace of Nikias (Thuc. 5. 25–31, etc.).

[15] For earlier defeats, cf. the death of Lysander at Haliartos in 395 (Xen. *Hell.* 3. 5. 19) and that by Chabrias at Thebes in 387 (Polyainos 2. 1. 1). For underlying patterns, see Hamilton 1997.

decline in the number of full citizens qualified to serve in the army. This in turn was probably the result of the unrestricted accumulation of land by the rich, causing the impoverishment of smaller landowners and their demotion from citizenship.[16]

In terms of evolving hegemony, the combination of more assertive regional identities in the later fifth century[17] and over-aggressive Spartan hegemony meant that upheaval was all the more violent when it came. It is no surprise, given the resulting collapse of Spartan hegemony, that the decade after Leuktra was one of the most turbulent in Peloponnesian history. This impression is not just a phantom created by the accidents of source survival or by Xenophon's interest in contemporary events;[18] the events of these years brought real, often radical, changes, some of them permanent. The power vacuum created by the toppling of Sparta from its position of supreme power opened the way for frequent episodes of *stasis* (internal civil conflict) and regime change (Chapter III).

Even before Leuktra there had been a climate of innovation. By 389 or earlier, for example, the first Achaean federation had been set up (with the power to grant citizenship, Xen. *Hell.* 4. 6. 1).[19] By the time Epameinondas invaded the Peloponnese in winter 370–369 and again in spring 369 – on the latter occasion reaching Laconia but avoiding a direct attack on Sparta and instead burning minor settlements on the way south to Gytheion, which was briefly besieged (6. 5. 32) – the 'Peloponnesian league' had begun to erode in the north, leaving Sparta with few allies there (6. 5. 29; 7. 2. 2).[20] Of these, Achaean Pellene was soon detached (on the unusual situation and sometimes independent behaviour of Pellene, see Sections II.3.a, V.3.d).[21] Already in 370 (so probably not yet under Theban influence)[22] the Arcadians had set up a federal state (Xen. *Hell.* 6. 5. 6).[23] Although the Thebans became patrons and protectors of the new western Arcadian 'capital' of Megalopolis ('Great City'), set up in the aftermath of Leuktra, the new *polis* has been described as 'essentially an Arcadian creation'.[24]

---

[16] Hodkinson 2000, 399–445.

[17] Funke 2009.

[18] Roy 1994, 205.

[19] Rhodes 1997, 106; Rizakis 2015, 121.

[20] Roy 1994, 191.

[21] See also incidents noted by Morgan and Hall 2004, 484–5 (*Inv. 240*).

[22] Date: e.g. Nielsen 2015, 250 (effective end in 363 BC, Nielsen 2015, 267).

[23] Roy 1994, 190, argues for late 370. On internal dynamics of the league, see also Kralli 2017, 9–24.

[24] Roy 1994, 193; see also Nielsen 2002, 414–55; Roy 2005; Nielsen 2015, 264–5. The decision to found Megalopolis is best placed after Leuktra: S. Hornblower 1990.

Though demographically a serious blow to a *polis* with shrinking manpower, the loss at Leuktra of 400 *Spartiatai* (out of the 700 present) and 600 other Lakedaimonian hoplites (Xen. *Hell.* 6. 4. 15) did not, as is popularly believed, neutralize Spartan power at a stroke. The dismantling of the remainder of the 'Peloponnesian league' by the armies of Thebes and its allies was a process that took several years. In the early stages, it entailed the removal from direct Spartan control of the farmland of central and western Messenia; but for a further generation Sparta held onto coastal Messenia with its perioikic harbour towns.

Theban domination also involved the creation of a fortified city at Ithome (later called Messene) in central Messenia, and the refortification of Mantinea in eastern Arkadia. Under Boiotian influence, Messene may have become the central place of a federation (see Section III.3.b). Mantinea was to be the leading fortress of eastern Arkadia, but did not necessarily have the economic muscle to outrank Tegea, probably the most prosperous *polis* there. The other new foundation, Megalopolis, brought together physically into one centre many small communities in western Arkadia, though the new city proved somewhat soluble. The 'three Ms', as we may call them, were clearly designed to block Spartan access by land to the rest of the Peloponnese and central Greece; to a large extent they were effective.[25]

Yet for another 180 years Sparta remained one of the major players in Peloponnesian affairs, at times a dominant one;[26] it was normally, for example, a threat to some of the Arkadian *poleis*. Nor was it always friendless: the Achaeans, for example, appear to have remained mostly loyal to Sparta well into the third century. Leuktra had made the first big dent in Spartan power, and accelerated the effects of declining citizen numbers and resources; but these trends were mitigated by the significant – albeit not always decisive – military force that the city could still sometimes deploy.[27] Sparta and the other Lakedaimonians retained considerable power to act at a distance, even without most of their former helots and allies. In 368, with the aid of twenty shiploads of troops sent by Dionysios I of Syracuse, they recaptured Karyai on their northern frontier and defeated Arkadia, Argos, and Messenia at the Tearless Battle in south-western Arkadia (Xen. *Hell.* 7. 1. 28–32). In 365, with reinforcements sent by Dionysios II after his father's death, they retook Sellasia (7. 4. 12), though in the next year over a hundred Spartans and *perioikoi* were taken prisoner from among a

[25] Nielsen 2015, 265–6.
[26] On the centrality of Sparta to Peloponnesian affairs in this period, see also Kralli 2017, xxii–xxxiii, 489–96.
[27] A point made even more forcefully – perhaps too strongly – by Tarn 1913, 65–6.

force besieged by the Arkadians at Kromnos in Megalopolitan territory (7. 4. 20–7).

The setbacks of the post-Leuktra years, therefore, did not in any way apply a guillotine to Spartan history or their capacity to pursue aggressive policies. The Lakedaimonians still entertained the ambition of dominating Peloponnesian and Greek affairs; whether the distribution of military and economic power would allow them to do so by traditional means remained to be seen. The Thebans had found it necessary to adopt a different approach – a new version of Sparta's 'delegated power from a distance', though based on democracy and federalism rather than oligarchy – but the very factor of distance, and Sparta's residual weight, proved insuperable; these problems being exacerbated by local tensions which may have been all the more virulent for the internal pressure built up under Spartan rule and now released.

II.2.c Waiting for the Macedonian (362–338)

Soon after the events just described, the geopolitics of Greece underwent a substantial shift with Macedonia's rise to pre-eminence. Initially, competition between central and southern Greek states continued under existing rules of engagement; but soon the burning questions for all involved were those of assessing the nature and weight of the Macedonian threat and deciding whether to work with or against the northern power. The next quarter-century would show the perils of miscalculation.[28]

In 363,[29] the splitting of the Arkadian *koinon* into two factions, one of them notionally under Theban protection, weakened Thebes' recently won influence, which was henceforth chiefly limited to Tegea and Megalopolis and was hampered by the intervening presence of the other towns. The Thebans attempted to restore their dominance over Arkadia, helping the Megalopolitans to bring back by force those who had returned to their former cities (Diod. 15. 94. 1–3);[30] but the division of Arkadia led to conflict[31] and ultimately in 362 to the indecisive battle of 'Second Mantinea', in which the Thebans defeated Sparta and Athens but Epameinondas was killed. On that day, Arkadians fought against Arkadians: on one side were ranged the anti-Theban Arkadians (the Mantineans playing a central role) together with the Eleians, Achaeans, Spartans, and Athenians; on the other

---

[28] Kralli 2017, 49–51, characterizes these years as 'weakness of all sides'.
[29] Date: e.g. Nielsen 2015, 267–8.
[30] Cf. Nielsen 2002, 493–7.
[31] Detailed account in Roy 1994.

the Tegeates, Megalopolitans, Argives, Sikyonians, and Messenians, among others.

After Second Mantinea, Xenophon's narrative ends and the picture (mainly from Diodoros, using Theopompos and others) is less clear for a time. The Spartans, with many *perioikoi* still at their disposal in coastal Messenia and the albeit truncated Laconia, remained the most powerful force; but they were hemmed in, were no doubt temporarily discouraged, and after the death of the towering figure of Agesilaos II in 360/59 were presumably reassessing their situation. They waited for a decade (as far as we can tell) before resuming their attempts to regain territory. In 353/2, they renewed their efforts to recapture northern Messenia, and temporarily overran Megalopolitan territory (Dem. 16; Diod. 16. 39. 1; Paus. 8. 27. 9–10). The Great City was aided by the Argives, Sikyonians, Messenians, and Thebans (Diod. 16. 39. 2) – but not by the eastern Arkadians. The Lakedaimonians captured Orneai in Argive territory, killed over 200 Argives, and plundered Arkadian Helissous (39. 4–5). The campaign ended indecisively with an armistice between the Lakedaimonians and Megalopolitans (39. 7);[32] they then remained mostly quiet for a time. Several sorties brought no lasting success, suggesting that the 'three Ms' remained an effective cordon.

For the next decade or more, the sources continue to suggest rivalry and violence between Peloponnesian states. Some were looking to safeguard themselves by projecting their interests more widely, such as Messene and Megalopolis, which were refused membership of the Delphic amphiktyony despite their alignment with the new ruler (initially perhaps regent) of Macedonia, Philip II.[33] Opposition to Philip even brought the two halves of Arkadia into alliance, though they were not reunited in one organization.[34]

Sparta's neutralization proved temporary (the city, after all, had never been captured) and, though the 'three Ms' did their job, Sparta's efforts at revival highlighted continuing divisions between groups of Peloponnesian communities. Sparta stood aside from the confrontation with Philip that led to defeat at Chaironeia in Boiotia in late summer 338. Other Peloponnesians did take part, particularly from the north and north-east; the Achaeans (and no doubt others) suffering heavy losses whose effects were still felt fifteen years later (Paus. 7. 6. 5).

---

[32] Griffith, in Hammond and Griffith 1979, 481.

[33] Ellis 1994, 765–6.

[34] Schol. Aeschin. *Ctes.* 83 (*IG* v. 2, p. 49).

II.2.d Retrospective of the Period down to 338

The story of the Peloponnese down to 338 is dominated by the break-up of Spartan hegemony and by decades of resulting turmoil as new relationships were forged, all too often through conflict. Spartan hegemony in the fifth century was delegated, relatively 'soft', and conservative; but regional identities now began to be expressed. After the Peloponnesian war this regionalization, combined with over-assertive policies on the part of the leaders of Sparta, made the collapse of Spartan hegemony, when it came, all the more complete. The Thebans perhaps modified Sparta's 'delegated power at a distance' approach, using the 'three Ms' (Messene, Megalopolis, and Mantinea); but adverse factors made its efficacy short-lived. Sparta's neutralization after Leuktra, however, proved temporary. Although hemmed in, the Spartans' efforts at self-recreation highlighted disunity among Peloponnesian communities, and thus the Peloponnese in the mid-fourth century was more fragmented than before.

The peninsula in this period recalls the 'anarchic' states society explored for the modern world by Bull[35] and for the early hellenistic period by Eckstein.[36] Unlike today, when, for all the limits of their effectiveness, international organizations inhibit to some extent the behaviour of states, in classical Greece no international law existed beyond one-off treaties (ratified by oaths and sacred rituals) and the general rules of a common religion and its short-term pronouncements (oracles, omens), or shared assumptions about what was acceptable in the context of violence and what was not. Both the general and the particular injunction could be ignored or politicized. Ambition was acceptable; pre-emptive attack often deemed reasonable; prudence, oaths, treaties, and the potential threat from an outside power almost the only restraints. Yet although the Peloponnese was more fragmented, new regional blocs of *poleis*, where they existed, gave relative protection or permitted relative freedom of action (as the 'Peloponnesian league' had done). This was obviously the case with the long-established Laconian bloc and the two Arkadian groupings; possibly with the Achaean *koinon* (about whose pre-hellenistic incarnation, though it is definitely attested, we know few details);[37] potentially with the Messenian federation if such an association existed (see Section III.3.b). An interesting further case in point is Triphylia, which under the leadership of the *polis* of Lepreon attached itself to the Arkadian league in the 360s (partly or chiefly

---

[35] e.g. Bull 1977.
[36] Eckstein 2007.
[37] Rhodes 1997, 106; Mackil 2013, 46–52, 62–3, 75–6; Rizakis 2015, 120–2.

for protection from Elis), adopting an Arkadian ethnic identity that became permanent (see Section I.2.b).

Already in the 360s, then, there were signs that new regional groupings or blocs might offer hope of a stability such as the so-called Peloponnesian league had offered; but until Chaironeia 'ever closer union' was deferred. In places, individual *polis* autonomy was thus pooled – whether voluntarily or by coercion – in the interest of security; but a strong trend towards federalism did not develop immediately. It would accelerate in the early hellenistic period, when Macedonian hegemony would sometimes mirror certain aspects of Spartan policy earlier – such as the identification and promotion of loyalists within a *polis* – but could also be far less conservative. Few of Philip II's successors seem to have attempted to promote a common cause in the Peloponnese, as Sparta had (see Section II.2.a); he himself did so.

II.3 Temporary Kings: The Early Macedonian Years (338–301)

The history of the Peloponnese under Philip and Alexander begins with a period of widespread submission, followed after an interval by hostile action, which in turn provoked repression; though commanders and kings would vary in the degree to which they tolerated local self-determination. The means of domination, or attempted domination, were sometimes similar to those used earlier by the Spartans, but sometimes more brutal. At times these interventions were to be the agents of disorder; at other times, external domination would offer some hope of stability.

II.3.a Philip and Alexander: Acquiescence, Revolt, and Reaction (338–323)

Philip II's settlement of Greece, and his general toleration of existing constitutions, held out the prospect of a reduction in disorder and violence; but not everyone was content.

After his victory at Chaironeia in 338, Philip II received the surrender of Megara and Corinth. The *poleis* of Achaea and the Argolic Akte had also opposed him. The Eleians, Argives, Arkadians, and Messenians, earlier his friends, had not actively supported him.[38] Sparta had not opposed him; but loyalty to, and fear of, Sparta had been key factors in Peloponnesian politics,

---

[38] Ellis 1994, 783.

albeit mediated through local relationships (Argos and Sikyon, for example, being perennially wary of Corinth). Now the states bordering Laconia – containing perhaps more than half of the peninsula's population – gained territory at Sparta's expense. Philip invaded Laconia, detached large parts of its perioikic territory, and handed them to Argos, Megalopolis, Tegea, and Messenia (Polyb. 9. 28. 7; 18. 14. 7).[39] Presumably on this account, he was honoured with a statue at Megalopolis (*SEG* 48. 521); no doubt with similar expressions of gratitude elsewhere.[40] The Spartans lost not only coastal Messenia but also what was left of their northern borderlands as well as the Thyreatis in the far north-east.[41]

Despite this violation, the Spartans were not cowed but stood aloof from the assembly, held at Corinth in 337, that enacted a peace treaty and an alliance (*symmachia*) between Macedonia and the participating Hellenes. The association is now often imprecisely called the 'league of Corinth' or 'Hellenic league'; more accurately the 'Hellenic alliance' (*SdA* 403; RO 76).[42] Philip perhaps tolerated the Spartans' absence to show that participation was voluntary, just as he claimed.[43] Their non-participation would also entrench the Messenian–Laconian division, enabling him to 'divide and rule' while Sparta was still fenced in by the 'three Ms' as buffer states.

Having spent some of his teenage years during the 360s as a hostage in Thebes, Philip understood the *polis* system. His intervention is naturally represented as beneficent by the second-century historian Polybios (Arkadian, Achaean, and anti-Spartan) in a speech he gives to Lykiskos, a pro-Macedonian Akarnanian, set in 211 (9. 33. 9–12). Lykiskos asserts that Philip entered Laconia under pressure from the other Peloponnesians, and did no harm but brought about a negotiated settlement. He is answering a speech by Chlaineas, an Aitolian, who urges the Lakedaimonians to take the side of Aitolia against Philip V of Macedonia and plays up the abuses committed by Alexander's successors (of which we shall see examples later). In a late book of his *History*, Polybios in his own voice, while criticizing the late fourth-century Athenian orator Demosthenes for his extreme opposition to Macedonia, takes a similar view to that of Lykiskos: those Peloponnesians who brought in Philip II were not traitors, for they acted not from self-interest but in the interest of their states, freeing lands conquered long

---

[39] Roebuck 1948; Shipley 2000a, 371.
[40] Lauter and Spyropoulos 1998, 445–7.
[41] Shipley 2000a, 386–7. See also Roebuck 1984 (= Roebuck 1948). The reallocations and their consequences are examined in detail by Kralli 2017, 61–8.
[42] Harding 1985, no. 99.
[43] Ellis 1994, 784.

before by the Lakedaimonians and enabling the peoples of the Peloponnese
'to draw breath again' (ἀναπνεῦσαι, 18. 14. 6). (See further section III.2.a.)
Whatever view we take of the choices that were made, they encapsulate the
dilemma faced by Peloponnesian elites – whether acting on behalf of one
polis or a group of *poleis* – cast adrift to some extent in a power-vacuum.[44]

To be sure, Philip's settlement imposed a certain degree of structure upon
the Peloponnese. His alliance was distinguished from other such associations by having a 'leader' (*hēgemōn*), a position he naturally occupied
himself, and a delegate assembly (*synedrion*) which could impose decisions
upon member cities if it chose. The text of the allies' oath, together with a
list of the members, is partly preserved in the very fragmentary inscription
already cited (RO 76; *SdA* 403), from which it is clear that the agreed terms
protected existing constitutions, implicitly both democratic and oligarchic
(some had taken their present form only after Chaironeia).[45] This protective spirit was later seen as a hallmark of Philip and Alexander's rule, and
became a precedent that could be invoked. In Laconia and its neighbours,
however, stabilization involved change rather than continuity, as we
have seen.

Despite Philip's benevolent attitude towards most Peloponnesian communities, immediately after his death the Arkadians, Argives, and Eleians
sent armies to the Isthmus in 336/5 as part of the first Greek attack on his
son and successor, Alexander III (Diod. 17. 8. 4–6).[46] Presumably this about-
turn reflected changes in internal political power balances. The Arkadians
were deterred by envoys from Alexander's viceroy in Greece, Antipater, and
withdrew on the grounds that they were 'compelled by the times' to serve
Alexander (Deinarchos 1. 20).[47] The unsuccessful Greek campaign ended
disastrously with the destruction of Thebes in late summer 335. Chaironeia
and Philip's Hellenic alliance had only temporarily dampened the fires of
opposition to Macedonia's new-found power; now the fate of the leading
Boiotian *polis* might have been expected to do so, but did not.

The presence of Peloponnesian troops among Alexander's army in Asia
Minor is noted by Arrian (*Anab.* 1. 17. 8); they included the Argive infantry
who garrisoned Sardis in 334,[48] as well as Greeks formerly in the Persian

---

[44] Cf. the acute analysis by Griffith, in Hammond and Griffith 1979, 474–84.

[45] O'Neil 1995, 103, notes that Philip's alliance contained both oligarchies and democracies.

[46] Campaigns of the southern Greeks against Macedonia after 338 are often called 'revolts' even
though they were (at least formally) allies, not subjects, of the Macedonians. 'Attack' and 'war'
are more appropriate terms.

[47] Hammond 1988, 59–60, does not adequately bring out the Arkadians' U-turn.

[48] Cf. Billows 1990, 38–9 and n. 69.

king's service, who are said to have been loyal to Alexander (3. 23). These troops were, in a sense, hostages for the good behaviour of their home cities. They are thought to have numbered several thousand, a substantial force if we consider that it did not include the Spartans.[49] The Spartans did not, however, remain inactive.

Perhaps fearing Spartan-led unrest, Alexander or Antipater may have stationed a military force in the Peloponnese under one Korrhagos (Aischines 3. 165);[50] or this may have been a response to the second attack on the Macedonians, launched in 331 under the leadership of Agis III of Sparta (r. 338–330). Without Athenian support, the campaign was unlikely to succeed. The Peloponnese suffered more than other parts of Greece, for in spring 330 Antipater invaded with an army of 40,000 (Diod. 17. 63. 1).[51] Agis was killed fighting alongside the other Greeks at Megalopolis; 5,300 Lakedaimonians (i.e. Spartiates and *perioikoi*) and allies of Sparta died (63. 2); presumably mostly allies in view of the high figure.[52] Fifty leading Spartiates were given to Antipater as hostages (73. 6), and the Lakedaimonians went quiet again, standing aside from the Lamian war a few years later (see Section II.3.b). Sparta was probably not, however, compelled to join the Hellenic alliance.[53]

Although Sparta after 331 has seemed to some historians 'a third-rate and inconsiderable Peloponnesian community'[54] and 'enfeebled beyond redemption',[55] that assessment does not take account of their enduring capacity for mobilizing and leading collective armies, their continuing ambition, and the evident determination of at least some leading Spartans to resist the entrenchment of Macedonian domination. Presumably this readiness to lead found willing followers among elites in *poleis* where Sparta's friends had not been eliminated. It is not many years before we see possible signs that the Spartans were willing to support military action, at least tacitly (see Section II.3.b and later).

The death of Darius III in 330, marking the Macedonian victory over the Persian empire, occasioned Alexander's standing down of his Hellenic allies, sent home with a collective bonus of 2,000 talents; many elected to

---

[49] Billows 1990, 40 n. 71.

[50] Aischines 3. 165 says that the Lakedaimonians and their mercenaries had 'destroyed the forces of Corrhagus'. Billows 1990, 194 n. 13, infers that Korrhagos was already in the Peloponnese before the Greeks attacked, but may be pressing the evidence too hard. See also Deinarchos 1. 34, referring to the war; Curtius 6. 1. 20, an account of the battle of Corinth.

[51] Hammond 1988, 85, 87.

[52] Rather than mostly *perioikoi* as in Cartledge and Spawforth 2002, 23.

[53] Cartledge and Spawforth 2002, 24–5.

[54] Cartledge and Spawforth 2002, 23.

[55] Bosworth 2012a.

remain in his service (Arrian 3. 19. 5–6).[56] About now, he is said to have installed tyrants in Messene (Ps.-Dem. 17. 4) and replaced a short-lived democracy at (normally oligarchic) Pellene with a tyranny under a certain Chairon (see Section III.2.b).[57] As Pellene, unlike other (and probably poorer) Achaean states, did not aid Agis' revolt (Aischines 3. 165), this tyranny may have preceded the anti-Macedonian campaign and may have deterred the people from taking part. It seems likely, however, that with these exceptions Alexander did not enforce 'regime change' widely, in contrast to some later commanders. Indeed, after his victory over Darius at Gaugamela in 331 he proclaimed that all Greek tyrannies were to be abolished and cities should live under their own laws (τὰς τυραννίδας πάσας καταλυθῆναι καὶ πολιτεύειν αὐτονόμους, Plut. *Alex.* 34. 2); a declaration others were to imitate.

As ever, the dilemma for southern Greek communities was whether to align themselves, even for protection against the Macedonians, with the Spartans, who despite occasional quiescence could be assumed to want to control the Peloponnese. Sparta might not, at present, be strong enough to dominate; but it might become so again. Was it worth expelling the Macedonians from the Peloponnese at the risk of seeing one's *polis* re-enter an unequal alliance with Sparta?

Events also showed that Philip and Alexander had no absolute preference for democracy, oligarchy, or tyranny; circumstances dictated their responses at the constitutional level, though in Asia Alexander appears to have favoured democracy because the Persians had favoured oligarchy.[58] Polybios (2. 41. 10) does not include Alexander among those who installed garrisons (though this is hardly evidence in Alexander's favour as Polybios also omits Antipater, who did install garrisons after the Lamian war). A general inclination to foster support by supporting democracy, however, is implied by events after Alexander's death, as we shall see.

II.3.b Further Unrest and Tighter Control (323–319)

Alexander's unexpected death at Babylon in summer 323 was followed by decades of warfare in Greece and western Asia among his generals, during which many southern Greeks fell victim to military campaigns; some being subjected to a control more invasive than under Philip and Alexander. Initially

[56] Bosworth 1994, 818.
[57] Morgan and Hall 2004, 484 (*Inv. 240*).
[58] O'Neil 1995, 103.

the generals acted in the name of the new joint kings, Philip III Arrhidaios (Philip II's only surviving son, Alexander's half-brother), thought by some unfit to govern,[59] and Alexander IV (Alexander's posthumous son), but within a few years they were both dead. Many parts of southern Greece changed hands several times, with casualties and economic losses on each occasion. The sources allow us to see much of the detail, giving a fuller narrative than at any time for nearly a century afterwards.

Alexander's death coincided with a third attack by the southern Greeks upon the Macedonians, leading to the Lamian war of 323–322, which was fought largely in Thessaly. This was partly provoked by the Exiles Decree of 324, in which Alexander ordered cities to take back political exiles,[60] which was felt by some to be intolerable. The failure of the campaign led to sterner repression. Diodoros (18. 11. 2) lists the Peloponnesian allies as Argos, Sikyon, Elis, Messene, and 'the inhabitants of the Akte', that is, the *poleis* of Argolis other than Argos and its dependencies (Pausanias 1. 25. 3–6 specifies Epidauros and Troizen, also adding Phleious). The Spartans, defeated a few years earlier, stood aside, perhaps fatally weakening the alliance. One might consider that they owed nothing to the Athenians, who had not helped Agis in 331. In the run-up to the war, however, Tainaron in Laconia provided Leosthenes of Athens with a base for a large force of mercenaries, many of them formerly in Alexander's service (Diod. 17. 108. 7; 111. 1–3; 18. 9. 2–3);[61] so the Spartans may have given tacit support to the preparations for revolt. (The Aristodemos episode in 314, see Section II.3.c, implies that Spartan permission was needed for recruiting activities at Tainaron.)

After defeating Athens and the southern Greeks in 322 – though the Aitolians fought on until 321 – Antipater installed a 'supervisor (*epimelētēs*) of the Peloponnese', one Deinarchos of Corinth (probably based in his home city and probably with military backup; Plut. *Phok.* 33. 3),[62] as well as garrisons. We have seen reason to doubt that such garrisons were common before the Lamian war; they would have made it almost impossible for the southern Greeks to launch their campaign, and in any case their imposition would have been incompatible with the aims and terms of Philip's Hellenic alliance. After the war, it was another matter, and Deinarchos may have been backed up with a detachment of troops which could be regarded as

---

[59] Carney 2001 accepts the mental infirmity but shows that Arrhidaios retained considerable agency as king.

[60] They may have included his own discharged soldiers: Cartledge 2016, 234.

[61] Hammond 1988, 107. On Tainaron as a Spartan base, not an international mercenary market as such, see Couvenhes 2008.

[62] Killed on Polyperchon's orders in 318, Plut. *Phok.* 33. 5. He is not the famous orator, also Corinthian but a metic at Athens (Suda s.v. Deinarchos conflates them).

a garrison. Polyperchon's later proclamation of restoring the constitutions that existed under Philip and Alexander – possibly an attempt to revive the Hellenic alliance[63] – implies that, where change occurred, it had been brought about by Antipater after the Greek defeat. Indeed, regime change at this date appears to have been widespread (see Section II.3.c). In light of the Greek attack on the Macedonians, power perhaps had to be enforced more crudely; Greek loyalty to the Hellenic alliance could no longer be taken for granted, or conjured up by threats of force made from a distance.

II.3.c The Subversion of Antipater's System and Growing Antigonid Power (319–301)

Antipater's attempt to 'pacify' southern Greece by force was disrupted by rivalry between other commanders. In 319, shortly before his death, he handed the regency of Macedonia, and effective leadership of the Hellenic alliance, not to his son Cassander (Kassandros) but to an older Macedonian, Polyperchon. In juridical terms, however, it was not Antipater's action but Cassander's violent response that made the logic of Philip's post-Chaironeia settlement unsustainable. That was perhaps unsurprising in the context of the warfare already under way among Alexander's generals in Egypt and Asia. Cassander's aspirations made the Peloponnese a springboard for those contesting control of northern Greece and Macedonia, inverting the previous geopolitical relationship.[64]

According to Diodoros, Polyperchon realized that Cassander could take over the cities of Greece from his father, since in some of them Antipater had planted garrisons while in others he had put his friends in charge of oligarchic constitutions (Diod. 18. 55. 2). In response to the threat from Cassander, Polyperchon proclaimed (in the name of Philip III) the cancellation of Antipater's measures against the cities that had fought against the Macedonians, and the restoration of 'the constitutions you had under Philip and Alexander' (56. 3).[65] This further confirms Alexander's generally *laissez-faire* attitude to constitutions in cities that remained loyal. Polyperchon also, however, followed the more high-handed example shown by the Exiles Decree by himself decreeing in 317 which cities were to take back their exiles as part of the restoration measures; though he allowed an exception for Megalopolis (56. 4–5). Conversely, he then ordered Argos

---

[63] Dixon 2014, 51.

[64] For Hieronymos of Kardia as a major source for Cassander's 'ruthless' energy, see J. Hornblower 1981, esp. 224–5.

[65] See also discussion by Billows 1990, 198–9.

to expel its former leaders from the time of Antipater, so that they could not hand the city over to Cassander (57. 1). Both measures amounted to support for democracy – or at least for those described as democrats – since the city-states had enjoyed it under Alexander, and this brought him the support of Athens; and despite his concession oligarchic Megalopolis remained sympathetic to Cassander (68. 3), as we shall shortly see. No doubt, however, Polyperchon was obliged to maintain or install garrisons in order to protect *poleis* from Cassander.

Polyperchon escalated his interference, ordering the cities not merely to expel but to put to death those who had been magistrates in Antipater's oligarchic regimes (Diod. 18. 69. 3) – though again this was part of his effort to restore constitutions to their earlier state. Most cities obeyed and made an alliance with him, but Megalopolis resisted; perhaps the only oligarchy strong enough to do so.[66] Diodoros describes in detail the resulting siege of Megalopolis (70. 1–72. 1), in which the Macedonians suffered heavy losses; we may suppose that many Peloponnesians were casualties on the Macedonian side. Although Polyperchon left a force in place to continue the siege, no more is heard of it and he presumably withdrew the army before the point at which Diodoros records (under the same year) the failure of the operation (74. 1). Polyperchon was perhaps more popular than Cassander among democrats, but his support came at a price; and his failure at Megalopolis weakened his appeal, as Diodoros observes in the context of Cassander's choice as governor of Athens in 317, the philosopher Demetrios of Phaleron (74. 4).

Also in 317, Philip III, under the influence of his powerful wife Eurydike, transferred the regency from Polyperchon to Cassander (Justin 14. 5), who was emboldened to launch a campaign in the Peloponnese. While he was away, Polyperchon invaded Macedonia with Olympias (mother of Alexander the Great) and put to death Philip and Eurydike (Diod. 19. 11. 1–7). Cassander was besieging Tegea when he heard the news (19. 35. 1), whereupon he agreed terms (of which we have no detail) with the citizens and hastened north to intervene. He would not be the last Macedonian commander who was forced to give up a Peloponnesian campaign in favour of pressing matters at home (see Section II.6).

In 316 Cassander took control of Macedonia and put Olympias to death in her turn (Diod. 19. 51. 1–6). Thereupon he decided on another Peloponnesian campaign (52. 5). Landing at Epidauros, which he doubtless pressed into submission, he forced Argos to adhere to his cause (54. 3),

---

[66] O'Neil 1995, 104.

gained the support of the cities of Messenia 'except for Ithome' (54. 4; i.e. the *polis* we generally call Messene), which may now have been allied to Polyperchon;[67] and secured Hermionis (the *polis* and territory of Hermion in Argolis) by negotiation (i.e. threats?). Returning to Macedonia, he left a garrison at the Isthmus (54. 4). His problem in the coming years, however, was keeping control of his power base in the south.

Cassander's next campaign forced Polyperchon and his son Alexandros (who was in charge of Corinth) onto the defensive; but in 314 they were still secure.[68] Help came from Alexander's former general Antigonos Monophthalmos ('One-eye'), based in Asia Minor, who sent Aristodemos of Miletos to forge an alliance with Polyperchon and raise a mercenary force against Cassander (Diod. 19. 57. 5). Aristodemos landed in Laconia, and with Spartan permission to recruit – presumably in Laconia, not only among Spartans – he came away with 8,000 soldiers from the Peloponnese (60. 1; so not only Laconians either). Although the Spartans had not, as far as we know, taken any steps against Macedonia since 331, this may be a sign that Kleomenes II and Eudamidas I, though little known to history, were not bereft of policies. Through Aristodemos, Antigonos appointed Polyperchon commander (*stratēgos*) of the Peloponnese (60. 1). At Tyre in Phoenicia, he issued his famous proclamation of Greek freedom (61. 3),[69] echoing that of Alexander after his victory at Gaugamela in 331 (Plut. *Alex.* 34. 2). In 313 he despatched fifty warships to the Peloponnese (Diod. 19. 62. 9).[70] Antigonos' strategy was evidently founded on a combination of financial inducements to potential recruits and a deliberate invocation of Philip and Alexander's earlier support for the *polis* system; it does not betoken a belief in the inherent superiority of democratic politics.[71]

This, as we shall see, did not prevent the Antigonids from imposing a garrison to keep a town loyal; the same pragmatism had been characteristic of Philip and Alexander. Cassander, on the other hand, is sometimes considered to have weakened his military effort by too readily supporting oligarchies 'and supplying them perforce with garrisons', in

---

[67] The failure to secure the support of Ithome is missed by Hammond 1988, 146, perhaps unaware that Ithome was the original name of Messene (see Shipley 2004b, 561–4 (*Inv. 318*). See further Chapter III n. 124. The story presumably confirms that the fortifications of Ithome–Messene were now complete. A Messenian–Macedonian treaty of *c.* 317 (*SEG* 47. 381; cf. 41. 320; 51. 456), was perhaps made when Polyperchon and his son Alexandros garrisoned Ithome in 317 (Diod. 19. 60. 1; 19. 64. 1; Themelis 1991, 86–7 no. 1).

[68] Billows 1990, 108, 111.

[69] Dillery 1995, 266.

[70] Billows 1990, 117 and n.

[71] On the Successors' use of the language of *polis* freedom, see Cartledge 2016, 234–5.

contrast to Antigonos who did so only out of necessity.[72] Polybios notes that Cassander (but also Demetrios, Antigonos' son) installed garrisons in the Peloponnese (2. 41). These years saw a number of notorious atrocities committed in his name. His general in Argos, Apollonides, captured Stymphalos and massacred hundreds of pro-Polyperchon democrats (Diod. 19. 63. 1–2, under 315/4). Cassander himself invaded the Peloponnese again, took Kenchreai, ravaged the territory of Corinth, seized two rural forts (φρούρια) where Alexandros had installed garrisons, and allowed the anti-Polyperchon faction in Orchomenos to massacre their opponents even though they had taken refuge in a sanctuary (63. 4–5).

Despite invading Messenia, Cassander temporarily gave up plans for a siege of the city when he found that Polyperchon had garrisoned it (Diod. 19. 64. 1). After installing a governor in Megalopolis and presiding at the Nemean games, he once more returned to Macedonia (64. 1). Alexandros sought to expel Cassander's garrisons, but was unexpectedly induced to desert his father and become Cassander's *stratēgos* in the Peloponnese (64. 2–4). A fleet sent by Seleukos (at this stage governor of western Asia, and allied to Antigonos) appeared at Kenchreai but left on learning of Alexandros' treachery (64. 4). Treachery by commanders seems a regular occurrence in these years (we shall see several examples later).

Cassander's Antigonid opponents, nominal upholders of Greek freedom, are not immune from charges of atrocities committed or condoned. We have noted that Polybios includes Demetrios among those who installed garrisons. Antigonos' envoy Aristodemos, having attacked and encircled Alexandros and the Eleians who were besieging Kyllene (Diod. 19. 66. 2, under 314/3), freed Patrai and Aigion from Cassander's garrisons, but allowed many citizens of Aigion to be killed while his army was looting the town (66. 2–3). In the same year, the fate of Dyme showed that brutality could be even-handed. Alexandros captured the town for Cassander with great slaughter, but provoked a decisive revolt by the survivors; they in turn, aided by the Antigonid force from Aigion, massacred their opponents (or possibly just the garrison; 66. 4–6). Alexandros was then assassinated at Sikyon (which he held); control of that city and of Corinth passed to his widow, the aptly named Kratesipolis ('Cityholder'), who suppressed opposition by crucifying some thirty citizens (67. 1–2).

Later Telesphoros, nephew of Antigonos, succeeding in expelling all of Cassander's garrisons except those of the late Alexandros at Sikyon and Corinth (Diod. 19. 74. 1–2, under 313/2).[73] In winter 312/1, however,

---

[72] Hammond 1988, 157.
[73] On the chronology of 312, see Billows 1990, 122 n. 52; cf. 225.

abandoning Antigonos' cause, he captured the *polis* of Elis, robbed the sanctuary of Olympia of 500 talents, and garrisoned Kyllene (87. 1–2). A further Antigonid commander, Ptolemaios or Polemaios, having 'razed' (κατασκάψας, lit. 'destroyed by digging') the fortifications of Elis erected by Telesphoros, 'liberated' that city, repaid the money Telesphoros had taken from Olympia, and negotiated the handover of Kyllene (87. 3).[74]

Antigonid forces now controlled nearly all the northern Peloponnese. Cassander, however, had not given up. Having disposed of the young Alexander IV in *c.* 310 (Diod. 19. 105. 2), in 309 he won Polyperchon his old enemy to his cause – just as he had earlier brought over Polyperchon's son Alexandros – sending him south as *stratēgos* of the Peloponnese (20. 28. 1–4). Polyperchon appears to have kept control of various mercenary garrisons; but in 308 Ptolemy, the Macedonian ruler of Egypt, 'liberated' Sikyon and Corinth from Kratesipolis (20. 37. 1; Polyainos 8. 58 says she handed it over against the wishes of her garrison) and attempted to revive the Hellenic alliance (Suda s.v. Δημήτριος ὁ Ἀντιγόνου).[75] Whether Ptolemy was interested in acquiring control of mainland Greece is debatable; probably a mixture of motives led him to intervene: pre-emptive harassment or distraction of Macedonia in its own 'back yard' may have seemed necessary to the security of Egypt and its own maritime possessions, while any opportunity to promote his reputation for success and benevolent patronage was not to be turned down lightly.[76] He does not, however, appear to have followed through: disappointed by the lack of support from a surely demoralized Peloponnese, he departed, leaving garrisons in those two *poleis* and allowing Cassander to keep the places he possessed (Diod. 20. 37. 2). Antigonos' position was weakened further by the desertion of Ptolemaios,[77] prompting him to launch, with his son Demetrios Poliorketes, the expedition that resulted in the liberation of Athens in 307 from the governorship of Demetrios of Phaleron.[78]

Alexander's legitimate heirs being dead, from 307/6 the leading Successors each adopted the title of *basileus*, 'king'. Antigonos I Monophthalmos and Demetrios I Poliorketes continued to harp upon the theme of Greek freedom. Their consistency, whether based on

---

[74] Billows 1990, 131. Telesphoros, surprisingly, reappears as an associate of Antigonos some years later.

[75] Billows 1990, 144–5 and n. 18; also 201.

[76] On the mix of Ptolemaic motives, cf. Shipley 2000b, 205–7. Bagnall 1976, 135, dates Ptolemaic tenure of Corinth and Sikyon to 308–303.

[77] Billows 1990, 145.

[78] Several years later, in 305, Polyperchon may have seized Corinth from Ptolemy: Hammond 1988, 176 – but wrongly citing Diod. 20. 100. 6.

conviction or on calculation, won them friends and civic honours.[79] In 304 Demetrios took Kenchreai (Plut. *Demetr.* 23. 1–3). Next spring (303) he 'liberated' Sikyon from Ptolemy (Diod. 20. 102. 2; Polyain. 4. 7. 3), refounding it on a new site (Diod. 20. 102. 2–4; Plut. *Demetr.* 25. 2).[80] Straight afterwards, he took Corinth from Cassander's general Prepelaos, garrisoning it at the request of the citizens (Diod. 20. 103. 1–3) – surely meaning the pro-Antigonid faction. It is, perhaps, from this date that we can begin to see the 'Fetters of Greece' (πέδαι Ἑλληνικαί) operating as an Antigonid chain of control comprising the four main harbours on the east coast – Corinth, Piraeus, Chalkis, and Demetrias – though they were not necessarily so named until a century later (by Philip V, according to Polyb. 18. 11. 5; cf. Livy 32. 37. 4, *compedes Graeciae*), by which time only three remained (Piraeus now being free; see Section V.1.c; cf. Plut. *Arat.* 16. 6; Strabo 9. 4. 14).

Demetrios moved on to 'liberate' Boura and another place with a garrison (φρουρά, Diod. 20. 103. 4), probably Skiros in south-eastern Arkadia.[81] Orchomenos was next on his list; with revealing ruthlessness, after the city's resistance was overcome with siege engines Polyperchon's garrison commander and eighty other opponents of the Antigonids were crucified in front of the walls, while 2,000 mercenaries were taken into Antigonos' army (103. 5–6). This hastened the surrender of 'those nearby occupying the forts' (presumably rural) and 'those garrisoning the *poleis*' (οἱ σύνεγγυς τὰ φρούρια κατέχοντες … οἱ τὰς πόλεις φρουροῦντες, 103. 7), which should mean the other Arkadian *poleis*. Continuing his triumphal progress, Demetrios went on to liberate Troizen[82] and Epidauros;[83] presided over the Heraia festival at Argos (Plut. *Demetr.* 25. 1–2); and may have

---

[79] On the frequency of honours to Antigonos and Demetrios, e.g. at Athens, and their probable spontaneity, see Billows 1990, 236 and n. 120. But B. exaggerates the originality and importance of Antigonos: see Derow 1993.

[80] Billows 1990, 170.

[81] 'Skyros' in the MSS of Diodoros (20. 103. 4); but the island in the Sporades can hardly be meant. Geer 1954, ad loc., notes Wesseling's suggestion of 'Skiros'. The only place of that name appears to be the possible town in N. Laconia (Shipley 2004a, 577), which may be identical with the Arkadian 'settlement' (*katoikia*) of Skiros 'near the Mainalians and Parrhasians' (Herodian, *On Orthography* 3. 2. 581. 23). It lay in a part of Sparta's perioikic territory given to Tegea by Philip II in 338 (Michel 452; Shipley 2000a, 373–4, 387).

[82] See McCabe's Halikarnassos no. 17, the honorific decree for Zenodotos, discussed at Billows 1990, 440 n. 120. Cyriac of Ancona recorded a corresponding decree at Troizen. Z., a citizen of Halikarnassos, had helped liberate Troizen from a garrison; the occasion is identified as Demetrios' campaign. See also Billows 1990, 208 and n. 54.

[83] *IG* iv² 1. 68 and 58. Billows 1990, 172 and n. 19 cites these, though 68 is evidence only because it was erected at Epidauros, while 58 only records Epidauros honouring a man also honoured at Athens as a member of Demetrios' court, see *IG* ii² 495.

'liberated' Elis.[84] Demetrios the 'liberator' was now in full control of the northern and central Peloponnese; control that was all the more secure for his personal presence (in partial contrast to the situation a generation later under Antigonos II Gonatas).

At the Isthmia of 302, Demetrios announced a new Hellenic alliance modelled on that of Philip, with a *hēgemōn* and council (*synedrion*; Diod. 20. 102; Plut. *Demetr.* 25. 3; cf. Diod. 20. 46 for his earlier plan). The new charter, like that of 337, is partly preserved (*IG* iv² 1. 68).[85] In its fragmentary text the names of the Eleians and Achaeans occur, but there must have been other members; it is not known whether Sparta was now among them. Despite Demetrios' occasional use of garrisons, the treaty left member cities autonomous and ungarrisoned[86] under their 'ancestral' constitutions, as in the earlier alliance, but required them to contribute military manpower, have the same friends and foes as Antigonos and Demetrios, and uphold their kingship. Macedonian control may have been firm: restrictions on calling magistrates to account were built into the constitution,[87] and a general 'in charge of common protection' was to be appointed.

Having swept across the northern Peloponnese with irresistible force, and doubtless dragooned political leaders in other *poleis* besides Orchomenos into loyal acquiescence, Demetrios was prepared now to adopt once more a public approach aimed at evoking the spirit of Philip and Alexander's alliance, and to earn himself plaudits for so doing.

II.3.d Retrospective of 338–301

Philip II's Hellenic alliance, and his general toleration of existing constitutions, seemed to augur more peaceful times; but first his death, then Alexander's departure for Asia, and finally Alexander's death all became the occasion for an attack on the Macedonians by the southern Greeks. Each attack failed, and the last provoked a U-turn in constitutional policy by Antipater; a repressive departure from the usual (though not consistent) Spartan and Theban policy of 'delegated power at a distance'. In the post-Lamian war climate, some of Alexander's immediate Successors

---

[84] Inferred from an instruction in the charter of the Hellenic alliance (see next note) which enjoins the Eleians to erect a copy of the document: *IG* iv² 1. 68 l. 136 (face B, fr. 5).

[85] *SdA* iii. 446; part trans. in Austin² 50; Bagnall and Derow 1981, no. 8; Harding 1985, no. 138; Ager 1996, no. 14; Canali de Rossi 2001, xvii no. 44 (giving addenda to *ISE* 44).

[86] Fr. 1 mentions the capture of garrisons by league members as warranting intervention; but this must refer to royal garrisons of a key nature, perhaps such as Corinth.

[87] Rhodes 2005, 7.

used not only garrisons but sometimes forcible political restructuring as instruments of domination, until Demetrios I – who since 314 had, with his father, proclaimed a more tolerant approach – set up a new Hellenic alliance in 301.

Submission, resistance, repression; but also structure and pacification: these had been the hallmarks of Philip II's settlement. The situation, as we have noted, created a familiar dilemma for those who were politically active in a *polis*: how to balance peace against independence. Alexander may have taken Greek forces into Asia partly as hostages for their cities' good behaviour; if so, it did not work. Despite unrest in Greece, however, he sent them home after the defeat of Darius (apart from those who wished to remain in his service) rather than dispose of them. Macedonian royal power in southern Greece after Chaironeia was a relatively light-touch affair, despite (or because of) the destruction of Thebes.

The Lamian war changed the terms of business between Macedonia and the southern Greeks. We now see garrisons and oligarchies being promoted by Antipater, with *polis* regimes owing loyalty to their external sponsor. This was to become a standard technique in the decades to come. Nevertheless, the decision of Polyperchon to win support by favouring constitutional reversal shows that the relationship between warlord and city was a dialogue; he preferred to influence the citizens, not coerce them if it could be avoided. It could not always be avoided, however, and the struggle between Polyperchon and Cassander in 319–314 was a particularly black period for the Peloponnese, with a second wave of misery in 314–312. The general population, not just the politically active, must have been desperate for some sort of peace.

Although we should not regard the Antigonids as inherently better behaved than others in this period, they contributed a measure of stability by generally adhering to their stated aim of respecting *polis* freedom. But Demetrios had to use considerable force in his triumphant campaign of the late 300s; and the best version of stability he could offer through his alliance's charter was to protect the interests of elite groups who were willing to keep their *polis* loyal, or at least neutral. This was, nevertheless, a situation involving dialogue and negotiation: *polis* leaders had to sign up to a code of conduct. It may be a case of one-sided diplomacy backed by the threat of force, but it was not the end of civic politics, such as had almost been brought about during Cassander's campaigns.

The pendulum swung between coercion and acquiescence, as it had under Spartan and Theban leadership; but all was still predicated upon the continuance of the *polis* system and of civic politics. This left considerable room for *polis* agency whenever the majority view of a citizen body changed. It is remarkable how many *poleis*, despite being forced or persuaded into Macedonian-sponsored alliances, despite having suffered in the wars of the Diadochoi, and despite the frequent imposition of garrisons, could still decide to send citizen soldiers against the Macedonians – and sometimes (as in 331, and subsequently in the early third century) to follow their old hegemon, Sparta, in so doing. To many, Spartan leadership may have seemed preferable to Macedonian coercion; perhaps on the principle that 'our masters then Were still, at least, our countrymen'.[88]

II.4 The Military Philosophers: Resistance and Reaction under the Antigonids (301–222)

The narrative of the first three-quarters of the third century forms the centrepiece of our historical study; but with the end of Diodoros' eighteenth book we enter a period devoid of continuous narrative sources apart from fragments of (that is, quotations from) contemporary authors and later retrospectives, chiefly Justin's useful epitome of Pompeius Trogus.[89] It is true that four *Lives* by Plutarch (*Demetrios, Pyrrhos, Aratos,* and *Agis–Kleomenes*) and, in less detail, passages of the second-century AD traveller Pausanias supplement the narrative. These are complemented by the piecemeal epigraphy; and from the 220s by the early books of Polybios (cited as 'P.' in the remainder of this chapter). On this basis, the present section attempts to lay a foundation for the discussion in Chapter III of issues including the degree to which military power rested upon garrisons and tyrannies; the aims of Macedonian rulers and whether there was a *pax Macedonica,* or indeed a *pax Achaica* later; whether Sparta's aims were still limited to imposing a more traditional *pax Laconica*; the behaviour of other states towards Sparta; and whether the pooling of sovereignty in the interests of security (or other interests) represented a partial or wholesale withdrawal from the political framework in which the *polis* was primary.

II.4.a First Interruption and Restoration of Antigonid Power (301–287)

Antigonid leadership of the new Hellenic alliance had been established for only a year or so when it was interrupted; though the hiatus would prove

---

[88] Byron, *The Isles of Greece*, 65–6 (quoted from Quiller-Couch 1900, 693).
[89] See Yardley *et al.* 2011, esp. appendix 5 (pp. 331–4) on what Justin leaves out.

temporary. In 301, at Ipsos in south-eastern Asia Minor, Antigonos and Demetrios were defeated, and Antigonos killed, fighting a coalition of the other leading Successors: Cassander, Lysimachos, and Seleukos. This resulted in the break-up of the alliance, leaving Demetrios with only a few coastal towns, chief among them Corinth.[90] At this point the city-states of the Peloponnese, some of them organized into blocs (most obviously Laconia; perhaps Messenia; in a different sense Eleia), presumably acted as wholly independent entities for a brief interval. Within three or four years, however, in 298 or 297, Cassander had died and Demetrios re-entered Greece. Before long, he controlled not only Corinth but also most of east-central Greece beyond the Isthmus, from Megara to Thessaly, and once more dominated Argolis, Achaea, and Arkadia.[91]

Around this time Pyrrhos of Epeiros, whom in 301 Demetrios had left to govern Greece (Plut. *Demetr.* 31. 2), attached himself to Ptolemy I of Egypt. In his place Demetrios appointed his son Antigonos (the future Antigonos II Gonatas), who appeared in this role in some part of Greece by 296.[92] When in 294 Demetrios captured Macedonia, Gonatas continued to govern southern Greece, though he does not appear to have tried to reconstitute the Hellenic alliance – a sign, perhaps, that his core interests lay outside the Peloponnese. These years represented the latest swing in Macedonian policy, back towards ruthless pragmatism, following Demetrios' more conciliatory gestures before Ipsos (see Section II.3.c). They also mark the beginning of temporally (though not spatially) continuous Antigonid domination of parts of the Peloponnese, especially in the north-east, until the 240s and perhaps, in places, until the early 220s.

Sparta has been absent from the narrative for some while (with only hints of tacit resistance: see Sections II.3.b, II.3.c), so it is doubtful whether (as Tarn claims) containment of Sparta was Demetrios' main aim in the Peloponnese.[93] Later in the 290s, however,[94] he seems to have tried to extend his mastery to the whole peninsula – an achievement Philip had never claimed despite invading Laconia – and focused his attention on Laconia and Messenia, both of which had perhaps stood aside from his Hellenic alliance of 302 (see Section II.3.c). After defeating Archidamos IV of Sparta (r. *c.* 305–*c.* 275) in a battle at Mantinea in 294 (Plut. *Demetr.* 35. 1; Polyain. 4. 7. 9), Demetrios

---

[90]   Tarn 1913, 11, is more positive ('a good deal of the Peloponnese'); cf. Will 1984, 101.
[91]   Tarn 1913, 50–1.
[92]   Tarn 1913, 20, citing *IG* xi. 2. 154A. 43–4 (296 BC), an Antigonos donating wood for a festival of Dionysos on Delos; *SEG* 48. 1033.
[93]   Tarn 1913, 66–8.
[94]   Will 1984, 105.

invaded Laconia and in a second battle killed 200 of the enemy and captured 500 (Plutarch does not specify how many of these 700 were Spartans, other Lakedaimonians, mercenaries, or allies). He then unsuccessfully besieged Messene (Plut. *Demetr.* 33. 2), which struck an alliance with Lysimachos either now or in the mid-280s (*SEG* 41. 322);[95] if now, it is the latter's first recorded involvement in the Peloponnese. Demetrios was prevented from consolidating his control of Sparta, however, as news of victories won by Ptolemy in Cyprus and Lysimachos in Asia Minor drew him away (35. 3–4).[96] Up to this point, he had adopted a more hard-line policy than before, dictated by military needs.

II.4.b Gonatas Meets Resistance (287–*c*. 267)

The next two decades saw the Antigonids apparently still in control of the northern Peloponnese, but seemingly doing little to combat the anti-Macedonian federation whose seeds were sown around 280 in Achaea; perhaps less troubled by it than by Pyrrhos' invasion in the late 270s.

In 287 Demetrios departed from Greece, for the last time as it turned out, to invade Asia Minor; he left Gonatas in charge,[97] but probably assigned him only enough manpower for defensive operations.[98] Athens, where the once popular Demetrios was now deeply disliked (if the moral narrative in Plut. *Demetr.* 26–7 is to be believed), had just revolted with partial success when Demetrios was captured by Seleukos; dying in captivity some years later.[99]

In the aftermath of his father's capture, Gonatas was concerned to defend the Antigonid fortresses. He retained Corinth and had the loyalty of Argos and Megalopolis ('of necessity', says Tarn: they needed protection against Sparta[100]). (The alliance between Messene and Lysimachos, previously mentioned, may instead belong in the years around 285.[101]) But when Pyrrhos abandoned Lysimachos and returned to Gonatas' side, it was northern Greece and Lysimachos that occupied Gonatas' attention.[102]

---

[95] *SEG* 41. 322 (*c*. 295?); cf. 45. 290; 51. 457 (*c*. 295 or *c*. 285?); Themelis 1990, 83–5, dates it 286–281; Matthaiou 1990–1 links it to Demetrios' attack on Messene (followed by Kralli 2017, 102–3), though at Matthaiou 2001, 229–31, he leaves the date open.

[96] Cartledge and Spawforth 2002, 31 (references at 238 n. 8).

[97] Tarn 1913, 92, 100–1.

[98] Tarn 1913, 103.

[99] Shipley 2000b, 124.

[100] Tarn 1913, 114.

[101] See n. 95 above.

[102] Tarn 1913, 115–18. The secret alliance between Gonatas and Pyrrhos is known from Phoinikides, *Auletrides*, fr. 1; see Hammond and Walbank 1988, 235 and nn. 2–3. (The statement of Eusebios that in 285/4 Gonatas took Sparta really refers to Doson in 222: Tarn 1913, 121 n. 21.)

Tarn assumes he was unpopular because he levied taxes upon the cities as Demetrios had done;[103] but there is no evidence for such a practice (see Section IV.2.b). We must also consider the question, discussed more fully in Chapter III, of how far Gonatas' power in the Peloponnese rested upon the systematic use of garrisons and tyrants; for now, we may note that it is hard to see a definite Antigonid policy in this respect before about the 270s, though Gonatas most probably maintained the tough stance towards the Greek *poleis* that his father had adopted in the 290s (see Section II.4.a).

In 281/0 a battle at Kouroupedion (or Koroupedion) near Sardis in western Asia Minor occasioned the death of Lysimachos directly, and indirectly that of Seleukos – the last two survivors among Alexander's generals. This conjunction of events, remote in space though it was, had an impact upon the Peloponnese, for it drew Gonatas away once again; this time to try to retake Macedonia. He was defeated at sea by Ptolemy Keraunos (exiled son of Ptolemy I),[104] an outcome which probably occasioned Sparta's first assault on Macedonian power in half a century. Also in 281/0, Areus I (r. 309–265) – who probably more than all other Spartan kings modelled himself on Alexander's Successors[105] – took the lead in promoting a further attack. Justin claims that 'more or less all the states of Greece' (*omnes ferme Graeciae civitates*, 24. 1. 2) rose against Macedonia; presumably a substantial number of Peloponnesians were involved.[106] Their only substantial achievement, however, was an attack on Aitolia,[107] a stratagem to avoid attacking Antigonos directly (24. 1. 3).[108] They failed to liberate Delphi from the Aitolians, however; and the venture collapsed after a costly defeat in Aitolia in which many Peloponnesians must have perished. Many states refused to give the Spartans any further aid, fearing that they wished to dominate the Peloponnese (*existimantes eos dominationem, non libertatem Graeciae quaerere*, 24. 1. 7)[109] – the eternal dilemma.

Another response to chaos in Macedonia – perhaps in concert with Areus' expedition – may have been the revival of the Achaean league as a federal union, which took place during the 124th Olympiad, 284–280 (P. 2. 41. 12); probably at the end of that quadrennium, in the aftermath of

---

[103] Tarn 1913, 115.
[104] Tarn 1913, 131.
[105] See e.g. Cartledge and Spawforth 2002, 28–37; Palagia 2006; more briefly, Shipley 2006a.
[106] Tarn 1913, 132–4, lists possible allies, but relies too much on inference. Kralli 2017, 119, argues that Isyllos' pro-Spartan hymn to Apollo Maleatas and Asklepios, inscribed at Epidauros (*IG* iv² 1. 128) and dated to *c.* 280, should precede Areus' defeat.
[107] Shipley 2000b, 125.
[108] See also Tarn 1913, 132–3.
[109] Tarn 1913, 133.

Kouroupedion. Polybios claims that the earlier league had operated a demo-cratic system, though the only evidence he gives is the abolition of the myth-ical kingship. In recent times, he says, the cities had fallen out with another and succumbed to Macedonian domination in the persons of Demetrios, Cassander, and Gonatas. Elsewhere he appears to imply that some of them had been under Macedonian domination (2. 41. 9–10; see Section III.2.c). Now the four westernmost *poleis*, those furthest from Gonatas' strong-hold at Corinth, took the initiative: first Patrai and Dyme, then Tritaia and Pharai. (The absentee in that district is Olenos, which probably still existed but may have been in decline.[110]) They were joined soon after by Aigion, Boura, and Keryneia. Polybios thus implies (though without specifics) that from the start the aim was to throw off kingly, specifically Macedonian, domination. We shall examine more closely in Chapter III the evidence for direct impositions by the kings. If there is any substance in the claims, the revival marks a break in their control of the northern Peloponnese, which in places had been almost continuous since the early 290s.

After their setback in 281/0, few Peloponnesians helped defend cen-tral Greece against an attack by the Galatai ('Gauls' or 'Celts') in 279; in some cases allegedly for fear of Spartan domination (Paus. 4. 28. 3 on the Messenians; 8. 6. 3 on the Arkadians; but at 7. 6. 7 he attributes their absence to indifference in view of the fact that the Galatai had no navy).[111] Among the Achaeans, only the Patraians sent a force, which suffered such heavy losses that their *polis* was reportedly 'dioikized', perhaps into settlements that had formerly been dependent *dēmoi* (Paus. 7. 18. 6 names Mesatis, Antheia, Bolina, Argyra, and Arba);[112] but it appears to have recovered before long, judging by Polybios' reference to the *chōra* of the *polis* in the 240s (4. 6) and by archaeological evidence (Sections IV.5.c, 6.a). The inva-sion of the Galatai,[113] however, led to Keraunos' death and in *c*. 277 to Gonatas' capture of Macedonia. Although he succeeded in holding on to his homeland – the start of over a century of continuous Antigonid rule there – it seems the Spartans continued to machinate against him: if Tarn is right, they established a relationship with Apollodoros, tyrant of Kassandreia in Chalkidike (Paus. 4. 5. 4), himself in contact with the new Seleukid king, Antiochos I (r. 280–261; Polyain. 6. 7. 2). This led nowhere, however, for Gonatas soon expelled Apollodoros from his city.[114]

---

[110] Morgan and Hall 2004, 483 (*Inv. 238*).
[111] Tarn 1913, 150.
[112] Morgan and Hall 2004, 477–8 (the *demoi*), 483–4 (*Inv. 239* Patrai), at 484.
[113] For a radical rethink of the invasion, and of the terms 'Galatai', 'Celts', and 'Gauls', see Campbell 2009.
[114] Tarn 1913, 172.

If it is correct to infer that the first four member *poleis* of the revived Achaean league – like the next two to join – had to divest themselves of (implicitly pro-Macedonian) governors or garrisons in order to combine, then it was perhaps after Demetrios' failure to return from Asia that Gonatas, following his father's example, sought to apply direct pressure to the northern Peloponnese through renewed impositions. The specific discussion of governors and garrisons in Chapter III, however, will suggest that Gonatas pursued such a policy only piecemeal and opportunistically; it would have been too costly, and indeed impractical, to attempt to impose a blanket system of puppet governors or 'tyrants'; he had more pressing concerns. We shall see, too, that there are some signs that the so-called tyrants of Peloponnesian *poleis* emerged from within their own citizen body. It is tempting to make a parallel with the Roman temporary magistracy of the *dictātor*, a man chosen by election or acclamation; the model had existed since at least the mid-fourth century, and perhaps recalls the archaic Greek role of *aisymnētēs* (arbitrator), a man brought in to resolve civil discord.

It is also intriguing to wonder why Gonatas did not, as far as we know, strike at the renascent league before its membership rose to ten with the accessions of Aigion, Boura, and Karyneia in 275 and of Leontion, Aigeira, and Pellene in 274. Either he could not muster the resources to act against it – perhaps because of more urgent business – or he did not think it worthwhile. In the latter case, it seems possible that from the Macedonian point of view it mattered little whether a city was kept friendly by a governor, with or without a detachment of infantry at his back, or was made quiescent – not actively hostile to Macedonian interests – by the realities of power relations. In any case, evidence concerning Pyrrhos' invasion of the Peloponnese (see the next paragraph) suggests that Gonatas' writ was still seen as running in substantial areas.

In 273,[115] Pyrrhos, having abandoned his campaigns in Italy and Sicily, and no longer Gonatas' ally, invaded the Peloponnese as a preliminary to assaulting Macedonia, as the early Successors had done – another testimony to the peninsula's significance for them, which perhaps was not so much positive (resources, manpower) as negative (its capacity to distract rulers and divert military resource if not kept inactive). At Megalopolis, he was met by envoys from Sparta (Plut. *Pyrrh*. 26. 20), whom he is reported to have told that he had come 'to liberate the cities under Antigonos' (ἐλευθερώσων τὰς ὑπ' Ἀντιγόνῳ πόλεις, 26. 10); if accurately reported, this implies that a substantial number were still seen as being under Macedonian domination,

---

[115] Date: Derow 2012b.

despite the tally of the Achaean league's members having reached double figures.[116] Other envoys came from Athens, Achaea, and Messene (Justin 25. 4. 4); the last of these helped Sparta against Pyrrhos shortly afterwards (Paus. 4. 29. 6), so these diplomatic missions are not evidence of any inclination towards Pyrrhos' cause.[117] The tide turned in Gonatas' favour in 272, in any case, when Pyrrhos treacherously attacked Sparta at the instigation of the exiled royal pretender Kleonymos (Plut. *Pyrrh.* 26. 9) but was defeated by the Spartans and Macedonians, cooperating for once (27–30); soon meeting his end while attacking Argos (31–4).

Gonatas had neutralized the danger from Pyrrhos in concert with the Lakedaimonians, and may have expected a time of calm in the Peloponnese. Antigonid power there, patchy and unsystematic as it appears to have been, may have been marginally diminished by the revival of an Achaean league; but Gonatas may not have been overly troubled by this development, so long as direct threats, for example to Corinth, did not materialize and the Ptolemies or Seleukids did not gain a foothold. Indeed, after the defeat of Pyrrhos it is possible that Gonatas' domination of the Peloponnese was reinforced, if Trogus (in Justin's summary) is correct in his claims:

> (1) After the death of Pyrrhos there occurred, not only in Macedonia but also in Asia and Greece, vast military campaigns. (2) For not only were the Peloponnesians handed over to Antigonos by treachery (*per proditionem Antigono traditi*), (3) but – since men variously felt fear or joy according to whether their particular cities had either hoped for assistance from Pyrrhos or had lived in fear of him – accordingly they either made an alliance with Antigonos or, because of hatred of one another, rushed into conflict.
>
> (Justin 26. 1. 1–3)

Talk of 'treachery' may refer, as Tarn suggests, either to Ptolemy II (r. 283–246) abandoning his interest in the Peloponnese for the time being, presumably for strategic reasons; or perhaps more likely to internal treachery within *poleis* by those ready to sacrifice independence in order to promote their own group's fortunes.

II.4.c Concerted Revolt and Harsh Response (*c.* 268–*c.* 252)

Spartan–Macedonian cooperation did not last; Antigonid power was soon subjected to another serious attack by Sparta among others; and

---

[116] Tarn consistently dismisses this, but perhaps insists too much.
[117] Tarn 1913, 269 n. 33.

the Ptolemies did indeed gain a beachhead. In the early 260s, probably in autumn 268,[118] an alliance of southern states launched a full-scale attack. Its failure was to have grave consequences for the Greeks. Modern scholarship calls the episode the Chremonidean war after the Athenian politician who proposed the relevant assembly decree.[119] The allies comprised Athens, Sparta, Elis (now post-tyranny), the Achaeans, five eastern Arkadian *poleis* (Tegea, Mantinea, Orchomenos, Phigaleia, Kaphyai; but not Megalopolis in the west), a number of Cretan towns,[120] and crucially Ptolemy II Philadelphos of Egypt (r. 283–246), who sought to check Gonatas' power in the Aegean.[121] Areus of Sparta, too, had his own ambition: the usual Spartan one of restoring Lakedaimonian hegemony in the Peloponnese.[122]

As far we can tell, the main action of the war was concentrated in the area from Attica to the Isthmus. Antigonid tenure of Acrocorinth blocked direct land contact between Athens and Sparta, and repeated Spartan attempts to force a passage were unsuccessful (Paus. 3. 6. 4–6). Gonatas raided the coastal demes of Attica, defended by Ptolemy's admiral Patroklos, whose main priority, however, seems to have been the Cyclades. Probably at this time,[123] Methana was occupied by the Ptolemaic navy as a base, and renamed Arsinoë;[124] part or all of its fortification wall was built or rebuilt about now.[125] It played an important surveillance role in the Saronic gulf,[126] and has been called part of 'Patroklos' ring around Attica'.[127] Under their new *ethnikon*, the people of 'Arsinoë in the Peloponnese' dedicated statues of Ptolemy II and Arsinoë II to Poseidon at Kalaureia (*SEG* 59. 367).[128]

---

[118]   Walbank 1984a, 236.

[119]   It is correctly viewed as an attack, not a revolt (Habicht 1997, 147). See now O'Neil 2008, dating the war from 268/7 to 262/1 or possibly 263/2.

[120]   *Syll.*³ 434–5; *IG* ii² 687; Austin² 61. Phigaleia is almost certain, cf. Φια[–, l. 39. Possible Cretan towns: Walbank 1984a, 236 n. 24. In *c.* C3f, perhaps not now, Messene made an alliance with five W. Cretan *poleis*: Aptera, Eleutherna, Sibrytos, Anopolis, and perhaps Phalasarna (*SEG* 60. 458; 58. 369; Themelis 2010, 60–2).

[121]   So Walbank 1984a, 237, following Will 1979, i. 180 ff.

[122]   Walbank 1988, 280. Tarn 1913, 293, sees the Spartans as recreating the Peloponnesian league; a fair point if we take the new association to be a network of alliances with Sparta, but Tarn probably means something more structured, given the usual view of the 'league' in his day. On the motives and interests of the Peloponnesian participants, see now Kralli 2017, 128–32.

[123]   Bagnall 1976, 135.

[124]   *IG* xii. 3. 466 = Foxhall *et al.* 1997, 273 no. 12; Gill *et al.* 1997, 74–5, where it is noted (74) that Patroklos may have chosen Methana as a base. Cf. Jameson *et al.* 1994, 87 (Ptolemaic from *c.* 268); 88 (reign of Ptolemy II); Bagnall 1976, 135–6.

[125]   Gill *et al.* 1997, 73; the site no. is MS103.

[126]   Tarn 1913, 341.

[127]   Bagnall 1976, 135.

[128]   Wallensten and Pakkanen 2009.

The Greek alliance broke up, however, after being defeated by Gonatas at Corinth (perhaps in 265/4) in a battle during which Areus lost his life (Plut. *Agis*, 3. 4; Trog. *Prol.* 26).[129] A recent reading of the war makes Ptolemy's caution about committing land forces to Greece a major factor in the campaign's failure.[130] Gonatas' victory led to the installation of a garrison in Athens (Paus. 3. 6. 6) and thirty-three years of direct Macedonian rule.[131] He followed up with a naval victory over Ptolemy near Kos (perhaps in 261),[132] which may have led to an Antigonid 'thalassocracy', or domination of the sea, in the 250s – a particularly obscure period.[133] We hear of no further Ptolemaic intervention in the Peloponnese until the next diplomatic move against Macedonia in the early 240s (see Section II.4.d) and subventions to Sparta in the mid-220s (see Section II.4.e). Corinth kept its Macedonian garrison, now commanded by Gonatas' half-brother Krateros.

Frustratingly, sources for the decade after the battle of Corinth are almost non-existent.[134] A Spartan attack on Megalopolis, in which the 'tyrant' Aristodamos repulsed king Akrotatos, may have occurred a few years after the battle.[135] The only other possible military incident involving Sparta at this time is an unsuccessful attack on Mantinea *c.* 250 (Paus. 8. 10. 5), whose genuineness is disputed. It is hard not to imagine that the defeat of the allies brought about an extension of Macedonian control, at least in the north-east and in parts of Arkadia.[136] Despite Gonatas' victory, however, it is evident that within a few years the Achaean league began to erode his power.

II.4.d The Achaean League Erodes Gonatas' Control (*c.* 252–239)

For whatever reasons, Gonatas was unable to stem the tide of Achaean league power permanently. Sikyon, after a series of 'tyrannies' or rather executive magistracies (Plut. *Arat.* 3–4; see Section III.2.b) that did not necessarily remove it from Antigonid control,[137] was 'liberated' in spring 251 from a

---

[129] Tarn 1913, 301. For the chronology, see Reger 1998, citing Dorandi 1991, 24–6, who in turn corrects Heinen 1972, 182–6; O'Neil 2008, 78–9, favours 265/4 for the battle.
[130] O'Neil 2008, esp. 83–9.
[131] Habicht 1997, 150.
[132] Walbank 1984a, 239–40. Reger 1998, reviewing Gabbert 1997, notes alternative dates.
[133] Walbank 1984a, 242–3.
[134] Tarn 1913, 311.
[135] Dated 260 by Tarn, acc. to Walbank 1933, 36; Walbank 1984a, 231, suggests *c.* 255.
[136] It is doubtful that the Arkadian league was revived: Nielsen 2002, 265; Nielsen 2015, 268), *contra* Tarn 1913, 359 n. 44.
[137] Walbank 1984a, 243.

governor who may have been seen as too friendly to Macedonia; the agent of change was Aratos, the 20-year-old son of a former leader of the city.[138] He had been an exile from boyhood, and his coup led to other, presumably anti-Macedonian, exiles being recalled (Plut. *Arat.* 9). To guarantee Sikyon's freedom, he enrolled it – presumably by persuading enough of the leading citizens to back the plan – in the Achaean league, even though the *polis* was Dorian (9. 6).[139] Cases such as this suggest that ethnic identity in federal leagues could have a primarily political value rather than denoting a (real or fictive) common ancestry.[140] (We return to regional identities at Section V.2.) The attachment of Sikyon to the league cannot have been welcome news for Gonatas, despite doubts raised on this point. It posed a clear threat to his possession of Corinth.

By 249, Gonatas' influence in the Peloponnese may have been confined to Argos and perhaps some small towns in Argolis.[141] At Corinth a son of Krateros, Alexandros, was now in charge but no longer sub-servient to Gonatas, carving out for himself a separate power base.[142] The Macedonian fleet based there was thus outside Gonatas' control.[143] After Alexandros' death, however, Gonatas took Acrocorinth by sub-terfuge from his widow, Nikaia, between 247 and 245 (Plut. *Arat.* 17. 4–6).[144] In midsummer 243, Aratos was able to return the compliment (18–23).[145] This put an end to simultaneous Macedonian control of all four 'Fetters'. Megara followed Corinth into the Achaean league (P. 2. 43. 5), where they were soon joined by Troizen and Epidauros (Plut. *Arat.* 24. 3; *IG* iv² 1. 70). In the context of this stage in Aratos' career, Polybios explicitly states that his overriding aims were 'the expulsion of the Macedonians from the Peloponnese, the suppression of the tyrants, and the re-establishment on a sure basis of the ancient freedom of every state' (P. 2. 43. 8).

Gonatas, however, may not have given up hope of controlling the nor-thern Peloponnese, for he allegedly made an agreement with the Aitolians

---

[138] Month of Daisios = Attic Anthesterion, Plut. *Arat.* 53. 5; Walbank 1933, 176, 202.
[139] Kralli 2017, 159–60, considers the motives of the league in admitting Sikyon.
[140] Beck 1997, 165–6.
[141] Tarn 1913, 366.
[142] Named 'king' in *IG* xii. 9. 212 from Eretria: Walbank 1984a, 247.
[143] Tarn 1913, 366.
[144] Tarn 1913, 372–3. Date: Walbank 1933, 178–9; Walbank 1984a, 250.
[145] Tarn 1913, 398–400, argues that there had been no hostility between the Achaeans and Gonatas, that he realized it was beyond his resources to retake Corinth and the *poleis* that followed it into independence. Both ideas are unconvincing; the latter in view of the Aitolian treaty.

to partition Achaea.[146] This plot (alleged by Lykiskos at P. 9. 34) prompted the formation of a coalition between Sparta, the Achaeans, and Ptolemy III of Egypt (r. 246–221), which may possibly be related to chariot victories won at Nemea and Olympia by Berenike, either Ptolemy's queen or a princess of the royal family, celebrated by the contemporary poet Poseidippos.[147] Events at Sparta over the following years, however, drove a wedge between that city and the Achaean league, hitherto its ally against the Macedonians.

The meteoric career of Agis IV (r. *c.* 244–241), the Spartan king in the Eurypontid line, is known chiefly from Plutarch's joint life *Agis and Kleomenes*, while the other subject of that joint *Life*, Kleomenes III (r. *c.* 235–222) of the Agiad dynasty, receives more nearly contemporary but hostile coverage from Polybios in his second book.[148] We shall return to Kleomenes later (Section II.4.e), but the two kings may be introduced together here.

We have seen time and again that even after severe defeats the Spartans did not see themselves as a spent force; but they still faced the problem of shrinking citizen numbers (see Section II.2.b). Increased reliance on mercenaries was one consequence; on Lakedaimonian *perioikoi*, another.[149] Both Agis and Kleomenes, like other leading men and women in the *polis*, were motivated by the desire to restore Sparta's hegemony, just as a number of their predecessors had been. To this end, they were prepared to embrace reform of debt and landholding – the first such proposals at Sparta, as far as we know – even at considerable personal cost to themselves and their peers, for the estates of richer families had clearly grown at the expense of the rest.[150] These schemes would reassign land to demoted Spartans and recruit *perioikoi* into the Spartiate citizen body from which the core of the Lakedaimonian army was drawn.

Perhaps fearing Agis' reformist tendencies, Aratos as leader of the Achaean league dissuaded him from meeting the Macedonians in battle at the Isthmus (Plut. *AK* 15).[151] When Agis returned home, he found that his proposals had been sabotaged by other rich citizens, and he was judicially murdered together with his mother and grandmother, influential supporters of his programme (*AK* 14–20). Agis' widow, Agiatis, was now given to Kleomenes, son of Agis' co-king, Leonidas, thus bringing the property of the Eurypontid royal

---

[146] Tarn 1913, 400–1.
[147] C. Austin and Bastianini 2002, nos. 82, 87; Cameron and Pelling 2012b (active 284–*c.* 250). On the identification see Thompson 2005; Dixon 2014, 94–5, opts for the queen.
[148] Shipley 2000b, 143–7; more detail in Cartledge and Spawforth 2002, 38–58.
[149] Shipley 2017a.
[150] Bresson 2016, 148–9, considers the possible numbers.
[151] Tarn 1913, 401.

line into the Agiad; but she is credited with making her first husband's ideals live again in her second, the future Kleomenes III. Sparta's underlying socio-economic, and thus military, problems remained severe; he would address them more ruthlessly when the time came (Section II.4.e). Even then, and after his defeat, the debate about possible remedies would continue to split the citizen body down to the reign of Nabis at the end of the third century.

At this time there was no inveterate enmity between Sparta and the league; they had fought Gonatas together in the 260s; but Agis' attempted reforms, though not revolutionary in the sense in which they have some-times been interpreted (see Chapter III), surely aroused wide interest across the Peloponnese, and may be considered symptomatic of wider stresses. A general concern must have been reawakened among civic elites, whether oligarchic or democratic, by any suggestion of land reform and debt can-cellation. These slogans could not mean the same in Sparta as elsewhere,[152] but a number of scholars have rightly emphasized the property-owning, oligarchic character of the Achaean league.[153] Aratos himself was a wealthy man from his early days;[154] later owning, for example, an estate, evidently of some size, in the territory of Sikyon or possibly Corinth (Plut. *AK* 40. 9) and, with his wife, property worth 60 talents (Plut. *Arat.* 19. 2). Any suggestion of land redistribution would alarm landed proprietors like himself; proposals to cancel debts would jeopardize the prospects of rich creditors. Both measures, as will be argued in Chapter III, extended only as far as the lower echelons of citizen bodies – themselves a privileged group. While they might apply to citizens of other *poleis*, such as resident aliens or, in Laconia, the free *perioikoi*, there was no suggestion of benefiting those beneath citizen status, such as slaves or free men too poor to qualify for citizenship. Nevertheless, they provoked enthusiasm in some quarters and consternation in others.

In 241, having avoided battle at the Isthmus, the Aitolians sacked Achaean Pellene, though Aratos claimed in his memoirs to have killed 700 of them there (Plut. *Arat.* 32. 3).[155] Tarn notes the Aitolians' ambitions in the western Peloponnese, evidenced by the ties they fostered with Elis, Phigaleia, and Messene as well as the later invasion of Laconia by which they aimed to restore those exiled after the fall of Agis (P. 4. 34. 9).[156] In spring 240 Aratos,

---

[152] Cartledge and Spawforth 2002, 40.

[153] Evidence assembled by O'Neil 1984–6; cf. Cartledge and Spawforth 2002, 43.

[154] Larsen 1968, 305–6.

[155] Probable peace treaty between Achaea, Aitolia, and Macedonia in 241/0 (Plut. *Arat.* 33. 1): Kralli 2017, 169.

[156] Tarn 1913, 382 n. 36. *Syll.*³ 472 (Schwyzer 1923, no. 71, *IPArk* 28), from Phigaleia: Messenian decree referring to Aitolian envoys. Messenian–Aitolian alliance: *SdA* 472; Walbank 1984a, 250, dates it to later 240s, perhaps 244.

who had earlier tried to kill the 'tyrant' Aristomachos I of Argos, unsuccessfully attempted to depose his son and successor Aristippos II (*Arat*. 25. 4–5)
and was fined by his own league.[157]

In Tarn's view this period marks the breakdown of Gonatas' system;[158]
but, as we shall see (Section III.2.c), it is hard to identify a system at all,
though there is a pattern in Gonatas' relations with civic leaders.

II.4.e Sparta's Resurgence and Further Defeat (239–222)

Gonatas was succeeded in 239 by his son Demetrios II. Even though the
Macedonians no longer controlled Corinth, it appears some tyrants were
able to lean on them for support. Demetrios appears to have acted vigor-
ously to shore up the remaining Antigonid presence in the Peloponnese;
but without the key stronghold he had limited scope for action. Instead
the Achaean league continued to grow with accessions of both western
and eastern Arkadian *poleis*: Heraia (Polyaen. 2. 36), probably Kleitor and
Thelphousa,[159] then Megalopolis (probably in 235; P. 2. 44. 5), and within
a year or two Orchomenos (*IG* v. 2. 344),[160] Mantinea, Tegea, and probably
Kaphyai (implied by P. 2. 46. 2).[161]

In 233 Demetrios invaded the Peloponnese, attacking the Achaeans;
at this time, unusually, allies of the Aitolians. It must have been on this
occasion that three of the newest members of the Achaean league – Tegea,
Mantinea, and Orchomenos – became instead members of the Aitolian
league;[162] evidently with Achaean permission during the Achaean–Aitolian
rapprochement of these years (P. 2. 46. 1). This bizarre-seeming move must
have been made as a security measure in face of Demetrios' aggression; perhaps with the consent of the *poleis*.

Under Gonatas' nephew Antigonos III Doson, king from 229, the major
power struggle in the Peloponnese would no longer be between the Achaeans
and the Macedonians, but between the Achaeans and the Spartans. Upon
Demetrios' death in 229, the tyrant of Argos – having perhaps enjoyed
his support – gave up power and became a general of the league (see
Section III.2.b); Polybios (2. 44) notes the demoralizing effect of the king's
death upon his adherents in the Peloponnese. The league's authority now

---

[157] Date: Walbank 1933, 204.
[158] Tarn 1913, 405.
[159] Mackil 2013, 107.
[160] Austin² 68.
[161] On these Arkadian accessions, see Kralli 2017, 180–8.
[162] They were 'in sympoliity with the Aitolians', τοῖς Αἰτωλοῖς … συμπολιτευομένας, when
       Kleomenes III seized them a few years later, P. 2. 46. 2.

extended over minor *poleis* in Arkadia and Argolis, including Hermion and Phleious. Within a few years, Kleomenes III would come close to re-establishing Spartan hegemony over the eastern Peloponnese. On the other side, Plutarch (*AK* 24. 8) tells us that Aratos' ambition was to bring into the Achaean league the Spartans, Eleians, 'and whichever Arkadians were inclined (προσεῖχον) towards the Lakedaimonians'; perhaps they were the only states unwilling to join.

Early in Kleomenes' reign, probably in 229,[163] after he had taken back from the Aitolians the eastern Arkadian *poleis* of Tegea, Mantinea, Orchomenos (P. 2. 46. 2), and perhaps Kaphyai[164] – the ephors sent him to seize the fort of Athenaion near Belbina, which had been one of Sparta's north-western dependencies until the intervention of Philip II but was now Megalopolitan; Plutarch justly calls it 'an entrance to Laconia' (*AK* 25. 1–2).[165] In response, the Achaeans resolved upon war (P. 2. 46. 4).[166] Aratos retook Kaphyai; in retaliation, Kleomenes captured Methydrion and ravaged the territory of Argos (*AK* 25. 7). In 227 he inflicted heavy defeats on the Achaeans near Mt Lykaion in Arkadia (26. 1; P. 2. 51. 3) and at Ladokeia in Megalopolitan territory (*AK* 26. 1; P. 2. 51. 3); the Achaeans in turn recovered Mantinea (*AK* 26. 1). Later in 227, Kleomenes was defeated at Leuktron near Megalopolis (27. 3) but captured Heraia and Asea (28. 5). We are not told how he administered the places he seized: whether by introducing reforms in the interest of one group within the citizen body, or, perhaps more likely, through the now usual technique of installing a garrison.[167]

Building on his military successes, Kleomenes now eliminated internal opposition (*AK* 29–31) as a prelude to a programme of institutional transformation similar to that which Agis IV had attempted. He arranged the assassination of four out of the five ephors (29), exiled eighty other citizens (31. 1), and enacted sweeping reforms (32) by which the core territory of the Spartan *polis* was redivided and many of the other Lakedaimonians (the *perioikoi*) brought into the Spartan citizen body (presumably without losing any land they owned in their home *polis*).[168] The Spartiate core of

---

[163] Talbert 2005, 241 n. 6 (Talbert 1988, 73 n. 1).

[164] Walbank 1933, 72–3, asserts that Kleomenes' deal with the Aitolians in 229 resulted in the transfer of these four cities to him, which they had acquired in 233 (this at p. 67). This may be an inference from the fact that Aratos attacked Tegea and Orchomenos in 229 or early 228 and later took Kaphyai (Plut. *AK* 25. 3 and 7). Date of 229: Walbank 1933, 206.

[165] Belbina: Shipley 2004a, 579 (*Inv.* 326).

[166] Walbank 1933, 206.

[167] Kralli 2017, 215, following Urban 1979, 168–9, points out the E. Arkadian *poleis* supported Kleomenes before his reforms at Sparta, and that there is no evidence of calls for reform there.

[168] Shipley 2017a.

the army, which had fallen to 700 or fewer[169] by the accession of Agis IV *c.* 244 (5. 4), was brought up to a strength of 4,000 (32. 1–2); the role of those who remained as *perioikoi* was probably formalized; and the traditional education (*agōgē*) was 'revived', or more likely redesigned. When, in the same year, his co-king, Archidamos V, died or was assassinated, Kleomenes ensured the elevation of his own brother Eukleidas to the vacant throne – the only occasion in Sparta's history, as Plutarch notes (32. 3), when both kings were from one family.[170] An alliance with Elis in the north-west of the Peloponnese, implied by later actions, was probably forged now.

The second phase of Kleomenes' military campaigns ranged further afield. In 226 he ravaged the territory of Megalopolis (33. 2), helped pro-Spartans in Mantinea expel their Achaean garrison, threatened Achaean Pharai, and defeated the league near Dyme and at Lasion,[171] expelling their garrison from the latter and handing the town to the Eleians (35. 5). His continuing successes induced Ptolemy III to transfer financial support from the Achaean league to Sparta (P. 2. 51). At this point in the narrative, Plutarch (*AK* 36. 1) reports an offer made by Kleomenes to the Achaean league to return their captives and 'places' (χωρία, probably towns and outlying forts) in return for making him their leader,[172] Aratos having resigned.[173] The Achaeans were minded to accept – the two states had been allies against Macedonia within living memory – but Aratos frustrated their wish by opening a channel of communication with Doson, secretly at first (37. 1–3); a refusal which Plutarch says spelled disaster for Greece.

As early as winter 227/6 (possibly even in late 229),[174] Aratos made contact with the king (P. 2. 47–50), and by early 225 agreement had almost been reached (*AK* 38. 2).[175] Polybios, in the voice of Chlaineas the Aitolian, comments on why Doson agreed to help the league, 'observing that his own domination (δυνάστεια) would not be firmly based if you [*the Spartans*] obtained the governance (ἀρχή) of the Peloponnese' (9. 29. 10). It is a telling comment; Polybios evidently believes that Antigonos now had little or no

---

[169]   'Not more than 700 Spartiates' (ἑπτακοσίων οὐ πλείονες Σπαρτιᾶται); not 700 *families*, as in the Loeb translation.

[170]   On the implications of the land reorganization, see Shipley 2017a.

[171]   Talbert 2005, 243 n. 29 (Talbert 1988, 82 n. 3) notes that the MS reading of Langon has been emended to Lasion.

[172]   παραδιδόναι … τὴν ἡγεμονίαν, sc. of the league, not of 'the Greeks' as in the Loeb translation.

[173]   If Kralli 2017, 244–5, is right to argue that Kleomenes would not have wanted the generalship of the league, this offer may have been made in the expectation that it would be declined.

[174]   Walbank 1933, 206.

[175]   Date: Walbank 1933, 207. Kralli 2017, 245, argues that the league's failure to retain Corinth, Orchomenos, and probably Heraia proves that it 'had lost control' of the situation.

power in the peninsula but foresaw problems if Sparta, rather than Achaea, should gain the hegemony. It is further evidence of the fundamentally precautionary nature of Antigonid intervention in the Peloponnese. The agreement entailed returning Corinth to Macedonian control.[176]

News of the realignment – formally a revival of Demetrios I's Hellenic alliance, as Polybios implies (2. 54. 4) – led Kleomenes to embark on the most aggressive, wide-ranging, and successful part of his campaigns (225–224), by which he briefly became master not only of Arkadia but also of the north-eastern Peloponnese and eastern Achaea (P. 2. 52). He expelled the Achaean garrison from Pellene, won the support of Pheneos and the fort of Penteleion, and by means of a surprise attack during the Nemean games was able to garrison Argos (Plut. *AK* 38. 6–8) – the first time Sparta had captured its ancient foe (39. 1). At Argos (and perhaps elsewhere?) he promised a reform programme including the cancellation of debts (41. 6), which induced the peoples of Kleonai and Phleious to join his cause (40. 1) and led Aratos to fear that Corinth might follow them (41. 2). Having secured Troizen, Epidauros, and Hermion, Kleomenes besieged Acrocorinth and ravaged Sikyonia (P. 2. 52; *AK* 40. 6–8). The renewal of the Heraclid leadership that might have made the Peloponnese great again – nostalgically lauded by Plutarch under the influence of Phylarchos (37. 2–4) – must have seemed certain to some.

Probably by early 224, however, a group in Argos, aggrieved at Kleomenes' failure to deliver reform, conspired to bring back the Achaeans (P. 2. 52–3; Plut. *AK* 41. 5–42. 5).[177] Fearing an invasion of Laconia, Kleomenes abandoned Corinth and Argos to the Macedonians (P. 2. 54) and retreated to Tegea, effectively giving up his new conquests at a stroke (*AK* 42. 7). Probably in late 224, Doson took Kleomenes' north-western forts at Aigys and Belbina. In spring 223 he recovered Tegea by siege, Orchomenos by assault, and Mantinea by siege, also receiving the surrender of Heraia and Thelphousa (P. 2. 54; *AK* 44. 1).[178]

Kleomenes, however, broke out of Laconia once more in a surprise attack. Having attacked Megalopolis three months earlier (P. 2. 55. 5; 9. 18. 1–4; or five months?),[179] he now devastated its urban centre (though he did

---

[176] Details are awaited of alliances concluded between Philip V and Greek states at the start of his reign; the texts, displayed at Corinth, were deliberately destroyed, perhaps by the Romans in 198: *AGOnline* ID 1883 (2010); *SEG* 48. 390; 61. 245.

[177] Date: Walbank 1933, 208.

[178] Date: Walbank 1933, 208.

[179] Walbank 1957–79, i. 258, shows that either P. has miscalculated or the number has been corrupted in transmission.

not occupy the city) after the citizens, influenced by the young Philopoimen among others, refused to take the city out of the Achaean league (P. 2. 55; Plut. *AK* 44–6). In spring 222 he ravaged Argive territory but failed to tempt Doson out to battle (P. 2. 64; *AK* 46. 5–8). When Doson did move, Kleomenes expelled the Macedonian garrison from the hill of Olygyrtos (or Oligyrtos) near Kaphyai in north-eastern Arkadia.[180] But the game was almost up: Ptolemy III cancelled his financial subventions (P. 2. 63), and ten days later Kleomenes' army was almost wiped out at Sellasia in northern Laconia (2. 65–9; *AK* 48–9).[181] Sparta's renewed military strength is made clear, ironically, by the casualty figures. Plutarch (49. 8) states that many (or 'most') of Kleomenes' mercenaries (ξένοι) were killed, along with all but 200 of the 6,000 Lakedaimonians present; if true, this represented almost one-third of the entire Lakedaimonian population (assuming that Kleomenes' reforms had successfully raised Spartiate numbers to 4,000 and that the defined number of the *perioikoi* was 15,000, as in Agis' plans twenty years earlier). There is some uncertainty about the text, however;[182] and in any case Justin (28. 4. 9) numbers the survivors as 4,000. At any rate, it was a disastrous outcome.[183]

Kleomenes escaped to Egypt, killing himself three years later after a futile attempt to overthrow Ptolemy IV (P. 2. 69; 5. 35–9; Plut. *AK* 50–8). Doson captured Sparta – the first invader to do so – but had to leave urgently to meet an Illyrian threat in the north, once again showing where the ultimate priorities lay for rulers of Macedonia. On his way north he is said to have restored the earlier form of government at Tegea (P. 2. 70), presumably installing a Macedonia-friendly regime. Once back in Macedonia, he unexpectedly died. Polybios understandably emphasizes the role of chance (2. 70; cf. *AK* 48): if Kleomenes had held out for a few more days, Sparta might have survived. Despite this counterfactual possibility, the Achaean league and the new Macedonian king, Philip V, would probably have achieved their desired outcome before many years had passed, in view of the overwhelming manpower and resources available to the Macedonians.

---

[180] Walbank 1957–79, i. 460, on Polyb. 4. 11. 5; cf. 4. 70. 1.

[181] Usually dated 222 or 221. Walbank 1933, 170–2, accepts arguments for a date of 223, but later adopts 222 (e.g. Walbank 1984b, 469; Walbank 1992, 173).

[182] The Teubner text (Ziegler 1971) reads τῶν ξένων <τοὺς> πολλοὺς λέγουσι καὶ <τοὺς> Λακεδαιμονίους ἅπαντας πλὴν διακοσίων, ἑξακισχιλίους ὄντας. The Loeb (Perrin 1921) lacks the supplements; Marasco 1983, 163 and 583–5, tacitly adopts them.

[183] Rightly emphasized by Marasco 1983, 583. He is unnecessarily troubled (584) by the 6,000 Lakedaimonians; the figure does not necessarily contradict the 4,000 of *AK* 32. 3, who are Spartans (in principle a subset); cf. Shipley 2017a. The *numbers* are certainly very high compared with Cl battles: Krentz 2005.

The immediate results of Sellasia were Achaean control of the Peloponnese and the end of the Spartan dyarchy (already modified in the direction of sole kingship by Kleomenes,[184] and by earlier kings such as Areus); the city's incorporation into Doson's Hellenic alliance (implied by P. 4. 24. 4);[185] and the placing of some of its last remaining northern *perioikoi* under Achaean protection, presumably within the league.[186] Despite this further reduction in perioikic territory, Polybios' view – expressed both in his own voice (2. 70) and in the speech of Lykiskos (9. 36. 4–5) – is that Doson treated the Lakedaimonians mildly. We have noted that in Polybios' opinion Doson feared Spartan control of the Peloponnese; but allowing for Polybios' Achaean bias, it is equally possible that Doson would not have wished to eliminate either of the potential hegemons but preferred to maintain a balance of power. Whether or not this is the case, his mild response looks like another attempt at soft, or delegated, power from a distance.

The issue of control of the Peloponnese appeared to have been settled; but, as so often in the periods covered by the present study, it was far from the end for Sparta as an active force. Within a very few years, it would again be a thorn in the side of the Achaeans and the Macedonians.

II.4.f Retrospective of 301–222

Ipsos had led to the rapid demise of the new Hellenic alliance and to new inter-Macedonian wars in the Peloponnese; Demetrios' policy hardening as he tried to achieve sovereignty over the peninsula. His ejection from the drama in 287 fomented further conflict among the Successors. A further Greek 'rising' in 281/0 forced his son Gonatas, too, into a harsher stance involving, when opportunities presented themselves, support for local governors ('tyrants' to their enemies). The 'forced marriage' of Sparta and Macedonia against Pyrrhos might have been expected to result in a more harmonious, even shared hegemony; but the Chremonidean war put paid to that, and may have provoked repression on Gonatas' part (unfortunately, the sources for *c.* 262–251 are very thin). For whatever reasons, it appears he was unable to stem the tide of Achaean league power for long. He lost Sikyon; eight years later Corinth. In response to Gonatas' death in

---

[184] See Marasco 2004 (*non vidi*). Also Shipley 2005a.

[185] Cartledge and Spawforth 2002, 57, following Walbank 1957–79, i. 470.

[186] Shipley 2000a, 377–9. Kralli 2017, 247–51, considers in detail Gonatas' awards of Spartan territory to Sparta's neighbours; and that the Sparta–Megalopolis arbitration referred to in *Syll.*³ 665 (*IvO* 47; C2b) took place immediately after Sellasia.

239, Demetrios II may have tried to boost pro-Macedonian governors, but without Corinth his scope for action was limited.

Macedonian intentionality and design must not be overstated; an important thread in the story is the retention of 'agency' by the Peloponnesian states. At Sparta, the reforms of Agis IV were blocked by internal forces, but were adapted and carried through in the 220s by the more ruthless Kleomenes III, who at one stage might have become leader of the Achaean league. Only Aratos' desperate U-turn and the league's alliance with Antigonos III Doson appeared to offer resolution of the 'eternal questions' of control of the Peloponnese and, for many, of Sparta; but after defeating the Spartans Doson treated them mildly – perhaps minded to divide and rule, as Philip may have been in 338, and not wishing to build up the Achaean league too far.[187] His Hellenic alliance of *c.* 223 can be seen as a new attempt at 'delegated power from a distance'.

An account of this period, in large part, must be effectively a commentary on the inadequate sources; it is not always possible to establish with certitude the configurations of alliances and alignments, or detect long-term continuities in particular states' external allegiances. The reconstruction attempted here suggests, however, that even with full evidence it would be unwise to suppose that one could draw lines on a map enclosing a Macedonian 'sphere of influence'; or that the period falls into defined phases (for example, of resistance and freedom); or that Gonatas pursued a systematic strategy of constitutional change. Nevertheless, it is possible to observe that Antigonid domination of the Peloponnese from soon after 301 (especially in the north and north-east) brought more order than chaos and continued the 'dialogue' model of king–*polis* relations. As already noted, Macedonian rulers appear to have alternated between harshness and mildness, though the former was more usual and our sources make clear that, at least at certain junctures, the Macedonians were seen as exercising conscious domination of a significant part of the peninsula: we may recall the telling words attributed to Pyrrhos (he came *to free* the Peloponnese, Section II.4.b) and Doson (fearing to *lose control* to Sparta, Section II.4.e).

The addition of the Achaean league to the existing blocs of city-states (eastern and western Arkadia) and centralized regions (Eleia, Messenia, Laconia, Argolis) appears to continue the earlier trend towards regional entities (the main exceptions being Sikyon and Corinth). It also seems to have tilted the balance of power against Macedonia. Federal and similar unions were not new; Spartan hegemony represented an alternative model,

---

[187]   Kralli 2017, 255, indeed, regards the league's success in 222 as illusory.

one that seemed preferable to some participants when compared with either Macedonian or Achaean domination (after a long period when Sparta was aligned with the league). At times, Sparta could be a focus for opposition. It represented, however, a different kind of threat to the autonomy of *polis* elites, whose interests Demetrios' league had attempted to safeguard; and it is the *polis* context, above all, that must be kept in mind despite the rise of multi-community unions: those groups among Peloponnesian elites who persuaded their fellow citizens to attack Macedonia again and again would not have done so if they had not been desperate to safeguard their own political freedom (as well as economic: see Chapter IV).

II.5 The Soldier's Art: Achaea between Macedonia and Rome (222–197)

The story of the post-Sellasia period is primarily that of the relationship between the Achaean league and Philip V of Macedonia, their ally for some twenty years from his accession in 221. The young king, as hegemon of Doson's Hellenic alliance (built around the Achaeans), could expect his partners to spare him some of the effort of keeping the Peloponnese quiet; but Doson's intervention, and the forcible reconstruction of Sparta, by no means spelled the end of unrest. Instead, a situation developed which reinforced separatist tendencies in areas such as Arkadia. The grit in the mechanism was internal tension between groups with differing interests within *poleis*, whether inside or outside the league. Internal schism at Sparta, for example – as later elsewhere – appears to reflect a clash between those who thought compliance with Macedonia under Achaean management the safest course, and those who preferred their *polis* to be independent, perhaps because they feared being marginalized or worse under the league. Additionally, pressing socio-economic tensions were a threat to stability, though it is important to read these precisely (see Chapter III).

An external factor in the shape of the Aitolian league gave the Spartans an opportunity to undermine Doson's settlement, and opened up new rifts within the peninsula which embroiled Philip in years of warfare. He might nevertheless have succeeded in maintaining control, but other agents – above all, Carthage and Rome – ultimately made it impossible. It was to be the last generation of Macedonian power in the Peloponnese; but that end could not be foreseen yet, and for a few years Philip seemed destined to take over the role of benevolent guardian.

II.5.a Aitolian Opportunism and Spartan Alienation (222–217)

Doson had revived the Hellenic alliance, in whose name the campaign of 222 against Sparta had been waged and which was designed to fence in the Aitolians.[188] Their response was predictable; but Polybios suggests (4. 7) that people in the Peloponnese thought their troubles were over and neglected military preparations, only to find themselves embroiled in a defensive war. Aratos had to act swiftly to restore the Achaeans' military capability. On the one side were the Hellenic alliance, supported by the Achaean league and officially Sparta; these 'Allies' (*socii* in Latin) have given their name to the 'Social' war (220–217). With Aitolia were ranged only Elis and – at first covertly – Sparta.[189]

The Aitolians had controlled the Delphic amphiktyony since 277, subsequently expanding their territory as far as the Maliac gulf in Thessaly. Living by raiding was nothing new for them (cf. P. 30 fr. 11), and Polybios comments that they had always presented a danger to the north-western Peloponnese (5. 3; cf. 4. 62); elsewhere he notes the vulnerability of that area to raids from the Adriatic, specifically Illyria (2. 5). More recently, they had cultivated close relations with *poleis* in the western Peloponnese, notably in Eleia and at Arkadian Phigaleia, which by 221 was a member of their league (4. 3. 6), doubtless against the wishes of some of its citizens.

Messenia, however, had been affected little by the war of Kleomenes (P. 4. 5. 5), appearing in Plutarch's life of the king principally as the place where in 223 the people of Megalopolis took refuge (*AK* 45. 2, 7–8). Now the Social war was provoked by Aitolian raids upon Messenia as well as Achaea (P. 4. 3–4, 6, 11–12);[190] this was sheer opportunism on the part of the Aitolians, observing Lakedaimonian 'alienation' (ἀλλοτριότης) from the Messenians (4. 5. 4). The raiding, combined with the enrolment into the Aitolian league of Phigaleia on Messenia's northern border, jolted the Messenians into taking part in the war (5. 4. 5). Spartans no doubt recalled the machinations in their interest by exiled Messenians in Megalopolis before its sack by Kleomenes (2. 55); these men had presumably not survived or were still excluded from their *polis*, which according to Polybios was strongly oligarchic around 220 (4. 31). These circumstances may have made the Spartans wary of Messene, though there may have been anti-Achaeans still in the *polis*.

At Sparta, despite the pro-Achaean government imposed after Sellasia, an anti-Macedonian view gained ascendancy, and soon the city was following

---

[188] Cartledge and Spawforth 2002, 61.

[189] Summary at Scullard and Derow 2012.

[190] Note also the stopover in 220, presumably with raiding, at Messenian Pylos by the Illyrian commanders Demetrios of Pharos and Skerdilaidas, Polyb. 4. 16.

an independent line. When the Achaeans declared war on Aitolia (P. 4. 13) and sought help from both Sparta and Messene (4. 15), the Spartans allegedly made secret overtures to the Aitolians (4. 16) in defiance of their new obligations;[191] they were to pursue an anti-Achaean strategy during the war except when compelled to behave otherwise. The Aitolians in their turn declared war, attempting unsuccessfully (4. 15–16) to detach Messene (and presumably other Messenian towns, perhaps more manipulable for having once been Lakedaimonian *poleis*) from the cause of the league; no doubt they were aware of anti-Achaeans within Messenia. In the north, the Aitolians renewed their attacks on the territories of Pellene and Sikyon; and in an infamous episode (4. 16–19) destroyed the north-western Arkadian city of Kynaitha, a member of the Achaean league, even though it was anti-Achaeans in the *polis* that had invited them in, after returning from exile and gaining the upper hand.[192]

Among the Messenians, as already noted, there were competing tendencies. They are castigated by Polybios (4. 31–2) for their reluctance to adhere to the allied cause, though like the Spartans they were eventually forced to declare their support in 218 (5. 3–4). In Sparta, however, despite a Macedonian garrison (20. 5. 12),[193] there had been *stasis* as early as 220 (4. 22–3), prompting some to urge Philip to 'hand over the state [πολίτευμα, i.e. Sparta] and the magistracies to his own friends' (4. 23) – a revealing example of how Macedonian power could be delegated. Despite what we can deduce was a significant group of pro-Achaeans in the city, its commitment to the Allies quickly proved hollow; at least, the anti-Macedonians kept the upper hand despite the continual recurrence of *stasis*, such as in 219 (4. 34) and 218 (4. 81), presumably pitting pro- and anti-Achaean factions against one another; the ephors of three successive years being killed or exiled. For the moment Philip stayed his hand, but a comment by Polybios, earlier in his account of the war, has interesting implications: he says Philip retained Orchomenos in contravention of the post-Sellasia settlement because it was strategically important for access to the interior of the Peloponnese (4. 6). Despite its humble status (it is not one of our 'top twenty' Peloponnesian *poleis* (in Section V.2.a) though it issued coins in the early and mid-fourth century: TABLE IV.3), Orchomenos does indeed control entry to and exit from the northern end of the eastern

---

[191] Polyb., however, makes this assertion in the course of general reflections on the situation (4. 16), so it may be an anticipation of the alliance developed at 4. 35. Walbank 1957–79, i. 463, doubts its truth.

[192] For reappraisal of the Kynaitha episode, see Kralli 2017, 179–80.

[193] There is a view that it was removed by 220; this may be an inference from the later outbreak of *stasis*. See Cartledge and Spawforth 2002, 61–2; Ehrenberg 1929, 1435.

Arkadian plain, and thus Sparta's main route to the north coast of the Peloponnese. The reality was, perhaps, that because of Sparta's unreliability Philip could not afford to relax his grip upon any of his strongpoints; though it would take a lot to make him attack Sparta directly.

The Spartans veered between a reluctant pretence of participation in the allied cause in 219 (P. 4. 33) and an unwillingness to abide by Doson's settlement; that is, different Spartans held opposing views.[194] The anti-Macedonian tendency became dominant; Sparta regained its dual kingship, elevating to one throne the young Agesipolis III (r. 219–215) under a regent; to the other a certain Lykourgos (r. 219–*c.* 212), who was allegedly unrelated to either royal house and had 'bought' his descent from Herakles with presents to the ephors (4. 35); he was perhaps from a non-royal Heraclid family (like the famous Lysander, Plut. *Lys.* 2. 1) but nevertheless related to the Eurypontid line.[195] The Spartans now moved to open hostility towards the Achaeans and their allies. Lykourgos attacked Argos' southern possessions, recapturing a string of former Lakedaimonian perioikic *poleis* in eastern Parnon (Polichna, Prasiai, Leukai, and Kyphanta) but failing to take the inland fort of Glyppia (or Glympeis) or the concealed harbour town of Zarax (P. 4. 36).

In 218, however, the Spartans once more behaved in contradictory fashion, presumably because of internal disagreements. First they were induced to change tack by following the lead of one Cheilon,[196] described by Polybios as a claimant to Lykourgos' throne who cultivated the support of the 'mass' (πλῆθος, 4. 81. 2–3) with promises of land redivision along Kleomenean lines. After securing the murder of the ephors, however, he failed to capture Lykourgos, only driving him into exile briefly before himself being forced to leave (4. 81. 9–10). Differences of view among Spartans – and perhaps among the wider community of perioikic Lakedaimonians, whose influence upon Sparta was probably growing during the late classical and early hellenistic periods[197] – may have corresponded to different economic interests and political allegiances within the propertied class. Rather than a division between 'hawks' and 'doves' both seeking Sparta's ancient goals, the confrontation may have been between pro- and anti-Achaeans.

---

[194] A 'vaguely Cleomenean political tendency' survives Sellasia: Cartledge and Spawforth 2002, 58.

[195] Walbank 1957–79, i. 484, on 4. 35. 14. Cartledge suspects the claim of fraud was a slur (Cartledge and Spawforth 2002, 62).

[196] Cartledge and Spawforth 2002, 64. The name Cheilon, equivalent to Chilon, was also that of Sparta's C6m lawgiver (e.g. Hdt. 1. 59); was it assumed?

[197] Shipley 2017a.

The anti-Achaean group may have included any of Kleomenes' new citizens who had survived Sellasia, if they had not been relegated to their former status. With Lykourgos back in charge, the Spartans, 'fearing Philip's presence' (4. 81. 11), demolished the Megalopolitan fort at Athenaion in south-western Arkadia (which he had captured earlier, 4. 60. 3), in order to prevent it being used against them.[198]

By now Philip had been in the Peloponnese for up to a year (since late 219, P. 4. 67). Aitolian violence in the territories of western Achaean towns (Dyme, Pharai, Tritaia, 59–60) included the seizure of the fort at Dymaiōn Teichos. In response to Philip's decision to take the campaign into Epeiros (61), the Aitolians sacked the Macedonian city of Dion (62); Philip responded with a series of victories in Aitolia (63–5). After returning to Macedonia to deter a Dardanian invasion (66), he suddenly reappeared at Corinth around midwinter (67) and launched a veritable *Blitzkrieg*: destroying an Aitolian force (68–9), capturing Psophis (once Arkadian, now Eleian; 70–2), Eleian Lasion, and Stratos in the territory of Arkadian Thelphousa, and restoring all three to the league as well as amassing booty from Eleia (73, 75). Arkadian Alipheira was taken from its Eleian–Aitolian garrison (78). Triphylian Typaneai, looted by its supposed allies from Aitolia, almost suffered the same fate as Kynaitha but survived to place itself in Philip's hands. So did Arkadian Heraia and Arkadian (now Aitolian) Phigaleia, the latter expelling its Aitolian garrison (79). Finally, he captured the remaining Triphylian towns, replacing an Aitolian garrison in the most important of them, Lepreon, with his own (80). By spring 218 he had retaken Dymaiōn Teichos, plundered Eleian territory once more (83), and appointed a commander for Peloponnesian affairs (ἐπὶ τῶν κατὰ Πελοπόννησον, 87).

To this sustained onslaught, Lykourgos responded by invading Messenia (P. 5. 17), which had now committed itself to the cause of the Allies (5. 4. 5); its capture would have isolated Triphylia and almost united the territories of the three anti-Macedonian powers (Aitolia, Elis, and Lakedaimon). Lykourgos' campaign was a failure, but he captured Arkadian Tegea (5. 17) and also Glyppia (20), which he had failed to take from the Argives in 219. The Eleians overran the territory of the long-suffering Dymaians (17); but in Laconia Philip finally attacked Sparta's southern *perioikoi* (19).[199] Ravaging of the land was followed by a direct assault on Sparta, but the city

---

[198] Pikoulas 1988b, 115–17; different from the Athenaion near Asea (Paus. 8. 44. 2–3), Pikoulas 1988b, 65–6.

[199] Shipley 2000a, 377–9, 381–3.

held out (21–4).[200] A further bout of *stasis*, or perhaps a dispute resolved politically, led to Lykourgos being exiled again, this time on suspicion of planning a tyrannical coup (29). 'Tyranny' is a familiar slur in this period; his plans may have been no more unpatriotic than Kleomenes' ruthless actions in the 220s, but perhaps fell victim to the perennial schisms inside Sparta. In winter 218/7 the Aitolians again raided coastal Achaea (30). In 217 Lykourgos, back in power, launched a second invasion of Messenia (91–2), seizing Kalamai, though an Aitolian attempt to join him was thwarted by the bravery of the people of Kyparissos (92).

Despite their uneven success, the Allies were gradually gaining the upper hand. A further Aitolian raid on Achaea was defeated (P. 5. 94), and the forces of Dyme, Patrai, and Pharai invaded Eleia (95. 7). To add to the continual episodes of plundering in the countryside, Philip's supposed Illyrian allies under Skerdilaïdas treacherously raided Achaea and began attacking merchant ships, including Macedonian, around the Peloponnese (95, 101). At this point in summer 217, however, Philip learned of Hannibal of Carthage's victory over the Romans at Lake Trasimene in Italy, and concluded peace at Naupaktos (103–5); partly under the impulse of mediation by East Greek states (Chios, Rhodes, Byzantion) and Ptolemy IV of Egypt, but also with a view to strengthening his hand in the Adriatic.[201]

Sellasia had made possible a new tutelary role for the Macedonians, and the young Philip at first won great popularity with the states of the northern and eastern Peloponnese which he led under the aegis of the Hellenic alliance. Polybios says, in a later context, that Philip had been 'as it were the beloved of the Greeks' (οἶον ἐρώμενος τῶν Ἑλλήνων, 7. 11). Garrisons were now at least as likely to be imposed by the Macedonians' enemies as by the king. Polybios even reports that in 218 Philip eliminated certain of his courtiers who sought to undermine Aratos and reduce Achaea to the same subjugated status as Thessaly (4. 76, 82, 84–7; 5. 1, 2, 25–6, 28). Policy considerations, however, imposed a limit upon his commitment to the Peloponnese; the reason for removing those advisers may have been that he had greater ambitions than merely to dominate that region.[202] Polybios may be right to speak of a transformation in Philip's personality at a later stage (7. 11–14; cf. 4. 77); but, as on many other occasions in this period, it was chiefly circumstances that compelled a Macedonian leader to resile from milder and at times supportive policies.

---

[200] Cartledge and Spawforth 2002, 63.
[201] Scullard and Derow 2012.
[202] On the transition from Doson, and on Philip's ambition, see Errington 1989b, 94.

Aitolian, and later Illyrian, aggression had given Sparta and Elis an opportunity to undermine Doson's settlement, embroiling the young king in continual warfare and eventually causing a decline in his celebrity. In terms of economic damage, the Social war had affected mainly the north and west of the peninsula, together with the small *poleis* of eastern Parnon; while eastern Arkadia, Korinthia, and Argolis had remained almost untouched. Conversely, Philip had successfully taken the war into Eleia, Triphylia, and Laconia and briefly into Aitolia and neighbouring areas, recouping some or all of the losses the Allies had incurred; but both Allied and enemy communities had suffered continual destruction and the removal of portable wealth and agricultural produce.

Although the war ended without resolution, the Allies were generally in the ascendant. Before long, however, the entry of a new factor would radically change the balance of power in Greece and indirectly add to disorder and suffering in the Peloponnese. It would also raise in a new form the perennial question of domination of, and stability in, the peninsula.

II.5.b From the Peace of Naupaktos to the Macedonians' Expulsion (217–197)

The interval between the Social war and the departure of the Macedonians began with most of the Peloponnese still divided between two blocs: the Achaean league (supported by Macedonia) on the one hand, embracing most of the peninsula; Sparta and Elis on the other, aligned with the Aitolians. Events are less well understood than for the preceding years, however, for Polybios' text is fragmentary after his fifth book, though it can be supplemented by Plutarch's *Aratos*, *Philopoimen*, and *Flamininus* as well as by Livy (cited as 'L.' in this chapter) where he adapts lost passages of Polybios. Five years after the war, however, Rome was caught up in Peloponnesian affairs, which in turn led to the involvement of Pergamon.

Although Lykourgos had stirred up the south-eastern Peloponnese and provoked serious retaliation from Philip in 218 before losing the towns in and beyond Parnon that he had briefly retaken, the Spartans may have kept their *perioikoi* in central and southern Laconia.[203] The years 217–207 have been characterized as obscure ones in Spartan history,[204] but it was probably

---

[203] This is a different view from that at Shipley 2000a, 378. Nabis' short-lived recovery of the *maritimi vici* in 193 (L. 34. 13. 1) would thus be reversing, not a recent dispossession, but a now well-established Argive suzerainty. We cannot be certain.

[204] Cartledge and Spawforth 2002, 64.

in 215 that Lykourgos expelled the young Agesipolis III (who reappeared later in Rome: P. 23. 6. 1; L. 33. 26. 14) and became sole ruler;[205] dying within a few years, however, for his son soon appears as king.

Oligarchic Messene, under hostile pressure from Aitolia and from its neighbours in Eleia and Laconia, had belatedly supported the Allies (Philip and Achaea). There had evidently been *stasis* leading to democratization, the 'notables' (ἀξιόλογοι) being banished and their land shared among new owners (P. 7. 10. 1). Probably the constitution was changed to Achaean-style moderate democracy, with Philip's encouragement. In 215 or 214, however, he invaded the long-suffering region, inflicted damage upon the *chōra*, and was reportedly urged by Demetrios of Pharos minded to seize Messene itself to complement his stronghold at Corinth; the citadels of Acrocorinth and Mt Ithome being the two horns by which the ox of the Peloponnese could be mastered (7. 10–14, esp. 12. 3).[206] Polybios makes the decline in Philip's popularity begin now. Aratos told the king to his face that his actions were treacherous; the king gave way (7. 12), but caused harm to Messenian territory later (8. 12; at 16. 16–17, P. castigates the errors of other historians on this episode).

Rome's first war against Philip, the 'first Macedonian war' (*c.* 212–205), was provoked by his negotiations with Hannibal. It was fought out mainly in north-western Greece, but also involved the northern Peloponnese in new troubles as Rome attacked Philip's Achaean and other allies, while he in turn carried the war into Eleia and north-western Greece, regions friendly to Rome. In 212, at the moment when the Romans were about to capture Syracuse in Sicily by siege and were negotiating an alliance with the Aitolians, the Syracusans made secret overtures to Philip; the fact that their envoy was a Lakedaimonian (L. 25. 23. 8–10; we are not told whether Spartan or perioikic) suggests some in Sparta saw their interests as bound up with those of the Allies. Attalos I of Pergamon also became involved on the Roman side, later (in 210) purchasing the island of Aigina after its capture by the Romans; he may have envisaged it as a counterweight to Ptolemy's naval base at Methana,[207] for the two are clearly visible from one another.[208]

At Sparta, the poorly documented rule of Machanidas began in or after 212 and lasted about four years;[209] he may have been regent for Lykourgos'

[205] Cartledge and Spawforth 2002, 62.
[206] Walbank 1957–79, ii. 56–61, esp. 56–7.
[207] Errington 1989b, 102.
[208] Derow 2012a.
[209] What we know is summarized by Volkmann 1969a and discussed by Cartledge and Spawforth 2002, 65–7.

son Pelops (cf. L. 34. 32. 1).[210] Like Kleomenes III and Lykourgos, he seems to have pursued a policy of direct aggression against Macedonia and Achaea. In 210, the Spartans had to decide whether to accept an alliance with the Romans, fellow allies of the Aitolians. Polybios (9. 28–39) dramatizes the issue in a formal debate at Sparta in which opposing speakers, Chlaineas from Aitolia and Lykiskos from Akarnania, review the history of Macedonian power in the Peloponnese since the time of their great-grandfathers, and whether the Macedonians have been a force for good or ill (cf. Sections II.3.a, II.4.d–e; III.2.c). Pragmatically, the Spartans concluded that they needed Rome's support against the Achaeans, renewed their alliance with the Aitolians, and were added (in the name of King Pelops) to the list of signatories to the recent Roman–Aitolian treaty (L. 34. 32. 1, in a later context). The military balance was thus tilted decisively against Macedonia and Achaea.[211]

Philip continued to aid the league against the Spartans and Aitolians; but in response to envoys from Alexandria, Rhodes, Athens, and Chios, he entered into discussions with a view to ending hostilities. Having attended an allied council at Aigion, at which the Aitolians demanded that the Achaeans return Pylos to the Messenians, now allies of Sparta, he presided at the Nemean games of 208, but interrupted his visit to repel Roman forces ravaging the territories of Sikyon and Corinth (on all this, see L. 27. 29. 9–31. 1–2). Back at Nemea, he made himself popular by removing his royal diadem and purple robe during the games, but harmed his reputation by abusive relationships with local women (P. 10. 26. 4; L. 27. 31. 4–8). On the positive side for Philip, however, Livy mentions (in a later context) that, after the Romans sacked and depopulated Dyme, Philip refounded it (32. 22. 5; cf. 27. 32. 11; Paus. 7. 17. 5); the city subsequently remaining pro-Macedonian. Furthermore, an expedition against the Romans in Eleia brought him and his allies copious amounts of booty (as during the Social war); but he was called away to North Greece to defend Macedonia from its neighbours, leaving only 2,500 troops to defend his allies (L. 27. 32. 1–10). Despite his absence, the Achaeans defeated the Aitolians and Eleians near Messene (27. 33. 5).

The Achaeans asked for Philip's help against Machanidas, once more encamped near Argive territory (P. 10. 41. 3; L. 28. 5. 5), prompting the king to return to the Peloponnese via Corinth and march towards Phleious

---

[210] Cartledge and Spawforth 2002, 65.

[211] This may be the occasion on which Damostratos of Sparta, who had helped resolve a dispute between Sparta and Messene, was honoured at Messene (*SEG* 47. 390 ~ 51. 477; C3; Themelis 1997, 108–12; P. 9. 28; 16. 13. 3).

and Pheneos (28. 7. 16). On learning, at Arkadian Heraia, that Machanidas
had attacked Elis but withdrawn to Sparta, he went on to an Achaean
council at Aigion (28. 7. 17), where he promised to hand control of Heraia
and the Triphylian towns to the league, and of Arkadian Alipheira to the
Megalopolitans, who claimed it (28. 8. 6); though the transfers of possession
did not happen for almost a decade. Once again, however, he was drawn
away by the demands of campaigns further north (28. 8. 10).

Also in 208, the Achaean commander Philopoimen equipped the Achaean
infantry with heavier armour (P. 11. 9–11; Plut. *Philop.* 9).[212] At some point
Machanidas must have captured Tegea, since in 207 he addressed his army
there before advancing on Mantinea (P. 11. 11. 2). The capture by so-called
Spartan 'tyrants' of the Belbinatis, their former north-western possession,
is attributed to Machanidas; it remained Spartan until *c.* 190 (L. 38. 34.
8).[213] Later in 207, however, the Achaeans defeated the Spartans heavily at
Mantinea, Philopoimen personally killing Machanidas,[214] and retook Tegea
(P. 11. 12–18). Polybios says 4,000 Lakedaimonians died and an even larger
number were captured (ἔτι πλείους, 11. 18. 10); as in the case of Sellasia
in 222, we are not told whether any of these were Kleomenes' new citizens who had retained their status, but in view of the very large figures it
seems likely that some had.[215] It has been claimed that the battle, known as
Third Mantinea, had a salutary effect on Spartan thinking;[216] but it no more
marked the end of Spartan aggression and hegemonic ambition than had
Sellasia, and was ultimately no more decisive.

Instead, the death of Machanidas brought to the throne Nabis (r. 207–192),
a younger contemporary of Kleomenes III.[217] Probably married to a niece
of Aristomachos II, the former 'tyrant' of Argos,[218] he maintained Sparta's
anti-Achaean, anti-Macedonian policy; and was ambitious, like Agis and
Kleomenes, to restore Spartan greatness through social and political reform.
Sparta's relations with its neighbours, other than Messenia, remained hostile;
but Nabis has been seen as a modernizer.[219] He minted coins bearing his name

---

[212] Larsen 1968, 375; M. F. Williams 2004.

[213] Cartledge and Spawforth 2002, 66; Ehrenberg 1929, 1437.

[214] On the maltreatment of Machanidas' body (after this, the first Achaean defeat of Sparta
without Macedonia's help) and the signal it was meant to send to Sparta, see Kralli 2017, 333.

[215] Walbank 1957–79, ii. 294 (on P. 11. 18. 10), does not comment on this point.

[216] Cartledge and Spawforth 2002, 67.

[217] Or he may have seized power on the death of Pelops, for whom he may have been regent as
Machanidas may have been earlier. See Cartledge 2012; Volkmann 1969b. On Nabis see esp.
Cartledge and Spawforth 2002, 67–79.

[218] Named Apia, rather than 'Apega' as at Polyb. 13. 7. 6; see Walbank 1979, 421 ad loc., citing
Wilhelm 1921; cf. Cartledge and Spawforth 2002, 54, 69.

[219] Cartledge 2012.

and possibly his portrait,[220] strengthened Sparta's fortifications (in and after 195),[221] and is said to have maintained a mercenary guard (P. 13. 6. 4; cf. 16. 13. 1–3), fine horses (13. 8. 3), and a palace (*regia*, L. 35. 36. 1); doubtless he aimed to put Sparta's image on a par with the post-Alexander Macedonian dynasties, as had Areus I. He probably exiled political opponents (e.g. 34. 26. 12; 36. 35. 7). More heinous allegations may be set out in increasing order of implausibility: that he extirpated the two royal families (despite being a Eurypontid himself), including the boy king Pelops (Diod. 27, fr. 1); assassinated Lakedaimonians in exile; made war on Megalopolis upon a trivial pretext; attracted criminals to his service and deployed them to cause trouble elsewhere in the Peloponnese; and operated a torture machine in the likeness of his queen (P. 13. 6–7). It is, however, accepted that he freed 'the slaves' (τοὺς δούλους, 16. 13; *servi* in L. 34. 31), probably meaning helots in Laconia, some of whom Kleomenes had allowed to buy citizenship but only during a military emergency (Plut. *AK* 44. 1).[222] The claim that he is freeing slaves and reallocating land to the poor is neither denied nor justified by Nabis in 195 in a speech in Livy (34. 31), though the terms Livy uses may reflect Polybian prejudice.[223] Nabis seems to have encouraged trade and was honoured as a benefactor at the key Aegean trading centre of Delos (*Syll.*[3] 584). Perhaps unsurprisingly, Polybios (13. 6–8) and Livy (esp. 31. 25) call him a tyrant; a judgement made easier, like the less credible allegations just noted, by his having broken a peace treaty (see later). Nabis was to be the last king of Sparta.

The Romans had left their Aitolian allies to do the main fighting, and by 206 Philip had forced the Aitolians to negotiate by attacking their common sanctuary at Thermon. In 205, when the Roman senate turned its attention back to Greek affairs after neglecting them for two years (L. 29. 12. 1), the peace of Phoinike was concluded. Livy's summary (29. 12. 12–14)[224] lists 'Nabis, *tyrannus* of the Lakedaimonians', among the signatories. As in the case of the Roman–Aitolian alliance, however, the entry may have been added after the event (but hardly with the title 'tyrant'!) to show the city's commitment to Rome or to secure protection against Philip.[225]

---

[220] Hoover 2011, 139 (comment); 142 nos. 608–9, AR (609 with ΒΑΣΙΛΕΩΣ ΝΑΒΙΟΣ, 'Of King Nabis'); 148 no. 635, AE (no portrait or legend).

[221] Kourinou 2000, 53 (stamped tiles of 'King Nabis'), 59–61, 277.

[222] Piper 1984–6; Cartledge and Spawforth 2002, 69, 70. For helots in Laconia, see Kennell 2003.

[223] e.g. 11, *quod servos ad libertatem voco, quod in agros inopem plebem deduco* ('that I am calling slaves to their freedom, that I am bringing the mass of poor men into the fields'); 14, *multitudinem servis liberandis auctam et egentibus divisum agrum* ('the mass increased by freeing slaves and the land divided among the needy').

[224] Austin[2] 80.

[225] Habicht 1997, 195–6; Shipley 2000b, 374.

Philip's interests now turned away from the Peloponnese, as he sought control of the Aegean and became involved in direct conflict with Pergamon. Despite the formal end of war, in 204 Nabis attacked Megalopolis (P. 13. 8. 4–7). In 201, he treacherously attacked his ally Messene, which only the proximity of Philopoimen's army deterred him from holding (16. 13. 3; 16. 16. 17).[226] In retaliation, after the Achaeans had declared war upon Sparta (L. 31. 25. 1), Philopoimen invaded Laconia in 200 and defeated Nabis (P. 16. 36–7), though he remained in power.

The campaigns by Philip in the Aegean and further afield stoked the fires of Roman concern and led to the second Macedonian war (200–197).[227] He attempted to retain the support of the Achaeans by offering them Orchomenos and repeating his earlier promise to make over to them Heraia and the towns of Triphylia, and to Megalopolis Alipheira (L. 32. 5. 4–5; cf. 28. 8. 6).[228] In 198, however, Attalos I of Pergamon induced the Achaeans to desert Philip for Rome, partly for fear of Nabis (32. 19–23). The league's choice seems to have been controversial at the time.[229] This second *volte-face*, reversing that of Aratos a generation earlier, represents a real turning-point in Mediterranean history. It left Philip isolated and sealed his fate. It also brought the Achaeans back onto the same side as the Spartans for the first time in decades; an uneasy situation for both, likely to result in the eventual incapacitation of one or the other.

In early 197,[230] Philip, under pressure from Rome to withdraw from southern Greece, told his governor in Corinth and Argos to offer the latter city to Nabis on a temporary basis; the two rulers agreed to seal their 'friendship' (*amicitia*) with marriages between Philip's daughters and Nabis' sons (L. 32. 38. 1–3).[231] Livy, doubtless following Polybios, presents Nabis as motivated only by a desire to plunder the city, and as feeling no commitment to Philip. Even more redolent of propaganda are the claims that, while confiscating the wealth of the richest Argives, Nabis ordered those who would not declare all their possessions to be tortured (32. 38. 7–8), and that his wife later robbed the rich ladies of their finery (P. 18. 17. 3–5; L. 32. 40. 11). Be that as it may, the key fact is that he proposed in Argos, just as Kleomenes had a generation earlier, reforms including debt cancellation and land redistribution. Livy attributes this to a desire to turn

---

[226] Further sources listed by Cartledge and Spawforth 2002, 246–7 n. 21.
[227] Errington 1989a, 244–8, 252–8.
[228] Walbank 1940, 97 and n. 1; 148 and n. 5.
[229] Eckstein 1987.
[230] Or 198: Errington 1989a, 276.
[231] Accepted by Chrimes 1949, 28; over-interpreted by Will 1979–82, ii. 158.

the common people against the aristocracy; but it is open to doubt whether Nabis' aims were so destructive. The measures were perhaps intended rather (as is argued in Chapter III) to bring to power a group of the elite who had not hitherto enjoyed the leadership of the *polis* and who would be loyal to a benefactor. If the parallel with reforms at Sparta can be extended, Nabis may well also have aimed to increase Argos' military manpower.

By accepting Philip's overtures Nabis did not intend to desert the Romans; such a U-turn would have been worthy of the Achaeans, and foolhardy, for Sparta had been consistently anti-Macedonian and pro-Roman since 210. Indeed, he at once arranged talks with Flamininus and Attalos, held in the territory of Mycenae,[232] at which he agreed to conclude an armistice with the Achaeans and not to help Philip (L. 32. 39. 10–11). Clearly, his overriding aim was to maximize Sparta's advantage, for he insisted on garrisoning Argos and refused to let the Roman commander Flamininus consult the people of the city to confirm that they had invited him in; but the question of Argos was left unresolved; and, while Attalos focused on cultivating Sikyon, Flamininus pressed the Macedonian governor of Corinth to surrender that city (L. 32. 40. 1–6).

It is credible that Nabis' dealings with Philip were an opportunistic feint designed to keep his options open while taking control, like Kleomenes, of an old enemy of Sparta. He paid dearly for his boldness. The defeat of Philip by the Romans at Kynoskephalai in Thessaly in summer 197, and Philip's consequent exclusion from central and southern Greece, marked the end of the Macedonian presence in the Peloponnese – and thus of our main narrative – but not the end of troubles for Sparta.

II.5.c Retrospective of 222–197

The last years of the Macedonians' involvement in the Peloponnese were a brutal time, despite what might have seemed to be the drawing of their sting by Aratos in the 220s. Delegation of control to the Achaean league should have meant that the king did not have to intervene directly – another variation on Macedonian hegemonic practice in the peninsula. Doson and Philip may have hoped that *polis* regimes would prove more stable within a federal union aligned with a Hellenic alliance under their military patronage, than when, as previously, they had been supported piecemeal with garrisons or by patronage of governors ('tyrants' to their enemies). The league, however,

---

[232] Livy's *haud procul urbe Mycenica* probably translates a Polybian reference to the *chōra* of Mycenae rather than to the town itself.

proved unable to control Sparta; the Hellenic alliance was quickly challenged by the Aitolians, exposing divisions and providing Sparta with new opportunities for seeking to revive its influence. Generally Philip could rely only upon the northern and north-eastern Peloponnese, watched from the stronghold above Corinth which he had reacquired in 222. Partly under the pressure of external forces, internal divisions within *poleis* and within regional blocs bedevilled any attempt at consistency. The war and its aftermath forced the hegemon to resile from hitherto mild and popular policies; and his aborted threat to Messene appears to have lessened his credibility.

Mediterranean strategic considerations, however, now played a greater role in the search for answers to the 'eternal questions', those of (for Macedonians) controlling the Peloponnese and (for the Peloponnesians) of restraining Sparta. When delegated control of the Peloponnese did not work, conflicts within the peninsula were a distraction and a drain on resources, especially once people's eyes were increasingly turned to the west. After a period when their interests diverged – and perhaps sensing that they no longer had a critical need for Philip's support – the Achaeans deserted the Macedonians. This ultimately led to the betrayal of Sparta by the Romans under Flamininus (remarkably similar to that by Philip II). Unsurprisingly, this unsatisfactory non-solution merely stoked the fires of intra-Peloponnesian conflict for another half-century.[233]

II.6 Control and Geostrategy

After the upheavals of the late fifth century, the peoples of the Peloponnese suffered further in the kaleidoscopic conflicts of the early fourth. The rest of that century was equally dangerous. Sparta's defeat in 371, and the humiliating Theban invasions of Laconia in the 360s, did not put an end to conflict; neither did Philip II's hegemony over southern Greece create a permanently pacified landscape or substantially rearrange the geostrategic dynamics. The 'long third century' of Macedonian domination (338–197) was rarely, if at all, characterized by a *pax Macedonica*. Cities continued to clash over territory. The old internal hegemon, Sparta, remained aggressive at times, competing for territory with Messene, Megalopolis, eastern Arkadia, and Argos and coming close to regaining a dominant position. Smaller centres of power survived in Arkadia, only briefly united in a larger association.

---

[233] For the view that Achaean power never replaced Spartan because it, too, remained reliant on external help, see Kralli 2017, 147–8.

The major *poleis* of the north-east remained individually powerful. From the 270s, the Achaean league rose to prominence, changing the balance of military resource to the disfavour of the Macedonians. Macedonian warlords and kings continually (though not continuously) projected power and exerted pressure from their base on the Isthmus, while another external power, Ptolemaic Egypt, interfered opportunistically, especially from nearby Crete.

Anti-Macedonian military campaigns were relatively frequent: some led by Sparta, notably the attack by Agis III; some enjoying Ptolemaic support, such as the Chremonidean war. Each one ended in disaster; but then the Achaean league began to grow in military weight, leading to changes of control in many states. Yet even the defeats of Sparta in 222 and 207 did not bring about the end of violent confrontation, which persisted after the establishment of Roman hegemony (not yet 'rule'). Even in the second century, Rome could not prevent regional problems from running out of control, though for decades Rome was the arbiter of disputes rather than of armed conflicts.

This chapter has attempted a new, comprehensive narrative for the Peloponnese in the late classical and early hellenistic periods, and has identified two 'eternal questions'. (*a*) For those powerful enough to aspire to hegemony over the peninsula, the issue was how control and stability could best be maintained. The response depended on the answers to two prior questions: in whose interests was control to be exercised, and how liberal or restrictive was that control to be? Hegemons appear to have responded differently at different times. (*b*) For states other than Sparta, the question was how Sparta could be prevented from re-establishing its dominance.[234] A further question arose at moments of opportunity and decision: how much local or internal power, if any, should Sparta be left with? The consistent response was 'a considerable amount', at least down to 195.

To Sparta's neighbours, the second question may have been uppermost. Many leading Spartans clearly wished to dominate the peninsula; perhaps to recreate a Peloponnesian league based on time-honoured networks among *polis* elites. This traditional model of *pax Laconica* appears to have commanded loyalty for a long time among certain Peloponnesians, particularly when the alternative was Macedonian domination. Even the Achaeans fought alongside Spartans at times. Others, however, may have seen no future for themselves under Sparta, which had always favoured friendly

---

[234] Though some, including certain Arkadian *poleis*, remained broadly loyal to Sparta: Kralli 2017, 130, 220, 493–4, etc.

oligarchies and had to some extent thrown away its reputation in the 390s. In the next chapter we shall examine what lay behind calls for constitutional change in Peloponnesian *poleis*, and how it may relate to the composition of citizen bodies. The divisions within them were perhaps responsible for making the prospect of old-style Spartan hegemony intolerable. It is perhaps no coincidence that the first moves in the formation of the new Achaean league were made well away from Macedonian-held Corinth, but also well out of reach of any possible Spartan influence.

On the question of 'pacification', Macedonia's interest seems to have been consistently focused on preventing assaults and distractions. Hence we see a strategy of delegated control and sometimes of more supportive patronage, though periods of milder rule usually proved unrealistic. Sometimes a king seems to have operated a policy of 'divide and rule', or of not destroying one of two potential hegemons. Some such thinking may explain why, like the Thebans in the 360s (who left Sparta with the coastal *poleis* of Messenia), neither Philip II nor Doson deprived Sparta of all its *perioikoi*, still less destroyed the *polis* of Sparta as the Spartans had destroyed Mantinea in 385, Philip II Olynthos early in his reign, and Alexander Thebes in 335. The Spartans themselves had refused to obliterate Athens in 404.

A positive analysis, of course, would see the Antigonids in the third century, like Philip II earlier, as wishing to be seen as champions of Hellenism (as long as Hellenism was biddable). For this reason, as much as reasons of economy, Macedonian kings attempted, when the geopolitical storms subsided, to operate a relatively 'hands off' policy in the Peloponnese. Many Peloponnesians and other Greeks may have admired Sparta for its leadership and sacrifices in the Persian wars, for overthrowing Athens' fifth-century empire, and latterly for repeatedly attacking the Macedonians; such historical considerations had not been present to save Mantinea or Thebes.

The relative priorities of Macedonian kings, as we have often noted, are shown by the number of occasions on which a ruler's attention was drawn away from this part of Greece, usually by affairs in northern Greece: namely, in 317 when Cassander was besieging Tegea (Section II.3.c); in the late 290s when Demetrios was campaigning in the southern Peloponnese and was distracted from news from the eastern Mediterranean (end of Section II.4.a); in the mid-280s when Gonatas left the south in the charge of Pyrrhos (Section II.4.b); in 222 when Doson could not stay to consolidate his victory at Sellasia (Section II.4.e); in winter 219/8 when Philip V went to fend off the Dardanians (Section II.5.a); in 208 when he rushed home from Eleia (Section II.5.b); and not long after, when he returned to Macedonia after forcing Machanidas to abandon an expedition (Section II.5.b).

On a larger scale, recent scholarship has also identified a perennial east-ward gaze on the part of Macedonian rulers from Cassander to Philip V, though it was steadier at certain times than at others.[235] Demetrios Poliorketes, for example, being determined to recover Asia, neglected security in Greece and reduced Greek freedom, but thereby jeopardized his greater aim. Gonatas learned from his father's failure and gave up the aim of recovering Asia, preferring as a compromise domination of the Aegean; to this end, he stubbornly restored his position in Greece and, as a result, survived what was in essence a Ptolemaic attack in the Chremonidean war. Gonatas' three successors maintained the Aegean focus, but realized that for this purpose it was necessary to prevent outbursts within Greece. After the peace of Phoinike, Philip V involved himself even more in the Aegean, which may have contributed to the Achaean decision to switch sides.

A different spatial pattern can be seen in Spartan history in these years: a prevailing interest in the western Peloponnese and north-western Greece, reflected in perennial alignment with Elis and Aitolia. In earlier periods, though also active throughout the eastern Peloponnese, Sparta had often maintained an almost proprietorial interest in the Olympic festival and, through its ally Corinth, in Adriatic networks. For Sparta, indeed, there were three land routes out of Laconia (since Taÿgetos impedes direct land travel into Messenia): the Eurotas–Alpheios furrow (also a way into Messenia if needed), the Orchomenos route (whose importance Philip V recognized), and the eastern route via Thyreatis and Argos (blocked after 338 except when Kleomenes and briefly Nabis controlled Argos).

In short, security considerations meant that the Macedonians needed to keep the lid on the Peloponnesians, and in particular prevent a revival of Spartan power unless it was balanced by Achaean; the Peloponnese was important to them instrumentally, not as an end in itself. Even the long-standing domination of Corinth, and the lavish investment in its amenities which they probably made,[236] are explicable in this light.

A compelling feature of this period, despite Macedonian power, is the degree to which – whether under external domination, Spartan overlord-ship, or the authority of a multi-*polis* association – the individual *poleis* retained a considerable degree of 'agency', of practical freedom to act as they chose; to act, that is, as politics within their decision-making body ebbed and flowed. A corollary of this is that within *poleis* and regional blocs, as already observed, division and competition were fundamental

---

[235] Buraselis 1982, esp. 177–9.

[236] Dixon 2014, 201–3: ship building yards, the Diolkos, water-supply; 207, Demetrios' attempt to build a canal.

dynamics of the geopolitical landscape. This is explored further in Chapter III, which examines the nature of politics in Peloponnesian communities, and enquires what effects if any Macedonian power had upon politics.

While he castigates the histories of Theopompos, Polybios concedes that Philip, Alexander, and their generals displayed 'courage (ἀνδρεία), love of toil (φιλοπονία), and in short virtue' (ἀρετή; 8. 10. 5); while even Alexander's immediate successors 'caused their own glory to be handed down in numerous memoirs' (παραδόσιμον ἐποίησαν τὴν ἑαυτῶν δόξαν ἐν πλείστοις ὑπομνήμασιν, 8. 5. 12). But he also, in the voice of Chlaineas the Aitolian, whipping up anti-Macedonian feeling in 211, characterizes the post-Lamian war period as one of abusive treatment of the Greeks by Antipater, with political officers hunting down anti-Macedonians (9. 29). Lykiskos the Akarnanian responds that Alexander's successors did both good and bad (9. 34). This polarity of interpretation is another issue which the examination of *polis* politics will help us explore.

II.7 Epilogue: 197–146

After Kynoskephalai, Flamininus continued in his attempts to ensure that Philip surrendered Corinth (P. 18. 11. 13). By a resolution of the senate the Greek states in Europe not held by Philip were to be free and 'use their own laws' (νόμοις χρῆσθαι τοῖς ἰδίοις), while those Philip held in Europe were to be surrendered to the Romans (18. 44. 2–3). According to Polybios, the Aitolians suggested that this meant that the latter group, in particular the three Fetters, were to be Roman possessions (18. 45. 1–6); but Flamininus persuaded the senate's commissioners in Greece that Rome must free them all. Accordingly, at the Isthmian games in summer 196 he proclaimed the freedom of those Greeks who were subject to Philip (18. 46. 5); that of the others being implied *a fortiori*, if Polybios reports his words accurately. Corinth, Triphylia, and Heraia were handed over to the Achaean league (18. 47. 10).

Aware, no doubt, that pacification of the Spartans was a key to Peloponnesian stability, Flamininus secured a mandate from the Panhellenic congress to attack them (L. 33. 45. 4), even though they had supported Rome against Philip V. Securing Achaean support on the pretext of liberating Argos (34. 22–4), he successfully invaded Laconia in summer 195 (34. 28–9) and removed much of what remained of perioikic territory from Sparta's control; it was probably soon after this that the league (*koinon*) of the Lakedaimonians was created.[237] In 193 Nabis attempted to retake those towns, but in 192 he was assassinated by Aitolian troops in Sparta (35. 35–6). Sparta fell to Philopoimen; apart from the imposition of a narrow oligarchy, the main innovation was its enrolment in the Achaean league (35. 37. 2). Once Messene and Elis followed in 191, the league was all-powerful.

Yet only three years after Nabis' fall, the aggrieved Spartans attacked hostile exiles at Las near Gytheion and declared Sparta's independence from the league; whereupon Philopoimen seized the opportunity to intervene once again with savage violence and abolish the constitution (L. 38. 30–4). Even so, the Spartans remained 'bad Achaeans' over the years to come; Messene, too (which had been a semi-detached league member at an earlier date: P. 4. 31–2), seceded on one occasion. Such demonstrations presented a now supremely confident Roman senate with opportunities to stop the Achaeans becoming too powerful; initially Rome's friend, the league became suspicious of Rome's motives and became suspect itself. According to Polybios, by the middle of the century the ordinary people of Greek states were among those most vehement in condemning Rome (e.g. 38. 12. 45). Arguments between the league and states such as Athens and Sparta led to diplomatic clashes with Rome, and ultimately to the Achaean war of 146. That resulted in the destruction of Corinth by Roman troops, and the abolition of the Achaean league. The main alternative to a traditional *pax Laconica* had failed.

---

[237] On the subsequent history of the *perioikoi*, see Kennell 1999.

III | Power and Politics

Now come tidings of … treasons, cheating tricks, robberies, enormous
villainies in all kinds, funerals, burials, deaths of princes, new discoveries,
expeditions, now comical, then tragical matters.
Robert Burton, *The Anatomy of Melancholy* (1621), preface (from Powell
1975, 272)

III.1 *Polis* Societies

Having examined events before and during the 'long third century', we
can now take a different path through the evidence. This chapter assesses
the balance between change and continuity in Peloponnesian politics, and
compares the extent to which it was affected by Macedonian power (III.2)
as opposed to internal factors (III.3).

Central to this account is the city-state or *polis*, the chief building-block
of Greek citizen society. If we are to reconstruct the internal dynamics of
a *polis*, we need to be clear about what a *polis* was and how it worked. The
following, very generalized discussion serves the purpose of ruling in, and
ruling out, certain possible explanations of fourth- and third-century politics, including *stasis* (civil conflict among citizens).

On the basis of literary and epigraphic sources down to the late fourth
century,[1] no minimum size or degree of independence was required for a
settlement to be called a *polis*. The preconditions were, rather, (*a*) that it be
a politically organized town and (*b*) that it have a rural territory or *chōra*.[2]
A settlement could be called a *polis* even if it was very small or if it belonged
to a larger entity such as a hegemonic league or federal state. If it belonged
to a federal state, or was dominated by a hegemonic state such as Sparta

---

[1] Esp. Hansen and Nielsen 2004b. Summary of Copenhagen Polis Project's findings: Shipley
2003; more fully Hansen 2004e (Danish), revised in Hansen 2006 (English). For possible
reservations, see Fröhlich 2010.

[2] For a more precise definition of this 'law' (in the sense of an observed regularity), jocularly
dubbed the *Lex Hafniensis de civitate* (Copenhagen law on the *polis*), see e.g. Hansen 1996, 28,
32–3; Hansen 2000b, 173; Hansen 2007, 13–14; Hansen 2004c, 34.

or Athens, it might be called a subordinate or 'dependent' *polis* (πόλις ὑπήκοος),[3] a phenomenon often seen in the Peloponnese. Naturally there is room for imprecise usage on the part of ancient writers, and the rhetorical manipulation of terminology; but the picture given by the archaic and classical sources is remarkably consistent. It is, furthermore, reasonable to assume, in the absence of contrary evidence, that no sudden change in terminology took place at or after the death of Alexander, though in the world of Successor dynasts we should expect an increase in the ideological use or misuse of words such as 'freedom' and 'independence'. Given these guidelines, it will be legitimate to see both small and dependent *poleis* as exhibiting broadly similar features to those found in large, independent ones, and to observe a tendency for internal political groupings to form in opposition to one another, each of which could cultivate relationships with external bodies and powers.

The realization that *polis* status was attributed to a range of communities of widely varying size and political complexion, including those that were part of multi-community entities, is in part a return to an earlier understanding. It also reflects a shift of interest by historians and archaeologists since the 1970s away from the greater powers that dominate the historical evidence, such as Athens, Sparta, and Thebes, towards the small, local, and secondary – in short, typical – settlements of Greece. Valuable insight has been gained into the social and political characters of middle- and lower-ranking political units, which do not necessarily conform to the templates offered by their better-known counterparts.[4] Even at lower levels there is no single typical *polis*, but everywhere variety.

What kind of citizen communities were these? For a minority of *poleis*, the nature of their internal politics and their constitutional form – whether democracy, oligarchy, or some form of one-man rule – are directly attested at one or more junctures during the classical and early hellenistic periods. For the majority, however, we lack direct evidence and must rely on inference from earlier history, associations with other *poleis*, or their general socio-economic character. Gehrke's stimulating study *Jenseits von Athen und Sparta: das dritte Griechenland* ('beyond Athens and Sparta: the third Greece')[5] offers some help here; attempting to sketch the social and economic characters of the less well-attested city-states, with a focus on the

---

[3] Hansen 2004g; Gschnitzer 1958, esp. 141–92; also Hansen 2006, esp. 63–5, 129–30.

[4] See esp. Gehrke 1986; Nielsen 2002, Nielsen and Roy 1999.

[5] The phrase 'the third Greece' is not meant to evoke the Third World. Gehrke 1986, 7, explains that he has in mind the older phrase *das dritte Deutschland*, denoting the small German states, as opposed to Austria and Prussia, before German unification in 1871.

Peloponnese. The study centres upon the archaic and classical periods, but, as we have already noted, we can legitimately extrapolate to the early hellenistic period unless there is reason to doubt a broad continuity of social formation. Gehrke groups the Peloponnesian states, other than the Spartan territories, as summarized in TABLE III.1. We can be broadly confident that a constitution ranging between limited democracy and moderate oligarchy was normal – both regimes characterized by visible decision-making and relatively wide participation – while one-man rule and full democracy were both the exception. Moderate democracy could mean what Gehrke calls *Bauerndemokratie*, 'farmer democracy' or 'peasant democracy' (cf. Section III.3.d); and the general range of constitutional forms reflects a broadly prosperous society secure in its agricultural and commercial resources.

Citizen societies, large or small, contained what may be thought of as vertical divisions, reflecting either divisions within a class of people of similar status (such as political factions) or divisions reflecting differing organization of areas of the Earth's surface. In the late classical period, for example, the majority of citizens of a *polis* and their families had their main residence within the urban centre while the same was not necessarily true of the rest of the population.[6] There were also, invariably, 'horizontal' divisions of status and wealth; as in every complex society, relationships of dependency and the influence of property played an important part. (We return to this theme when we review the archaeological evidence for landscape change in Chapter IV.) Such differences in privilege and influence may be called horizontal, like the layers in a sponge-cake.

Besides free citizens and their families the population would include chattel slaves; there might be a 'semi-free', serf-like group, typically resident in the *chōra*.[7] The importance of both slave and semi-free to production and military service may have been considerable, though their numbers may have varied greatly. To focus for the moment on the semi-free (those 'between free and slave', in the words of a late commentator drawing on classical or hellenistic sources):[8] besides the well-known Spartan helot system (which endured in Laconia at least until the reign of Nabis, see Section II.5.b), other evidence for semi-free groups in the Peloponnese refers mainly to the north-east. At Sikyon, the *korynēphoroi* ('club-bearers') or *katōnakophoroi* ('sheepskin-tunic wearers') are attested

---

[6] Hansen 2004a, 11–16; Hansen 2004b, 74–9.
[7] See esp. Lotze 1959; Ducat 1990 (helots); Ducat 1994 (Thessalian *penestai*).
[8] Pollux, *Onomasticon* 3. 83, compiled in C2 AD, though the extant text derives from a C9 AD epitome.

Table III.1. *Gehrke's classification of Peloponnesian* poleis

Category	Cities Assigned by Gehrke	Comments
important agrarian states[a]	Elis	Also Sparta.[b] Other than Sparta, all those in this class have an important maritime component.
middling agrarian states	Phleious Argos main Arkadian *poleis*: Mantinea, Tegea, Megalopolis	
middling agrarian states with significant maritime component	Corinth	
middling and smaller agrarian states with maritime component	Sikyon (coastal) Achaean *poleis*[c] minor Argolic *poleis* (Hermion, Halieis, Troizen, Methana, Epidauros)	Also small coastal *poleis* of Eleia and Triphylia.
poorer agrarian states, with or without limited maritime component	smaller Arkadian *poleis*	Also inland, smaller *poleis* of Eleia.

[a] The categories are from headings at Gehrke 1986, 96, 107, 116, 136, 150. For Elis, see Gehrke 1986, 103–4 (with nn. at 186); Phleious, 107–8 (187); larger Arkadian *poleis*, 109–13 (187); Argos, 113–16 (187–8); Corinth, 128–33 (190–1); Sikyon, 138–40 (191–2); Achaia, 144–7 (192); Halieis, 148–9 (193); minor Argolic *poleis*, 149, at (*f*); smaller Arkadian *poleis*, 151–4 (193).

[b] Gehrke excludes Sparta in accordance with the decentralizing aims of his study; we may reasonably assign it (even after 369) to the first category as an 'important agrarian state'.

[c] One might relegate the more remote inland *poleis* of Achaia to the fifth category.

for the fourth century.[9] The Argive *gymnētes, gymnēsioi* ('naked ones'), or *perioikoi* ('dwellers around', 'circumhabitants')[10] are known from late evidence but probably existed in classical or hellenistic times. The Epidaurian *konipodes* ('dustyfoots') are mentioned by Plutarch and others.[11] Although we lack similar evidence for Achaea, Eleia, and Arkadia, it is possible that such groups existed there, since those that are attested are each recorded so rarely, despite their potential economic importance, that others may have existed without leaving any trace.[12] Their existence may have defused potential resentment on the part of poor free men, whether or not excluded from formal politics. If their life was anything like that of Spartan helots – though perhaps not subject to declarations of war like those made regularly by the Spartan ephors (Plut. *Lyc.* 28. 4) – it was better than that of a chattel slave and probably involved family life, religious activities, and other forms of association – short of political organization.

This view of divisions in Peloponnesian communities has important implications for politics, such as what issues might motivate different groups and where discord and tensions might arise. All politics involves either compromise or the willing or unwilling relinquishing of certain viewpoints. Not only is a *polis* itself not unitary, it is not a sentient organism. A *polis* has no intentions; it can take no decisions except as the result of interaction between its multiplicity of members. Time and again, historical enquiry reveals, or implies, the existence of multifarious individuals and especially groups pursuing their own interests and competing to see their point of view prevail. When 'a *polis*' changed sides or adopted a new constitution, it will usually have been because one group among the politically was able to outvote, disarm (literally or metaphorically), deter, expel, or annihilate another. Indeed, it is often such groups, rather than a *polis* as a whole, that seek to maximize advantage from a relationship with an external force such as a hegemonic *polis* or strong neighbour.[13] Belonging to a group (a *stasis* in the sense of 'party') may sometimes have been more important than

---

[9] Theopompos, *FGrHist* 115 F 176.

[10] This term was used for free citizens of dependent *poleis* of Elis (earlier) and Sparta (to C2e). In Crete, however, it appears to refer to semi-free serfs like the helots (Arist. *Pol.* 2. 1271b 1–1272a 1).

[11] Plut. *QG* 291 d–e; Hsch. s.v. κονίποδες.

[12] Shipley 2002a, 178–9. For the equation of Chian *therapontes*, Lakedaimonian helots, Argive *gymnēsioi*, Sikyonian *korynēphoroi*, and Italiote Pelasgoi see Steph. Byz. s.v. Χίος (originally compiled in the LR period but drawing on Ar–Hl sources). For the equation of Lakedaimonian helots, Thessalian *penestai*, Cretan *klarōtai* or *mnōïtai*, Mariandynian *dōrophoroi*, Argive *gymnētes*, and Sikyonian *korynēphoroi*, see Pollux, *Onomasticon* 3. 83.

[13] Hansen 2004f, 124, 128.

membership of a *polis* in shaping political behaviour.[14] The fact, therefore, that a group attaches to itself – or has attached to it by contemporaries – a label like 'democrats' or 'oligarchs' may not necessarily reflect a high level of ideological commitment.[15] It may rather be evidence of the need to sub-scribe to a particular model of politics in order to gain traction.

The internal dynamic between groups is part of a wider structure, that of long-lasting inter-*polis* networks; particularly between members of elites, who in all probability continued to sustain the ties of guest-friendship (*xenia*) and inter-marriage across *polis* boundaries that we know well from the archaic and classical periods. Sparta, for example, regularly aided those in other states who were formal 'guest-friends' (*xenoi*) of Spartans.[16] Membership of an 'international' group, in this sense, may have carried at least as much political meaning for some men as membership of their *polis* or of a group within it.

III.2 Garrisons, 'Tyrants', and Macedonian Power

We saw in Chapter II that frequent warfare and its attendant effects were partly the result of the actions and ambitions of Macedonian commanders or kings. These warlords also attempted, to varying degrees, to direct or restrict the actions of political communities, for example, by installing garrisons; but although we know almost no specifics of any of these garrisons, the evidence suggests that the practice was commoner in time of war. Whether in war or in peace, some garrisons were presumably put in place to support one of those political leaders about whom our sources often use terms such as 'tyrant' (*tyrannos*) or 'tyranny' (*tyrannis*). Tyranny in ancient Greece can be defined as the exercise of government over a *polis* by one citizen in breach of normal practice; sometimes, perhaps normally, backed up by force. It was not necessarily a suspension of the rule of law, and probably no man, at least in our period, ever held the official title *tyrannos*; so the label is likely to be a slur on the part of a hostile source. Accordingly we will sometimes qualify these terms with inverted commas or use circumlocutions such as 'one-man rule' or 'governorship'.

Until the mid-fourth century, as far as we know, one-man rule had not occurred in the Peloponnese since the archaic period. It made a

---

[14] Hansen 2004f, 125.
[15] Cf. Roy 1994, 206.
[16] See e.g. Cartledge 1982; Hodkinson 2000, 349–50.

reappearance with short-lived regimes at Sikyon and Corinth in the 360s and again at Sikyon in the 340s (TABLE III.2); it reappeared occasionally under Philip and Alexander, and occurred more often thereafter. In Chapter II we considered the evolution of techniques of external control applied successively in the fourth and third centuries by the Spartans, Thebans, Macedonians, and Achaeans. Under Macedonian domination there was a new emphasis upon garrisons and 'tyrants'. There is, however, an issue of reliability, since the majority of sources are hostile to the men and regimes involved and offer sweeping and damning verdicts on the state of Peloponnesian politics for large parts of the 'long third century'. In this section we seek to establish how widespread the phenomenon of one-man rule was; whether it had a single cause or multiple causes; to what extent the Macedonians were responsible; and how 'tyrants' relate to garrisons. We set out the evidence before addressing these questions.

III.2.a Garrisons and 'Tyrants' Before Chaironeia (338)

A brief resurgence of short-term regimes called tyrannies by the sources may be observed in the aftermath of Leuktra: at Corinth under one Timophanes (brother of the famous general Timoleon) and at Sikyon under the populist Euphron (on these, see further Section III.3.b). Closer in time to our study period, probably during the early part of Philip II's reign, a pro-Macedonian citizen of Argos, whom the Athenian orator Hypereides names Mnesias, installed as *archōn* (chief magistrate) in Troizen a certain Athenogenes, who proceeded to expel certain citizens, presumably anti-Macedonians (Hyp. 5 = *Against Athenogenes*, 31).[17] Mnesias is probably the 'Mnaseas' whom Demosthenes, writing in 330, lists among men who unpatriotically promoted Macedonian interests in their *polis*:

> Because of their own shameful greed they cast aside the common good, each group tricking and corrupting (διαφθείροντες) the citizens until they were enslaved – the *Thessalians* by Daochos, Kineas, and Thrasydaios; the *Arkadians* by Kerkidas, Hieronymos, and Eukampidas; the *Argives* by Myrtis, Teledamos, and Mnaseas; the *Eleans* by Euxitheos, Kleotimos, and Aristaichmos; the *Messenians* by the sons of that enemy of the gods (θεοῖς ἐχθροῦ) Philiadas, namely Neon and Thrasylochos; the *Sikyonians* by Aristratos and Epichares; the *Corinthians* by Deinarchos

---

[17] Athenogenes' title depends on the restoration [ἄρχω]ν, which in view of the space available seems likely.

Table III.2. 'Tyrannies' in the Peloponnese, 371–197, by date

	Dates	Tyrant	Sponsors	Notes	Evidence
371–338					
Sikyon	368–365	Euphron	Thebans	'democratic coup'	Xen. *Hell.* 7. 1. 44–6; 7. 2. 11–15; 7. 3. 2–12
Corinth	366	Timophanes	Thebans?	*Inv. 227*	Arist. *Pol.* 1306a 21–4
Sikyon	c. 340	Aristratos		*Inv. 228;* tyranny ends when pro-Macedonian group installs narrow oligarchy or joint tyranny	Dem. 18. 48, 295; 'tyrant', Plut. *Arat.* 13. 1–3
Sikyon	c. 340?	Epichares		mentioned once, with Aristratos	Dem. 18. 295
338–323					
Troizen	c. 338–?	Athenogenes	**Mnesias/ Mnaseas of Argos**	installed as *archon*	Hypereides, *Oration* 5; Dem. 18. 294
Pellene	c. 334–?	Chairon	**Alexander**	*Inv. 240*	Ps.-Dem. 17. 10; Paus. 7. 27. 7; Ath. 11. 119. 509 b
Messene	c. 334–?	Neon, Thrasylochos (ss. Philiades)	**Alexander**		Ps.-Dem. 17. 4

(continued)

Table III.2. (*Cont.*)

	Dates	Tyrant	Sponsors	Notes	Evidence
323–297					
Megalopolis 297–239	312–?	Damis	**Cassander**	installs *epimelētēs*	Diod. 19. 63. 4–64. 1
Patrai?	pre-*c.* 281/0?	?	Gonatas??	expels a tyrant to refound Achaean *koinon* with Dyme?	Polyb. 2. 41. 12
Dyme?	pre-*c.* 281/0?	?	Gonatas??	expels a tyrant to refound Achaean *koinon* with Dyme?	Polyb. 2. 41. 12
Tritaia?	pre-*c.* 281/0?	?	Gonatas??	expels a tyrant to join Achaean *koinon*?	Polyb. 2. 41. 12
Pharai?	pre-*c.* 281/0?	?	Gonatas??	expels a tyrant to join Achaean *koinon*?	Polyb. 2. 41. 12
Karyneia	pre-281/0?–*c.* 275/4	Iseas	Gonatas?	resigns	Polyb. 2. 41. 14
Boura	pre-281/0?–*c.* 275/4	?	Gonatas?	deposed by citizens	Polyb. 2. 41. 14
Argos	*c.* 272	**Aristippos I**	Gonatas?	tyranny inferred by Walbank 1988, 273 (cf. 266); he is probably f. Aristomachos I	Plut. *Pyrrh.* 30. 2

Argos	272 or earlier–**Aristomachos I** c. 235 or 229–8	Gonatas?	probably s. Aristippos I (Volkmann 1964a; Walbank 1984a, 247; Walbank 1988, 273); for family tree see *HCP*; resigns to become Achaean league general		Plut. *Pyrrh.* 30. 2
Elis	272–c. 272	Aristotimos	**Gonatas**	assassinated (*KP* s.v.); Walbank 1988, 272	Paus. 5. 5. 1; 6. 14. 11; Plut. *Mor.* 250 f–253 e; Just. 26. 1. 4, 10
Sikyon	c. 271 or later– c.251	predecessor(s) of Kleon			Plut. *Arat.* 2. 1
Sikyon	c. 271 or later– c. 251	Kleon			Plut. *Arat.* 2. 1; Paus. 2. 8. 1–3
Sikyon	c. 271 or later– c. 251	*archontes* Timokleidas and Kleinias, then K. alone		Kleinias is f. Aratos	Plut. *Arat.* 2. 1
Sikyon	c. 264–252	Abantidas	Gonatas??		Plut. *Arat.* 2. 2
Leontion	c. 260?	?	Gonatas??	refounds *polis*, possibly as base for tyrant (see n. 29 below)	Strabo 8. 7. 5
Hermion	c. 260?–c. 229 Xenon		Gonatas?		Polyb. 2. 44. 6

(continued)

Table III.2. (Cont.)

	Dates	Tyrant	Sponsors	Notes	Evidence
Phleious	c. 260?–c. 229	Kleonymos	Gonatas?		Polyb. 2. 44. 6
Megalopolis	c. 255–c. 250	Aristodamos 'the Good'		repels Spartan attack; followed by democracy; assassinated by two philosophers. Volkmann 1964c; Walbank 1988, 272–3 (contra Walbank 1984a, 231)	Plut. Ag.–Kl. 3. 7; Paus. 8. 27. 11, 30. 7, 32. 4, 35. 5, 36. 5; Polyb. 10. 22. 2; Plut. Philop. 1. 4; Diog. Laert. 4. 31
Sikyon	252–251	Paseas	Gonatas??		Plut. Arat. 3. 4
Sikyon	251	Nikokles	Gonatas?		Plut. Arat. 9. 3
Argos	c. 240–235	**Aristippos (II)**	Gonatas?	elder s. Aristomachos I; repels Aratos 235 (Walbank 1984b, 447); daughter marries Nabis. See Volkmann 1964b.	Plut. Arat. 25. 4–29. 5
239–197					
Sparta	c. 235–222	[Kleomenes III]	–	called 'tyrant' by hostile sources	Polyb. 2. 47. 3, etc.
Orchomenos	?–c. 234	Nearchos	Demetrios II?		SdA 499

City	Name	Sponsor	Dates		Reference
Megalopolis	Lydiadas	Demetrios II?	?–234 or 229/8	resigns to become Achaean league general	Polyb. 2. 44, 4. 77
Argos	Aristomachos (II)	Demetrios II?	?–228?	younger s. Aristomachos; 'sprung from tyrants' (Phylarchos ap. Polyb. 2. 59. 5), so > 1 ancestor was tyrant; succeeds brother Aristippos (II) c. 235 (Walbank 1933, 186–7; Walbank 1957, 238; Walbank 1984b, 455–6; Volkmann 1964d); resigns to become Achaean league general	Polyb. 2. 44, 59–60
Sparta	[Lykourgos]		219–c. 218	[exiled c. 218 on suspicion of desiring tyranny]	Polyb. 5. 29
Sparta	[Machanidas]		c. 208/7	'tyrant' in hostile sources	e.g. Polyb. 13. 6–8; Livy 27. 29. 9
Sparta	[Nabis]		207–192	'tyrant' in hostile sources	e.g. Polyb. 4. 81, 13. 6; Livy 29. 12. 14
Argos, Corinth	Philokles	**Philip V**	?–197	Philip's governor (*Corintho Argisque praeerat*)	Polyb. 18. 17; Livy 32. 38. 2–9

Key: f. = father of; s. = son of

City names are in **bold** at first occurrence only. Sponsors' names are in **bold** if positively attested.

and Demaretos; the *Megarians* by Ptoiodoros, Helixos and Perillos; the *Thebans* by Timolaos, Theogeiton, and Anemoitas; and the *Euboeans* by Hipparchos, Kleitarchos, and Sosistratos.

(*On the Crown* = Oration 18. 295)

Demosthenes thus names twenty-seven individuals from ten *poleis* or regions, mainly in the Peloponnese; there are precisely two or three from each region, and among the Argives is Mnaseas though not Athenogenes.

To this Polybios responds, perhaps with reference to Philip V's handing over of Argos to Nabis:[18]

> (1) So while one would praise Demosthenes in many respects, one would criticize him in this: that he randomly and unwisely hurled the bitterest blame at the most famous of the Greeks, (2) saying that in Arkadia Kerkidas, Hieronymos, and Eukampidas were traitors to Greece because they fought on the side of Philip; likewise … [*he repeats most of Demosthenes' list, including Mnaseas*] (5) and has enumerated several others, naming them by their city.
>
> Yet all the aforementioned men had many obvious reasons for acting in defence of their own rights, especially those from Arkadia and Messene. (6) For they, by drawing Philip into the Peloponnese and humiliating the Lakedaimonians, first caused all the people living in the Peloponnese to breathe again and seize the notion of freedom; (7) second, by taking back the land and cities which the Lakedaimonians had seized, in the era of their success, from the Messenians, Megalopolitans, Tegeates, and Argives, strengthened their own fatherlands, as is generally agreed. …
>
> (9) Now if they had done these things while admitting a garrison from Philip in each fatherland, or abolishing the laws and depriving their fellow citizens of liberty and free speech in the service of private greed or power, they would merit this appellation [*sc. of traitor*]. (10) If, however, in protecting the rights of their fatherlands they had a different judgement about affairs – thinking that different things were beneficial for Athenians and for their own cities – they ought not on this account to be called traitors by Demosthenes. … (13) For the Athenians, the result of their resistance to Philip was to experience the greatest calamities after being defeated in the battle at Chaironeia.

(Polyb. 18. 14. 1–13)

Although Mnaseas may have wielded executive power in Argos, and Athenogenes apparently did so in Troizen, while Aristratos is referred to as one of the previous 'tyrants' by Plutarch (*Arat.* 13. 1–3, referring to the reign

---

[18] So Walbank 1957–79, ii. 564–5, ad loc.

of Philip II), this does not prove that they or the other men were uncon-
stitutional sole rulers. Indeed, tyranny is not the point of Demosthenes'
remarks: he simply presents these men as having successfully persuaded
their fellow citizens to adopt a pro-Macedonian stance. Polybios' words
are, indeed, clear evidence that the cities in question were not, at that time,
garrisoned by Philip II. His statement about continuity of the rule of law
equally implies that these men were not tyrants. Nevertheless, the evidence
for Athenogenes and probably that for Mnesias shows that the template for
pro-Macedonian executive magistracy existed before 338. The role seems to
have fallen to home-grown talent, presumably drawn from the local citizen
elite; its holders were not outsiders, 'parachuted in'.

III.2.b Garrisons and 'Tyrants' from Chaironeia to Kynoskephalai (338–197)

As we saw earlier (Sections II.3.b–c), at the end of the Lamian war Antipater
broke with Philip and Alexander's practice and installed garrisons and
in some places oligarchies, as well as a 'governor' or 'superintendent'
(*epimelētēs*) of the Peloponnese. This represented a much harsher line
than Philip had followed in 338; the charter of his Hellenic alliance had
promised the retention of traditional constitutions. Antipater's impositions
also opened the way for others – in the first place his chosen successor,
Polyperchon – to gain the favour of the Greeks by promising what Philip
had. It should be noted that it was not tyrannies that Antipater introduced,
but oligarchies; this episode, despite the vitriolic language which Polybios
attributes to Chlaineas the Aitolian (9. 29), offers no precedent for the possible use of tyrants by the Macedonians – which in many cases, as we shall
see, is by no means conclusively attested or, if attested, transparent in nature.

  The evidence for tyranny and especially garrisons in the long third century is patchy, often little more than passing mentions or indirect hints.
This is probably because the history of Hieronymos of Kardia ended at or
soon after Pyrrhos' death, while that of Phylarchos on a later period was less
trustworthy; both are known only from quotations.[19]

Garrisons After 338 (with or without Evidence of Tyranny)

As we saw earlier (Section II.3.c), the war between Cassander and the
Antigonids in the Peloponnese – lasting from *c.* 312 to *c.* 303, and fought

---

[19] Walbank 1988, 274.

chiefly in the north but also in Messenia – involved the placing of garrisons in numerous towns. The specific occasions need not be repeated; suffice it to note that among those garrisoned, and when necessary fortified, by one side or the other were (at various times) Orchomenos, Messene, Patrai, Aigion, Dyme, Sikyon, Corinth, Kyllene, Elis, Troizen, Epidauros, various rural forts, and probably Skiros in northern Laconia or south-eastern Arkadia.[20] An unpublished inscription (*SEG* 37. 280) documents a Macedonian garrison at Argos between 315 and 303.[21] References to the 'liberation' of a *polis* should usually imply that it had been garrisoned, for example, Boura in 303; while general statements about a commander garrisoning the *poleis* of a region suggest – what we would assume in any case – that they routinely left a detachment of soldiers to stabilize places they had captured or wished to prevent from falling into other hands. This does not necessarily mean that they interfered directly in internal politics, though even the presence of a garrison might influence the choices of a political body.

In the eastern Argolid in the mid-270s, the Spartan pretender and former regent Kleonymos 'liberated' Troizen from a garrison set up (perhaps in 278) by Krateros, the Macedonian governor of Corinth and half-brother of Gonatas. Kleonymos

> sent over the walls certain missiles upon which was written that he had come to liberate their state. Simultaneously he sent back some prisoners who had been persuaded to his side, in order that they should denigrate Krateros. By this scheme, internal unrest was aroused among those in the besieged city …
>
> (Frontinus, *Stratagems*, 3. 6. 7)

The passage is striking:[22] Kleonymos not only induces captured citizens to change sides, but deliberately exploits the tendency of even a relatively small *polis* to divide into factions.

Other episodes of warfare in the succeeding decades presumably involved the imposition of garrison detachments; but the sources are thin. The next well-attested episode is Kleomenes III's war against the Achaean league in the 220s, when we see garrisons imposed regularly by one or both sides. Locations include Mantinea, Lasion, Pellene, and Olygyrtos, in all of which the Achaeans installed garrisons to prevent pro-Spartan elements taking power; and Argos, where Kleomenes III installed a force (see Section II.4.e).

---

[20] For the last, see Chapter II, n. 81.

[21] Cf. *SEG* 50. 357; 60. 985 ad fin.

[22] Frontinus makes Cleonymus an Athenian, but Polyainos 2. 29. 1 calls him king of the Lakedaimonians.

As in other wars of this period, however, a detachment of troops is likely to have been installed in any captured, or vulnerable, settlement or rural fortification, such as the towns Kleomenes captured or which joined his cause (including Kleonai, Phleious, Troizen, Epidauros, Hermion, Tegea, Orchomenos, Mantinea, Heraia, and Thelphousa). In some cases, the imposition of Spartan control may have been accompanied (or preceded) by a new group among the citizens of the town taking power.

The Macedonian garrison set up in Sparta by Antigonos III in 222 remained after his death (Section II.5.a). Philip V's retention of Orchomenos (Polyb. 4. 6) was presumably effected through a garrison. His Peloponnesian campaigns against the Aitolian league on behalf of his Achaean allies involved frequent capture of cities and the substitution of enemy garrisons with his own. The subsequent wars involving Lykourgos, Machanidas, and Nabis of Sparta will likewise have entailed military occupation of minor places (Section II.5.b). We have no positive evidence that the democracy–oligarchy polarity was a factor in such cases, except perhaps at Argos, where Nabis enacted social reforms (Sections II.5.b, III.3.d). Nor is there any evidence to link these episodes to the installation of tyranny – anyway an unthinkable action for Achaeans though they did impose a 'military governor' (lit. '*stratēgos* of the *polis*') on Kynaitha when the pro-Achaean party gained the upper hand (Polyb. 4. 17. 5).

'Tyrannies' After 338

The evidence is here reviewed in approximately chronological order. We shall avoid the unqualified use of the prejudicial term 'tyrant' at this stage, except when quoting an ancient source. The evidence (also in TABLE III.2) supports the existence of between twenty-one and twenty-six governors of different kinds in eleven to sixteen *poleis* between 338 and about 229, with no definite examples thereafter (other than that the Spartan kings and regents are called 'tyrants' by hostile sources).

Late Fourth Century. According to the oration *On the Treaty with Alexander* attributed (perhaps wrongly) to Demosthenes and set in 334, Alexander had recently restored 'the sons of Philiades' as tyrants (*tyrannoi*) in Messene in violation of the general peace terms (Ps.-Dem. 17. 4; 'restoring', καταγαγών, may not necessarily mean reviving an earlier tyranny, rather bringing the men back from exile). They will be the Neon and Thrasylochos of whom Demosthenes himself complains (in *On the Crown*, just quoted) that they sacrificed their city's independence to Philip. These may have been the first applications of the 'governorship template' in the Peloponnese.

This and other sources refer to Alexander elevating one Chairon, an Olympic wrestling champion, to a *tyrannis* (tyranny) in Achaean Pellene (Ps.-Dem. 17. 10; Paus. 7. 27. 7; Athenaeus 11. 509 a–b). Athenaeus mentions atrocities committed by him.

Finally, it is reported that at Megalopolis around 312 Cassander installed an *epimelētēs* ('superintendent') named Damis (Diod. 19. 63. 4–64. 1).

Sikyon: First Half of Third Century. Following its fourth-century experience of 'tyranny', and after an interval of up to about seventy years, Sikyon had at least seven governors of some kind in the half-century to 251, though some or all of these may have operated within the existing oligarchic constitution. None was necessarily in the Macedonians' pockets; but Plutarch, describing the city's liberation, says Aratos brought back men exiled 'in the time of the earlier tyrants' (ἐπὶ τῶν ἔμπροσθεν τυράννων). In some cases their exile had taken place some fifty years before (οἷς μακρὰ μὲν ἡ πλάνη καὶ ὁμοῦ τι πεντηκονταετὴς ἐγεγόνει, *Arat*. 9. 5), which could take us back to Cassander's time or, for those absent for a shorter time, to the early days of Gonatas' governorship of the Peloponnese (*c*. 296–*c*. 277). Plutarch also refers to Sikyon as (*a*) 'exchanging tyrant for tyrant' (τύραννον ἐκ τυράννου μεταβάλλουσα) until the death of (*b*) one Kleon (*Arat*. 2. 1; Paus. 2. 8. 1–3), whose rule may have begun just after autumn 272;[23] the implication is that there was at least one governor before him, indeed probably more than one; and that the sequence began some years before 272 (hence we label Kleon '*b*' here). Either way, some link with Cassander in or before the early 290s, or Gonatas from the mid-290s onwards, seems plausible (and it may be relevant to recall that Cassander had sponsored the 'superintendency' of Demetrios of Phaleron in Athens in 317–307, and allegedly the more recent regime of Lachares at Athens in the early 290s).

After the death of Kleon, says Plutarch, the Sikyonians chose (εἵλοντο) as *archontes* (chief magistrates) (*c*) Timokleidas and (*d*) Kleinias, father of the future Achaean leader Aratos (*Arat*. 2. 1);[24] upon his colleague's death Kleinias remained in office alone until his assassination in 264. It is unclear whether or not this period is to be regarded as one of democracy or oligarchy; certainly Plutarch implies that Kleon's death marked an end of continuous one-man rule, but a dual co-magistracy under the title of archonship looks like a modification or suspension of normal politics.[25] The author of a major study of Greek federalism goes so far as to comment

[23] Griffin 1982, 79.

[24] Walbank 1988, 273–4, discussing (at 274 n. 2) the slightly different version of events in Paus.

[25] Tarn 1913, 268, 361.

that Aratos' father and uncle 'probably were as much tyrants as the rest', while recognizing that probably no man ever called himself a tyrant.[26] Kleinias must have maintained friendly links with both Macedonia and its enemy Egypt, since later the young Aratos, in exile at Argos, was said to be corresponding with 'the kings who were his friends and his paternal guest-friends' (φίλοις οὖσι καὶ ξένοις πατρῴοις, *Arat.* 4. 2). One of Kleinias' aims may have been to keep Sikyon safely neutral. If Kleon had been aligned with Macedonia, the change represented by the appointment of co-archons may be that the political class in the *polis* was putting a distance between itself and Gonatas; something the king did not, or could not, prevent. Such an independent stance may have been Kleinias' legacy to Aratos.

(*e*) Kleinias' assassin – and brother-in-law (Plut. *Arat.* 2. 2) – Abantidas 'made a *tyrannis* for himself' (*Arat.* 2. 2) but was killed in 252 (so after about a dozen years in power) by two intellectuals, named Deinias (perhaps the historian from Argos, *FGrHist* 306) and Aristoteles (a philosopher). Coincidentally or not, Aristodamos of Megalopolis was also assassinated by two philosophers in the same year (see later).

(*f*) Abantidas' father, Paseas, succeeded to the position for a short while.

(*g*) He in turn was killed and was replaced by Nikokles, whom Aratos expelled four months later, in spring 251, in a coup that was reportedly bloodless (Plut. *Arat.* 9. 3), though Aratos tried to capture and kill the young son of Abantidas, his own father's murderer (2. 2). We have no direct evidence that these men had links with Macedonia, but the royal stable (τὰς ἵππους τὰς βασιλικάς, 6. 2) was located in Sikyonian territory, suggesting that Nikokles – and perhaps his two predecessors, and/or the earlier predecessors of the co-archons – enjoyed at least amicable relations with Gonatas.

Plutarch gives many enlivening details of Nikokles' rule and fall, presumably taken from Aratos' memoirs. Nikokles sent spies into Argos to observe Aratos (*Arat.* 6. 5). Aratos would later restore eighty men exiled by Nikokles, and 500 more exiled in the time of his predecessors (ἐπὶ τῶν ἔμπροσθεν τυράννων, 9. 4), presumably meaning either Abantidas and Paseas or those who wielded power before Timokleidas and Kleinias. Nikokles possessed substantial military force (τοσαύτην δύναμιν, 6. 5), and at the time of Aratos' coup in 251 there was a 'general's headquarters' (στρατήγιον) in the city as well as a force of mercenaries (μισθοφόροι, 8. 5). After the coup, Aratos knew that Antigonos was envious and wished to possess the city (it is 'begrudged', φθονουμένην, by him), which was still riven with disorder and *stasis* (9. 5).

---

[26] Larsen 1968, 306.

(*h*) Provocatively, we might add Aratos himself to the list. Strabo, indeed, does so (8. 6. 25), commenting that the city 'always had decent men for tyrants, of whom the most renowned was Aratos' (ἀεὶ τοὺς τυράννους ἐπιεικεῖς ἄνδρας ἔσχεν, Ἄρατον δ᾿ ἐπιφανέστατον). Since he later worked against 'tyrants' elsewhere, it might seem natural not to see him as one; but he is also portrayed repeatedly as having 'a position of personal power', and as taking major political decisions purely upon his own responsibility;[27] so it would make sense to see both him and other sole rulers simply as governors.

Some of this paints what might be thought a predictable picture of the workings of pro-Macedonian oppression; yet things are not that simple. Even before the liberation, Aratos had been in touch with his enemy Gonatas, as well as with Ptolemy II of Egypt, hoping for practical aid from both (Plut. *Arat.* 4. 3). After the coup he received a donation of 25 talents from 'the king' (11. 2), probably meaning Gonatas.[28] The relationship to Macedonia of a governor such as Nikokles – or indeed a leader like Aratos – was not straightforward. While Nikokles was supported by Gonatas, the support was patently not unconditional: the king was willing to consider abandoning him in favour of another man, even a *prima facie* enemy, who could more reliably ensure the city's neutrality if he could not deliver active support. After his protégé's overthrow, he tried to buy the new leader's loyalty with money that, as he well knew, might be used to hire troops to fight against him.

All this being so, it is impossible to think that the choice between alternative leaders was necessarily based on ideological distinctions; that a 'pro-Macedonian' orientation meant the same thing in every case, or was necessarily exclusive; or that Macedonian policy was designed to build a new political order conforming to a specific philosophy or programme. 'Tyranny', constitutional governorship, and even the suspension of normal business were all manifestations of traditional *polis* politics and factionalism; an element of proper procedure, albeit more oligarchic than democratic, is not excluded. Yet however 'correct' the process by which a governor acquired executive power, he would have enemies somewhere in the *polis*, and the label of 'tyrant' would be attached to him however virtuous his exercise of authority.

---

[27] Griffin 1982, 81.

[28] A few lines later (12. 1), Aratos resolves to sail to Egypt and seek subventions from Ptolemy. This is surely what prompted translators such as Langhorne and Perrin to take the unspecified βασιλέως at 11. 2 to be Ptolemy; but the king mentioned most recently in the text is Gonatas (9. 3; cf. 6. 2), and A.'s decision would surely have been unnecessary if Ptolemy was already generously supporting his campaign.

Achaea: Second Quarter of Third Century. In Achaea, it is possible that the four *poleis* that founded the revived Achaean league – Patrai, Dyme, Tritaia, and Pharai – had deposed Macedonian-sponsored governors in order to do so; we have no evidence for this, but it is a reasonable guess, given that a few years later the citizens of Boura killed a 'tyrant' in order to join the league (*c.* 275/4) and the 'tyrant' Iseas resigned at Karyneia (Polyb. 2. 41. 14). It is not known how long these rulers had exercised power, or whether they had been elected to an office, emerged informally, or were imposed by an outside power; but the likelihood is that they were in some sense pro-Macedonian, or at least supported by Gonatas, if their removal was necessary to enable a newly dominant group among the politically active citizens to attach their *polis* to the league.

At some date, says Strabo (8. 7. 5), Gonatas 'founded' (i.e. refounded) Achaean Leontion, which may imply that he garrisoned it or installed a sole ruler.[29]

Elis: 272. At Elis, the notorious Aristotimos, who seized power after the death of Pyrrhos (272), is said to have been helped to do so by Gonatas. Pausanias (5. 5. 1) names his father and grandfather, which implies that he was from a distinguished family,[30] and says Gonatas 'helped him prepare the things he needed for the attack' (συμπαρασκευάσαντος αὐτῷ τὰ ἐς τὴν ἐπίθεσιν), presumably in the form of hardware or manpower on a small scale.[31] Plutarch devotes the longest of the twenty-seven stories in his *Bravery of Women* to the women and citizens who suffered outrages but ultimately killed Aristotimos (*Mulierum virtutes*, 15 = *Mor.* 250 f–253 e).[32] Aristotimos may have issued coins before and during his rule, though the case is unproven.[33] In this account he 'was strong because of Antigonos' (ἴσχυε δι' Ἀντιγόνου) and stayed in power by relying on an armed force of

---

[29] Strabo 8. 7. 5, modified by the palimpsest. See Walbank 1957–79, i. 231 (on Polyb. 2. 41. 7–8); Rizakis 1995b, 308, following Baladié 1978, 206 n. 3. Hl fortifications: Morgan and Hall 2004, 483 (*Inv. 237*).

[30] Justin (26. 1. 4) calls Aristotimos *princeps*, either meaning that he was already a 'leading citizen' or referring to his new status.

[31] As Walbank 1988, 272, notes (*contra* Tarn 1913, 279), Justin's failure to say that Gonatas helped him to power does not trump Paus.; Justin's reworking of Trogus here is very jejune.

[32] A Delphic proxeny decree for Kyllon son of Kyllon from Alis (i.e. Elis) probably honours the leading conspirator but mentions no events (*FdD* iii. 3. 191 = *Syll.*³ 423 (²920)).

[33] Head 1911, 424–5, notes that the legend API is not necessarily his name. Walker 2004, 70 (with 71–2 nos. 211–16), considers it possible, but notes that they seem to have been struck over a long period of C3a, and that the same letters are on earlier and later coins including p. 61 no. 153 (*c.* 340 BC; Hoover 2011, 90 no. 387). Hoover 2011, 92 no. 401 (AR stater or didrachm, *c.* 280–*c.* 260), 100 no. 458 (AR hemidrachm or triobol, *c.* 280–*c.* 264), does not discuss the matter.

'mixed barbarians' (βαρβάροις μιγάσι); even if this last comment reflects hostile propaganda, it indicates that his soldiers were, at any rate, not citizens of Elis or other southern Greek *poleis*, but either Macedonians or non-Greeks. One of their commanders is named Leukios and may have been Italian (Lucius?). Plutarch says 800 exiles fled to Aitolia (cf. Justin 26. 1. 5–6). Aristotimos was assassinated after a few months in power,[34] when the exiles were encamped in Eleian territory and Krateros was sending him military assistance (Plut. *Mor.* 253 a).

Megalopolis: Second and Third Quarters of Third Century. At Megalopolis, (*a*) a certain Aristodamos, a former citizen of Phigaleia adopted into a prominent local family, took an executive position early in Gonatas' reign. He is called 'tyrant' by Plutarch (*Ag.–Kl.* 3. 7) and Pausanias (8. 27. 11; 8. 36. 5), but was remembered as 'The Good' (χρηστός, Paus. 8. 27. 11), and probably not only because he defeated the Spartans under Akrotatos in the 260s or early 250s. Many public buildings at Megalopolis were still linked to his name hundreds of years later (8. 30. 7; 8. 32. 4; 8. 35. 5) – their quantity suggesting a lengthy reign – and his grave-mound was pointed out to visitors (8. 36. 5).[35] In about 252 he was assassinated by two philosophers,[36] one named Ekdemos (Polyb. 10. 22. 2) or Ekdelos (Plut. *Philop.* 1. 3; *Arat.* 5. 1; 7. 4, 6; Paus. 8. 49. 2), the other Demophanes (*Philop.* 1. 3; Polyb. 10. 22. 2), Megalophanes (Paus. 8. 49. 2), or possibly Diophanes (father of the mid-second-century Achaean league general Diaios).[37]

(*b*) Later – Pausanias says two generations later (8. 27. 12), a clear mistake – Lydiadas son of Eudamos became another apparently patriotic 'tyrant' of Megalopolis, though he gave away the *polis* of Alipheira to the Eleians as part of some 'private acts' (πρός τινας ἰδίας πράξεις, Polyb. 4. 77. 10), perhaps in return for help in taking power.[38] Later, probably in 235,[39] he resigned and became an admired leader of the Achaean league (2. 44. 5; Paus. 8. 27. 12).[40] Publicly honoured in his lifetime at Lykosoura by the citizens of Kaphyai (*IG* v. 2. 534),[41] after his death in battle against Kleomenes III in 227 (Polyb. 2. 51. 3) he was posthumously honoured in his home city, as we know from an inscribed

---

[34] Four (*quinto mense*, Justin 26. 1. 10) or six (μῆνας τυραννήσαντα ἕξ, Paus. 5. 5. 1).
[35] Chronological details: Walbank 1988, 272–3.
[36] Tarn 1913, 357–9.
[37] The identification with Diophanes is proposed by Lauter and Spyropoulos 1998, 448; see Stavrianopoulou 2002, 139 n. 67 (at p. 140).
[38] Walbank 1957–79, i. 531 ad loc.
[39] Walbank 1936, 66, with references.
[40] On the implications of Megalopolis' admission to the league, see Kralli 2017, 178.
[41] The inscription on the statue base confirms his father's name as Eudamos.

exedra of about the 180s on which earlier honours for his father and himself were inscribed (*SEG* 52. 445–7). His son Aristopamon was honoured at Megalopolis in 227 (*SEG* 36. 379),[42] while Aristopamon's son in turn, another Lydiadas, enjoyed the same good fortune in the early second century (*SEG* 48. 524). Clearly Lydiadas' deeds did not hold the family back; in fact, the reverse.

Although the editor proposes to identify Eudamos, father of Lydiadas, with the assassin of Aristodamos elsewhere named Ekdemos or Ekdelos, this sits oddly with the fact that both 'tyrants' were honoured long after their death.[43] Whatever the truth of that identification, both Aristodamos and Lydiadas had a good press and did not suffer *damnatio memoriae*. There is no report that either man committed atrocities, or any direct evidence that their 'tyranny' had Macedonian support. Given the Achaean league's opposition to one-man rule, however – Aratos is credited with ending the tyrannies at Argos, Hermion, Phleious, and Megalopolis (Strabo 8. 7. 3)[44] – and Megalopolis' absence from the ranks of the allies in the Chremonidean war,[45] it is reasonable to assume that Aristodamos was an obstacle to the free movement of Areus and the Spartans, which would at least be welcome to Gonatas.[46]

Argos: Second Quarter of Third Century to 229. At Argos, a series of three or more likely four men from one family were leaders of the *polis* over several decades (since they share just two names, we number them each I or II; see FIGURE III.1).

(*a*) The family's domination probably began in the 270s or 260s with Aristippos I, who at the time of *stasis* in Argos during Pyrrhos' invasion (273–272) 'seemed to treat Antigonos as a friend' (ἐδόκει χρῆσθαι φίλῳ τῷ Ἀντιγόνῳ, Plut. *Pyrrh.* 30. 2). He shares the name of Aristippos II, and is probably his grandfather. If he held office as his probable grandson did later, it would explain why Phylarchos (Polyb. 2. 59. 5) describes Aristomachos II (soon described under (*d*)) as 'descended from tyrants', plural;[47] Aristippos, however, is not called a tyrant in any source.

---

[42] Taeuber 1986.
[43] Stavrianopoulou 2002, 138–43, esp. 139 n. 67.
[44] For a reassessment of Aratos' supposed principled opposition to tyranny, see Kralli 2017, 170–1.
[45] O'Neil 2008, 83.
[46] Tarn 1913, 298, suggests that by 267, when Areus I marched north to attack the Macedonians, Megalopolis and Argos may not have been under Macedonian tyrants, as there is no mention of their delaying him; plainly a weak argument. *CAH*² vii/1 table (p. 503) places the beginning of Gonatas' system of tyrants too late, at 245.
[47] See Walbank 1984a, 231, modified at Walbank 1988, 273.

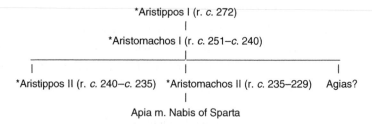

Aristippos I (r. c. 272)

Aristomachos I (r. c. 251–c. 240)

*Aristippos II (r. c. 240–c. 235)   *Aristomachos II (r. c. 235–229)   Agias?

Apia m. Nabis of Sparta

* Likely or attested sole ruler

Figure III.1. Probable family tree of the Argive 'tyrants'

(*b*) The first member of the family to be called a tyrant is Aristomachos I, probably a son of Aristippos I. He founded his rule before or after 251,[48] perhaps succeeding his father after an interregnum since in the 250s Sikyonian and Megalopolitan exiles were able to plot against their own 'tyrants' while living in Argos (Plut. *Arat.* 5. 3; 6. 2);[49] though perhaps governors of different cities could be enemies. He was honoured at Athens (then under Macedonian rule) when Gonatas was attacking his rebel nephew Alexandros in Corinth; this is at least suggestive of a pro-Macedonian stance.[50] Aristomachos, having survived an assassination plot devised by Aratos, was murdered 'by slaves' around 240 (Plut. *Arat.* 25. 1–4).

(*c*) Aristomachos' elder son Aristippos II succeeded him and repulsed more than one attack by Aratos (25. 4; 27. 1–28. 3). In doing so he was apparently aided by his popularity among his fellow citizens; it is glossed as subservience by Plutarch, but he is using the hostile Aratos as his source (25. 4). Aristippos in turn plotted against Aratos, allegedly with the support of Gonatas (25. 6), who supported him in power (26. 1). He was killed in about 235 trying to retake Kleonai from the Achaeans (29. 1–4).[51]

(*d*) The second son of Aristomachos I, Aristomachos II – the one 'descended from tyrants' – immediately took control (Plut. *Arat.* 29. 4), an incident alluded to in an inscription from Nemea;[52] but upon the death of Demetrios II of Macedonia in 229 he was induced by Aratos to relinquish power (Polyb. 2. 60. 5).[53] This suggests that he had enjoyed

[48] Walbank 1984a, 247.

[49] Walbank 1988, 296–8. Tarn 1913, 280 n. 13, wonders whether Aristomachos could have been in power during the Chremonidean war, when Areus of Sparta appears to have had considerable freedom of movement (but presumably after 267, cf. n. 46 above); but has perhaps not considered the possibility that the dynasty was discontinuous.

[50] *IG* ii² 774; *ISE* 23; Walbank 1984a, 248.

[51] Walbank 1984b, 447–9.

[52] Bradeen 1966, 323–6 no. 6, reading [Ἀγί]ας Ἀρ[ιστ]ομάχου at l. 25 and suggesting this is the Agias who aids Aristomachos II at Plut. *Arat.* 29. 6 and that he is another brother.

[53] On the chronology, see Walbank 1933, 186–7. On Aratos' motives, see Kralli 2017, 170–1, 176.

Macedonian support in some fashion, and now felt exposed. Like Lydiadas of Megalopolis, he received league protection and was elected general for 228/7 (2. 44. 6; 2. 60. 4; Plut. *Arat.* 27–9; 35. 5; Paus. 2. 8. 6).[54] Later, however, he withdrew from the campaign against Kleomenes, allegedly tortured and executed eighty upper-class opponents, and on being captured was put to death cruelly by the Achaeans; admired by the pro-Spartan historian Phylarchos, he is unsurprisingly reviled by Polybios (2. 59. 5–60. 8).[55] His daughter Apia was almost certainly given in marriage to Nabis of Sparta.

Orchomenos, Hermion, and Phleious, Third Quarter of Third Century to c. 229. The admission of Arkadian Orchomenos to the Achaean league in *c.* 234 took place under Demetrios II. The terms, partially preserved in an inscription (*SdA* 499; *Syll.*³ 490; *IG* v. 2. 344),[56] include an amnesty for one Nearchos and his sons, presumed to have been the governor of the *polis*;[57] perhaps up to the moment of its accession.

The dictatorships of Xenon at Hermion and of Kleonymos at Phleious ended with their resignations and their cities' admissions to the league in *c.* 229. They are otherwise unknown.

We do not know how long any of the last three individuals held power, or whether any of them was Macedonian-sponsored; but the coincidence of the resignation of the last two with the death of Demetrios II suggests that they had depended in some measure, and at least in the recent past, upon Macedonian support.

[Laconia: 230s to 192]. The epithet 'tyrant' is applied polemically to Kleomenes III by Polybios, to Machanidas by Livy, and to Nabis by both. In fact, the lack of credible attestations of tyrants after 229 is noteworthy – and unsurprising, for this was the acme of Achaean league power, when one-man rule was deprecated.

III.2.c Garrisons and 'Tyrants': A Balance-sheet

If we turn to the interpretation of garrisons and sole rulers, we may consider whose purposes they served and the extent to which the Macedonian installation of, or support for, sole rulers was part of a deliberate strategy.

---

[54] The statue dedicated at Epidauros by Apia daughter of Aristippos and Aristomachos (II?) son of Aristo[machos (III?)] cannot be closely dated; *SEG* 29. 377 gives *c.* 255–229 (previously *IG* iv² 1. 621; *SEG* 25. 416); Mandel 1979; also *SEG* 1. 77; *IG* iv. 1111.

[55] Walbank 1984b, 455, 456.

[56] Austin² 68 = BD 30.

[57] Accepted by Mackil 2013, 259–60, 462–6 no. 39.

The Case Against Macedonia

Polybios' view is uncompromising. In one of his briefer statements on the subject of Macedonian rule, he sees major Greek *poleis* as having succumbed to *force majeure* rather than as being to blame for their loss of freedom, in contrast to a later period of submission to Rome: 'at certain times the men of Chalkis, Corinth, and certain other *poleis* obeyed the kings in Macedonia, and received garrisons, because of the natural excellence (εὐφυΐαν) of their locations' (38. 4. 3).

In two other key passages, he makes fuller and more specific statements about Macedonians who, he says, oppressed the Greeks not only with garrisons but also with tyrannies. The first passage, early in the *Histories*, is in his own voice:

> (9) In the period following that of Alexander, but earlier than the Olympiad just mentioned [284–280], they [the Achaeans] fell into such discord and such a bad condition, especially because of the kings from Macedonia, that all the cities were divided among themselves and pursued their own interests in opposition to one another (ἐναντίως τὸ συμφέρον ἄγειν ἀλλήλαις).
>
> (10) What happened as a result of this was that some of them came to be garrisoned (τὰς μὲν ἐμφρούρους αὐτῶν γενέσθαι) by Demetrios and Cassander, and subsequently by Antigonos Gonatas, while some also [or 'even'] had tyrants imposed upon them (τὰς δὲ καὶ τυραννεῖσθαι) [*sc.* by Gonatas]; for this man appears to have planted the greatest number [or 'a very great number'] of sole rulers (πλείστους γὰρ δὴ μονάρχους οὗτος ἐμφυτεῦσαι δοκεῖ) among the Greeks.[58]
>
> (2. 41. 9–10)

The word translated as 'the greatest number' (πλείστους) could mean 'the largest number' (that is, Gonatas set up more tyrannies than the other rulers) or only 'very many'. Either way, Gonatas is represented as the main patron of tyrants. The words that follow may, furthermore, suggest that whereas Demetrios and Cassander used garrisons but not tyrants (or used tyrants but rarely), only Gonatas used both (or did so more often than the others); but it is possible that Polybios' words should not be pressed so hard. The limited nature of his claim in one respect should, however, be noted: the charge is not that Gonatas installed tyrants in every city that he controlled or was aligned with

---

[58] Both Paton's version and Shuckburgh's ignore δοκεῖ and wrongly make the last clause a comparative statement. Paton's addition of 'by the latter', corresponding to my 'this man', is justified by sense and context.

him. Nor is it necessarily that he was particularly prone to support tyranny *in the Peloponnese*, for Polybios ends his statement with 'among the Greeks'. A crucial point, not always given due emphasis, is that Polybios clearly testifies that Achaea before *c.* 281/0 was divided internally – the *poleis* 'began to act against others' interests'; it is hard to imagine that he has anything in mind other than that, while some Achaean *poleis* before 281/0 were aligned with Macedonia, others were opposed. To what extent the former group was actively managed by the Macedonians is a question worth posing.

A third passage of Polybios, making a slightly different distinction, comes in the speech he puts in the mouth of Chlaineas the Aitolian in the setting of 211. After reminding his Spartan audience how, after Alexander's death, Antipater hunted down and killed anti-Macedonians, Chlaineas turns to the period that followed:

> (5) And as for the deeds of Cassander and Demetrios, and moreover (σὺν δὲ τούτοις) those of Antigonos Gonatas, who does not know of them? ...
> (6) Some of these men by bringing garrisons (οἱ μὲν φρουρὰς εἰσάγοντες) into the cities, others by planting tyrants (οἱ δὲ τυράννους ἐμφυτεύοντες), ensured that no city escaped the ignominy of being enslaved (οὐδεμίαν πόλιν ἄμοιρον ἐποίησαν τοῦ τῆς δουλείας ὀνόματος).
>
> (9. 29. 5–6)

The language of slavery has appeared earlier in Polybios' text, when he says the league combated 'those who either themselves or through the kings attempted to enslave their native cities' (2. 42. 3). Importantly, Chlaineas' statement is not specifically about the Peloponnese (though the sentences that follow refer to Sparta's aspirations to hegemony); nor is this passage definite evidence that each ruler used either garrisons or tyrannies but not both together. Similarly, the verb translated in the second and third passages as 'plant' (ἐμφυτεύω)[59] cannot be taken as firm evidence that these rulers usually or always set up a new tyranny, as opposed to supporting a man already in power; both statements are made by 'speakers' – Polybios and Chlaineas – who seek to lay grave charges at the Macedonians' door and may be exaggerating.

Imprecise and rhetorical as these passages are, it is inescapable that Polybios expresses himself more negatively about Gonatas than about other Macedonians.

---

[59] It is nowhere else used of the installation of a tyranny, but the suggestion (Tarn 1913, 279 n. 8) that Polyb. may be echoing Aitolian rhetoric is too speculative: the word is standard in LCl Greek (e.g. Thphr. *CP* 1. 6. 1).

The Case for the Defence

In evaluating Polybios' principal claims – first, that the Macedonian rulers 'enslaved' the cities; second, that Gonatas was the one most enamoured of such a policy – we may conveniently start from the sceptical assessment by Tarn, which, though a century old, is one of the most detailed studies and continues to exercise influence.[60] We are now in a position to review its strengths and weaknesses; some of the latter have been noted by others.[61]

In his passionate, book-length apologia for the king, Tarn doubts (probably rightly, as we shall see) that Gonatas was responsible for a blanket imposition of tyranny. He is on less firm ground when he argues that after 287 the future king set up no new tyrannies but only left existing garrisons in place (so as not to appear weak) and supported friends already in power. This policy, in his view, was based on the realization that puppet regimes would be unreliable;[62] but we have seen examples of long-lasting regimes that presumably brought about stability, a thing Gonatas undoubtedly desired (cf. Section II.4.f).[63] The rarity of evidence for Gonatas actually installing a tyrant in power is striking.

It is with greater plausibility that Tarn rejects Polybios' picture of enslavement. He is skating on thin ice again, however, in suggesting that Gonatas was merely following Alexander's humane policy of supporting 'protected native rulers' in the former Persian empire.[64] Tarn admits that the circumstances were totally different. If a precedent were sought, there were others closer to home, such as in the behaviour of Philip II and Alexander; or one could appeal to the regime of Euphron at Sikyon (*c.* 368–*c.* 366), whose populist or even democratic credentials are evident.

Tarn attempts to underpin his awkward compromise, and save Gonatas' reputation, by limiting the scope of his 'protected tyrants' policy to a few major *poleis*: Elis, Argos, and Megalopolis.[65] But whereas he discounts the possibility that rulers of the smaller *poleis* of Hermion, Phleious, and Orchomenos were pro-Macedonian because the evidence is vague,[66] we

---

[60] Tarn 1913, 113–14, 198, 301–2, and esp. 277–85.

[61] Explicitly, Reger 1998; implicitly, Walbank 1988, 274.

[62] Tarn 1913, 277–8.

[63] Tarn 1913, 281 n. 20 says support for tyrannies 'is the one single [*sic*] fact about Antigonos that our anti-Macedonian tradition has invariably managed to remember'; but the late source he cites (Eusebios, *Chronikon*) says only, 'It was he who mastered Hellas by force (ἐγκρατῶς χειρωσάμενος)', which may simply refer to the Chremonidean war (Schoene *et al.* 1866–75, i. 237–8).

[64] Tarn 1913, 278, cf. 198.

[65] Tarn 1913, 280.

[66] Tarn 1913, 279–80.

have seen that it is reasonable to infer from the chronology that they were so; the same is true of Boura and Keryneia earlier. Tarn denies links between another secondary power, Sikyon, and the Macedonians; this, too, we have shown to be implausible.[67] At Tarn's third city, Megalopolis, by contrast, there is not even the suggestion of evidence for Antigonid intervention (which does not, of course, prove that it did not happen).

Tarn asserts that Polybios is not convinced of the truth of what he makes Chlaineas say, supporting this by claiming that Polybios uses the words 'it is said'. This is untrue; no such phrase stands in the passage of book 9 we have quoted. Polybios does use 'appears' (δοκεῖ) in the passage from book 2; but that verb need not imply real doubt, and means rather 'is likely'.[68] It may be that Polybios is not unsure whether Gonatas installed many tyrannies and garrisons, but uncertain about whether he installed more than other rulers.

In a more persuasive argument for Gonatas' mildness, Tarn rightly observes that some of the tyrants of Argos, though Macedonian-sponsored, appear to have enjoyed strong support from within their *polis*. The same may have been the case elsewhere. Having proposed that Gonatas deliberately sought 'not merely to establish his own party in power in such of the cities as were necessary to him, but to aid the leading man of that party to rule the city as a "tyrant" ', however, Tarn at once undermines his position by doubting that in every case Gonatas 'actually installed them, or was responsible for their seizure of power'.[69] Yet of his three relevant tyrants, one (Aristotimos of Elis) was certainly, and another (Aristippos I of Argos) was probably, installed with his help. Tarn has perhaps momentarily forgotten his suggestion that Gonatas interfered actively in only three places.[70]

While seeking to present Gonatas as a ruler of unusual moral integrity, Tarn is forced to accept that he fell short of the best standards of the day and risked the hostility of the Greeks; but argues at considerable length that the king was forced to support tyrants in order to protect Macedonia.[71] To argue thus is to ignore that at least some, perhaps all, so-called tyrants must have had support within their *poleis*, and that there may have been disagreements about what kind of freedom, and whose, was most valuable – an observation

---

[67] Although strictly it is true that 'there is no evidence that Abantidas or any other Sikyonian tyrant had ever been a nominee, an ally, or a friend of Antigonos' (Tarn 1913, 395 n. 4), the argument from plausibility retains force.

[68] δοκεῖ need not connote serious doubt: cf. LSJ s.v., II. 5, '*to be reputed*, c. inf.'

[69] Tarn 1913, 278.

[70] Since we do not believe this, we cannot follow Tarn 1913, 278, in taking the words 'those attempting to dissolve laws and ancestral constitutions' in the Chremonides decree (*IG* ii² 687. 14–16) as referring only to 'general support' rather than the installation of tyrants.

[71] Tarn 1913, 281–5.

that brings to mind Polybios' own warning against condemning those who sought a *modus vivendi* with Macedonia. This, too, sits oddly with Tarn's attempt to limit Gonatas' policy to a few strategic *poleis*.

Finally, since Tarn claims that Gonatas' tyrant strategy was applied only rarely, is it odd that he credits the king with an economic motive, arguing not only that the *poleis* themselves paid for being garrisoned, but that additional financial levies were imposed on them. Aside from the contradictory way of proceeding, while the evidence for the second proposition is slightly stronger than for the first, neither will prove compelling.

A Reassessment

How does Polybios' claim that Gonatas was the greatest imposer of tyranny measure up against the cases reviewed? We have seen definite or possible evidence for 'tyrants' in up to eighteen *poleis* (excluding Sparta). The evidence for garrisons peters out in the mid-third century, perhaps partly because of the deficiencies of the sources. Can a garrison often have existed without a tyranny, or vice versa? Whatever the answer, the evidence for 'tyranny' intensifies rather than declines.

Of the cases listed – ranging from the reign of Philip II to that of Antigonos III – nearly all are explicitly, or can presumptively be, associated with Macedonian 'support', actual or potential; that support being, however, of different content and degree. The clearest exceptions are Kleinias at Sikyon, who appears to have steered a diplomatic middle course (and whose son, Aratos, was no friend of Macedonia during the first half of his career), and presumably therefore Kleinias' co-archon, Timokleidas. Other 'tyrants' have a positive image in the sources, but this does not rule out a pro-Macedonian orientation.

Furthermore, most of the attested or inferred episodes of one-man rule fall between the 280s and *c.* 240, during Gonatas' governorship of the Peloponnese and his subsequent occupancy of the Macedonian throne. During these years, we have evidence for fifteen to twenty governors in nine to thirteen *poleis*. This may, however, partly reflect the nature of the evidence for that period (not least that of Polybios himself) or even simply Gonatas' longevity: he had about fifty-seven years in which to support governors and garrisons. Likewise, the rarity of one-man rule before *c.* 300 may partly reflect the fact that Cassander had relatively few opportunities to change the constitution of a *polis*; while Demetrios I, the other man specifically accused by Polybios, is unlikely to have openly violated his and his father's declared principle of leaving constitutional arrangements alone (Section II. 3.c), at least until after the collapse of his Hellenic alliance following the defeat at Ipsos in 301. Indeed, despite Polybios' second and third passages, we lack any evidence to link Demetrios to specific instances of one-man rule.[72]

If Gonatas remains the probable prime mover, how do we read his conduct? The evidence already falls well short of a blanket policy or totalitarian system, let alone the suppression of *polis* politics. As Walbank observes, it does not suggest that in any strong sense Gonatas 'rested his power in the Peloponnese on pro-Macedonian tyrants'.[73] His judicious reconstruction is more nuanced than Tarn's, but our earlier reading of the evidence may add further precision.

Walbank judges that Gonatas exercised a general policy in favour of one-man rule only after losing Corinth in 243; before the Chremonidean war his policy had been 'more eclectic, with some tyrants, some garrisons, and here and there a tolerated neutrality, and with Craterus' troops on Acrocorinth to oversee and coordinate'.[74] This, however, seems not to give enough weight to the long sequence of one-man rulers at Sikyon from about the 290s on; to the evidence from the time of Gonatas' governorship of the Peloponnese; to the divisions in Achaea before *c.* 281/0 attested by Polybios, which probably centred around each *polis*'s stance towards Macedonia; to the Argive 'dynasty' that began in the 270s or 260s; or to the difficulty Gonatas would have had in operating a 'tyrant policy' at all after the loss of Acrocorinth in 243. Walbank's balanced description of Gonatas' early reign seems equally applicable to the later years,[75] and it is hard to see a definite change-point.

Once Demetrios had recaptured the Peloponnese in 298 or 297 and put Gonatas in charge – himself campaigning against Sparta and Messene – it may have made sense to set up governors, or at least garrisons, in certain towns to keep control of them. (Changes in the Antigonids' approach were discussed at Sections II.4.a–b.) Demetrios' departure from Greece in 287, Pyrrhos' defeat in 272, and the end of the Chremonidean war in the late 260s are further contexts in which Gonatas might have considered imposing political governors or supporting existing governors. We have seen reason to suspect, for example, that up to six Achaean *poleis* had governors by 281/ 0. Not all attested tyrannies in the mid-third century, however, were necessarily his creations; and many endured for up to a decade after his death,

---

[72] Larsen 1968, 216, considers the period from 294 on the likeliest context for any Demetrian tyrannies.

[73] Walbank 1988, 272–4 (quotation, 274).

[74] Walbank 1988, 274.

[75] Walbank 1988, 274.

as Demetrios II appears to have fought a rearguard action, attempting to rebuild some of Macedonia's influence; but without tenure of Corinth he was swimming against the tide (see Section II.4.e). Nor does it appear that Gonatas was wedded to one-man rule as a uniform solution to the problem of control; indeed, to enforce regime change would contradict his primary concern for stability. The use of a senior Macedonian figure, rather than a local governor, to direct affairs at Corinth tells the same story. At times, however, Gonatas' attention was drawn away from the south, such as after Kouroupedion, which created an opportunity for the Achaeans to shift the scenery.

We can go further in offering a positive rather than critical analysis. The consensual interpretation does not supply all the answers. It appears that most one-man rule in the early hellenistic Peloponnese was connected, to a greater or lesser extent, with Macedonian domination; yet it also had a 'home-grown' character, perhaps reflecting the political culture of each *polis*. Patently these 'tyrants' do not fit Aristotle's picture (*Politics* 5. 10) of tyranny as either the result of the overthrow of the elite by a champion of the masses or a modification of high office or kingship; neither do they conform to Polybios' cyclical model (6. 7) in which tyranny follows monarchy.[76] A man whom others call *tyrannos* seems generally to have been more of a governor or 'superintendent' (to invoke Demetrios of Phaleron's title of *epimelētēs*), drawn from the local citizenry and very likely possessing hereditary wealth, who sought to preserve stability, security, and the interests of the political elite (or their part of it), not impose a new order. Some may have been military commanders with additional civil responsibilities, or men appointed to a special magistracy under oligarchic or democratic procedure. To some extent they resemble Rome's *dictātores*, retired magistrates reappointed for a fixed term to resolve a crisis;[77] or the central figure in Aineias Taktikos' *Poliorketika* (*Siege Matters*), a military generalissimo with power to issue orders to the civilian population of his *polis*.[78] At an earlier epoch, a similar role had sometimes been performed by leading men in Greek *poleis* under Persian rule (see, for example, the list at Hdt. 4. 138).

Polybios, as we saw, may mean us to understand that more cities were garrisoned than had governors imposed on them. His words leave open the possibility (to be assumed *a priori* in any case) that kings might install a garrison where there was no governor; it is hard to imagine them installing a governor without giving him garrison protection. Where a governor

---

[76] Cf. Hahm 2000.

[77] Cf. Kalyvas 2007 for the Roman *dictator* as, in origin, designed to suppress internal conflict.

[78] On Aineias, see Whitehead 1990; Pretzler and Barley 2017.

held power independently of Macedonian support, he might not need a military guard.

The *modus operandi* of a garrison is scarcely attested. One can imagine it being commanded by a Macedonian officer, or a non-Macedonian officer from another *polis* in royal employ, or a local *stratēgos* (like Aineias Taktikos' general); any of whom might also wield political authority over the *polis*. As for the footsoldiers, Polybios' word 'introducing' (εἰσάγοντες, 9. 29. 6) may indicate that citizens did not police their own town; and in the only cases where we have any information we hear of Aristotimos' 'barbarians' and Nikokles' 'mercenaries'. We do not know who paid the soldiers – the king, or members of the local community? What was its impact upon local politics, and was it politically proactive or purely reactive?

It makes sense, in the light of our discussion of the internal make-up of *poleis*, to consider that some governors were the product of city politics.[79] What we might have assumed was a series of one-man regimes imposed from outside may be, rather, an example of the natural condition of a citizen body: that of being divided into groups with different interests and allegiances, each seeking to maximize their advantage, even at the cost of the *polis*'s freedom. In such a scenario, it may have been a case of the elite pursuing their normal style of politics. If the governor had a track record of supporting Macedonia, he must have belonged to a group of citizens who welcomed his elevation and felt part of the new regime.

We cannot assume that the Macedonians were particularly concerned about the political inclination of a governing group, such as whether it was democratic or oligarchic. A committed democrat was, of course, unlikely to accept the role of governor; but how many of the elite were so philosophically committed? The fact, however, that over the long third century the Successors (like Philip and Alexander) sometimes supported democratic constitutions, sometimes oligarchic, and sometimes one-man rule suggests that they had no ideological aim of actively promoting one-man rule as such.

Hardly any of these governors spoilt their reputations by savage acts. Some earned admiration rather than incurring hatred: Aristodamos was remembered as The Good, while Kleinias and Lydiadas (elected magistrates) appear to have been patriots; the fact of having such a man for a father – or even being a kind of *tyrannos* himself – was apparently not held against Aratos. Several led their city's army into battle and enjoyed good posthumous reputations. They might even be rehabilitated so far as to

---

[79] Cf. the perceptive discussion of Lewis 2009, 111–17.

serve as generals of the Achaean league (a pattern observed by Aristainos of Megalopolis as chief commander in the 190s, speaking to the Romans and Nabis: Livy 34. 33. 2). (A parallel may be drawn with Douris, 'tyrant' of Samos in the early third century, who after demitting office *c.* 280 appears to have lived on safely in his *polis*, writing his histories.[80]) Given all this, it seems unlikely that governors were often, if ever, elevated by the Macedonians in the face of overwhelming hostility. Only a few – Aristotimos, Nikokles and his predecessors, and Aristomachos II – are alleged to have committed atrocities, and then only against other members of the elite. Such acts, or a violent end to their rule, may reflect the normal course of *polis* politics rather than an embittered response to Macedonian (or home-grown) oppression, let alone to a Macedonian programme or ideology. To be sure, if they were seen as backed by the Macedonians, it would be the anti-Macedonians that opposed them; but more for the fact of losing freedom than (in most cases) because of downright oppression. As Polybios saw, however, freedom might sometimes have to take second place to the safety of the *polis* or economic considerations.

Indeed, a governor's relationship to a supportive Macedonian king may not have been wholly passive. One of his important roles will have been to mediate between city and king, a role performed in many parts of the hellenistic world by diplomatic envoys and by the king's official 'friends'. It would be easy to dismiss governors as puppet rulers or destroyers of civic values. The task of safeguarding the *polis*'s interests and satisfying the king's desire for stability could hardly be carried out by an individual unless he had a group of like-minded men backing him. He may, indeed, have been put forward by them as their candidate for the role, on the basis that he would preserve whichever external alignment of the *polis* they preferred. Even when a *polis* was anti-Macedonian or neutral, the creation of a sole ruler – perhaps through the device of a special civic office as at Sikyon – may represent the (temporary) victory of one of the competing groups, which in other circumstances could have taken the form of violent *stasis*.

This model of 'consensual tyranny', of the governor as delegate – while it may not have operated everywhere – assumes that such a regime had no ideological programme other than (*a*) the maintenance of a particular stance *vis-à-vis* external powers and (*b*) opposition to political rivals within the *polis*; either of which could be presented as the prevention of revolution (see Section III.3.d) and be used to justify selective exile or executions. A sole ruler may have been popular or unpopular with the broad swathe of

---

[80]   Kebric 1974; Shipley 1987, 175–81, with caveats of Dalby 1991 and Lund 1992, 120–4.

citizens, but popularity was probably not a prerequisite for holding power; it was the support of an elite group that mattered.[81] Indeed, in *poleis* such as Sikyon one-man rule appears to have become culturally embedded, with no necessary connection to Macedonia. The extent to which tyrannies there 'began' and 'ended' may be questioned; it may be better to see the successive governors, the two elected co-archons, and their eventual successor Aratos as men cast in the same aristocratic mould.[82]

It is hardly possible to know the exact geographical reach of Macedonian power at any given time; the evidence is fragmentary, and scholars have generally avoided the question. Errington argues that it was firmly established and did not break down until the early second century;[83] but this is too definite, for the situation is largely unclear and was certainly not uniform in space or time. Macedonian domination of the northern Peloponnese was not a monolithic institution; there were no 'Macedonian areas' and 'non-Macedonian areas' with discrete boundaries.

Finally, it is worth unpicking what support for Macedonia may have meant. We cannot assume that a governor who accepted support from Gonatas, even in the form of a garrison, was in all other respects 'pro-Macedonian'. A lack of deep-seated or ideological commitment to the Macedonian 'cause' may be deduced in the cases, at least, of those so-called tyrants who demitted office, were straightaway rehabilitated, and became senior commanders in the Achaean league.

Of course, every form of regime, including one-man rule, was affected by the presence of Macedonian power, in the sense that every *polis* had to reach some accommodation with Macedonia or else find other protection – which brought its own risks. In any case, the main potential guardians, before the rise of the Achaean league, were Sparta and Egypt, neither of which could be relied upon consistently. To quote Walbank, 'though not every tyrant was Gonatas' man, once in power a tyrant would be likely to look to Macedon'; conversely, Gonatas was likely to remind existing governors of his capacity to help them, as he reminded Aratos in 251.[84] As for 'the cause', it is difficult to see what that could mean other than stability; a guarantee of neutrality could be enough to save a *polis* from active intervention. We have no evidence that allies of Macedonia – even under the

---

[81] On the increasing domination of early Hl politics by elite citizens, see e.g. Shipley 1987, 211–17, 221–4; Shipley 2000b, 96–102; IV.7.c below, and Chapter V, *passim*; Cartledge 2016, ch. 14, e.g. pp. 234–6.

[82] Lewis 2009, 114, comments: 'clearly Aratus was attempting to restore his family's place at the heart of civic politics'.

[83] Errington 1990, 237.

[84] Walbank 1957–79, i. 233 (on Polyb. 2. 41. 10).

Hellenic alliance in its several incarnations – swore to uphold the exclusive and universal authority, or the ambition, of the *hēgemōn* as against those of Alexander's other successors.

Suppose for a moment that the Greeks used flagpoles. Whose flag would have been hoisted over a *polis*, whatever its alignment? Surely not the Macedonian flag, or that of the governor's family, or his party; but the flag of the *polis* itself.

III.3 Politics and *Stasis*

We have seen how the Macedonians sometimes intervened forcefully in *polis* politics. Internal disharmonies also played an active part in events, potentially limiting or reinforcing the effects of external domination. The most obvious reflection of the fractured *polis* is the widely attested phenomenon of *stasis*: violent internal confrontation between groups of citizens wishing to align the constitution with their own preferences and interests. A group might even be willing to sacrifice the *polis*'s freedom in exchange for its own freedom to govern (whether in the interests of change or of stability).[85] Like the overall socio-economic relationships within a *polis*, the tradition of political violence might be deeply rooted; some communities seem to have had a propensity for it. To this extent, political developments were in part a continuation of existing behaviour rather than the result of Macedonian domination.

This section will consider the frequency and nature of political confrontation and civic violence, whether there was a rising trend, and the factors driving both. Rather than attributing events primarily to external force or to ideological programmes, an answer more in line with Section III.2 will be offered, in terms of the interaction of these factors with existing and often long-standing divisions within *poleis*, and with traditional political practices, sometimes deep-rooted. The relative impact of these and other factors will be seen to have varied according to particular circumstances.

The *Poliorketika* of Aineias Taktikos is evidence for a mind-set in which the absence of civic peace and the presence of mercenaries were both accepted as normal.[86] The existence of a large 'floating population' of mercenaries, or potential mercenaries, many of them exiled from their *polis* as a result of *stasis*, is a significant feature of the late classical and early hellenistic

---

[85] Hansen 2004f, 124, 128.

[86] M. M. Austin 1994, 530–1; Hansen 2004f, 124. On Aineias generally, see Pretzler and Barley 2017. The identification of the author with the Stymphalian general is accepted by Whitehead 2002, 10–13.

periods, even if we allow for the exaggerated rhetoric of conservatives like Isokrates.[87] Not only the rootless, however, served for money: Spartans, for example, even kings and their relatives, acted as mercenaries, often outside Greece, in an effort to boost the *polis*'s dwindling funds. The existence of increased numbers of mercenaries in Greece[88] was one of the results of frequent civil strife in southern Greece. It is true that Greece had always exported men, and the existence of mercenaries may also be evidence of population growth; but it would be simplistic to attribute the rise of mercenary service to over-population when political, and geopolitical, factors were certainly at work. We shall examine later whether this had economic consequences.

Unfortunately, the evidence for the internal history of Peloponnesian *poleis* in the third century is less plentiful than for the fourth. For the fourth, it often includes detailed evidence of internal cleavages, both vertical and horizontal (cf. Section III.1), and of their consequences. The greater part of the evidence is contemporary, whereas much of the (sparser) evidence for the third century comes from later writers looking back with hindsight or *parti pris*. It will be assumed here, as elsewhere, that the structural characteristics of a *polis* society changed only slowly – except at times of crisis, but not even a crisis necessarily has long-term effects – and that it is legitimate to reconstruct third-century conditions partly by extrapolation from preceding generations, unless there is contrary evidence.

The phenomenon of *stasis* is generally presented by the sources as a conflict between democrats and oligarchs. Like other political labels, however, 'democracy' and 'oligarchy' could have their meanings changed, and could be represented as more transparent or stable in content than they really were; they could evolve with changing circumstances. We shall return to these issues; for the moment simply considering events as they are reported.

The ancient sources for some episodes of *stasis* report, or presuppose, strident calls for radical change, particularly for the cancellation of debts and the redistribution of land. This feature has sometimes been identified as a revolutionary tendency or a reflection of class conflict; such claims deserve close examination.

We focus first on events before 338 in order to characterize politics in those *poleis* for which we have evidence.[89] Two main themes emerge: internal

---

[87] M. M. Austin 1994, 534. On 'outsiders' in C4 Greece, see McKechnie 1989.

[88] They did not gather at Tainaron, which was not a 'mercenary market' as such, but a Spartan base (Chapter II, n. 61): Couvenhes 2008.

[89] The narrative of Roy 1994, 189–94, 197–200, 203–6, gives due weight to the long-term political inclinations of states.

division, particularly expressed either in terms of democracy versus oligarchy or in terms of 'revolutionary' views; and external relations, particularly with hegemonial powers and neighbours. As with tyranny, we need to cast our gaze back to an earlier time in order to understand the long-term temper of different states.

III.3.a Political Divisions and *Stasis* Before Leuktra (371)

In a number of *poleis* we can trace constitutional changes and internal conflicts in some detail between the mid-fifth and the mid-fourth century. The relevant sources (mainly Thucydides, Xenophon, and Diodoros) report many episodes of *stasis*; some internal conflicts were conducted by proxy, an outside power sustaining one party. After reviewing the various circumstances, we shall suggest a range of explanatory factors behind communities' constitutional orientations. The sources regularly portray *stasis* as taking place between democrats and oligarchs. (We shall examine what that may mean in more detail at Section III.3.d.)

We begin by treating hegemonic Sparta on its own, as the dominant Peloponnesian state until the early fourth century. As is well known, it had a mixed constitution with a dual kingship ('dyarchy' in scholarship), elderly councillors appointed for life, and an assembly.[90] It is often described as an oligarchy; this is simplistic. Despite social divisions, political contestation rarely seems to have spilled over into violent *stasis*, though in the perioikic *polis* of Kythera there were divisions at one time: in 424, after the Athenians defeated the Kytherians and set up a base there, they felt it was prudent to remove certain men (Thuc. 4. 57. 4) – presumably those still loyal to Sparta as opposed to their own collaborators. In *c.* 399 a conspiracy within Sparta itself was allegedly organized by one Kinadon, who had apparently been demoted from full Spartiate status. He was quoted as saying that he would mobilize not only the helots but also the *perioikoi* against the state (Xen. *Hell.* 3. 3. 5, etc.); his hopes, if accurately reported, were exaggerated, for the latter, and even the former, were overwhelmingly loyal to Sparta. Externally, in terms of their domination over the Peloponnese outside Lakonike, the Spartans seem to have rested confidently on support from their external allies, without at first seemingly exerting strong pressure in favour of oligarchy. During and after the Peloponnesian war, however, they began to take a harder line; perhaps because increasing numbers of politically active citizens in those states were questioning whether their *polis*'s

---

[90] For the Spartan *polis* see, in brief, Shipley 2004a, 587–94 (*Inv. 345*).

traditional support for Sparta was in their long-term interests. We shall discuss the increasing politicization of regional identities in Chapter V.

States Normally Oligarchic Before Leuktra

Several states during the period of Spartan domination were persistently oligarchic.

The stability of Corinth may reflect the role of large-scale traders and the prosperity of the *polis*, though the elite was probably not a commercial class as such.[91] Yet divisions surfaced in the early fourth century. Though allied to Sparta, the city was enabled by size, distance, and a strong navy to be critical of its senior partner (e.g. Thuc. 1. 68–71). Anti-Spartan sentiment grew in the 390s in response to Sparta's autocratic behaviour in the Peloponnese and Aegean. The Corinthian war led to a full breach: after massacres by those wishing to change Corinth's relationship to Sparta, an alliance was formed and eventually isopolity (common citizenship) with democratic Argos was agreed. The King's Peace of 386 reversed the innovations: but it is uncertain whether agitation for democracy played any part in events, or that Corinth became briefly democratic (see further Section V.3.e).[92] The tyrant Dion of Syracuse (d. 354) is said to have admired Corinthian oligarchy (Plut. *Dion*, 53. 4); and it has been observed that the city, with its poor haul of inscribed decrees, appears to have developed participatory institutions only to a limited degree. Its fourth-century assembly may have had a restricted membership.[93]

Corinth's neighbour Sikyon, too, was consistently oligarchic, perhaps reflecting its limited but productive territory, its earnings from seaborne trade (it lay at one end of an important land route), a relatively broad farmer class, and a narrow aristocracy.[94] Here too, however, tensions can be detected. In 417, following the peace of Nikias, the moderate oligarchy was made more exclusive by joint Spartan–Argive intervention (Argos was briefly an oligarchy at the time), perhaps to prevent the kind of democratization that had occurred at Mantinea (see later). Even so, the Sikyonian

---

[91] Corinth as *polis*: Legon 2004, 465–8 (*Inv. 227*); see generally Salmon 1984.

[92] Salmon 1984, 355–6, points out (*contra* Gehrke 1985, 82–7) that Diod. 14. 86. 1 contains no reference to democrats unless one accepts (with the Loeb editor) an improbable emendation to the text. Others accept that Corinth was briefly democratic: e.g. Griffith 1950; E. W. Robinson 2011, 22–3.

[93] Rhodes 1997, 72–3.

[94] Sikyon as *polis*: Legon 2004, 468–70 (*Inv. 228*); Gehrke 1986, 138–9.

regime was not extreme, and its subsequent stability suggests broad-based support among farmer hoplites.[95] A democratic coup failed in 375 or 371/0 (Diod. 15. 40. 4); but there was further trouble after Leuktra.

The western Arkadian *polis* of Phigaleia, like Sikyon and the Achaean *poleis*, did not change its constitution in this period, but may have had its existing oligarchy made narrower by the Spartans after the peace of Nikias was signed between Athens and Sparta.[96] Yet among Arkadian places it was perhaps the most remote from Sparta; why were the Spartans nevertheless determined to keep control? The answer perhaps lies in Phigaleia's proximity to the vulnerable frontier (before the creation of Triphylia) between Spartan-controlled Messenia and Eleia, which was anti-Spartan at this time. Geostrategic importance presumably focused Spartan attention on the area, at least while they were powerful enough to act at so great a distance.

In eastern Arkadia, Tegea, unlike its neighbour and competitor for water resources (Thuc. 6. 65. 3–4) Mantinea, was more or less consistently oligarchic.[97] Linked to Sparta since the mid-sixth century in the famous anti-Messenian treaty set up by the river Alpheios (Plut. *QG* 292b 5–11), the *polis* was probably a moderate oligarchy in the early fifth century. Even here, however, social divisions were sometimes acute. The Spartan victory over several Arkadian *poleis* at the battle of Dipaia (early 460s) led to the ravaging of Tegea's territory – but not the estates of the rich, who appealed to the victors (Polyain. 2. 10. 3). As a result the oligarchy may have become narrower, enjoying Spartan protection against Mantinea and its allies in 420–418 and surviving a coup attempt launched by anti-Spartan moderates in 418 (Thuc. 5. 62. 2; 5. 64. 1–2). The hard-line oligarchs remained in power for a generation, perhaps creating a build-up of resentment.[98]

States Disputed between Democracy and Oligarchy Before Leuktra

Other Spartan-dominated states witnessed tension between democracy and oligarchy, in each case resolved in favour of the latter.

The inland *polis* of Phleious,[99] a 'middling agrarian state', is an extreme case of politics being affected by external forces, though geographical

[95] Gehrke 1985, 146–7.
[96] Phigaleia as *polis*: Nielsen 2004a, 527–8 (*Inv. 292*); Gehrke 1985, 127.
[97] Tegea as *polis*: Nielsen 2004a), 530–3 (*Inv. 297*).
[98] Gehrke 1985, 152–3.
[99] Phleious as *polis*: Piérart 2004, 613–14 (*Inv. 355*).

factors probably also played a part: the city lay on a strategic land route to the north coast (see Section V.3.d). In the early fourth century the *polis* was a democracy dominated by the numerous farmers. As at Corinth, Sparta's actions after the Peloponnesian war provoked resentment, leading to the expulsion of pro-Spartans in the mid-390s. The Phleiasians held back from supporting Sparta in the Corinthian war, but an Athenian attack drove them back into the Spartan camp. While a Spartan garrison was accepted, however, the constitution remained democratic, though a few years later, in 381, Sparta forced the *polis* to take back the exiles.[100] Later the reinstated men appealed to Sparta to secure their rights and were punished by the other Phleiasians; this led to a twenty-month siege by King Agesilaos of Sparta, the expulsion of the democrats, and the imposition of a moderate oligarchy in 379.[101] While Sparta had tolerated democracy by Sparta for a while, the increasingly vulnerable hegemon of the pre-Leuktra period took a different view. Despite Phleious' democratic tradition, the force of circumstance seems to have caused oligarchy to put down deep roots, as its later history shows.

The Achaean *poleis* may have been forced by the Spartans in 417 to replace their smallholder democracies with oligarchies (Thuc. 5. 82. 1);[102] if so, these were probably moderate regimes with relatively large hoplite electorates in relation to their, mainly rather small, populations.[103]

Mantinea in eastern Arkadia, Tegea's northern neighbour, had been a moderate oligarchy earlier in the fifth century,[104] but probably between 425 and 423 adopted a democratic constitution (Thuc. 5. 29. 1);[105] in Gehrke's terminology, a 'farmer democracy'. It remained an ally of Sparta; but the relationship between the two was uneasy, as one might expect of a city competing with two others (Tegea and Orchomenos) for the soil and water of the same upland plain. After the battle known as First Mantinea in 418, in which Sparta defeated Argos, Athens, Mantinea, and others, Mantinea and Sparta concluded a thirty years' peace (417), and Mantinea's constitutional situation endured without interference for the time being. In 385, however, after the treaty had expired, the Spartans broke up the *polis* 'four ways, just as they used to live in olden days' (τετραχῇ, καθάπερ τὸ ἀρχαῖον ᾤκουν,

---

[100]   Date: Cartledge 1987, 372.
[101]   Gehrke 1985, 127–30.
[102]   Rhodes 1997, 106, qualifies this event with 'perhaps'. On the *poleis* of Achaia, see Morgan and Hall 2004 (*Inv. 229–44*).
[103]   Gehrke 1986, 145.
[104]   Mantinea as *polis*: Nielsen 2004a, 217–20 (*Inv. 281*).
[105]   E. W. Robinson 2011, 34–40, regards much earlier dates as possible.

Xen. *Hell.* 5. 2. 7); that is, into the *kōmai*, 'villages', to which Xenophon refers just after. The Spartans spared the democrats, but some fled to Athens.[106] (See further Section III.3.b.) The case of Mantinea, like that of Elis, proves that under certain circumstances moderate democracy could exist within the Spartan network of alliances, but is another example of the harder line taken by the hegemon in the early fourth century.

Stasis is also reported in 421 in Arkadian Parrhasia, a sub-region of non-*poleis* on the borders of Lakonike.[107]

States Normally Democratic Before Leuktra

A third group of *poleis* were usually democratic in the generation or two before Leuktra.

In the classical period Troizen,[108] despite its proximity to Athens, which it faced across the Saronic gulf, was normally an ally of Sparta, though many Athenians took refuge there during Xerxes' invasion (Hdt. 8. 41. 1; ML 23) and from 460/59 Athens held the city for fourteen years (Thuc. 1. 115. 1; 4. 21. 3). Already around 369, though still loyal to Sparta (Xen. *Hell.* 6. 2. 3; 7. 2. 2), it had an assembly and a probouleutic council (preparing draft resolutions for the assembly);[109] so its constitution may well have had been democratic from well before Leuktra, perhaps under Athenian influence.

One consistently democratic *polis* was Argos;[110] but it preserved its constitution only after episodes of extreme violence in 418–414 and 370. As we have seen (Section I.2.b), it was a primarily agrarian state with no significant maritime element and a high proportion of farmers.[111] Consistently with that profile, it appears from just before the Persian wars to have been a broad hoplite oligarchy. Then the Argives gave refuge to the people of Tiryns, expelled from their *polis* by former Argive serfs, and a democracy was created in which the former Tirynthians presumably remained an identifiable group, strong guarantors of the new order. As at Athens, opponents of democracy worked within the system. Argos tended to side with Sparta's enemies for reasons of safety: the two cities were inveterate foes, the Argives having lost the Thyreatis to Sparta (perhaps in the mid-sixth century). Rather than join the Greek alliance against Persia in the

---

[106] Gehrke 1985, 101–5.
[107] Gehrke 1985, 126 (wrongly categorizing Parrhasia as a single *polis*).
[108] Troizen as *polis*: Piérart 2004, 615–17 (*Inv. 357*).
[109] On *probouleusis*, see Andrewes 1954; Rhodes 1997, ch. 3.
[110] Argos as *polis*: Piérart 2004, 602–6 (*Inv. 347*).
[111] Gehrke 1986, 113–15.

480s led by Sparta and Athens, they medized; later tending to side with democratic Athens, though in 451 prudence dictated a peace treaty with Sparta. In 421, however, they were induced by several of Sparta's allies who did not accept the peace of Nikias to make a separate treaty (Thuc. 5. 28). Several years of unrest, and the brief ascendancy of pro-Spartan oligarchs who made a new peace with Sparta (5. 77–9), ended in 414 with the expulsion of 300 pro-Spartans and the restoration of democracy; this is best read as internal *stasis* based on power politics among the elite rather than as class conflict.[112] From now on, the democracy seems to have been stable for over forty years; from 392 to 386 the city enjoyed joint citizenship with Corinth, even though the latter was probably still oligarchic. In general, the Argives were militarily and economically strong enough to resist Spartan pressure; but despite the strong democratic tradition the relationship with Sparta modified the political dynamic. Argos was in an unusual position, lying in a region not normally united under the hegemony or one *polis* and therefore containing a complex web of inter-*polis* relationships. At certain moments a proportion of the dominant hoplite class presumably changed their views on how to pursue their interests or guarantee safety; but their commitment to democracy was deeply rooted.

In Elis during the archaic period, the large class of landed aristocrats had operated a moderate oligarchy;[113] yet a democratic *polis* was created by synoikism in 471 (probably under the influence of Themistokles of Athens). This presumably moderate regime appears to have endured despite Elis' normal alignment with Sparta; that alliance, however, was broken from 420 to *c.* 394. The nadir was reached with a two-year Spartan–Eleian war around 400, during which an oligarchic coup was narrowly avoided (the plotters escaping to Sparta) but Sparta removed the southern *perioikoi* from Eleian control and set up an independent Triphylia. Despite these setbacks, however, the democratic system remained in place, and by 394 the Eleians had renewed their alliance with the Lakedaimonians[114] even though they still desired to regain their southern territories.[115] Elis proved less capable than Argos of withstanding Spartan pressure; paradoxically, after the end of Spartan hegemony it proved still less able to do so, as we shall see. The *polis*'s ability to protect its democratic constitution, however, perhaps reflects a wider stability, perhaps related to a relative lack of harbours and external

---

[112] Gehrke 1985, 24–31.
[113] Elis as *polis*: Roy 2004, 494–8 (*Inv. 251*); Gehrke 1986, 103–4.
[114] Roy 2004, 495.
[115] Gehrke 1985, 52–4.

trade;[116] most wealth took the form of land and livestock, with little scope for growth.

Summary

In the half-century before Leuktra, especially after *c.* 400, intervention by the Spartans in Peloponnesian communities was increasingly frequent, and the correlation between oligarchy and a pro-Spartan orientation has considerable validity. Only three relatively powerful *poleis* appear to have been normally democratic; in others, determined attempts to replace oligarchy were frustrated by the Spartans. The more consensual habits of the 'Peloponnesian league' had been gradually sacrificed under the pressure of wider conflict during and after the 'Athenian war' of the late fifth century.

Among the factors that may help account for the democratic or oligarchic complexion of a *polis* down to Leuktra, proximity to another *polis* of a particular constitutional type does not seem pre-eminent. More influential was Spartan intervention, sometimes motivated by strategic importance to the hegemon. The breadth or narrowness of the elite, broadly reflecting a *polis*'s resources, also provided the underlying tenor of political traditions.

III.3.b Political Divisions and *Stasis* from Leuktra to Chaironeia (371–338)

After Leuktra, there was undoubtedly an increase in the frequency of *stasis*.[117] Just five years after Sparta's defeat, the Athenian pamphleteer and rhetoric teacher Isokrates, adopting the voice of Agesilaos' son Archidamos, a future king of Sparta (r. 360–338), correlates freedom from Spartan domination with democracy while condemning the latter:

> (64) And I believe that not only the general mob (ὄχλον) in the Peloponnese but also the democratic faction (δῆμον), which we believe to be most hostile to us, now longs for our patronage (ἐπιμέλειαν). For after they deserted us, none of their expectations was fulfilled; but instead of freedom the opposite has happened. For having destroyed the best men among them, they have encountered the worst of the citizens. Instead of independence (αὐτονομίας), they have fallen victim to many terrible crimes (εἰς πολλὰς καὶ δείνας ἀνομίας ἐμπεπτώκασιν) … (68) More men have been exiled from one city than previously from the whole Peloponnese.
>
> (Isocrates, *Archidamos* (Oration 6), 64–8)

---

[116] On the harbours, see Antonopoulos 2015.
[117] Roy 1994, 204–8.

A similar story of Sparta's former allies rushing to adopt democracy is told
by Diodoros, whose main source here is Ephoros, a pupil of Isokrates.[118] He
tells us that, as Spartan control weakened (either shortly before or shortly
after Leuktra), the *dēmos* everywhere rose against Spartan oligarchies:[119]

> (1) After the granting of independence (αὐτονομίαν) to the citizen bodies
> (δήμοις), the cities fell into great chaos and civil conflicts (*staseis*); espe-
> cially those in the Peloponnese. For, having been accustomed to oli-
> garchic constitutions, but now employing injudiciously (ἀπειραγάθως)
> the opportunities of democracy, they began to exile many of their
> good men and, launching spurious lawsuits against them, to condemn
> them. Wherefore, falling into civil conflicts, they imposed expulsions
> and public confiscations of estates, especially upon those who during
> the Lakedaimonians' hegemony had been prominent representatives of
> their fatherlands. (2) For in that period those men had treated the citi-
> zens imperiously; so that later the democratic mob (δημοτικὸς ὄχλος),
> regaining its freedom, remembered its grievances.
>
> (Diod. 15. 40)

States Normally Oligarchic between Leuktra and Chaironeia

Yet some *poleis* bucked the supposed trend, including allies of Sparta that
remained staunchly oligarchic, though not without episodes of *stasis* or
attempted constitutional change.

   Phleious, where support for local democracy had been fatally undermined
by the Spartans' earlier actions (cf. Section III.3.a), is once again an unusual
case. Xenophon (*Hell*. 7. 2. 1–2) is at pains to emphasize how loyal the
Phleiasians were to Sparta – perhaps the dominant families knew that if
they lost their strongest external support they would be overwhelmed by
their enemies. Democracy was not always, if ever, a spontaneous creation
based on grass-roots support; it could emerge from competition between
groups, or be imposed or fomented by outsiders; so it was here, by those
seeking to build a bloc of states with a particular orientation. For in 370
Argos, Arkadia, and Elis tried to ensure that Phleious remained anti-
Spartan by giving assistance to democratic exiles, probably settled on Mt
Trikaranon on the frontier with Nemea (then under Argive control). The
moderate oligarchy imposed earlier by Sparta repelled this assault as well as
a second, launched a few months later by the democrats, who had relocated

---

[118] Sacks 2012.
[119] Diod. places this under 375/4, as does Roy 1973; but these events are often dated after Leuktra
    (Roy 1994, 189).

to Argos. In or before 366 the Argives gave them Trikaranon as a fortified base; but after a separate peace in 365 it became part of the Argive state (7. 4. 11) – perhaps with the consent of the exiled Phleiasians.[120] At least three externally sponsored attempts to reintroduce democracy had now failed. Once again, Phleious' strategic location may have attracted this high level of outside intervention.

At Corinth, the traditional oligarchy (cf. III.3.a, c) endured, apart from a brief 'tyranny' under Timophanes in 366/5 (Arist. *Pol.* 1306a 19–26; Diod. 16. 65. 2–9) – perhaps initiated for security reasons, since Aristotle attributes his rise to mistrust of the common soldiers in wartime.[121]

At Sikyon, change was stifled; the relatively narrow but widely supported oligarchy (cf. Sections III.3.a, c) remaining loyal to Sparta (Xen. *Hell.* 6. 4. 18, cf. 7. 1. 44). When Epameinondas captured the city during his second Peloponnesian campaign (spring 369), he may sensibly have decided not to install democracy.[122] The strength of local tradition is evidenced paradoxically by the depth of support for Euphron, hitherto a leading pro-Spartan oligarch, who set himself up as an anti-Spartan *democrat* in order to establish a personal rule or tyranny (Xen. *Hell.* 7. 1. 44–6), though he probably had the interests of the *polis* at heart given what happened subsequently. In summer 366 the army of the democratic Arkadian league, with Theban support, expelled him, whereupon he placed the city in the hands of the very Spartans whom he had abandoned – yet then, with Athenian help, exploited the confrontation between the returning oligarchs and the *dēmos* to take back power. In early 365 he was assassinated by a Sikyonian opponent while negotiating at Thebes in central Greece. Buried in the *agora* of Sikyon, he was later heroized as the city's founder. Clearly he enjoyed considerable support among the citizens. Later, before the battle of Chaironeia (338), in which Sikyon played no part, a pro-Macedonian group led by Aristratos and Epichares seized power and may have installed a narrower oligarchy or joint tyranny.[123] In general, Sikyon remained true to its oligarchic past; it also exemplifies the malleability of political slogans.

A *polis* that appears not to have become democratic when we might have expected it to do so is the new foundation of Ithome, later known as Messene.[124] We are not told what constitutional arrangements were put in

[120] Gehrke 1985, 130–1. Heraia: Nielsen 2004a, 513–14 (*Inv. 274*). Orchomenos: Nielsen 2004a, 523–5 (*Inv. 286*).
[121] Gehrke 1985, 87; Salmon 1984, 384–5.
[122] Roy 1994, 191.
[123] Gehrke 1985, 147–50; cf. Plut. *Arat.* 13. 1.
[124] Messene as *polis*: Shipley 2004b, 561–4 (*Inv. 318*). On the chronology of the names, see Luraghi 2015, 286–8.

place in the areas of Messenia that became independent after Leuktra. Since the Thebans did not introduce democracy everywhere – not in Sikyon, for example – it is uncertain what they may have, or would have, chosen to do, or encouraged others to do for themselves, if Ithome was viewed as a single *polis*;[125] but there may from the start have been a Messenian federal league (*koinon*),[126] including those former perioikic *poleis* of the Lakedaimonians (mostly inland) that did not remain part of Lakonike until *c.* 337 (as the coastal *poleis* did).[127] Harbour dues imposed by Kyparissos in the third century (*IG* v. 2. 1421),[128] and coins issued by Mothone in the late fourth century (though no other *polis* apart from Messene does so before the early second century: TABLE IV.3), are evidence of *polis* status but are equally compatible with federal association. While the most recent study (n. 127) is rightly cautious on the federal question, however, it identifies a late third- to early second-century phase of Messenian *poleis* attempting to break free of control by the central settlement, implying at least a strongly unipolar landscape. The same tension may be implied earlier by Cassander's failure to secure the support of Ithome–Messene in 316, alone among Messenian *poleis*; it may reflect a residual pro-Spartan sentiment in these former perioikic *poleis*.

The evidence for a Messenian federation is insubstantial and indirect, apart from one very late third-century inscription. What is apparent, however, is that there was some sort of formal association among the *poleis*, and that Ithome–Messene dominated it. If it was a federal *koinon*, one might expect it and its members to have adopted democratic constitutions like those in the Arkadian league. The text of an earlier alliance between Pisa, Sikyon, and Messene (*SEG* 49. 466, fr. B; 365/4 BC) forbids 'overthrowing (a) constitution or the *dāmos*'; the latter term is restored, however,[129] so this is not evidence that the constitution of Messene, as opposed to the other parties, was democratic. By the late third century the *polis* was viewed as one of the most oligarchic in the Peloponnese (cf. Polyb. 4. 31–2);[130] its ephors (ἔφοροι), attested in the 290s or 280s, may have been oligarchic rather than democratic officials.[131] Perhaps the process of setting up the new

[125] *SdA* 285a; Roy 1994, 205–6.

[126] Lazenby 1972, 90.

[127] Federal Messenia: Shipley 2004b, 561–4 (*Inv. 318*), at 562; Luraghi 2015 (C3l–C2e separatism at 293–4).

[128] See also Bresson 2016, 308, dating it C4 or C3 and citing Dareste *et al.* 1891–5, ii. 340–3 no. xxxiv; *Syll.*³ 952; Pleket 1964, no. 8; also Migeotte 2001.

[129] [ὅπλ]α ἐπιφέρηι ἢ πο[λιτείαν ἢ τὸν δᾶμον (?) καταλύηι], ll. 4–5; ὅπλα ἐπιφ[έρηι ἢ πολιτείαν ἢ τὸν δᾶμον (?) κατα]λύηι, ll. 9–10.

[130] Rhodes 1997, 86.

[131] They swear the oath for the alliance with Lysimachos, dated 286–281 by Themelis 1990; *c.* 295/4 by Matthaiou 1990–1. On their status, see Luraghi 2015, 287.

state under Theban supervision had encouraged the self-identification of a strong propertied elite, so that an oligarchic constitution was adopted from the start or introduced later by some process we cannot trace. Messenia was a region whose very meaning had been rewritten, and whatever was done was bound to be a departure from a non-political past. Other states and regions seem to have been affected less seriously by the new geopolitical circumstances.

States Disputed between Democracy and Oligarchy between Leuktra and Chaironeia

Other states saw conflict between democrats and oligarchs resolved in favour of the status quo.

In Achaea, where some *poleis* had been forcibly oligarchized by Sparta in 417 (Section III.3.a), Epameinondas' third invasion of the Peloponnese (367 or 366)[132] led to the imposition by the Thebans of 'harmosts' (*harmostai*, coordinators) in cities. Although this office had been used by the Spartans after 403 to impose narrow oligarchies upon Athens' former allies, the new harmosts allegedly expelled the 'best men' (*beltistoi*), meaning the rich, and set up democracies in place of existing oligarchies (Xen. *Hell*. 7. 1. 43).[133] The exiles quickly seized back control, however, and the *poleis* were once more aligned with Sparta,[134] and oligarchic.[135] (See further Section III.3.c.)

Elis, like Sikyon, went against the supposed democratic trend after Leuktra. When, in 365/4, the traditional democracy was in conflict with the democratic Arkadian league over possession of Triphylia, Eleian oligarchs (last seen in the Spartan war) seized civil and military magistracies and worked with exiled Arkadian oligarchs to attack a league stronghold at Lasion in Akroreia, provoking an Arkadian invasion and the capture of Olympia. In tit-for-tat invasions and rebuffs, the Eleian oligarchs were supported by others from Achaea (including Pellene, the main Achaean *polis*) and by the Spartans, while the Arkadians were supported by exiled Eleian democrats. After failing to install democracy, the Arkadians instead made Olympia into an independent though short-lived *polis* under the name of Pisa.[136] The oligarchy now established at Elis

[132] Lazenby 2012 implies 367.
[133] Errington 2012, 4.
[134] Roy 1994, 198.
[135] Rhodes 1997, 106. Gehrke 1986, 146, considers that the Achaeans themselves threw out the democracies, though we must bear in mind that changes of constitution were usually the wish of only one faction.
[136] Pisa as *polis*: Roy 2004, 500–1 (*Inv.* 262).

remained in place until *c*. 350, when after a reconciliation the constitution apparently reverted to a moderate democracy with institutions devised by the Platonist philosopher Phormion of Athens.[137] External pressures had at times destabilized the democracy;[138] on the other hand, this was the second occasion on which a major democratization took place seemingly without bloodshed, suggesting that political cleavages within the broad landed aristocracy were not so severe as in places under greater stress. (See further Section III.3.c.)

States Normally Democratic between Leuktra and Chaironeia

Some states, however, did move towards democracy or retained a democratic habit.

At Argos (Sections III.3.a; 3.c), the traditional democratic culture protected the constitution from change, but once again only after extreme violence. Even before the arrival of the Thebans in 370, an oligarchic plot provoked a popular backlash so violent that the democratic leaders could not control it. In a notorious episode known as the *skytalismos* ('bludgeoning', 'clubbing'), over 1,200 of the better-off citizens – surely a greater number than could seriously be regarded as oligarchs – were killed; some democratic politicians were swept up in the maelstrom (Diod. 15. 57. 3–58. 4; Aen. Tact. 11. 7–8 may describe the same episode).[139] This is more likely to be an extreme example of 'regular' politics, in a *polis* under threat from Sparta, than of class conflict; the confiscation of the dead men's property, for example, was not, as far as we know, followed by its redistribution. The *polis* remained true to its old allegiances; intervening, for example, in Sikyon in support of Euphron's democratic takeover, presumably in order to strengthen the anti-Spartan alliance. A number of Argive exiles, however – presumably oligarchs – fought for Sparta during Epameinondas' invasions.[140] Argos thus resisted pressure that might have led to constitutional change; maintaining its position of independence from Sparta, but not immune from pro-Spartan agitation or internal schism.

In Arkadia, at oligarchic Tegea, perhaps because of its location, the formula 'pro-Spartan equals oligarch, anti-Spartan equals democrat' holds more strongly than in most places. In the wake of Leuktra, *stasis* broke out in Tegea over whether to surrender sovereignty to the

[137] Gehrke 1985, 54–6.
[138] E. W. Robinson 2011, 32–3.
[139] Piérart 2004, 602–6 (*Inv. 347*), at 604. The men executed, not lynched: Gehrke 1985, 32.
[140] See generally Gehrke 1985, 31–3; Gehrke 1986, 115.

Arkadian league then being formed; the supporters of the traditional constitution were defeated and some 800 took refuge in Sparta (Xen. *Hell.* 6. 5. 10), from where they continued to oppose the league; presumably the city was democratized.[141]

At Phigaleia, where the oligarchy had been made more exclusive by the Spartans (Section III.3.a), a revolution took place, before or after Leuktra, that involved throwing off a regime seemingly dependent on Spartan backing; it may have been accompanied by democratization (Diod. 15. 40. 2).[142] Pro-Spartans were exiled; from a base in Heraia they attacked the *polis* during a festival of Dionysos (festivals were always a good time to attack a *polis*), but were driven off and, like the Tegeate oligarchs, took refuge at Sparta.[143]

As early as 370 the people of Mantinea (Section III.3.a), 'dioikized' into villages fifteen years earlier, reconstituted their democracy against the wishes of Agesilaos, and welcomed back their exiles (Xen. *Hell.* 6. 5. 3–5). The reborn *polis* became one of the leading members of the new Arkadian league.[144] A traditional constitutional preference for democracy was thus upheld against the odds, presumably with majority support.

Megalopolis was founded as a democracy;[145] that was also the tenor of the new Arkadian league founded soon after Leuktra at the instigation of Lykomedes of Tegea (Diod. 15. 59. 1), plainly in order to guarantee Arkadian security from Sparta. The league had a plenary assembly, open to all citizens of member *poleis*, and a publicly funded standing army. Unfortunately, the cost of the latter quickly destabilized the league; disappointing the poorer citizens, who had benefited the most, and strengthening the hand of oligarchs and pro-Spartans. The leaders were divided over whether to seek support from distant Thebes or from nearby Elis, and arguments over the uses of sacred funds (Xen. *Hell.* 7. 4. 33) and the making of treaties led to the league's break-up. An anti-Theban group led by Mantinea was now allied with Elis, the Achaean *poleis*, and Athens. Opposed to it was a pro-Theban group of Tegea, Megalopolis, Asea, Pallantion, and minor *poleis* whose inclusion Xenophon (7. 5. 5) attributes to the fact 'that they were small and surrounded by these others' (i.e. the large *poleis*).[146] The twofold schism

---

[141] Diod. 15. 59. 1–3 says over 1,400 fled from *stasis* in Arkadia, but seems to have Tegea in mind since he implies that 600 fled to Pallantion – apparently the group of Tegeates who Xen. *Hell.* 6. 5. 9 (giving no number) says were tricked into leaving a temple at P. and subsequently executed.

[142] See n. 96 above. Arkadian league's commitment to democracy: E. W. Robinson 2011, 41–4.

[143] Gehrke 1985, 127.

[144] Gehrke 1985, 105.

[145] Megalopolis as *polis*: Nielsen 2004a, 520–2 (*Inv. 282* Megale polis).

[146] Gehrke 1985, 155–8.

would bedevil Arkadia for generations. Interesting also is the appearance on opposite sides of Tegea and Mantinea, both now democratic but historical enemies; similarly, the alliance between oligarchic Elis and democratic Mantinea. Similar constitutional orientation did not necessarily drive states into each others' arms.

At Heraia, the non-violent change from election to sortition (drawing of lots; Arist. *Pol.* 5. 3. 1303a 13–16) may indicate a change from oligarchy to democracy under Arkadian league pressure *c.* 369 (cf. Xen. *Hell.* 6. 5. 11, 22).[147]

Summary

To sum up the decades before Chaironeia: despite, or because of, the removal of Spartan hegemony we see many short-term upheavals – many of which will have involved *stasis* – but limited evidence of permanent changes. Overall, the pattern of democracy and oligarchy after Leuktra, albeit attested only for a minority of *poleis*, does not bear out Isokrates' claim. There were attempts to move from oligarchy to democracy after Leuktra, but they met with limited success outside Arkadia; some states reverted to type, that is, to oligarchy. The latter tradition remained strong, and the states in question were now independent rather than kept in being by Sparta. Since groups opposed to change could no longer rely on Spartan backing, it seems that where they regained, or retained, power it was because they commanded relatively wide support within a *polis*. In the north and west of the peninsula especially, there was little sustained support for democracy, perhaps because the *poleis* had enjoyed a certain freedom of action, lying as they did at a great distance from Sparta (although the Spartans had at times coerced Phigaleia and defeated Elis). Proximity rarely explains constitutional preference; distance more often does so; but most of all deep-rooted tradition, not least in places with established loyalty to Sparta. Sparta's role in harbouring oligarchic refugees strengthens the correlation between democracy and resistance to the former hegemon; but this correlation had not always been so strong, and may reflect a hardening of attitude in Sparta. In all cases, such outcomes depended upon the ambition and strength of particular groups within *poleis*. Neither did states with similar constitutions necessarily display a friendly disposition towards one another; while those whose political systems differed were not necessarily thereby made into enemies.

[147] Gehrke 1985, 70.

Sparta's own conduct varied between a preference for oligarchy alongside tolerance of democratic allies down to about the mid-fifth century, and a greater insistence on oligarchy during and after the Peloponnesian war. Adaptability, and the tensions within the *polis*, can be seen in the change of policy; later rulers, as we argued in Chapter II, were aware that techniques of control needed to be adapted to suit different circumstances.

III.3.c Political Divisions and *Stasis* After Chaironeia (338–197)

After Chaironeia, the evidence does not allow us to trace many internal conflicts in detail. For 323–301 we have some detailed accounts of episodes in Diodoros; after that, the only surviving continuous narrative is Justin's version of Trogus; while Polybios' full coverage begins only with the late third century. After Alexander's death there is a fundamental change in the narrative: *stasis* may have been no less common, but now seems to have been sparked more often by external force than by internal politics. The same is true of constitutional change.

Alexander seems to have favoured democracy, which for some states' dominant elite will have been an unwelcome prospect. When we hear that Antipater planted garrisons and oligarchies (Diod. 18. 55. 2), or that Polyperchon announced a reversion to Alexander's arrangements (18. 56. 3), we may imagine that the effects on *poleis* were similar to those associated with outright *stasis*. Polyperchon, like Alexander, expected cities to take back their exiles (18. 56. 4–5), many of whom were presumably democrats; to expel other men (18. 57. 1), doubtless including oligarchs; and later to execute certain pro-Antipater elements (18. 69. 3), again probably oligarchs.

It is likely that whenever a city was captured or 'liberated', there were at least two main factions, even if they are not identified in the sources; one or both groups potentially being willing to sacrifice the city's freedom. If such factions could not be identified in advance of a city's capture, the new – though often very temporary – masters would find men willing to exercise power on their behalf. Sometimes it is through apparently liberal proclamations that we glimpse the unhappy normality: in the years preceding the formation of his new Hellenic alliance in 302 Demetrios I more than once proclaimed himself to be campaigning for Greek freedom. After expelling Cassander from Attica, for example, 'he gave their freedom to the Greeks on this side of Thermopylae' (Plut. *Deme.* 25. 2); in 304 Rhodes was to be 'autonomous and ungarrisoned' (Diod. 20. 99. 3); his campaign against Cassander in 303 was to be fought in order to 'free the Hellenes'

(20. 102. 1); at Sikyon he declared he had restored its 'freedom' (20. 102. 2). The text of the 302 alliance (Schmitt, *SdA* 446)[148] refers more than once to 'peace' as a goal (e.g. ll. 22, 67) and presents itself as an alliance between the Antigonids and 'the *poleis*' (e.g. l. 13) or 'the *Hellenes*' (e.g. ll. 4, 84).[149] The fact that Demetrios thought it necessary to spell out beneficent and universal aspirations suggests that he needed to allay fears prompted by bitter experience of his rivals. However, the nature of many episodes may explain why the sources less often portray confrontation in terms of democracy versus oligarchy than in the preceding period; the choice will now have been sometimes between adherence to one external power rather than another. This is particularly true if the Macedonians displayed no determination to campaign for any particular constitutional form (cf. Section III.2.c).

After the accession of Gonatas, at the start of the period that Rostovtzeff calls 'the balance of power' (*c.* 276–222), the historical record is patchy but glimpses of the flow of events confirm that *stasis* continued to occur regularly. In the absence of evidence we can sometimes only infer the socioeconomic character of a *polis* from that in the better-documented fourth century; even if there were unrecorded changes of constitution, there were in most *poleis* deep-seated preferences that would often prevail. The geopolitics of this period, however, were new, and this has implications for the nature of internal divisions. Whereas before the Chremonidean war southern Greece was often the scene of conflicts between rival Macedonian commanders (including Pyrrhos), afterwards there was a single Macedonian hegemon who was challenged by groups of *poleis* or a single powerful *polis* such as Sparta.

More than once in the third century, as we saw in Chapter II, a number of communities took joint action against the Macedonians and, despite a lack of detailed sources, we may infer the existence of intra-*polis* divisions. Justin says that 'more or less all the states of Greece' (24. 1. 2) rebelled after Kouroupedion in 281/0; a little over a decade later a broadly based alliance launched the Chremonidean war. On such occasions, and also when a tyrant or governor took power (whether in the Macedonian interest or not) or resigned or was ousted, it is likely that the *polis*'s decision to turn in a new direction was the outcome of political contestation, with or without violence – it being unimaginable that all active citizens wanted identical

---

[148] The text in Schmitt, *SdA* represents a major revision of that in *IG* iv² 1. 68.

[149] See W. S. Ferguson 1948 for a decree of the Athenian tribe Akamantis of *c.* 302, referring to individual agreements between *poleis* and Demetrios which 'made them free and autonomous' (ll. 8–9) and preceded the Hellenic alliance.

outcomes. Of course, we cannot usually see the detailed processes. The existence of exiles, whom we have seen mentioned a number of times, is also evidence of political conflict, not always violent. Apparent demands for revolutionary or radical reform might point to a different schism within citizen bodies, to which we shall return.

The rather attenuated record of specific episodes of constitutional change and *stasis* after Chaironeia is worth compiling, though the picture is more piecemeal than before.

Argos, previously democratic but at the cost of repeated bloodletting, continued to suffer from violence under the warring Diadochoi. Polyperchon took steps against supporters of Cassander, at a time when according to Diodoros (18. 57. 1, 69. 3–4) murder and exile were rife in the Peloponnese. A few years later Cassander took over the city and based a general there. Later it was on the Antigonid side for many years, perhaps during all four 'tyrannies' discussed at Section III.2 (*c.* 272–*c.* 229), finally joining the Achaean league. The promise of political reform, held out by Kleomenes III and implemented by Nabis a generation later, suggests a community as deeply divided as before.

Oligarchic Corinth, home of the Hellenic alliance in its several incarnations, played a special role as the southernmost 'Fetter of Greece'. Despite being a great strategic prize, it seems to have retained its traditional constitution down to and beyond its enrolment in the Achaean league in 243.[150] Its citadel of Acrocorinth, garrisoned continuously from 338, changed hands repeatedly but was usually managed by a senior Macedonian. The first was Alexandros son of Polyperchon, who switched his allegiance to Cassander *c.* 312 (Diod. 19. 64. 2–4); the next was Alexandros' widow Kratesipolis, who executed internal opponents (19. 67. 1–2); later Ptolemy I of Egypt held it (308–303); then Cassander's general Prepelaos. Finally the Antigonids kept hold of the city for many years: from 303 Demetrios I; then Gonatas from *c.* 297. From 261 it was governed by Gonatas' half-brother Krateros; then Krateros' son, another Alexandros, who began to pursue an independent policy from Gonatas; then the latter's widow Nikaia, from whom Gonatas regained the city by trickery only to lose it again to Aratos in 243. At that point it joined the Achaean league and became autonomous for the first time since Philip II's reign (Plut. *Arat.* 23. 4), but apparently not democratic. At each change of control, there were probably expulsions and restorations; but as far as we know no change of constitution, despite the presence of anti-Macedonian activists.

---

[150] Dixon 2014, 200.

At Sikyon, changes of governor were certainly sometimes accompanied by *stasis*; Aratos' father was assassinated, for example, and he himself was sent into exile as a boy in the 260s; after liberating Sikyon he secured the recall of fellow exiles, presumably anti-Macedonian. The city may have become democratic as a member of the Achaean league, but its politics probably remained elite-centred.

In Achaea, where democracies had been replaced by oligarchies in the late fifth century and then restored, Pellene was a democracy when Alexander imposed a 'tyrant' (Ps.-Dem. 17. 10). During the war of Cassander, Dyme was polarized between two factions, one hostile to and one supportive of Cassander's general Alexandros son of Krateros (Diod. 19. 66. 4–6); there is no mention of democracy or oligarchy. The smaller *poleis* surely experienced some of the same things but are largely below the radar of ancient writers. Polybios' general reference to discord within the earlier instar of the Achaean league before 280 (2. 41. 9) implies that the *poleis* had been afflicted by *stasis*. The league's refoundation was accompanied or followed by the overthrow of several 'tyrants', implying the resolution of some political process but with attendant violence in some cases. As the Achaean league consolidated its power, however, there seems to have been a decline in *stasis*, except when a city was captured by, or from, the league; the league itself sometimes used force to change the situation in a *polis*.

Elis, previously democratic and characterized by a spirit of compromise (Sections III.3.a–b), changed hands several times in the wars of the Diadochoi and briefly suffered during Gonatas' reign under a brutal tyrant who expelled many opponents. Otherwise, the *polis* appears to have avoided serious *stasis*, perhaps because of the basic stability of its social relations, which may have fostered a capacity to reinvent the community's self-image without having resort to violence.

In Arkadia, Stymphalos was the scene of a massacre of democratic supporters of Polyperchon by Cassander's general Apollonides in 312 (Diod. 19. 63. 1). At Orchomenos, Cassander allowed his supporters to massacre his opponents (19. 63. 5). At Megalopolis, the original democracy must have been abolished at some point; it was an oligarchy under Polyperchon; the restoration of democracy *c.* 252 followed the assassination of Aristodamos the Good. We hear of Megalopolitan exiles at Argos in the 250s; and of Messenian exiles at Megalopolis in connection with the events of the 220s (Polyb. 2. 55. 3). During the Social war, Kynaitha was a victim of *stasis* exacerbated and exploited by the Aitolians (Section II.5.a).

At Messene, oligarchic by the late third century and perhaps from its foundation, there appears to have been *stasis* leading to democratization around the time of the Social war, involving the expulsion of 'notables' (see Section II.5.b). It is another case of external conflict leading to internal instability.

Finally, in Laconia, despite frequent attacks and invasions, Sparta with its tripartite constitution seems to have escaped internally generated violence for much of the period. Disputes among claimants to a throne were a time-hallowed tradition, and the fall of Agis IV can be seen as a continuation of normal politics among a narrow elite, which led to the exile of some of his supporters (as we can infer from Polyb. 4. 34. 9; 9. 34. 9). Kleomenes III, in turn, exiled his opponents (e.g. Plut. *Ag.–Kl.* 31. 1), procured the deaths of ephors, and temporarily reconstituted Spartan domination over much of the Peloponnese; but after his fall Sparta was much more prone to *stasis* involving, for example, the elimination or exile of ephors. The successive careers of King Lykourgos (twice briefly exiled), the regent Machanidas, and King Nabis were similarly troubled. *Stasis* took a particular form in the unusual circumstances of Sparta, with its mix of monarchy (technically dyarchy until 215), oligarchy, and democracy; there are no signs that any group wished to change the constitution or put the city under foreign control until after Sellasia, when there were pro-Achaean elements.

III.3.d The Role of Ideology

Democracy and Oligarchy

Stasis continued to plague the Peloponnese during the wars of the early Successors. For the more stable decades of Gonatas' rule, however, the sources less often portray factional opposition in terms of democracy versus oligarchy. While a wider range of politicians may have identified themselves as democrats, some may have supported limiting the franchise; those in favour of still more exclusive voting lists may increasingly have eschewed the label of oligarch.[151] There are still, however, enough references to states being democratized, alongside a prominent reference to late third-century Messene as oligarchic, to show that, while there had been a certain convergence, opposing groups still sought support from different constituencies. The key political issue was the same as before.

---

[151] O'Neil 1995, 104.

There were, however, no 'movements' in the modern sense: there were interest groups with broad social and political preferences (the limit of the franchise, for example). The Macedonians did not promote one particular constitutional form but, depending on the time and place, wanted military success or security or both. They did not pursue regime change in the service of ideology, but in order to keep their opponents, or potential opponents, out of power. Moreover, the vastly increased influence of outside powers after 338 changed the nature of oligarchic–democratic opposition, and probably relegated ideological or philosophical issues to second place. Internal politics was now part of a much greater game involving powerful players elsewhere.

Every community contained groups with different interests and views, and *stasis* must often have occurred without leaving any trace in our evidence. When the sources present the situation as a conflict between democracy and oligarchy, did these words mean the same in different *poleis*? Was *stasis* motivated by political theory or ideological orientation, or by contingent or local factors? Did Macedonian power play a role in how internal struggles were represented, and how they developed?

In the classical period, democracy normally involved (*a*) a sovereign assembly; (*b*) rotation of office with fixed periods of tenure; (*c*) the removal of all minimum property qualifications for citizenship or magistracies (public offices), with certain exceptions such as state treasurer; (*d*) detailed scrutiny of the financial accounts of magistrates.[152] In a few cases, which we may call radical democracies – such as Athens – there might also be (*e*) public pay for jury service, assembly attendance, military or naval service, and so on; (*f*) extensive use of sortition to appoint councillors and magistrates, with only a limited use of election by ballot (e.g. for the highest military commands). Especially in the latter form, democracy gave political rights to poor citizens, not ordinarily considered to have the means and leisure to play a part in politics; but did not necessarily subsidize them so that they could do so.

An oligarchy, in contrast, usually maintained (*a*) the sovereign assembly and (*b*) rotation of office, but typically retained minimum levels of property, or more likely of income, to qualify a man for citizenship, membership of the decision-making assembly or council, and office-holding. We can be sure that in any *polis* described as oligarchic the constitution formally reflected the interests of those with property – whether rich or only moderately well off, and whether a small minority, a large one, or even,

---

[152] Sherwin-White 1978, 176; Rhodes 1997, 533.

occasionally, a majority of the free population. Election would be used more widely, sortition less often if at all. Aristotle classifies oligarchies according to the degree to which property ownership was concentrated: the larger the landed estates, the more a citizen body would tend to be narrow, self-perpetuating, and not subject to the rule of law (*Politics* 1293a 12–34). Thus, in practice, oligarchic *poleis* were societies in which the size of the voting body as a proportion of the number of free, home-born men tended to vary according to the degree to which the agricultural territory was in the hands of a larger number of families.[153]

Thus oligarchy was not necessarily government by the very rich; neither was it government without assemblies, councils, and magistrates.[154] It was constitutional government, to adapt Aristotle's formulation, by and for the *euporoi* or 'well-resourced' – those with a certain level of disposable funds; often a larger group than the *plousioi* or 'wealthy'.[155] It excluded from full political rights (if not necessarily legal citizenship) the *aporoi* or 'unresourced' – not the poor alone, but a wider group including those with significant amounts of property but no ready income; men, perhaps, who could not fulfil Xenophon's prescription in his philosophical dialogue *Oikonomikos* (*Household Manager*) for what the citizen of the richest class should do with his wealth:

> (2. 5) 'First', answered Sokrates, 'I see that you are required to make many large sacrifices ... Second, you are obliged to host many foreigners, and on a grand scale. Third, to provide meals and benefactions to the citizens, otherwise you would be bereft of allies. (2. 6) Then again, I realize that the *polis* not only imposes great expenses upon you now – maintaining horses, paying for choruses, presiding over the *gymnasion*, accepting presidencies – but if a war begins I know it will impose warship commands and similarly large contributions that you will scarcely endure them.'
>
> (2. 5–6)

From a Western, twenty-first-century perspective we might assume that oligarchy was an oppressive form of government and a hotbed of tension and ideological opposition. This was often not the case. It is possible, indeed likely, that political conflict in Greek *poleis* could arise not from protest by the poor, but from the grievances of those who were not quite *euporoi* and were thereby debarred from full participation, but were well able to express their dissatisfaction. Not all those without the vote may have desired democracy

---

[153] For these points, see Ostwald 2000b.
[154] Rhodes 1997, 75–6, 85–6, 92.
[155] Ostwald 2000a; cf. Ostwald 2000b.

as such; many may simply have wanted more land so that they and those at their level could join the voting body or hold office under the existing rules. Where we do hear calls for change, we may be hearing protests by the *aporoi* – not the poor, but the almost well-off. The existence in several parts of the Peloponnese of semi-free labouring classes (see Section III.1) may have mitigated the grievances of the poorest free men, who despite their lack of income enjoyed more privileges than the semi-free.

Analysis of decrees passed by the Greek states has shown that a *polis* that called itself a democracy was not necessarily more democratic than one that did not.[156] Oligarchy and democracy correspond to two overlapping ranges of points on the same spectrum of property distribution. The system usually in place in many of the classical *poleis* of the Peloponnese has been called 'moderate' (*gemäßigte*) oligarchy,[157] but this approximates to 'moderate' democracy, typically what Gehrke calls a 'farmer democracy' or 'peasant democracy' (*Bauerndemokratie*, cf. Section III.1). Prosperity made stable oligarchy more likely (as at Sikyon and Corinth), but by and large it was moderate oligarchy.

In the period before Leuktra, whether a politician advocated democracy or oligarchy did not simply reflect his economic position (despite Aristotle's later typology), and *stasis* is not necessarily evidence of a clash between economic ideologies or between rich and poor. In any case, *polis* politics both then and later was chiefly the business of the elite; competing groups perceiving themselves to be advantaged or disadvantaged. One's political stance was not determined purely by global economics or class interests, but by how those factors interacted with others such as one's status, the level of one's ambition, and above all the situation of one's *polis vis-à-vis* other powers. At Elis, indeed, some form of democracy was compatible with the existence of a strong landed elite, and confrontation between democrats and oligarchs could be non-violent. As Roy remarks, 'on occasion the two factions could both pursue their political aims within a given constitution', suggesting again that this was not an ideological struggle in which one side aimed at a new social or legal order.[158] Anti-oligarchic politics was probably only partly based on devotion to certain principles and a particular definition of 'freedom'; it was also an outgrowth of local circumstances. Thus, for example, it may have been one thing to be a democrat in Argos, with its peculiar ethnic mix and history of bloody conflict; quite another in Sikyon at the time of Euphron.

---

[156] Rhodes 1997, 531–6.
[157] Gehrke 1986, e.g. 63–5, 104; in more detail Shipley 2005b, 325–6.
[158] Roy 1994, 206.

At Athens, early hellenistic politicians whose careers we can trace tend to be consistent in their policy positions;[159] but it is not usually possible to tell whether this consistency was born primarily from adherence to reasoned principles or primarily from loyalty to a political or kinship grouping; probably both played a part. Nevertheless, it is not necessary to go as far as Hahm, who claims that the distinction between democracy on the one hand, and aristocracy or oligarchy on the other, disappeared.[160] (Hahm also claims that monarchy was now seen as the only alternative to democracy; but this seems to embody a misunderstanding of the nature of *polis* politics, for a city did not become a 'monarchy' by virtue of being under the control of a Macedonian king.) We have already seen enough evidence to reject the observation as a description of actual practice; it may be a truer description of abstract theories (such as those in certain passages of Polybios). It assumes a fundamental change in the meaning of 'democracy', which Hahm implicitly takes to have occurred almost immediately after the death of Alexander; but much recent research rejects so radical a change, at least for the early or middle hellenistic period. A growing body of scholarship has also shown that democracy (though not the radical democracy of fifth- and fourth-century Athens) lasted in many Greek cities down to the first half of the first century BC.[161] Not only does Strabo (9. 1. 20) say that Demetrios of Phaleron, Athens' governor under Cassander, did not destroy democracy, he says the Athenians preserved democracy right down to the Mithradatic war. We must give such assertions full weight.

One difference between classical and hellenistic democracy was that few *poleis* (and none in the Peloponnese) instituted pay for citizens; in the Achaean league only members of the federal council appear to have been paid.[162] On the other hand, a sign of continuity in political practice is that, as new work has emphasized, political oratory retained its importance in hellenistic city-states.[163]

---

[159]   Bayliss 2011, e.g. 103, 107–8, 211, 214.

[160]   Hahm 2000.

[161]   e.g. Crowther 1992; Rhodes 1997, 532–6 (warning that 'democracy', while still used in a strong sense, was sometimes debased); Grieb 2008; Carlsson 2010. Cf. Bresson 2016, 149 (cf. 218) for 'democracy' in the Hl period as more often synonymous with the rule of law and the absence of one-man rule; Cartledge 2016, ch. 14 (pp. 231–46), for the stronger view that during C3 δημοκρατία (*dēmokratia*) came to mean something more like the Roman *respublica*. Assembly politics remained central to 'democratic' *poleis* of the Hl, non-radical kind, which perhaps approximated to Aristotle's ideal *politeia* and not to oligarchies.

[162]   O'Neil 1995, 116–17: citizen pay attested only at Rhodes and Iasos.

[163]   See papers in Kremmydas and Tempest 2013, esp. Rubinstein 2013, Chaniotis 2013; also Shipley 2013a.

The Lack of 'Revolutionary' Ideologies

We have seen that the democracy–oligarchy polarity was not a matter of organized political 'movements' or membership associations. Some scholars, however, believe that ideology of a different kind was an important factor in political confrontation. Radical calls for measures such as cancellation of debts and redistribution of land recur in similar forms on a number of occasions and may have been justified on the basis of a philosophy. Some scholars have seen them in terms similar to modern ideologies such as collectivism, socialism, or communism.[164]

One of the most widely cited studies of class conflict in late classical and hellenistic Greece is that of Fuks.[165] He identifies a large increase in the reported cases of *stasis* after the early fourth century, and attributes it to the growth of a rural 'proletariat' after 400. This in turn, he argues, was exacerbated in the generations after Alexander by the expansion of Greek trading horizons, which led to more 'economic polarity': falling wages and higher prices. He also argues for increasing 'revolutionary consciousness', particularly in the third century.

There are problems with this analysis. The apparent increase in *stasis* may simply reflect changes in the quantity and nature of the written sources. Historians are no longer confident that they can identify trends in prices across the Greek world, preferring to emphasize regional and short-term factors.[166] That being so, we can say nothing about prices and wages in the Peloponnese in the absence of documentation.[167] We no longer take for granted that reliance on regular wage labour (as opposed to payments for specific tasks) played a significant part in Greek economies. *Stasis*, it is now clear (and the examples in the preceding pages confirm), was often unconnected with any 'social-economic revolution'; it could reflect simply rivalries among the elite. Rather like Beloch's *republikanische Bewegung* ('republican movement') or Freeman's 'federal movement', for Fuks the notion of class

---

[164] For the invocation of communism and socialism in this context, see von Pöhlmann 1893–1901; replaced by *Sozialismus* alone in the title of later editions, von Pöhlmann 1912 and von Pöhlmann 1925. Mitchison's excellent novel about Sparta under Kleomenes III (Mitchison 1931) is skewed by her view of him as a proto-socialist, perhaps fostered by her association with historians such as H. T. Wade-Gery and A. J. Toynbee.

[165] Fuks 1974–5.

[166] Cf. esp. Reger 1994.

[167] Documents recently discovered at Argos may provide a chink of light, if they cover the Hl period. Whitley 2003–4, 19–20: 120–50 bronze plaques of C4e and possibly C4c relating to the treasury of Athena, suggesting that the sanctuary acted as a central bank. See also *SEG* 41. 284 (citing Kritzas 1992, 231–40), bronze plaques with financial details from Argos, one of *c.* 300 BC.

consciousness and revolutionary fervour in C3 Greece 'seems ... to take on a supernatural existence of its own'.[168]

Fuks takes several phenomena to be aspects of the new revolutionary tendency. None is problem-free. Leaving aside (*a*) the events at Syracuse in 356 and (*b*) the reaction of the *demos* to Roman hegemony in the first half of the second century as outside the chronological scope of this study, the so-called populist tyrannies such as (*c*) that of Apollodoros at Kassandreia in Macedonia (280–276; e.g. Diod. 22. 5. 1–2), who distributed the land of the rich among 'the poor' and incited 'household slaves and the craftsmen from workshops' (οἰκέτας καὶ τοὺς ἀπὸ ἐργαστηρίων τεχνίτας, Polyaen. 6. 7. 2) to rebel, must be treated more circumspectly than they are by Fuks. Diodoros' τεχνῖται are hardly 'factory workers', as Fuks translates with modern overtones; hardly an urban proletariat. Encouraging domestic slaves and relatively poor men is a fairly common phenomenon in the hellenistic period (seen later, for example, in the revolt of Aristonikos of Pergamon), and is attested earlier; a would-be ruler, desperate for military backing, seeks support wherever he can. Apollodoros, notably, did not rouse agricultural slaves or the poorest free men.

(*d*) In the *skytalismos* at Argos, rich conspirators against the democracy brought the wrath of the *dēmos* upon the heads of all the propertied class, including the leading democrats; to see this as one political ideology triumphing over another is to go beyond the evidence.

(*e*) Fuks identifies 'party-political' reform movements, citing Aitolia in 205–204 as an example. But, without going into detail, there is little resemblance in these events to what we can recognize as political parties or movements.

(*f*) Finally, Fuks includes among examples of revolutionism the Spartan kings Agis IV and Kleomenes III, who, he believes, pursued economic and social equality.[169] Their programme is better seen, however, as a charter for 'traditional' citizenship, the hoplite army, and the restoration of Spartan hegemony.[170] Plutarch's portrayal of moral decadence in Sparta (*Ag.–Kl.* 3. 1, etc.) is anachronistic and probably reflects the anxieties of the elite in Gracchan and late republican Rome. The question remains to what extent, during his brief domination of the eastern Peloponnese, Kleomenes sought to foment revolution inspired by political and social aims. He captured

---

[168] Walbank 1933, 2 (referring chiefly to Beloch).

[169] Cf. Fuks 1962, 165.

[170] I therefore give a different emphasis to Agis' plans from Cartledge 2016, 239, who sees him as the 'unlikely champion' of the distressed poor of the Peloponnese or at least 'willing and able to exploit that distress'.

some eighteen *poleis* at one time or another. Fuks states that at least ten, and probably more, are said by the sources to 'have tied up their fate with Kleomenes' revolutionary Sparta'.[171] Without doubt there were pro-Spartans in every *polis*, as there were in Sikyon (Plut. *Arat.* 39. 4; 40. 1) and Corinth (40. 1); but the motives of such men were not necessarily ideological. Of the two groups just named, Plutarch says they conspired with Kleomenes 'on account of their desire for private power' (ἰδίων ἐπιθυμίᾳ δυναστειῶν, *Arat.* 40. 1; cf. 40. 2). The pro-Spartan group may have been particularly popular in Phleious (39. 5), but this is not evidence of revolutionary enthusiasm for social justice. Still less does surrender imply radicalism: Heraia and Thelphousa voluntarily put themselves in Kleomenes' power (Polyb. 2. 54), but only after Mantinea had been terrorized into submission.

One of the most general statements in this connection is by Plutarch:

> A movement (κίνημα) of the Achaeans had occurred, and the cities became keen to revolt. The citizen bodies (δήμων) conceived hopes of land distribution and cancellations of debts (νομήν τε χώρας καὶ χρεῶν ἀποκοπάς); while the top men (πρῶτοι) in many places were unhappy with Aratos and some felt angry that he had brought the Macedonians into the Peloponnese. Uplifted by these these factors, Kleomenes invaded Achaea ...
>
> (*Ag.–Kl.* 38. 6)

Even this is problematic. Plutarch's term 'movement' (κίνημα) does not imply an organized, international network of activists; it is, rather, a set of actions or events.[172] As we saw earlier, while redivision of land may have been of concern to all citizens, cancellation of debt was chiefly of interest to the well-off. Plutarch even invokes the ambition of the elite, who were not about to give up power; and dismisses all pro-Spartan movements as based on a failure to understand Kleomenes' true motives.[173] Both Agis and Kleomenes exploited social stresses in Sparta and elsewhere; but their so-called programme, while offering fair treatment for those on the margins of the propertied hoplite class, did not aim at justice for the poorest in the

---

[171] Fuks 1974–5, 74 n. 27, without references but noting that Polyb. (no ref.) says only that Megalopolis and one other *polis* 'were not affected by the revolutionary commotion'. Yet at 2. 55 Polyb. explicitly says (though wrongly) that M. and Stymphalos were the only places where Kleomenes *did* find support.

[172] For κίνημα as 'political movement', see LSJ s.v. A.2.a, citing e.g. Polyb. 5. 29. 3; but there it is appropriately translated 'serious trouble' by Paton.

[173] For a summary of untenable views about the motives of Agis and Kleomenes, see Cartledge and Spawforth 2002, 39. They include 'Beloch's notion of a struggle between Spartan capitalists and landlords'; cf. Walbank 1933.

polis, let alone the semi-free and unfree who were not members of it. It also aimed at re-establishing the Spartans' domination over their neighbours (as we saw in the case of Nabis).

The Macedonians, for example through treaties (such as the charter of the Hellenic alliance), sought to prevent radical changes such as debt cancellation and land redistribution. But it seems unlikely that calls for such measures were supported specifically by the poor, such as Fuks's wage labourers. They arose, rather, from the concerns of the propertied and perhaps chiefly of those who had property but were not quite *euporoi* (in the sense of having a ready cash flow). They may have included men who had borrowed cash against land (e.g. for social expenditure such as on weddings) and feared they would be ousted from the upper or middle wealth stratum of their city, or had already been demoted from the political class by their opponents as the result of loss of income (as at Sparta) or constitutional change. What we do not see is organized cooperation between groups in different *poleis*, which would be a precondition for a revolutionary movement such as Fuks posits.

Calls for 'revolutionary' measures probably, therefore, reflect the same kind of internal divisions as *stasis* and the democracy–oligarchy confrontation. Only rarely were the resentments that could provoke such calls exploited systematically by outsiders; in fact chiefly, as far as we can see, by Kleomenes III and Nabis. Mostly such calls were prohibited by the terms of inter- and intra-state agreements. The 'tyrants' or governors of this period, as we argued earlier, probably did not exploit them; most of them not achieving power through populism.

Explanations in terms of political ideologies do not adequately account for the nature of civil conflict. The calls for change of which we hear were probably made, not by the most disadvantaged, but by groups among the propertied classes seeking privileges within a largely unchanged political and economic system rather than seeking to build an entirely new social order. Equally, the prohibitions upon such measures reflect the traditional domination of *polis* (and therefore league) politics by the elite.

III.4 Political Continuities

The introduction to this chapter posed questions about the degree of political change and the balance between internal and external causes; in particular, the role of Macedonian power. To assess how oppressive Macedonian domination was, it is vital to understand correctly the nature of *polis* politics and of the broad relationship between a *polis*'s social make-up, natural resources, and political traditions. To this end, we have considered the vertical and horizontal divisions within late classical and early hellenistic *poleis*, and have emphasized the central importance of internal groups – particularly among the politically active members of *polis* elites – as well as linkages between members of elites in different *poleis*. Macedonian generals and later kings varied in the degree of severity with which they approached Peloponnesian communities. In general, Philip II and Alexander III tended not to employ either garrisons or 'governors', a term preferable to the 'tyrants' of the sources; Antipater, however, followed a harsh line after the Lamian war. The nature of *polis* politics, and the evidence for these governors, suggest that they tended to emerge from the local elite and acted, to a large extent, like magistrates exercising special command of the city and its forces; Polybios' castigation of the Macedonians who imposed 'tyrannies' is probably tendentious and partisan, except in one or two extreme cases. The Antigonids operated through garrisons and governors only in the light of local circumstances, rarely initiated a governor's regime, and did not attempt the blanket imposition of any particular constitutional ideology. Conversely, governors' internal role was not ideological, and their relationship to Macedonia not uniform.

Likewise, internal divisions within Peloponnesian *poleis* were not necessarily more glaring or destructive than before the death of Alexander; and were not to any great extent exacerbated by any Macedonian policy, though the wars of the early Successors tended to increase political polarization. Political opposition in the long third century tended to centre around the *polis*'s relationship or potential relationship to an external hegemon, rather than around the democracy–oligarchy contrast; let alone the 'revolutionary' ideologies that some scholars have claimed to detect.

In short, as in Chapter II, it is the continuing importance of *polis* politics that stands out clearly. Since the Macedonians were not aiming to build a new social or political system, or to run the Peloponnese as any kind of 'province', it is not surprising that continuity is more salient than change. Indeed, in the area of politics there were not as many changes as we might have predicted given Macedonia's military dominance; those that occurred were driven largely by internal factors, though the actions of hegemonic powers may have accelerated or intensified some trends. External agencies, such as Sparta or Macedonia, did not point in a consistent political direction or act always in the same way; communities were often able to manoeuvre within existing relationships to secure maximum advantage. A community's identity is not unitary or static; it is made and continually remade through discourse – a discourse between more than one voice, unless some be silenced – as well as by internal contestation. Likewise, neither prosperity nor geography completely determines a *polis*'s constitution or development; most of the evidence is consistent with local tradition having played a prominent role in maintaining continuity (albeit sometimes with interruptions). All the factors mentioned, however, played a part: external force, regime change, diplomatic negotiation, the economic base, proximity and distance, and local tradition. They were no less evident during the subsequent Roman takeover of Greece.[174]

Because of the proportionally large size of propertied elites in some Peloponnesian cities, oligarchy was probably, in most cases, based on a relatively wide franchise – akin to moderate democracy (Aristotle's *politeia*). Yet at the same time it is undeniable that, in any contest for political support, it will have been democracy that held out the prospect of a greater number of free men being involved in public decisions. The leader of an attempted coup at Corinth in 366/5 (see Section III.3.b) had support from the poor. In some cases democracy evidently had practical consequences, such as for those Arkadians who for a brief period gained employment in their federal army, until it proved unaffordable. Thus, where a city seems habitually to have been an oligarchy, one may ask whether it was easier to keep certain groups out of politics (or the assembly, or public office), muting their voice for the time being, if the 'in-group' of those eligible was relatively wide than if it was relatively narrow. Since resentment fuels activism and militates against a preference for the status quo,[175] it is hard to avoid concluding that where *stasis* was common or particularly bitter, it was fuelled by the relative narrowness, or perhaps the closed nature, of the in-group rather than by the virulence of any oppression meted out to the out-group. Indeed, as argued earlier, it may not have been the poorest in society, but those just outside the dominant in-group or recently excluded from it, whose resentment led to democratic–oligarchic polarization.

Nevertheless, a general centrist tendency is notable; it probably reflects the *poleis*' common character as 'agrarian states' in Gehrke's terminology. 'Reverting to type', though a biological metaphor that we should be cautious of using, does capture the frequency with which certain features recur in the political balance within a *polis*, whether habitually democratic or oligarchic. There are several explicit cases in which a *polis* experiences a 'double

[174] Gruen 1984 repeatedly emphasizes the particularism of Greek local conflicts and the way in which local rivals exploited relationships with outside powers; cf. Shipley 1987; Sherwin-White 1978.
[175] Scruton 2006, 150–2, 154–6.

change of constitution' within a short space of time.[176] It seems likely that if democracy offered 'more of you' a share in government, this rarely if ever meant 'all of you'. It did not necessarily mean a permanent redistribution of wealth or power, even though democrats might exile some rich men – just as tyrants or oligarchs might.

While, however, the 'default value' of moderation, in democracy or oligarchy, can be observed or inferred, *stasis* was endemic and political division reflects a structuring principle of *polis* society that operated with the greatest frequency at times of stress, other than in the largest and most stable cities such as Athens and Sparta.[177] The Arkadian experiment, perhaps informed by the experience of the Boiotians, who knew something of federalism, might be thought to have failed because of the excessively particularist behaviour of some Arkadian *poleis*. Yet the same tendency towards group rivalry, sometimes leading to internecine strife – a tendency often blamed for the supposedly (but probably not) cataclysmic effects of the Peloponnesian war[178] – has been identified as Greece's 'lifeblood' rather than, as some would have it, its worst national characteristic.[179] It is certainly inseparable from the classical and early hellenistic *polis*.[180]

Among the factors that affected *polis* freedoms and political orientations under Macedonian domination were, of course, Macedonian military power (before and during the period of stable Antigonid rule) and ideological polarization (grounded to some extent in wider currents of philosophical and social change). But it is not evident that there was more, or bloodier, *stasis* than before; and the sufferings of the Peloponnese were not due solely to external factors. A greater role in fomenting disorder may have been played by traditional internal divisions. The chief spur to political strife seems to have been the deeply embedded ambitions of groups within local elites and their tendency since at least archaic times – except when, possibly, checked by laws, decrees, oaths, or agreements – to advance their material interests within civic landscapes. They also made common

---

[176] Hansen 2004f, 125.

[177] Hansen 2004f, 125 (Sparta), 128 (Athens).

[178] Scruton 2006, 195, refers to the war as Greece's collective suicide. Such quasi-Thucydidean exaggeration is common; but Too 2008, reviewing Osborne 2007, is not convinced that there was a 'cultural revolution' at Athens after the war; and Cartledge 2001 refrains from imposing homogeneity upon the after-effects of the war.

[179] Gruen 1984, 437. An example of the older, negative view is W. S. Ferguson 1911, 2: 'the city-state was the cause of manifold ills […] and thus forbade the formation of a single nation'.

[180] Kralli 2017, 311, notes that Polyb. 5. 106. 3–6 says 'all Peloponnesians are fond of hegemony and liberty' (my trans.), but limits its applicability to the Achaean league and Sparta, each seeking to dominate the other. Hegemony was not a realistic aim for other states.

cause with elite groups in other *poleis* in order to safeguard their position mutually, so that both inter-regional and intra-regional factors are at work.

If there was more continuity than upheaval in the practice of politics under Macedonian domination, it remains to be seen whether economic life and landscapes underwent any greater change. What do we make of Polybios' claim that the Peloponnese was 'ruined' by the kings and by warfare? Was life for the majority better or worse by the end of Macedonian involvement? And how does this bear on the Achaean league's performance, or that of other states and organizations? Next we shall look at possible economic impacts of Macedonian rule, and economic developments more generally. The same question about relations between external and internal factors will arise.

IV | Economies and Landscapes

Hermes, I stand here by the windy orchard
at the joining of ways near the grey shore,
offering tired men a break from the road.
The spring pours out its cold, pure water.

Anyte of Tegea, *Greek Anthology* 9. 314

IV.1 Questions of Evidence

IV.1.a A Glass Half-Empty?

Now that it is clear that the political aims of the Macedonians in the Peloponnese were limited, we can extend our investigation to economic change and continuity, and the possible economic effects of Macedonian power, in order to clarify, if possible, whether people were worse off, better off, or in much the same state by the end of the early hellenistic period.

Historians have rarely enquired after the economic condition of the Peloponnese at this time,[1] and have tended to echo the damning judgements of ancient authors. Polybios, above all, in the context of his comments on the limited quantity of movable wealth in the Peloponnese, refers to past times 'when the affairs of the Peloponnesians had been utterly ruined (κατέφθαρτο) by the kings in Macedonia, but still more (ἔτι δὲ μᾶλλον) by the succession (συνέχεια) of wars against one another' (2. 62. 4). By 'the kings' he is unlikely (given the narrative in Chapter II) to mean Philip II and Alexander III, or the non-royal Successors such as Antipater or Cassander, and most probably has in mind the Antigonids. He gives no indication here (though he does to some extent elsewhere, as we saw in Chapter III) of what kind of damage the kings are supposed to have inflicted, and it is interesting that – perhaps motivated by animus against specific states – he rates this damage as less serious than that caused by local wars.

---

[1] Cf. the call by Rizakis 1991 for research on Achaean societies and economies. On Polyb. as a source for economic history, see Davies 2013.

As we shall see, the written sources are problematic; at least, a weight has sometimes been placed on them that they will not bear. Much, therefore, must be based upon other evidence of a 'tracer' character; or upon inference from the general state of Greece both now and in the preceding century. Little attempt has been made hitherto to quantify epigraphic activity or to synthesize archaeological evidence; but new data may facilitate progress. Numismatics, by contrast, has made great strides in recent years. By combining the written sources with other evidence, we can hope to generate a new account of the early hellenistic Peloponnese.

IV.1.b Economic Decline?

First it is necessary to elucidate a number of negative assessments, and examine whether the evidence sustains them; particularly in regard to the impact of war and *stasis*, and in regard to claims that the economy suffered from localism, under-development, and demographic decline.

As noted in Section I.1.b, it is commonly assumed that Greece was in a poor state after the Peloponnesian war, suffering population collapse and a disastrous economic climate.[2] For example, in one of the stronger expressions of this view Rostovtzeff presents a dark picture of conditions after *c.* 400, centring on the notions that Greece could not feed itself and that there was widespread poverty, proletarization, and unemployment, all of which worsened in the second half of the fourth century.[3] His thesis is that agriculture and manufacturing became increasingly technological during that century, and that therefore changes in the economy can only be explained by changes in 'the conditions of the market for Greek agricultural and industrial products'.[4] He uses the archaeology of other regions of the Mediterranean and Black sea (such as finds of Greek fine-ware pottery, amphoras, and so on) to argue that these areas were less dependent on the Greek homeland than before. He presents no evidence specific to the Peloponnese, however.

Several general objections may be made. (*a*) We no longer view Greek states in general – as opposed to members of elites – as predominantly dependent for their survival or prosperity upon income from exports of manufactured goods. Rather, the preponderance lay in, for example, the production of primary commodities for local consumption and their

---

[2] For a more nuanced view, see Kallet 2000, 196: 'The war left the Hellenic world weakened economically *in the short term at least*' (emphasis added).

[3] Rostovtzeff 1941, 90–126.

[4] Rostovtzeff 1941, 104.

exportation (usually in a preserved or processed form), with middleman trade and other generators of private profit playing a central role. (*b*) The general absence of regular, year-round wage labour vitiates the use of terms such as 'proletarization' and 'unemployment'. (*c*) The view that agriculture became significantly more technological in the fourth century[5] seems to overstate the implications of the limited evidence. It perhaps rests on the general scaling up of production detected in specific parts of Greece, such as Macedonia, but not others; on the initial introduction, but not yet widespread use, of new equipment such as the rotary grain-mill and the *trapetum*-style olive-press (to use its Latin name);[6] and on the simple fact that the second half of the fourth century was the period when writers such as Aristotle and Theophrastos began to classify natural organisms and analyse their management.[7] The archaic and classical centuries may have seen a gradual improvement in agricultural knowledge and to some extent in technology;[8] the third century may be the time when such technology began to move forward more rapidly in the hellenistic world; but this process is likely to have been haphazardly distributed across the Greek eastern Mediterranean. It is far from clear that such changes would have had any significant impact on Peloponnesian economies by the start of the post-Alexander period, and therefore unnecessary to conjure up adverse market conditions.

Another view is that things deteriorated economically because of wars and *stasis*; but political–military conditions were not necessarily more unsettled in the first half of the fourth century than they had been earlier. It is by no means clear that the possible economic and demographic effects of the Peloponnesian war – or indeed other wars – were long-lasting. Casualties, for example, could have been replenished within a generation by families deciding to rear more children,[9] or by admitting new citizens (cf. Section IV.1.c). Settlements reported as destroyed were not necessarily wiped out completely; many such (not all) were, as far as the archaeological evidence goes, occupied without interruption or resettled almost at once. As Alcock notes with reference to the later hellenistic period, warfare affected different regions in different degrees.[10] In Greek history generally, trade was not

---

[5] Accepted by Rizakis and Touratsoglou 2011, 17, without elaboration.

[6] Bresson 2016, 196: rotary mill adopted from W. Mediterranean in Hl times; 195–6, *trapeta* seen in Greece from C4m or C4l but not yet widespread.

[7] On innovations in Hl agriculture, see Thompson 1984.

[8] See generally Bresson 2016, 161–71.

[9] Cf. Roy 1999 on Arkadians' long-term strategies; Bresson 2016, 49–51, on families' reproductive strategies.

[10] Alcock 1993, 149.

necessarily interrupted by war,[11] and geopolitical factors may sometimes have led to trade in new directions. Short-term devastation of cultivated land (apart from the destruction of fruiting trees) can be remedied relatively quickly, if sufficient manpower is available (see Section IV.2.c). Recent work casts further doubt on the pessimistic view: Bresson, for example, argues for a general economic downturn, not after the Peloponnesian war but as a result of the Macedonian conquest of southern Greece – and then only for Athens and adjacent regions forming its economic sphere, such as central Greece and certain islands; other parts of the Aegean world seem to have prospered from the third century onwards.[12]

Fuks, as we saw in Chapter III, identifies an increase in civil war after the early fourth century.[13] *Stasis* was frequent, to be sure, but some of the increase may reflect changes in the nature of the source evidence. Furthermore, it is not clear that *stasis* was provoked by economic processes such as proletarization or impoverishment rather than by existing political behaviours; that *stasis* sprang from ideological convictions; or that *stasis* itself brought about economic change. If there were economic changes, they are equally likely to have been the result of long-term trends that worked themselves through irrespective of political events.

A recent, more detailed assessment of the economic condition of the hellenistic Peloponnese paints almost as dark a picture as Rostovtzeff.[14] On the basis of the almost wholly negative factors that they invoke, the authors conclude that while the Peloponnese did not necessarily decline in absolute terms during the last three centuries BC, it missed out on the benefits of positive economic developments under way elsewhere and suffered a relative decline that only the *pax Romana* would reverse.[15] Their observations and claims will be tested in the following pages, particularly with respect to the early hellenistic period, as far as the evidence allows.

First, we may examine the literary evidence that the authors adduce. A story in Pausanias (4. 35. 6–7) has been taken as evidence that the

---

[11] As assumed by Siebert 1978, 198–9 (referring to 'une "économie de guerre"', 199). Kramer 2013, 290, however, points out that Eastern Sigillata A pottery was developed in Seleukid N. Syria or Cilicia precisely at a time of frequent conflicts (C2m); on possible reasons for its introduction, see Shipley 2018. Rizakis and Touratsoglou 2011, 20, concede that in the Hl Peloponnese there was disposable wealth, despite the wars.

[12] Bresson 2016, 60–3 and 202–3.

[13] Fuks 1974–5, 59–61.

[14] Rizakis and Touratsoglou 2011; cf. Rizakis 2001a on post-146. For a similar view, see Siebert 1978, 191–202, referring mostly to C3l and later.

[15] Though Rizakis 1995a, e.g. 223–4, 235–6, argues for economic depression from LHl onwards; and Rizakis 2014 for increasing rural deprivation in the EImp period.

productive sector was biased towards regional or local markets.[16] Set in the late third century or later,[17] it concerns Illyrian pirates who put in at Messenian Mothone, bought local wine for the asking price, sold their own wares in return, and then 'seized many men and even more of the women' and took them away. Although wine is the only local produce mentioned, to assume that it was the only item for sale, and was produced purely for the local market, is unwarranted.[18] (Even if those assumptions were well-founded, they would not demonstrate economic decline.) Neither does the fact that the visitors paid the price that the locals asked constitute evidence that the inhabitants were unused to trading with foreigners; rather, in the narrative context, it illustrates the Illyrians' deceitful behaviour.

Aristotle's story (*Rhet.* 1365a, 1367b) about an Olympic victor who had earlier portered dried fish from Argos to Tegea suggests that small-scale, intra- and inter-regional traffic was normal; indeed, fish could be a luxury item.[19] Yet this isolated anecdote – apart from the fact that it lacks any chronological context[20] – does not bear at all upon the question whether large-scale or long-distance trade also had an important role.[21]

As an example of such long-distance trade, indeed, the vast store of Hermionian purple (reportedly 5,000 talents' weight, some 130 tonnes) found at Sousa by Alexander has been cited;[22] but it is clear from the main source (Plut. *Alex.* 36. 2–3) that the dye was believed to have been delivered in the archaic period, or at various times from then on, and preserved.[23] Indeed, though at times purple-making was important to both Hermion and nearby Halieis (cf. Section I.2.b), the latter *polis* was partly or wholly abandoned in the first half of the third century, suggesting that the craft was no longer sufficiently profitable for that community. The evidence for purple at hellenistic Epidauros, though not

---

[16] Rizakis and Touratsoglou 2011, 21.

[17] The episode should postdate *c.* 232, as Paus. sets it after the fall of the Epeirote monarchy (4. 35. 5).

[18] The inference might be thought justified because Paus. says the visitors 'asked them to bring wine to their ships; and when a few men came to bring it, they bought it'; but this need not imply that the locals were not ready and waiting at the harbour when the Illyrians appeared.

[19] Möller 2011, though with reference to Attica.

[20] Though the epigram quoted looks Cl rather than earlier.

[21] As it is by Rizakis and Touratsoglou 2011, 21.

[22] Rizakis and Touratsoglou 2011, 21 (also citing Strabo 3. 16. 4, an error, perhaps for Arr. *Anab.* 3. 16. 7 though the purple is not mentioned there).

[23] Bresson 2016, 362, rightly rejects (with comparative evidence) the suggestion that the hoard was of purple *cloth* rather than dye; and argues that it was delivered over a long period, not all at once in C6l.

yet closely dated, may indicate that the latter town replaced Halieis as a producer.[24]

Questions about whether the export trade in general from the Peloponnese was under-developed and whether, if so, this had deleterious effects on the economy are better addressed through archaeology. One long-distance export attested in written sources, for example, is red marble (*rosso antico*) from the Tainaron peninsula (cf. Strabo 8. 5. 7); but its widespread use across the Mediterranean does not seem to antedate the middle or late hellenistic period.[25] (On Peloponnesian trade, see further Section IV.8.)

In the scales against the purportedly negative evidence we may place testimonies such as that of Livy (34. 29. 3) that Gytheion in 195 – while still a perioikic dependency of Sparta – was 'a strong city, endowed with a great number of citizens and other inhabitants and with all equipment necessary for war'.

In short, the pessimistic claims about the Peloponnesian economy in the fourth and third centuries, thus far, have been shown to have little support from written sources. Other evidence, primarily archaeological, will be examined later in this chapter.

IV.1.c Demographic Decline?

It has been suggested that in the late classical and hellenistic periods a demographic crisis caused a decline in rural cultivation, increasing inequality in land ownership, a rise of 'excessive' pastoralism, and an increase in frontier disputes between *poleis*.[26] Why, however, should a falling population have those consequences rather than, say, larger shares of land for all, less competition with neighbouring communities over borderlands, and so on? Indeed, what would constitute 'excessive' pastoralism as opposed to, say, flourishing pastoralism?

A prior question, however, is how reliable the notion of a 'demographic crisis' is. Several texts are cited in support of this proposition.[27] In a notorious passage, Polybios asserts that in his day the whole of Greece was suffering from a lack of children and manpower, the abandonment of cities and productive land, and a moral crisis in which people preferred to spend their wealth and avoid having children rather than leave their money to

---

[24] *AGOnline* ID 1458 (2000); Morgan 2009–10, 40.
[25] P. Warren 2012; Baladié 1980, 203, 207, 248. The earliest example cited by Baladié 1980 (207) is a Delian inscription granting proxeny to Nabis (*IG* xi. 4. 716).
[26] Rizakis and Touratsoglou 2011, 24–5.
[27] Rizakis and Touratsoglou 2011, 24.

heirs (36. 17. 5–10).[28] The last, moral charge is one he has already laid at the door of the late third-century Boiotians; adding that they abandoned fighting, ceased to administer the justice system, and were persuaded by their leaders to subsidize the poor (20. 4–6).[29] Both passages recall his allegation – not necessarily of any demographic relevance – that for two or three generations down to his day certain Eleian landowners had preferred 'the life of the fields' to participation in politics, while continuing to enjoy the privileges of citizenship (4. 73. 5–74. 2).[30] In the absence of supporting evidence, none of these assertions can be trusted as evidence of the scale of change, particularly before 200.[31] They may conceal short-term political and military factors that affected elite behaviour in specific states at specific times; but their extreme tone arouses a suspicion of prejudice against particular persons or groups among Boiotians, Eleians, or Greeks as a whole.[32] That is not to say that certain real phenomena do not lie behind Polybios' statements[33] – he may, for example, have had information about shrinking citizen registers in specific cities[34] – but it will be wise to test the notion against other evidence (see Section IV.3.c, specifically on Eleia).

Warfare might be assumed to have taken its toll of population levels, but for how long? Despite the bleak catalogue of kilodeaths in the narrative (Chapter II), we cannot automatically assume that population levels were affected in the long term.[35] (For examples of short-term losses, see Section IV.2.c.) There seems to have been no shortage of Peloponnesian troops. Emigration from Greece has been thought to entail adverse economic

---

[28] Austin[2] 99.

[29] Austin[2] 102; 'probably coloured by Achaean prejudice', M. M. Austin 2006, 202 n. 4. Müller 2013 shows that the passage is a literary construct.

[30] Austin[2] 103.

[31] Shipley 2000b, 30; *contra*, Rizakis 2004, 21–2. Alcock 1993, 148, envisages 'some level of population loss' in the *later* Hl period.

[32] Cf. M. M. Austin 2006, 195 ad loc.

[33] Bresson 2016, 61–2, argues in favour of accepting the claims by Hl and later sources of demographic decline in Greece. The case seems far from closed. He notes that we do not find such statements in Cl sources; but the changing concerns and philosophical outlook of writers could explain that. A speaker in Plut.'s dialogue *On the Cessation of Oracles* (*Mor.* 413 f–414 a) says civil wars and other conflicts have caused a lack of manpower (ὀλιγανδρία) to the point that one could not raise 3,000 soldiers in Greece; this obviously ignores social factors and the non-militarized nature of Roman Achaia.

[34] Reger 2003, 335, makes a similar distinction between falling population (which he is inclined to doubt) and falling citizen numbers. Grandjean 2006, 196, suggests that calls for the redistribution of land imply that there was no lack of persons; rather, as suggested above (III.4), they reflect an increasingly skewed distribution of ownership among existing citizens and, in some cases, the possible exclusion, or demotion, from citizenship of those with limited holdings.

[35] Summary of casualties with numbers: Shipley 2008a, 57.

consequences. Parts of rural Greece have, notoriously, always exported young men; this need not reduce a home population permanently.[36]

There were, of course, local problems. Human populations, like others, are capable of replenishing losses within a number of years, or preventing a short-fall, by changing reproductive strategies; even without modern contraceptive techniques, people in pre-industrial societies could quite readily decide to limit or increase their rate of reproduction.[37] Other measures could also be taken. In the late third century, for example, remedies for lack of manpower were put in hand by Macedonian rulers, both in the Peloponnese and elsewhere. Philip V pressed the people of Larisa in Thessaly to admit new citizens for the good of the *polis* (*Syll.*[3] 543 = *IG* ix. 2. 517);[38] but despite his stated desire that the land should be more extensively cultivated – 'that the city be strong and the land not be, as now, shamefully left fallow' (χερσεύεσθαι; l. 30) – this is not necessarily evidence that the population was falling in absolute terms; it may be, rather, that the king decided that civic exclusivity needed curbing; the existing elite being perhaps unwilling to contemplate allowing others, such as resident foreigners, to take charge of farmland.

Some political attempts to mitigate population loss were ineffectual.[39] Some were aimed at specific short-term problems rather than at a widespread and persistent shortage of population, as may be the case at Achaean Dyme where in *c.* 219/8, after a period of warfare, citizenship was shared with 'new settlers' (ἔποικοι), and with a similar measure at Achaean Tritaia around the same time; both probably under the aegis of Philip V.[40] The granting of land rights to non-citizens is also attested, as when Orchomenos joins the league *c.* 234 (*Syll.*[3] 490 = Austin[2] 68). The repopulation of Mantinea by the Achaeans in 223 followed the destruction of a league garrison, the recapture of the city, the enslavement of most citizens (Polyb. 2. 58. 4–15, cf. 2. 56. 6), the execution of leading men, and the renaming of the *polis* as Antigoneia (Plut. *Arat.* 45. 4–6).[41] The attempts of

[36] Roy 1999, 347–9. On the ever-present potential for a demographic explosion in ancient Greece, see now Bresson 2016, 49–51.
[37] Sallares 1991, 86, 89–90, 129–60, etc.
[38] Part in Austin[2] 75.
[39] Rizakis and Touratsoglou 2011, 24.
[40] Rizakis 1990b studies attempts to replenish the citizen bodies of Dyme (*c.* 219/8) and perhaps Tritaia (C3d), probably at time of Philip V's campaign in 219 and perhaps sponsored by him.
[41] Full references at Cohen 1995, 123. Some cases of new residents postdate 197: e.g. Epidauros (*IG* iv[2] 1. 28 ~ *SEG* 47. 344, 52. 335; with Jameson *et al.* 1994, 566–7), 146 BC, though the text may be evidence of in-migration rather than the rectification of falling citizen numbers. For Stymphalos, Rizakis and Touratsoglou 2011, 24, citing no source, refer to new settlers probably installed by the league; but if this refers to the sympolity of Stymphalos and Lousoi (*IG* v. 2. 358), the text refers only to mutual citizenship.

several Spartan rulers (Agis IV, Kleomenes III, Nabis) to augment the core citizen body were responses to the problems caused by the dysfunctional system of social exclusion rather than to reproductive failure and absolute, population-wide demographic loss as such. While ancient criticisms of communities for neglecting their demographic health may well be tendentious, top-down measures to replenish citizen numbers may reflect other factors than a long-term net reduction in population, and do not necessarily indicate structural economic problems.

Politics, too, might be thought to have reduced, or rather displaced, available manpower without the necessity to invoke a failure to reproduce. In the fourth century, the supposedly large numbers of exiles in Greece was sometimes portrayed as evidence of socio-economic breakdown; but the claim was exaggerated and, in the case of Isokrates of Athens, politically motivated.[42] Even though there are examples of *stasis* leading to the relocation of exiles to another *polis*, such as Eleians at Sparta, Corinthians in Argos and Athens, Sikyonians in Argos, and more generally Peloponnesians in Egypt,[43] we do not hear the same rhetoric about social chaos. This may partly be because, for communities such as the Arkadians, mercenary service was not the result of social collapse or a desperate last resort for those excluded from their *polis*,[44] but a normal social strategy with benefits such as the amelioration of competition for inheritances.[45] Furthermore, there is no indication that the presence of exiles from other *poleis* was resented, at least until the question of sharing citizen privileges arose (as at Larisa).

IV.1.d Beyond 'Growth'

One of the problems with previous assessments is the unspoken assumption that 'economic growth' would have been a good thing, its absence bad; furthermore, that its presence or absence could be detected. Von Reden pointedly asks whether scholars, while no longer glorifying the Western market economy, do not still worship growth.[46] Without going too deeply into questions about 'the ancient economy', the present study assumes that caution is required in applying modern economic terminology to ancient

---

[42] McKechnie 1989, esp. 22–8.

[43] Vasdaris 2004.

[44] McKechnie 1989, 1–15, argues that the growing numbers of such men facilitated the rise of Macedonian power (whose effects, however, he overstates). As Fisher 1989 points out in his review, mercenaries were also recruited from within city-states.

[45] Roy 1999, 346–9.

[46] von Reden 2010, 11.

Greece.[47] This is not to revert to the position of Finley, who believed the economy was characterized by small surpluses and a near-total absence of wage labour and long-distance trade, and that economic development was subordinated to, or even held back by, social relationships and status considerations.[48] Today the importance of a wide range of profit-oriented activities in classical Greece 'beyond agriculture' is fully acknowledged, as is the possibility of overall growth in some sense of that term (though in general we could expect to observe only the consequences of growth rather than the process itself);[49] and while social relations were extremely influential, contrasting modes of economic activity probably coexisted in any ancient society, operating at different scales and only in some respects bound by political, cultural, or geographical frontiers.[50]

Greek economies, particularly at *polis* level, were not 'managed' or directed in any way that a British chancellor of the exchequer would recognize as economic. While an elite citizen, even in earlier days, could aspire to improve the value of an estate with a view to selling it at a profit (Xen. *Oik.* 20. 22–5), and individual producers could 'play the market' by, for example, withholding goods until prices rose,[51] hellenistic states did not aim at 'growth' in the modern sense – which must be distinguished from 'profit' – but operated, rather, in three economic modes: direct capture of resources; protection of commerce; and attempts to control the supply of goods in pursuit of their strategic aims.[52] None of these implies the manipulation of economic instruments, such as money supply or tax rates, for purposes such as increasing the velocity of money in circulation, controlling prices and wages, or encouraging investment.[53] In the absence of most of the economic metrics available to authorities today, such top-down manipulation was scarcely imaginable.

---

[47] Davies 2005, 127–9; more cautiously than his editors, who embrace modernizing concepts, e.g. 'growth' and 'per capita output', under the influence of New Institutional Economics. See e.g. Morris and Manning 2005, 34; Morris 2007 and other papers in that volume. Human Development Index: Scheidel 2010. Cartledge 2002a is an important earlier survey of the issues.

[48] Finley 1973; characterization by Morris and Manning 2005, 12–14; Morris 2007, 2–4.

[49] See e.g. papers in Mattingly and Salmon 2001. Economic growth and decline during the Ar to ER periods are a major focus of Bresson 2016; the evidence may be evaluated independently of the appeal to New Institutional Economics, which postulates that action-limiting institutions are a precondition of development.

[50] Davies 2005, 130–4.

[51] Bresson 2016, 171.

[52] On these modes, see Davies 2013, 328–33.

[53] On the quantity theory of money, see e.g. J. L. Hanson 1961, 361–3.

That is not to say that if we had much more extensive and representative data (which we probably never will have) we could not identify positive or adverse trends in wealth distribution, market conditions, prices, and so on. Even if those phenomena occurred in a recognizable form, however, they would probably result mainly from extremely local processes; many goods, for example, will never have reached a recognizable market.[54] Moreover, why should the absence of growth necessarily imply immiseration of part or all of the population?

What may be easier to detect, and what will have created a sense of economic well-being for some people, are events such as large gifts of cash by internal or external donors to *poleis* and sanctuaries. Other flows of value, while not directly attested, can be confidently assumed to have existed, such as the arrival of the accumulated earnings of mercenaries returning from abroad; salaries paid to troops stationed locally; and profitable trade deals by landowners and shippers. Any of these might in principle lead to the greater availability of cash in private hands and perhaps, through local monetary transactions, enable a wider cross-section of the population in turn to buy more goods, or goods of higher value and quality. Equally, however, these processes might be arrested and relative hardship result. Yet, even supposing we could identify[55] a rise or fall in, for example, the total quantity of money, household artefacts, or public amenities within a settlement or region, this would not tell us how the benefits or disbenefits were distributed across society.[56]

In the rest of this chapter we shall evaluate the available evidence for settlement, construction, material culture, and money in the light of what has emerged in previous chapters, such as the internal dynamics of *poleis*, the degree to which communities could exercise 'agency', the strength of continuity in political traditions, and the limited aims of the Macedonians. (The question of growth will be kept in view; we return to it in Section IV.7.c.)

IV.1.e Resource Complementarity

The Peloponnese was not uniform in its natural endowments. It might be expected that the fundamental geographical character of an area – relief, geology, climate, and so on – would exercise a determining role upon

---

[54] Davies 2005, 128.

[55] Morris and Manning 2005, 23, and Morris 2007, 4–7, attempt to calculate for the *longue durée* of Roman antiquity.

[56] Cf. Hobson 2012, 24–32, for the risk that 'growth' may blind us to inequality.

economies and societies. Certain areas, for example, are (and presumably were) more suited to agriculture, such as the alluvial and Neogene zones of Korinthia–Sikyonia, the wide Eleian lowlands, the southern part of the West Arkadian plain, the two plains of Messenia, the Eurotas valley, and the plain of Argos. Lesser pockets of good land include the coastal shelf of Achaea, various inland and coastal basins of Laconia,[57] the Thyreatis (disputed between Sparta and Argos in the archaic and classical periods), and lowland parts of eastern Argolis (including Methana with its volcanic soils).[58] The mineral wealth of the Peloponnese is limited: the peninsula as a whole lacks silver ores; iron was extracted in south-eastern Laconia;[59] but there are no ores in Arkadia (see Section I.2.b), making the region wholly dependent on metal imports. All communities lacked some resource, and all depended upon trade with one another to fill the gaps.[60]

On the basis of topography and resources, one might expect Korinthia–Sikyonia, Eleia, Laconia, Messenia, and Argos to predominate over Achaea, Arkadia, and the rest of Argolis. But while environmental possibilities may constrain, they also evoke responses and open up possibilities, depending on the state of technological development at a given time.[61] This is why a mountain environment such as Arkadia will not necessarily have an impoverished economy.[62] Nor are the same regions always dominant: in the late Bronze Age, certain Argolic communities were among the richest in Greece, while in the late classical and hellenistic periods it was sometimes Arkadia (after 369) or Achaea (after *c.* 251) that gave impetus to political currents. In a relatively prosperous society such as third-century Greece, all regions had well-established trade links, and mutual interdependence and exchange were the norm. Connectivity is thus critical, including links between regions and other links to the world outside the Peloponnese; these will be examined.

What kind of economies are likely to have existed? To begin to build an answer, we should first recall that the Peloponnese was made up of culture regions, which we have already met (see Section I.2.a): Argolis, Korinthia, Sikyonia, Achaea, Eleia, Triphylia (for a time in the fourth century), Arkadia, Messenia, and Laconia. The fragmentation of the peninsula is mirrored in its dialects – now known to exhibit more local variation in and

---

[57] See esp. Shipley 1992.
[58] This formulation seems more precise than that at Shipley 2006b, 28.
[59] Cartledge 2002b, 78; Treister 1996, 21, 29, 144.
[60] Cf. Mackil 2013, 264–74.
[61] Febvre 1925, e.g. 73–7, 85–90, 171–81, 223–5, 235, 360–8.
[62] Roy 1999, 323–4, 326, citing Forbes 1996, Gehrke 1994, etc.

after the fourth century than was previously thought[63] – and by the varied constitutional arrangements at most periods. With variations over time, these regions, and the city-states within them, are likely to have formed the primary framework for the regulation of market-related activities.

By the classical period, marked regional differences in economic strategies and structures, as opposed to natural resources, were already deeply embedded. Corinth, with its harbours on two seas, had become an important trade centre by archaic times, with a tradition of high-quality craft production including a pottery industry that exploited the accessible clays of the coastal shelf. The wider north-eastern Peloponnese, too, was home to multiple political centres and international sanctuaries, all well connected by land and sea, and thus the setting for a continual movement of people and a continual exchange of commodities and knowledge. The documents from the rebuilding of Apollo's temple at Delphi after 373/2 illustrate the disproportionate role played by craftsmen from this area, attesting to a plentiful supply of skilled and mobile labour in those communities – some of which, indeed, had made very large contributions to the rebuilding costs.[64] Moreover, men from other parts of the Peloponnese and southern Greece seem to have made up a majority of skilled craftsmen working on construction projects at Epidauros in the fourth and third centuries.[65] We do not have similar evidence from the southern Peloponnese, where at least down to the fourth century traditional agriculture may have been more dominant in the economy, particularly where unfree labour was used. Together with Eleia, where evidence suggests a rather static picture of land use (see Section IV.3.b), Laconia and Messenia form something of a contrast with the north-east; trade may have been relatively less important to them.

One factor that may have facilitated the exchange of complementary resources and ideas between the regions is the network of ancient 'tramlines' for wheeled traffic that has been identified in recent decades (for details see Section V.3.c). Some of them may have been made under the direction of Sparta as head of the 'Peloponnesian league';[66] others may reflect the aspirations of independent communities such as Argos.[67] There is so far no consensus as to whether the network had primarily a military or a commercial role; a combination of both is likely.

---

[63] See papers in Minon 2014a.
[64] Davies 2001, 218–23.
[65] Burford 1969, e.g. 198–203, 212–21 (*c.* 370 BC), 230.
[66] As argued by Pikoulas 1999a; Pikoulas 2012 (Laconia).
[67] The view of Tausend 2006 with reference to Argolis; cf. Shipley 2008b. Further traces: Lolos 2011, 93–179 *passim* (Sikyonia); Marchand 2009 (Kleonaia).

Although the evidence is suggestive rather than conclusive, it is clear from the distribution of resources that we should not expect to find that Peloponnesian economies were homogeneous – a point not highlighted in previous studies. This finding would be consistent with the frequency of monetary transactions using coins, which was similarly disparate; a factor to which we shall turn later (in Section IV.7).

IV.1.f. Digression: Natural Forces?

A possible factor in economic development is natural processes affecting the landscape. While environmental changes took place or can be inferred (alluviation, sea-level changes), however, substantial effects cannot be detected, other than two natural events (earthquake and volcano) which probably had limited and local effects.

Earthquakes are a well-known feature of Peloponnesian, particularly Laconian, history.[68] Although there are no specific reports relating to the early hellenistic period, the north of the peninsula in the fourth century had seen seismic events with long-lasting ramifications. The seismically generated destruction of the Achaean coastal *poleis* of Helike and Boura in 373 is first mentioned by Polybios (2. 41. 7).[69] Boura was refounded by the citizens who were absent at the time of the disaster and thus survived (Paus. 7. 25. 8–9).[70] Helike had probably been the location of the Achaean league's federal shrine; if so, that was moved to Aigion, even though (from new evidence) Helike was rebuilt as early as the late fourth century and reached a peak of prosperity in the third and second;[71] it had, for example, a substantial dye-works.[72] The destruction of a temple at *Áno Mazaráki* (Achaea) by earthquake and fire *c.* 400–*c.* 350 – though cult deposition resumed and lasted until the fourth century AD – may be related to the same seismic events.[73] The destruction of a classical country house at *Áno Sychainá* (Achaea) in the fourth century, attributed to earthquake followed by fire,[74]

---

[68] Laconia: Cartledge 1976.

[69] Baladié 1980, 145–53; Lafond 1998. Helike was allegedly 'swallowed up' (καταποθείσης, from καταπίνω) 'by the sea', Polyb. 2. 41. 7; destroyed by earthquake and 'wave' (κῦμα, Diod. 15. 48. 1–3, and Strabo 1. 3. 18, 8. 7. 1) or 'overwhelmed' (κατεκλύσθη, Strabo 8. 7. 2); along with cliffs (Poseidippos, fr. 20 in C. Austin and Bastianini 2002); earthquake followed by wave causing flood (κῦμα), Paus. 8. 24. 12 (salt-corroded ruins visible, 8. 24. 13). It did not collapse into the sea, but was ruined and covered by a lagoon: Blackman 2001–2, 38–40.

[70] Morgan and Hall 2004, 481: almost continuous LAr–R occupation at *Kástro*.

[71] Whitley 2003–4, 32.

[72] Katsonopoulou 2011.

[73] Blackman 2000–1, 38–9, at 39.

[74] Not '*Ano Sykaina*' as in French 1992–3, 24. Cf. Pikoulas 2001a, no. 3996.

should not necessarily be linked to the events of 373.[75] A case of seismicity evidenced only in archaeology is that of late fourth-century Corinth, where buildings in the town and at the Isthmia sanctuaries were apparently damaged by an earthquake; presumably it will have affected Sikyon and other nearby towns too.[76] Otherwise, however, there is no reason to support that seismic activity had any wider impact on the Peloponnese in our period.[77]

The eruption of the Methana volcano during the reign of Antigonos Gonatas (Paus. 2. 34. 1)[78] might be assumed to have affected the history of the surrounding region; but most earthquakes and volcanic eruptions are thought to have no long-lasting impact upon human societies.[79] Without specific evidence, we should not necessarily expect to see effects of the eruption beyond the immediate environs of the Methana peninsula (Strabo 1. 3. 18 implies that huge boulders were hurled 20 *stadia*, which is 2½ miles).

Turning to an environmental change that may be modified by human action, we may note that theoretical writers of the age were well aware of coastal aggradation caused by alluviation (e.g. Ps.-Skylax, 34. 3; Thphr. *HP* 5. 8. 3), as well as of water management, implied by legends about Herakles' exploits in Arkadia.[80] While we should not imagine that widespread deforestation was a necessary prelude to agriculture – the notion of a primevally forested Greece is false[81] – it is possible that the long-term expansion of plough-land led to increased redeposition of soil along the lower parts of major watercourses. We have no specific ancient reports relating to the Peloponnese in this period, but it is likely that the coastline was advancing in places such as the lower plains of the Alpheios and Eurotas.[82] At present, however, it is not possible to relate such assumed changes to historical events, and only tentatively to long-term social developments such as the earlier spread of settlements throughout Eleia.

We can therefore exclude natural disasters and geomorphological processes as significant influences on the economy of the Peloponnese in the long third century.

---

[75] On the relationship between seismic events and the archaeological record, see Helly 1998. Buck and Stewart 2000, similarly, argue for caution in relating written sources to seismic data.

[76] Dixon 2014, 117,

[77] Bresson 2016, 32–3, similarly regards the economic impact of earthquakes as limited.

[78] Baladié 1980, 157–63.

[79] Zangger 1998.

[80] Herakles' interventions in landscapes: Salowey 1994. Rivers as human constructs and as material culture: Edgeworth 2011.

[81] Rackham 1996, refuting Hughes 1983; Hughes 1994.

[82] Progradation of Helos plain: Wagstaff 1982; Wagstaff 1979. Alluviation in Elis: Fouache 2000, 77–131 (Elis), 169–92 (plain of Argos); Kraft *et al.* 2005 (Elis).

IV.2 Violence and Economies

To get as close as we can to a balanced assessment of Peloponnesian economies, we should consider external factors. First, we will look at the negatives. The military–political data tend to follow the sources – being consequently more plentiful for 338–301, 229–197, and to some extent the 260s – but while being aware of the gaps one should observe that a number of *poleis* suffered repeatedly from casualties or depredations, to the extent that one may legitimately ask whether their economy suffered as a result; though it is also important to ask how this might have come about.

IV.2.a Frequency and Distribution of Conflict

War often led to destruction in towns and their countrysides, and some places suffered repeatedly. Direct consequences of warfare, including casualties, might be limited to certain localities and times; but sometimes the frequency of violence across a wider landscape is notable. In the revolt of Agis III in 331–330, for example, the Peloponnese suffered more than most parts of Greece after being invaded by Antipater's huge army. Consequences might also be felt away from home: the Lamian war of 323–322 was mostly fought out north of the gulf of Corinth and in the Aegean,[83] but Peloponnesian manpower was heavily involved.

As the narrative in Chapter II makes clear, the years 338–301 brought violence to most of the peninsula on a scale and with an intensity comparable, for example, to those of the 360s. Let the reader imagine a recent thirty-seven-year period, such as 1980–2017, and populate it with the same kinds and numbers of wars, sieges, massacres, and invasions – all within an area the size of Wales or Massachusetts. The threat of invasion, sack, and massacre continually hung over many communities. Every region was affected in some way, particularly after 323. Nearly all the large settlements were caught up in the turmoil of the Diadochic wars, some of them more than once. The struggles between Cassander and his Antigonid opponents, for example, led to the capture of a number of towns, massacres in several *poleis*, and executions and *stasis* in others. The 300s, too, saw cities occasionally change sides, which must usually have meant capture by force resulting in casualties; one of the worst atrocities was the crucifixion of eighty anti-Antigonid partisans at the almost powerless *polis* of Orchomenos.

---

[83] Will 1979, 29–33.

Over the next eight decades (300–222), the frequency of conflict varied; and though nearly all parts of the peninsula were again affected, Macedonian power is likely to have had its strongest impact in the north-east because of the existence until 243 of the Acrocorinth garrison (Chapter III). Finally, the quarter-century after Sellasia (221–197) was unpleasant for many communities; the last generation of Macedonian involvement being marked by two intense periods of warfare (220–217, 208) that had impacts across all regions.

On the other hand, the level of outside intervention varied, as did the asperity of royal policy. Certain areas also suffered less at certain times than others. In Eleia and Messenia, if we consider the early hellenistic period as a whole, there are fewer known instances of major military activity. In the setting of 221, indeed, Polybios makes Dorimachos of Aitolia comment that Messenia is the only region of Greece (evidently meaning the Peloponnese) not to have been plundered during the Kleomenean war (4. 5. 5). The historian later comments in his own voice (4. 32. 3–6) that, while the Messenians' 'marginality' (παράπτωσις) from theatres of action protected them, it also led them to withhold commitment from both Arkadia and the anti-Spartan cause. It is indeed remarkable that Kleomenes apparently did not try to seize territory in Messenia; perhaps he simply had more pressing concerns. Dorimachos, in the passage cited, describes the region as unguarded (just as Peloponnesians in general let their guard drop after Sellasia, 4. 7). As with Eleia (4. 73. 6–8), Polybios gives us the impression of a region that had gained economically from enjoying a relatively peaceful life in the third century. Now, however, in winter 221/0, Dorimachos led the Aitolians into Messenia for an unprovoked plundering expedition. Eleia, too, suffered repeated plundering in the following years, chiefly at the hands of Philip V.

Some places, however, attracted trouble because of their strategic location. The frequency with which major cities like Megalopolis and Mantinea are caught up in military campaigns reflects, of course, their inherent wealth and fortified presence; itself partly the result of their location on natural major routes. Under certain conditions Messenia could also be strategically crucial: in 214 Philip, already in possession of Corinth, was minded to seize Messene in order to gain complete control of the Peloponnese (see Section II.5.b). It is more interesting, perhaps, when second-rank *poleis* are targeted for their strategic significance. We noted earlier Philip V's retention of Orchomenos, which lies on a key route north from Sparta. Further north, Pellene, commanding a valley running down to the gulf of Corinth, was often a focus of Macedonian interest. Kynaitha surely suffered its terrible

fate partly because of its commanding position *vis-à-vis* western Achaea.[84]
Conversely, the rarity with which the harbours of the eastern Parnon sea-
board feature in the narrative (Prasiai and Zarax only in 219; Epidauros
Limera apparently never, despite its growing importance, see Section IV.5.c)
suggest the area's secondary importance to generals.

Polybios, noting Illyrian raids on Elis and Messenia in 231, comments
that Eleia and Messenia had long been vulnerable to the Illyrians because of
their open coastline and the inland locations of their towns (2. 5. 1–2). In the
second half of the third century, an additional threat to the north-western
and western Peloponnese was posed by the rise of the Aitolian league. In
the context of Aitolian raids from a base in Kephallenia in 213, Polybios
notes that the island commands the maritime approaches to both west-
central Greece and the north-western Peloponnese (5. 3. 9–10). Polybios
makes it a general truth that (in the era before 167) the Aitolians 'had been
accustomed to living by plunder and such illegality' (30. 11. 1; cf. 'off those
nearby', 4. 3). Their moral reputation has been restored by recent studies,[85]
but they were undoubtedly a perennial thorn in the side of those in the
northern and western Peloponnese. On several occasions during the Social
war of 220–217 the Aitolians or their associates plundered various parts of
the northern and north-western Peloponnese and Messenia.[86] Both Philip
V in Eleia (4. 83) and Aitolia (5. 8–9), and the Achaeans in Eleia (5. 95),
responded in kind. The frequency of ravaging in the north and west by the
Aitolians and Illyrians (nine episodes in fourteen years at one stage in the
late third century) may have had economic and demographic consequences
in these parts.

Although every region of the Peloponnese was affected by conflict at one
or more stages, the distribution of violence varied. In general, however, it
appears to have been the northern half of the peninsula that suffered the
most: at first the north-east, at the end of the period the north-west. Nor
was violence limited to the larger centres.

IV.2.b Economic Effects of Royal Policy

Tarn detects an economic rationale for pro-Macedonian tyrannies, claiming
in the first place that a tyrant would have to pay for his own garrison;[87] but
this is pure speculation. At least one tyrant's garrison was staffed wholly or

[84] Walbank 1936, 66, calls it 'a permanent threat to the inhabitants of the coast'.
[85] e.g. Grainger 1999.
[86] Polyb. 4. 6; 4. 67; 4. 79; 5. 30; 5. 94; 5. 95; specifically on Lousoi, 4. 18. 10–11; 4. 25. 4; 9. 34. 9.
[87] Tarn 1913, 113–14.

partly by non-Greek mercenaries rather than by Macedonians of the king's standing army or by citizens of the *polis*; no source, however, tells us who paid Aristotimos' 'barbarians' (see Section III.2.b). We have no evidence for the make-up of any other garrison; it is no more than a plausible suggestion that a Corinthian woman buried in Macedonia during the third century was married to a former member of the garrison in her home town.[88]

Regarding garrisons in general, we have no evidence that the cost was ever offset by tribute or other contributions from a *polis*.[89] There was not necessarily, therefore, a flow of resource out of a local community, and quite possibly an inflow if the soldiers' pay came from outside the Peloponnese and some of it was spent locally. The frequency with which silver coins of Gonatas are found in and around Corinth (see Section IV.7.b) may suggest that, in that case at least, the Macedonian treasury footed the bill at least in the first instance.

A related question is whether Macedonian kings, particularly Antigonos Gonatas, extracted funds from cities in other ways, such that we might view it as a form of tribute. Tarn makes a circumstantial case that Gonatas did so on the basis that his father, Demetrios I, had received large sums from Euboia (Diog. Laert. 2. 140), from either Athens or Thessaly (Plut. *Demetr.* 27. 1–2), and from some Aegean islands.[90] It is true that by the terms of the Hellenic alliance of 302, for example, cities were obliged to pay sub-stantial cash sums if they failed to contribute the prescribed numbers of cavalry, hoplites, light-armed soldiers, or seamen (Schmitt, *SdA* no. 446, ll. 95–8); but this is a different case from that of an occupied city. On the other hand, in view of their limited size and territory most of the towns of the northern Peloponnese cannot have been very remunerative places to have under one's control, apart from the busy trading centre of Corinth and perhaps Argos and Sikyon. Polybios estimates the entire movable wealth of the Peloponnese in his day, excluding slaves, as worth less than 6,000 talents (2. 62. 1–5); if there were *c.* 130 *poleis*, that gives an average of *c.* 46 talents per *polis*. (How many men in the 'average *polis*', one wonders, possessed

[88] Dixon 2014, 181 and n. 77, citing *LGPN* iii A, s.v. Eutychis 10.
[89] The orders of Philip V about provisioning his garrisons, published at Chalkis, Kynos, and elsewhere, in which the *oikonomoi* (finance officers) of the cities are treated as under his command (Hatzopoulos 1996, 36–8 no. 13 = Hatzopoulos 2001, 151–3 nos 1. I–II), are not necessarily relevant to the Peloponnese under his predecessors. For uncertainty about the financing of garrisons in Hl Asia Minor, see Couvenhes 2004, esp. 92–6.
[90] *Syll.*³ 390 (Austin² 256; *c.* 280 BC) documents Ptolemy I's remission of taxes as he took over the league of the Islanders from Demetrios (cf. *RC* 14 = Austin² 259, *c.* 262/1 BC, referring to Miletos). On Gonatas' policy, see Tarn 1913, 113 n. 4.

wealth greater than one talent?) The movable wealth of one large *polis*, Megalopolis, was worth no more than 300 talents at the time of Kleomenes' attack, though a majority of the free population and slaves had fled (2. 62. 9); as noted, he gives the same figure, but *including* slaves, for the lesser *polis* of Mantinea when it was sacked shortly afterwards (2. 62. 12). The smaller *poleis* of Achaea and Argolis were surely not comparable to those Arkadian centres in population or assets. Major ports such as Piraeus and Corinth, with their capacity to levy tolls, and agricultural heartlands such as Thessaly, will have been much more important to the king, for both economic and military reasons.

If Gonatas could risk throwing away 25 talents in a speculative attempt to bribe Aratos (see Section III.2.b), it seems unlikely that he was so desperate for cash that he would invest money and *matériel* in capturing second- and third-rank *poleis* in the hope of raising additional income from them, given his more pressing concerns in North Greece and elsewhere. Any direct extraction was probably limited in scale. It seems that direct benefit to the royal treasury was at best a marginal factor in kings' decisions; we cannot assume, therefore, that Macedonian domination, where it operated, had any direct or pronounced effects on the local economy.[91] A study of Gonatas' coinage has reached a similar view.[92] There may have been indirect effects; if so, they were probably mostly small-scale.[93]

On a more positive note: to the extent that communities relied on external subventions to support their military ventures (such as Ptolemy III's gifts to the Achaeans and later to Kleomenes, Section II.4.e), and perhaps occasionally their building projects, outside powers may have represented a source of injected capital, some of which will have found its way into towns and sanctuaries. The archaeological evidence suggests that the northern Peloponnese benefited most. Indeed, the presence of garrisons or naval bases in and around the Peloponnese may to some extent have stimulated local cash economies.

IV.2.c Economic Effects of Conflict

Although the authors of a largely pessimistic study cited earlier acknowledge the availability of wealth even in a time of frequent warfare, and concede that worsening economic performances began in the first half of the

---

[91] For similar remarks, cf. Shipley 2000b, 130–1.
[92] '[T]he exercise by the Antigonids of pro-active economic and administrative control was limited' (Panagopoulou 2000, abstract).
[93] Dixon 2014, 77, 82, 90, 208, doubts whether the Antigonids taxed Corinth.

third century, they also argue that frequent warfare inhibited economic development.[94] Some evidence could be adduced in support of this view. The suggestion has been made that Corinth's economy suffered during the wars of the early Successors, with fewer records of Corinthian craftsmen abroad and archaeological evidence suggesting the disruption of the ceramics industry for a brief period.[95] Earlier, however, we suggested that war does not necessarily disrupt trade (Section IV.1.b); it can even encourage it. One might reasonably suppose that Argos' finances were stretched at various times during the long third century, given the frequency of military confrontations and the cost of building the rural towers that guarded the *chōra* (see Sections IV.5.a–b). Polybios (as part of an emotive critique of another historian) connects Macedonian power and inter-*polis* wars to the relatively modest 300 talents of booty taken by Kleomenes from both Megalopolis and Mantinea (see Section IV.2.b). More directly and more usefully, though it lies outside our period, he explains Messene's three-year exemption in the 180s from contributing to Achaean league funds by the recent devastation of its *chōra* (24. 2). On the other hand, a review of the consequences of warfare (see Section IV.1.b and later in this subsection) suggests that effects on local economies were generally intermittent and limited, though capable of being exaggerated by tendentious sources. It has been argued that the effects of warfare worsened as the victors, no longer content with victory, habitually engaged in destroying crops;[96] but this was also a feature of the classical period.[97]

Similarly, a claim is made that piracy adversely affected agriculture and trade.[98] Piracy – which we need not tie to a particular definition – evinces strong sentiments in the sources,[99] but was far from being constant in time, ubiquitous in space, or wide-ranging in its effects; and is not always easy to differentiate from trade. We saw earlier (Sections II.5.a; IV.2.a) that Polybios refers to a long tradition of Illyrian raids on the north-western Peloponnese; but in the long third century, at least, such ventures were not indiscriminate and were moderated through diplomatic institutions,[100] as were those of the Aitolians. Illyrian and Aitolian raiding in this area is most frequently evidenced in the late third and second centuries. Only in the late

[94] Rizakis and Touratsoglou 2011, 20 and 24–6 (more positive).
[95] Dixon 2014, 90–1.
[96] Rizakis and Touratsoglou 2011, 26.
[97] See e.g. Foxhall 1993, with a less apocalyptic view of the results of damage than V. D. Hanson 1982 ~ V. D. Hanson 1998.
[98] Rizakis and Touratsoglou 2011, 26.
[99] On Polybian distortion of Aitolia, see Scholten 2000, e.g. 3–6, 275–95 *passim*.
[100] Limits of C3 Illyrian piracy: Davies 2004, 122–3.

hellenistic period (roughly the first century BC) are there signs that pirat-
ical raids around the coast were having adverse demographic effects, as may
be implied by the creation of Roman veteran settlements partly intended
to revive towns whose population had shrunk.[101] There is, for example, no
evidence of towns being relocated inland for protection from piracy, as
happened in the early medieval period. In the third and second centuries, at
least, coastal towns that suffered from depredations appear to have bounced
back in the second.

A better candidate for an economically disruptive force is political
massacres such as those in 312 at Stymphalos (Diod. 19. 63. 1), Orchomenos
(19. 63. 4–64. 1), and Dyme (19. 66. 4–6). By removing a proportion of the
landowning or commercial elite, such evil deeds may have interfered with
existing economic activities. On the other hand, in most of these cases the
casualties may have represented only a small fraction of the elite, and any
vacant land or workshops may have come into the hands of their opponents
for whom they would be profitable.

More serious, at least in the short term, were pitched battles, which though
rarer than the capture or sack of towns could involve far greater losses. Heavy
casualties were suffered, for example, by the Greek allies at Megalopolis
in 331 (at the hands of the Macedonians); by the Lakedaimonians at
Mantinea in the late 290s (against Demetrios I); by the Lakedaimonians
again at Sellasia in 222 (at the hands of Doson and the Achaeans), when
5,800 casualties are reported; by the Achaeans in three battles in 227–226
(against Kleomenes III); by the Eleians near Messene in 208 (fighting with
the Aitolians against the Achaean league); and by the Lakedaimonians at
Mantinea *c.* 208 (at the hands of the Achaeans), when 4,000 were allegedly
killed. As noted earlier, however (Section IV.1.c), short-term demographic
reverses can be made good relatively quickly.

The occurrence of a major battle in a *polis*'s territory could bring about
a combination of the worst effects of both hostile and friendly forces. The
presence of two armies for a period of days or weeks would be a major drain
on resources and exacerbate the normal, indiscriminate effects of military
indiscipline. Both sides might forage, requisition, or compulsorily purchase
food to supplement the soldiers' diet. Supply trains would need fodder
and water in large quantities for any pack animals.[102] Normal land use was

---

[101]   e.g. Octavian's probable settlement of veterans at Stymphalos (H. Williams 2012); plantations
of settlers at Dyme in 67, 44, and EImp times (Rizakis 1990a). Rizakis and Touratsoglou 2011,
24, note Pompey's installation of former pirates at Dyme (App. *Mith.* 96. 444; Plut. *Pomp.* 28.
7; Strabo 8. 7. 5).

[102]   Cf. Engels 1978, though details of his calculations have been questioned.

interrupted where each army was encamped; a potential battlefield might be cleared of crops. Afterwards, a victorious invading army might well indulge in mass looting and violence against the population; slaves might be seized, citizens enslaved or massacred. Fugitives from the defeated side, if not residents of the locality, might wander about the countryside, robbing the locals (or being hidden and fed by them) and potentially behaving with ill-discipline. The effects of hundreds or thousands of cremations or burial – such as the Achaeans, numbering up to 500, interred in a mass grave after the battle of Kaphyai (Polyb. 4. 12. 8; 13. 1–3) – might affect the feasibility or permissibility of cultivation and pasturage for an indefinite period.[103]

Any invasion or siege, especially one that ended in a town's capture, will have entailed negative effects on the urban or rural landscape, which will have varied in severity and duration. The activities leading to these effects are expressed by a number of key terms in Greek, such as πορθέω (I destroy, sack, plunder), λάφυρα (booty, spoils), δηόω (I ravage), καταφθείρω (I destroy), and λήζομαι (I commit piracy).[104] Translations into English, however, often seem to treat them as if they were interchangeable; so when one sees verbs such as 'foray', 'forage', 'lay waste', 'ravage', 'plunder', 'pillage', or nouns such as 'raid' and 'booty', one must verify which Greek words lie behind them. In what follows, these activities are gathered together to give an overall picture of the human and physical damage caused by military activity.

The impacts of such events on urban landscapes are rarely reported in detail (an exception is the Aitolians at Dyme, Diod. 19. 66. 4–6). They could include temporary or enduring changes in the status and distribution of settlements. Modern studies speak of cities being 'taken' or 'seized'; this bland formulation may often mask large-scale violence, casualties not being restricted to fighting troops. Likewise, a group 'seizing power' in a *polis* will often, as we have seen, have meant internecine killing.

Besides the impacts upon towns, it is worth focusing on the countryside. The presence of hundreds or thousands of armed men, perhaps with a baggage train, probably along a well-frequented route – particularly if they stopped anywhere for one or more nights – might leave a trail swept clean of crops and perhaps of people, though littered with discarded material and waste of all kinds. Incidental effects such as residues from fires, cooking

---

[103] On the effects of burning on soils, see Delano Smith 1996, 170–4. On the effects of armies, cf. Siebert 1978, 199 n. 3.

[104] For the multivalency of λήζομαι, which need not refer to naval activity, see MacDonald 1984.

refuse, and human waste should not be overlooked. In a wider zone of disorder either side of the army's track, locals might well abandon their farms. Siege warfare would exacerbate the problem. In the vicinity of encampments, there might be – as a matter of policy, or on soldiers' private initiative – the intensive thieving of foodstuffs, the killing, raping or enslavement of any civilians unfortunate enough to be in the way, damage to farmhouses and stores, the seizure of mature crops, and wanton damage to immature crops. This last may have had only limited economic costs in view of the tendency for landholdings to be fragmented and the difficulty of wiping out an entire harvest (other than perhaps in grapes);[105] but the destruction of rural installations such as olive-presses would impose severe costs. Assaults on the lands of the rich could be a political weapon: the fifth-century author of the Pseudo-Xenophontic *Constitution of the Athenians* (2. 14) observes that those with wealth or land are most likely to treat with the enemy.

Even an allied army passing through, or settling in to raise a siege, might cause short-term damage. Food, for example, might be requisitioned or forcibly purchased. Polybios describes Philip V in Arkadia as 'advanc[ing] on Psophis through the territory of Kleitor, collecting missiles and ladders from the towns he passed through'; this being allied territory, one would dearly like to know whether he paid for them.[106] The Spartans' good conduct in other states' territories while on campaign under Agis IV was noted, presumably because it was thought exceptional (Plut. *Ag.–Kl.* 14). There might, however, be sporadic violence even on the part of supposed allies; on one occasion, the Aitolians were expected to show restraint but (if Polybios is to be believed) did not do so:

> While making their march through the lands of the Patraians, Pharaians, and Tritaians, they acted as if they wished to commit no injustice against the Achaeans; but since the mass of them were incapable of keeping off the land because of their addiction to profit (τὰς ὠφελείας), they damaged and abused it as they proceeded through it, until they made it to Phigaleia.
> (Polyb. 4. 6. 9–10)

Many of these effects were probably localized or short-term, or both. If repeated or prolonged, however, such encounters could have more serious consequences. It is pertinent to recall Polybios' statement that in 223/2 the Megalopolitans 'had lost most of their men from the (sc. eligible) age-groups in the battle at Mt Lykaion and the later one at Ladokeia' (2. 55. 2).

---

[105]   V. D. Hanson 1982 (~ V. D. Hanson 1998), refined by Foxhall 1993.
[106]   Shipley 2008a, 57.

While Macedonian power may, predictably, have had its strongest impact in the north-east (including eastern Achaea), kings and commanders may have been careful not to damage irremediably the landscapes and communities they hoped to control and patronize. The north-west was probably affected more by its relationships with Aitolia and Illyria. Taking the peninsula as a whole, the frequency of violence is striking, particularly in certain regions, and the large size of some armies and the duration of certain campaigns should be borne in mind; but since some economic or demographic effects may have been of short duration, neither war nor piracy can wholly account for any economic effects we may detect. Can other evidence illuminate whether underlying economic structures were adversely affected by the recorded episodes of violence?

IV.3 Rural Survey Data

In attempting to understand changes in rural settlement,[107] we shall take account as far as possible of the elements of choice and response, while bearing in mind the economic implications (if any) of the data. (For further methodological discussion, see Section IV.3.d.) We shall focus particularly on 'intensive' field surveys,[108] of which at least eleven have taken place since the early 1980s including no fewer than four in Argolis (TABLE IV.1) but unfortunately none in Eleia or Triphylia. We shall not ignore the results of non-intensive ('extensive') surveys. Together the projects represent a data set unavailable to most earlier scholarship. Given the problems of reading survey data, however, caution must be exercised.[109] In what follows, we shall avoid taking an increase or decrease in archaeologically attested activity in the countryside as straightforward evidence of prosperity or impoverishment, pending the summative analysis. Although our starting-point is the identification of economic change and continuity, we will find that the evidence bears on other questions too (we return to some of these in Chapter V). In general, it will be important to consider both external factors (such as Macedonian power) and internal causes (such as *polis* politics and social structures) in attempting to account for the data.

---

[107] Complementary discussions in Shipley 2000b, 29–31; Shipley 2001–2, 435–6; Shipley 2002a, 180–5; Shipley 2002c, 41; Shipley 2002d, 312–16.

[108] For characterizations of intensive as opposed to non-intensive (often unhelpfully called 'extensive') survey, see Alcock 1993, 33–7; Stewart 2013, 7–12.

[109] On the particular problems of Hl data from the Peloponnese, see Bintliff 2008. Rizakis and Touratsoglou 2011, 24, pass general comments on the survey data.

Table IV.1. *Archaeological survey projects*

ARGOLIS	* Argolid Exploration Project	§ Jameson *et al.* 1994, superseding van Andel and Runnels 1987	
	* Methana Survey	§ Mee and Forbes 1997	partly urban
	* Nemea Valley Archaeological Project	§ Wright *et al.* 1990; Cherry *et al.* 1996–2000 (on-line outline)	other papers on prehistory, post-Hl; includes Phleious urban survey
	‡ Phleious Survey	Alcock 1991	see previous entry
	* Berbati–Limnes Archaeological Survey	§ Wells 1996; Hjohlman *et al.* 2005	
	Kleonai	† Mattern 2013, 331	
KORINTHIA– SIKYONIA	† Sikyonia Survey	§ Lolos 2011; also Lolos 2005	
	‡ Sikyon Survey	Lolos *et al.* 2007	*AGOnline* ID 107 (2006), ID 289 (2007), ID 1422 (2009)
	* Eastern Korinthia Archaeological Survey	Tartaron *et al.* 2006 (overview); Caraher *et al.* 2010 (fortifications)	other papers cover R and later
ACHAIA	*† Western Achaia Survey	§ e.g. Dalongeville *et al.* 1992; Rizakis 2000	Dyme–Patrai area
	*/† Aigialieia Survey	Whitley 2006–7, 32; *AGOnline* ID 1925 (2010)	Aigeira area
ELEIA	† Peneios Valley survey	H. S. Robinson 1968; Karwiese *et al.* 1968 (esp. Howell at 178–83); excavation, Ellis Jones 1970	
TRIPHYLIA	‡ Triphylia Survey	*AGOnline* ID 2079 (2010), ID 1513 (2009)	territories of Samikon, *Gýllos* (Hypana?), Epitalion, *Ágios Ilías* (Pyrgos?), Lepreon, Makiston

Table IV.1. (*Cont.*)

ARKADIA	† Eastern Arkadia	Howell 1970	
	* Asea Valley Survey	§ J. Forsén and Forsén 2003	
	* Megalopolis Survey	Roy 1983; Lloyd *et al.* 1985; Roy *et al.* 1992	
	* Norwegian Arcadia Survey (Tegea area)	e.g. Cracolici 2005; Ødegard 2005	rural and urban, in Tegea area
MESSENIA	† Five Rivers Survey	Lukermann and Moody 1978	
	† Minnesota Messenia Expedition	§ McDonald and Rapp 1972	research aims mainly prehistoric
	* Pylos Regional Archaeological Project	§ Davis *et al.* 1996–2010 (on-line data set); Davis *et al.* 1997 (overview); Davis 1998 ~ Davis 2008; Alcock *et al.* 2005 (ancient periods)	other papers on methodology, prehistory, post-R
LACONIA	* Laconia Survey	§ Cavanagh *et al.* 1996 (data), Cavanagh *et al.* 2002 (interpretation)	
	* Boiai–*Elaphónisos* Survey	E. Mantzourani, unpublished report	ID 1927 (2010)

* intensive   † non-intensive   ‡ largely/wholly urban survey
§ substantially or fully published
The *Berbáti–Límnes* survey will sometimes be abbreviated to '*Berbáti*'.

We first summarize the relevant results by chronological phase. (The new survey of ancient Aigila, modern *Andikýthira*, is omitted by reason of the island's location closer to Crete than to Laconia.)[110]

IV.3.a Late Classical Survey Data

The fourth century, in some parts of Greece, sees a peak in rural settlement numbers, or the prolongation of such a peak. We review the results of Peloponnesian field surveys in *periplous* order once more.

[110] For the Hl pottery, see esp. A. W. Johnston *et al.* 2012; Tsaravopoulos *et al.* 2014.

Archaic–classical maxima occur in the north-east: in Korinthia and at Kleonai in Argolis,[111] though in southern Argolis the upturn is delayed until the very end of the classical period; a rise in the number of small farms occurring around 350.[112] Data from Nemea[113] suggest that numbers peak in the classical and early hellenistic phases. In Eleia and Triphylia, a relatively dense spread of nucleated settlements appears to have existed in classical times. Few of those can be tied to an ancient name;[114] this may partly reflect our incomplete knowledge of Eleian *poleis*, but most of the *c*. 37 unnamed sites in Eleia and the *c*. 8 in Triphylia may have been non-*poleis* forming a relatively dense settlement pattern.[115] Preliminary results from Arkadian Megalopolis point, as at Nemea, to a fourth- and third-century peak.[116] At Arkadian Asea[117] and Messenian Pylos,[118] an upturn in site numbers is observed in about the fourth century.

The picture is not, however, uniform. At *Berbáti* in Argolis, the fourth-century pattern suggests relatively dispersed settlement.[119] In the Laconia Survey area – situated within the north-eastern part of Sparta's *chōra* – there is a sharp fall in site numbers around the mid-fifth century and a further decrease in the fourth.[120] The data thus paint a picture of contrasts for the fourth century, with a general upturn in rural settlement but not in the Laconia Survey area, or everywhere in Argolis.

IV.3.b Hellenistic Survey Data

In some areas, the hellenistic data do not definitely indicate either change or continuity. In Sikyonia, the results of non-intensive survey do not present a clear picture for the early part of the period, though they point to a classical maximum and a fall in the late hellenistic.[121] Similarly, a non-intensive survey of eastern Achaea indicates a fall in numbers from hellenistic to Roman, and discontinuity between the two periods, but does not reveal

---

[111] Bintliff 1997, 4, no. 14, citing Sakellariou and Faraklas 1971; etc. On Corinth, see also Engels 1990, esp. 82, 157–8.
[112] Jameson *et al.* 1994, 383, 393–4.
[113] Wright *et al.* 1990, 616–17.
[114] Roy 2004, 489–90; Nielsen 2004b.
[115] The densely settled Cl landscape of Eleia is noted by Osborne 1987, 127. For *poleis* and other settlements in Eleia, see Roy 2004; for Triphylia, Nielsen 2004b.
[116] Aupert and Ginouvès 1989, 149; Lloyd 1991, 189–90.
[117] Tomlinson 1994–5, 12; J. Forsén *et al.* 1996, 91; B. Forsén 2003.
[118] Davis *et al.* 1997, 455–6.
[119] Stewart 2013, 52.
[120] Shipley 2002c, 41; Shipley 2002a, 187.
[121] Lolos 2011, 329–30, cf. 367–8.

trends within the hellenistic period.[122] The Five Rivers Survey in south-central Messenia does not identify a clear trend between the classical and hellenistic periods.[123]

In the hellenistic period, sometimes more specifically the early hellenistic, some areas exhibit high numbers of rural settlements, similar to those of the fourth century. In eastern Korinthia up to the year 2000, for example, the surveyors found hellenistic or classical–hellenistic material at a majority of findspots.[124] In Eleia and Triphylia, the relatively dense classical distribution appears to persist; the non-intensive Peneios Valley Survey found a number of hellenistic sites, possibly including a tile kiln and a farmhouse.[125] Although we do not have the same level of detail as is provided by intensive survey in other regions, we may view Eleia as a landscape that had altered little.[126] At Arkadian Asea, settlement numbers remain elevated for most of the hellenistic period.[127]

In other areas, the hellenistic period appears to usher in site creation.[128] In Argolis, at *Berbáti*, there is a wave of new settlement around 300 at the edges of the inhabited area,[129] which the surveyors link to the refoundation of nearby Mycenae. The *chōra* of Methana sees a slight increase in site numbers, despite the eruption of the volcano (see Section IV.1.f),[130] and the area remains relatively intensively worked in the third century, perhaps because of the presence of a Ptolemaic base.[131] In western Achaea, the data from Dyme suggest a significant recolonization of the landscape in the early or middle hellenistic period; the evidence for low-level rural habitations is considered reliable.[132] At Messenian Pylos, the fourth-century increase in rural

---

[122] Stewart 2013, 78–9.

[123] Harrison and Spencer 1998 = Harrison and Spencer 2008, 160, imply that the Five Rivers Survey identified Hl farmsteads, apparently new since Cl times. This contradicts Lukermann and Moody 1978, 96–7, who note that Cl and Hl finds were hard to distinguish and, following McDonald and Hope Simpson 1972, 145, warn that the Hl sites may also have been occupied in Cl times.

[124] Gregory and others 1998 (no longer active); see now e.g. Caraher *et al.* 2006, e.g. p. 17 table 1 (*Kromna–Perdikaria* area).

[125] Fraser 1969–70, 14–15.

[126] The C4l abandonment of a cemetery at Skillous (Parlama 1972; cf. H. W. Catling 1972–3, 17–18) probably has no bearing on this.

[127] J. Forsén *et al.* 1996, 91–2; J. Forsén and B. Forsén 2003, 334; Stewart 2013, 56–7.

[128] Rizakis and Touratsoglou 2011, 24, regard this as a bright spot in their largely bleak portrayal.

[129] Penttinen 1996a, at 229, 271–2, 279–81.

[130] Gill *et al.* 1997.

[131] Stewart 2013, 47.

[132] Lakakis and Rizakis 1992c, 68–9 (citing sites 11, 16, 20, 34, and 42, though only the last four have definite Hl material according to the site catalogue, Dalongeville 1992), 70; Petropoulos and Rizakis 1994, 190–2 (tables 1–2), 198; Petropoulos 1994, 405–24. Note, however, the warning by Gill 1994, that some so-called R sites in the survey of W. Achaea may be Hl; cf. Stewart 2013, 77.

settlement continues; the strong showing of rural sites is accompanied by a greater level of coastal activity and presumably growing trade; and sites are generally larger than those seen in 'surges' in other regions, with fewer possible small farms.[133] The Laconia Survey data point to the recolonization, around 300, of marginal land abandoned in the fourth century, with new small and medium-sized sites being occupied; though on the basis of their assemblages it appears that few of these sites were primarily residential farmsteads.[134] (Once again, however, the increase in site numbers should not necessarily be taken as evidence of the economic well-being of a community.)

In some regions, dense rural settlement has been linked to urban expansion or revival. It is claimed that Dyme and its territory flourished in parallel.[135] The case may be the same with Sparta: the early hellenistic city was expanding, the open spaces within being filled in. In addition, the Laconia Survey identified a satellite settlement just north of Sparta, apparently growing in the hellenistic period;[136] rescue excavation has since revealed late classical–early hellenistic buildings linked to a cult complex destroyed in the late third century (perhaps after the battle of Sellasia).[137]

In the areas so far reviewed, then, there is generally an upturn in rural site numbers, and some evidence of urban growth. In one region, southern Argolis, there is evidence of increasing site size consistent with the rise of larger estates.[138]

In other places, the number of rural sites falls at some stage during the hellenistic period. Some surveys do not permit conclusions to be drawn about trends within the period. In eastern Korinthia, for example, we cannot see any effects of the destruction of Corinth in 146 in the wider *chōra*.[139] The same is true, understandably, of non-intensive surveys such as that of the Peneios valley. Other surveys point to the reduction in site numbers but do not allow us to date it precisely: such is the case at Nemea,[140] around Megalopolis,[141] in the latter's southern territory,[142] and in the area

---

[133] Davis *et al.* 1997, 456–7; Stewart 2013, 69–71.

[134] Shipley 2002d, e.g. 283–6, 310–12, 322; modified by Stewart 2013, 40–2.

[135] Lakakis and Rizakis 1992c, 70 and n. 10.

[136] Site H45 *Geladári*: Shipley 1996b, 355–7, with map at 354; Shipley 2002d, 266 (finds mainly Hl–R), 293 (contraction in R).

[137] Eleftheriou and Skagkos 2010–13, esp. 536–7 (LCl–Hl structures), 537–47 (R funerary complex); the buildings are clearly visible on Google Earth (image dated 26 Oct. 2013) at 37° 07' 07" N, 22° 24' 58" E.

[138] Though note Shipley 2002a, 184–5: no significant alteration in site size in Laconia or Methana.

[139] Millis 2006 rejects some of the evidence for partial occupation of Corinth during 146–44 BC.

[140] Wright *et al.* 1990, at 616–17.

[141] Roy *et al.* 1989, at 149; Lloyd 1991, at 189–90.

[142] Pikoulas 1988b, 231–2.

of Patrai.[143] Elsewhere, however, a downturn appears early. In southern
Argolis, even though the late Classical rise comes later than elsewhere,
there is a marked fall in the numbers of small farmsteads only a couple of
generations later, perhaps as early as *c.* 250;[144] we may recall that the *polis*
of Halieis in this area is thought to have been abandoned by *c.* 280 (though
see Section V.3.e).[145] At *Berbáti* the drop is thought to have occurred by
200, possibly leaving only one site in the valley.[146] Finally, in some places a
decline does not appear to happen until after the early hellenistic period.
On the Methana peninsula, the downturn is modest and appears not to
begin until the late second century.[147] In the *chōra* of Dyme, contraction
begins in the late hellenistic period,[148] just as expansion began later here
than elsewhere. Similarly, around Sparta there is no firm evidence of a
decline in rural sites until the first century BC,[149] when some created early
in the period may have been abandoned.[150]

It is difficult to avoid using terms with positive or negative connotations
such as 'decline' and 'upturn'; but they are here used without prejudice to
the possible implications for society and the economy, particularly agriculture. It is not obvious that a fall in the number of farmsteads necessarily means a fall in cultivation, let alone that shrinking rural settlement
means economic decline.[151] At *Berbáti*, for example, the third-century
fall in site numbers is accompanied by a probable increase in estate size
(which continues later), with more diversified agriculture a likely component.[152] Equally, the fall in rural site numbers should be interpreted
in the light of greater nucleation at the nearby *polis* of Mycenae; but it is
debatable whether the construction of rural towers like that at *Pyrgoúthi*
in the *Berbáti* valley is evidence of the breakdown of central authority, or
of tighter central control.[153] At Arkadian Asea, too where the central settlement diminishes in size,[154] more than one interpretation is possible: it may

[143] Papagiannopoulos and Zachos 2000, 145–6.
[144] Jameson *et al.* 1994, 383–4, 391, 393–4, etc.
[145] Stewart 2013, 63–4.
[146] Stewart 2013, 52–3; Penttinen 1996a, 271 (two sites) with 281 ('basically only one site').
[147] Gill *et al.* 1997; data reinterpreted by Stewart 2013, 47.
[148] Lakakis and Rizakis 1992c, at 68–9, 70; Petropoulos and Rizakis 1994, at 190–2 (tables 1–2), 198.
[149] Shipley 2002d, esp. 274–88, 310–12, 322–6.
[150] Stewart 2013, 41–2.
[151] As assumed by Rizakis and Touratsoglou 2011, 26.
[152] Stewart 2013, 52–3.
[153] Penttinen 2005, 119.
[154] J. Forsén *et al.* 1996, 91; J. Forsén and B. Forsén 2003, 334.

have been an unusual *polis* with fragmented or even quasi-federal settle-ment;[155] or it may have switched in and out of *polis* status (with implications for civic organization) after being absorbed into Megalopolis in the mid-fourth century.[156]

IV.3.c Survey Data in a Social Context

Trends

In principle, rural settlement data ought to be crucial for addressing the question posed earlier, of whether the Peloponnese was in a better eco-nomic condition in *c.* 200 than at the start of Macedonian involvement. The construction of chronology from field survey data, and the interpretation of changing numbers of small rural sites, are admittedly complex problems.[157] Survey data cannot, however, be interpreted in isolation from evidence for changes in, for example, political systems, elite culture, land ownership, or warfare, imprecise as that evidence may be. Three key features of the data, however, stand out.

The first is the generally high level of rural occupation throughout the 'long third century'.[158] There is no reason to posit a general withdrawal from the countryside. Change of that kind is more likely to have occurred in the later second century or even later, when it would parallel the decline in public architecture noted below (see Section IV.5.d). This compels a revision of existing views. On the basis of limited published data at the time when she was writing,[159] Alcock posits a progressive abandonment of rural sites from the second half of the third century onwards; the beginning of a process that produced the characteristic landscape of Roman Greece, with limited rural residence and large elite estates. She presents this change as taking place largely under Roman domination; but, since the full weight of Roman power was not felt in Greece as early as the late third century, concedes that other reasons for the change may have included the actions of hellenistic rulers, or a desire on the part of some country-dwellers to move into towns,

---

155 Stewart 2013, 56–8.
156 That absorption is itself uncertain: Nielsen 2004a, 510 (*Inv. 267*).
157 See e.g. papers in Francovich *et al.* 2000; Alcock and Cherry 2004 with Stewart 2005; also Shipley 2002a, 180–2.
158 Rizakis and Touratsoglou 2011, 24, see both survey and excavation data as showing that there was no abandonment and that some new farmsteads were set up (sc. in EHl). While I agree that the C3 picture is, on the whole, not negative, their observation does not explicitly take account of regional differences.
159 Only two intensive surveys: Nemea Valley Archaeological Project; Western Achaia survey. The latter appeared only just before Alcock 1993.

perhaps for security.[160] With many more surveys now published, and in the light of Stewart's recasting of the raw data, we can see that the thesis of a widely distributed rural downturn beginning before *c.* 200 is hard to sustain. Cases of decline are rare enough to weaken the hypothesis that general change took place so early.

Second, despite the problems of interpreting survey data, it is clear that regional variation in the nature and timing of landscape changes is a strong characteristic of the Peloponnese. This alone may fatally weaken the hitherto orthodox view that hellenistic Greece was the victim of 'decline and depopulation'.[161]

A third point, related to this, is that the detailed evidence for some regions, when set in the context of wider social and economic developments, points to variation at a sub-regional scale, so that contrary trends may appear within a constricted area. We shall consider this next.

When all this material is examined and put together, we shall see that survey data do not, in fact, give any definite answer to overall questions about the economic well-being, or otherwise, of the Peloponnese; but point to more subtle, and arguably more interesting, changes and continuities (see Section IV.3.d).

Intra-regional Variation

Intra-regional variation is most obvious in Argolis, the only region where we have intensive survey data from different *polis* territories. On the one hand, the change in the *Berbáti–Límnes* valley to a single main settlement – and perhaps a single estate – by *c.* 200 BC[162] parallels the decline of small rural sites in the eastern Argolis (Akte), where Halieis and most third-order sites around it disappear. Yet, within the Akte, sites around Hermion increase in number, and the *polis* may even have overtaken Troizen in population during the third quarter of the third century, perhaps as a result of the actual relocation of inhabitants.[163] Furthermore, while the frequency of land arbitrations suggests there may have been increased pastoralism in the eastern Akte,[164] there seems to be an upswing in activity further west, with the

---

[160] Alcock 1993, 218 and 113 respectively. These two concessions are also highlighted in a review by Woolf 1994.

[161] Stewart 2013, 113.

[162] Penttinen 1996a, 229, 271–2, 279–81.

[163] Jameson *et al.* 1994, 395.

[164] See Jameson *et al.* 1994, 397, 567; Dixon 2003 (Achaean league–Arsinoë, i.e. Methana, 243–228); Dixon 2005 and Dixon 2014, 146–8 (Corinth–Epidauros, 242/1); Dixon 2001 (Epidauros–Hermion, 175–172); cf. Dixon 2000, ch. 1.

revival of Mycenae, the refoundation of Asine, and the new fortifications at Nauplion. There are signs of a rise in site numbers around the Argive plain. Thus a recession in some areas may be balanced by immigration and urban growth elsewhere – a shift in population *density*, not necessarily a loss of *people*. This evidence is suggestively paralleled by the distribution of epigraphic finds (Section V.2.d), which suggests a shift of political activity from east to west within Argolis between the third century and the second.

In Korinthia, the evidence for Kromna, a non-*polis*, might be read as indicating its abandonment after the early hellenistic period; but more probably points to a shift in the focus of agricultural activity away from the central place.[165]

Within Achaea, the replacement of Olenos as a local centre by Dyme may have drawn settlement away from the *Alissoú–Kamenítsa* area, which declines in hellenistic–Roman times while Dyme's core territory is actively settled.[166]

In Eleia, the apparent continuation of flourishing rural settlement seems consonant with Polybios' observations (4. 73–4) on Eleia's rural elite who run the *polis* for their own advantage – he puts it in terms of the town-dwellers looking after the country folk, but presumably it is the latter that are dominant – and spend most of their time in the countryside. The data suggest a reinforcement of the scatter of sites across the *chōra* that was already a feature of archaic and classical Eleia. The seeming increase in rural occupation in at least part of western Elis may indicate a shift of activity away from some of the perioikic areas that had been lost temporarily in the first half of the fourth century. This in itself need have had no effect on elite prosperity.

In Laconia, within the northern territory of Sparta, shifts of activity can be observed between the three sectors of the survey area (defined by geology and topography), such as a net movement of settlement numbers and estimated population towards the schistic soils of the northern sector.[167]

Explanations of Change

The phenomena requiring explanation, therefore, are not only the apparent general strength of rural settlement in the early hellenistic period[168] and the subsequent downturn in some (not all) areas, but also the different

[165] Tartaron *et al.* 2006, 500–1 with 503–4.
[166] Papagiannopoulos and Zachos 2000, 144–5.
[167] Shipley 2002d, 309–10.
[168] Rizakis and Touratsoglou 2011, 24.

characters and trajectories of different regions and sub-regions. What might explain such phenomena?

We saw earlier (Section II.3.b–c) that late fourth-century warfare concentrated in the north-east; subsequently, under Antigonid rule, it occurred in all regions except Eleia and Messenia; finally, under Achaean domination it was widespread, with the added complication of Aitolian, Messenian, and Illyrian raiding in the north-west. A possible link between the wars of the Diadochoi and the early downturn in rural sites in southern Argolis is at first sight tempting; but as that downturn does not take place until about the mid-third century, even later at *Berbáti*, it seems a tenuous connection at best. Parts of western Achaea certainly suffered in those early wars; yet the countryside seems thickly settled. Likewise, while the delayed fall in settlement around Dyme could reflect the fact that western Achaea apparently did not suffer severely in war until the late third century, it could be a coincidence. We could link the apparent success of Eleian rural sites in the third century with the fact that this region, too, escaped the worst of the violence at the start of the period; but firmer evidence would be needed to posit a causal connection. In Messenia, we might wish to associate the apparent absence of rural abandonment at Pylos with the fact that the region escaped serious plundering until after the Kleomenean war, as noted earlier. Counter-instances are not hard to find, however. Settlement in Sparta's north-eastern *chōra*, for example, appears to suffer no lasting effects from the many invasions of Laconia.

If warfare and its direct effects cannot alone account for landscape changes, perhaps the indirect consequences of warfare may be considered. Was there, perhaps, a gradual flight from the *chōra* in certain areas because of a sense of insecurity, such as we see in the late Roman period in western Europe? But in that context the flight was away from the rural villas of the ruling elite to fortified towns that offered better security and protection.[169] In our period, protection would presumably be sought primarily within the walls of a fortified settlement from the start. In any case, a general perception of danger cannot explain the upturn in rural settlement in parts of the early hellenistic Peloponnese. What we see, rather, is a reduction in site numbers in some areas with no necessary reduction in overall population; and in some cases shifts of population from one *chōra* to another.

If neither the direct nor the indirect effects of warfare provide a convincing explanation of settlement changes, alternatives (not mutually exclusive) present themselves. One might look for evidence of direct economic

---

[169]   Christie 2004 (definition of 'insecurity' at 16); Scott 2004, 55–9.

intervention from Rome and Italy affecting the *chōra* directly, as is generally
believed to have happened in the middle and late hellenistic period (second
and first centuries BC). Roman or Italian traders were increasingly active
in the Adriatic by the 230s,[170] and while they were probably not present in
significant numbers in the Aegean world or the eastern Mediterranean until
the late second century,[171] we can imagine that developments in the Adriatic
economies in some way influenced the agricultural economies of southern
Greece. Alternatively, changes in Peloponnesian settlement patterns may in
some way reflect wider changes in trade across the post-Alexander eastern
Mediterranean. We shall return to these points.

A distinctly tempting possibility, in line with Chapter III, is that the
changes partly reflect internal causes, such as the working through of social,
economic, or political processes that began earlier and were not necessarily
related to external circumstances. With this in mind, it is relevant to ask
what effects the increasing domination of civic affairs by elites[172] may have
had upon rural landscapes. In some regions it is possible that changes in
the sizes of sites, or in the area controlled by each, reflect increased elite
domination of landholding, with variation between regions.[173] The rise of
consolidated elite estates has been mooted as a feature of, particularly, the
period after 146, which may be characterized as a time when elite land ownership was often disrupted.[174] Extreme domination of the rural landscape
by luxury 'villas', however, tends not to be seen before the early Imperial
period.[175]

Literary evidence for elite landholding is inconclusive. The 'excellent
farm' (ἀγρὸς καλός) of Philopoimen, located 20 stades (only *c.* 2½ miles, 4
km) from his home city of Megalopolis, where 'labourers' (ἐργάται) work
the vines and tend the animals (Plut. *Philop.* 4. 1–4), cannot be invoked
as evidence of a new phenomenon of extra-urban luxury residences; need
it be substantially different from the estate of Ischomachos in Xenophon's
Oikonomikos, written around 360?[176] The 'small steading (ἐπαύλιον) called
Chyron's' near Messene, raided by the Aitolians in 221 (Polyb. 4. 3–4), with

---

[170] Davies 2004, 125–7.
[171] Lawall 2006, 275 n. 56, citing Hasenohr and Müller 2002 (general), Follet 2002 (Athens),
        Müller 2002 (Boiotia), Rizakis 2002 (Macedonia). Rizakis 2001b notes that in the Caesarian
        colonies the role of *negotiatores* varied: strong at Corinth, doubtful at Patrai, non-existent
        at Dyme.
[172] Cf. Chapter III, n. 81 above; IV.7.c below; Chapter V, *passim.*
[173] Shipley 2008a, 66.
[174] Alcock 1993, 72–80.
[175] Alcock 1993, 63–71. For cash-cropping in C2m Italy, see von Reden 2010, 53.
[176] Pomeroy 1994, 8. Lloyd 1991, 190, over-translates ἀγρὸς καλός (4. 3) as 'fine estate'.

its labourers (οἰκέται) and livestock (κτήνη), is not known in detail and does not sound like a luxury residence.[177] Nor do we know whether the 'house' (οἰκία) that Aratos owned 'in Corinth' (ἐν Κορίνθῳ) in the late third century (Plut. *Arat.* 41. 4) was urban or rural, or its scale.

Archaeology, however, does point to a possible increase in site size in certain regions at certain times.

(*a*) Some of the evidence relates only to a later period and cannot necessarily be retrojected to the third century. In Argolis, Arkadian transhumants may have been installed at Troizen around 146; taken together with archaeology, this may point to poor Epidaurians leaving in search of a better life or seeking different work, combined with larger estates with more non-citizens and slaves working on them.[178] This trend may not have been common to the whole of Argolis, however; and may not have been evident as early as the third century. A rise in transhumance in other regions is not to be excluded *a priori*; whether this has implications for inter-*polis* relationships is a question to which we will return.

In Achaea, it was probably not until during and after the first century BC, under the Roman occupation, that larger 'villas' arose, particularly on the coastal shelf around Patrai, once the Roman colony had been founded.[179] Possible evidence of elite estates in hellenistic times comes from Achaean Dyme, where one or possibly two sites are identified as large hellenistic farmsteads or villas; one has third-century pottery, but the evidence is so far inconclusive.[180] Perhaps somewhat later, as Roman influence culminates, there are possible signs in western Achaea of the amalgamation of landholdings into fewer, larger estates and a possible shift towards monocropping, implying a greater interest in the market than before on the part of the elite.[181]

(*b*) More relevant are the data from the end of the classical period and the early hellenistic. In southern Argolis after *c*. 350, the new spread of sites is thought by the surveyors to reflect increased olive cultivation (though this has been questioned)[182] and greater involvement in wider networks, probably accompanied by an increase in estate size and perhaps in pastoralism.

---

[177] ἐπαύλιον connotes no specific size, though as a diminutive form of ἔπαυλις (LSJ s.vv.) it could certainly refer to a modest establishment.

[178] Jameson *et al.* 1994, 397, 565–7.

[179] Rizakis 1997, 28–9.

[180] Dalongeville *et al.* 1992, 68–9 with table at 61, where site Araxos E (Hl) is marked as 'ferme, villa rustica'; a C3 kantharos was found (142). (At 61 Lakkopetra G is, tentatively, so marked; but at 184 it is a Cl–Hl–R 'petite ferme'.)

[181] Papagiannopoulos and Zachos 2000, 145.

[182] By Acheson 1997, 181.

Analysis of typical sites in different surveys confirms that those in southern Argolis tend to be larger than those in, for example, Methana and Laconia.[183] The shift in agricultural preference, however, need not imply commercial mono-cropping of the olive, and on present evidence there is nothing to connect it with elite domination of land ownership.[184]

In Arkadia, the prominence of middle-sized sites (0.25–1.00 ha) in the territory of Megalopolis would be consistent with a shift towards single-estate settlement.[185]

A more complex situation emerges in Messenia, where the Pylos survey has suggested the emergence of a rich, presumably landowning class alongside dispersed small farmsteads, now making their first appearance.

Finally, in Laconia, specifically in the north-eastern portion of Sparta's *chōra*, the classical falls in site numbers invite a local explanation in terms of Sparta's specific historical trajectory, such as its notorious shortage of citizens (*oliganthrōpia*).[186] The surveyors suggest that these sites may have been occupied by dependent poor citizens or free non-Spartiates (*hypomeiones*, 'inferiors') under the patronage of the rich, as a remedy for *oliganthrōpia*;[187] this trend possibly intensifying in some areas in the late third and early second centuries.[188] Such steps are imaginable under a king like Areus I (II.4.b–c), anxious to maintain Sparta's military strength while integrating it into wider networks.[189] If this reconstruction is right, we should interpret the evidence of increasing involvement of 'Lakedaimonians' in farming in the late fourth century (implied by Arist. *Pol.* 2. 5. 1264a 10–11) as referring either to the installation of small farmers by elite patrons (in the marginal land of the Laconia Survey area or elsewhere) or to the rise of large estates (not attested in the area specifically surveyed, where hellenistic sites generally have a low level of material wealth, but perhaps taking place elsewhere in Sparta's *polis* territory). A re-analysis of the raw data for the early hellenistic sites set up on marginal land in the north of the *chōra*, indeed, suggests a shift towards more intensive cultivation or cash-cropping.[190] Into

---

[183] Shipley 2002a, 184–6.

[184] Stewart 2013, 63–4. Acheson 1997 takes a different line, relying on inferred 'land pressure' for which the evidence seems unclear, but rightly rejects any simplistic version of the commercial explanation as the driving force behind settlement change (cf. Jameson *et al.* 1994, 383–4, 391, 393–5, etc.; cf. van Andel and Runnels 1987, 109–10).

[185] Lloyd 1991, at 189–90; Roy *et al.* 1989, esp. 149; J. Roy, pers. comm. (2001); Roy *et al.* 1988, 179–82; Lloyd *et al.* 1985, at 217.

[186] R. W. V. Catling 2002, 235–40, 243–8.

[187] Shipley 2002a, 189–90, 191.

[188] Shipley 2002d, 321–6.

[189] For Sparta in relation to the wider world of C3, see Shipley 2009.

[190] Stewart 2013, 91–2.

this picture we could fit the third-century inscription found on the east bank of the Eurotas, listing citizens belonging to the south-east part of the city (just across the river) who donated money to improve the water supply (*SEG* 40. 348),[191] presumably on their own landholdings.

In all these regions, the data have been shown to be susceptible to a context-specific reading reflecting the regional evidence – including written sources, treated with all possible caution – rather than a one-size-fits-all, over-arching model such as Macedonian 'imperialism' or economic intervention by Macedonians or, later, Italians. It is, however, a reasonable assumption that one of the motors for landscape change was very often competition and ambition among the *polis* elite. Although the data do not conclusively dictate a significant shift towards estate-based agriculture, they are consistent with such a possibility.

IV.3.d Economic Implications of Survey Data

To return to the main question of this chapter, that of changes in the level of prosperity and the distribution of wealth: it is now clear that rural site numbers cannot stand proxy for the general state of an economy. Given the problems of 'reading' survey data – and the absence of any direct evidence for population size, even at urban centres – it is impossible to be sure whether the more active deposition of artefacts on farmland, or the cultivation of a larger total area, betokens a thriving society and economy, or one under pressure; full employment, or a shortage of resources forcing the uptake of marginal land; a buoyant population, or dispersal from shrinking, or growing, urban centres. Conversely, does a drop in rural settlement indicate less activity, economic problems, even catastrophe; a restructuring of agriculture or land ownership; a change in the wider economy of the hellenistic world with potentially beneficial results; or even an economic upturn that allowed more people to opt for residence in the city and enjoy its amenities? (Similarly, it has been observed that while land tenure may have been reorganized in early Roman Greece, abandonment of land may have been a largely local phenomenon.[192])

---

[191] Cf. *SEG* 50. 406. The inscription records a dedication to (Artemis) Eulakia in honour of an official called a ὑδραγός ('water-bringer') and his two assistants, found between Menelaion and Aphysou; the donors are from the obe of Kynosoura, the nearest part of Sparta (ed. pr. Peek 1974). Cf. Robert and Robert 1976, 467–8 no. 267. The text mentions an ἀνυδρία, 'absence of water', i.e. drought.

[192] Woolf 1994, 420.

Two modern examples may illustrate the difficulty of reading the 'health' of an economy from rural settlement. Samos in the first half of the twentieth century was the most densely populated eastern Aegean island, particularly after an influx of refugees from Turkey; at this time (if not earlier) all available land was under cultivation, even at altitude.[193] In such a case, would archaeological evidence of increased rural site numbers and/or new small farms indicate economic problems or success? Conversely, in the era of agricultural industrialization supported by European Union subsidies in the 1980s, Laconia saw the crude modification of many rural hill-slopes by bulldozer, high and wide terraces being created (without the traditional supporting masonry wall to guard against erosion and collapse) for olive cultivation in previously uncultivated areas; despite the lack of deposition of new material culture, the farmers in question were enjoying a rise in income, though arguably jeopardizing the long-term viability of the land. Other scenarios could be imagined; the point is that on its own the evidence of rural deposition of artefacts does not necessarily indicate the general state of things.

The different trajectories of regions and sub-regions are likely to be explicable in terms of local circumstances, even if we cannot confidently identify precise causes. We should not assume that changes in settlement patterns are necessarily forced upon a population; they may be strategic options or the result of internal politics. Local culture plays its part. The fourth-century story of how the Mantineans 'asked the Athenian cavalry to help if they were able, since all their animals and their workmen (ἐργάται) were outside the city, with many of the free children and old people' (Xen. *Hell.* 7. 5. 15), gives a flavour of a complex social organization whose archaeological signature cannot be easily predicted.[194]

A characterization of the overall economy of the early hellenistic Peloponnese cannot be 'read off' from survey results in a simple fashion, but must be sought by combining survey data with other evidence. For the 'long third century', the survey data, in the context of what we now believe about social and economic change, tends to indicate – *but only in a limited number of places* – first, a net shift of settled population from countryside to town (which need not imply actual migration; towns can grow from a number of causes); second, a degree of reorganization of land ownership

---

[193]   Cf. Admiralty 1944–5, i. 386–7, 478; ii. 20–1; iii. 542, 544–6.

[194]   Lloyd 1991, 190, surely rightly, takes this as evidence for residents of the town 'commuting daily to the fields'. The reference to 'free citizens' suggests that at least some of the 'workers' were unfree – not all, since the younger men were also out of town.

and agriculture in favour of elites.[195] They also suggest that landscape change was not radical; more far-reaching developments were to take place in the second and first centuries, developments in which Roman imperialism played its part. To the limited extent that both trends are real, the driving force behind them was probably elite ambition of the same kind that drove change in the classical period.

What survey data cannot do is demonstrate the health or sickness of 'the economy'. Rather, how we adjudge the state of 'the economy' on the basis of other evidence can be used to help explain the survey data.

IV.4 Epigraphy in a Landscape

One of the few quantifiable bases for regional comparison is the number of inscriptions from each region. The numbers of these known from *c.* 369 to *c.* 100 BC (ignoring small objects and texts dated simply 'hellenistic') point to significant differences in epigraphic output, perhaps reflecting differences in political culture. The data summarized in TABLE IV.2 are drawn from the main epigraphic corpora,[196] despite the obvious reluctance one feels to rely on dates given by early editors.[197] They have to some extent been standardized, a certain degree of precision being sacrificed to permit comparison between regions.[198] The figures are thus open to reinterpretation and should be regarded as provisional; for this reason, no precise data within the regional totals are given.

The record is, of course, subject to non-random factors. Archaeological exploration varies in its completeness, and only certain parts of certain centres (e.g. Messene, Corinth) have been intensively investigated. The presence of a major international shrine, such as the sanctuary of Zeus and Hera at Olympia or the Asklepieion at Epidauros, may attract epigraphic activity

---

[195] Bresson 2016, 149, identifies the concentration of land in fewer hands as a trend in the Hl period.

[196] Argolis: *IG* iv and iv² 1. Laconia, Messenia: *IG* v. 1. Arkadia: *IG* v. 2. Achaia: Rizakis 1998. Korinthia, Sikyonia: *IG* iv; Meritt 1931; Kent 1966. All regions: *SEG* vols 1–61 (the main source for Eleia–Triphylia); Rhodes 1997. *IvO* was not searched, as the Eleian data were already overwhelmingly olympiocentric.

[197] Some early editors of *IG* did not assign a date to every text; many texts, both dated and undated, have never been restudied; without detailed reanalysis one cannot know whether editors applied the same criteria to different inscriptions.

[198] Texts dated simply Hl are excluded. Those with cross-century dates, e.g. C4–C3, are divided between centuries (usually 0.5 each). More precise dates are simplified: e.g. C3e becomes C3. Some C4e inscriptions are ignored. Minor objects such as stamped tiles and ceramic graffiti are not counted; otherwise, no account was taken of genre (e.g. gravestone, decree).

away from nearby cities (for this reason, major sanctuaries are included as well as city-states). Clearly, too, one is not comparing like with like: the data for Messenia, for example, are undoubtedly heavily influenced by the special role of the central place and the generous haul of new inscriptions from the recent Messene excavations; while Arkadia and Argos already contained a plethora of well-established *poleis* before the hellenistic period, many of which had already acquired the 'epigraphic habit'.

Despite these caveats, the data-set gives broad-brush indications of the relative pace of epigraphic activity. Students of Corinthian inscriptions, for example, have concluded that the near-absence of civic documents in the classical and hellenistic periods is due not to the Roman sack of 146 but to a genuine absence of the epigraphic habit.[199] The scarcity of Eleian inscriptions outside Olympia, even from the *polis* of Elis, also seems real. Other *poleis*, however, have inscriptions in single figures and it would be rash to analyse their individual fortunes on this basis. Aggregating the data for groups of *poleis*, or a region, may be more valid.

In the fourth century, Argolis (Argos and eleven other sites, with nearly 100 inscriptions) is the source of around 41 per cent of known Peloponnesian inscriptions, followed by Arkadia with 21 per cent; together representing three-fifths of the total. Laconia and Korinthia–Sikyonia (the latter a small region, though presumably densely populated) each produce twenty to thirty texts (*c.* 11 and *c.* 10 per cent respectively); Messenia, Eleia–Triphylia, and Achaea barely make double figures (5–6 per cent each).

In the third century, the total of inscriptions known rises by some 40 per cent.[200] Argolis' share falls slightly, but is still over one-third of the total. Arkadia, still in second place, sees its share increase to nearly one-third; and the near-doubling of its absolute numbers to close to 100 is reflected in many Arkadian communities, as epigraphically active *poleis* become more so; close to twenty *poleis* have yielded third-century inscriptions, as opposed to just over ten in the fourth century. In Messenia the number of texts more than doubles, no doubt because of the prestige and rapid urbanization of the new capital city; the region now accounts for around one-eighth of the Peloponnesian total. Achaea and Korinthia–Sikyonia have similar shares to before, while the relative contributions of Laconia and Eleia–Triphylia decline (*c.* 6 and *c.* 3 per cent respectively).

Although the second century is not our concern here, it may be noted that the contribution of Argolis drops sharply at that time while those of

---

[199] Kent 1966, 1; Rhodes 1997, 73; Dixon 2014, 6.

[200] This is at least partly the result of not counting some specifically C4e texts; on the other hand, this is partly offset by counting all texts dated simply as C4, some of which may be C4e.

Achaea, Laconia, and especially Messenia roughly double. In each of the last three regions, several *poleis* produce inscriptions for the first time.

Although the percentages indicated possible trends, they do not take us far. Can the strength of the 'epigraphic habit' be in any degree a proxy measure of economic success? While Argolis, Arkadia, and to some extent Messenia head the field, it is difficult to make such a case in any detail, as other evidence suggests that the north-east of the peninsula may have been more economically innovative in the long third century (see Section IV.8). Moreover, the epigraphic data show no exact correlation with other indicators. If the data suggest anything, it is increased political activity at *polis* level in third-century Arkadia and Messenia – a sign of the continued vitality of the *polis*, perhaps – with a relative downturn elsewhere.

The habit of erecting inscriptions is, of course, partly a reflection of ideology and aspiration; while epigraphy is not inherently democratic,[201] the erection of collective decisions is inherently political. The respect in which the numbers of inscriptions may potentially have economic implications is that there is an expense involved in carving stone, and resources must be available for this purpose. To go further and examine whether these epigraphic also track the general level of economic activity, we should need more quantitative data, above all from archaeology. Such data, however, are at present inadequate to the task. In the absence of clear pictures of this kind, we may get more out of the epigraphic data by looking at the internal dynamics of regions, such as the degree to which a central place dominates (see Section V.2.d).

IV.5 Built Landscapes

We turn, therefore, to the material record, beginning with the record of monumental building, in order to characterize the level of activity in early hellenistic times as compared with the preceding period. (Supplementary evidence comes from the few urban surveys carried out, notably at Phleious, or from data gathered from town sites within mostly rural surveys: TABLE IV.1.) Complete documentation is beyond the scope of this study, but even a summary tells a consistent tale. Occasionally the archaeological record is supplemented by literary and epigraphic evidence.[202]

---

[201] Hedrick 1999, 425; cf. Oliver 2003 for Athenian decrees under the oligarchy of 321/0–319/8.
[202] For reasons of space, archaeological data are sometimes cited from digests such as 'Archaeology in Greece' (in *Archaeological Reports* or *Archaeology in Greece Online*) or the Copenhagen *Inventory* (Hansen and Nielsen 2004b).

Table IV.2. *Approximate numbers of inscriptions by region*

	C4	C3	C2
Argolid	95	114	44
Arkadia	48	92	80
Korinthia–Sikyonia	22	31	27
Eleia–Triphylia	13	10	11
Messenia	15	37	59
Laconia	25	20	29
Achaia	13	19	38
Totals	**231**	**323**	**288**

IV.5.a Construction Projects of Late Classical Date

We begin with urban and peri-urban construction projects. In the late classical period, the Peloponnese seems to have been a centre of innovation in urban grid-planning.[203] Towns were also founded, rebuilt, or reshaped in Argolis (Kleonai),[204] Achaea (Boura, re-erected after the earthquake of 373: Paus. 7. 25. 8–9),[205] Triphylia (Lepreon,[206] Euaimon,[207] and from survey data Samikon and Typaneiai),[208] Arkadia (Megalopolis,[209] Stymphalos;[210] also Mantinea, restored after 371),[211] and Messenia (possibly at Prote Island;[212] above all at Ithome, where the first steps were taken in building up the spectacular civic centre of Messene).[213] The Messenian towns or *poleis* of Kolonis/Kolonides (Plut. *Philop.* 18. 3; Paus. 4. 34. 8, 12)[214] and

---

[203] Donati and Sarris 2016. The rectilinear plan of Tegea may be earlier, however: Whitley 2006–7, 23–4. Bresson 2016, 45, speculates on the possible environmental and health benefits of rectilinear planning.

[204] Possible extension of city in C5s or C4: *AGOnline* ID2076 (2010); ID2409 (2011).

[205] Morgan and Hall 2004, 480–1 (*Inv. 233*).

[206] Building programme from C4 on: Nielsen 2004b, 543–4 (*Inv. 306*), at 544.

[207] New *polis* site by C4m, including vast theatre: Nielsen 2004a, 511 (*Inv. 269*).

[208] Triphylia Survey: *AGOnline* ID1513 (2009). Samikon and Typaneiai (located at *Platianá*) may have been elevated to *polis* status in C4 or later, though as settlements they existed earlier: Nielsen 2004b, 542.

[209] e.g. Nielsen 2004a, 520–2 (*Inv. 282*); Tsiolis 1995 (cited by *SEG* 45. 350).

[210] C4m city plan: Blackman 1996–7, 22–3.

[211] e.g. Nielsen 2004a, 517–20 (*Inv. 281*), esp. 520. Watchtowers: Pikoulas 1995, nos. 38–41.

[212] LCl or Hl fortification enclosing 2.8 ha: LN 129; Valmin 1930, 141–5.

[213] Shipley 2004b, 561–4 (*Inv. 318*), esp. 563–4. C4m epigraphic documents confirm the pace of development, e.g. *SEG* 45. 297, 45. 310 (cf. 49. 420+), 45. 410. C4 temple: *AGOnline* ID2085 (2010).

[214] Shipley 2004b, 556–7; Lazenby and Hope Simpson 1972, 89; Lukermann and Moody 1978, 96.

Korone[215] may have been founded after 369 for security against the remaining Lakedaimonian *perioikoi* in the region. The civic centre of Argos gained new buildings,[216] as did Corinth,[217] Aigeira,[218] and Messenian Pylos.[219] Laconian Geronthrai (*Geráki*) expanded onto its acropolis.[220] The majority of known buildings at Phleious are archaic and classical, and the urban survey points to intensified use of the site in the classical period.[221]

Theatre building took place at Arkadian Tegea (*IG* v. 2. 6 = RO 60),[222] Messenian Thouria,[223] and, most spectacularly for visitors today, at Epidauros in Argolis.[224]

Apart from, presumably, large numbers of residential structures in the above-mentioned new or growing settlements, houses are attested or can be inferred at Argolic Halieis,[225] Achaean Aigeira,[226] and Arkadian Gortys[227] and possibly Lousoi.[228]

Urban fortification or the renovation of town walls in the late classical period is attested (with varying degrees of confidence and at various scales) at Argolic Hermion[229] and Kleonai,[230] Achaean Leontion,[231] and in Eleia at *Vrestó* (perhaps ancient Pteleia),[232] as well as at several Arkadian *poleis*[233]

---

[215] Shipley 2004b, 561 (*Inv. 316*); Valmin 1930, 178, dates repairs to the fortification wall to the 360s.

[216] Barakari-Gléni and Pariente 1998. C4–Hl street: *AGOnline* ID3819 (2001).

[217] South Stoa (C4m): Broneer 1954.

[218] C4m guest-house: Whitley 2006–7, 49–50; *AGOnline* ID149 (2006); ID339 (2007); ID895 (2008); ID2971 (2011).

[219] LN 130.

[220] Langridge-Noti and Prent 2004; E. Langridge-Noti, pers. comm.; Whitley 2005–6, 40; Whitley 2006–7, 27; Crouwel *et al.* 2005; Crouwel *et al.* 2006; Morgan 2007–8, 36–7; and other reports in *Pharos*.

[221] Alcock 1991, 458–9; also 452 fig. 15.

[222] Nielsen 2004a, 530–4 (*Inv. 297*), at 532.

[223] *AGOnline* ID1503 (2009) (C4).

[224] Piérart 2004, 606–8 (*Inv. 348*), at 608.

[225] Jameson *et al.* 1994, 83: peak of urban settlement C4b–C4c; walls C4; towers exist by C4m.

[226] Mosaic house: Blackman 1999–2000, 44; Blackman 2000–1, 38. Dining-house: Whitley 2002–3, 40. Both C4m or earlier.

[227] Nielsen 2004a, 512 (*Inv. 271*): post-370.

[228] C4 or C3 houses: Nielsen 2004a, 516–17 (*Inv. 279*), at 517; H. W. Catling 1984–5, 23; H. W. Catling 1985–6, 28; H. W. Catling 1988–9, 33–4. Fortification: Nielsen 2004a, 516–17 (*Inv. 279*), at 516.

[229] Walls C4, possibly C4l: Piérart 2004, 609–10 (*Inv. 350*), at 610, citing Jameson *et al.* 1994.

[230] Walls may precede Argos' C4l takeover of Kleonai: Piérart 2004, 610–11 (*Inv. 351*), at 611.

[231] LN 44, with refs.

[232] LN 102–3, with refs; Shipley 2004b, 551, citing McDonald and Rapp 1972, no. 701, and Pikoulas 2001a, 110, no. 754 (mistyped as 504).

[233] HALOUS: Nielsen 2004a, 512 (*Inv. 272*). ORCHOMENOS: F. E. Winter 1989, 195 (dated C4c). PHENEOS: Nielsen 2004a, 527 (*Inv. 291*). PHIGALEIA: Nielsen 2004a, 527–8, no. *292*, at 528

and at *Nisí Agíou Andréa* in the Thyreatis (possibly ancient Anthana; formerly Laconian, now Argive).[234]

Information about urban and peri-urban cult sites in late classical times is plentiful, partly because of the biases of earlier exploration and partly because civic investment was often directed towards sanctuaries. Besides the major urban sites already mentioned, notable examples include the temples of Hippolytos and Asklepios at Troizen in Argolis,[235] a small temple at Corinth,[236] a long public building at the cemetery there,[237] and the huge temple of Athena Alea at Arkadian Tegea,[238] not to mention new sanctuary buildings erected in other towns in Argolis,[239] Achaea,[240] Triphylia,[241] and Arkadia.[242]

Although few data from perioikic Laconia have been cited earlier, the evidence of increased numbers of gravestones from inland Geronthrai (e.g. *IG* v. 1. 1119, 1121, 1138) and of a proxeny decree from coastal Kyphanta (*IG* xii. 5. 542) are testimony to civic politics and the ability of some communities to fund an epigraphic habit.

Outside towns, there is less evidence for construction in the late classical period. There is also a noticeable dearth of above-ground religious structures, other than at major sanctuaries, and the archaeological record is dominated by fortifications and towers, which increase in number after the end of Spartan domination. Examples include a network of mostly fourth-century towers in Argolis – including many designed to protect the region against invasion by members of the Peloponnesian league, or via friendly

---

(C4m). PSOPHIS, rather earlier: Nielsen 2004a, 529 (*Inv. 294*) (C5d/C4a?). Maher 2012 dates most Arkadian *polis* fortifications C4e.

[234] *AGOnline* ID2435 (2010), fortification dated C4l.

[235] LN 72, with refs; Meyer 1975b, 984; cf. financial accounts, *IG* iv. 823.

[236] Dixon 2014, 111 (C4l/C3e), 113 fig. 5.1 ('naiskos'), cf. 117; *Corinth Excavations* (http://corinth.ascsa.net, last accessed 30 May 2017), C4 temple, converted into aedicula in C3.

[237] *AGOnline* ID101 (2006); Whitley 2006–7, 13–14. Cemetery in use mainly C4l–C3e: *AGOnline* ID2494 (2004).

[238] Not before C4s, Blackman 1996–7, 36. Sophistication of columns, etc.: Pakkanen 1998. C4m building regulations: *IG* v. 2. 6; RO 60.

[239] METHANA: C4 and later sanctuary of Apollo Phytalmios (*SEG* 47. 330; Forbes 1982, 45–6).

[240] PELLENE: C4 temple (Meyer 1972c, 601).

[241] LEPREON: C4b temple, Nielsen 2004b, 543–4 (*Inv. 306*), at 544. MAKISTON: C4e temple, LN 102.

[242] LYKOSOURA: C4 temple, Meyer 1969a, 820. PHIGALEIA: C4 sanctuary of Athena and Zeus, Blackman 1997–8, 51; cf. *SEG* 46. 448 (52. 457+), statue base of deities. GORTYS: C4 Asklepieion with stoa, LN 47–8; Nielsen 2004a, 512 (*Inv. 271*).

Korinthia[243] – as well as rural fortifications in Korinthia–Sikyonia[244] and in the territory of Arkadian Kleitor.[245]

As for cult sites, cult deposition continued at Achaean *Áno Mazaráki* despite the earlier destruction of the temple,[246] while the Argolic site of *Berbáti–Límnes* received a new temple.[247] Also in Argolis, a hilltop temple west of Nauplia was built or renovated during the fourth century.[248] To these may now be added the lower sanctuary of Zeus on Mt Lykaion, where important buildings were erected in the second quarter of the fourth century; the sanctuary remaining in active use until the first century.[249] Most of the known building projects, however, were at the sanctuaries of international importance with which the Peloponnese was notably well endowed, such as those at Epidauros,[250] Isthmia,[251] Nemea,[252] and Olympia.[253]

A possible farm structure is reported in rural Eleia.[254]

IV.5.b Construction Projects of Late Classical or Early Hellenistic Date

A number of urban projects are dated to the second half of the fourth century; examples can be found in Argolis (Methana,[255] Orneai),[256] Achaea

---

[243] Pikoulas 1996–7; see also Piteros 1996–7a; Piteros 1996–7b; cf. Lord 1939; and esp. now Tausend 2006 with extended review of Shipley 2008b. C4 towers at *Ákova* and *Várda*: Blackman 1997–8, 29.

[244] See generally Gauvin 1983; Lolos 2011, 181–267.

[245] Nielsen 2004a, 515–16 (*Inv. 276*), 515; Pikoulas 1999b, 144–53.

[246] Blackman 2000–1, 38–9.

[247] Blackman 1997–8, 29–30.

[248] *Prophitis Ilias* near *Kivéri*: ID291 (2000).

[249] Romano and Voyatzis 2015.

[250] Asklepieion: rebuilding (C4m), e.g. Burford 1969, 53–6; LN 61–2; Lembidaki 1996–7; building accounts, *SEG* 24. 278 (cf. 25. 383–409), etc.; houses, Blackman 1997–8, 31; Corinthian pottery, Lambrinoudakis 1978; well, Blackman 1997–8, 31. Apollo Maleatas sanctuary, altars: *SEG* 33. 303–4 (35. 311); 41. 303.

[251] Stadium (C4e), Reinmuth 1967, citing *IG* iv. 203. 24; Paus. 2. 1. 7; repairs to temple of Poseidon, French 1991–2, 11; roof works, French 1990–1, 15–17.

[252] C4 building programme: e.g. Miller 1994; bath, Blackman 1996–7, 22; landscaping, Blackman 1999–2000, 26; Blackman 2000–1, 24.

[253] Echo Colonnade, Blackman 2001–2, 47; many statue-bases, e.g. *SEG* 14. 357 (29. 417+; *c.* 390–380), 30. 429 (C4s), 40. 387 (C4), 46. 478 (49. 480; C4s–C3f); stadium, LN 98; South Stoa (C4m), *AGOnline* ID2077 (2010).

[254] At *Triandafylliá*, large C4–C3 'agricultural residence' with contemporary graves, *AGOnline* ID2509 (2010).

[255] Acropolis wall: Piérart 2004, 611 (*Inv. 352*).

[256] City wall: Piérart 2004, 612–13 (*Inv. 354*), at 613, citing Pritchett 1980, 25–7; Pikoulas 1995, 267–70.

(Aigion, cf. Diod. 19. 66. 3),[257] and Arkadia (Stymphalos),[258] Of similar date are the theatre at Arkadian Orchomenos (probably)[259] and cult buildings at Kalaureia,[260] Alipheira,[261] Gortys,[262] Pheneos,[263] and Thouria.[264] Other projects may be either late classical or early hellenistic. Programmes of fortification or wall renovation in this date range are identified in Argolis (Argos),[265] Eleia (Lasion),[266] Arkadia (Pheneos,[267] *Káto Lousoí*),[268] Messenia (Kalamai[269] and Prote),[270] and Laconia (Zarax, cf. Polyb. 4. 36. 5).[271] A road in Argos is dated to this time,[272] as is a grave peribolos.[273] A cemetery at Triphylian Phrixa was in use in the late classical and early hellenistic periods.[274]

Extra-urban projects dated, with greater or lesser certainty, to the second half of the fourth century include two at Epidauros,[275] a new retaining wall for the Altis precinct at Olympia, and the Philippeion erected there by Philip II.[276] Projects that may be either fourth- or third-century include a possible cult building at Epidauros,[277] the Leonidaion at Olympia,[278] temples at *Perivólia* in Eleia,[279] and at *Kallianí Gortynías*[280] and *Arachamítai*

---

[257]   City wall (by C4l): Morgan and Hall 2004, 480 (*Inv. 231*), citing Diod. 19. 66. 3.

[258]   City wall (C4m/C4l): Nielsen 2004a, 529–30 (*Inv. 296*), at 530.

[259]   Built by C4l, Voyatzis 1999, 147.

[260]   C4s building at Poseidon sanctuary: Blackman 1999–2000, 22; Whitley 2003–4, 13–14.

[261]   C4s sanctuary of Asklepios: Nielsen 2004a, 509–10 (*Inv. 266*), at 510; Alevridis and Melfi 2005, 264 (C4s); Jost 1985, 81.

[262]   C4s baths at 2nd Asklepieion: Nielsen 2004a, 512 (*Inv. 271*).

[263]   C4l–C3e pavement as Asklepeion: *AGOnline* ID4510 (2009).

[264]   Doric temple of Asklepios and Hygieia, finds beginning in C4: *AGOnline* ID3314 (2012), ID2083 (2010).

[265]   Fachard 2016, 79 (C4l–C3e). EHl salient: *AGOnline* ID2635 (2011).

[266]   Blackman 1998–9, 44 (C4/C3e).

[267]   *AGOline* ID5051 (2015), dated post-345; cf. ID4510 (2009); Kissas 2013.

[268]   Acropolis fortified: C4/Hl (French 1991–2, 22); C4, Nielsen 2004a, 516–17 (*Inv. 279*), at 516.

[269]   If correctly identified with *Elaiochóri* (f. *Giánnitsa*, see Pikoulas 2001a, 146 no. 1106): Shipley 2004b, 556; Valmin 1930, 40–4, esp. 41 (walls dated post-BA on archaeological, and C3 on historical, grounds by Noack 1894, 481–5).

[270]   LN 129; Valmin 1930, 141–5.

[271]   Pre-219 date implied by Polyb. 4. 36. 5; post-274, Cartledge and Spawforth 2002, 34; from my autopsy, may be C4. Gate inscription regulating access to fortress: *SEG* 60. 418 (unpublished).

[272]   French 1990–1, 20; Blackman 1996–7, 23–4; Blackman 1997–8, 28–9.

[273]   Morgan 2009–10, 27–8.

[274]   *AGOnline* ID4295 (2005).

[275]   'Epidoteion': Lembidaki 2002, 129–33. Sacred precinct Y: Lembidaki 2002, 123–9.

[276]   Altis wall post-C4m: Blackman 2000–1, 46. Iconography of Philippeion: e.g. Carney 2007; Palagia 2010.

[277]   Lembidaki 2002, 133–6.

[278]   Dedication on Leonidaion, C4s–C3f: *SEG* 46. 478 (49. 480).

[279]   C4/C3 temple on road to Bassai: LN 99.

[280]   LN 48.

(Artemis Lykoatis in the territory of Lykoa)[281] in Arkadia. Otherwise they are mostly fortifications, notably a possible network of forts in the *chōra* of Messene;[282] other rural forts (in addition to those cited at Section IV.5.a) are known in Argolis,[283] including towers in the *chōra* of Phleious;[284] in Triphylia possibly at Lepreon;[285] and in Arkadia.[286] In Korinthia, a network of late classical–early hellenistic rural forts was probably designed, like their Argive counterparts, to prevent an army moving south from the Isthmus.[287]

IV.5.c Construction Projects of Early Hellenistic Date

In the first half of the hellenistic period,[288] no new towns are created; but in Argolis the town of Asine, reputedly destroyed by the Argives *c.* 700 BC, had nevertheless seen fortifications built in the classical period; presumably it was not recognized as a *polis* until its refoundation in or after *c.* 300, after which it prospered until at least the second half of the second century.[289] Sikyon moved to a new site (Diod. 20. 102. 3; initially named Demetrias), soon endowed with buildings such as theatre, temple, council-house, and stoa as well as a possible palaestra;[290] a new cemetery was opened,[291] and the city's existing temple has an early hellenistic building phase.[292] A nearby quarry may have been opened during the third century.[293] In Achaea, the rebuilt Helike flourished in the hellenistic period (see Section IV.1.f),[294] and a new upland settlement of

---

[281] Predecessor of Rectangular Building I: *AGOnline* ID 2422 (2011); B. Forsén 2016.

[282] LCl/EHl, Shipley 2004b, 563, with refs.

[283] Cl/Hl forts at *Kazárma* (LN 64) and *Koiláda* (LN 64–5); LCl/Hl, *Lychnári* bay, Morgan 2008–9, 15; C4/C3, at *Moní Zoödóchou Pigís* near Nauplia, *AGOnline* ID 4410 (2005).

[284] Towers: Gauvin 1992; Gauvin 1997, Gauvin and Morin 1997.

[285] Judging from the photograph at *AGOnline* ID 1513 (2009), one tower is LCl/EHl.

[286] LOUSOI: possible tower on road, C4/Hl?, French 1993–4, 17. TEGEA: 2 fortified watchtowers, Nielsen 2004a, 530–3 (*Inv. 297*), at 531; Pikoulas 1995, 253–5 nos. 42*, 43. *Vlachorrápti Gortynías*: fortress, LN 55, citing Charneux and Ginouvès 1956.

[287] Caraher and Gregory 2006.

[288] I include structures reported as 'Hl' if they are not specified as C2, post-*c.* 150, C1, or LHl (noting them as such), most of which are likely to precede C1 or 146.

[289] Cl fortifications (end C5–C4f, rebuilt in Hl): Blackman 2001–2, 25 (cf. French 1990–1, 21). Stamped tiles: Penttinen 1996b, 163–5. Prosperity to at least C2s: Penttinen 1996b.

[290] Lolos *et al.* 2007, 273 (summarizing earlier discoveries); 285, 288 (preponderance of Hl material); overview at Lolos 2011, 274–86. EHl (?) *bouleutērion*, C3b (?) gymnasium of Kleinias: Barber 1995, 329; LN 86 with refs. C3 stadium, stoa: Barber 1995, 329. C3e (?) theatre: Legon 2004, 470, citing Rossetto and Sartorio 1994, ii. 291–2. Stoa confirmed as EHl: *AGOnline* ID 4429 (2013).

[291] Cemetery: *AGOnline* ID 4518 (2008).

[292] *AGOnline* ID 2487 (2011).

[293] *AGOnline* ID 1421 (2000).

[294] Hl dye-works: Katsonopoulou 2016, incl. 239–40 (much EHl–MHl pottery).

hellenistic date at *Óasi*, south of Aigeira.[295] Above all, perhaps, Messene underwent spectacular architectural development,[296] which continued into the late third or early second century with the early phases of the spring-house.[297]

Improvement of the urban centre, typically including houses, streets, fortifications, a theatre, a stoa, or a combination of these, occurred at other places in Argolis (Argos,[298] Kleonai,[299] Mycenae,[300] and Phleious,[301] where urban survey also points to a further increase in deposition of material in the hellenistic period).[302] At Corinth, various monumental enhancements took place, perhaps to be credited to the Antigonids.[303] Other urban enhancements are seen in Achaea (Aigeira,[304] Aigion,[305] Dyme,[306]

---

[295] *Panagía* at *Oási*: *AGOnline* ID1590 (2000) (Hl); cf. Morgan 2009–10, 66.

[296] Walls pre-316: Kaltsas 1989, 14. C3 fountain: Tomlinson 1994–5, 24. Hl houses: LN 127. Rizakis and Touratsoglou 2011, 17, infer economic growth. Stoa: *AGOnline* ID3315 (2012); Whitley 2004–5, 31.

[297] Reinholdt 2009.

[298] Barakari-Gléni and Pariente 1998, 168. C3m peak of prosperity, another after Nabis' defeat: Barakari-Gléni and Pariente 1998, 169–70, 175. C4l renovation of walls: Barakari-Gléni and Pariente 1998, 168. C3s house: Barakari-Gléni and Pariente 1998, 171–3. C3a theatre: Barakari-Gléni and Pariente 1998, 170, 175. Hl workshops: Barakari-Gléni and Pariente 1998, 173–4. EHl theatre: Barakari-Gléni and Pariente 1998, 175. City's greatest extent, C3m: Barakari-Gléni and Pariente 1998, 171–3, 175. EHl streets: Barakari-Gléni and Pariente 1998, 168–9 (also Hl, *AGOnline* ID3845 (2004), ID1445 (2000)); Banaka-Dimaki 2002, 112–13. EHl renovation programme: *AGOnline* ID3043 (2012). Houses, other buildings: e.g. *AGOnline* ID1432 (2000) (Hl); ID1447, ID1443 (2000).

[299] Hl complex of buildings: *AGOnline* ID111 (2006).

[300] Refounded post-290: Klein 1997, 292. C3 fountain house, small theatre, renovation and extension of city wall: Klein 1997, 292. Hl public buildings, cemetery, houses: Klein 1997, 256–7, 292; generally oriented upon theatre, *AGOnline* ID1430 (2009). Hl dye-works: Bowkett 1995.

[301] Most public buildings post-300: Piérart 2004, 613–14 (*Inv. 355*), at 614. Hl walls: *AGOnline* ID3887 (2002).

[302] Alcock 1991, 458–9; also 453 fig. 16. Note, however, that the admittedly low-resolution data at Alcock 1991, 452–4 figs 15–17 and pp. 461–2, suggest similar population levels in Cl and Hl Phleious, increasing in ER.

[303] C3 columns at fountain, NW stoa, S stoa rebuilt pre-146: Barber 1995, 199. Theatre modified *c*. 300: Stillwell 1952, 131–2. Possible Antigonid building programme: Dixon 2014, 137–8.

[304] Hl town plan: French 1993–4, 20. C3 dining-house: Whitley 2002–3, 40; Whitley 2003–4, 32). Hl buildings: Blackman 1996–7, 41. Fortifications ('by C2'): Whitley 2002–3, 40. Hl Peripteros: Blackman 1996–7, 41. C3e expansion of public guest-house: *AGOnline* ID2971 (2011), ID895 (2008), ID339 (2007), ID149 (2006); Morgan 2007–8, 43.

[305] *Bouleutērion* by C3: Morgan and Hall 2004, 480 (*Inv. 231*); Polyb. 11. 9. 8. Theatre by C3m: Gogos 2001. Hl houses: *AGOnline* ID5024 (2006). Substantial Hl structure: Whitley 2004–5, 38.

[306] Post-314 grid-plan: Lakakis and Rizakis 1992b, 94, 98 (?). C3–C1 buildings of declining quality: Lakakis and Rizakis 1992b 100, cf. Rizakis and Lakakis 1988. Fortifications: Lakaki-Marchetti 2000, 114, cf. 81. Substantial EHl structures: *AGOnline* ID3905 (2001), ID1540 (2000); Whitley 2004–5, 36; Morgan 2009–10, 59.

Patrai),[307] in Eleia (at Elis),[308] in Triphylia (Epitalion),[309] and in several *poleis* in Arkadia. Megalopolis was renovated after its sack by Kleomenes III (Polyb. 5. 106. 3; cf. 2. 55. 4; 5. 93. 5).[310] At Tegea, literary and archaeological evidence shows the urban centre to have been active down into the second century.[311] At Teuthis there is more archaeological evidence of domestic activity than in classical times.[312] The cemetery at Phigaleia contains elaborate rock-cut tombs showing the influence of Macedonian royal burials.[313] There is evidence of building activity in Messenia (Kyparissos).[314] In Laconia, two town sites developed strongly in the third century (Geronthrai,[315] Sparta);[316] development at Sparta includes a bridge across the *Magoúla*, a tributary of the Eurotas.[317] Epidauros Limera became the main town in south-eastern Laconia.[318]

A theatre is perhaps the building that most clearly indicates that a civic and political culture exists in a *polis*. Among places already noted, theatres were built early in the third century at Argos, Sikyon, and Elis, in the mid-third century at Aigion, and some time in the third century at Mycenae; while remodelling of the theatre took place at Corinth around 300,[319] and rebuilding of that at Tegea in the early second century (*c.* 170, Livy 41. 20).

[307] Hl projects include houses (Tomlinson 1995–6, 15; Blackman 1996–7, 42), a new cemetery (Blackman 2001–2, 42); a public building with two phases (Tomlinson 1994–5, 17–18); roads (French 1990–1, 29, *AGOnline* ID1579 (2001); Tomlinson 1994–5, 17–18; Blackman 1998–9, 39; Blackman 2001–2, 40); and a stoa (French 1991–2, 22). EHl walls: Morgan 2009–10, 61. C4s–C3l site: *AGOnline* ID1556 (2000); Morgan 2009–10, 62. Various Hl projects: Whitley 2004–5, 36–7; 'imposing' Hl buildings on the main N–S street; *AGOnline* ID3935 (2002).
[308] *AGOnline* ID337 (2004).
[309] New site in Hl: Nielsen 2004b, 543 (*Inv. 305*), also 540.
[310] Rebuilt after Kleomenes' sack: Baladié 1980, 319 (inferring from Polyb. 5. 106. 3?). New work included the C3b stoa of Aristodamos, rebuilt C2f (Whitley 2003–4, 26).
[311] *Agora* operating in C3: *SEG* 22. 280 (59. 815+). C2b theatre: Livy 41. 20. Hl pottery workshops: Blackman 2000–1, 32.
[312] Nielsen 2004a, 533 (*Inv. 298*), citing Pikoulas 1986, 116 (= Pikoulas 2002, 200); French 1990–1, 25 (Hl pottery).
[313] Blackman 2001–2, 47; C3m–C2m, Arapogianni 2005.
[314] *AGOnline* ID5550 (2007).
[315] New acropolis wall, C3: Blackman 1998–9, 31; also e.g. Prent 2002, Langridge-Noti 2009. C3 houses, including 12-roomed C3m building: Blackman 2001–2, 30; Whitley 2002–3, 33. Hl street: Whitley 2003–4, 28.
[316] C3 house: Blackman 1999–2000, 41. C3 water-pipes: Kourinou 2000? C3 in-fill between villages: Kourinou 2000, 89–95, 279–80, 285. EHl monumental tombs: Raftopoulou 1998, 134. Hl buildings: Blackman 1997–8, 36–7; Blackman 2000–1, 34, 35–6; Blackman 2001–2, 33, 34; Whitley 2002–3, 29–30. Walls: Kourinou 2000? General Hl expansion implied: Whitley 2006–7, 37.
[317] Morgan 2008–9, 32 (C4l/C3).
[318] Zavvou 1996–7, 504.
[319] Stillwell 1952.

In addition to these cases, house-building is attested, or can be inferred, at other sites in Argolis (Epidauros),[320] Achaea (Aigion,[321] Patrai,[322] Dyme),[323] Arkadia (Asea,[324] Mantinea,[325] Orchomenos,[326] Stymphalos,[327] Lousoi),[328] and Messenia (Kyparissos,[329] Pylos).[330] Hellenistic workshops including a weaving establishment and coroplastic workshops have been found at Argos,[331] a potter's workshop at Aigion,[332] and olive-processing installations at Dyme.[333]

Programmes of fortifying cities or renovating city walls, dated after *c.* 338 with reasonable certainty, are attested in many *poleis* besides those already mentioned: namely, in Argolis (Nauplion,[334] Asine,[335] Troizen),[336] Achaea (probably Leontion),[337] Eleia (Elis itself, cf. Diod. 19. 87. 2–3),[338] Arkadia (Gortys,[339] Heraia,[340] Pallantion,[341] Kleitor,[342] Teuthis,[343] Thisoa,[344] and

---

[320]   Blackman 1997–8, 31.

[321]   *AGOnline* ID1586 (2000): EHl deposit and Hl building.

[322]   *AGOnline* ID5001 (2006).

[323]   *AGOnline* ID5018 (2006); ID3906 (2001).

[324]   Hl houses: Blackman 2000–1, 31. Note also C3l lower city wall: J. Forsén *et al.* 2005. Possible shrinkage of town from C3e, perhaps due to existence of Megalopolis: B. Forsén 2003, 260.

[325]   French 1990–1, 26.

[326]   Domestic settlement well into Hl: Nielsen 2004a, 523–5 (*Inv. 286*), at 524, citing Hiller von Gaertringen and Lattermann 1911, 20. Cf. also *SdA* 499 (*c.* 234), implying sales of house-plots at Orchomenos (though not specifically house-building at this time).

[327]   Blackman 1997–8, 28; Blackman 2001–2, 22. Hl stage-building: E. H. Williams 2005.

[328]   EHl stoa: Whitley 2003–4, 33, 35.

[329]   Hl houses, cemetery: LN 125.

[330]   LN 130, with references; MME #9.

[331]   *AGOnline* ID1442 (2000); Morgan 2009–10, 32; other evidence of weaving, Morgan 2009–10, 27. Hl workshops: Whitley 2004–5, 20–2 (Hl); cf. *AGOnline* ID3819 (2001), ID3853 (2001). Coroplastic: *AGOnline* ID1433 (2000).

[332]   *AGOnline* ID3921 (2001) (Hl).

[333]   *AGOnline* ID3901 (2001) (Hl).

[334]   Acropolis wall: Meyer 1972a. Harbour wall: Whitley 2002–3, 26.

[335]   *AGOnline* ID4414 (2005); C3 stamped tile, Whitley 2004–5, 26.

[336]   Walls mainly C3: Meyer 1975b, 984. Hl tower: Jameson *et al.* 1994, 26 fig. 1. 8.

[337]   Morgan and Hall 2004, 483 (*Inv. 237*); Strabo 8. 7. 5 with Baladié 1978, 206, based on the palimpsest; Walbank 1957–79, i. 231; Rizakis 1995b, 308; Baladié 1978, 206 n. 3. Walls presumably by Gonatas, so C3m (rather than C4 as in Leekley and Noyes 1976); destroyed C3l.

[338]   *Kaloskopí* acropolis: Roy 2004, 494–8 (*Inv. 251*), at 498. Theatre: Hl, Hellenic Ministry of Culture 1995–2001; *c.* 300, Roy 2004, 498, citing Glaser 2001 (without page no.) and Rossetto and Sartorio 1994, ii. 207.

[339]   Part of city wall adapted by Demetrios I: Ginouvès 1994, citing Ginouvès 1959, 15 (and 17 fig. 18). MHl baths: Ginouvès 1959 (cf. Shipley 2000b, 334).

[340]   Nielsen 2004a, 513–14 (*Inv. 274*), at 513 (not Cl, *pace* Jost 1985, 76–7).

[341]   New stoa (Hl); walls postdating Cassander's siege of 318: *AGOnline* ID2418 (2009).

[342]   Walls *c.* 300: Polyb. 4. 19. 3; Nielsen 2004a, 515–16 (*Inv. 276*), at 515, citing F. E. Winter 1989, 199 (c. 300); Blackman 1998–9, 38–9. Two Hl phases: Petritaki 2005.

[343]   Hl, not C4: Nielsen 2004a, 533 (*Inv. 298*), citing Pikoulas 1986, 113 = Pikoulas 2002, 197.

[344]   Nielsen 2004a, 534 (*Inv. 301*), C3; Jost 1985, 212 n. 1.

before the reign of Philip V possibly Psophis: Polyb. 4. 70. 10), Messenia (Korone,[345] Pylos,[346] perhaps Thouria),[347] and Laconia (Geronthrai,[348] perhaps Gytheion).[349]

Cultic construction in and around towns was mostly small-scale, but included work at sanctuary complexes in, for example, Megalopolis[350] and Messene,[351] and new temples in Argolis (Halieis,[352] Troizen,[353] Mycenae),[354] Arkadia (Asea,[355] Kaphyai,[356] Lousoi,[357] Stymphalos,[358] Thisoa),[359] and Laconia (Sparta;[360] possibly Tainaron).[361]

A probable treasury excavated in Messene may be that mentioned by Plutarch (*Philopoimen*, 19) with reference to the early second century, and may date to the third.[362]

Away from towns, early hellenistic projects are again mostly fortifications. These occur in all parts of the peninsula. Examples include, in Argolis, the isolated tower (*c.* 300 BC) at *Berbati–Límnes*,[363] another tower (last quarter of fourth century) at *Tsérpho* near ancient Tyros in Kynouria (a Lakedaimonian area before *c.* 338, now Argive); in Achaea, the outlying fort at Dymaiōn Teichos;[364]

---

[345] Cl or Hl: LN 129, with refs. Hl buildings: Kalogeropoulou 1962.

[346] LN 130. Hl fortifications: LN 130. Large Hl cemetery: LN 131.

[347] Identified with *Ellinikó* (C4l/C3e). Walls probably C4: *AGOnline* ID888 (2008); or Hl, Whitley 2004–5, 31.

[348] Blackman 1998–9, 31.

[349] Town walls Hl though not closely dated, Whitley 2006–7, 40.

[350] C4d sanctuary of Zeus Soter: French 1993–4, 17–18; Gans and Kreilinger 2002, 188; Lauter 2005.

[351] Besides the spectacular urban Asklepieion (C2e, French 1991–2, 26, with Tomlinson 1994–5, 24), note the temple of Artemis Limnatis and Laphria (?) on Mt Ithome (C3l, Themelis 2004a, 152–4).

[352] Bergquist 1990; temple not Cl but Hl (presumably EHl, as Halieis abandoned C3m).

[353] LN 72 with refs.

[354] C3, Klein 1997.

[355] LN 46 with refs.

[356] Hl Doric temple: French 1990–1, 25.

[357] Blackman 2000–1, 31; small LCl temple renovated in EHl, new larger peripteral temple in EHl: Whitley 2004–5, 27–8; Whitley 2005–6, 48; Whitley 2006–7, 30–1; Morgan 2007–8, 33–4; Morgan 2008–9, 28–9.

[358] LN 86.

[359] LN 54.

[360] Small Hl temple, LN 113 (Waldstein 1894). Hl rebuilding of Artemis Orthia temple: Dawkins 1929, 32–4. The (new?) Artemis Kyparissia sanctuary is most active in Hl (Kourinou-Pikoula 1992; cf. *SEG* 45. 284; 46. 2359; 50. 395–405), as is that of Artemis Issoria (Paus. 3. 14. 2; Kalogeropoulou 1969–70, 414; Kourinou 2000, 212–13).

[361] LS LL210, remains of temple of Poseidon Tainarios.

[362] Whitley 2006–7, 28; *SEG* 58. 397.

[363] Blackman 1997–8, 29–30.

[364] Polyb. 4. 59. 5 etc.; with nearby tower at *Karavóstasi* (Lakakis and Rizakis 1992a, 116), may date from Social war.

in Arkadia, at Theisoa[365] and Kynaitha;[366] and in Laconia, the upland fort of Glyppia, which antedates Philip V's invasion (Polyb. 5. 22. 11).[367] Another rural tower, at *Ágios Dimítrios* near Epidauros,[368] is dated to the hellenistic period.

Extra-urban cultic construction is again concentrated at major non-*polis* sanctuaries[369] (Epidauros,[370] Nemea,[371] Isthmia,[372] Olympia).[373] Alcock identifies a hellenistic decline in votive activity at rural cult sites, though there are exceptions.[374] In terms of construction projects, however, both the late classical and the early hellenistic period have yielded evidence of many undertakings.[375] Examples include a 'temple-form grave monument' east of Olympia;[376] early hellenistic monumental tombs at *Dáphni* near ancient Elis;[377] a stoa and the earlier phases of the 'Rectangular Building' at the sanctuary of Artemis Lykoatis in central Arkadia;[378] and a cultic structure near Kleonai.[379]

A farm building with an early hellenistic phase has been found near Patrai,[380] and a hellenistic building of uncertain function at *Staphidókambos* in western Eleia.[381]

---

[365] Five or more 'isolated patrol stations' probably postdate C4m: Pikoulas 2008; *AGOnline* ID870 (2008).

[366] *Kalávryta, Kástro*: foundations of Hl city wall with dated finds, *AGOnline* ID4381 (2005).

[367] Shipley 2004a, 574 (not a *polis*).

[368] *AGOnline* ID4415 (2005).

[369] I give only salient examples in this and the next three notes.

[370] Asklepieion: propylon, *gymnasion, c.* 300, and EHl retaining wall of incubation hall (Lambrinoudakis 1987–8); Hl water supply (Peppa-Papaïoannou 1992). Apollo Maleatas sanctuary: Hl terrace, *peribolos* wall (Blackman 2000–1, 28).

[371] Innovative C4l architectural programme (French 1990–1, 18); Hl heroön of Opheltes (Blackman 1997–8, 27); temple of Zeus, 330–320 (Meyer 1972b).

[372] East gateway, *c.* 300 (French 1990–1, 15); Hl *temenos* of Poseidon temple (Tomlinson 1995–6, 10).

[373] EHl water-channels around Philippeion (Blackman 2000–1, 46); Hl predecessor of SW Building (French 1992–3, 28); Hl stoa, poss. athletes' quarters (Blackman 1999–2000, 50–1); Hl altar(s) to Artemis (*SEG* 38. 369; 46. 473; 46. 477; 55. 547); Hl fountain-house (Schauer 1997). Ptolemaic dedication: *AGOnline* ID2973 (2012); ID1514 (2009); Hl well (Whitley 2004–5, 33–5).

[374] Two small temples near *Koúrnos* in S. Laconia (one C1, the other C2l or C1): J. E. Winter and Winter 1983; Shipley 1996a, 306 no. LL205 with further refs.

[375] My EHl includes some buildings simply dated Hl in reports, as archaeologists often terminate the Hl period at 146 or 100 BC. Most monuments called Hl in preliminary reports are probably EHl or C2f at latest, finds and structures of C2s–C1 being called R; e.g. Lakaki-Marchetti 2000, 118–19, differentiates LHl material at Dyme from C1; and Blackman 1996–7, 42, refers to C1f structures at *Kallitheókambos* (Achaia) as R.

[376] At *Stenó* (*Palaiochóri*): *AGOnline* ID4315 (2014) (C3–C2).

[377] At *Vrína*: *AGOnline* ID1530 (2000).

[378] Hl stoa, *AGOnline* ID753 (2008), ID302 (2007), pottery C3d–C1f. EHl phases of 'LHl Rectangular building': *AGOnline* ID3257 (2012).

[379] At *Ágios Vasíleios*: *AGOnline* ID1426 (2009) (Hl); cf. Whitley 2005–6, 24.

[380] At *Voudéni*: *AGOnline* ID1593 (2000) (EHl); occupied from LAr to ER, Whitley 2004–5, 36.

[381] *AGOnline* ID4314 (2005).

IV.5.d Economic Implications of Construction Projects

Apart from the dependent *poleis* of Laconia and the minor *poleis* of Messenia, the active building works are widely distributed, with no clear regional biases. To attempt to identify more specific patterns, without knowing the exact chronology or funding sources of projects, would be unwise.

This evidence shows, however, that many communities had resources available for such projects sufficiently often to rebut any description of the Peloponnese as chronically depressed.[382] Temples and other public edifices required substantial outlay.[383] Many urban sites continued to develop, despite the depopulation suspected by earlier historians, and despite the fact that some cities were dependent on Macedonian patronage or on membership of larger organizations. That is not to say that the data should be read in a wholly positive sense. Many projects must have been put in hand because wartime damage needed to be made good. Some may have been made possible by the support of a dynast or king whose motives were more strategic than altruistic; a large proportion of the cost falling upon members of the local elite. Nevertheless, most undertakings surely required approval by local civic institutions, even if the original initiative came from higher up. Indeed, since in some respects this era sees the greatest investment in Peloponnesian architecture of any ancient period, with the possible exception of the second century AD, we should credit many *poleis* with the capacity to exercise choice rather than simply respond passively.[384]

A reason for the relative infrequency of new large-scale works may be that, unless damaged beyond repair, they did not need to be built twice: once a *polis* had a central temple or circuit wall, it did not need another. Many small *poleis*, however, erected new temples and fortifications. The frequency of renovation and repair work, alongside these new structures, tells against a decline in *polis* culture, let alone the abandonment of politics in favour of either 'introversion' or individualism.[385] *Gymnasia* and theatres are far from being a withdrawal from *polis* thinking, though they may perhaps be evidence of a change in it;[386]

---

[382] Cf. Shipley 2005b, 322; Shipley 2008a, 55. On the scale of labour and resources involved in temple-building, see Salmon 2001. More negative view: e.g. Rizakis and Touratsoglou 2011, 27.

[383] Costs of temples: Salmon 2001; cf. Davies 2001.

[384] Rizakis and Touratsoglou 2011, 19–21, 27.

[385] Negative view: Rizakis and Touratsoglou 2011, 25–6, 27.

[386] Negative view: Rizakis and Touratsoglou 2011; note 'spiritual bankruptcy' (πνευματική πτώχευση), 27.

the *gymnasion* was precisely the setting for the cultural formation of the elite,[387] and several records survive of men serving as gymnasiarchs.[388] Assemblies and oratory remained at the core of politics down to the first century BC.[389] *A fortiori*, the early hellenistic period, with its numerous decrees of honours to citizen benefactors, is part of a golden age of *polis* politics, continuing the classical tradition of public debate, political competition, and aspiration to honours.[390] Nor can these features of the data be connected with the spiritual or moral crisis supposedly illustrated by the rise of the cult of the goddess Tyche, personification of Fortune.[391] The mistake of viewing the hellenistic period as one when citizens withdrew from traditional religion or indulged in superstition has been addressed elsewhere.[392]

In all probability, it was after the effective Roman takeover of southern Greece in the mid-second century BC that *polis* politics began to change; certainly it was very different in tone by the end of the Republic and after the formation of the province of Achaia in the late first century. In the second century, there is also a fall in public building work,[393] and by the first century the scope for debate about questions concerning the very survival of the *polis* was more limited. But throughout the earlier hellenistic period, and for some time after, we see a great deal more continuity than change; and *polis* architecture (both urban and rural) is still a manifestation of *polis* culture. Built landscapes, though in many places affected by warfare, were not passive reflections of trends but the product of choices whereby communities or groups of communities – in pursuance of their leaders' competitive ambitions, or in response to circumstances – were able to improve their surroundings. Commitment to the *polis* endured.

---

[387] Not necessarily the site of most formal education: Scholz 2007. *Gymnasia*: Epidauros *c.* 300 (Lambrinoudakis 1987–8); Mycenae (?) (Klein 1997, 256–7); Troizen *c.* C3e (*IG* iv. 754); Sikyon ('gymnasium of Kleinias', C3), Meyer 1975a; Patrai (?) (French 1991–2, 22); Messene (inscriptions, Blackman 1996–7, 49; C3/C2 dedication to Hermes, *SEG* 41. 361, 43. 154). Messene honours a gymnasiarch: *SEG* 52. 401 (C2).

[388] CORINTH: *Corinth* viii. 3. 30 (C3e). THOURIA: *IG* v. 1. 1386 (*c.* C2). KYTHERA (C3): *IG* v. 1. 938 with *SEG* 11. 897. TAINARON (C2/C1): *SEG* 22. 304 (60. 416).

[389] See papers in Kremmydas and Tempest 2013, esp. Rubinstein 2013.

[390] See e.g. Shipley 2013a, esp. 364–5. Bresson 2016, 215, stresses the inherent link between benefaction and the city-state culture.

[391] Another suggestion of Rizakis and Touratsoglou 2011, 27.

[392] e.g. Shipley 2000b, 155–6, 160–2, 170, 173–5. Potter 2003, similarly, gives pride of place to continuity (or continuous development) rather than change in Greek religion of this period. Mikalson 1998, esp. 288–323: individualism arose within, not in opposition to, traditional Athenian religious practice.

[393] Shipley 2005b, 322.

IV.6 Material Culture

IV.6.a The Non-Ceramic Record

A hindrance to any investigation of the economy in fourth- and third-century Greece, and *a fortiori* in the Peloponnese, is the near-total absence of synthetic work on material culture that might illustrate the nature of household assemblages, patterns of circulation within and between regions, rising and falling prosperity, or changes in household organization;[394] and even of studies of the development of particular pottery styles across the peninsula. Despite this, we can make some headway by drawing together the piecemeal evidence for movements and stylistic developments in ceramics; and may be able to detect economic innovation as well as engagement between regions, and between the Peloponnese and the outside world.

In the matter of internal household organization, a start has at least been made. A recent study notes several pieces of evidence: the tyrant Aristodemos of Argos is said to have used a portable bed (Plut. *Mor.* 781 d–e); Antiochos IV gave a curtain or hanging to the temple of Zeus at Olympia (Paus. 5. 12. 4); and a bathing-basin was used at the Mysteries of the Great Gods at Andania in Messenia (referred to in the famous sacred law).[395] The household archaeology of the hellenistic Peloponnese, however, has not yet been drawn together systematically, though luxury items of furniture and other material culture have sometimes been noted.[396]

There is clear evidence of active sculpture and terracotta workshops. For example, sculptural terracottas were made at the sanctuary of Demeter and Kore in Corinth until the end of the fourth century or a little later.[397] Most pre-Roman sculpture in Corinth is from the early hellenistic period and belongs to a cosmopolitan range of styles.[398] In Arkadia, clay statuettes were made at Lousoi,[399] and Tegea continued to have a lively sculptural tradition,[400] as in the fourth century.[401] In the third century, the aristocracy of

---

[394] For a first attempt, see Rotroff 2006.

[395] Andrianou 2009, 65, 100, and 119 respectively. Latest edition: Gawlinski 2012. Dates proposed for the text are 91 BC and AD 24.

[396] Andrianou 2009 notes stone bed- and table-supports at a sanctuary (pp. 35, 52), a poros bed in a chamber tomb (p. 45), and C4/C3 loomweights (p. 105), all from Corinth. Later items: Hl–R loomweights at Nemea (pp. 104, 105); C2c luxury storage box from Patrai (pp. 71, 78).

[397] Bookidis 2010.

[398] Sturgeon 1998.

[399] Mitsopoulou-Leon 2005.

[400] Levendi 1993, 123.

[401] e.g. Waywell 1993; Despinis 1993.

Messene developed a tradition of monumental family tombs.[402] In Laconia, the carving of palmette stelae continued into the fourth century or early hellenistic period,[403] and at Sparta itself there are numerous grave-reliefs from the late third century to Roman times.[404] A Peloponnesian tradition of sculptured capitals continued from the classical period into the hellenistic, including examples at Tegea.[405] Other stelae were produced in Achaean workshops, as well as a limited quantity of precious-metal jewellery.[406]

A house at Aigeira has a pebble mosaic of the mid-fourth century.[407] One occurs in a third-century *naiskos* at Aigeira,[408] another is a late hellenistic mosaic at Tainaron.[409] Mosaic floors (both pebble and tessellated) occur in hellenistic houses at Sparta.[410] None of the mosaics located by the non-intensive Sikyonia Survey was dated to this period,[411] but an early hellenistic villa outside the walls of Argos has a mosaic floor[412] and a hellenistic mosaic is reported at Kleonai.[413] A hellenistic pebble mosaic has been found at Aigion,[414] together with others of hellenistic–Roman date[415] including one in a hellenistic workshop.[416]

A hellenistic–Roman bronze workshop has been identified south-east of the central settlement of Argos.[417] On the other hand, the earliest evidence for gold-working appears to be at Patrai in the second half of the second century.[418]

While this section has not attempted a full survey of craft production, the examples show that the Peloponnese was far from isolated, far from devoid of active, innovative craftwork. There seems to be no obvious regional pattern.

IV.6.b Pottery

We can perhaps go further by focusing on the ceramic data. The Peloponnese received limited coverage in the nine Scientific Meetings on

---

[402] Fröhlich 2008.
[403] Delivorrias 1993, 214.
[404] Papaefthymiou 1993.
[405] Karageorga-Stathakopoulou 2005, 131, 134–5.
[406] Rizakis and Touratsoglou 2011, 20, 21.
[407] Blackman 1999–2000, 43–4, with Blackman 2000–1, 38, and Blackman 2001–2, 36–7.
[408] Madigan 1991, 509; cf. French 1993–4, 20.
[409] Moschou 1975, 175 with 174 fig. 7.
[410] Raftopoulou 1998, 127.
[411] See Lolos 2011, 273–4, 287, 324, 437, 523 for earlier and later mosaics.
[412] Blackman 1996–7, 23–4.
[413] Morgan 2009–10, 26.
[414] LN 32.
[415] Blackman 1996–7, 41.
[416] Blackman 1999–2000, 44.
[417] Blackman 1996–7, 23–4.
[418] Petropoulos 2005b, 20.

Hellenistic Pottery (1986–2012),[419] and has only just begun to be explored synoptically.[420] In a few instances, however, it is possible to assess historical implications. Certain ceramic assemblages point to differences between town and country life, such as those from rural farmhouse sites in the Methana Survey and a few town houses excavated at Halieis; black-glazed ware being ubiquitous on rural sites, figured ware almost absent.[421] At *Ráchi* near the Isthmia sanctuary, the house assemblages are adjudged simple.[422] The Laconia Survey data point to the generally modest resources of small farms on marginal land.[423] Furthermore, there are enough data from excavations and surveys to allow us to explore in outline the movements of pottery and the transmission of stylistic influences.

Regional Developments

In Argolis, pottery exports from Argos decline from the late third century, though the city subsequently becomes the centre of mould-made bowl production in the Peloponnese (many of its wares turning up at the Epidauros sanctuary);[424] an Athenian workshop even opens a 'branch office' at Argos towards the end of the 'long third century'.[425] At the town site of Epidauros, expanding in this period, grave-goods from the late fourth to early first centuries show links with Corinth, Argos, Attica, Aigina, and Asia Minor; there are imports from the first three places alongside local production, though imports decline in the second half of the second century.[426] Late fourth- and early third-century finds from the *propylon* of the 'Gymnasium', however, are more local; predominantly Corinthian with only a few Attic and Laconian and no Argive or Aiginetan.[427] At Asine, there is evidence of either the importation of fine ware from Argos or stylistic influence from that direction.[428] Argolis thus displays a mixed picture, with limited and in

---

[419] A point made more fully at Shipley 2008a, 61–3. The 7th Scientific Meeting on Hellenistic Pottery, at Aigion in 2005 (*7th Hellenistic Pottery Meeting*), was the first to cover the Peloponnese in depth; the conference 'album' (Kypraiou 2005) provides an overview. If the table at Shipley 2008a, 61 fig. 2a, were updated to reflect later meetings, the proportion of papers on the Peloponnese would fall from 11 per cent to 9 per cent, largely because of a boom in Black sea archaeology.

[420] Cf. remarks of Petropoulos 2005a, 26.

[421] Foxhall 2004, esp. 260–1.

[422] Anderson-Stojanović 2004, 628–30.

[423] R. W. V. Catling 2002, 187–95; Shipley 2002d, 269, 273–4; Stewart 2013, 14, 42.

[424] Banaka-Dimaki 2005, 128, 129.

[425] Rotroff 2013; evidence includes C3d–C2e stamps used in both *poleis*.

[426] Proskynitopoulou 2000, esp. 401–2. Study of finds has focused mainly on C2s.

[427] Danali 1994, 268–9.

[428] Zehbe 1988.

some respects declining interaction with places outside the Peloponnese. At Halieis, fourth-century deposits show that the *polis* was actively trading with Attica, Argos, and Corinth.[429]

Turning to Korinthia–Sikyonia, at *Ráchi*, in the lower, earlier fill (late fourth–early third century) of the South Slope Cistern the largely Corinthian amphoras accompany mainly local but also Attic pottery; in the later, upper fill (latter half of third century), imported amphoras are more common than Corinthian, but imported pottery less plentiful; the settlement as a whole has few 'Megarian' mould-made bowls.[430] Here potters, probably local, made their own versions of functional wares found elsewhere in Korinthia, for local use rather than mass production.[431] Material in use when the site was destroyed *c.* 200 includes fewer imports than in the late fourth and early third centuries;[432] most of the West Slope ware is local.[433] At this site, at least, the picture is of increasing localism. At Corinth itself, there is evidence of Macedonian pottery, perhaps reflecting the permanent garrison.[434] At a burial site in Sikyon, pottery of the last quarter of the fourth century shows the influence of Macedonian metalwork.[435]

In Achaea, scientific analysis of pottery from Patrai and Dyme confirms the use of local clays.[436] At Dyme, tomb pottery dated to the second half of the fourth century and the first half of the third shows a combination of local manufacture with influences from large production centres in Attica, Corinth, and Elis.[437] At Keryneia, third-century pottery shares some features with that of the western Peloponnese and of Argos.[438] Cemetery material at Patrai similarly testifies to a local workshop,[439] possibly related to others in western Greece;[440] grave-goods of the second half of the fourth century show links with Eleia, central Greece, and Corinth. Although the number of tombs declines in the third century, from the late part of that century new local forms predominate (albeit tracking wider developments and showing links with Peloponnesian centres such as Messenian Pylos and

[429] Bresson 2016, 363; Ault 1999.
[430] Anderson-Stojanović 1997.
[431] Anderson-Stojanović 2004, 628–30.
[432] Anderson-Stojanović 2011.
[433] Anderson-Stojanović 2000, esp. 382.
[434] Drougou and Touratsoglou 2013.
[435] Krystalli-Votsi 1997.
[436] Rathosi 2005.
[437] Vasilogamvrou *et al.* 2011.
[438] Dekoulakou 2011.
[439] Kolia and Stavropoulou-Gatsi 2005.
[440] A. Kyriakou 2011.

Argos); there are now strikingly few imports.[441] At Aigion, early hellenistic cemetery finds point to mainly or wholly local production;[442] this may be part of a pattern in which *polis* size correlates with the level of external interaction.

In Eleia, it is not yet possible to distinguish securely the products of the *polis* of Elis from those of the rest of the region.[443] A probable import, in the shape of a kantharos form found widely in Apulia and Campania, is also common in the western Peloponnese, chiefly at Elis and (Messenian) Pylos, but nowhere else in mainland Greece.[444] At Elis itself, there were important workshops for painted and relief pottery[445] as well as black-glazed; many of the latter being of types that also occur at Olympia.[446] Pottery was made both for distribution within Eleia and for local use.[447] Lamps are local but have typological links with Achaea, other nearby regions, Athens, and Corinth.[448] Finds from the south stoa at Elis (now dated late in the second quarter of the third century or to the third quarter) are predominantly local fine wares blending long-lived local shapes with variants of foreign types, while the West Slope ware has a local character;[449] an earlier study, though now superseded in details, emphasizes the strength of local tradition.[450] The 'Homeric beakers' of Elis are likely to be local rather than Macedonian.[451] Pottery from the 'tomb of Philemena' at *Bouchióti* (third quarter of third century) is local and largely conservative, like that from other peripheral workshops of third-century Greece.[452] At Olympia, the second-century pottery from a well is largely local.[453] Pottery production in Eleia seems mostly focused on local (intra-regional) consumption, but follows trends developing elsewhere, of which Eleian potters were clearly aware. Whether this 'conservatism' is a sign of adverse conditions is a question to which we shall return.

In Arkadia, early hellenistic pottery at Lousoi shows links with Corinth, Olympia, Athens; Asia Minor and Argos featuring in the second century.[454]

[441] D. Kyriakou 1994, 193–5.
[442] Papakosta 2005; Papakosta 2011.
[443] Rogl 1997, 321 n. 34.
[444] Alexandropoulou 2011.
[445] Vasilakis and Koutsoubeliti 2011.
[446] Georgiadou 2000.
[447] Leon-Mitsopoulou 1994, esp. 166–9.
[448] Iliopoulos and Kanellopoulos 2011; Katsarou and Mourtzini 2011.
[449] Kastler 2000, esp. 411.
[450] Kastler 1997 (note disclaimer at 23).
[451] Rogl 1997.
[452] Themelis 1994, 157; cf. *SEG* 46. 456 (52. 1977) with Stroud ad loc.
[453] Schauer 1997, 24, 30.
[454] Mitsopoulou-Leon 2000 [1989], 23–8 *passim*.

Everyday pottery includes Corinthian lamps and Argive and Corinthian relief cups, but also moulds confirming local production of long-petalled cups.[455] About 12 per cent of relief ware is imported, mostly from Argos but also from Achaea and areas north of the gulf of Corinth, including Phokis; there are scarcely any influences from the south; and there is evidence of local production of most household, ritual, and architectural ceramic objects, as well as (in the second century) plaques similar to Eastern Sigillata A and Campana C.[456] At Tegea, preliminary survey results point to plentiful classical–hellenistic production with limited imports from the eastern Peloponnese (Laconia, Corinth, perhaps Argolis).[457] Evidently Arkadia was a less isolated region than Eleia; or perhaps its 'isolation' took a different form.

In Messenia, scientific analysis of material from hellenistic Messene confirms the regular production of large storage jars using local clay.[458] There is also source evidence to help build a picture of lively interaction. The region had third-century trade links to Alexandria (e.g. the horse-dealer Nikagoras, Polyb. 5. 37–8); Italian imports are known from the last quarter of the fourth century, probably arriving through Pylos and Kyparissos (cf. e.g. *IG* v. 2. 1421, a third-century law of Kyparissos on harbour dues). Funerary material from Pylos, indeed, has links with the western Peloponnese, Rhodes, Athens, Pergamon and Macedonia.[459] Yet at Messene itself, one important early hellenistic deposit is seen as pointing to a conservative, insular society;[460] while most of the material from the fill of the fountain-house of Arsinoë is from workshops within the city.[461] Again, then, the picture varies with distance from international networks and routes; and the question arises once more: how did the citizens of Messene pay for their spectacular architectural programme?

In Laconia, excavation at Skandeia (*Kastrí*), the ancient harbour town of Kythera, yielded few hellenistic finds.[462] At Geronthrai, by contrast, early hellenistic stew-pots conserving an earlier tradition, as well as Laconian cups, are found alongside mould-made bowls in a regional variety showing awareness of wider Greek fashions; while black-glazed *Plakettenvasen* (vases with appliqué decoration) suggest a link with an Alexandria–Crete–Taras

[455] Mitsopoulou-Leon 1990.
[456] Rogl 2004.
[457] Cracolici 2005.
[458] Giannopoulou and Kiriatzi 2008.
[459] Danali 2011.
[460] Themelis 2004b, 427–9 ~ Themelis 2005, 97.
[461] Giuliani 2011.
[462] A. W. Johnston *et al.* 2014, 18, 19, 42.

trade route.[463] At Sparta, pottery from one elite tomb, in use from the mid-third to the late second century, reflects contacts with Asia Minor, Crete, Athens, Mytilene, and possibly Boiotia and Macedonia, though the largest proportion is from a local workshop producing for local markets; the few imports being considered to reflect sporadic visitors rather than systematic trade, and certain types widespread in Greece are absent.[464]

The data point to declining interaction in parts of the northern Peloponnese, while Laconia, Messenia, and perhaps Arkadia seem especially to enjoy increasing international links.

Networks

To summarize the evidence: in Argolis, there seems to be more interaction with the Aegean world than there is in the gulf of Corinth; links with the rest of the Peloponnese are also becoming stronger. Assemblages vary in character between sites and contexts, however. In Korinthia, finds are predominantly of local manufacture, indicating a possible shift in the balance of production, not necessarily of outside trade in other goods. In Achaea, the material seems more cosmopolitan the larger the centre. Small centres (including pre-Roman Patrai) reveal wares either of local character or linked stylistically to the gulf and to central and western Greece. That is also the case in Eleia (including Elis and Olympia), where the pottery has a strongly regional character – at first sight, perhaps, surprisingly given the international profile of the Olympics; such outside links as exist are with the gulf of Corinth and Athens. Novel styles influenced by those of other regions seem to be preferred to actual imports. In Arkadia, Lousoi displays links with the northern Peloponnese and central Greece rather than with the southern Peloponnese; as one might expect in a landlocked region, there is (as yet) no sign of material brought from outside the Peloponnese, though some middle hellenistic plaques may have Italian connections. Only coastal Messenia and parts of Laconia reveal links with further-off parts of the eastern Mediterranean. The city of Messene has a strongly localized material record; the Messenian coastal towns are more cosmopolitan. Laconian pottery shows more awareness of external styles than in Eleia and Messenia, and is more closely linked to the wider Aegean world, Alexandria, and Magna Graecia than to the Peloponnese.

---

[463] Langridge-Noti and Prent 2011.
[464] Raftopoulou 2000 *passim*, esp. 425.

The archaeological evidence reviewed here demonstrates that there were active material-cultural links both between regions of the peninsula and between the Peloponnese and the outside world. The claimed isolation of the peninsula is once again disproved.[465]

The evidence of cultural links has not, however, deterred scholars from claiming – usually with reference to a period later than the 'long third century' – that there was a decline in the quality of ceramics. For example, Peloponnesian pottery in general is said to have become inferior in the middle or late hellenistic period, with slips and decoration being abandoned.[466] It is with reference to the Roman period (*c.* first century BC and after) – not the hellenistic – that petrographic analysis of lamps from western Achaea identifies lower standards of clay preparation and less well-controlled firing conditions.[467] It would be wrong, therefore, to infer hastily a general decline in quality before the middle or late hellenistic period. It is true that pottery in the important sealed deposit at Messene, as early as *c.* 290, is viewed as adhering to older forms and showing 'unstable modelling, cheap matt glaze', derivative copying of forms produced in major centres, and the avoidance of decoration and polychromy; all of which is taken to be evidence of conservatism.[468] Assuming this is true, one might explain it by the relative youth of the *polis* of Messene and of its regional organization; the resources needed to construct its superlative monumental civic centre not yet having been accumulated by the elite. On the other hand, the Laconia Survey found that some hellenistic wares have a softer fabric and more variable slip quality than archaic and classical wares,[469] which might uphold the suggestion of a fall in technical attainment. Changes in different wares, however, take place at different times: as early as the late classical period or even earlier, for example, roof tiles from the Laconia Survey undergo a change in technique to a less hard fabric, a thinner paint.[470] In Laconia in general, some classical forms are favoured well into the hellenistic period; a general change of style occurring only in the first century BC – later than in some regions.[471] Finally, some styles display high technical prowess: at Sparta from around the second quarter of the second century, for example, mould-made bowls were manufactured which, while borrowing

---

[465] The isolation of Messenia asserted by Tarn and Griffith 1952, 111–12, is refuted by the ceramic evidence, as Themelis 2005, 95, notes.

[466] Petropoulos 2005a, 26, referring to C2s.

[467] Rathosi 2005, 543–4.

[468] Themelis 2004b, 428–9 ~ Themelis 2005, 97.

[469] Visscher 1996, 92.

[470] R. W. V. Catling 1996, 86.

[471] Visscher 1996, 91.

some motifs from elsewhere, show an originality of conception that justifies the inclusion of their workshop-owners' names among their decorative elements.[472]

More importantly, it is far from self-evident that something we may perceive as a change in quality has anything to do with overall social or economic conditions. It is rash to infer *economic* decline from an apparent reduction in *technical* accomplishment; the manufacture of less durable objects can sometimes go hand in hand with economic 'growth' in the form of increased output at reduced unit cost – as in the modern economy.

Some scholars posit economic under-development on the basis of what they see as an 'introverted' pottery industry, reflected in conservatism of style and a relative lack of production for 'export'; most pottery being aimed at 'local' consumption, imports of non-Peloponnesian wares limited in quantity.[473] They concede that there are exceptions, such as Argive bowls destined for export, and so-called Eleian *lekythoi* (albeit not necessarily Eleian-made)[474] that circulated through the western Peloponnese and reached Aitolia and Akarnania. Similarly, the standard study of Peloponnesian mould-made bowl workshops, which began operating in the late third century, explains the limited extent to which they reflect new foreign styles (such as Campanian ware) in terms of the endurance of a primarily agricultural economy dominated by conservative elites;[475] this is consistent with the analysis adopted here, but the author acknowledges that there was a surprising number of active local workshops,[476] which could just as well be a sign of economic security and of well-funded elites as of 'under-development'. Indeed, influences from other parts of the eastern Mediterranean did penetrate certain inland areas; presumably through a mix of middle-distance sea crossings (e.g. western Crete to Gytheion) and *cabotage* around the coasts.[477]

The survey of ceramic evidence suggests that while pottery is, in the present state of knowledge, insufficient as an indicator of economic well-being, it has much to tell us about networks and regional characteristics. A recent study argues persuasively that 'pottery does not merely depict economic networks but illuminates many aspects of social interactions between and

---

[472] Zavvou 2005.

[473] Rizakis and Touratsoglou 2011, 20, using 'local' to refer to what in the present work are called the regions of the Peloponnese.

[474] Petropoulos 2005a, 23.

[475] Siebert 1978, esp. 196–7.

[476] Siebert 1978, 279.

[477] For the importance of *cabotage* (coastal tramping), see e.g. Arnaud 1992; specifically in Hl period, Élaigne 2013, 227–8.

within ancient societies'.[478] It therefore seems appropriate, having argued that pottery cannot tell us certain things, to look for what it can tell us. The suggestion has been made that the Peloponnese was broadly divided between a western technological 'zone' and an eastern, with part of Achaea in each and Arkadia in an uncertain position.[479] The western zone in the fourth and third centuries extended to Kephallonia, Ithaca, Aitolia, and Akarnania and had links with Epeiros and southern Italy. The data we have reviewed, however, also point to two cross-cutting divisions, giving four 'Peloponneses':

(*a*) (1) We can characterize Eleia, smaller places in Achaea and Arkadia, and inland Messene as generally conservative in their ceramics; we may not necessarily follow those who psychologize this feature as 'inward-looking'. (2) In contrast, Corinth, Dyme, the Messenian harbours, and inland Laconia (including at least one perioikic *polis*) display active links with the outside world; Corinth possibly less so after *c.* 300.

(*b*) (1) As against a northern and north-western culture sphere along the gulf of Corinth, including parts of the western Peloponnese, there is (2) a southern sphere where stylistic links with the eastern Mediterranean and Magna Graecia are stronger. Geographical location, ancestral trading contacts, and traditional sea routes will have much to do with these patterns.[480] The patterns themselves may bear little relation to overall economic 'development'.

IV.7 Coin Production and Monetization

IV.7.a Coinage and Money

One institution that may have had the potential to unite the different regional economies is, of course, money. It has been noted that historians have paid insufficient attention to how coinage may illuminate not only the economies of the hellenistic Peloponnese but also the landscape;[481] in this section we shall assess what the evidence of coins can, and cannot, tell us.

---

[478] Riedel 2013 (quotation from 371).

[479] Petropoulos 2005a, 25, arguing that not enough pottery from Arkadia has been published to decide the question. On the W zone, see also Themelis 2004b, 427 ~ Themelis 2005, 96.

[480] Petropoulos 2005a, 25, drawing a parallel with the Mycenaean and Geometric periods.

[481] Grandjean 2007, 19–20; Grandjean 2006, 198–9 (at 210–11 she suggests using hoards to define 'regions').

The level of monetization[482] at the start of the period and for some time after is thought to have been low in the sense that most coins were high-value and of silver, relatively few states coined at all, and fewer still adopted fractional silver or lower-value bronze. Posthumous issues in the name of Alexander, in the large denominations such as the silver tetradrachms (4-drachma coins, typically around 17 g in weight) that dominate the numismatic record,[483] were adopted later than elsewhere, around 300.[484] During the early part of the period there were few substantial coinage issues anywhere.[485] The extreme case is, famously, Sparta, where no coinage was minted until the reign of Areus,[486] who, probably in connection with the Chremonidean war, issued tetradrachms in his own name on the Attic standard, accompanied by a silver obol (one-sixth of a drachma) on the Aiginetan. In another conflict a generation later, Kleomenes III issued both silver and Sparta's first bronze (the largest being a probable *hexachalkon* or half-obol).[487] In Messenia, only one *polis* other than Messene issued coins before they joined the Achaean league in the early second century, and that only briefly (Mothone in the late fourth century).[488] Few hoards of the period have been found in Messenia (which may be a positive indicator, pointing to relatively infrequent or brief warfare),[489] and the use of coinage seems almost entirely restricted to the chief *polis* of Messene and the harbour towns of Pylos and Kyparissos,[490] though Mothone issued bronze coinage in about the late fourth century (TABLE IV.3).

If Peloponnesian communities were not great users of coinage, what would this imply about the economy – particularly in the south-eastern Peloponnese, where until well into our period the Lakedaimonians must

---

[482] For 'levels of monetization', and rural monetization, see Hollander 2006, 315–16.

[483] On 'Alexanders', see Howgego 1995, 49–51.

[484] Rizakis and Touratsoglou 2011, 22 (for Peloponnesian hoards, see large foldout preceding p. 17).

[485] Implied by Grandjean n.d. [2008]. It should be noted that the fact that a *polis* does not issue coins is not necessarily evidence for the suppression of freedom by an outside power: Meadows 2001, esp. 62.

[486] Bresson 2016, 270, interestingly comments 'There was no room for a transparent instrument of exchange in this hierarchized, inegalitarian city-state'. He over-interprets the sources, however, in assuming a positive decision not to coin after the Peloponnesian war: Xen. *Lak. pol.* 7. 5–6 and Plut. *Lyc.* 9. 1–2 refer only to the 'Lykourgan' system, while the issue debated in C4e at Plut. *Lys.* 17 concerned the use of foreign coins.

[487] Areus and Kleomenes: Grunauer-von Hoerschelmann 1978, 1–20, 112–16, pls 1–4 (Gruppen I–VI); Hoover 2011, 142–54. *Hexachalkon* (?): Grunauer-von Hoerschelmann 1978, 16–19, 114–15, pl. 3, Gruppe IV (8–13 g); Walker 2006, 215 nos. 843–4; Hoover 2011, 145 no. 621 ('Denomination A/B').

[488] On the C2 AE issues of the league, see J. A. W. Warren 2007 with Kroll 2007.

[489] Duyrat 2011, 431, cautions against simple links between hoarding and warfare.

[490] Grandjean 2006, 203.

have relied on currencies issued by other states? The question is not a straightforward one, since market trade was able to exist without coinage, so that there is no necessary correlation between the frequency of coin issues and the strength of an economy.

An important strand of recent scholarship rightly stresses the non-commercial roles of Greek coinage. Until at least the classical period, coinage is sometimes claimed to have had more to do with culture than with quotidian purchases or what one might call 'shopping';[491] but it is important to distinguish the political content of symbols on coins from their possible roles in commerce or in the transfer of value, which has far greater scope than market activities. Alexanders may have continued to be struck partly in order to link a *polis*'s identity to a 'safe' past rather than to any contemporary regime such as the Diadochoi (or later the Romans). Such ideological statements would not, however, imply that the currency itself was not primarily monetary in its aims. Furthermore, 'money' is not limited to coinage – any commodity can be used as a standard of exchange.[492] (Nor was precious metal used primarily for coins; only a minority of gold and silver was ever minted.)[493]

If coinage were to be deemed a primarily non-commercial institution, it could not inform us directly about the state of 'the economy' if by that we mean such features as *per capita* levels of production, trade, and consumption and whether these were rising, falling, or stable. Indeed, it is doubtful that any realistically obtainable evidence could so inform us, since those phenomena – modern constructs that they are – were not the subjects of ancient data-collection. Nevertheless, without having to choose between the modernizing model of the ancient economy and its minimalist counterpart, is it not possible to situate coinage both in the sphere of cultural expression and in that of financial transactions? In our period, the non-market-based uses of coinage might include reimbursements of expenses to officials, pay for mercenaries, the purchase of services by the *polis* from local or foreign third parties, loans, payment of duties and taxes, and the funding of monuments and festivals, as well as the convenient transportation of large sums of cash by investors or merchants for their commercial dealings.[494] Nevertheless, a radical shift in scholarship has been under way

---

[491] See generally von Reden 2010, 3–11. C4 coinage still more about culture than economy: Grandjean 2003, 65.

[492] von Reden 2010, 3–6; Hollander 2006, 316.

[493] de Callataÿ 2006, esp. 64–7.

[494] For similar observations on the Seleukid empire, where tetradrachms were mainly for payments by or to the state, see Aperghis 2001.

for a number of years that recognizes that Greek coins at all periods had an important commercial role that may have been primary.[495] This rethink has been prompted partly by a greater awareness of smaller denominations, which we shall consider in the next subsection and which almost certainly did facilitate trade in some way. Additionally, the all-pervading 'culture of credit' in Greek society – on a significant scale where the elite is concerned – may have 'increas[ed] the number of monetary transactions and, in modern parlance, "consumer spending",[496] even without the more sophisticated instruments of credit that started to develop in the later hellenistic and Roman periods.

IV.7.b Ranges of Values

What, then, do coin issues tell us about economic conditions? It may be that the information varies with the denomination.

(*a*) The large denominations most useful in such transactions are strongly over-represented in hoards:[497] most third-century coins from the Peloponnese are large silvers such as tetradrachms, probably minted in connection with specific military events such as the Chremonidean war or major building programmes such as at Messene. Alexanders were evidently used for high-value or mass transactions by states that lacked their own currency. In contrast, it is likely that most or all everyday exchanges and purchases were carried out in kind or by informal credit and deferred reciprocity.[498]

Large silver coins, such as the Alexanders already mentioned, or staters (didrachms, 2-drachma coins) of non-Peloponnesian states militarily involved in the peninsula, are *prima facie* evidence for the sporadic injection of large sums of cash into local economies – for example, by one-off transactions on the part of a *polis* or by the actions of internal or external benefactors – and for the occasional disbursement of large sums by states. These may have included the issue of coin in bulk for distribution to mercenaries, who are thought to have received their wages proper in arrears and in silver, their living expenses in advance and in bronze.[499] A mercenary with

---

[495] Cf. e.g. Mackil and van Alfen 2006, e.g. 203.

[496] von Reden 2010, 11, 12, 27, and esp. 94–5 (quotation, 95).

[497] Howgego 1995, 88.

[498] Rizakis and Touratsoglou 2011, 21–2. For a caution about the use of the term 'barter', which tends to characterize hostile encounters between groups, see von Reden 2010, 27.

[499] Salary: μισθός, μισθοί. Living expenses: σιτήρεσιον, Ps.-Dem. 50. 10; τροφή, Aen. Tact. 13. 2; σιταρχία, σιταρχίαι, Ps.-Arist. *Oik.* 1351b 11–15, etc. In Hl times the term ὀψώνιον superseded μισθός, Polyb. 1. 66. 3 etc. Full references: Psoma 2009, 4.

the ancient equivalent of a roll of banknotes in his hand might spend part of his earnings on entertainment, consumables, and small-scale luxuries, boosting the income of some members of the local community;[500] but save the greater part of his wages for the day when he hoped to return home. He might thus take his remaining funds out of a host *polis*'s economy[501] – a loss that might, however, be offset by citizens of the same *polis* returning from service abroad. A merchant importing a shipload of grain could make a profit of hundreds or thousands of drachmas in a single day, at irregular intervals; the short-term effects on the economy might be limited: he might host a dinner party to celebrate, but save most of the profit for reinvestment or for major outlays such as buying land or a house,[502] giving his daughter a dowry, or donating money to the *polis* for a festival or diplomatic mission. At any rate, thanks to what might be considered a 'trickle down' effect, large silver denominations do potentially point to certain kinds of activities in the *polis* economy and a certain boost to the velocity of monetary circulation.

(*b*) Middle-sized silver denominations, also frequent in the numismatic record, may be said to comprise the drachma and its primary divisions: the hemidrachm or triobol (½ dr.), trihemiobol (¼ dr.), and obol ($^1/_6$ dr.), the last weighing typically 0.8–0.9 g (all are combined with larger silvers in TABLE IV.3). Examples include issues from Sikyon, Argos, and Phleious from the late fifth century to the late fourth.[503] Scholars sometimes regard them as petty cash;[504] but how low was their value?

Estimating the purchasing power of ancient currency is not easy, but we need some sort of 'fix' on the material if we are to assess the possible effects of the circulation of coins. That such coins are not, in fact, 'loose change' is suggested by the evidence for typical daily payments of 1 drachma or 2–3 obols to Athenian citizens in the classical period;[505] the increases in some

---

[500] On the possible impact of mercenaries' pay on local economies, see Couvenhes 2006, esp. 419–25.

[501] Howgego 1995, 98–9; cf. Couvenhes 2006, 424–5 (lack of direct evidence for economic impact of returning mercenaries).

[502] Existence of a market in landed properties in Cl Attica: Xen. *Oik.* 20. 22–3.

[503] Rizakis and Touratsoglou 2011, 22–3.

[504] e.g. Rizakis and Touratsoglou 2011, 23–4.

[505] *Daily fees.* (*a*) Jury service: 2 ob. (C5m), 3 ob. (C5l; Arist. *Ath. pol.* 27. 3–4). (*b*) Architect's fee: 1 dr. (C5s; Salmon 2001, 202, citing *IG* i³ 476. 60–1, 266–8; cf. 33–46, sawyers; 131–4, carpenters). (*c*) Craftsmen on C5 public projects: similar level, though varied (Randall 1953). (*d*) Rowing in trireme on campaign: 1 dr. (implied, Thuc. 6. 8. 1). (*e*) Erechtheion workers: unskilled, 3 ob.; skilled, 1 dr. (*IG* i³ 475). (*f*) Allowance for ambassadors: 2–3 dr. excessive (Ar. *Ach.* 65–7, 90, 159, 161, 602). (*g*) Not using cash to get provisions in a village (Ar. *Ach.* 33–6). (*h*) Two jurors, given 1 dr. coin between them as no ½ dr. coins are left, go to fish market to change it into obols (Ar. *Wasps*, 788–9); this need not imply an obol was 'small change' – we do not know what it would buy, and smaller AR fractions existed (Hoover 2014,

of these payments over time, incidentally, need not reflect inflation and the devaluation of coinage so much as the tendency for citizens to reward themselves handsomely.[506] In the light of these data, one might equate a drachma with what, in England today, a skilled craftsman such as an electrician might earn for a full day's work on a private house; perhaps in the region of £200. This would make a tetradrachm worth the better part of a thousand pounds – the price of a rather old secondhand car – and even an obol tens of pounds.

Those are mere guesses, and a comparison of ancient living costs with modern can never be accurate; but they make the point that the commonest coins surviving from the Peloponnese at this time, silver hemidrachms (triobols) and above, were not 'small change' but represented sums that a person would not spend casually or often. Their frequent survival testifies to a spectrum of cash transactions that were perhaps more local but still relatively high-value; they probably involved mainly members of propertied groups but extended well beyond the one-off or prestige movements of capital for which larger denominations were suitable. They may have included such payments as craftsmen's fees for private commissions, private purchases of consumable luxuries, and so on. The frequency of mid-sized silvers is a further indication that certain significant areas of economic activity were far from quiescent.

(*c*) We have noted the probability that most small-scale transactions took place without coinage; but between capital transfers and luxury acquisition on the one hand, and cashless exchange on the other, there was – as has recently become clear (TABLE IV.3)[507] – a significant gap filled by smaller coins, either silver fractions of the obol or heavier bronze coins with lower nominal values. (Larger bronzes such as staters feature only later, in the second century and after.[508]) The benchmark was the *chalkous* (meaning simply 'bronze'), usually one-twelfth of an obol (sometimes one-eighth), typically weighing about 2 g; together with its multiples the *dichalkon*

489–91 nos. 1668–88, esp. 491 no. 1686, C5s *tetartēmorion* = ¼ ob.). (*i*) Assembly pay: 1 ob. (from *c*. 400), soon 2 ob., then 3 ob. (*Ath. pol.* 41. 3). (*j*) Good income for citizen: ½ dr. (Xen. *Poroi* 3. 9–10). (*k*) Cost of renting slave miner from Nikias (C5l): 1 ob. (Xen. *Poroi* 4. 14). (*k*) *Boulē* pay: 5 ob. (C4l), assembly pay now 1 dr., 1½ dr. for special session (*Ath. pol.* 62. 2). (*l*) Eleusis sanctuary workers (320s): unskilled, 1½ dr.; skilled, 2–3 dr. (*IG* ii² 1672).

[506] See also Rhodes 1981, 691.

[507] Largely thanks to the series of vast auction sales of the collection of 'BCD' (see I.1.c): e.g. Numismatik Lanz 2001 (Corinth); Walker 2004 (Olympia); Walker 2006 (rest of Peloponnese). For the representativeness of these collections, as far as medium and smaller denominations are concerned, see Walker 2006, [5–6].

[508] Grandjean 2007, 28 (e.g. drachmas in Boiotia). LHl donation of AE staters to citizens of Aiolian Kyme: Picard 2006.

(double *chalkous*), *tetartēmorion* or *trichalkon* (¼ ob.), *hexachalkon* (½ ob.), and *tritetartēmorion* (¾ ob.; sometimes contracted to *tritartēmorion*). Because of variations in weight, however, a bronze coin's intended denomination is not always certain.[509]

Already in the late fifth century, Pheneos, Sikyon, and Phleious had issued bronze alongside silver, perhaps under the stimulus of the western colonies with which they had links; Argos and Tegea may also have coined both metals at that time. During the Peloponnesian war (431–404), the Athenians had temporarily issued silver-plated bronze (see later), but they did not issue bronze regularly until the mid-fourth century.[510] At a later period, bronze gradually replaced silver in many Peloponnesian *poleis*, the last known fractional silver being that of Phleious in the late fourth century, though larger silver coins continued to be made.[511] Bronzes are likely to be under-represented in hoards, however, since silver, being more valuable, would more often be hidden away. The question immediately arises, therefore, of how often lower-denomination coins were met in everyday life. We should remember that they are not 'small change': on the equivalences just posited, a *chalkous* might be worth a few pounds sterling in today's money; and the *chalkous* was not divided before the middle hellenistic period,[512] setting a limit to potential monetization.

The increased use of bronze is at first sight a major change in the monetary economy; but what, if any, economic effects can it have had? It has generally been supposed that it is only when bronzes are introduced that Greek coinage takes on a fiduciary aspect, leading to a possible increase in market-driven pricing. If any Greek issues constitute a fiduciary coinage[513] – one whose monetary value is greater than that of its metal content – it is surely this bronze currency.[514] But precious-metal coins also had a degree of fiduciarity, as is shown by the coexistence of different weight standards, and the frequent imprecision of coin weights; what mattered was that an appropriate authority had certified the coin's value.[515] As early as the late archaic period, a few communities used silver fractions, whose weight

---

[509] Hoover 2011, lxx, is more conservative than e.g. Walker 2006 in identifying coins of particular weights with particular fractions of the obol.

[510] Psoma 1998, 20.

[511] See also Picard 2007 ~ Picard 1989.

[512] The half-*chalkous* ($^1/_{144}$ dr.), for example, may have been introduced at Messene (with a weight of *c.* 1 g) only in C2s or C1e: Grandjean 1996, 694–5; Grandjean 2003, 189–90 nos. 669–73 (C2s); Hoover 2011, 131 nos. 592–3 (C2s). (Tully 2014, 29, rules it out for C4 Paros.)

[513] Psoma 1998, 19. Bronze was a full-weight coinage in Etruria and Rome from C6 and at Rome until C3 (Howgego 1995, 7).

[514] In C4l Athens, 1 talent of uncoined AE cost 61 dr. in AR coin: Murray 1985.

[515] Picard 2013, 73–4.

was inevitably variable given their minuscule size.[516] Similar coins have been identified in Macedonia and parts of southern Greece from the first half of the fifth century onwards.[517] To this extent, then, the economy had already been affected by fractionalization and fiduciarity before the introduction of bronze coinage. The balance may have shifted towards greater monetization in the fourth and third centuries; particularly since coins, issued mainly at irregular, often lengthy intervals rather than continually, must have remained in circulation for many years.[518] The balance, however, shifts only slowly and, as already noted, reaches a temporary limit with the *chalkous* despite its clear potential for further subdivision (it is wider and heavier than a silver obol).

If fractionalization proceeded slowly despite the already partly fiduciary character of coinage, does this imply economic 'under-development' or a missed opportunity? Or, to turn that question on its head, what was the incentive for states to adopt small denominations?

(*a*) There is no evidence of deliberate attempts to manipulate prices or the volume of trade.

(*b*) Fiduciary currencies were sometimes emergency measures, one possible motive being a difficulty of obtaining silver during wartime,[519] which probably explains the silver-plated bronzes of late fifth-century Athens,[520] the exceptional iron coins of Argos[521] and Tegea,[522] and the bronzes issued by the fourth-century Athenian general Timotheos while on campaign (Ps.-Arist. *Oik.* 2. 1351a 1). But the same explanation is unlikely to account for other small denominations.

(*c*) Some bronzes appear to have been issued in connection with military campaigns such as (presumably) those of Kleomenes III; at this period

---

[516] A famous example is the C6l hoard from Kolophon in Ionia (Kim 2001), with its 24ths and 48ths of a stater (½ and ¼ ob. respectively). Such cases are best treated as exceptional measures in unusual circumstances, rather than as pioneering instances of everyday 'small change'. See Kim 2002, 47; Kim and Kroll 2008, though he supposes they were in daily use in the market. Arist. *Pol.* 3. 4: at Kolophon the rich had 'formerly' been the majority of the citizens, thanks to their landholdings; was silver devalued by its ubiquity? Alternatively, was the huge issue, of which – given the number of dies – this hoard was a tiny part, intended for a one-off purpose such as a military campaign?

[517] Psoma 2013, 57–9.

[518] Cf. e.g. the Megarian AR trihemiobol of C4b, 'commonly found in rather worn condition' (Walker 2006, 22 no. 5); or the Phleiasian AR trihemiobol of C4e/C4m in a C3m hoard (Walker 2006, 47 no. 115). Other examples include Walker 2006, 86 no. 305; 90 no. 316; 93 no. 325; 97 no. 337, all from Sikyon.

[519] Grandjean 2007, 27; plus Walker 2006 for Argos and Tegea.

[520] Kroll 1976, *contra* Giovannini 1976.

[521] Hoover 2011, nos. 693–4.

[522] Hoover 2011, no. 1055.

Sparta minted both silver and bronze, perhaps for the system of dual payments to soldiers. Non-local bronzes were, in fact, used in some parts of the Peloponnese at times; renewed attention has been paid recently to bronzes issued by Macedonian kings, from the late fifth century on, to pay soldiers' subsistence expenses: bronzes of Cassander and Demetrios I have recently been found at Stymphalos, and elsewhere in eastern Arkadia others of Demetrios have been found at a site near modern *Trípoli* and at Orchomenos.[523] Surprisingly, given the length of his reign, bronzes of Antigonos II Gonatas are rare in hoards;[524] but they occur regularly in the Corinth excavations.[525] The bronzes of Antigonos III and Philip V found at Corinth, though fewer, are likely to be connected to military events.[526] Although this uneven picture may partly reflect inconsistent publication practice and scholars' lack of interest in, and limited knowledge of, Greek bronze coinage until recently, their frequency in and around Corinth suggests they enjoyed a primarily local circulation, and is most easily explained by the long-term presence of a Macedonian garrison. It has also been noted that bronzes generally circulated over limited distances[527] and may have been legal tender only within a given territory.[528] A similar scenario may be imagined for other garrison sites.

(*d*) Other small-denomination coinages, not necessarily fiduciary, may have been issued for administrative convenience;[529] designed, perhaps, to facilitate already occurring transactions for which drachmas, staters, and tetradrachms were impractical. They could, for example, simplify the process of taxation, which was not a general practice but was imposed on goods entering a harbour, typically at a rate of 2 per cent.[530]

It does not seem justifiable, therefore, to assume that a fiduciary coinage by itself, with all its limitations, would be designed to stimulate the economy, whether locally or more widely. Fractional or low-denomination issues as whole, however, might increase the velocity of transactions and

---

[523] Weir 2007; Psoma 2009, 23–4.

[524] Psoma 2009, 24, cites two coins from *Kato Klitoria* (near *Tripolis*), 1 each from Argos and Corinth, and two from *Lechainá*.

[525] Psoma 2009, 24, referring to their discovery 'very frequently in the excavations of Corinth and other sites in the Peloponnesus', but citing only publications from Corinth.

[526] Psoma 2009, 25, again referring to 'the Peloponnesus' but citing only coins from the Corinth excavations.

[527] Psoma 2009, 9.

[528] Psoma 2013, 61.

[529] See Picard 1987, referring to C4 Thasos. Cf. Picard 2001: by C2, Thasos is using AE issues for local expenditure, AR for external.

[530] For examples of fractional sums levied at Alexandria, see e.g. *PCZ* 59012 (Austin² 298), 259 BC.

perhaps facilitate wider ownership of capital. They may also have led to more complex price-setting in places where they were used. If fractions were minted in one *polis*, that is no reason to assume that their adoption would encourage 'monetization' in others, or in other regions; as noted earlier, bronzes tended to circulate locally, and different ranges of economic activities existed in different regions. Despite the possible effects of monetization noted here, however, it would be too simplistic to infer from the minting of low denominations or fiduciary coinage that a particular region was on average more prosperous than others. A greater impact on available monetary wealth may have been made by the importation of silver; while it is the concentration of minting in certain *poleis* that marks them out as having greater volumes of economic activity.

IV.7.c Economic Implications of Money

TABLE IV.3 shows where and when various denominations were issued. Several features may be noted.

(*a*) The occurrence of minting is extremely patchy; this may be illustrated by the near-total absence from the table of Sparta (which minted only occasionally, and not before the later part of Areus' reign); of all but one of the other Laconian *poleis* (despite the fact that some left Spartan control in 369, 338, 222, or 195); and of the minor Messenian *poleis* (which may have been federated under the central *polis* after 369).

(*b*) Certain peaks of production, such as those of the Arkadian league in the mid-fourth century, Kleomenean Sparta in the late third, and the Achaean in the mid-second, may have had a military purpose.

(*c*) After the large bronze issues of the Achaean league in the mid-second century, Peloponnesian minting ceases almost completely, which puts something of a positive gloss on the 'long third century'.

(*d*) More importantly for our purposes, some *poleis* dominate the picture with the near-continuity of their minting activity over a long period. By simplifying the data in the table, we can observe the introduction of fractional silvers (i.e. fractions of an obol) and the transition from silver to bronze taking place at widely differing dates. The introduction of small silver denominations occurs most often before 400, but is wholly absent from Achaea and Corinth and is seen nowhere after the mid-fourth century (except possibly in Phleious).

Judging by the recorded types, one of the earliest *poleis* to stop minting silver was Arkadian Psophis – not a *polis* one would necessarily have assumed to be an economic power-house; it appears to have stopped in the

Table IV.3. *Silver and bronze coinage minted in the Peloponnese*

		C5l	C4e	C4m	C4l	C3e	C3m	C3l	C2e	C2m	C2l
ARGOLIS	Argos	SHb	shb	SHb	sB	SB	sb	Sb	Sb	SB	sb
	Epidauros			s	sb	Sb	Sb	B		S	s
	Halieis	b	b	SB	b						
	Hermion			sb	Sb	sb	sb	B			
	Kleonai	sh			B					B	
	Methana			B				B			
	Phleious	SHB	shb	shb	shb	B			S	B	
	Troizen	SH	S	h	SB	b	B				
KORINTHIA	Corinth	S	SB	SB	SB	SB	B	SB	Sb	SB	
	Tenea									B	
SIKYONIA	Sikyon	SHB	h	ShB	SB	Sb	b	SB	S	SB	
ACHAIA	Aigeira			B					b	SB	
	Aigion								B	SB	
	Dyme			s	sB	b	b	B	s	sB	
	Helike		B								
	Kallistai									B	
	Keryneia									B	
	Patrai								S	B	
	Pellene			Sb	SB	b	b	S		SB	
ELEIA	Elis/Olympia	SH	SH	SH	Sb	Sb	sB	sb	Sb	SB	
TRIPHYLIA	Hypana									B	
ARKADIA	Alea		SB							B	
	Alipheira									B	
	Asea									B	
	Dipaia									B	
	Gortys									B	
	Helisson									B	
	Heraia	Sh	Shb	B	sb	sb	sb			B	
	Kaphyai						b	b		SB	
	Kleitor	s	s	B	sb	sb				SB	
	Lousoi									SB	
	Mantinea	Sh	h	SB	sB	B	b		S		
	Megalopolis			SB	sb	sb		S	S	SB	
	Methydrion		B								
	Orchomenos		B	Sb						B	

Table IV.3. (*Cont.*)

		C5l	C4e	C4m	C4l	C3e	C3m	C3l	C2e	C2m	C2l
	Pallantion	s	s							B	
	Pheneos	sB	S	SB	b	b	b			SB	
	Phigaleia									B	
	Psophis	sh		b	b		b	b		B	
	Stymphalos		S	SB						B	
	Tegea	SHb	s	SB			b	b	b	B	
	Teuthis									B	
	Thaliades			B							
	Thelphousa			SB							
	Thisoa									B	
MESSENIA	Asine									B	
	Kolonides									B	
	Korone								S		
	Messene			SB	b	b	b		SB	sB	sB
	Mothone				b						
	Thouria										b
LACONIA	Kythera								b		
	Sparta						S	SB	S		

S = middle–large silver (obol and upwards) definitely/probably of this phase (lower-case = possibly of this phase)

H = fractional silver (hemiobol or smaller) definitely/probably of this phase (lower-case = possibly of this phase)

B = bronze definitely/probably of this phase (lower-case = possibly of this phase)

The gold coinage of Pisa (extant only in the 360s) is omitted (Hoover 2011, nos. 547–8).

Sources: Walker 2006; for Korinthia, Numismatik Lanz 2001 (online version) and Hoover 2014, 518–42; further information from Hoover 2011, including the C2m rather than C2e dates for Achaean league bronzes (Hoover follows J. A. W. Warren 2007); additional information on Olympia from Walker 2004; checked against Classical Numismatic Group 2009.

late fifth century and replaced its coinage in the mid-fourth with a series of bronzes, the first of several such down to the mid-second. Elis ended its silver issues in the mid-fourth century; they were succeeded by bronzes from the late fourth to the mid-second. Phleious ended its silver series a little later, in the late fourth century, but had already introduced bronzes before almost any other Peloponnesian *polis*, in the late fifth, and continued to coin bronze until the late second century, when Messene was the only other *polis* issuing coins. The other pioneering adopter of bronze was Sikyon; but unlike Phleious it continued to coin silver almost continuously down to the mid-second century. Corinth produced a near-continuous series of coins down to the mid-second century (ending at or before the time of its destruction), with silver and bronze coexisting at many periods. Other *poleis* to issue large silver down to the third or second century were Dyme and Pellene in Achaea, and Heraia, Mantinea, Megalopolis in Arkadia (details in the table); but all coined bronze as well from the mid- or late fourth century onwards. Among the cities so far named, by far the commonest date for the adoption of bronze was the mid-fourth century.[531] Another city that began then and carried on down to the mid-second century was Messene. This raises interesting questions about the possible consequences of the ending of Spartan hegemony.

Most of the cities that dominate the table are ones we would have considered powerful or prosperous on other grounds, but in some cases, such as Psophis, the coins reveal a status that the written sources do not; the picture being confirmed in several cases by the number of separate issues.[532] The over-representation of the north-east (before the massive outburst of minting by the greatly enlarged Achaean league in the second century) invites explanation in terms of proximity to major trade centres and routes. The evidence outlined here is enough to confirm that the Peloponnese was not a backwater; there was plenty of activity, though it may have been concentrated in certain regions. A recent observer notes that one can no longer talk of a general hellenistic decline across Greece;[533] we can now claim the same specifically for the Peloponnese. Although quantitative data are not yet available, and despite the general impression that there was less big money around than in certain other corners of the post-Alexander world, there was more than enough to support the life of the *polis*. There may possibly

---

[531] Pergamon adopted AE in C4: Marcellesi 2010.

[532] Types may be counted in Hoover 2011 (Peloponnese except Corinth); Numismatik Lanz 2001 (Corinth), now with Hoover 2014 including Corinth. An impression of relative prominence may also gained by a perusal of Walker 2006.

[533] Grandjean 2006, 210.

have been a *relative* falling behind in comparison with Athens or the major
new cities of the Greco-Macedonian world – calculations of the total quantities of booty acquired during the expansion of the Roman empire suggest
that the eastern Mediterranean was far richer in precious metal than the
western part[534] – but this does not mean there was hardship or fundamental
economic problems. Nor is there any sign in the numismatic evidence
that the Macedonians were interested in the economic exploitation of the
Peloponnese; Philip II, for example, did not stop cities minting their own
coins.[535]

The very fact that the reduced Aiginetan weight standard becomes dominant in the Peloponnese between 280 and 210, replacing the Attic,[536] while
it was presumably partly a cost-cutting tactic,[537] implies both engagement
between regions and their involvement in wider networks. While we do
not see 'cooperative coinage' arrangements between the mid-fourth century and the mid-second, the absence of counter-marking (the addition
of marks subsequent to a coin's first issue in order to re-validate it) before
the mid-second also suggests the widespread acceptance of 'foreign' currency and a consensus about equivalences.[538] If the very sporadic character
of *polis* issues is not an artefact of the archaeological record, the possible
use of itinerant coiners should be noted; it might reflect a similar sharing
of resources and decision-making. On the other hand, since our sample
undoubtedly under-represents the number and size of actual issues, a still
more dynamic picture should probably be conceived; in this connection, a
recent study suggests that the island *polis* of Paros minted at least 10 kg of
bronze per year in the hellenistic period.[539]

Presumably the nearest thing to economic 'growth' that we can identify
is not more efficient production or an increased volume of agricultural or
manufactured outputs, but precisely (*a*) occasional large-scale injections of
cash from outside sources (e.g. kings), as well as on a smaller scale and more
often by traders and mercenaries; and (*b*) the presumed accumulation of
wealth by *polis* elites, resulting from their increasing domination of society.
Clearly there was no radical transformation, such as one might expect if
there was a great influx of bullion to this peninsula; but money from both
sources may have circulated more quickly, not because of monetization as

---

[534] de Callataÿ 2006, 44–5.
[535] Picard 1990.
[536] Grandjean and Nicolet-Pierre 2008.
[537] Mackil and van Alfen 2006, 204 n. 11.
[538] For 'cooperative coinages', see Mackil and van Alfen 2006.
[539] Tully 2014, 31.

such, but chiefly because of increased networking and the greater inter-penetration of *polis* communities, especially at elite level.

Commentators have argued that a major change took place some time after the end of the Macedonian presence in the peninsula in 197, and particularly after the effective consummation of Roman power in 146; and have agreed that an economic decline began (or a further decline took place) at a time when Romans and Italians were intervening in Greek economies in greater numbers, from around the late second century[540] or somewhat later, when the Roman civil wars were in full swing. Yet the minting of coinage was at a much higher level in the later hellenistic period;[541] and monetization is thought to have accelerated in the second century, at the point when the structure of land ownership began to be reorganized in certain places under elite pressure[542] – a change that scholars tend to look on as bad for society, though in light of the rural settlement data (see earlier) this is contestable. It is also said that in the second century Rome did not manage the economic affairs of its Greek allies closely; the eastern Mediterranean remained a separate sphere.[543] If so, any innovations in Peloponnesian coinages may have been generated internally, not as the result of external pressure. On the basis of what has been said about monetization, however, we shall also have to look at the social and economic changes of the 'long third century' to see whether processes that the Romans are thought to have initiated had actually begun earlier. Were they pushing at an open door? Was the door being pushed open, not by them, but by *polis* elites?

Minting shows marked variability in space and time. Specifically, it suggests that Argos, Corinth, Sikyon, Elis, Messene, and a limited number of Argolic and Arkadian *poleis* were among the communities most actively engaged in trade and experiencing the sorts of flows that made coinage advantageous. Conversely, Achaea and Laconia may mostly have used other states' coins. Overall, the evidence points to an active commercial economy, as does the adoption of the lighter Aiginetan standard. Numerous injections of high-value monies can also be identified, though economic innovation – perhaps occurring at a lower level of magnitude than in the eastern kingdoms of the hellenistic world – depended equally on local, presumably elite-led initiatives.

[540] Similarly, Petropoulos 2005a, 26: systematic Italian trade initiatives begin in C2s.
[541] Grandjean 2007, 20–1.
[542] Grandjean 2006, 211; Grandjean 2007, 28.
[543] Picard 2010.

IV.8 Economic Interactions

The evidence of rural survey, epigraphy, urban archaeology, pottery, and coinage adequately rebuts the notion of absolute economic decline. To refine that 'headline' message: we have argued for a slight increase in monetization but no direct evidence of a stimulus to the productive economy; denominations developing through internal evolution, but external benefactions augmenting the supply of silver. We have observed a wide range of building work. The rural economy may fairly be described as active in general; given the positive overall picture, it may be taken as indicating agricultural productivity rather than desperate expansion into marginal areas. There was a slight change in the balance of settlement patterns towards towns, and in some areas (not all) a partial restructuring of land ownership. Finally, traders and producers engaged actively with wider Mediterranean networks.

Consistent with this positive picture, perhaps, are the widely distributed origins of the three best-known Peloponnesian poets of the age: Mnasalkes of Sikyon (third century), one of whose probable epigrams, recently discovered, evokes the landscape of the north-eastern Peloponnese;[544] Alkaios of Messene (*c.* 200),[545] and the remarkable Anyte of Tegea (early third century), noted for introducing nature and animals into the epigrammatic genre.[546] Doubtless the tip of the literary iceberg, they suggest (what we might have assumed *a priori* or inferred from the classical and early hellenistic history of these cities) a well-established culture of *elite education*.[547] The ubiquity of inscribed documentary prose, and the relatively wide distribution of verse epigrams – created and consumed locally if not necessarily composed by local authors – supports that picture.[548] Equally striking is the constellation of Peloponnesian historians, around ten of whom were probably active in the long third century, with *ethnika* including those of Argos, Sikyon, Sparta (or Lakedaimon), Megalopolis, and perhaps more surprisingly Lepreon. Second-century authors from Troizen, Elis, and Tegea extend the geographical spread (TABLE IV.4).

---

[544] Mackail 1906, 317–18; Gow and Page 1965. New epigram (Pergamon, *c.* 230–220): *SEG* 39. 1334, 46. 1590; Kerkhecker 1991; Lehnus 1996.

[545] Mackail 1906, 319; Gow and Page 1965; Cameron and Pelling 2012a with recent bibliography.

[546] Mackail 1906, 311–12; Gow and Page 1965; Gutzwiller 1993; de Cerio Díez 1998b; 1998a; Roy 2009a (C3e date).

[547] Elite education, presumable in any case, is firmly implied for C11 by a list of ephebes from Messenian Asine, *SEG* 57. 365. For *gymnasia*, cf. n. 387.

[548] A selection of those assigned EHl dates would include *SEG* 11. 343 (55. 408; 59. 341; Argos, C3); *SEG* 37. 280 (50. 357; 60. 985; Argos, 303); *SEG* 25. 418 (Epidauros, 218), for Philip V;

Specific evidence, however, points to differences between different areas of the Peloponnese, as we have seen. The evidence of coinage identifies the north-east (Argolis, Corinth, Sikyon), Elis, Messene, and parts of Arkadia as being among the communities actively engaged in trade; the traditional regions not listed are Achaea, Triphylia, Arkadia, and Laconia. Evidence suggestive of urban growth, or at least a net shift of population from country to town, similarly occurs in the north-east, at three Argolic *poleis*, but elsewhere too, at Achaean Dyme and at Sparta. Possible evidence of increased rural estate size comes once again from the north-east, at Argolic *Berbáti*, but also from Arkadian Megalopolis and Messenian Pylos. Thus far, it is perhaps no surprise, given the earlier history and favourable geographical locations of the Argolic cities and those on the gulf of Corinth, that these areas seem most closely integrated into wider Greek networks. Ceramic evidence, on the other hand, points to increasing localism of production in the north-east, while the southern half of the Peloponnese seems to have enjoyed more active overseas links.

Despite these differences, most of the peninsula seems to have been the setting for active trade and construction, as well as experiencing relatively active rural settlement. How did people pay for imports, especially those that reached areas like Laconia and Messenia from distant parts of the eastern Mediterranean; and how did communities pay for building works? Phenomena such as monumental construction, elite benefaction, and mercenary employment imply the short-term and occasional availability of large sums of 'new' money. Some of it will have found its way into the hands of the less well-off; especially if those with disposable wealth spent some of it in marketplaces. If the most reasonable inference is not decline but general well-being – either modest growth or a sustained level of activity – the simplest explanation is that elite and middle-income members of *poleis* were at least as actively involved in commerce as before, if not more so. Such a trend is not directly attested in the sources; but, if real, it would entail that at least some manufacturers were not producing primarily for local consumption.[549] Beyond such generalizations, we cannot yet see whether productive regimes changed, or the status of those 'semi-free' labouring populations whose shadowy existence in some regions may have been a major economic underpinning of civic life (Section III.1).

SEG 30. 391–2 (51. 1508; 54. 1074; Epidauros, post-324), for Gorgos of Iasos; *SEG* 27. 40 (61. 272; Hermion, *c.* 265–255), for an Olympic victor; *SEG* 39. 334 (Corinth, C4l), for Diogenes the Cynic; *SEG* 28. 437 (Dyme, pre-210); *SEG* 47. 390 (51. 477; Messene, C3, perhaps *c.* 210); *SEG* 36. 365 (Sparta, *c.* C4s–C3f); *SEG* 42. 332 (Sparta, *c.* 200).

[549] As Rizakis and Touratsoglou 2011, 20, claim.

Table IV.4. *Peloponnesian historians, C4–C1*

FGrHist no.				
94	ARGOS	Iason	*Περὶ Ἑλλάδος, Ἀρχαιολογία Ἑλλάδος*, etc.	C4s?
131	SIKYON	Menaichmos	History of Alexander's time, *Ὀλυμπιονῖκαι*, etc.	C4l
308	ARGOS	Dionysios	?	C4/C3
306	ARGOS	Deinias	*Ἀργολικά*	C3m
231	SIKYON	Aratos	*Ὑπομνήματα*	C3l
598	SPARTA	Kleomenes III	oration on the constitution ap. Plut. (written by Sphairos?)	C3l
161	MEGALOPOLIS	Ptolemaios	*Περὶ τὸν Φιλοπάτορα*	C3l
176	LAKEDAIMON	Sosylos	wrote on Hannibal	C3l
319	LEPREON	Harmodios	*Περὶ τῶν κατὰ Φιγάλειαν νομιμῶν vel sim.*	C3?
595	LAKEDAIMON	Sosibios the Lakōn	*Χρόνων ἀναγραφή, Περὶ τῶν ἐν Λακεδαίμονι θυσιῶν*, etc.	*c.* C3s–C2f
173	MEGALOPOLIS	**Polybios**	*Ἱστορίαι*, also *Περὶ Φιλοποίμενος, Numidian War*	C2f
838	TROIZEN	Aristotheos	wrote ἐν[κώ]μια εἰς Ῥωμαίους τοὺς κοινοὺς τῶν Ἑλλήνων εὐεργέτας (decree of Delphians)	*c.* 158/7 BC
821	TROIZEN	Zenodotos	Wrote about Rome	*c.* 150 BC
414	ELIS	Aristodemos	Olympic victors' list?	C2c
589	LAKEDAIMON	Molpis the Lakōn	*Λακεδαιμονίων πολιτεία*	C2s/C1f
316	TEGEA	Araithos or Ariaithos	*Ἀρκαδικά*	Hl ('vor Apollodor', Jacoby)
310	ARGOS	Sokrates	*Ἀργολικά* and work on cults	C1
503	SIKYON	Diogenes	*Τὰ περὶ Πελοπόννησον*	Hl?
606	TROIZEN	Hegias	wrote about Herakles	Hl?
591	SPARTA	Aristokrates the Spartiate	*Λακωνικά*	C2 BC–C1 AD
587	LAKEDAIMON	Nikokles the Lakōn	*Λακώνων πολιτεία*	pre-C1m ('vor Didymos', Jacoby)

To pay for imports, they must have offered something in return; and apart from pottery (either as trade good or container) the most obvious object of trade is primary or processed comestibles. Ancient literary sources are notoriously reticent about specific objects of trade, but Thucydides indicates its central importance when he makes the Corinthians warn their allies inland about the threat Athens' naval power poses to the 'bringing down of your seasonal produce' (τὴν κατακομιδὴν τῶν ὡραίων) to the coast with a view to trade (1. 120. 2). If we wish to reconstruct Peloponnesian exports in the early hellenistic period, we have little alternative to extrapolating from the few commodities whose export is specifically known, or inferred, with reference to the classical period. Corinth, for example, was known for its perfumes, bronzes, and textiles among other exports;[550] Arkadia for timber – sometimes handled by Sikyonian middlemen[551] – as well as agricultural produce and medicinal herbs;[552] we may infer that Arkadian textiles were exported; the late archaic poet Pindar refers to woollen cloaks as prizes in a contest at Pellene (*Nem.* 10. 44–5). Perishable items may have been carried in the amphoras manufactured at Corinth and elsewhere (see Section IV.6.b). Beyond that, it is possible that more specialized produce found its way to the wider eastern Mediterranean; one thinks of the rather more luxurious commodities recorded in cargo lists from third-century Egypt, which among other things document wine (in different grades), grape syrup, olive oil, dried figs, honey, cheese, nuts, preserved game, salt fish, sponges, and of course pottery; many of these items are attributed to a specific place though most of the those are in the Aegean and further east.[553] Whether the importation of 'Laconian' (Λακωνικά) fig-shoots to third-century Alexandria (*P. Cairo Zeno* 59839) is evidence of trade with the Peloponnese, however, must be doubtful; the name could simply denote a botanical variety, as in Theophrastos (*Hist. Pl.* 2. 7. 1; 2. 8. 1), rather than a geographical origin.

To this extent, then, Peloponnesian traders and financiers participated successfully in the wider processes of social, economic, and cultural change across the eastern Mediterranean world, characterized by greater trade, connectivity, and exchange.[554] (Further investigation of inter-community networks follows in Chapter V.)

---

[550] Salmon 1984, 117–20, 135–6.

[551] Meiggs 1982, 430–2; Davies 2001, 222.

[552] Roy 1999, 335, 339–40.

[553] See esp. *PCZ* 59012 (n. 530 above).

[554] On possible evidence of 'proto-capitalism' in this period, see Bintliff 2014.

V | Region, Network, and *Polis*

Harmodios the Lepreate, in his work On the Customs among the Phigaleians, *says that the Phigaleians became drink-lovers (φιλοπότας) because they were neighbours of the Messenians and were accustomed to travelling abroad.*

Harmodios of Lepreon (*FGrHist* 319) F 2

V.1 Factors in Change and Stability

V.1.a The Interplay of Continuity and Change

In Chapter II we identified the varying strategies adopted by hegemonic powers – successively Sparta, Thebes, Macedonia, and the Achaean league – in response to two 'eternal questions': how to control the disparate communities of the peninsula, and how to restrain or circumvent the Spartans' perennial desire to dominate their neighbours. Evidence for brutal oppression or violent atrocities relates mostly to the wars of the early Diadochoi; they are not always attributable to Macedonian actors.

Chapter III argued that the Macedonians installed garrisons and supported governors ('tyrants') opportunistically rather than systematically,[1] and that there was broad constitutional continuity. *Stasis* was frequent at times in certain places; but so it had been before. Traditional divisions within *poleis* may have held greater sway over most people's lives than external factors. There was no ideologically based revolutionism or general protest on the part of poor citizens or those without citizen status.

Chapter IV argued that neither Macedonian domination nor warfare, more frequent at certain times than at others, need have had severe or long-lasting economic effects on landscape or population, except in a few places; and that broadly the economic condition of the Peloponnese was sound. It is undeniable that, even leaving aside wartime atrocities, the short- and medium-term effects of external powers' actions or of wars upon

---

[1] Cf. Mackil 2013, 97, EHl kingship as 'improvisational'.

individuals and communities were sometimes grievous. Polybios more than once paints a pessimistic picture (see e.g. Sections III.2.c, IV.1.a), and insists (2. 62) that the movable wealth of the *poleis* in the late third century was much smaller in quantity than another historian, Phylarchos, claimed; possibly he had access to factual data to support these assertions, but it is impossible to concur with his view that the Peloponnese was 'ruined' by a combination of the Macedonians and local warfare. The evidence of rural survey is broadly consistent; in some areas we see no widespread changes in the countryside, though this may sometimes be for lack of data. The data that we do have point to a relative shift of population to towns in certain regions, and a limited increase in the elite domination of land ownership; these trends imply neither economic improvement nor decline. Local factors influence the record strongly. Neither can the large numbers of mercenaries implied and attested for this period be regarded as a negative consequence of Macedonian power or policy. Monumental construction and material culture point to active engagement with the wider world by producers and traders; an interest sometimes manifested in stylistic innovation. Archaeological evidence thus tends to disprove claims of widespread impoverishment; and what some historians have taken as evidence of decline is insubstantial. Finally, the increase in the use of smaller coin denominations in some areas is at least compatible with, and moreover may have promoted, a greater velocity of local market transactions, tending to contradict the idea that the Peloponnesian economies were severely degraded.

This summary of Chapters II–IV has highlighted discontinuity in hegemonic control; the limited effects of Macedonian domination and of warfare; the importance of city-state politics; and the relatively positive state of Peloponnesian economies though with variations between *poleis*, regions, and in some cases wider geographical units.

The remainder of this chapter considers why continuity and perhaps modest improvement – rather than radical change or, as some have claimed, economic and social ruin – were the salient features of the early hellenistic Peloponnese. To try to understand possible factors promoting or inhibiting change, the discussion focuses on the peninsula as a natural and human landscape, considering the different spatial scales at which change and continuity may have been manifested, how spatial units at those several scales are constituted, and how they interacted.

We focus first on the extent to which the attainment of Macedonian goals – which, as we have already seen (Sections II.6, III.3.c, III.4), were somewhat circumscribed – may have been blunted by geography, tradition, and the decisions of political communities. After re-examining the limits of change, the evolution of Macedonian strategy, and the ways in which landscapes and traditions may have obstructed attempts to impose change from above, we turn to a more positive agendum: how did the Peloponnese work, and how might this account for its development? To this end, we consider (V.2) the relative importance of local, *polis*-based, regional, and Peloponnesian identities and frames of action, and enquire whether a regional analysis correlates significantly with patterns of development. Having explored the limits of regionalism, we turn (V.3) to relationships between *poleis* and the importance of intra- and inter-regional communications. The Conclusion (V.4) considers how the continuing primacy of the *polis* can be accounted for by the social and political complexion of Peloponnesian societies. In some areas of activity it is likely to have been a community's elite (whether constituted by property ownership or by economic activity), or a subset of it, that initiated responses to forces bearing upon the community, including actions in relation to communities and regions outside their own.

V.1.b Macedonian Aims

A narrative résumé will help us focus on the nature, and changing character, of the Macedonians' approach to the Peloponnese, and on the limits of their power and goals.

Philip II and Alexander III principally sought acknowledgement of their status as hegemon, undertakings of loyalty from the Greeks for the sake of stability, and support for their campaign in Asia. They and their governors seem to have been concerned chiefly to create a solid platform of support, for example, by requiring the expulsion or readmission of certain men. But interaction of Macedonian power with Peloponnesian communities was not a unipolar, one-way encounter: the model of 'delegated power at a distance' required *poleis* to contribute and consent, and thus issues of external relations needed to be sorted out through internal *polis* politics.

That consent, moreover, was not universal. The refusal of many communities to accept Philip II's settlement as final led to repressive measures by Antipater, though some of these were abrogated by Polyperchon. The wars of the early Successors inflicted severe damage on parts of the Peloponnese, but were less about establishing imperial or colonial rule than about using the peninsula as a springboard for assaults on Macedonia. They gave rise to a situation in which cities had to steer a dangerous course between competing warlords, with a high expectation that calamity might ensue. Some commanders, however, modified their approach in the light of changing circumstances.

The establishment of Antigonos II Gonatas' dominance obviated, for the most part, the need for *poleis* to walk a tight-rope, though the Pyrrhos–Kleonymos episode should not be forgotten and the Ptolemies at times competed for the loyalty of communities. The Antigonids seem to have wanted above all to prevent trouble arising in the Peloponnese. This may explain why the refoundation and initial expansion of the Achaean league appear to have elicited no military response from Macedonia. Even a generation later, Gonatas' first reaction to the overthrow of 'his man' in Sikyon was not to attack the league but to try to corrupt the city's new leader, Aratos. His response suggests a non-ideological, ad hoc strategy based on separate relationships with individuals and communities; not an overall design.

Despite Gonatas' victory in the Chremonidean war, it is unclear whether he was able to tighten his hold upon the northern Peloponnese during the 250s. The negative effect, from his point of view, of the independence of Corinth – intermittent from 251, more enduring from 243[2] – was exacerbated by the accessions of Epidauros, Megara, and Troizen to the league, further dividing the Macedonians' stronghold in Attica from their friends in the north-eastern Peloponnese and Megalopolis.[3] Gonatas' successor, Demetrios II, may have been able to reassert some degree of influence by supporting *polis* governors; after his death in 229, however, the Achaean league effectively excluded the Macedonians from the Peloponnese for several years.

The resurgence of Sparta under Kleomenes III gave Antigonos III Doson the chance to build a relationship with the Achaeans, adopting a new form of 'delegated power at a distance'. The battle of Sellasia opened a new phase in the Macedonian relationship with the Peloponnese, as Philip V took over Doson's new Hellenic alliance and adopted, for a time, a protective role towards his allies; garrisons were more likely to be installed by his opponents than by him. The last years of the Macedonian presence saw further cooperation with the Achaeans, more limited intervention by the hegemonic power (once Philip had been warned off Messene), but eventually his exclusion by the Romans. The league was his principal and last ally; yet, as the preceding chapters show, Tarn is wrong to regard the league in this era as 'a bit of the Macedonian empire broken off and fitted with a new constitution',[4] on the grounds that each of its main cities had one or more

---

[2] It lasted until the forging of the Achaean–Macedonian pact in 224. Walbank 1984a, 251.
[3] Walbank 1984a, 251.
[4] Tarn 1913, 407.

Macedonian-sponsored tyrants. The Achaeans were their own men, capable of flexibility in choosing and dropping partners.

The Macedonians' domination of southern Greece was not seamless in time; for even where their power was brought to bear, its operation was interrupted at several junctures. Neither was its operation spatially continuous: in Attica, for example, the kings at times controlled the Piraeus without controlling Athens, and did not always hold the fortified outlying demes; while in the Peloponnese, from their base in Corinth their power radiated only part-way across the peninsula.

Although the kings responded forcefully to successive attacks, they do not appear to have had plans to take over the Peloponnese – in any case an unachievable aspiration, as we shall argue (Section V.1.c). They seem to have been largely reactive, intervening only when attacked or when an ally was attacked; doing what was needful to ensure that the peninsula was not a hotbed of unrest.[5] Neither did the kings actively seek the obliteration of Sparta. Only when the successes of Kleomenes III threatened to weaken the Achaean league and recreate Sparta's Peloponnesian hegemony did Doson commit an army;[6] even then he did not destroy Sparta, whose continued existence allowed a 'divide and rule' strategy to be pursued, but also may have been measured against a humane criterion relating to the kings' desire to be the patrons of Hellenism. The fact that in the early years of Philip V's reign his guardian, Apelles, is said to have wished to reduce the Achaeans to the condition of the Thessalians (Polybios 4. 76) shows that a difference was seen to exist between the levels of control exercised in the two areas;[7] and the very fact that Apelles was prevented from doing so (5. 1) is a sign of the king's desire to act as protective patron rather than imperial overlord. Polybios alleges a psychological change in Philip's conduct after the Social war; be that as it may, it seems that once he was deeply embroiled in the renewed struggle of the Achaeans against Sparta, Elis, Aitolia, and later Rome, he was the first Macedonian for nearly a century to try to reshape the political geography of the peninsula.

While the dominant group in the Corinthian elite seems to have been consistently pro-Macedonian,[8] Antigonid policy does not appear to have aimed at building a new social order at Corinth, or at creating a cultural bloc of wider geographical scope in which elites would identify the interests

---

[5] Similarly, Rostovtzeff 1941, 36; Walbank 1992, 91.

[6] On Gonatas' 'wary neutrality' towards the Aitolian and Achaean leagues in the 240s, see Walbank 1984a, 255.

[7] See Griffith 1979, 259–95, for close Macedonian control and taxation of Thessaly in C4s.

[8] Dixon 2014, e.g. 199–200.

of Macedonia as their own. Macedonian rule was not usually, perhaps never, totalitarian in character. There is, for example, no evidence of any attempt to foster ruler-worship of the kind seen elsewhere in the early hellenistic period. We see no systematic attempt to force *poleis* to change constitution, as had happened repeatedly in the late fourth century. Macedonian-style bureaucracy was not imposed; the map of land ownership was not redrawn, and there is no evidence of grants of communities and their revenues to the king's friends (as in parts of Seleukid Asia Minor)[9] or of land to veterans (as in western Achaea and north-western Greece following the Roman civil wars of the first century BC). We have also seen that Antigonid policy was not, or not primarily, economic in intention. Furthermore, although the Peloponnese was not in decline or ruined, the relatively modest scale of its resources would have minimized any temptation the Macedonians might have felt towards interventionism. If control of Corinth brought in revenue, that will have been a bonus; but without direct evidence it would be unwise to situate Macedonian concern for Corinth purely or primarily in economic motives.[10]

Thus the Peloponnese should not be thought of as a Macedonian province, let alone a 'possession' or even a 'back yard' like Thessaly. Except, perhaps, during the wars between the early Diadochoi, it was important less for its resources than in relation to the security of Macedonia and in relation to the kings' wider geostrategic concerns. Thus, first, the repeated phenomenon of commanders and kings abandoning campaigns here for urgent business in the North (Section II.6) shows where the Peloponnese ranked among their ultimate priorities. Second, keeping the lid on southern Greece was part of a grander strategy of ensuring that the events on Macedonia's southern flank would not distract the ruler from his overriding aim: that of facing down the Seleukids and Ptolemies in Asia Minor and the Aegean. Control of the Isthmus, and through it as much of the Peloponnese as was feasible, or rather necessary, was not only a means of preventing internal disruption within, or on the borders of, territory that the Macedonians wished to keep in a placid state. It was also a means of preventing other powers, principally the Ptolemies, from gaining access to central Greece. To protect the strongpoint of Corinth, it was necessary to exert some pressure upon the adjoining regions of Sikyonia, Argolis, and Achaea, though this did not require the imposition of direct rule. It was useful to leave Sparta in existence (as Philip II had) in order to keep its

---

[9]   Bresson 2016, 150, also finds no evidence of land grants by Macedonian rulers in S. Greece.
[10]   On the importance of Corinth to Macedonian strategy, see e.g. Walbank 1984a, 230.

neighbours in line. There is little evidence, however, that Gonatas deployed significant naval power specifically against places in the Peloponnese; it was aimed, rather, against the Ptolemaic fleet based in the Aegean and (from the 260s) at Methana. Since Gonatas and his two successors had bigger fish to fry than the often unruly Peloponnesians, subjection to Macedonia was not an immediate danger to all communities at all times; only sporadically, and mainly in the north. *A fortiori*, the risk of domination by more distant powers (e.g. Aitolia, the Ptolemies, Epirus, or Illyria) was still more limited, while other major players in the early hellenistic firmament (Pergamon, the Seleukid empire) scarcely feature in events. Even the Ptolemies, relatively active in this part of the Greek world, appear to have had no real desire to capture the Peloponnese, but rather sought to distract the Antigonids by exploiting pressure-points such as Methana and the Cycladic islands.[11]

The unnecessary application of force at a great distance could be costly and self-defeating. An external power was better advised to work with each community – usually, perhaps invariably, through its elite – and to pay careful attention to assembly politics, the need for effective rhetoric, and so on. Thus Macedonian aims were necessarily adapted to circumstances, like the geographical focus or focuses of their activity at any given time. Phases of harsher and milder treatment, therefore, do not simply correspond to the differing personalities of commanders; most of them modified their policy at least once in areas such as *polis* constitutions, garrisons, and military collaboration.

Limited though Macedonian aims were, they were not without impacts. We shall consider presently some further reasons why those impacts were not more severe; first, we may note that the action of Macedonian power was not just a one-way process but depended on the choices made by a local community. Alignment with, or dependence upon, an external or internal power (Macedonia, Egypt, the Achaean league) may not have been without its advantages, though obviously the same was not true when this power was an aggressive one such as the Aitolian league. In cases such as Macedonia or Egypt, however, subordination to or alignment with a foreign power, be it temporary or permanent, could bring benefits to a *polis* or *koinon* in terms of stability, though it might favour one group of citizens over others. Thus, for example, the Ptolemaic takeover of Methana (Section II.4.c), which must previously have been independent (since it minted its own coins in the late fourth and early third centuries) and which is perhaps connected with the Chremonidean war, may have constrained local

---

[11] See generally Bagnall 1976.

politics; the town, now renamed Arsinoë, probably gained protection against Argos. Even changing the time-hallowed name of a *polis*, as when Sikyon became Demetrias under Demetrios I and Mantinea was redesignated Antigoneia by Doson, may have seemed to some a price worth paying. Diodoros (20. 102. 2) says the name Demetrias did not prove permanent; but the name Antigoneia lasted into the Roman period.[12] Even in economic terms, while the presence of a garrison might impose a cost upon the rich and any others to whom they passed this on, the presence of soldiers with money to spend may also have stimulated a local economy. Finally, as well as ensuring protection for a *polis* or a group within it, the renaming of a city in honour of a king or his relative may sometimes have been accompanied by royal funding for building initiatives; to this extent, culturally and economically, the loss of freedom could be mitigated.

V.1.c A Resistant Landscape

As already hinted, the attainment of even the limited goals of the Macedonians was blunted; alternatively, they were scaled down to reflect the potential difficulty of managing, let alone micro-managing, the Peloponnese and the limited rewards to be expected from such efforts. Their strategy may have evolved to reflect this. As already noted, action at a distance poses difficulties for hegemonic states. The most obvious factor militating against close Macedonian control was the sheer distance from the river Peneios (their frontier with Thessaly) to Corinth, which even by modern roads is 290 miles (470 km), a march of many days – ancient armies usually moved slowly.[13] The effect of distance was partly offset by possession of Acrocorinth; but that stronghold is perhaps to be seen as important chiefly as a link in maritime, not terrestrial, communications, Corinth being the southernmost in a chain of garrisoned harbour cities, the 'Fetters' (Section II.3.c). In a sense the control of harbours shortens distances: Pseudo-Skylax (56–65) implies a sailing distance from Corinth to the northern limit of Thessaly of some 2,000 stades (*c.* 250 mi, *c.* 400 km), which might be covered in as little as two days and two nights in ideal conditions. The Macedonian foothold in the Peloponnese thus takes on a more 'Aegean-facing' aspect; control of Corinth is not necessarily evidence of an intention to manage the Peloponnese closely.

---

[12] Antigoneia: Rhodes 1997, 87 (AD 125).

[13] Campbell 2009, 200–3, argues for an average of *c.* 9 mi (14 km) per day for a Hl army.

None of the post-Alexander kingdoms, not even Macedonia, was in a position to contemplate close management of the Peloponnese or its tight integration into a structure of domination. Egypt is much further away than Macedonia, though Libya is only *c.* 260 miles (*c.* 420 km) from the south-eastern extremity of Laconia; a few days' sailing broken by convenient landfall in western Crete. The Seleukid and Pergamene centres in Asia Minor were closer than Egypt – the list of distances appended to Pseudo-Skylax's *periplous* (113)[14] gives the crossing from Cape Malea via Crete to Rhodes as around 4,000 stades (*c.* 450 mi, *c.* 700 km) or a week's voyage; that from Attica to Mykale as shorter, around 2,400 stades (*c.* 270 mi, *c.* 420 km) or four to five days – but between them and the Peloponnese lay a plethora of 'goodly states and islands'. Moreover, the Peloponnese was not one of the, as it were, seismic zones of tectonic plate collision between Pergamon and the Seleukid empire on the one hand and Macedonia on the other; those lay rather in Thrace, the northern Aegean, and east-central Greece. More direct threats were posed from across the gulf of Corinth by Aitolia, and by Epeiros and Illyria beyond it; Polybios, as we saw (Section IV.2.a), comments on the perennial vulnerability of the north-western Peloponnese to raiding from west-central Greece. Yet even these proximate dangers were mitigated by the size of the Peloponnese and by the nature of its landscapes and societies. The actions of nearby non-Peloponnesian states also had the potential to impede Macedonian ambitions in the Peloponnese. Relations with Achaea became of critical importance after the Aitolians, habitually anti-Macedonian, took control of the Delphic amphiktyony in 277 and then – after taking the allied side in the Chremonidean war of the 260s[15] – extended their sphere of influence east to the Malian gulf,[16] which gave them the power to obstruct land travel down the east coast of Greece.[17] This redoubled the importance to Gonatas of the 'Fetters'.

Distances within the Peloponnese meant that the costs and uncertainties of any military intervention would increase rapidly the further a scene of action lay from Corinth. In the mid-fourth century, the distance from Boiotia to western Arkadia had presented an ultimately insuperable difficulty for the Thebans. Even from the Macedonian strongholds of Piraeus and Acrocorinth, much of the Peloponnese was not only at an inconvenient distance but also topographically difficult of access. In round numbers, the Peloponnese has a maximum north–south extent of 140 miles (220 km);

---

[14] Possibly nearly contemporary with the main text, written in the 330s. Shipley 2011, 201–11.
[15] Walbank 1984a, 241–2.
[16] Walbank 1984a, 234.
[17] Cf. Martinez-Sève 2011, 24–5, maps for 260, 246, and 222 BC.

roughly the same from west to east. Its longest dimension is on the diagonal: 160 miles (255 km) from Cape Araxos in the north-west to Cape Malea in the south-east; even the shorter diagonal, from the Isthmus to Cape Akritas in Messenia, is 110 miles (175 km). These figures, however, take no account of dissected relief, which made road distances considerably longer. A table of estimated travel times for the Roman period shows that the Peloponnese was a larger space than today; the journey on foot from Mothone to Corinth taking over a week, that from Patrai to Boiai up to two.[18] Under these conditions, one may readily understand why the forced march of Philip V's army in 218, which reached Sparta only four days after leaving the island of Leukas, stunned his enemies (Polyb. 5. 18).[19]

The influence of distance is not constant: it depends where the centres of power lie. With reference to the late Bronze Age, with Minoan power intruding at Kythera and major Mycenaean 'palace' centres in Argolis, Messenia, and possibly Laconia, one might define different places as 'remote'; Arkadia, for example. In classical times, with wealth from Greek trade flowing mainly into Athens and Corinth, one could have viewed Eleia with its single main harbour, subjugated Messenia, and near-landlocked Laconia as remote. Spartan interventions in Eleia were rare. In our period, the relative isolation of Messene from the Isthmus seems to have spared it a deal of trouble. We may speculate that the distance of Patrai and its neighbours from Corinth may explain why it was the westernmost Achaean *poleis*, rather than the eastern, that revived their league at the end of the 280s – possibly deposing Macedonian-supported governors (Chapter III) – and why Gonatas does not seem to have responded with force despite the relative weakness of these *poleis*. The remoteness of the towns of the Malea peninsula and western Messenia from their respective regional centres stands out clearly. In principle, one might suppose that these areas of the far south would have benefited less from the economic opportunities created by Alexander's conquests in the wider eastern Mediterranean than the possibly more cosmopolitan centres along the gulf of Corinth. But they were also, in principle, hard to control from Corinth with the toolkit available to early hellenistic commanders; and remoteness can be overcome by active movement. The other side of the coin for these places was their proximity to

---

[18] Sanders and Whitbread 1990, 347 table 5 (based on Peutinger Table): Corinth–Mothone 2,760 minutes or 8 days (at 6 h walking per day); Boiai–Patrai 4,700 minutes or 13 days. Another working of the data: Shipley 2008a, 59 fig. 1.

[19] To discussion at Shipley 2008a, 60 and n., I would add that Polyb. specifies that Philip reached Lechaion the day after he sailed from Leukas, and Sparta after 4 days' march (1–2 days faster than the Peutinger Table implies for Corinth–Sparta).

alternative centres of power and trade; or to places on the way to such centres. For Laconians, for example, Crete served as a stepping-stone to Rhodes and Alexandria. (See Sections IV.6.a–b for evidence of extra-Peloponnesian trade links.) Pseudo-Skylax appreciates this special relationship, interrupting his coastwise circuit of the Peloponnese, after describing Lakedaimon, with a detour to Crete and the Cyclades (47–8) before resuming with Argolis. We have seen that these eastern contacts are reflected in a flow of third-century innovations in material culture (Section IV.6.b).

Local rivalries, such as between Tegea and Mantinea, will have made management yet more difficult (see further Section V.3.a). Local memory – the sense of 'how we do things here' – probably acted as a powerful brake upon external interference – except, perhaps, in the rare cases where most or all of a *polis*'s population was replaced by new settlers. Constitutions tended to revert to their customary form; if there was lasting change, it was either secured by external force or tended to mask essentially unaltered social relations. Such conservatism was not, of course, hard-wired into the minds of the citizens. It was, we must suppose, maintained and continually reinforced at the level of intra- and inter-community relationships. More intangibly, the strength of local tradition was an inhibiting factor upon any intended exercise of power, especially given the other constraints upon kings' actions. One such was the deep-rooted (and probably intensifying) domination of *polis* politics by the elite;[20] we see this with particular clarity in the Achaean league.[21] This domination may have made it harder to impose by force a widespread reshaping of constitutions. The opportunistic rather than systematic use of local governors shows that some Macedonians saw the wisdom of working with rather than against the grain of political societies, in contrast to some of Alexander's immediate successors.

It might be supposed that federalism was the most important political feature of the Greek states in this period, and that it represented – particularly in its Achaean incarnation – a valiant effort to shore up the city-states system by providing a counterweight to the post-Alexander kingdoms, especially Macedonia and the growing power of the Achaean league.[22] From that position it would be a logical step to assume that federalism minimized the political, social, and economic impacts of external power. If, however, Macedonian aims were limited to begin with, it may not be the case that the

---

[20] O'Neil 1995, 114–16. This seems more secure than his claim (116–19) that poor citizens were less active in democracy than before. Cf. n. 48 below.

[21] O'Neil 1984–6.

[22] The starting-point for a study of federalism is now Beck and Funke 2015; several of its chapters are cited in the present work.

Achaean league was, as a consequence of its policies, responsible for the preponderance of continuity over change. The league was, after all, powerful
for less than half the duration of our study period. If it was to any degree
responsible for damping down change, it may have been so only because of a
more general characteristic of *polis* society; a feature of their persisting socio-
economic make-up leading the elites in different *poleis* to cooperate in preserving their social position and power. One could equally make a case for
seeing the Achaean league as an active, rather than purely reactive, force. We
have already commented on the league's possible role in inhibiting change;
but it may be that the league was not simply designed, and run by its leaders,
in order to preserve, but to effect change – to take power away from the
Macedonians; later, to neutralize Sparta; additionally, and later still, to draw
a geopolitical map of a kind not seen before.[23] Later in this chapter, we shall
attempt to show at which level or levels the leaders of *poleis* were most active,
and in what community's interests they were pursuing their ambitions.

In short, the Macedonians' capacity for effective action was limited by factors
such as distance, relief, local relationships, and perhaps most importantly *polis*
tradition (the last proactively maintained and contested through internal *polis*
politics) and sometimes the active policies of leagues. Viewing the history in
terms of geography and space allows us to see more clearly that the effects of
external power were different at different times, and that the Macedonians'
aims were limited by several factors: their wider strategic interests; the relative
lack of any economic incentive to expend substantial resources and manpower
in the Peloponnese; and obstacles, both geographical and social, that would
have made any attempt at root-and-branch change impracticable. It is not,
therefore, a case simply of 'natural' resistivity in landscape and society; there
was active self-determination by the subordinate community.

V.2 A Peloponnese of the Regions?

The Peloponnese was rarely quiet, despite alternating phases of harsher and
milder rule on the part of hegemonic powers responding to the two 'eternal
questions': how to control the Peloponnese, and how to block Spartan ambition. Despite this near-continuous stress, we see broad continuity in politics as well as in landscapes, demography, and economy. Whereas studies
of the hellenistic period habitually assume that there were fundamental

---

[23] Kralli 2017, 149, 495–6 (citing Walbank 1984b, 459), judges that the league expanded too
   rapidly for techniques of harmonious integration or skilful leadership to be developed.

shifts in culture and society after Chaironeia, the present investigation has shown that, with local exceptions, there was probably no radical or lasting upheaval. Indeed, the picture that emerges is relatively positive. Other than by the top-down application of power and resistance to it, in what ways can we account for the balance between change and continuity? Having established the limits of Macedonian strategy and why its impacts were limited, we may turn to possible explanations of change and continuity in more dynamic terms. Having raised the question of elite initiative at a level above their *polis*, we may ask to what extent developments were influenced by regional processes. Might additional features of the 'long third century' be revealed if we considered the peninsula as a set of regions?

V.2.a The Contribution of Scale

In examining this interplay of forces it may be helpful to consider four spatial scales: peninsula, region, *polis*, and locality. The simplistic presentation in some modern works, implying that the period was entirely dominated by the rise of the 'leagues', raises the question of the scale or scales at which change or continuity can be observed. Historians have tended to think at the widest scale by default – for example, in terms of spatially undifferentiated effects of Macedonian oppression upon the Peloponnese – and consider smaller-scale processes only in passing. One may easily conceive, however, that both change and continuity could be accounted for by the internal dynamics between peninsula, region, *polis*, and sub-*polis* locality; or a combination of two or more of these.

A particular feature of the narrative is the interplay between *polis* and region. The actions of a *polis* were sometimes subsumed within collective action by a group of *poleis*; the most important such association, the Achaean league in its enlarged form, altogether transcending definition as a culture region. In the preceding chapters, we have often grouped the data according to the traditional regions; but if we are to consider whether regions were active entities expressing processes of change, or conservatism, not seen at *polis* level, we need to clarify what we mean by a region, and what questions it is legitimate to pose about development at this scale.

'Region', of course, corresponds to no particular Greek word but is a modern tool of analysis, one that can seem frustratingly slippery: definitions of the term itself, and of related terms, are contested, as is their utility.[24]

---

[24] See e.g. R. J. Johnston 1996; 1991, esp. 132. I do not have in mind the sense of 'region' often seen in political science, that of a legally constituted territorial division of a nation state whose

In principle, dividing a study area into regions (whether empirical or theoretical) may help to clarify processes of change.[25] It is often a problem,
however, to know where to set boundaries between regions as defined –
a question rarely confronted in the study of ancient history.[26] There is no
essence of the term 'region' that tells us how large the area so defined should
be.[27] What is the most useful scale at which to divide a landscape into parts
and ask the geographer's classic question, 'why do places differ'?[28] A serviceable definition of a region may be *one of a set of bounded parts of a spatial entity* (a region, in other words, representing the highest or 'first' level
of division) *which may itself be divided into smaller entities* ('second-level'
subdivisions, or sub-regions). The size of a region may defined in relation
to the particular inquiry.[29] When considering the Peloponnese within a
larger entity such as the Roman province of Achaia, one would be justified in writing of the whole peninsula as a 'region'; for present purposes,
when we are trying to understand how the peninsula works in its entirety,
it is more appropriate to use 'region' for its first-level divisions. (In a
broad sense, 'region' is rightly almost as flexible as 'place' – a term some
geographers prefer,[30] perhaps because it is more indeterminate and value-
free. It is more useful, however, to regard 'places' as non-contiguous loci of
attachment, 'fields of care', connected by the 'spaces' between them.[31] For
present purposes, 'region' is more useful.)

It emerges from our definitional exercise that, in an investigation of
the Peloponnese as a whole, it is essential to consider its regions in relation to one another, but also as potentially containing dynamic interaction
between their internal components. At any of our four levels (locality, *polis*,
region, peninsula), the components of a division will in principle influence

interests are often at odds with the central power of the state – a phenomenon that cannot
be imagined in the pre-R Peloponnese. Nor do I have in mind the use of 'region' and its
derivatives familiar from works on economic planning at the level of 'developing' states.

[25] Cf. Elton and Reger 2007a, 13: 'a region that looks perfectly stable at a given time […] need not
stay that way'.

[26] A welcome exception is Elton and Reger 2007b on Asia Minor (cf. n. 25 above). There is little
discussion of regionalism as such in Horden and Purcell 2000.

[27] In one recent publication, different authors write of a 'dry region' of Laconia (Rackham 2002,
115), 'the Pylos region' within prehistoric Messenia (Cavanagh and Crouwel 2002, 149), 'the
survey region' itself (R. W. V. Catling 2002, 153), 'the wider region of Laconia and Messenia'
(R. W. V. Catling 2002, 163), and the south-eastern 'region' of the survey area (Shipley 2002d,
164). There is no necessary inconsistency here.

[28] See e.g. R. J. Johnston 1991, 131, 133, 145.

[29] Elton and Reger 2007a, 13.

[30] R. J. Johnston 1991, 132.

[31] Tuan 1974, 241–5. The concept of 'field of care', regrettably, was not taken over into the book of
the same title, Tuan 1977.

each other and thus modify the impact of the unit of which they form part upon units at the adjacent level above or below; influencing the situation in an upward as well as a downward direction.

Our earlier geographical overview (Section I.2.b) shows that in terms of population and territory certain centres had, in principle, the capacity to dominate others. (See TABLE I.1.) There were about seven major *poleis*: in *periplous* order Argos, Corinth, Sikyon, Elis, Megalopolis, Messene, and Sparta. A second tier comprises around a further thirteen; the list cannot be authoritative but might include three in Argolis (Epidauros, Troizen, and Phleious because of its numismatic tradition and despite its small *chōra*), three in Achaea (Dyme, Pellene, and perhaps Aigion), and from three to seven in Arkadia (Heraia, Mantinea, and Tegea, as well as perhaps Pheneos, Psophis, Kleitor with its large *chōra* and numismatic tradition, and Stymphalos with a small *chōra* but new urban plan). The total estimated area of the *chōrai* of the 'Big Seven' is around 2,300 sq mi (6,000 sq km), nearly 30 per cent of the land mass of the Peloponnese; much of the rest being mountainous terrain, some perhaps belonging to no *polis*. The territories of the next thirteen *poleis* add up to roughly 1,500 to 1,900 sq mi (3,800–4,800 sq km), though probably nearer the lower figure.

Size of *chōra* is not, of course, an adequate measure of a *polis*'s importance. Sometimes the correspondence seems clear: Achaea's *poleis* probably had the smallest total *chōra* of those of any region, and neither any individual *polis* nor the entire *koinon* was ever powerful before the second half of the third century. On the other hand, a *polis* might punch above its weight because of its relationships or special advantages in location or resources. Some *poleis* wielded greater influence than their territory would seem to warrant, such as Corinth and Sikyon; no doubt because of trade factors. Others gained influence from their role in a region: Messene may have acted as hegemon over other *poleis* in its region; we hear little of them, and the region appears to have become rather strongly unified. Sparta spoke for a perioikic community occupying several thousand square kilometres; even after the repeated losses of borderlands in and after the 360s, a tightly knit regional community could mobilize great power.

Not all political–military blocs were co-extensive with traditional culture regions: the Achaeans became powerful only when their *koinon* transcended its ancestral geographical, cultural, and even ethnic boundaries; first incorporating, and then being dominated by, non-Achaean *poleis* such as Dorian Sikyon and Arkadian Megalopolis. Even the Arkadians, with their vast total *chōra*, wielded power as a regional entity only briefly; individual large or medium-sized Arkadian *poleis* more often affecting the course of events. Moreover, the traditional ethnic regions are not the only potential explanatory divisions of the peninsula: the coinage record (see Section IV.7.c) suggests that the north-east was particularly strong in economic terms; partly perhaps in virtue of its many harbours located on major shipping routes.

So we have particularly strong *poleis*, an influential 'top twenty'; but across the range of settlement sizes a variety of *poleis* acting singly or in concert. As often, the initiatives and relationships that promoted change and continuity will usually have lain with *polis* elites or groups within them; or, in the case of a league, with its leading men. The latter tended to be drawn from the leading *poleis*, and may have represented their own community's interests as much as, or more than, those of the association in which they held office.[32]

V.2.b Peloponnesian Identity

What degree of unity did the Peloponnese possess? As a peninsula, it lends itself to being treated as an entity for some purposes; but in pre-Roman sources its unity is usually implied, or asserted, only in passing.

The Spartans, during the period of their hegemony, had sometimes attempted to foster a pan-Peloponnesian identity. This was, at least sometimes, more political than ethnic: 'Peloponnesians' could include any allies of the Lakedaimonians ('members of the Peloponnesian league' in scholarly parlance), whether inside or outside the peninsula.[33] This over-arching identity may have been seen as serving the Spartans' own interests and was rarely articulated except when it was deemed that security required urgent joint action,[34] as in 480–479. No other 'supra-region' of Greece gave rise even to this degree of collective identity.[35]

Perhaps unsurprisingly, given the Spartans' role in the matter, expressions of Peloponnesian identity appear to have become less frequent, in contrast to those in Sicily or Italia (Greek southern Italy).[36] No author before Strabo (see Section I.1.b), indeed, attempts to characterize the Peloponnese as an entity. Instead, it is treated as a group of highly differentiated ethno-regional units occupying contiguous spaces, which in turn form parts of Hellas. Thus Pseudo-Skylax, describing the coastal areas of the world accessible to

---

[32] O'Neil 1984–6; O'Neil 1995, 114–16.
[33] de Sainte Croix 1972b, 103, 104, and esp. 188.
[34] Pretzler n.d. [2008].
[35] Vlassopoulos n.d. [2008].
[36] Vlassopoulos n.d. [2008].

the Greeks, makes two passing allusions to the Peloponnese as a unity, but does not let this distract him from his primary schema in which the world accessible to the Greeks was composed of regions made up of *poleis* – the regions being defined either ethnically or politically, as in this extract:[37]

> (40) From here begins the Peloponnese. … (41) And after Corinth is Sikyon, a *polis*. … (42) And after Sikyon the Achaeans, an *ethnos* … (55) And after Epidauros is the territory of the Corinthians … and the Isthmus … Here the Peloponnese ends. And the Corinthians also have territory outside the Isthmus.

(Note that in this representation part of Korinthia is outside the Peloponnese.) Modern studies are generally based upon one or more of these conventional regions. Only Argolis is presented by Pseudo-Skylax as a plurality of separate *poleis* each with its own *chōra* (see Section I.2.b).

In the absence of a strong sense of Peloponnesian identity before the Imperial period, we may regard Plutarch's statement (*Ag.–Kl.* 37. 2) that Kleomenes III was trying to 'restore' the greatness of the Peloponnese as mildly anachronistic; the king himself might not have put it in those terms, other than perhaps for rhetorical purposes.

In contrast to the final phase of Sparta's classical hegemony, expressions of Peloponnesian unity are less apparent in the literary evidence than are those of regional identities. But how strongly did those regional identities influence behaviour and development, as compared with *polis* identities?

V.2.c Regional Unity and Inter-relatedness

We next examine how the traditional regions were constituted; then their inter-relationships. In using the culture regions as units of analysis, we are imposing a certain artificiality by juxtaposing areas that may have had different degrees or kinds of unity, or none. That being so, do regions display distinctive characteristics or follow unitary trajectories? Did they influence one another? To describe the landscape thus is not to subscribe to geographical determinism, except in a negative sense; landscape inhibits historical change or facilitates it but does not, in the usual sense of the word, *cause* it.

Some of the traditional regions have 'natural' boundaries defined by terrestrial features; others are less obviously demarcated, or less obviously

---

[37] On the Peloponnesian chapters, see Shipley 2011, 118–24, 128–31.

united (see Section I.2.a). Politically, too, regions varied in their degree of unity:

(*a*) Some regions were inherently indivisible, having but one *polis*; but these were of small extent, namely Korinthia and Sikyonia, which remained separate throughout our period (though in the early fourth century Corinth briefly combined with Argos to form a single *polis*). Their permanent separation is remarkable, given that they are in full view of one another, and separated by no more prominent feature than the river Nemea, a seasonal torrent. Both were regarded as belonging to the Dorian *ethnos*.

(*b*) In some multi-*polis* regions, political unity was intermittent or incomplete. In Argolis, the components were strongly united only at certain periods, and although the geographical term Argolis could include the dissected and mountainous Akte peninsula, Argive political identity (expressed by the ethnic Ἀργεῖος–*Argeios*) was never extended to all the people of the region.[38] Argos itself, in the western plain, does not seem normally to have controlled the Akte, parts of which looked away from it towards the Saronic gulf. Pseudo-Skylax, as we saw earlier (Section I.2.b), simply divides the Akte between different *poleis*, not bringing them together under any ethnonym or regional name: first Argos, including 'in it' coastal Nauplia and 'in the interior' Kleonai, Mycenae, and Tiryns (49), evidently as dependencies; then Epidauros (50. 1; 54), Halieis (50. 2), Hermion (51. 1), Troizen (52. 1), and Kalaureia (52. 2).

(*c*) Some multi-*polis* regions were politically more homogeneous, at least in certain periods; no particular *polis* or *poleis* standing out as dominant and a 'flat' set of relationships prevailing. Such is the case with, for example, Achaea, even though certain *poleis* were larger or more powerful at certain periods (such as Pellene). The 'flatness' is expressed by, for example, the choice of a roughly central, rather than powerful, city to house the common sanctuary: probably Helike down to its destruction in 373, thereafter Aigion.[39] On the other hand, in the era of the first Achaean league in the fifth century, it appears that more powerful Achaean *poleis*, such as Patrai and Pellene, could act independently on occasion (Thuc. 2. 9. 2; 5. 52. 2).[40]

(*d*) Finally, in other multi-*polis* regions most of the city-states were usually not independent but were in a relationship of 'dependency' with a larger *polis* in their region, such as Sparta, Elis, or after *c.* 369 Ithome–Messene; or were members of a federal state (*koinon*), as in Arkadia in the

---

[38]   On the scope of these names, see Piérart 2004, 599–600, 602–3.
[39]   Morgan and Hall 2004, 482 (*Inv. 235*).
[40]   Morgan and Hall 2004, 474.

mid-fourth century and possibly Messenia (Section III.3.b). These organ-
izational structures were certainly based upon the conventional divisions
of the peninsula, and gave greater unity to regions; in the case of Laconia
it was an increasingly attenuated region, yet the size and population of the
collective territory repeatedly allowed the Lakedaimonians to try to dominate their neighbours.

(*e*) In Arkadia down to the late fourth century, a level of sub-regional
units stood between the ethnic culture region and the *poleis*. These included
the Eutresians, Kynourians, Mainalians, and Parrhasians. Each comprised a
number of small settlements, probably including small *poleis*, in a given area,
which had a common religious cult, adopted a sub-regional *ethnikon* which
sometimes replaced the *polis*-ethnic, and were militarily organized. Their
history appears to have ended soon after the foundation of Megalopolis.[41]
As well as these sub-regional unities, Arkadia contained local hegemonic
leagues led by Tegea and Mantinea in the fifth century, and possibly Kleitor
from an earlier date.[42]

A region may be advantaged or disadvantaged by its location, depending
on the criteria applied, and by historical circumstances. The eastern Argolid
may have been affected positively by the prosperity of nearby Corinth,
Attica, and Aigina. But Argos seems not to have attracted much maritime
trade,[43] even though control of the Nemean festival will have brought an
influx of people and currency every two years. Corinth controlled the most
important sea and land routes by virtue of its location on the Isthmus, as
well as the Isthmian games in alternate years (between the Nemean); it
was the only Peloponnesian state besides Epidauros to benefit from two
coasts (cf. Ps.-Skylax, 40; 55), having harbours on the gulf of Corinth and
on the Saronic arm of the Aegean. Korinthia thus benefited from a location
that uniquely favoured trade; but this made it a prize for external powers.
Sikyon, rich enough in the archaic period to build a treasury at Delphi,
may have benefited from land and sea trade to a degree not far short of
Corinth but similarly became a strategic place to be fought over. Achaea was
exposed to the sea but scarcely accessible from the south; one might regard
it as disadvantaged except in terms of coastal traffic, and its *poleis* were not
powerful to the same degree as the 'Big Seven'. Eleia was fertile and good for
horses, but vulnerable by sea from the north-west and by land from the south
and east; yet despite this and its lack of harbours it was home to the Olympic

[41] Nielsen 1996; Nielsen 2002, ch. 7 (271–307) and appendixes 4–6 (537–43); more briefly,
Nielsen 2015, 256–7.
[42] Nielsen 2002, 364–74.
[43] Tomlinson 1972, 7; Gehrke 1986, 113–14.

festival and became a frequent destination for travellers. Messenia was vulnerable from the north, which may explain the Spartans' keen interest in its harbours down to the fourth century (they allowed immigrants, for example, to set up perioikic coastal towns, e.g. at Asine); equally, harbour towns such as Kyparissos and Mothone clearly attracted interest from the outside world, a further possible explanation for Spartan interest.

Thus, while we might tend to assume simplistically that some areas were disadvantaged by their location – Eleia as an undefended region, Arkadia as (usually) landlocked, Messenia as remote, Laconia as isolated, and so on – such an assumption may be unfounded at a given epoch. In fact, location is inseparable from accessibility, since most settlements were situated on communications routes. Contact with the outside world is possible even for a small coastal settlement or one far inland, as the cases of Messene and Geronthrai show. More importantly, this sketch illustrates how we must presume that regions' development took place in a context; but not only a context in which regions adjoined one another. An equally valid interface is that between coast and hinterland. Epidauros enjoyed huge patronage by visitors and saw a lot of development, as did coastal Isthmia but also inland Nemea and Olympia. Some inland *poleis* clearly thrived, such as Megalopolis. Inter-dependency of settlements, not of regions as such, is in fact the norm; and this will include settlements on opposite sides of a body of water, such as the gulf of Corinth or the Saronic gulf. Prosperity and military success are not geographically determined (though geography may favour or discourage certain things); they depend partly on geography, but partly also on the external connectivity of a settlement or area at a given epoch – which is itself a function of human movement.

Certain traditional regions are defined 'naturally', but they vary in their degree of internal geographical, political, cultural unity. Apparent locational advantages of regions seem not to correspond to different patterns of development. In sum, regional entities neither had a monopoly of supra-*polis* association, nor exerted particularly strong influence on communities' development.

V.2.d Centralization within Regions

In accordance with the definition of region offered earlier (Section V.2.a), the interactions between elements within in a region played an important role in their geopolitical fortunes, and possibly in their economic development. As well as potentially reflecting differences in resources, quantified epigraphic data (Section IV.4) can suggest power relationships and differing regional profiles.[44]

In the fourth century, in most regions epigraphy is strongly centralized. In Messenia four-fifths of known inscriptions are from Ithome–Messene; in Eleia–Triphylia three-quarters from Olympia; in Laconia over half from Sparta. Unsurprisingly perhaps, most inscriptions in Korinthia come from its only *polis*. Achaea, admittedly with small numbers of texts, is bimodal, with two-thirds of known inscriptions coming from two centres, Patrai in the west and Pellene in the east. Argolis is multi-centred but epigraphy is concentrated in a few places; three-fifths of the texts coming from two sites, Epidauros (town and sanctuary)[45] and Argos; most of the remainder from two more, Troizen and Nemea. Only Arkadia is strongly decentralized, little over one-third of texts coming from Tegea and the other two-thirds from nine other *poleis*, led by Megalopolis and Mantinea.

The third-century data reveal a continued concentration of epigraphy in some areas. Centralization remains strong in Messenia, more than four-fifths of inscriptions coming from the central *polis*. In Achaea, though it is again bimodal, Dyme replaces Pellene and the west virtually monopolizes the data. Centralization may have an archaeological aspect, as in Laconia, where the inland central place of Sparta coalesced into an urban entity during the third century; or in Messenia, where the central *polis* developed spectacularly despite its supposedly remote position (Section V.1.c); Messene's rapid growth was presumably not purely, if at all, the result of financial or material contributions from outside powers, but chiefly or wholly of the pronounced political monocentrism of this region, which appears to have allowed this *polis* to mobilize resources and accumulate the benefits of trade on behalf of much of the south-western Peloponnese. Elsewhere, however, there are some signs of dispersal and the dissemination of the 'epigraphic habit'. In Argolis, while three sites (Argos, Troizen, Epidauros) still account for three-quarters of all texts, there is epigraphic activity for the first time at Mycenae, Methana, and Nauplia. In Arkadia the number of epigraphically active *poleis* rises from just over ten to closer to twenty.[46]

In the second century, inscriptions in Korinthia–Sikyonia, western Arkadia, and western Achaea are more concentrated; in the last area perhaps surprisingly, given that nearly all the Achaean league *poleis* issued

---

[44] Data presented at Shipley 2005b, 327–8, and updated from later volumes of *SEG*. On the data, see IV.4 init.

[45] It is not always possible to attribute inscriptions specifically to the town as opposed to the Asklepieion or the sanctuary of Apollo Maleatas; they have been combined.

[46] Shipley 2005b, 328.

coins, many for the first time, during the first half of the century (TABLE IV.3). In other regions epigraphy is more dispersed and many *poleis* catch the 'epigraphic habit', especially in Arkadia, Messenia, and Laconia; in the last two, this picture is consistent with the break-up of hegemonic structures under Roman domination.[47] Where epigraphy is dispersed, it may sometimes be right to infer a desire by local communities – presumably their elites or the leaders of the elite – to assert their status. This would appear to confirm the enduring liveliness of local politics, as Polybios' narrative of the first half of the century implies.[48]

The *polis* remains the main locus of epigraphic display, apart from a few prominent religious sites. Overall, continuity is the main feature of the data. Our survey suggests that during the third century there was no radical change in the role of central places. Centralization within regions, at any rate, was not demonstrably higher in the third century, and no significant change can be seen in the internal dynamics of regions before the second. On the other hand, the persistent importance of centres within some regions reflects a world in which the traditional cultural regions are no less important than before as frameworks for expressions of *polis* and regional identity. But to what extent did regionality govern processes of interaction and change?

V.2.e Limits of Regional Specificity

Given its variety and relative lack of unity, the peninsula is unlikely to have seen all its parts develop in parallel. In the present state of knowledge, however, it is hard to identify accurately socio-economic differences between regions. We do not yet have enough archaeological data to illuminate in detail the distinct characteristics, if any, of most regions. Even supposing we had more evidence, and could generalize more securely about a region's economy or social character, or arrive at quantitative averages for key measures, it would not necessarily show whether the communities in a region were developing in parallel, in response to each other, or independently from one another.

We have no *a priori* reason to assume that a region (other than the single-*polis* regions of Korinthia and Sikyonia) would behave as an economic bloc. There is a danger of making history too 'smooth' because of deficient

---

[47] Shipley 2005b, 328.
[48] This tells against the view of O'Neil 1995, 117, that public interest in politics declined; cf. n. 20 above.

evidence.[49] More impressionistic indicators do not suggest that change was structured along regional lines. There are, for example, the two (or four) Peloponneses implied by ceramic networks (Section IV.6.b); this distinction cuts across conventional regional boundaries. The concentration of architectural investment in certain places does not seem to correspond to political–cultural regions but may have in each case a local explanation (e.g. at Messene and Olympia).

Federalism testifies to some degree of regional unification in Arkadia, albeit briefly; more successfully in Achaea. In such a case we may be justified in attributing some sort of fellow-feeling – or at least coordination of behaviour – to at least a sizeable percentage of citizens across a region's *poleis*. Yet even in strongly unified regions (Messenia, Laconia, perhaps Eleia and western Arkadia), and *a fortiori* in less unified ones, *polis* communities may have evolved independently to a great extent.

To the extent that regions were endowed with significant meaning, they did not necessarily persist in a given form. There is a diachronic dimension. In order to understand the potential impact of identities, whether of regions or at other scales, it is important to remind ourselves that none of them exists by nature.[50] Although they may to some degree map onto geography and may embody genuine, long-standing traditions, they continue to be expressed only because people – generally those with the greatest influence – assert that they exist and take steps to enact and thus prove their existence, for example through repeated rituals. Some old Greek identities, such as the supra-regional Pelasgian,[51] fell into abeyance in historical times – were for some reason no longer useful – while others were sustained and nourished through the archaic and classical periods and continued to be articulated in the hellenistic. After the Persian wars, we see the rise of politicized regional identities: Messenian identity, for example, may have been constructed by exiles,[52] while from the late fifth century other parts of the peninsula were increasingly 'ethnicized'.[53] Indeed, greater emphasis upon expressions of regional identity went hand in hand with their increasing politicization.[54] The greater politicization of certain regions, too, will have militated against parallel development.

---

[49] Broodbank 2013, 23.
[50] A fundamental study is Hall 1997, developed further in Hall 2002.
[51] See e.g. Sourvinou-Inwood 2003.
[52] Luraghi 2009b.
[53] Funke 2009; Ulf 2009; E. W. Robinson 2009, also seeing this as part of a reaction against Spartan domination.
[54] Cavanagh and Roy n.d. [2008]; Funke and Luraghi 2009, to be read with Siapkas 2010, whose strictures about the use of archaeology may be taken as a call for historians and archaeologists to engage more fully with the material culture of the Peloponnese; see IV.6 above.

An essentialist danger is to be guarded against: that of positing 'an' identity for a traditional region. Only if, hypothetically, all members of a society agreed on what its 'identity' was could one perhaps speak of a completely common identity; given the cleavages within Peloponnesian *poleis*, let alone the variation within regions, the likelihood of this having happened is vanishingly small. Since the conventional culture regions had political aspects, their scope and boundaries could be changed under certain circumstances. Sometimes change was imposed, as when Lydiadas of Megalopolis gave Arkadian Alipheira to the Eleians (Polyb. 4. 77. 10), or when Augustus later gave Messenian Kardamyle to Sparta (Paus. 3. 26. 7). In our period, Lakedaimonian *perioikoi* whose *polis*, on the orders of an external power, was incorporated into Messenia or made subject to Megalopolis or Argos, must have been expected to give up the Lakedaimonian aspect of their identity and adopt another. Identity could also be fashioned or adjusted more benignly, albeit in the interest of (or at the behest of) an outside power or on the initiative of a ruling or dominant elite. This is not to say that such an identity could not command wide allegiance on the part of a wide cross-section of society and entail the suppression or self-effacement of alternative viewpoints. One such case may be the creation of Triphylia in the 390s by the Spartans, out of a group of 'liberated' Eleian *perioikoi*, and its rebranding in the 360s as part of Arkadia, an identity which, in the case of the leading *polis* of Lepreon at least, seems to have been maintained down to the Roman period (Paus. 5. 5. 3).[55] Psophis is another example of ethnic boundary-crossing, switching from Arkadian to Eleian identity in the late third century (see Section II.5.a; Polyb. 4. 70). Phigaleia appears to have switched voluntarily from Arkadia to the Aitolian league in or before 222 (Polyb. 4. 3. 6), presumably power changed hands in the *polis*. Another example of 'elastic ethnicity' is the enlargement of the Achaean league beyond Achaeans – or, as it might be viewed, the takeover of Achaean identity by others. There was, in fact, a fourth-century precedent for extending league membership beyond a regional ethnicity, for in or before 389 Aitolian Kalydon and Naupaktos had been enrolled in the Achaean league (Xen. *Hell.* 4. 6. 1, 14).[56]

The potential for artificiality is shown with particular clarity if we ask in what the unity of Arkadia subsisted. From a topographical point of view, the region naturally divides into an eastern and a western half, as it did politically after the break-up of the Arkadian league; yet this geographical fissure was

---

not an impediment to a common Arkadian identity. From another point of view, Arkadia could comprise five or more entities, as when the sub-regional groupings of minor *poleis* carried particular weight in the fourth century.[57] Pan-Arkadian identity was thus a cultural and political claim rather than a topographical or genealogical one; but it was not usually expressed more forcefully than the *polis* identities within it. Indeed, there were several potential layers of identity: Nielsen perceptively analyses the components of ethnicity both at an Arkadian and at a sub-regional level – in terms of, for example, collective name, claimed kinship, shared history and culture, territorial foundation, and more subtly solidarity[58] – while noting that none of these was at odds with a claim of over-arching Hellenic identity.

To judge from the evidence of inscriptions, the traditional culture regions were distinguished by their dialects in the archaic and classical periods. While the broad ethno-linguistic division between Dorian and Ionian identity was in large measure politically constructed,[59] it did correspond to linguistic groups. Within those, there were real dialect differences corresponding to regions, even if the correct classification of some dialects is still uncertain.[60] Strikingly, however, during the late classical to middle hellenistic periods there was already linguistic standardization in the Peloponnese under the influence of Attic Greek, though it did not proceed at the same pace or in the same way in every place, and involved a Doric *koina* (common language) as well as the Ionic *koine* dominated by Attic features.[61] Attic forms, together with the Ionic (or Milesian) alphabet adopted at Athens in 403/2, spread first to Epidauros and then other Argolic *poleis* by the mid-fourth century; as at Athens, it was used here for official business.[62] Eleian dialect gains Attic features from the late fifth century and loses distinctive features between the fourth and the second century, as outside influences grow[63] – a confirmation that this region, too, was not isolated.[64] In Messenia, the replacement of local forms by standardized Doric takes place gradually from the late fourth or early third century to the second, a change attributed to the area being opened up to outside influences;[65] the same process takes

---

[57] Nielsen 2002, 271–307; also Nielsen 1995.
[58] Nielsen 2002, 48–52 (Arkadian), 272–8 (the 'tribal' communities); on components of identity, see Smith 1986.
[59] Alty 1982.
[60] Woodard 2008, 50–72, esp. 50–2.
[61] Colvin 2014; Crespo 2014.
[62] Nieto Izquierdo 2014.
[63] Minon 2008; Minon 2014b.
[64] Minon 2014b.
[65] Lanérès 2014.

a little longer in Arkadia, where catalogues of ephebes (young soldiers) are strictly in local dialect until the late third century, though other kinds of text begin to show change by then.[66] Even in Laconia, a supposedly conservative region, interaction with Attic can be detected from the fourth century BC, local forms being fully replaced by *koine* (a standardized Greek dialect) by the first century BC.[67]

Where regional or federal identity was strong, was *polis* identity less so? We do not normally refer to *polis* identity in ethnic terms (the ancient term *ethnikon* for a citizen's '*polis* surname' appears likely to have been a, regrettably ambiguous, post-classical invention);[68] but it existed alongside other identities that a citizen of a Peloponnesian state might perceive himself to have, identities we may think of as 'nested' and all of which can be described as ethnic. So it is with many European communities today, for example, in those nation states – the majority – within which there exists a plurality of dialects, historical identities, and distinct, long-established languages. Besides the ancient examples already mentioned, we may recall the Arkadian *polis* of Kynaitha, a member of the Achaean league, which according to Polybios deserved its fate because the citizens had neglected traditional Arkadian music and dance (4. 19. 13–21. 11); whether or not his strictures were justified or even relevant, they indicate the depth of commitment to one's *polis* that a devotee of the Achaean league, even in the mid-second century, could expect to see manifested.

The common feature in these examples appears to be that the fact of *polis* identity being articulated, and the way in which it was articulated, did not change, even if some *poleis* changed their supervening regional identity. Rather, *polis* identity was sometimes combined with a higher-level identity. The latter, however, continued to be constructed by decisions taken by *poleis*, which remained the forum in which meanings were put into regional structures. It was usually with individual *poleis* that external powers, for example, had to deal directly; and it is hard to see how regional structures, other than federal, could channel or drive change. Uniform development within a multi-*polis* region is unlikely, in any case, because regions were still agglomerations of separate *poleis*; it was still at *polis* level that decisions were taken about most matters; some diplomatic and military decisions being

---

[66]   Dubois 2014 (to C1).

[67]   Alonso Déniz 2007, e.g. 178, 462–3; Alonso Déniz 2014, 146, 152–3, 178 (abstract).

[68]   I can find no pre-Hl examples, and none of the adjective ἐθνικός before Polyb. (e.g. 2. 44. 5) and Strabo (e.g. 2. 3. 1); Demetrios of Phaleron's *Letter* to King Ptolemy about the Jews (Hercher 1873, 218) may not be genuine. Most attributions of ἐθνικόν to pre-Polybian authors are in Steph. Byz., *Ethnika* (c. C6 AD, but we only have a later precis); while he often cites Ar–Cl sources (e.g. Hekataios, Theopompos), his classificatory terms, e.g. ἐθνικόν, may not be theirs.

taken by *poleis* even while they were members of a federation. The *polis* presumably retained primary jurisdiction over the organization of commerce, including such matters as the running of harbours and markets and the entitlement of citizens or resident aliens to trade; also in the conduct of euergetism, architectural construction, and so on. An account framed in terms of regions does not explain enough.[69]

A striking example of *polis* localism is the probably third-century writer Harmodios of Lepreon from whom Athenaeus (4. 31 = *FGrHist* 319 F 1) quotes anecdotes about Phigaleian gluttony. In his *Customs at Phigaleia*, says Athenaeus, Harmodios described the copious amounts of food supplied by the grain-officer (σίταρχος) to members of the city's dramatic choruses ('each day three pitchers of wine, a bushel and a half of barley-meal, five pounds of cheese'), and the supplementary contribution by the *polis* authorities in the form of three sheep and all the cooking and dining equipment. Furthermore, he asserted that at all their meals the Phigaleians would give hungry young men extra broth, barley-cakes, and wheaten bread, 'for such a young man was held to be manly (ἀνδρώδης) and a thoroughbred (γενναῖος), since hearty eating (πολυφαγία) was admired and praised among them'. In another fragment (F 2 = Ath. 10. 59. 442b) he tells us that they became great drinkers (φιλοπόται) because they were neighbours of the Messenians and were accustomed to travel abroad (ἀποδημεῖν ἐθισθέντες). The tone recalls the partially extant humorous sketch of the cities of central Greece written around 270 by an author known as Herakleides Kritikos.[70] Was the Lepreate – a citizen of a *polis* which, as we saw, was once Eleian but then Triphylian and finally Arkadian – merely documenting interesting anthropological curiosities, or was he having fun at the expense of old-style, mountain-dwelling Arkadians?

Whatever Harmodios' intention, the passage encapsulates the interplay between localism and the wider view, and shows both *polis* culture and the intellectual 'internet' of the day to be as active as ever, if not more so. Local and regional groups could see themselves as part of a much bigger Hellenic entity that gave validity to their cultural practices or rendered them eccentric. Pseudo-Skylax expresses the view that Hellas extends wherever Greeks live, but that there is a core of 'continuous Hellas' in the southern Balkan peninsula and a wider, discontinuous Hellas everywhere else.[71] If Harmodios wrote – wherever he did write – for an audience outside his

---

[69] Cf. Pébarthe 2007, 1438, reviewing Descat 2006: possible regional differences should not blind us to the potential impact of wider currents of change.

[70] I follow the dating of Arenz 2006.

[71] Shipley 2011.

native Triphylia or Arkadia, as seems likely, it was an audience interested in the *polis* and in its place in the wider construction of Greekness; and clearly implies, like the evidence for dialect change, that the Peloponnese was a theatre of continual movement: interaction between places within it, interaction with the world outside.

V.3 A Peloponnese of the *Poleis*

Our examination of regions has made clear the importance of decisions taken by individual political communities within them, even within a league structure. We now consider further aspects of how the components of regions interacted: principally *poleis* in their territories.

V.3.a Good and Bad Neighbours

The constitutional form of a *polis* seems to have depended partly upon whether it could make its own decisions or was under the control of outsiders; partly on the geostrategic factors that made outside intervention more likely or less likely; and partly upon its size, wealth, and distance from powerful neighbours. While we argued (Section III.3.a) that geographical proximity could not be used to account for a *polis*'s often long-standing constitutional complexion, considerations of distance may be more usefully invoked to explain the geopolitical circumstances in which *poleis* found themselves. Phleious seems to suffer more than its share of external interference, perhaps because of its location on a strategic route (see Section III.3.a). Tegea and Mantinea, neighbours competing for the same natural resources, had different relationships with Sparta: Tegea (closer to Sparta) having an oligarchy installed by Sparta in the mid-fifth century and protected from Mantinea, so that the *polis* remained pro-Spartan in the early fourth century; after Leuktra the Mantineans forcibly democratized Tegea and expelled 800 oligarchs (Section III.3.b); but at Second Mantinea the two were on opposite sides (Section II.2.c). Phigaleia's marginal position in the far west of Arkadia perhaps enabled the *polis*, despite Spartan concern with the Eleian frontier in the late fifth century (Section III.3.a), to break with Sparta later (Section III.3.b) and subsequently to leave the Arkadian league for the Aitolian (Section V.2.e). Distance from Corinth probably enabled the westernmost Achaean *poleis* to take the initiative in refounding the Achaean league (Section II.4.b). The relatively small *polis* of Orchomenos was not enrolled in the Arkadian league because its citizens hated the Mantineans (Xen. *Hell.* 6. 5. 11); later, because of its situation on an important route, it drew unwelcome attention from Philip V (Section II.5.a). Distance from Sparta was surely a factor in the almost unparalleled disloyalty – perhaps under duress – of some of the Messenian *perioikoi* during the helot revolt of the 460s (Thuc. 1. 101. 2) and of some *perioikoi* in northern Laconia during the first Theban invasion a century later (Xen. *Hell*. 6. 5. 24–5).

A settlement – whether *polis* or non-*polis* – could be dependent upon (subordinate to) a nearby *polis*. Argos dominated the nearest Argolic settlements, as it had before – particularly Nemea and Phleious – but not those of the Akte further off. Halieis' dependency on Hermion has been noted earlier. Mases was another dependency of Hermion; Eileoi perhaps became another during the Classical period and was then abandoned.[72] Several places around Argos became *kōmai* of the city.[73] Tiryns and Mycenae were taken over in the first half of the fifth century, though Mycenae was later revived (if settlement was in fact interrupted; see Section I.2.b). Kleonai, which controlled Nemea, was annexed by Argos in about the late fourth century but continued to administer the Nemean games until the early third, as it did again in the late third.[74] Some Arkadian centres, likewise, had local spheres of dependency (see Section V.2.c), while in Achaea Patrai had dependent settlements (Section II.4.b). The most prominent example of a dominant relationship over subordinate *poleis* is that between Sparta and its *perioikoi* (see Section I.2.b). Other towns, too, became dependent upon Sparta during the war of Kleomenes, notably Argos, which was lost soon afterwards; some twenty-five years later, however, Nabis accepted it as a gift from Philip V, retaining it for four years (Section II.5.b).

When not effected by force, military–political alignments between *poleis* will often have been based upon personal and familial interactions such as guest-friendship (*xenia*) or trade conducted or managed by members of a *polis*'s elite. When forcibly created, a relationship of alignment or subordination will sometimes have operated through compliant members of the elite who had pre-existing ties to citizens of the dominant *polis*.

V.3.b Routes and Connectivity

Elite initiatives created, and depended upon, networks and travel along land and sea routes, including key river valleys.[75] We have seen that

---

[72] Jameson *et al.* 1994, 30–1, 376.

[73] On the meaning of *kōmē*, see Hansen 1995; at Argos, unusually, it was a political subdivision of a *polis*.

[74] Buraselis 2013.

[75] As the book went to press I was alerted to Bonnier 2016, a detailed study of valley routes connecting the Corinthian gulf towns to S. Achaea and N. Arkadia.

Peloponnesian communities were not blank canvases for the inscribing of Macedonian power, but participants in a relationship – one of many that a ruler of Macedonia had to sustain – to which they brought their own momentum, or inertia. The building of identities, and the negotiation of relationships, depended on movement: flows of people, information, and resources between important settlements (chiefly *poleis*) and non-urban sanctuaries.[76] This may, in principle, help to account for observed changes and continuities. Archaeological evidence is not yet to hand in sufficient quantity to allow us to reconstruct networks of routes in detail; but flows will have taken place along a multi-scale complex of unmade local paths, man-made roads, 'natural' land routes, and established sea routes. Thus we can begin to infer patterns of movement from what we know of these routes.

It used to be thought that long-distance transportation of goods and people in the ancient world was economically viable only by sea; but recent work has restored land travel to its due prominence.[77] This is especially relevant within a sizeable land mass; indeed, land transport was the only option for movement into, out of, or through Arkadia, landlocked except for the post-Leuktra corridor to the sea via Lepreon (2½ mi or 4 km from the sea), or other inland areas. The fact that several of the major population centres of other regions, such as Messene, Elis, and Sparta, were at a considerable distance from their own principal harbour – indeed, Kyllene, the Messenian harbours, and those in Laconia were nowhere near the main inland settlement – made land travel not merely necessary but positively life-giving. Faced with the evidence that some Peloponnesian places were almost two weeks' walk from one another,[78] we might think some towns remote; but we have seen how the effect of supposed remoteness is mitigated in a deeply interconnected landscape, especially with patterns of trade shifting their focus on a secular basis (cf. Sections V.1.c, V.3.d). The fragmentation of the landscape by mountain ranges (cf. Section I.2.a) further exacerbated the costs imposed by distance. Obstacles presented by relief, however, were offset by a small number of crucial natural routes that channelled traffic and helped endow certain communities with strategic value.

---

[76] On flows see e.g. Davies 2005.

[77] Albeit mainly for high-value goods: Bresson 2016, 84. For the history of this debate, see Laurence 1998, 129–36.

[78] Sanders and Whitbread 1990.

V.3.c Routes and Scale

In the past generation it has become a matter of principle that in investigating changes at the widest scale in the ancient Greek world we neglect the local at our peril. As already noted, historians and archaeologists have achieved a new understanding of smaller, more typical Greek settlements.[79] We must keep in mind the importance of extremely local phenomena at the level of 'micro-environment';[80] the 'connectivity' which, at a grand level, links regions of the Peloponnese and of the Mediterranean, also links localities. Another facet of this working principle is that, while from an ecological or environmental point of view one is entitled to ignore the urban–rural boundary for certain investigative purposes,[81] one need not abandon the city as a useful unit of analysis.

An *a priori* typology of Peloponnesian routes might take different forms, and not all kinds of frequented travel-ways in the landscape can be detected archaeologically in the present state of knowledge. For the sake of argument, however, the following schematic hierarchy may serve (and leads to an important claim).[82]

(*a*) Communications within the *chōra* of a *polis* may have had the greatest significance for most inhabitants on a day-to-day basis. Unfortunately, this is also the aspect for which we have the least evidence. At the lowest level, one may conceive of field paths and seasonally dry watercourses that would require no, or very little, investment of *matériel* or labour to keep them serviceable. These have a kind of counterpart in the unclassified or unmetalled roads marked on modern maps (coloured yellow or left unshaded, for example, on those of the British Ordnance Survey). In the Greek context, they may be imagined as facilitating local movement between and around different localities in the agricultural and pastoral countryside, including isolated built structures.

(*b*) At a slightly higher level were roads between non-*polis* settlements, or between these and the nearest town. This is one level of the hierarchy that we sometimes see in Pausanias' accounts of his movements between towns and villages in the Antonine era. British readers may equate them roughly with modern 'B roads' (shaded brown on OS maps), not designed for long

---

[79] See e.g. Gehrke 1986; and the work of the Copenhagen Polis Centre.
[80] Horden and Purcell 2000, e.g. 83, 94; cf. their 'microecologies', e.g. 80, 85; 'microregions', e.g. 123, 296–7.
[81] Horden and Purcell 2000, esp. 89–96.
[82] For a similar division of routes into levels, see Lolos 2011, 93–7.

journeys. In the post-medieval Greek uplands, they could include the cobbled or rock-cut, sometimes walled *kalderímia* (singular *kalderími*; this Greek form of a Turkish name may derive from καλὸς δρόμος, 'good road') that typically connect villages, rural chapels, monasteries, and sometimes mountain tops many are still in use. Their distinctive form has no obvious counterpart in antiquity; but this could be partly an artefact of preservation or incomplete investigation.[83]

Meaning and value coagulate around routes at any scale and however little they are used; but it may be imagined that minor routes of the two kinds described, being used on a daily or hourly basis, collected the greatest 'density of meaning'.[84] Largely undetectable today other than by inference from contours, stream-beds, or later use, they will have covered almost the whole landscape at a density even greater than those middle- and long-distance 'rough roads', cart-tracks, bridle-paths, and mule-paths compiled in the first world war edition of the British Admiralty's handbook to Greece.[85] It is, of course, impossible to reconstruct the internal organization of an ancient *chōra* in detail. When, however, Pausanias describes his journeys through a *polis*'s territory, we may assume that he is usually following paths of great antiquity, given that the network of nucleated settlements had changed little since classical times.

These less elaborate routes were the chief means by which relationships in the vicinity of settlements were created and maintained, and information and goods circulated. While we tend to concentrate on 'arterial' routes and do not normally have specific evidence for their 'capillary' counterparts, a local route can sometimes be inferred from a sequence of small outlying fortifications. In the north-eastern Peloponnese, for example, classical and hellenistic towers may have housed garrisons or signal stations guarding agricultural land or out-of-town routes: for example, in the Sikyonia[86] or along the Corinth–Argos road in the Kleonai area.[87] In Laconia, the *Kelephína* valley shows evidence of the regular spacing of farmsteads in this period,[88] which may well have been viewed as a community of some

---

[83] For the possibility that some *kalderímia* are ancient (perhaps of R date), see Baldwin Bowsky and Niniou-Kindeli 2006, 414, 415, 427.

[84] Tuan 1977, 182.

[85] Admiralty n.d. [1918], 179–635, at 398–635 nos. 53–95 (Peloponnese), many referring to or crossing Arkadia and documented with mileages. This work remains to be exploited in the study of ancient geography. Other important data such as journey times are collected by Leake, esp. Leake 1830.

[86] Caraher *et al.* 2010, 409–10, citing Lolos 1998, 233–4, for a tower overlooking a route to the Stymphalos area. See also Lolos 2011.

[87] Marchand 2009.

[88] Shipley 2002d, 284–5, 312.

kind; the river valley will have served as a line of communication between outlying settlements, just as it served Philip V as a surprise 'back road' to Sparta. Future work could build upon intensive and non-intensive field survey data, combined with site assemblages and natural topography, to begin to reconstruct local communication networks. For most of the Peloponnese, however, a clear understanding of the hierarchy of minor settlements within *polis* territories has not yet been achieved.

(*c*) The next level in our imagined branching network, the approximate equivalent of Britain's 'A roads' connecting towns,[89] is partly represented by many discoveries of parallel wheel-ruts, with a standard distance of 1.4 m between them, cut into the bedrock at certain places on routes between major settlements and sanctuaries.[90] The network is plausibly dated to approximately the archaic or classical period. Most of these 'roads' – perhaps better visualized as the ancient equivalent of tramlines – have been found in the eastern half of the Peloponnese, though this may simply reflect where the majority of fieldwork has been carried out (see Section IV.1.e).

This evidence of substantial investment of material and labour further strengthens the notion that, away from the coasts, land travel was a central fact of life. Rather than being the creation exclusively of the Spartans in the era of the 'Peloponnesian league',[91] it seems likely that these waggon roads resulted from initiatives by a range of communities, presumably for economic as much as military reasons.[92] The archaeological signature of these roads is seen only on rocky ground – such construction was not necessary in level terrain, and if any investment took place there it has not yet been identified. The technique is the same whether a road connects places within a region, in different regions, or inside and outside the Isthmus. Constructed roads, in general, ran between *poleis* or important sanctuaries, and are not to be thought of as having been devised in order to connect regions as such. Major *poleis* and sanctuaries were where the most important markets operated; where pottery finally 'landed' after being transported from abroad; where money was minted and presumably mostly spent; and from where the road network was organized.[93]

(*d*) At inter-regional level, military intervention flowed chiefly along a few major conduits determined by relief: first, along the north coast, whether

---

[89] Many, however, have now been upgraded and no longer pass through towns.

[90] Pikoulas 1990; 1999a; 2001b; 2012 (with Shipley 2014); and references his earlier studies cited therein.

[91] As argued by Pikoulas 1999a, 306–8.

[92] See Tausend 2006 (with Shipley 2008b).

[93] On these 'tram-lines' and towers in Argolis, see Tausend 2006.

by road or sea; second, the diagonal Corinth–Argos–Megalopolis–Messene route passing through eastern and western Arkadia; third, the natural highway formed by the perennial (but non-navigable) rivers Alpheios and Eurotas, whose headwaters adjoin one another in Arkadia, creating a virtual furrow bisecting the Peloponnese on the other diagonal, from Eleia to Laconia.[94] It offered, in principle, a good short cut if one was moving between the north-west and anywhere to the south or vice versa; though for longer journeys a sea voyage might be faster. The route facilitated Spartan access to Olympia on the Alpheios – a dedication there by a Lakedaimonian athlete even refers to the exact distance between the two places (*IvO* 171, *c.* 316 BC) – as well as military expeditions against Eleia and Messenia. It is surely no accident that after Leuktra the new Arkadian city of Megalopolis was planted along this route, or that the fortification known as Athenaion near Belbina aroused such concern in the minds of Spartans and their enemies (Section II.4.e). It intersects with the Argos–Messene route, but its southern stage leading into Laconia is longer than the more easterly, perhaps more arduous approach via the Thyreatis which Philip V used in 218 in order to surprise the Spartans (Polyb. 5. 18. 10–19. 1). The existence of these routes was doubtless well known to outside powers; Ptolemy III may have had Spartan access to the Isthmus in mind when he subsidized Kleomenes III. Philip V's concern to hold on to Orchomenos has already been linked (Section II.5.a) to its location on this route – indeed, it stands at the junction of the easier route from Argos with the route to and from Pellene on the north coast.

(*e*) 'Trunk routes' also include those expressed as 'coastal sailings' (*paraploi*) in the coastal description by Pseudo-Skylax. These may mitigate the apparent remoteness of a place. Kyllene, for example, looked in two directions, linking the northern Peloponnese not only with the Adriatic but also with Messenia and places beyond. Given the relative ease of movement along the north and west coasts of the Peloponnese, the option of travelling by sea was usually preferable,[95] unless coastal communities could use naval force to block a route, as the maritime *poleis* in Achaea may sometimes have been able to do. The east and south coasts are a different matter: often steep to access, and dangerous in onshore winds. But they are better endowed with natural harbours than much of the north and west; and though the dangers of the southern capes, particularly Malea, were notorious, their impact on the actual frequency of journeys may be doubted.[96] Sailors, well

---

[94]   Admiralty 1944–5, iii. 157.
[95]   Freitag 1999, 271–2, 323–5.
[96]   Woodward *et al.* 2012.

aware of the dangers, could shelter in coves or behind islets (as in Pseudo-Skylax 108. 2–3, referring to NW Africa), or give the cape a wide berth by crossing to and from Kythera, whose importance for the Cretan route may have been enhanced by the fact that it avoided Cape Malea.

(f) We cannot view routes within the Peloponnese in isolation from links to places outside it. In Chapter IV we noted the existence of ceramic links between places here and, for example, Athens and Alexandria. Other links extended in many directions.[97] One such was the sea voyage across the gulf of Corinth from Aigion to the coast of Lokris, or diagonally to Delphi in Phokis a little further east and from there via Kirrha to central Greece and Thessaly. The short crossing from Eleia to Aitolia brought the Peloponnese into close contact with north-western Greece. In Eleia itself, Kyllene was a staging post to the Ionian islands and thence to the Adriatic and Italy.[98] In another direction, the cities of the Argolic Akte were in active contact with the other side of the Saronic gulf. The apparent growth of Boiai, the south-easternmost *polis* on the Laconian gulf, in hellenistic and Roman times can hardly be explained other than by trade with Kythera and Crete, and indirectly with Libya and Egypt.[99] The importance of the Isthmus of Corinth for both land and sea travel has always been appreciated.[100] These and other connections brought cultural information, for example, in the form of people or goods, to the starting-points of routes into the Peloponnese, and equally transmitted it in the opposite direction. This information was unevenly distributed when it reached its first or final destination; but, in any community, those persons most active in long-distance dealings were surely aware of the wider networks of the eastern and central Mediterranean. Such extra-Peloponnesian communications were indispensable to the activities and ambitions of elite groups.

Of routes at different scales, the more local may have carried more traffic in aggregate, but are the least visible archaeologically. At the upper level – inter-*polis* routes – the evidence for artificial improvement (e.g. chiselled wheel-ruts) implies elite- and state-led interest in their creation and maintenance, probably for both exchange and military purposes. The claim promised at the start of this subsection is this: that the inter-*polis* routes, those connecting regions, and those joining the Peloponnese to mainland Greece – that is, routes (c) to (f) – are all the same kind of

---

[97] On crossings to other land masses, see Shipley 2006b, 40.
[98] Freitag 1999, 274–5.
[99] Archaeological evidence for Cl–Hl Boia(i) is lacking, but the *polis* existed at least from C4m, Shipley 2004a, 579–80 (*Inv. 327*), and issued coins in R times, Head 1911, 433.
[100] See most recently Pettegrew 2016; and various papers in Kissas and Niemeier 2013.

route. That is, they are not to be thought of as linking regions as such, or as mere components in much longer chains of communication (like modern motorways); they do not bypass, but invariably connect, *poleis* or major extra-urban sanctuaries.

Where roads required investment of labour, it was probably organized, in most cases, by *poleis* rather than by supra-*polis* organizations. In the next subsection we shall ask whether the network of routes can be differentiated on a regional basis.

V.3.d Connectivity and Regions

A consideration of the different kinds of roads will show whether regions varied in their degree of internal and external connectivity, not forgetting connectivity by sea (cf. Section V.3.b); but also confirms that regions were not the only divisions that were significant in the development of the Peloponnese.

The lowlands of western Argolis were an important channel for the movement of people and goods from prehistory onwards; the area was the setting for the Bronze Age central place, Mycenae. The mostly mountainous character of the Akte to the east will have obliged inhabitants to use inshore boats often; western Argolis, however, was more penetrable – yet perhaps rarely penetrated, because of the protecting mountains around the coastal plain and because of the habitual prosperity of the main settlement.

When making for, or starting from, the north-eastern Peloponnese, one could use the low-lying Corinth–Argos road (if one's way was not barred), and combine this with sections of the network linking Phleious, Stymphalos, Nemea, and other places that gave access to the southern part of the East Arkadian plain. If one was barred from Korinthia, one might follow the Asopos valley running down to Sikyon from Phleious; the prominence and evident prosperity of the latter town, as well as its generally pro-Spartan stance in the classical period, is doubtless related to its location on this route.[101] Since the route was a way to bypass Corinthian control, it was in the Corinthians' interest to maintain good relations with Sikyon. Another alternative was to follow the valley running down from prosperous Pellene in Achaea to its harbour at Aristonautai, at one time Sparta's primary access to the gulf of Corinth.[102] Pellene itself has been identified as a

---

[101] Kralli 2017, 99–100, notes evidence of close social and economic ties between Sikyon and Stymphalos in the 300s; cf. Taeuber 1981; *IPArk* 17.

[102] Freitag 1999, 256.

market centre for Arkadia (cf. Section II.3.a),[103] which is a reminder that these routes were not just ways of getting from *A* to *B*, but were actively maintained for economic reasons too.

Important routes thus clustered in Argolis, including the short crossings to the north coast of the gulf of Corinth at the point where the western Boiotian shore gave access to central Greece. All these considerations, and the presence of the Isthmus, help to explain why places in the north-east feature so often in the military narratives, especially of the early decades of our period; but geography did not wholly determine economic development.

In Achaea, most *poleis* did not control important routes into the interior, for the majority of valleys led only into the mountains of northern Arkadia. An important exception is the valley of the river Erasinos (or Bouraïkos, Paus. 7. 25. 10), debouching in the *chōra* of Keryneia; its source near upland Kynaitha adjoins that of the river Kleitor, which after passing the *polis* of that name merges with the Aroanios (flowing down from near Lousoi) and joins the Ladon, eventually reaching the prosperous *polis* of Heraia on the Alpheios not far east of Olympia. This represents the longest continuous pass, albeit an arduous one, through the middle of the northern mountain massif. The harbours of Achaea, meanwhile, offered the possibility of hindering movement along the gulf, and controlled further crossings into mainland Greece. The mountainous nature of Phokis to the north may partly explain why it was the coastal towns of the eastern and western ends of the gulf that saw the greatest development.

Lying centrally as it does, one might expect Arkadia's principal towns to have played key roles in communications; but in the era before the motor engine its contours will have heavily influenced the degree of connectivity in different parts.[104] Political conditions permitting, movements between Arkadia and Laconia (via Tegea, or via Megalopolis along the Alpheios and Eurotas) or Messenia (again via Megalopolis) were easy, as was the descent into Argolis, the shortest route to which begins not far from Mantinea (only a short day's ride from Argos).[105] Some upland *poleis* of northern Arkadia enjoyed relatively easy access to specific *poleis* in Achaea, and recent study points to regular traffic between them despite the steep contours; this is what one would expect, given the number of *poleis* situated in this upland environment. Location upon a strategic route could favour the development of a place: Lousoi in northern Arkadia was an important stop on a

---

[103] Freitag 1999, 256.
[104] See excellent discussion by Baladié 1980, 265–77.
[105] Gehrke 1986, 109–13, on Mantinea and Tegea, stresses their connectivity.

land route to and from the gulf of Corinth,[106] and as already noted (Section IV.2.a and earlier in this section) Kynaitha's position on a long and crucial route attracted the wrong kind of attention.[107] Tegea gained added importance in or before Strabo's day because of its position on a main route giving access to Eleia and north-western Greece.[108] Study of ancient route networks stresses the role of Megalopolis as a node of communications for the whole Peloponnese;[109] before its foundation this role may have been played by western *poleis* such as Gortys and Lykosoura, which tended to lie just above the Alpheios–Eurotas route. The strategic importance of this district clarifies the Spartans' determination to keep hold of the Athenaion near Belbina,[110] a fort in the area of the headwaters of the Eurotas.

The greater importance of the eastern Arkadian plain, in comparison with the western, reflects its position on routes to the Isthmus. Polybios' remark about Philip V keeping control of Orchomenos, at first sight surprising given the modest status of that *polis* and its restricted *chōra*, is easily explained in this light.[111] '[D]ifficulty of access did not deter visitors'. Classical sources, sometimes distracted by their concentration on Sparta, probably under-represent the frequency with which armies traversed northern Arkadia.[112]

Communications within Messenia are facilitated by a route avoiding the Aigaleion range, though travelling directly across the range is not difficult as the parallel passes are not particularly lofty. Messenian communications with Triphylia, Eleia, and western Arkadia are simple, those with Laconia less so. In antiquity, the narrow and arduous *Langáda* pass through the central part of the Taÿgetos range – the route taken by the modern motor road – was probably not much used; most traffic will have passed around the north end of the range or rounded Cape Tainaron by ship.

Because of Taÿgetos on the west and the broken massif of Parnon to the east, Laconia is usually thought of as well protected, but the entries from the north (cf. Section V.3.c), especially from Tegea, are not arduous and the wide Eurotas valley offered no impediment other than the marshland around Helos (Ἕλος, 'Marsh') where aggradation has now moved the coast forward several kilometres since antiquity.[113] It is not, then, surprising that the Lakedaimonians were so concerned about their borderlands.

---

[106] Mitsopoulou-Leon 2000, 21.
[107] Mitsopoulou-Leon 2000, 21.
[108] Baladié 1980, 333.
[109] Sanders and Whitbread 1990.
[110] Or Bel(e)mina; Shipley 2004a, 579 (*Inv. 326*).
[111] Shipley 2008a, 62.
[112] Roy 1999, 323.
[113] Wagstaff 1979.

Implicitly we have viewed routes synchronically; but their course, and importance, may have altered as a result of natural changes in a landscape which we are unlikely to know about. An exception to this generalization is the submersion of Helike in Achaea in 373,[114] which will have modified routes in the immediate vicinity; as will the relocation of Sikyon. Routes may also change as roads are improved or the technology of transportation evolves. Control of Sikyon was prized by commanders in the early hellenistic period, when it repeatedly suffered attack (as well as at earlier, such as twice at the hands of the Athenians early in the Peloponnesian war: Thuc. 1. 108. 5; 1. 111. 2) or political intervention; the city nevertheless remained powerful.

Connectivity, therefore, like distance, need not have a constant value.[115] Routes between *poleis* (whether in one region or different regions) can illuminate the military–political narrative, provided that we take account of changing circumstances. In broad terms, warfare and trade tended to concentrate in the north-eastern Peloponnese, while the relative importance of long-distance contacts may have been greater in the south.

A study of the late Roman road network[116] has revealed a corridor of 'connectivity' running from Nemea via Megalopolis to Arkadian Leuktra, which had been an obscure place in earlier periods.[117] Once sea connections are factored in, this corridor extends west to Olympia and Kyllene and includes the north coast, making a circuit around the northern Peloponnese. In both cases central Arkadia, Messenia, and Laconia appear poorly integrated into the network; but when the Peloponnese is combined into the route network of mainland Greece as a whole, the corridor lengthens as far as Corinth, which now becomes the best-connected place, followed by Patrai, Argos, Epidauros, Kyllene – and, perhaps surprisingly, Boiai and Messenian Pylos. Some details of this network will have been specific to a post-hellenistic period; but it may encourage us to look for similarly complex connections for periods in which they are not explicitly documented. In terms of accessibility, attractiveness to trade, and utility as a centre of power, remote places with good sea or land connections are likely to have fared better than one would expect. In each period, however, particular circumstances will modify the *a priori* scheme; remoteness from the sea, for

---

[114] e.g. Soter and Katsonopoulou 2011.

[115] Cf. Bresson 2016, 79–80: it is one thing to assert the importance of connectivity, another to identify its level.

[116] Sanders and Whitbread 1990.

[117] Leuktron appears in Sanders and Whitbread 1990, 343, table 4, under its medieval name of *Leondari*; this is anc. Leuktra or Leuktron in NW Laconia (in SW Arkadia after C4m), not anc. Leuktron or Leuktra in SE Messenia.

example, may have protected Sparta from attack, but only in periods when southern Laconia was under its control or when, after 195, the former *perioikoi*, though independent of Sparta, were nevertheless closely connected with, and even aligned with, their former hegemon.

In all these cases, geopolitical conditions and local or regional initiative (by political entities or individuals) could counteract the limitations, or negate the advantages, of location. The north-eastern Peloponnese in general saw more warfare and trade; but the south enjoyed its own connections with different commercial centres, and possibly more changes in material culture styles.

V.3.e Changes in the Landscape of *Poleis*

How did this landscape of *poleis* change between the late classical period and the early second century? Following the indications noted earlier (Section III.1), it is sometimes possible to see a place beginning, or ceasing, to be explicitly or implicitly represented as a *polis* in ancient evidence (which is necessarily incomplete and may be unreliable or contradictory) or, in the absence of textual evidence, as losing or gaining physical features characteristic of a *polis*. Thus, for example, it appears that settlements in Achaea began to be acknowledged as *poleis* only during the fifth century.[118] The causes of the first appearance, disappearance, and reappearance of towns are varied; as are the concomitants of status change, which may range from complete physical relocation to partial evacuation, as well as different kinds of synoikism.[119] Each change into, or out of, *polis* status meant a shift in the internal dynamics of a region and of the *chōra* of that *polis*. In rare cases, it could entail abandonment and the physical relocation of a population – if not killed or sold into slavery, they would need to find new homes – while a change in the constitutional relationship between a settlement and its neighbours may have had effects on local culture that were viewed negatively or positively depending on the observer.

To see whether the political landscape in the third century was particularly subject to disruption, we can once again compare an earlier time.

Changes to Poleis in the Fourth Century

It appears that the first two-thirds of the fourth century had seen a number of cases of *polis* formation and status change.

---

[118] Morgan and Hall 2000.
[119] Demand 1990.

A city's independence could be altered by agreement. At Corinth in 392, for example, after a revolution a short-lived 'isopoly' was formed with Argos (Section III.3.a). It probably did not, as some have believed, involve the abolition of either *polis* (despite the emotive language of Xen. *Hell.* 4. 4. 6 on the removal of boundary markers), nor was it 'a refreshing attempt to break free of the constraints of the particularism of the city'.[120] It may, rather, have been a preferable solution to the radical option of federal union.[121]

Completely new *poleis* could be created. The break-up of the 'Peloponnesian league' after 371 presented an opportunity for *polis* formation in some regions. Megalopolis and Ithome (later Messene) were the most impressive foundations; both grew into elaborate urban environments.[122] Other evidence for *polis* formation or demotion is piecemeal. Keryneia, listed as a member of the fourth-century Achaean league, appears to have been recognized as a *polis* for the first time during that century.[123] Eleian Pylos was destroyed after Leuktra (a date supported by archaeology);[124] while the wars of the 360s resulted in the short-lived experiment of making Olympia an independent *polis* by the name of Pisa.[125] In other cases it is uncertain whether a change of status occurred before or after 338, as with the downgrading or disappearance of Argolic Orneai[126] and Achaean Aigai.[127]

The creation of a new central place, as at Ithome and Megalopolis, might be assumed to have had a profound impact on local autonomy and, at least in the short term, on settlement patterns. In the case of Megalopolis, however, the evidence points to limited long-term demographic impact even if formal union was achieved. The dynamics of relationships between major *poleis* and sub-regional groupings kept some *poleis* out of the synoikism.[128] Pausanias lists the many communities synoikized to form Megalopolis, but modern assessments suggest that few were abandoned, at any rate

---

[120] Salmon 1984, 360–2, rebutting Griffith 1950, 252–6; Hamilton 1972, 37; Hamilton 1979, 252, 253; etc.

[121] Salmon 1984, 357–62.

[122] Ithome already a settlement before *c.* 369: inferred by Luraghi 2015, 288, though the evidence cited (Luraghi 2008, 124–7) is only for an Ar–ECl sanctuary.

[123] Morgan and Hall 2004, 482–3 (*Inv. 236*).

[124] Roy 2004, 501–2 (*Inv. 263*), at 502.

[125] Roy 2004, 500–1 (*Inv. 262*). For an Eleian–Pisatan conflict of C4 (rather than Ar), see Möller 2004.

[126] Apparently a *kōmē* by LHl, Strabo 8. 6. 17. Cf. Piérart 2004, 612–13 (*Inv. 354*), at 612.

[127] Last attested at some date between *c.* 370 and C3e. Morgan and Hall 2004, 478–9 (*Inv. 229*), at 479.

[128] Roy 2005.

permanently.[129] Pausanias, indeed, goes on to say that some entered the new union unwillingly, while those people of Trapezous who survived a massacre by their fellow Arkadians (!) even emigrated to the Black sea (8. 27. 6). Notoriously, Megalopolis saw some of its population drift back to their original homes (Diod. 15. 94. 1–2).[130] The vast majority of *poleis* in the jurisdiction of Megalopolis remained in existence, though perhaps with interruptions or changes of status unrecorded in the sources and invisible to archaeology; few of them ever issued coins before the mid-second century (TABLE IV.3).

The detail is worth setting out, not only in order to understand the nature of Megalopolis but because of what it suggests about the strength of the *polis* tradition in Arkadia. Trapezous may have been exceptional in losing *polis* status (Paus. 8. 27. 5).[131] More typical is faraway Kleitor, whose absorption may have been purely formal or temporary; while it provided one of the ten *oikistai* ('founders') of Megalopolis, it continued to exist (or was soon revived) as a *polis*, perhaps with its own dependent settlements (both *poleis* and non-*poleis*),[132] and issued coins down to the late fourth or early third century. Even towns close to Megalopolis did not necessarily disappear: Lykosoura is said to have resisted incorporation (Paus. 8. 2. 6) and may have become a dependent *polis* of Megalopolis, as may Lykaia and Trikonoloi.[133] Others that appear to have survived as settlements or even *poleis* include Oresthasion, Alipheira,[134] Eutaia, Gortys, Methydrion (though it ceased to mint coins after the early fourth century), Thisoa, Helisson (to at least 352), Asea (to at least the late third century, possibly the mid-second), Teuthis (into hellenistic times), and perhaps Dipaia (possibly a dependent *polis* of Orchomenos before the creation of Megalopolis). Pallantion may not have been incorporated despite the original intention to do so,[135] though like Methydrion it did not issue coinage after the late fifth or early fourth century. Even some of Sparta's former north-western *perioikoi* may have persisted as separate settlements within

---

[129] Grunauer-von Hoerschelmann and Scheer (in Lauffer 1989, 411–12 s.v. Megalopolis) are wrong to claim that the city's foundation entailed the 'desolation' (*Verödung*) of a wide upland area.

[130] Diodoros refers incorrectly to the city's desertion as early as 362. See Demand 1990, 114.

[131] Nielsen 2004a, 535 (*Inv. 303*).

[132] Nielsen 2004a, 515–16 (*Inv. 276*), at 515 (still a *polis* in C4m).

[133] Nielsen 2004a, 517 (*Inv. 280*).

[134] Nielsen 2004a, 509–10 (*Inv. 266*), at 509; Paus. 8. 26. 5 says only part of the population went to Megalopolis and the city was not abandoned; Megalopolis controls it in Polyb. 4. 77. 10, but it is a *polis* in *SEG* 25. 447 (C3l).

[135] Nielsen 2004a, 526 (*Inv. 289*).

Arkadia.[136] In some cases political synoikism may have been effected by the transfer of rituals rather than population; by simply relocating a cult statue in order to set up a new 'branch office' of a cult or inaugurating a periodic procession between the old venue and the new. While some rural sanctuaries declined, many continued in use.[137] Thus the foundation of Megalopolis had only a limited impact on the wider settled landscape.

On the negative side, there are examples of demographic disruption so radical that we may suspect that there was little or no continuity between the old *polis* and the new. Thus the installation of democracy at Tegea by the Mantineans in the 360s was accompanied by a bloody coup that resulted in some 800 persons emigrating (Section III.3.b) – surely a large proportion of the *demos*.

Changes to Poleis in the 'Long Third Century'

When we turn to the 'long third century', we find that a small number of *poleis* and other settlements appear to have been abandoned. Achaean Olenos, identified with an archaic to early hellenistic site at *Skágia*, disappeared (or at least ceased to be a *polis*) between 280 and Polybios' day; it appears to have been absorbed by nearby Dyme (Strabo 8. 7. 1), apparently with the physical relocation of the inhabitants. Patrai was briefly dioikized in 279 as a result of losses sustained in fighting the Celts or Gauls when they attacked southern Greece (see Section II.4.b). In Eleia, Makiston may have ceased to exist by 219 – presumably after the battle that took place there, if the inscription from Messene listing casualties is evidence of its continued existence.[138] The evidence for settlement at Elaious, a non-*polis* in Argolis, also runs out in the third century.

Some abandonments, however, may not be all that they seem to be. In Achaea, Helike was submerged in 373 but excavation has revealed a flourishing hellenistic town (Section IV.1.f). In Argolis, the *polis* of Halieis, possibly at times a dependency of nearby Hermion, appears from archaeo- logical evidence to have been partly evacuated – possibly by stages, or with phases of desertion and revival. At Halieis, the peak of activity seems to be in the second and third quarters of the fourth century, and built structures appear to end *c.* 330, but there are also early third-century finds. The city

---

[136] Whether Kromnos (first settled C5m?) did so is uncertain; archaeology does not show whether it was abandoned in C4 or later (Pikoulas 1988b, 161–4; H. W. Catling 1982–3, Touchais 1983, 764–7).

[137] Demand 1990, 115; Nilsson 1951, 18–25; Jost 1985.

[138] Blackman 1996–7, 49; *SEG* 51. 493 (47. 406); but not listed at Polyb. 4. 77. 9, referring to 219.

is thought to have been abandoned *c.* 280, perhaps after being sacked by the exiled Spartan Kleonymos, with a possible transfer of population; yet the archaeologists who suggest this also report later 'squatter' occupation.[139] The *ethnikon* of Halieis is recorded at Epidauros in 220/19 (*IG* iv² 1. 42. 10–11), and it is possible that a small fishing town remained in existence, perhaps as a non-*polis*.[140]

Abandonment could also be reversed. Dyme, which may have existed as a synoikized *polis* only from the fifth century and had perhaps been fortified first in 314,[141] was captured in 208 by the Romans, who sold the population into slavery; but not long afterwards Philip V refounded the city (Section II.5.b), after which it flourishes archaeologically. At least one other substantial settlement, Mycenae, destroyed by the Argives in the fifth century (Diod. 11. 65) but still apparently extant in the late fifth (Thuc. 1. 10), was revived some time after 290[142] and is recorded as a *kōmē* (civic subdivision) of Argos in the third century (cf. *SEG* 13. 238, cf. 52. 331), surviving until its late hellenistic abandonment.[143] Several other *poleis* were removed to new sites, most famously Sikyon by Demetrios Poliorketes.[144] The reason for Hermion's removal, during the second or first century, to a site about half a mile (1 km) west of its original location (cf. Paus. 2. 34. 9–10),[145] is unknown. Leontion was refounded by Gonatas at some point (Strabo 8. 7. 5). Whether relocation of an existing *polis*, even to a site considered more advantageous, was welcome to all its inhabitants may be doubted.

The regions that saw the largest number of changes in the statuses of settlements were Laconia and Argolis, followed by Achaea. Arkadia also displays instability in the physical existence or subordination of *poleis*. To judge by the surviving evidence, however, Messenia seems to have escaped major disruption until the late third century; in this it was not typical.

Change could be for the better. Kalaureia enjoyed a period of independence from Troizen in the third century,[146] for reasons we cannot detect – presumably to do with the aspirations of certain groups among the politically active. A settlement could also be elevated to *polis* status, as was Tenea near

---

[139] Jameson *et al.* 1994, 88–9, cf. 436–7 (also 394–5).

[140] Compare the modest foundation by Tirynthians settling in Halieis (Baladié 1980, 267).

[141] Synoikism by 460: Morgan and Hall 2004, 481–2 (*Inv. 234*), at 481.

[142] Klein 1997, 256–7, 292; Wace *et al.* 1921–3. On the *kōmai* of Argos, see Hansen 1995.

[143] Wace *et al.* 1921–3 implies its C2s abandonment, though Vertsetis 1996–7 says the name disappears only in C1 AD.

[144] Freitag 1999, esp. 241–3, 312.

[145] Piérart 2004, 609–10 (*Inv. 350*), at 610.

[146] Jameson *et al.* 1994, 86.

Corinth in the third century.[147] It is possible that Arkadian Asea changed from *polis* to non-*polis* and back again (see Section IV.3.b). Two *poleis* might merge, presumably for reasons of security or economy, as Stymphalos and Lousoi did in the first half of the third century (*IG* v. 2. 358; *SdA* 560). Forcible intervention in *polis* space by the Macedonians, across the Greek world as a whole, has been claimed as a characteristic of the early hellenistic period, in contrast to the reigns of Philip and Alexander;[148] but both purely formal synoikisms and actual shifts of population may sometimes have been initiated at local level. Changes of status may be forced upon people or chosen by them; in the third century specifically, one motive may have been the policy of a league to which the *polis* belonged or into which its leaders wished to take it.

Since more than 10 per cent of *poleis* in the Peloponnese underwent a change of status at some point during the early hellenistic period, the historical narrative may have given the impression of a deeply unstable landscape. But urban relocation, synoikism, and partial evacuation had often happened before, not only because of warfare. Change was not necessarily more common in the long third century than it had been earlier. The changes we observe were spread unevenly over a long continuum of time, and cases of radical dislocation were relatively few. Alteration of political status was a normal feature of the landscape of settlements because the *polis* was a political, internally contested community competing for space with its neighbours. Status change affected mostly smaller *poleis*, while major *poleis* and major festivals generally continued as before. As with the traditional regional identities, this points to the preponderance of continuity. It also tells against the idea of regional identities being expressed in ways that entailed major consequences. The city-states system was labile, but the *polis* remained the principal framework for changes in political landscapes.[149]

V.4 The Persistent and Permeable *Polis*

Building on the earlier findings, such as the limited political and economic impacts of Macedonian power, we have shown (Section V.1) that the aims of the Antigonids were limited – necessarily, because of the physical and social

---

[147] Legon 2004, 462.

[148] Demand 1990, ch. 12, esp. 158–64.

[149] Cf. Larsen 1955, 103: 'Greek formal political theory was so dominated by the city-state that even a laudation of a federal state took the form of a claim that it was almost a polis' (cf. Polyb. 2. 37. 11).

landscape and their wider strategic interests – and were periodically modified in light of circumstance. We have argued (Section V.2) that regional
identities were less important than *polis* identities, and regions not tightly
integrated to the point where (with the exception of single-*polis* regions)
they can have behaved as social and economic blocs; though there is some
reason (Section V.3) to see the south, somewhat surprisingly, as affected
by long-distance economic linkages to a greater degree. While networks
at different scales were actively constructed and maintained by elites, the
greatest inputs to networks were still made at *polis* level.[150] The continued
primacy of the city-state is largely due to elite initiative, focused not only on
diplomacy but probably also on commerce.

At several points we have emphasized that the Peloponnese and its
peoples were not passive subjects, a blank slate on which powers inscribed
themselves. Change was certainly imposed from outside on occasion; but,
having shown in more than one way that the effects of Macedonian power
were generally limited, we should view changes and continuities in politics,
economy, and landscapes partly as the results of active choices by communities, usually *poleis* though sometimes federal states.

From the data reviewed earlier, it is likely that few explicit choices
affecting the landscape or economy were made either at regional level or at
that of the locality. An example of decisions possibly taken below *polis* level
may be seen in the data from the northern sector of the Laconia Survey,
which may be tentatively interpreted as evidence that demoted Spartans
may have subverted the system or exploited opportunities to try to re-
establish their credentials. In general, however, it was at *polis* level that key
decisions continued to be taken. The scope for agency was greatest here; it
could act upon politics, identity, and inter-*polis* and extra-Peloponnesian
links. Outreach beyond a *polis*'s territory, or beyond the Peloponnese,
was also achieved largely through decisions by *poleis*, and presumably the
men involved in commerce operated primarily as citizens of their *polis*
even when it belonged to a league, though diplomatic missions might be
conducted in the name of the federation. To the plentiful evidence for the
continued vitality of the *polis* may be added the fact that at least twenty-four
poleis minted coinage during the 'long third century' (TABLE IV.3), always
in their own name. Within the Peloponnese, the *polis* remained the primary
agent, or mediator, of both change and continuity.

---

[150] Kralli 2017, ch. 9 (pp. 399–488), is an important study of relationships between specific
poleis, as expressed through institutions such as festivals, proxeny, *theorodokia*, and honorific
decrees.

Earlier (Section III.1) it was remarked that a *polis* was not a sentient being. It did not literally choose: members of the community chose, under the influence chiefly of men active in public life. Identity was (as discussed earlier) negotiable; it may not have been singular even in sub-*polis* settlements; at higher levels, *a fortiori*, it was fluid and labile across space and time, varying between groups, at individual and group level, and in different social contexts. Indeed, it has been argued that 'the state', at least in Greek history, is a hypostatization of what was really a set of fluid relationships.[151] Inscribed records of civic transactions are invariably framed as if *polis* identity was homogeneous and commanded universal assent; but beneath this veneer of unanimity lay a political society in flux. Was every civic decree passed by unanimous vote? Was any?

Both innovation and conservatism were the product of a political process. The search for change and continuity has led us to look at the plural and often diverse elements making up political communities. These include formal and informal status groups, factions, landscape areas with varying resources and settlement patterns, and so on. They could include a partly or wholly new population, in cases where a citizen body had been depleted, exiled, or sold into slavery. International politics was conducted by and between such groups.

Whenever we use a collective noun to attribute acts to agents, such as 'the Stymphalians', we mask the diversity of views that undoubtedly existed, as well as the political processes leading to decisions of a community. The history of civil strife within *poleis* offers many examples of factions with different views; even in normal times, politics was characterized by division. A faction could itself harbour conflicting views, and the absence of modern-style party organizations may have allowed members of factions to change their allegiance more easily, making any such association potentially unstable.[152]

Since the most influential element in dealings within and between *poleis* will normally have been members of the elites of those *poleis*,[153] we should take into account the sources of their power and the manner of their dominance. The pressures for and against innovation were created by contestation among those with the greatest material stake in the fortunes of the state, whether they belonged to the richest group or stood just outside the inner elite. Elite power within a *polis*, however, was not simply a matter of

---

[151] Routledge 2013, 26 (quoted by De Angelis 2015).
[152] On parties as suppressing the individual conscience, see Weil 2014 (trans. of Weil 1957).
[153] On increasing domination of politics by the elite, see e.g. O'Neil 1995, 114–20.

birth or land ownership as such; its actualization not simply a matter of securing majority support in the assembly. The active exploitation of inter-*polis* links and extra-Peloponnesian networks was also a vital aspect of elite construction and maintenance. We suggested earlier that Peloponnesians were increasingly active in long-distance trade networks. It is reasonable to suggest that the men with most to gain from cooperation between *poleis* were also involved in commercial relationships,[154] both within and without the Peloponnese.

Aristotle's famous dictum that the *polis* exists for the sake of 'the good life' (τὸ εὖ ζῆν, lit. 'living well', *Pol.* 1. 2. 1252b 30) presumably reflects a widespread attitude on the part of *polis* members; certainly the more privileged among them, but quite possibly the greater part – citizen status itself bringing considerable privileges. The more prosperous citizens, even if a minority, would view their lifestyle – including the fulfilment of onerous obligations for the benefit of all, with only a distant prospect of civic honours at some future date – as the norm and not the exception. This would, in their eyes, define the worth of the *polis* and their value to it, and justify whatever diplomatic and military steps they might deem necessary in order to preserve this 'good life', which they might rate as good for the *polis* and therefore as more valuable than the freedom of their opponents, who simply by opposing them were a threat to the good life and thus to the *polis*.

Conserving a way of life, paradoxically, can require innovation and – given that circumstances do not remain static – the invention of new forms of organization. Something often seen as a defining feature of the early hellenistic period is the formation of federal leagues and their rise to power. Given the inherent limitations of Macedonian power in the Peloponnese, the constraints upon its efficacy, and its limited aims, rulers' policies may have had the unintended consequences of sparking the refoundation of the Achaean league and creating favourable conditions for the expansion of the Aitolian. There is a temptation to see the formation of federations as a progressive step, aimed at preserving the *polis* system from dissolution and thus preserving freedom within *poleis*.[155] Supra-*polis* organizations are often thought to have offered the best defence against outside powers. Many factors play a part in explaining why and where federal states arose: geography, geopolitical circumstances, the strength of *polis* identity, the nature of internal politics, and so on. Some leagues were formed ostensibly to

---

[154] Mackil 2013 rightly stresses the economic role of federations, but tends to marginalize divisions within *poleis*.

[155] Thus Mackil 2013, 407, writes of the federation as protecting the *polis*. The question immediately arises, *cui bono?*

protect freedom. Messenia, for example, may have become federal after Leuktra; if so, it is natural to suppose that the intention was to strengthen the region's defences against Sparta. At some point between *c.* 369 and *c.* 338, indeed, the coastal *polis* of Korone may have been refounded under Theban patronage (Paus. 4. 34. 5) precisely in order to disrupt Spartan control of southern Messenia.[156] In the case of the Arkadian league, we are expressly told that it was set up in order to prevent a revival of Spartan domination (Paus. 8. 27. 1).

Even if we accept that the Achaean league began as an anti-Macedonian venture, however, we need not accept Polybios' teleological encomium that makes the league as good as the perfect *polis* while embracing the whole Peloponnese – in other words, replacing the member states of the union as citizens' primary source of identity and focus of allegiance. If there is any truth in this idea, which is debatable, it cannot have been so before the first half of the second century – which is also the time when epigraphic outputs point to changes in the degree of centralization in some regions. But enrolment in a federal state might not be to the benefit of all citizens: it might, for example, involve the execution or expulsion of one group and the entrenchment of another in power. If elite members of different *poleis* were willing to cooperate with one another in military and diplomatic dealings at a level above that of a single territory, their motive – especially in an unstable world – was surely not merely geopolitical security but also the securing – as individuals or as groups – of their own participation in certain cultural roles and of their social standing. The partial surrender of autonomy involved in taking one's *polis* into a federal association could thus be seen as a worthwhile sacrifice by certain persons; the alternative being to cede supremacy within the *polis* to their hated opponents under one external hegemon or another.

As evidence of the continuing importance of the *polis*, both in terms of citizens' identity and in terms of managing the wider Peloponnesian environment, one need hardly do more than point to the active investment by *poleis* in both urban sanctuaries and cult places within their rural territory. A 'federal' shrine like that at Aigion was not in neutral territory (as if it were an ancient Australian National Territory or District of Columbia) but firmly under the control of a *polis*, as of course Olympia had always been. Other *polis* sanctuaries, like that of Artemis Lykoatis in the *chora* of Lykosoura – whether the latter was independent or subordinated to Megalopolis some 7 km away – acted as a focus for local, regional, Peloponnesian, and even

---

[156] Roebuck 1941, 34; Demand 1990, 111; Shipley 2004b, 561 (*Inv. 316*).

Mediterranean-wide participants. As new research extends the field of hellenistic sanctuaries beyond the great and favoured architectural environments like Pergamon and Athens,[157] we shall be better placed to understand
how convergence at state and inter-state festivals knitted together local
and more extended networks of communities – with implied commercial
benefits in addition.

At one point, Tarn casts the Achaean league in a negative light, claiming,
first, that it never evolved beyond its anti-Macedonian mission and ended
up serving the ambitions of Aratos:[158]

> [I]ts possibilities of usefulness in the history of Greece were severely
> conditioned and limited from the first. It never had any chance of revivi-
> fying Greece as a whole; it had not the driving force even to withstand
> Kleomenes.

Yet he contradicts himself twice within the next few paragraphs: claiming,
second, that the league was hampered in its aim of unifying the Peloponnese
by the permanent opposition of Sparta, Elis, and Messene (though, as we
have seen, periods of Spartan–Messenian hostility alternated with periods
of alignment); third (a few lines later), that it 'prevented the unification
of the Peloponnese' by neutralizing Kleomenes III![159] The last suggestion
contains a grain of truth – that, because of individual ambitions, opportunities were missed to unite the energies of the league and of Sparta, and
thereby fulfil the original motive for the league's foundation – but the first
of the three formulations is the most accurate, since the league, despite its
successes, could not field a force capable of defeating Sparta and had to rely
on Macedonia to do so.

As for Tarn's second formulation, is it even correct to say that the league
had as its aim the *unification* of the Peloponnese? Its anti-Macedonian
goal surely did not require that. Cooperation between *poleis*, therefore –
or the pooling of sovereignty – reflects the same characteristic of the *polis*
itself as we have identified: the traditional political–economic role of the
elite and their self-conception. Federation, therefore, did not necessarily
aim – at least at the outset – at replacing the *polis*; indeed, in this light a
koinon looks less like a 'federation'. True, it presupposed an existing sense of
regional identity grounded in time-hallowed myths, which was sometimes
endowed with a political meaning and was a precondition of success; but

---

[157] Melfi and Bobou 2016 contains a core of case studies from the Peloponnese, set in a wider
   Greek, Adriatic, and Aegean context.
[158] Tarn 1913, 406.
[159] Tarn 1913, 407.

league loyalty depended upon a prior, and deeper, attachment to one's city-state. Despite the innovative form of early hellenistic *koina*, their strong executives, run by members of *polis* elites and dominated by men from the largest *poleis*,[160] reflected the deep-seated, broadly conservative traditions of the peninsula.[161]

The Antigonids, like the rulers of the other major hellenistic kingdoms, seem to have supported *polis* values and invested in the city-states system. Given the new global order and the pre-existing importance of inter-state networks, however, it was almost inevitable that the legal and political boundaries of the *polis* would become more permeable. We see, for example, citizens possessing land in *poleis* other than their own: Aratos, for example, owned a house (οἰκία) at Corinth (Plut. *Arat.* 41. 4). The admission of Orchomenos to the Achaean league was accompanied by a rule requiring buyers of real estate in the city to hold it for twenty years; perhaps designed to prevent outsiders from engaging in property speculation. By the late hellenistic period, leading Spartans would own land in the territories of other *poleis* of southern Laconia[162] and Arkadia.[163] But increasing permeability did not entail the immediate abandonment of *polis* identity.[164] Whether the *polis* and the city-states system could survive the further consolidation of the Achaean *koinon* and the establishment of Roman rule was a question that would be answered only after the Macedonians had left the Peloponnese.

---

[160] McKechnie 1989, 1–15, argues that the *polis* ceased to be all-determining, identifying (at p. 5) a contradiction between an elite ideology still framed in terms of the *polis* and the reality of depleted independence; but he overstates the loss of independence and the effects of Macedonian power.

[161] On democracy in Hl federations, see O'Neil 1995, 121–33, though he exaggerates the differences between Cl and Hl democracy.

[162] Asopos on the mainland: Lane 1962, with *SEG* 22. 310; island of Kythera given to Eurykles by Augustus, Dio 54. 7. 2 (cf. Strabo 8. 5. 1); likewise Thouria, Paus. 4. 31. 1; Kardamyle, Paus. 3. 26. 7. Cf. Bowersock 1961, 112–13, 116.

[163] Megalopolis honours members of Eurykles' family: *IG* v. 2. 541–2. Cf. Spawforth 1978, 253; Alcock 1993, 78.

[164] Bresson 2016, 215–16 (with nn. 45–6 on p. 488), argues that the city-states system was intrinsically connected with exclusive landholding.

Works Cited

Acheson, P. E. (1997), 'Does the "economic explanation" work? Settlement, agriculture, and erosion in the territory of Halieis in the late classical–early hellenistic period', *JMA* 10. 2: 165–90.

Admiralty, Naval Intelligence Division (1944–5), *Greece*. 3 vols. [London]: Naval Intelligence Division.

(1945), *Greece*, iii: *Regional Geography*. [London]: Naval Intelligence Division.

(n.d. [1918]), *A Handbook of Greece*, i: *The Mainland of Old Greece and Certain Neighbouring Islands*. London: HMSO.

Ager, S. L. (1996), *Interstate Arbitrations in the Greek World, 337–90 BC*. Berkeley–Los Angeles and London: University of California Press.

Alcock, S. E. (1991), 'Urban survey and the polis of Phlius', *Hesperia* 60. 4: 421–63.

(1993), *Graecia Capta: The Landscapes of Roman Greece*. Cambridge University Press.

Berlin, A. M., Harrison, A. B., Heath, S., Spencer, N., and Stone, D. L. (2005), 'The Pylos Regional Archaeological Project, part VII: historical Messenia, Geometric through late Roman', *Hesperia*, 74. 2: 147–209.

and Cherry, J. F. (eds) (2004), *Side-by-Side Survey: Comparative Regional Studies in the Mediterranean World*. Oxford: Oxbow.

Alevridis, S., and Melfi, M. (2005), 'New archaeological and topographical observations on the sanctuary of Asklepios in Alipheira', in E. Østby (ed.), *Ancient Arcadia* (Athens and Sävedalen, Sweden: Norwegian Institute at Athens/Åström), 273–84.

Alexandropoulou, A. (2011), 'Ο ηλειακός υψίπους κάνθαρος', in *7th Hellenistic Pottery Meeting*, 613–22, pls 261–4.

Alonso Déniz, A. (2007), 'Estudios sobre la aspiración de /s/ en los dialectos griegos del I milenio', PhD thesis. Universidad Complutense de Madrid.

(2014), 'L'esprit du temps: koiné, dialecte et hyper-dialecte dans les inscriptions agonistiques du sanctuaire d'Artémis Orthia à Sparte', in S. Minon (ed.), *Diffusion de l'attique et expansion des koinai dans le Péloponnèse et en Grèce centrale* (Geneva: Droz), 141–68.

Alty, J. H. M. (1982), 'Dorians and Ionians', *JHS* 102: 1–14.

Anderson-Stojanović, V. R. (1997), 'A third century BC deposit from the south slope cistern in the Rachi settlement at Isthmia', in *4th Hellenistic Pottery Meeting*, 13–19, pls 1–10.

(2000), 'Corinthian West Slope pottery from Isthmia', in *5th Hellenistic Pottery Meeting*, 381–5, pls 203–4.

295

(2004), 'Dinner at the Isthmus: hellenistic cooking ware from the Rachi settlement at Isthmia', in *6th Hellenistic Pottery Meeting*, 623–30, pls 303–6.

(2011), 'Pottery from destruction deposits of the Rachi settlement at Isthmia ca. 200 BC', in *7th Hellenistic Pottery Meeting*, 117–22, pls 51–4.

Andrewes, A. (1954), *Probouleusis: Sparta's Contribution to the Technique of Government (an Inaugural Lecture delivered before the University of Oxford on 25 May 1954)*. Oxford University Press.

Andrianou, D. (2009), *The Furniture and Furnishings of Ancient Greek Houses and Tombs*. Cambridge University Press.

Antonetti, C. (2012), 'Il trattato fra Sparta e gli Etoli Erxadiei: una riflessione critica', in S. Cataldi, E. Bianco, and G. Cuniberti (eds), *Salvare le poleis: costruire la concordia, progettare la pace* (Alessandria: Edizioni dell'Orso), 193–208.

Antonopoulos, K. V. (2015), 'Τα ηλειακά λιμάνια Κυλλήνης και Φειάς και ο ρόλος τους στους Ολυμπιακούς Αγώνες της Αρχαιότητας', *Historika*, 5: 183–204.

Aperghis, G. G. (2001), 'Population – production – taxation – coinage: a model for the Seleukid economy', in Z. H. Archibald, J. Davies, V. Gabrielsen, and G. J. Oliver (eds), *Hellenistic Economies* (London and New York: Routledge), 69–102.

Arapogianni, X. (2005), 'Οι ελληνιστικοί τάφοι της Φιγάλειας', in L. Kypraiou (ed.), *Ελληνιστική κεραμική από την Πελοπόννησο* (Athens: Ypourgeio Politismou), 83–94.

Archibald, Z. H., Davies, J., Gabrielsen, V., and Oliver, G. J. (eds) (2001), *Hellenistic Economies*. London and New York: Routledge.

Davies, J. K., and Gabrielsen, V. (eds) (2005), *Making, Moving and Managing: The New World of Ancient Economies, 323–31 BC*. Oxford: Oxbow.

Davies, J. K, and Gabrielsen, V. (eds) (2011), *The Economies of Hellenistic Societies: Third to First Centuries BC*. Oxford University Press.

Arenz, A. (2006), *Herakleides Kritikos, Über die Städte in Hellas: eine Periegese Griechenlands am Vorabend des chremonideischen Krieges*. Munich: Herbert Utz/tuduv.

Arnaud, P. (1992), 'Les relations maritimes dans le Pont-Euxin d'après les données numériques des géographes anciens', *L'Océan et les mers lointaines dans l'Antiquité = REA* 94. 1–2: 57–77.

Ault, B. A. (1999), 'Koprones and oil presses at Halieis: interactions of town and country and the integration of domestic and regional economies', *Hesperia*, 68. 4: 549–73.

Aupert, P., and Ginouvès, R. (1989), 'Une toiture révolutionnaire à Argos', in S. Walker and A. Cameron (eds), *The Greek Renaissance in the Roman Empire* (London: Institute of Classical Studies), 151–5, pls 57–9.

Austin, C., and Bastianini, G. (2002), *Posidippi Pellaei quae supersunt omnia*. Milan: LED.

Austin, M. M. (1994), 'Society and economy', in *CAH*, 2nd edn, vi: *The Fourth Century BC*, 527–64.

(2006), *The Hellenistic World from Alexander to the Roman Conquest: A Selection of Ancient Sources in Translation*, 2nd edn. Cambridge University Press.

Avraméa, A. (1997), *Le Péloponnèse du IVe au VIIIe siècle: changements et persistances.* Paris: Centre de Recherches d'Histoire et de Civilisation Byzantines.

Bagnall, R. S. (1976), *The Administration of the Ptolemaic Possessions outside Egypt.* Leiden: Brill.

and Derow, P. S. (1981), *Greek Historical Documents: The Hellenistic Period*, 1st edn. Chico, CA: Scholars Press.

Baladié, R. (ed.) (1978), *Strabon, Géographie, v: Livre VIII.* Paris: Les Belles Lettres/ Association Guillaume Budé.

(1980), *Le Péloponnèse de Strabon: étude de géographie historique.* Paris: Les Belles Lettres.

Baldwin Bowsky, M. W., and Niniou-Kindeli, V. (2006), 'On the road again: a Trajanic milestone and the road connections of Aptera, Crete', *Hesperia*, 75. 3: 405–33.

Banaka-Dimaki, A. (2002), 'Cult places in Argos', in R. Hägg (ed.), *Peloponnesian Sanctuaries and Cults* (Stockholm: Svenska Institutet i Athen), 107–16. Trans. J. van Leuven.

(2005), Ἑλληνιστική κεραμική ἀπό τό Ἄργος', in L. Kypraiou, *Ἑλληνιστική κεραμική ἀπό την Πελοπόννησο* (Athens: Ypourgeio Politismou), 126–42.

Barakari-Gléni, K., and Pariente, A. (1998), 'Argos du VIIᵉ au IIᵉ siècle av. J.-C.: synthèse des données archéologiques', in A. Pariente and G. Touchais (eds), *Ἄργος καὶ Ἀργολίδα: τοπογραφία καὶ πολεοδομία/Argos et l'Argolide: topographie et urbanisme* (Paris: Ypourgeio Politismou, D´ Ephoreia Proïstorikon kai Klasikon Archaiotiton/École française d'Athènes), 165–78.

Barber, R. L. N. (1995), *Greece*, 6th edn. London and New York: A. & C. Black/W. W. Norton.

Bayliss, A. J. (2011), *After Demosthenes: The Politics of Early Hellenistic Athens.* London: Continuum.

Beard, M., and Henderson, J. (2000), *Classics: A Very Short Introduction.* First published 1995. Oxford and New York: Oxford University Press.

Beck, H. (1997), *Polis und Koinon: Untersuchungen zur Geschichte und Struktur der griechischen Bundesstaaten im 4. Jh. v. Chr.* Stuttgart: Steiner.

and Funke, P. (eds) (2015), *Federalism in Greek Antiquity.* Cambridge University Press.

Beloch, K. J. (1886), *Die Bevölkerung der griechisch-römischen Welt.* Leipzig: Duncker & Humbler.

Bergquist, B. (1990), 'Primary or secondary temple function: the case of Halieis', *OAth* 18: 23–37.

Billows, R. A. (1990), *Antigonus the One-eyed and the Creation of the Hellenistic State.* Berkeley–Los Angeles and London: University of California Press.

Bintliff, J. L. (1997), 'Regional survey, demography, and the rise of complex societies in the ancient Aegean: core–periphery, neo-Malthusian, and other interpretive models', *JFA* 24. 1: 1–38.

(2008), 'The Peloponnese in hellenistic and early Roman imperial times: the evidence from survey and the wider Aegean context', in C. Grandjean (ed.), *Le Péloponnèse d'Épaminondas à Hadrien* (Bordeaux and Paris: Ausonius and De Boccard), 21–52.

(2014), 'Mobility and proto-capitalism in the hellenistic and early Roman Mediterranean', in E. Olshausen and V. Sauer (eds), *Mobilität in den Kulturen der antiken Mittelmeerwelt* (Stuttgart: Steiner), 49–53.

Birgalias, N. (2003), 'The Peloponnesian league as a political organization', in K. Buraselis and K. Zoumboulakis (eds), *The Idea of European Community in History*, ii: *Aspects of Connecting Poleis and Ethne in Ancient Greece* (Athens: National and Capodistrian University of Athens/Greek Ministry of Education and Religious Affairs), 19–26.

Blackman, D. J. (1996–7), 'Archaeology in Greece 1996–97', *AR* 43: 1–125.

(1997–8), 'Archaeology in Greece 1997–98', *AR* 44: 1–128.

(1998–9), 'Archaeology in Greece 1998–99', *AR* 45: 1–124.

(1999–2000), 'Archaeology in Greece 1999–2000', *AR* 46: 3–151.

(2000–1), 'Archaeology in Greece 2000–2001', *AR* 47: 3–144.

(2001–2), 'Archaeology in Greece 2001–2002', *AR* 48: 1–115.

Bolmarcich, S. (2005), 'Thucydides 1.19.1 and the Peloponnesian league', *GRBS* 45. 1: 5–34.

Bonnier, A. (2016), 'Harbours and hinterland networks by the Corinthian gulf: from the archaic to the early hellenistic period', in K. Höghammar, B. Alroth, and A. Lindhagen (eds), *Ancient Ports: The Geography of Connections* (Uppsala: Acta Universitatis Upsaliensis), 65–94.

Bookidis, N. (2010), *The Terracotta Sculpture*. Princeton: American School of Classical Studies at Athens.

Bosworth, A. B. (1994), 'Alexander the Great part 1: the events of the reign', in *CAH*, 2nd edn, vi: *The Fourth Century* BC, 791–845.

(2012a), 'Agis III', *OCD*⁴ 39.

(2012b), 'Hieronymus 1', *OCD*⁴ 684.

Bowersock, G. W. (1961), 'Eurycles of Sparta', *JRS* 51: 112–18.

Bowkett, L. C. (1995), *The Hellenistic Dye-works*. Oxford: Oxbow.

Bradeen, D. W. (1966), 'Inscriptions from Nemea', *Hesperia*, 35: 320–30.

Bresson, A. (2014), 'The ancient world: a climatic challenge', in F. de Callataÿ (ed.), *Quantifying the Greek Economy and Beyond* (Bari: Edipuglia), 43–62.

(2016), *The Making of the Ancient Greek Economy: Institutions, Markets, and Growth in the City-states*. Princeton and Oxford: Princeton University Press. Trans. S. Rendall.

Broneer, O. B. (1954), *The South Stoa and its Roman Successors*. Princeton, NJ: American School of Classical Studies at Athens.

Broodbank, C. (2013), *The Making of the Middle Sea: A History of the Mediterranean from the Beginning to the Emergence of the Classical World*. London: Thames & Hudson.

Buck, V. A., and Stewart, I. S. (2000), 'A critical appraisal of the classical texts and archaeological evidence for earthquakes in the Atalanti region, central mainland Greece', in W. J. McGuire, D. R. Griffiths, P. L. Hancock, and I. S. Stewart (eds), *The Archaeology of Geological Catastrophes* (London: Geological Society), 33–44.

Bull, H. (1977), *The Anarchical Society: A Study of Order in World Politics*. London: Macmillan.

Buraselis, K. (1982), *Das hellenistische Makedonien und die Ägäis: Forschungen zur Politik des Kassandros und der drei ersten Antigoniden im ägäischen Meer und in Westkleinasien*. Munich: Beck.

—— (2013), 'On the Nemean games in the hellenistic period: the vicissitudes of a Panhellenic festival through war and peace', in N. Birgalias, K. Buraselis, P. Cartledge, and A. Gkartziou-Tatti (eds), *War–Peace and Panhellenic Games – Πόλεμος–ειρήνη και πανελλήνιοι αγώνες: In Memory of Pierre Carlier* (Athens: International Institute of Ancient Hellenic History 'Sosipolis'/Institut du Livre/Kardamitsa), 169–88.

Burford, A. (1969), *The Greek Temple Builders at Epidauros: A Social and Economic Study of Building in the Asklepian Sanctuary, during the Fourth and Early Third Centuries* BC. Liverpool University Press.

Bury, J. B. (1898), 'The double city of Megalopolis', *JHS* 18: 15–22.

Cameron, A. D. E., and Pelling, C. B. R. (2012a), 'Alcaeus (3)', *OCD*⁴ 50.

—— (2012b), 'Posidippus (2)', *OCD*⁴ 1195.

Campbell, D. R. J. (2009), 'The so-called Galatae, Celts, and Gauls in the early hellenistic Balkans and the attack on Delphi in 280–279 BC', PhD thesis. University of Leicester.

Canali de Rossi, F. (2001), *Iscrizioni storiche ellenistiche*, iii. Rome: the author.

Caraher, W. R., and Gregory, T. E. (2006), 'Fortifications of Mount Oneion, Corinthia', *Hesperia*, 75. 3: 327–56.

—— Nakassis, D., and Pettegrew, D. K. (2006), 'Siteless survey and intensive data collection in an artifact-rich environment: case studies from the eastern Corinthia, Greece', *JMA* 19. 1: 7–43.

—— Pettegrew, D. K., and James, S. (2010), 'Towers and fortifications at Vayia in the southeast Corinthia', *Hesperia*, 79. 3: 385–415.

Carlsson, S. (2010), *Hellenistic Democracies: Freedom, Independence and Political Procedure in Some East Greek City-states*. Stuttgart: Steiner.

Carney, E. D. (2001), 'The trouble with Philip Arrhidaeus', *AHB* 15. 1–2: 63–89.

—— (2007), 'The Philippeum, women, and the formation of a dynastic image', in W. Heckel, L. Tritle, and P. Wheatley (eds), *Alexander's Empire: Formulation to Decay* (Claremont, CA: Regina Books), 27–60.

Cartledge, P. A. (1976), 'Seismicity and Spartan society', *LCM* 1. 1: 25–8.

—— (1982), 'Sparta and Samos: a special relationship?', *CQ* 76(n.s. 32). 2: 243–65.

—— (1987), *Agesilaos and the Crisis of Sparta*. London: Duckworth.

—— (2001), 'The effects of the Peloponnesian (Athenian) war on Athenian and Spartan societies', in D. R. McCann and B. S. Strauss (eds), *War and Democracy: A*

Comparative Study of the Korean War and the Peloponnesian War (Armonk, NY, and London: M. E. Sharpe), 104–23.

(2002a), 'The economy (economies) of ancient Greece', in W. Scheidel and S. von Reden (eds), *The Ancient Economy* (London and New York: Routledge and Edinburgh University Press), 11–32.

(2002b), *Sparta and Lakonia: A Regional History 1300–362 BC*, 2nd edn. London and New York: Routledge.

(2012), 'Nabis', *OCD*⁴ 994.

(2016), *Democracy: A Life*. Oxford: Oxford University Press.

and Spawforth, A. J. S. (2002), *Hellenistic and Roman Sparta: A Tale of Two Cities*, 2nd edn. London and New York: Routledge.

Catling, H. W. (1972–3), 'Archaeology in Greece, 1972–73', *AR* 19: 3–32.

(1982–3), 'Archaeology in Greece, 1982–83', *AR* 29: 3–62.

(1984–5), 'Archaeology in Greece, 1984–85', *AR* 31: 3–69.

(1985–6), 'Archaeology in Greece, 1985–86', *AR* 32: 3–101.

(1988–9), 'Archaeology in Greece 1988–89', *AR* 35: 3–116.

Catling, R. W. V. (1996), 'The archaic and classical pottery', in W. Cavanagh, J. Crouwel, R. W. V. Catling, and G. Shipley, *Continuity and Change in a Greek Rural Landscape: The Laconia Survey*, ii. *Archaeological Data* (London: British School at Athens), 33–89.

(2002), 'The survey area from the Early Iron Age to the classical period (*c.* 1050–*c.* 300 BC)', in W. Cavanagh, J. Crouwel, R. W. V. Catling, and G. Shipley (eds), *Continuity and Change in a Greek Rural Landscape: The Laconia Survey*, i. *Methodology and Interpretation* (London: British School at Athens), 151–256.

Cavanagh, W. G., and Crouwel, J. (2002), 'The survey area in the prehistoric periods', in W. Cavanagh, J. Crouwel, R. W. V. Catling, and G. Shipley, *Continuity and Change in a Greek Rural Landscape: The Laconia Survey*, i: *Methodology and Interpretation* (London: British School at Athens), 121–50.

Crouwel, J. H., Catling, R. W. V., and Shipley, D. G. J. (1996), *Continuity and Change in a Greek Rural Landscape: The Laconia Survey*, ii: *Archaeological Data*. London: British School at Athens.

Crouwel, J. H., Catling, R. W. V., and Shipley, D. G. J. (2002), *Continuity and Change in a Greek Rural Landscape: The Laconia Survey*, i: *Methodology and Interpretation*. London: British School at Athens.

and Roy, J. (eds) (n.d. [2008]), *Being Peloponnesian* (Nottingham: Centre for Spartan & Peloponnesian Studies, University of Nottingham).

Chaniotis, A. (2013), 'Paradoxon, enargeia, empathy: hellenistic decrees and hellenistic oratory', in C. Kremmydas and K. Tempest (eds), *Hellenistic Oratory: Continuity and Change* (Oxford University Press), 201–16.

Charneux, P., and Ginouvès, R. (1956), 'Reconnaissances en Arcadie: fortifications de Paliocastro, Saint Nicolas et Hellenico', *BCH* 80: 522–46.

Cherry, J. F., Davis, J. L., and Mantzourani, E. (1996–2000), 'The Nemea Valley Archaeological Project archaeological survey: internet edition'. 15 Dec. 2002.

Chrimes, K. M. T. (1949), *Ancient Sparta: A Re-examination of the Evidence.* Manchester University Press.

Christie, N. J. (2004), 'Landscapes of change in late antiquity and the early Middle Ages: themes, directions and problems', in *Landscapes of Change: Rural Evolutions in Late Antiquity and the Early Middle Ages* (Aldershot: Ashgate), 1–37.

Classical Numismatic Group (2009), *The BCD Collection of Coins of the Peloponnesos, Part II*. Lancaster, PA., and London: Classical Numismatic Group.

Cohen, G. M. (1995), *The Hellenistic Settlements in Europe, the Islands, and Asia Minor*. Berkeley–Los Angeles and London: University of California Press.

Colvin, S. (2014), 'Perceptions synchroniques des dialectes et de la koiné', in S. Minon (ed.), *Diffusion de l'attique et expansion des koinai dans le Péloponnèse et en Grèce centrale* (Geneva: Droz), 19–28.

Couvenhes, J.-C. (2004), 'Les cités grecques d'Asie Mineure et le mercenariat à l'époque hellénistique', in J.-C. Couvenhes and H. L. Fernoux (eds), *Les Cités grecques et la guerre en Asie Mineure à l'époque hellénistique* (Paris: Presses Universitaires François-Rabelais), 77–113.

(2006), 'La place de l'armée dans l'économie hellénistique: quelques considérations sur la condition matérielle et financière du soldat et son usage dans les marchés', in R. Descat (ed.), *Approches de l'économie hellénistique: 4mes rencontres sur l'économie antique, Saint-Bertrand-de-Comminges, 2004* (Saint-Bertrand-de-Comminges: Musée archéologique départemental de Saint-Bertrand-de-Comminges), 397–436.

(2008), 'Le Ténare: un grand marché de mercenaires à la fin du IVe siècle?', in C. Grandjean (ed.), *Le Péloponnèse d'Épaminondas à Hadrien* (Bordeaux and Paris: Ausonius and De Boccard), 277–315.

Cracolici, V. (2005), 'Pottery from the Norwegian Arcadia Survey: a preliminary report', in E. Østby (ed.), *Ancient Arcadia* (Athens and Sävedalen, Sweden: Norwegian Institute at Athens and Åström), 123–9.

Crespo, E. (2014), 'Diffusion de l'attique et développement de koinai dans le Péloponnèse (1re moitié du IVe siècle av. J.-C.)', in S. Minon (ed.), *Diffusion de l'attique et expansion des koinai dans le Péloponnèse et en Grèce centrale* (Geneva: Droz), 57–68.

Crouwel, J. H., Prent, M., and Thorne, S. M. (2006), 'Geraki: an acropolis site in Lakonia. Preliminary report on the twelfth campaign (2006)', *Pharos* 14: 1–14.

van der Vin, J., and Smits, L. (2005), 'Geraki: an acropolis site in Lakonia. Preliminary report on the eleventh season (2005)', *Pharos* 13: 3–28.

Crowther, C. V. (1992), 'The decline of Greek democracy?', *JAC* 7: 13–48.

Curtius, E. (1851–2), *Peloponnesos: eine historisch-geographische Beschreibung der Halbinsel*. 2 vols. Gotha: Justus Perthes.

Dalby, A. (1991), 'The curriculum vitae of Duris of Samos', *CQ* 85(n.s. 41). 2: 539–41.

Dalongeville, R. (1992), 'Les sites archéologiques', in R. Dalongeville, M. Lakakis, and A. D. Rizakis (eds), *Le Bassin du Péiros et la plaine occidentale* (Athens: Kentron Ellinikis kai Romaïkis Archaiotitos, Ethniko Idryma Erevnon), 171–222.

Lakakis, M., and Rizakis, A. D. (eds) (1992), *Le Bassin du Péiros et la plaine occidentale*. Athens: Kentron Ellinikis kai Romaïkis Archaiotitos, Ethniko Idryma Erevnon.

Danali, K. (1994), Ἡ ἑλληνιστικὴ κεραμικὴ ἀπὸ τὸ πρόπυλο τοῦ "γυμνασίου" στὸ Ἀσκληπιεῖο τῆς Ἐπιδαύρου', *AEph* 133: 255–98.

(2011), Ἑλληνιστική κεραμική από τον τάφο 3 του τύμβου της Τσοπάνης-Ράχης στην Πύλο', in *7th Hellenistic Pottery Meeting*, 107–16, pls 47–50.

Dareste, R., Haussoullier, B., and Reinach, T. (1891–5), *Recueil des inscriptions juridiques grecques*. 2 vols. Paris: E. Leroux.

Davies, J. K. (2001), 'Rebuilding a temple: the economic effects of piety', in D. J. Mattingly and J. B. Salmon (eds), *Economies beyond Agriculture in the Classical World* (London and New York: Routledge), 209–29.

(2004), 'Demetrio di Faro, la pirateria, e le economie ellenistiche', in L. Braccesi (ed.), *La pirateria nell'adriatico antico = Hesperìa*, 19: 119–27.

(2005), 'Linear and nonlinear flow models for ancient economies', in J. G. Manning and I. Morris (eds), *The Ancient Economy: Evidence and Models* (Stanford, CA: Stanford University Press), 127–56.

(2013), 'Mediterranean economies through the text of Polybios', in B. Gibson and T. Harrison (eds), *Polybius and his World: Essays in Memory of F. W. Walbank* (Oxford and New York: Oxford University Press), 319–35.

Davis, J. L. (ed.) (1998), *Sandy Pylos: An Archaeological History from Nestor to Navarino*. Austin, TX: University of Texas Press.

(ed.) (2008), *Sandy Pylos: An Archaeological History from Nestor to Navarino*, 2nd edn. Princeton, NJ: American School of Classical Studies Publications.

Alcock, S. E., Bennet, J., Lolos, G. G., and Shelmerdine, C. W. (1997), 'The Pylos Regional Archaeological Project, part I: overview and the archaeological survey', *Hesperia*, 66. 3: 391–494, pls 85–92.

Alcock, S. E., Bennet, J., Lolos, G. G., Shelmerdine, C. W. and Zangger, E. (1996–2010), 'The Pylos Regional Archaeological Project: internet edition'. 12 Nov. 2013.

Dawkins, R. M. (1929), 'The history of the sanctuary', in R. M. Dawkins (ed.), *The Sanctuary of Artemis Orthia at Sparta* (London: Council of the Society for the Promotion of Hellenic Studies/Macmillan), 1–51, pls 1–6.

De Angelis, F. (2015), review of B. Routledge, *Archaeology and State Theory*, in *BMCR* 2015.04.37.

de Callataÿ, F. (2006), 'Réflexions quantitatives sur l'or et l'argent non monnayés à l'époque hellénistique: pompes, triomphes, réquisitions, fortunes de temples, orfèvrerie et masses métalliques disponibles', in R. Descat (ed.), *Approches de l'économie hellénistique: 4mes rencontres sur l'économie antique, Saint-Bertrand-de-Comminges, 2004* (Saint-Bertrand-de-Comminges: Musée archéologique départemental de Saint-Bertrand-de-Comminges), 37–84.

de Cerio Díez, M. D. (1998a), 'La evolución de un género: elementos estructurales de los epigramas dedicados a animales de Ánite de Tegea', *Emerita*, 66: 119–49.

(1998b), 'Tipología formal y función estilística de la referencia a la muerte en los epigramas funerarios de Ánite de Tegea', *Faventia*, 20. 1: 49–73.

de Sainte Croix, G. E. M. (1972a), 'The "constitution of the Peloponnesian league": a summary', in *The Origins of the Peloponnesian War* (London: Duckworth), 339–40 (appendix 18).

(1972b), *The Origins of the Peloponnesian War*. London: Duckworth.

Dekoulakou, I. (2011), Ἑλληνιστικὴ κεραμικὴ ἀπὸ τὴν Κερύνεια Ἀχαΐας', in *7th Hellenistic Pottery Meeting*, 35–6, pls 1–2.

Delano Smith, C. (1996), 'Where was the "wilderness" in Roman times?', in G. Shipley and J. B. Salmon (eds), *Human Landscapes in Classical Antiquity: Environment and Culture* (London and New York: Routledge), 154–79.

Delivorrias, A. (1993), 'Λακωνικὰ ἀνθέμια', in O. Palagia and W. Coulson (eds), *Sculpture from Arcadia and Laconia* (Oxford: Oxbow), 205–16.

Demand, N. H. (1990), *Urban Relocation in Archaic and Classical Greece: Flight and Consolidation*. Bristol: Bristol Classical Press.

Derow, P. S. (1993), review of R. A. Billows, Antigonus the One-eyed and the Creation of the Hellenistic State, in *CR* 107(n.s. 43). 2 (1990): 326–32.

(2012a), 'Philip (3) V', *OCD*⁴ 1129.

(2012b), 'Pyrrhus', *OCD*⁴ 1245.

Descat, R. (ed.) (2006), *Approches de l'économie hellénistique (4ᵐᵉˢ rencontres sur l'économie antique, Saint-Bertrand-de-Comminges, 2004)*. Saint-Bertrand-de-Comminges: Musée archéologique départemental de Saint-Bertrand-de-Comminges.

Despinis, G. (1993), 'Ἕνα σύμπλεγμα ἐφεδρισμοῦ ἀπὸ τὴν Τεγέα', in O. Palagia and W. Coulson (eds), *Sculpture from Arcadia and Laconia* (Oxford: Oxbow), 87–97.

Dickinson, O. T. P. K. (2012), 'Tiryns', *OCD*⁴ 1486.

Dillery, J. (1995), *Xenophon and the History of his Times*. London and New York: Routledge.

Dixon, M. D. (2000), 'Disputed territories: interstate arbitrations in the NE Peloponnese, ca. 250–150 BC', PhD thesis. Ohio State University.

(2001), 'IG IV².1.75+ and the date of the arbitration between Epidauros and Hermion', *ZPE* 137: 169–73.

(2003), 'Hellenistic arbitration: the Achaian league and Ptolemaic Arsinoe (Methana)', in E. Konsolaki-Giannopoulou (ed.), Ἀργοσαρωνικός: Πρακτικὰ 1ου Διεθνοῦς Συνεδρίου Ἱστορίας καὶ Ἀρχαιολογίας τοῦ Ἀργοσαρωνικοῦ, ii (Athens: Dimos Porou), 81–7.

(2005), 'Epigraphy and topographical survey: the case of the Corinthian–Epidaurian border in the hellenistic period', in N. M. Kennell and J. E. Tomlinson (eds), *Ancient Greece at the Turn of the Millennium – La Grèce antique au tournant du millénaire: Recent Work and Future Perspectives – Travaux récents et perspectives d'avenir* (Athens: Canadian Archaeological Institute at Athens), 137–44.

(2014), *Late Classical and Hellenistic Corinth: 338–196 BC*. London and New York: Routledge.

Donati, J. C., and Sarris, A. (2016), 'Evidence for two planned Greek settlements in the Peloponnese from satellite remote sensing', *AJA* 120: 361–98.

Dorandi, T. (1991), *Ricerche sulla cronologia dei filosofi ellenistici*. Stuttgart: Teubner.

Dreyer, B. (1999), *Untersuchungen zur Geschichte des spätklassischen Athen: 322–ca. 230 v. Chr.* Stuttgart: Steiner.

Drougou, S., and Touratsoglou, I. P. (2013), 'Die hellenistische Keramik Makedoniens außerhalb des Landes', in N. Fenn and C. Römer-Strehl (eds), *Networks in the Hellenistic World: According to the Pottery in the Eastern Mediterranean and Beyond* (Oxford; BAR), 47–57.

Dubois, L. (2014), 'Dialecte et langues communes en Arcadie à l'époque hellénistique', in S. Minon (ed.), *Diffusion de l'attique et expansion des koinai dans le Péloponnèse et en Grèce centrale* (Geneva: Droz), 87–96.

Ducat, J. (1990), *Les Hilotes*. Paris: École française d'Athènes.

(1994), *Les Pénestes de Thessalie*. Paris: Les Belles Lettres.

(2008), 'Le statut des périèques lacédémoniens', *Ktema*, 33: 1–86.

Duyrat, F. (2011), 'Guerre et thésaurisation en Syrie hellénistique, IVe–Ier s. av. J.-C', in T. Faucher, M.-C. Marcellesi, and O. Picard (eds), *Nomisma: la circulation monétaire dans le monde grec antique* (Paris: École française d'Athènes), 417–31.

Eckstein, A. M. (1987), 'Polybius, Aristaenus, and the fragment "on traitors"', *CQ* n.s. 37: 140–62.

(2007), *Mediterranean Anarchy, Interstate War, and the Rise of Rome*. Berkeley–Los Angeles, CA: University of California Press.

Edgeworth, M. (2011), *Fluid Pasts: Archaeology of Flow*. London: Bristol Classical Press/Bloomsbury Academic.

Ehrenberg, V. (1929), 'Sparta: Geschichte', *RE²* iii. 2. 1373–1453.

Élaigne, S. (2013), 'Éléments d'évaluation des échelles de diffusion de la vaisselle de table au IIe siècle avant J.-C. dans le monde hellénistique', in A. Tsingarida and D. Viviers (eds), *Pottery Markets in the Ancient Greek World (8th–1st Centuries BC)* (Brussels: Université libre de Bruxelles, Centre de Recherches en Archéologie et Patrimoine), 213–28.

Eleftheriou, E. P., and Skagkos, N. I. (2010–13), 'Βουτιάνοι Λακωνίας, Ἐκκλησιές: η ανασκαφική έρευνα, I', *Ὅρος* 22. 5: 535–60.

Ellis, J. R. (1994), 'Macedonian hegemony created', in *CAH*, 2nd edn, vi: *The Fourth Century BC*, 760–90.

Ellis Jones, J. (1970), 'Excavations in the Peneios valley', *ADelt* 25. B (Chr.). 1: 197.

Elton, H., and Reger, G. (2007a), 'Introduction', in H. Elton and G. Reger (eds), *Regionalism in Hellenistic and Roman Asia Minor* (Bordeaux: Ausonius), 11–16.

(eds) (2007b), *Regionalism in Hellenistic and Roman Asia Minor (Trinity College, Hartford CT, 22–24 August 1997)*. Bordeaux: Ausonius.

Engels, D. W. (1978), *Alexander the Great and the Logistics of the Macedonian Army*. Berkeley–Los Angeles, CA: University of California Press.

(1990), *Roman Corinth: An Alternative Model for the Classical City*. First published Chicago University Press, 1990. London and New York: Routledge.

Errington, R. M. (1989a), 'Rome against Philip and Antiochus', in A. E. Astin, F. W. Walbank, M. W. Frederiksen, and R. M. Ogilvie (eds), *CAH*, 2nd edn, viii: *Rome and the Mediterranean to 133 BC*, 244–89.

(1989b), 'Rome and Greece to 205 BC', in A. E. Astin, F. W. Walbank, M. W. Frederiksen, and R. M. Ogilvie (eds), *CAH*, 2nd edn, viii: *Rome and the Mediterranean to 133 BC*, 81–106.

(1990), *A History of Macedonia*. Berkeley–Los Angeles and London: University of California Press.

(2012), 'Achaean confederacy', *OCD*[4] 4–5. Trans. C. Errington.

Ethniki Statistiki Ypiresia (1986?), *Συνοπτική στατιστική επετηρίδα 1985–1986 – Concise Statistical Yearbook 1985–1986*. Athens: Ethniki Statistiki Ypiresia tis Ellados/National Statistical Service of Greece.

Fachard, S. (2016), 'A decade of research on Greek fortifications', in M. Stamatopoulou, 'Archaeology in Greece 2015–2016', *AR* 62: 1–132, at 77–88.

Febvre, L. (1925), with L. Bataillon, *A Geographical Introduction to History*. First published 1922. London: Kegan Paul, Trench, Trübner & Co. Trans. E. G. Mountford and J. H. Paxton.

Fenn, N., and Römer-Strehl, C. (eds) (2013), *Networks in the Hellenistic World: According to the Pottery in the Eastern Mediterranean and Beyond (Proceedings of the International Conference held at the Universities of Cologne and Bonn, February 23–26, 2011)*. Oxford: Archaeopress.

Ferguson, J. (1973), *The Heritage of Hellenism*. London: Thames & Hudson.

Ferguson, W. S. (1911), *Hellenistic Athens: An Historical Essay*. London: Macmillan.

(1948), 'Demetrius Poliorcetes and the Hellenic league', *Hesperia* 17: 112–36.

Finley, M. I. (1973), *The Ancient Economy*, 1st UK edn. London: Chatto & Windus.

Fisher, N. R. E. (1989), review of P. McKechnie, *Outsiders in the Greek Cities in the Fourth Century BC*, in *CR* 41. 2: 394–7.

Follet, S. (2002), 'Les italiens à Athènes (IIe siècle av. J.-C.–Ier siècle ap. J.-C.)', in C. Müller and C. Hasenohr (eds), *Les Italiens dans le monde grec: IIème siècle av. J.-C.–Ier siècle ap. J.-C. Circulation, activités, intégration*. Athens: École française d'Athènes), 79–88.

Forbes, H. A. (1982), 'Strategies and soils: technology, production and environment in the peninsula of Methana, Greece', PhD thesis. University of Pennsylvania.

(1996), 'The uses of the uncultivated landscape in modern Greece: a pointer to the value of the wilderness in antiquity?', in G. Shipley and J. B. Salmon (eds), *Human Landscapes in Classical Antiquity: Environment and Culture* (London and New York: Routledge), 68–97.

Forsén, B. (2003), 'The archaic–hellenistic periods: conclusions', in J. Forsén and B. Forsén, *The Asea Valley Survey: An Arcadian Mountain Valley from the Palaeolithic Period until Modern Times* (Stockholm: Svenska Institutet i Athen), 247–71.

(2016), 'Artemis Lykoatis and the bones of Arkas: sanctuaries, and territoriality', in M. Melfi and O. Bobou (eds), *Hellenistic Sanctuaries: Between Greece and Rome* (Oxford University Press), 40–62.

Forsén, J., and Forsén, B. (2003), *The Asea Valley Survey: An Arcadian Mountain Valley from the Palaeolithic Period until Modern Times*. Stockholm: Svenska Institutet i Athen.

Forsén, B., and Karlsson, L. (2005), 'Recent research concerning the walls at Asea', in E. Østby (ed.), *Ancient Arcadia* (Athens and Sävedalen, Sweden: Norwegian Institute at Athens and Åström), 307–19.

Forsén, B., and Lavento, M. (1996), 'The Asea Valley Survey: a preliminary report of the 1994 season', *OAth* 21: 73–97.

Fouache, É. (2000), *L'Alluvionnement historique en Grèce occidentale et au Péloponnèse: géomorphologie, archéologie, histoire*. Athens: École française d'Athènes.

Foxhall, L. (1993), 'Farming and fighting in ancient Greece', in J. Rich and G. Shipley (eds), *War and Society in the Greek World* (London and New York: Routledge), 134–45.

(2004), 'Small, rural farmstead sites in ancient Greece: a material cultural analysis', in F. Kolb and E. Müller-Luckner (eds), *Chora und Polis* (Munich: Oldenbourg), 249–70.

Gill, D., and Forbes, H. A. (1997), 'Inscriptions of Methana', in C. Mee and H. Forbes (eds), *A Rough and Rocky Place: The Landscape and Settlement History of the Methana Peninsula, Greece* (Liverpool University Press), 269–77 (appendix 2).

Francovich, R., Patterson, H., and Barker, G. (eds) (2000), *Extracting Meaning from Ploughsoil Assemblages*. Oxford: Oxbow.

Frangakis-Syrett, E., and Wagstaff, J. M. (1992), 'The height zonation of population in the Morea c. 1830', *ABSA* 87: 439–46.

Fraser, P. M. (1969–70), 'Archaeology in Greece, 1969–70', *AR* 16: 3–31.

Freitag, K. (1999), *Der Golf von Korinth: historisch-topographische Untersuchungen von der Archaik bis in das 1. Jh. v. Chr.* Munich: Tuduv.

French, E. B. (1990–1), 'Archaeology in Greece 1990–91', *AR* 37: 3–78.

(1991–2), 'Archaeology in Greece 1991–92', *AR* 38: 3–70.

(1992–3), 'Archaeology in Greece 1992–93', *AR* 39: 3–81.

(1993–4), 'Archaeology in Greece 1993–94', *AR* 40: 3–84.

Fröhlich, P. (2008), 'Les tombeaux de le ville de Messène et les grandes familles de la cité à l'époque hellénistique', in C. Grandjean (ed.), *Le Péloponnèse d'Épaminondas à Hadrien* (Bordeaux and Paris: Ausonius and De Boccard), 203–27.

(2010), 'L'inventaire du monde des cités grecques: une somme, une méthode et une conception de l'histoire [review of Hansen–Nielsen, *Inventory*, and Hansen, *Polis*]', *RH* 312. 3 [655]: 637–77.

Fuks, A. (1962), 'Agis, Cleomenes and equality', *CPh* 57: 161–6.

(1974–5), 'Patterns and types of social-economic revolution in Greece from the fourth to the second century BC', *AncSoc* 5–6: 51–81.

Funke, P. (2009), 'Between Mantineia and Leuktra: the political world of the Peloponnese in a time of upheaval', in P. Funke and N. Luraghi (eds), *The Politics of Ethnicity and the Crisis of the Peloponnesian League* (Washington, DC: Center for Hellenic Studies), 1–14.

Funke, P. and Luraghi, N. (eds) (2009), *The Politics of Ethnicity and the Crisis of the Peloponnesian League* (Washington, DC: Center for Hellenic Studies.

Gabbert, J. J. (1997), *Antigonus II Gonatas: A Political Biography*. London and New York, NY: Routledge.

Gans, U. W., and Kreilinger, U. (2002), 'The sanctuary of Zeus Soter at Megalopolis', in R. Hägg (ed.), *Peloponnesian Sanctuaries and Cults* (Stockholm: Svenska Institutet i Athen), 187–90.

Gauvin, G. (1983), 'Corinthian fortifications of the classical and hellenistic periods', in D. R. Keller and D. W. Rupp (eds), *Archaeological Survey in the Mediterranean Area* (Oxford: British Archaeological Reports), 257–9.

(1992), 'Les systèmes de fortification de Kléonai et Phlionte à la période classique–hellénistique', in S. van de Maele and J. M. Fossey (eds), *Fortificationes antiquae* (Amsterdam: Gieben), 133–46.

(1997), 'La tour phliasienne au sud du Polýphengo', in J. M. Fossey (ed.), *Proceedings of the 1st Montreal Conference on the Archaeology and History of the North East Peloponnesos* (Amsterdam: Gieben), 29–43.

Gauvin, G. and Morin, J. (1997), 'Quelques sites préhistoriques à la périphérie des plaines de Cléonées et Phlionte: une note', in J. M. Fossey (ed.), *Proceedings of the 1st Montreal Conference on the Archaeology and History of the North East Peloponnesos* (Amsterdam: Gieben), 1–13.

Gawlinski, L. (2012), *The Sacred Law of Andania: A New Text with Commentary*. Berlin and Boston: de Gruyter.

Geer, R. M. (ed.) (1954), *Diodorus of Sicily*, x: *Books XIX. 66–110 and XX* (Cambridge, Mass.: Loeb Classical Library).

Gehrke, H.-J. (1985), *Stasis: Untersuchungen zu den inneren Kriegen in den griechischen Staaten des 5. und 4. Jahrhunderts v. Chr.* Munich: Beck.

(1986), *Jenseits von Athen und Sparta: das dritte Griechenland und seine Staatenwelt*. Munich: Beck.

(1994), 'Bergland als Wirtschaftsraum: das Beispiel Akarnaniens', in E. Olshausen and H. Sonnabend (eds), *Grenze und Grenzland: Stuttgarter Kolloquium zur historischen Geographie des Altertums 4, 1990* (Amsterdam: Hakkert), 71–7.

Georgiadou, A. (2000), 'Hellenistische Keramik aus Elis', in *5th Hellenistic Pottery Meeting*, 386.

Giannopoulou, D., and Kiriatzi, E. (2008), 'Understanding the technology of large storage jars: raw materials and techniques in hellenistic and modern Messenia', in Y. Facorellis, N. Zacharias, and K. Polikreti (eds), *Proceedings of the 4th*

Symposium of the Hellenic Society for Archaeometry (Oxford: Archaeopress), 335–47.

Gill, D. W. J. (1994), review of R. Dalongeville, M. Lakakis, and A. D. Rizakis, *Le Bassin du Péiros et la plaine occidentale,* in *CR* 44. 1: 111–12.

—— and Vickers, M. J. (2001), 'Laconian lead figurines: mineral extraction and exchange in the archaic Mediterranean', *ABSA* 96: 229–36.

Foxhall, L., and Bowden, H. (1997), 'Classical and hellenistic Methana', in C. Mee and H. Forbes (eds), *A Rough and Rocky Place: The Landscape and Settlement History of the Methana Peninsula, Greece* (Liverpool University Press), 62–76.

Ginouvès, R. (1959), *L'Établissement thermal de Gortys d'Arcadie.* Athens and Paris: École française d'Athènes and de Boccard.

—— (1994), 'Macedonian dedications outside Macedonia', in R. Ginouvès and M. B. Hatzopoulos (eds), *Macedonia: From Philip II to the Roman Conquest* (Princeton University Press), 192–219.

Giovannini, A. (1976), 'Athenian currency in the late fifth and early fourth century BC', *GRBS* 16: 185–90.

Giuliani, A. (2011), 'Hellenistic pottery from the fountain-house of Arsinoë in Messene [poster]', in *7th Hellenistic Pottery Meeting,* 766.

Glaser, F. (2001), 'Das Theater von Elis und das Problem einer hölzernen Skene', in V. Mitsopoulos-Leon (ed.), *Forschungen in der Peloponnes* (Athens: Österreichisches Archäologisches Institut), 253–6.

Gogos, S. (2001), 'Das Theater von Aigeira: ein Beitrag zur Chronologie des Zeus-Heiligtums', in V. Mitsopoulos-Leon (ed.), *Forschungen in der Peloponnes* (Athens: Österreichisches Archäologisches Institut), 79–87.

Gomme, A. W. (1937), 'The end of the city-state', in *Essays in Greek History and Literature* (Oxford: Basil Blackwell), 204–48 (ch. 11).

Gow, A. S. F., and Page, D. L. (1965), *Hellenistic Epigrams* (The Greek Anthology, 1–2). 2 vols. Cambridge University Press.

Grainger, J. D. (1999), *The League of the Aitolians.* Leiden: Brill.

Grandjean, C. (1996), 'Le kappa de l'inscription IG V 1, 1532 et les fractions du chalque en Messénie à l'époque hellénistique', *REG* 109. 2: 689–85.

—— (2003), *Les Messéniens de 370/369 au Ier siècle de notre ère: monnayages et histoire.* Paris: de Boccard.

—— (2006), 'Histoire économique et monétarisation de la Grèce à l'époque hellénistique', in R. Descat (ed.), *Approches de l'économie hellénistique: 4mes rencontres sur l'économie antique, Saint-Bertrand-de-Comminges, 2004* (Saint-Bertrand-de-Comminges: Musée archéologique départemental de Saint-Bertrand-de-Comminges), 195–214.

—— (2007), 'De la drachme au denier', *Revue européenne des sciences sociales,* 45. 137: 19–30.

—— (2008a), 'Introduction', in C. Grandjean (ed.), *Le Péloponnèse d'Épaminondas à Hadrien* (Bordeaux and Paris: Ausonius and De Boccard), 11–17.

(ed.) (2008b), *Le Péloponnèse d'Épaminondas à Hadrien (Colloque de Tours 6–7 octobre 2005)*. Bordeaux and Paris: Ausonius and De Boccard.

(n.d. [2008]), 'Unity and diversity in the hellenistic Peloponnese: Sparta's allies and their regional identity', in W. G. Cavanagh and J. Roy (eds), *Being Peloponnesian* (Nottingham: Centre for Spartan & Peloponnesian Studies, University of Nottingham), ch. 5.

and Nicolet-Pierre, H. (2008), 'Le décret de Lykosoura en l'honneur de Damophon et la circulation monétaire dans le Péloponnèse aux IIIe–IIe siècles avant notre ère', *Ktema*, 33: 129–34.

Green, P. M. (1998), review of P. J. Stylianou, *A Historical Commentary on Diodorus Siculus Book 15,* in *BMCR* 1999. 10: 11.

Gregory, T. E., and others (1998), 'Eastern Korinthia Archaeological Survey', http://eleftheria.stcloudstate.edu/eks (updated 26 Nov. 2001). Accessed 25 Feb. 2003.

Grieb, V. (2008), *Hellenistische Demokratie: politische Organisation und Struktur in freien griechischen Poleis nach Alexander dem Grossen*. Stuttgart: Steiner.

Griffin, A. (1982), *Sikyon*. Oxford: Clarendon Press.

Griffith, G. T. (1950), 'The union of Corinth and Argos (392–386 BC)', *Historia* 1: 236–56.

(1979), 'The reign of Philip the Second', in N. G. L. Hammond and G. T. Griffith, *A History of Macedonia*, ii: *550–336 BC* (Oxford: Clarendon Press), 203–698 (= Part II).

Gruen, E. S. (1984), *The Hellenistic World and the Coming of Rome*. 2 vols. Berkeley-Los Angeles and London: University of California Press.

Grunauer-von Hoerschelmann, S. (1978), *Die Münzprägung der Lakedaimonier*. Berlin: de Gruyter.

Gschnitzer, F. (1958), *Abhängige Orte im griechischen Altertum*. Munich: Beck.

Gutzwiller, K. J. (1993), 'Anyte's epigram book', *SyllClass* 4: 71–89.

Habicht, C. (1997), *Athens from Alexander to Antony*. Cambridge, Mass., and London: Harvard University Press. Trans. D. L. Schneider.

Hahm, D. E. (2000), 'Kings and constitutions: hellenistic theories', in C. J. Rowe and M. Schofield (eds), *The Cambridge History of Greek and Roman Political Thought* (Cambridge: Cambridge University Press), 457–76.

Hall, J. M. (1997), *Ethnic Identity in Greek Antiquity*. Cambridge University Press.

(2002), *Hellenicity: Between Ethnicity and Culture*. University of Chicago Press.

Hamilton, C. D. (1972), 'The politics of revolution in Corinth, 395–386 BC', *Historia* 21. 1: 21–37.

(1979), *Sparta's Bitter Victories: Politics and Diplomacy in the Corinthian War*. Ithaca, NY, and London: Cornell University Press.

(1997), 'Sparta', in L. A. Tritle (ed.), *The Greek World in the Fourth Century: From the Fall of the Athenian Empire to the Successors of Alexander* (London and New York: Routledge), 41–65.

Hammond, N. G. L. (1988), 'From the death of Philip to the battle of Ipsus', in N. G. L. Hammond and F. W. Walbank, *A History of Macedonia*, iii: *336–167 BC* (Oxford: Clarendon Press), 3–196.

—— and Griffith, G. T. (1979), *A History of Macedonia*, ii: *550–336 BC*. Oxford: Clarendon Press.

—— and Walbank, F. W. (1988), *A History of Macedonia*, iii: *336–167 BC*. Oxford: Clarendon Press.

Hansen, M. H. (1995), 'Kome: a study in how the Greeks designated and classified settlements which were not poleis', in M. H. Hansen and K. A. Raaflaub (eds), *Studies in the Ancient Greek Polis* (Stuttgart: Steiner), 45–81.

—— (1996), 'Πολλαχῶς πόλις λέγεται (Arist. Pol. 1276a23): the Copenhagen inventory of poleis and the lex Hafniensis de civitate', in M. H. Hansen (ed.), *Introduction to an Inventory of Poleis* (Copenhagen: Kongelige Danske Videnskabernes Selskab/Munksgaard), 7–72.

—— (ed.) (2000a), *A Comparative Study of Thirty City-state Cultures: An Investigation Conducted by the Copenhagen Polis Centre*. Copenhagen: Kongelige Danske Videnskabernes Selskab/Reitzel.

—— (2000b), 'A survey of the use of the word polis in archaic and classical sources', in P. Flensted-Jensen (ed.), *Further Studies in the Ancient Greek Polis* (Stuttgart: Steiner), 173–215.

—— (ed.) (2002), *A Comparative Study of Six City-state Cultures: An Investigation Conducted by the Copenhagen Polis Centre*. Copenhagen: Kongelige Danske Videnskabernes Selskab/Reitzel.

—— (2004a), 'The concept of the consumption city applied to the Greek polis', in T. H. Nielsen (ed.), *Once Again: Studies in the Ancient Greek Polis* (Stuttgart: Steiner), 9–47.

—— (2004b), 'Introduction', in M. H. Hansen and T. H. Nielsen (eds), *An Inventory of Archaic and Classical Poleis* (Oxford University Press), 3–154.

—— (2004c), 'The inventory of poleis', in M. H. Hansen, 'Introduction', in M. H. Hansen and T. H. Nielsen, *An Inventory of Archaic and Classical Poleis*, (Oxford University Press), 3–154, at 23–38.

—— (2004d), 'The perioikic poleis of Lakedaimon', in T. H. Nielsen (ed.), *Once Again: Studies in the Ancient Greek Polis* (Stuttgart: Steiner), 149–64.

—— (2004e), *Polis: den oldgræske bystatskultur*. Copenhagen: Museum Tusculanums Forlag.

—— (2004f), 'Stasis as an essential aspect of the polis', in M. H. Hansen, 'Introduction', in M. H. Hansen and T. H. Nielsen, *An Inventory of Archaic and Classical Poleis* (Oxford University Press), 3–154, at 124–9.

—— (2004g), 'A typology of dependent poleis', in M. H. Hansen, 'Introduction', in M. H. Hansen and T. H. Nielsen, *An Inventory of Archaic and Classical Poleis* (Oxford University Press), 3–154, at 87–94.

—— (2006), *Polis: An Introduction to the Ancient Greek City-state*. Oxford University Press.

(2007), 'Was every polis town the centre of a polis state?', in M. H. Hansen (ed.), *The Return of the Polis: The Use and Meanings of the Word Polis in Archaic and Classical Sources* (Stuttgart: Steiner), 13–51.

and Nielsen, T. H. (2004a), 'Indices', in M. H. Hansen and T. H. Nielsen (eds), *An Inventory of Archaic and Classical Poleis* (Oxford University Press), 1253–1396.

and Nielsen, T. H. (2004b), *An Inventory of Archaic and Classical Poleis (An Investigation Conducted by the Copenhagen Polis Centre for the Danish National Research Foundation)*. Oxford University Press.

Hanson, J. L. (1961), *A Textbook of Economics*, 3rd edn. London: Macdonald & Evans.

Hanson, V. D. (1982), *Warfare and Agriculture in Classical Greece*, 1st edn. Pisa: Giardini.

(1998), *Warfare and Agriculture in Classical Greece*, 2nd edn. First published 1982. Berkeley–Los Angeles and London: California University Press.

Harding, P. W. (1985), *From the End of the Peloponnesian War to the Battle of Ipsus*. Cambridge University Press.

Harrison, A. B., and Spencer, N. (1998), 'After the palace: the early "history" of Messenia', in J. L. Davis (ed.), *Sandy Pylos: An Archaeological History from Nestor to Navarino* (Austin, TX: University of Texas Press), 147–62 and fig. 70 on p. 146.

(2008), 'After the palace: the early "history" of Messenia', in J. L. Davis (ed.), *Sandy Pylos: An Archaeological History from Nestor to Navarino*, 2nd edn (Princeton: American School of Classical Studies at Athens), 147–62 and fig. 70 on p. 146.

Hasenohr, C., and Müller, C. (2002), 'Gentilices et circulation des Italiens: quelques réflexions méthodologiques', in C. Müller and C. Hasenohr (eds), *Les Italiens dans le monde grec: IIème siècle av. J.-C.–Ier siècle ap. J.-C. Circulation, activités, intégration* (Athens: École française d'Athènes), 11–20.

Hatzopoulos, M. B. (1996), *Macedonian Institutions under the Kings*, ii: *Epigraphic Appendix*. Athens: Kentron Ellinikis kai Romaïkis Archaiotitos, Ethniko Idryma Erevnon.

(2001), *L'Organisation de l'armée macédonienne sous les Antigonides: problèmes anciennes et documents nouveaux*. Athens: Kentron Ellinikis kai Romaïkis Archaiotitos, Ethniko Idryma Erevnon.

Head, B. V. , with Hill, G. F. Macdonald, G., and Wroth, W.. (1911), *Historia Numorum: A Manual of Greek Numismatics*, New and enlarged edn. Oxford: Clarendon Press.

Hedrick, C. W., Jr. (1999), 'Democracy and the Athenian epigraphical habit', *Hesperia* 68. 3: 387–439.

Heinen, H. (1972), *Untersuchungen zur hellenistischen Geschichte des 3. Jahrhunderts v.Chr.: zur Geschichte der Zeit Ptolemaios Keraunos und zum chremonideischen Krieg*. Wiesbaden: Steiner.

Hellenic Ministry of Culture (1995–2001), 'Odysseus', www.culture.gr (updated 2001).

Helly, B. (1998), 'La sismicité est-elle un objet d'étude pour les archéologues?', in E. Olshausen and H. Sonnabend (eds), *Naturkatastrophen in der antiken Welt: Stuttgarter Kolloquium zur historischen Geographie des Altertums 6, 1996* (Stuttgart: Steiner), 169–89.

Hercher, R. (ed.) (1873), *Epistolographi Graeci*. Paris: Firmin Didot.

Hiller von Gaertringen, F., and Lattermann, H. (1911), *Arkadische Forschungen: aus dem Anhang zu den Abhandlungen der königl. preuß. Akademie der Wissenschaften vom Jahre 1911*. Berlin: Akademie der Wissenschaften/G. Reimer.

Hjohlman, J., Penttinen, A., and Wells, B. with Bassiakos, Y., Theodorakopoulou, K., Granger-Taylor, H., Isaksson, S., Lymberakis, P., Mylona, D., Ntinou, M., Sarpaki, A., and Syrides, G. (2005), *Pyrgouthi: A Rural Site in the Berbati Valley from the Early Iron Age to Late Antiquity (Excavations by the Swedish Institute at Athens 1995 and 1997)*. Stockholm: Paul Åström.

Hobson, M. S. (2012), 'The African boom? Evaluating economic growth in the Roman province of Africa Proconsularis', PhD thesis. University of Leicester.

Hodkinson, S. J. (2000), *Property and Wealth in Classical Sparta*. London and Swansea: Duckworth and Classical Press of Wales.

Holford-Strevens, L. (2005), *The History of Time: A Very Short Introduction*. Oxford and New York: Oxford University Press.

Hollander, D. (2006), 'Coins in the countryside? Gauging rural monetization', in C. C. Mattusch, A. A. Donohue, and A. Brauer (eds), *Common Ground: Archaeology, Art, Science, and Humanities (Proceedings of the 16th International Congress of Classical Archaeology)* (Oxford: Oxbow), 315–17.

Hoover, O. D., with Walker, A. S. (2011), *Handbook of Coins of the Peloponnesos: Achaia, Phleiasia, Sikyonia, Elis, Triphylia, Messenia, Laconia, Argolis, and Arkadia. Sixth to First Centuries* BC. Lancaster, PA, and London: Classical Numismatic Group.

(2014), *Handbook of Coins of Northern and Central Greece: Achaia Phthiotis, Ainis, Magnesia, Malis, Oita, Perrhaibia, Thessaly, Akarnania, Aitolia, Lokris, Phokis, Boiotia, Euboia, Attica, Megaris, and Corinthia. Sixth to First Centuries* BC. Lancaster, PA, and London: Classical Numismatic Group.

Horden, P., and Purcell, N. (2000), *The Corrupting Sea*. Oxford and Malden, MA: Blackwell.

Hornblower, J. (1981), *Hieronymus of Cardia*. Oxford University Press.

Hornblower, S. (1990), 'When was Megalopolis founded?', *ABSA* 85: 71–9.

Houby-Nielsen, S. (1997), 'Grave gifts, women, and conventional values in hellenistic Athens', in P. Bilde, T. Engberg-Pedersen, L. Hannestad, and J. Zahle (eds), *Conventional Values of the Hellenistic Greeks* (Aarhus University Press), 220–62, pls 8–14.

Howell, R. J. (1970), 'A survey of eastern Arcadia in prehistory: with some notes on classical topography', *ABSA* 65: 79–127.

Howgego, C. J. (1995), *Ancient History from Coins*. London and New York: Routledge.

Hughes, J. D. (1983), 'How the ancients viewed deforestation', *JFA* 10: 437–45.

(1994), 'Forestry and the ancient economy in the Mediterranean region in the time of the Roman empire in the light of historical sources', in B. Frenzel (ed.), *Evaluation of Land Surfaces Cleared from Forests in the Mediterranean Region during the Time of the Roman Empire* (Mainz: European Science Foundation/ Akademie der Wissenschaften und der Literatur), 1–14.

Iliopoulos, D., and Kanellopoulos, D. (2011), Ἑλληνιστικά λυχνάρια από την πόλη της Ἠλιδος [poster]', in *7th Hellenistic Pottery Meeting*, 739–46, pls 299–302.

Jameson, M. H., Runnels, C. N., and van Andel, T. H. with Munn, M. H. (1994), *A Greek Countryside: The Southern Argolid from Prehistory to the Present Day*. Stanford University Press.

Johnston, A. W., Quercia, A., Tsaravopoulos, A. N., Bevan, A., and Conolly, J. (2012), 'Pots, piracy and Aegila: hellenistic ceramics from an intensive survey of Antikythera, Greece', *ABSA* 107: 247–72.

Slane, K. W., and Vroom, J. A. C. (2014), 'Kythera forty years on: the pottery from historical Kastri revisited', *ABSA* 109: 3–64.

Johnston, R. J. (1991), 'A place for everything and everything in its place', *TIBG* 16. 2: 131–47.

(1996), 'Region', in A. Kuper and J. Kuper (eds), *The Social Science Encyclopedia*, 2nd edn (London and New York: Routledge), 729–31.

Jones, J. E., *see* Ellis Jones, J.

Jost, M. (1985), *Sanctuaires et cultes d'Arcadie*. Athens and Paris: École française d'Athènes and de Boccard.

Kallet, L. (2000), 'The fifth century: political and military narrative', in R. Osborne (ed.), *Classical Greece* (Oxford University Press), 170–96.

Kalogeropoulou, A. G. (1962), Ἀνασκαφὲς καὶ εὑρήματα τοῦ 1962 στὴν Πελοπόννησο', *Πελ.* 5: 348–63.

(1969–70), Ἀρχαιολογικὰ Πελοποννήσου', *Πελ.* 7 [1970]: 407–18.

Kaltsas, N. (1989), *Ancient Messene*. Athens: Greek Archaeological Service.

Kalyvas, A. (2007), 'The tyranny of dictatorship: when the Greek tyrant met the Roman dictator', *Political Theory*, 35. 4: 412–42.

Karageorga-Stathakopoulou, T. (2005), 'Τα επίκρανα της Τεγέας', in E. Østby (ed.), *Ancient Arcadia* (Athens and Sävedalen, Sweden: Norwegian Institute at Athens and Åström), 131–8.

Karwiese, S., Howell, R. J., Ducrey, P., Vandenabeele, P., Hamdorf, F. W., Beschi, L., and others (1968), Σωστικαὶ ἀνασκαφαὶ εἰς Ἦλιδα', *ADelt* 23. B (Chr.) 1: 174–94.

Kastler, R. (1997), 'Abriss zur hellenistischen Keramik von Elis', in *4th Hellenistic Pottery Meeting*, 21–3.

(2000), 'Die Keramik der Südhalle von Elis und die Problematik der regionalen Keramikchronologie der Region Elis', in *5th Hellenistic Pottery Meeting*, 403–16, pls 211–14.

Katsarou, C., and Mourtzini, T. (2011), Κεραμική με ανάγλυφη διακόσμηση από την Ἦλιδα [poster]', in *7th Hellenistic Pottery Meeting*, 747–60, pls 303–10.

Katsonopoulou, D. (2011), 'The hellenistic dye-works at Helike, Achaea, Greece', in C. Alfaro, J.-P. Brun, P. Borgard, and R. Pierobon Benoit (eds), *Textiles y tintes en la ciudad antigua* (València and Naples: University of Valencia, CNRS, and École française de Rome), 237–42.

——— (2016), 'Selinous: history and iconography of a river in the area of ancient Helike, Achaea, Greece', *NAC* 45: 17–25.

Kebric, R. B. (1974), 'A note on Duris in Athens', *CPh* 69: 286–7.

Kennell, N. M. (1999), 'From perioikoi to poleis: the Laconian cities in the late hellenistic period', in S. J. Hodkinson and C. A. Powell (eds), *Sparta: New Perspectives* (London: Duckworth and Classical Press of Wales), 189–210.

——— (2003), 'Agreste genus: helots in hellenistic Laconia', in N. Luraghi and S. E. Alcock (eds), *Helots and their Masters in Laconia and Messenia: Histories, Ideologies, Structures* (Washington, DC: Center for Hellenic Studies and Harvard University Press), 81–105.

Kent, J. H. (1966), *The Inscriptions: 1926–1950*. Princeton: American School of Classical Studies at Athens.

Kerkhecker, A. (1991), 'Zum neuen hellenistischen Weihepigramm aus Pergamon', *ZPE* 86: 30–2.

Kim, H. S. (2001), 'Archaic coinage as evidence for the use of money', in A. R. Meadows and K. Shipton (eds), *Money and its Uses in the Ancient Greek World* (Oxford University Press), 7–21.

——— (2002), 'Small change and the moneyed economy', in P. Cartledge, E. E. Cohen, and L. Foxhall (eds), *Money, Labour and Land: Approaches to the Economies of Ancient Greece* (London and New York: Routledge), 44–51.

——— and Kroll, J. H. (2008), 'A hoard of archaic coins of Colophon and unminted silver (CH I.3)', *AJN* 20: 53–103.

Kissas, K. (2013), 'Ἡ φενεατική πεδιάδα: τα αποτελέσματα των πρόσφατων ερευνών της Αρχαιολογικής Υπηρεσίας', in K. Kissas and W.-D. Niemeier (eds), *The Corinthia and the Northeast Peloponnese: Topography and History from Prehistoric Times until the End of Antiquity* (Munich: Hirmer), 437–42.

——— and Niemeier, W.-D. (eds) (2013), *The Corinthia and the Northeast Peloponnese: Topography and History from Prehistoric Times until the End of Antiquity (Proceedings of the Conference organized by the Directorate of Classical and Prehistoric Antiquities, the IZ' Ephorate of Classical and Prehistoric Antiquities, and the German Archaeological Institute, Athens, held at Loutraki, March 26–29, 2009)*. Munich: Hirmer.

Klein, N. L. (1997), 'Excavation of the Greek temples at Mycenae by the British School at Athens', *ABSA* 92: 247–322, pls 49–59.

——— (2002), 'Evidence for the archaic and hellenistic temples at Mycenae', in R. Hägg (ed.), *Peloponnesian Sanctuaries and Cults* (Stockholm: Svenska Institutet i Athen), 99–105.

Kolia, E.-I., and Stavropoulou-Gatsi, M. (2005), 'Το βόρειο νεκροταφείο των αρχαίων Πατρών: οικόπεδα οδών Νόρμαν–Κωνσταντινουπόλεως και

Κατερίνης 14–16᾽, in L. Kypraiou (ed.), *Ελληνιστική κεραμική από την Πελοπόννησο* (Athens: Ypourgeio Politismou), 47–58.

Kourinou, E. (2000), *Σπάρτη: συμβολή στή μνημειακή τοπογραφία της (διδακτορική διατριβή).* Athens: Horos.

Kourinou-Pikoula, E. (1992), ῾Ενεπίγραφα ἀναθηματικά ἀνάγλυφα ἀπὸ τὴ Σπάρτη (περίληψις)᾽, in *4th Peloponnesian Congress,* ii, 207–8.

Kraft, J. C., Rapp, G., and Gifford, J. A. (2005), ῾Coastal change and archaeological settings in Elis᾽, *Hesperia* 74. 1: 1–39.

Kralli, I. (2017), *The Hellenistic Peloponnese: Interstate Relations: A Narrative and Analytic History, from the Fourth Century to 146 BC.* Swansea: Classical Press of Wales.

Kramer, N. (2013), ῾Überlegungen zur Eastern Sigillata A᾽, in N. Fenn and C. Römer-Strehl (eds), *Networks in the Hellenistic World: According to the Pottery in the Eastern Mediterranean and Beyond* (Oxford: BAR), 283–92.

Kremmydas, C., and Tempest, K. (eds) (2013), *Hellenistic Oratory: Continuity and Change.* Oxford University Press.

Krentz, P. (2005), ῾Casualties in hoplite battles᾽, *GRBS* 26 (1): 13–20.

Kritzas, C. V. (1992), ῾Aspects de la vie politique et économique d'Argos au Ve siècle avant J.-C.᾽, in M. Piérart (ed.), *Polydipsion Argos* (Athens: École française d'Athènes), 231–40.

Kroll, J. H. (1976), ῾Aristophanes' πονηρὰ χαλκία: a reply᾽, *GRBS* 17. 4: 329–41.

— (2007), review of J. A. W. Warren, *The Bronze Coinage of the Achaian Koinon,* in *JHS* 129: 192–3.

Krystalli-Votsi, P. (1997), ῾"Κλειστό σύνολο" πυράς μέσα σε πειόσχημο ταφικό μνημείο της αρχαίας Σικυώνας᾽, in *4th Hellenistic Pottery Meeting,* 20.

Kypraiou, E. (ed.) (2005), *Ελληνιστική κεραμική από την Πελοπόννησο.* Aigio: Ypourgeio Politismou, ST´ Ephoreia Proïstorikon kai Klasikon Archaiotiton.

Kyriakou, A. (2011), ῾Οι υδρίες από τη Στενόμακρη Τούμπα της Βεργίνας [poster]᾽, in *7th Hellenistic Pottery Meeting,* 821–32, pls 335–6.

Kyriakou, D. (1994), ῾Ελληνιστικὴ κεραμικὴ ἀπὸ τὸ νεκροταφεῖο τῆς Πάτρας᾽, in *3rd Hellenistic Pottery Meeting,* 185–95, pls 127–41.

Lafond, Y. (1998), ῾Die Katastrophe von 373 v.Chr. und das Verschwinden der Stadt Helike in Achaia᾽, in E. Olshausen and H. Sonnabend (eds), *Naturkatastrophen in der antiken Welt: Stuttgarter Kolloquium zur historischen Geographie des Altertums 6, 1996* (Stuttgart: Steiner), 118–23.

Lakaki-Marchetti, M. (2000), ῾Σωστικές ανασκαφές στην Κάτω Αχαγία᾽, in A. D. Rizakis (ed.), *Δύμη και Δυμαία χώρα – Dymé et son territoire* (Athens: Kentron Ellinikis kai Romaïkis Archaiotitos, Ethniko Idryma Erevnon), 113–21.

Lakakis, M., and Rizakis, A. D. (1992a), ῾Deux forteresses dans le N.-O. du Péloponnèse et le système de défense achéen᾽, in R. Dalongeville, M. Lakakis, and A. D. Rizakis (eds), *Le Bassin du Péiros et la plaine occidentale* (Athens: Kentron Ellinikis kai Romaïkis Archaiotitos, Ethniko Idryma Erevnon), 101–23.

(1992b), 'Dymé, cité achéenne: son histoire à la lumière des fouilles récentes', in R. Dalongeville, M. Lakakis, and A. D. Rizakis (eds), *Le Bassin du Péiros et la plaine occidentale* (Athens: Kentron Ellinikis kai Romaïkis Archaiotitos, Ethniko Idryma Erevnon), 77–100.

(1992c), 'Les grandes étapes de l'occupation du sol de l'Âge de Pierre à l'époque contemporaine', in R. Dalongeville, M. Lakakis, and A. D. Rizakis (eds), *Le Bassin du Péiros et la plaine occidentale* (Athens: Kentron Ellinikis kai Romaïkis Archaiotitos, Ethniko Idryma Erevnon), 59–75.

Lambrinoudakis, V. K. (1978), 'Σχέσεις Ἐπιδαύρου καὶ Κορίνθου ὑπὸ τὸ φῶς τῶν ἀνασκαφῶν', in *1st Argolic Congress*, 28–36.

(1987–8), 'Excavation and restoration of the sanctuary of Apollo Maleatas and Asklepios at Epidauros', in *3rd Peloponnesian Congress*, ii, 298–304.

Landuyt, F., and Shipley, D. G. J. (2003), 'Laconia Survey inscriptions', www.csad. ox.ac.uk/Laconia/ (last accessed 4 Aug. 2017)

Lane, E. (1962), 'An unpublished inscription from Lakonia', *Hesperia*, 31. 4: 396–8.

Lanérès, N. (2014), 'Le messénien: un dialecte introuvable?', in S. Minon (ed.), *Diffusion de l'attique et expansion des koinai dans le Péloponnèse et en Grèce centrale* (Geneva: Droz), 117–39.

Langridge-Noti, E. (2009), 'Continuity, connections and change in hellenistic pottery from Geraki, Laconia', in W. G. Cavanagh, C. Gallou, and M. Georgiadis (eds), *Sparta and Laconia: From Prehistory to Pre-modern* (London: British School at Athens), 225–33.

and Prent, M. (2004), 'Preliminary report on the hellenistic material from the Dutch excavations at Geraki (Geronthrai) in Laconia', Archaeological Institute of America Annual Meeting abstract www.archaeological.org/webinfo.php? page=10237&searchtype=abstract&sessionid=&paperid=241 (accessed 1 June 2005).

and Prent, M. (2011), 'Deposition and chronology in hellenistic deposits at Geraki, Laconia', in *7th Hellenistic Pottery Meeting*, 135–46, pls 57–60.

Larsen, J. A. O. (1955), *Representative Government in Greek and Roman History*. Berkeley–Los Angeles, CA: University of California Press.

(1968), *Greek Federal States: Their Institutions and History*. Oxford: Clarendon Press.

Lauffer, S. (ed.) (1989), *Griechenland: Lexikon der historischen Stätten von den Anfängen bis zur Gegenwart*. Munich: Beck.

Laurence, R. (1998), 'Land transport in Roman Italy: costs, practice and the economy', in H. M. Parkins and C. J. Smith (eds), *Trade, Traders and the Ancient City* (London and New York: Routledge), 129–48.

Lauter, H. (2005), 'Megalopolis: Ausgrabungen auf der Agora 1991–2002', in E. Østby (ed.), *Ancient Arcadia* (Athens and Sävedalen, Sweden: Norwegian Institute at Athens and Åström), 235–48.

Lauter, H. and Spyropoulos, T. G. (1998), 'Megalopolis: 3. Vorbericht 1996–1997', *AA* 1998: incl. 417–48.

Lawall, M. L. (2006), 'Consuming the west in the east: amphoras of the western Mediterranean in the Aegean before 86 BC', in D. Malfitana, J. Poblome, and J. Lund (eds), *Old Pottery in a New Century: Innovating Perspectives on Roman Pottery Studies* (Catania and Rome: 'L'Erma' di Bretschneider), 265–86.

Lazenby, J. F. (1972), 'The literary tradition', in J. F. Lazenby and R. Hope Simpson, 'Greco-Roman times', in W. A. McDonald and G. R. Rapp, Jr., *The Minnesota Messenia Expedition: Reconstructing a Bronze Age Regional Environment*, (Minneapolis, MN: University of Minnesota Press), 6, 81–99, at 81–93.

—— (2012), 'Epaminondas', *OCD*[4] 507–8.

—— and Hope Simpson, R. (1972), 'Greco-Roman times: literary tradition and topographical commentary', in W. A. McDonald and G. R. Rapp, Jr. (eds), *The Minnesota Messenia Expedition: Reconstructing a Bronze Age Regional Environment* (Minneapolis, MN: University of Minnesota Press), 81–99.

Leake, W. M. (1830), *Travels in the Morea*. 3 vols. London: John Murray.

Leekley, D., and Noyes, R. (1976), *Archaeological Excavations in Southern Greece*. Park Ridge, NJ: Noyes Press.

Legon, R. P. (2004), 'Megaris, Korinthia, Sikyonia', in M. H. Hansen and T. H. Nielsen (eds), *An Inventory of Archaic and Classical Poleis* (Oxford University Press), 462–71.

Lehnus, L. (1996), 'On the metrical inscription found at Pergamum (SEG 39.1334)', *CQ* 46. 1: 295–7.

Lembidaki, E. (1996–7), 'Χθόνια ἱερὰ στὸ Ἀσκληπιεῖο τῆς Ἐπιδαύρου: ἕνα παράδειγμα', in *5th Peloponnesian Congress*, ii, 305–23.

—— (2002), 'Three sacred buildings in the Asklepieion at Epidauros: new evidence from recent archaeological research', in R. Hägg (ed.), *Peloponnesian Sanctuaries and Cults* (Stockholm: Svenska Institutet i Athen), 123–36.

Leon-Mitsopoulou, V. (1994), 'Keramik der klassischen und nachklassischen Zeit aus der Stadt Elis', in *3rd Hellenistic Pottery Meeting*, 159–73, pls 89–105.

Levendi, I. K. (1993), 'Τα αγάλματα της Υγείας και του Ασκληπίου στο ναό της Αθηνάς Αλέας στην Τεγέα', in O. Palagia and W. Coulson (eds), *Sculpture from Arcadia and Laconia* (Oxford: Oxbow), 119–27.

Lewis, S. (2009), *Greek Tyranny*. Exeter: Bristol Phoenix Press and University of Exeter Press.

Lloyd, J. A. (1991), 'Farming the highlands: Samnium and Arcadia in the hellenistic and early Roman periods', in G. Barker and J. Lloyd (eds), *Roman Landscapes: Archaeological Survey in the Mediterranean Region* (London: British School at Rome), 180–93.

—— Owens, E. J., and Roy, J. (1985), 'The Megalopolis survey in Arcadia: problems of strategy and tactics', in S. Macready and F. H. Thompson (eds), *Archaeological Field Survey in Britain and Abroad* (London: Society of Antiquaries of London), 217–24.

Lolos, G. A. (1998), 'Studies in the topography of Sikyonia', PhD thesis. University of California, Berkeley.

—— (2005), 'The sanctuary of Titane and the city of Sikyon', *ABSA* 100: 275–98.

with Koskinas, A., Kormazopoulou, L., Zygouri, I., Papathanassiou, V., and A. P. Matthaiou, A. P. (2011), *Land of Sikyon: Archaeology and History of a Greek City-state*. Princeton, NJ: American School of Classical Studies at Athens.

Gourley, B., and Stewart, D. R. (2007), 'The Sikyon survey project: a blueprint for urban survey?', *JMA* 20. 2: 267–96.

Lord, L. E. (1939), 'Watchtowers and fortresses in Argolis', *AJA* 43. 1: 78–84.

Lotze, D. (1959), *Μεταξὺ ἐλευθέρων καὶ δούλων: Studien zur Rechtsstellung unfreier Landbevölkerungen in Griechenland bis zum 4. Jahrhundert v. Chr.* Berlin: Akademie-Verlag.

Lukermann, F. E., and Moody, J. (1978), 'Nichoria and vicinity: settlements and circulation', in G. R. Rapp, Jr. and S. E. Aschenbrenner (eds), *Site, Environs, and Techniques* (Minneapolis, MN: University of Minnesota Press), 78–112.

Lumley, J. (2011), *Joanna Lumley's Greek Odyssey*. DVD. London: British Broadcasting Corporation.

Lund, H. S. (1992), *Lysimachus: A Study in Early Hellenistic Kingship*. London and New York: Routledge.

Luraghi, N. (2008), *The Ancient Messenians: Constructions of Ethnicity and Memory*. Cambridge University Press.

(2009a), 'The helots: comparative approaches, ancient and modern', in S. Hodkinson (ed.), *Sparta: Comparative Approaches* (Swansea: Classical Press of Wales), 261–304.

(2009b), 'Messenian ethnicity and the free Messenians', in P. Funke and N. Luraghi (eds), *The Politics of Ethnicity and the Crisis of the Peloponnesian League* (Washington, DC: Center for Hellenic Studies and Harvard University Press), 110–34.

(2015), 'Traces of federalism in Messenia', in H. Beck and P. Funke (eds), *Federalism in Greek Antiquity* (Cambridge University Press), 285–96.

and Alcock, S. E. (eds) (2003), *Helots and their Masters in Laconia and Messenia: Histories, Ideologies, Structures*. Cambridge, MA, and London: Centre for Hellenic Studies and Foundation of the Hellenic World.

MacDonald, B. R. (1984), 'Λῃστεία and λῄζομαι in Thucydides and in IG I³ 41, 67, and 75', *AJPh* 105. 1: 77–84.

McDonald, W. A., and Hope Simpson, R. (1972), 'Archaeological exploration', in W. A. McDonald and G. R. Rapp, Jr. (eds), *The Minnesota Messenia Expedition: Reconstructing a Bronze Age Regional Environment* (Minneapolis, MN: University of Minnesota Press), 117–47.

and Rapp, G. R., Jr. (eds) (1972), *The Minnesota Messenia Expedition: Reconstructing a Bronze Age Regional Environment*. Minneapolis, MN: University of Minnesota Press.

Mackail, J. W. (ed.) (1906), *Select Epigrams from the Greek Anthology: Edited, with Revised Text, Translation, Introduction, and Notes*, New edn. London: Longmans, Green & Co.

McKechnie, P. (1989), *Outsiders in the Greek Cities in the Fourth Century* BC. London and New York: Routledge.

Mackil, E. (2013), *Creating a Common Polity: Religion, Economy, and Politics in the Making of the Greek Koinon*. Berkeley–Los Angeles, CA: University of California Press.

—— and van Alfen, P. G. (2006), 'Cooperative coinage', in P. G. van Alfen (ed.), *Agoranomia: Studies in Money and Exchange Presented to John H. Kroll* (New York: American Numismatic Society), incl. 204–35.

Madigan, B. C. (1991), 'A transposed head', *Hesperia*, 60. 4: 503–10.

Maher, M. P. (2012), 'The fortifications of Arkadian poleis in the classical and hellenistic periods', PhD thesis. Vancouver: University of British Columbia.

Mandel, J. (1979), 'À propos d'une dynastie de tyrans à Argos: IIIᵉ siècle avant J.-C.', *Athenaeum*, n.s. 57: 293–307.

Marasco, G. (1983), *Commento alle biografie plutarchee di Agide e Cleomene*. 2 vols. Rome: Edizioni dell'Ateneo.

—— (2004), 'Cleomene III fra rivoluzione e reazione', in C. Bearzot and F. Landucci Gattinoni (eds), *Contro le 'leggi immutabili': gli Spartani fra tradizione e innovazione* (Milan: Vita e Pensiero Università), 191–207.

Marcellesi, M.-C. (2010), 'Adoption et diffusion de la monnaie de bronze dans le monde égéen: une évolution économique et institutionnelle', in B. Virgilio and others (eds), *Studi ellenistici*, 24: 255–71.

Marchand, J. C. (2009), 'Kleonai, the Corinth–Argos road, and the "axis of history"', *Hesperia* 78. 1: 107–63.

Martinez-Sève, L. with Benoit-Guyod, M. (2011), *Atlas du monde hellénistique (336–31 av. J.-C.): pouvoirs et territoires après Alexandre le Grand*. Paris: Autrement.

Mattern, T. (2013), 'Kleonai: neue Forschungen in einer Stadt des "dritten Griechenlands"', in K. Kissas and W.-D. Niemeier (eds), *The Corinthia and the Northeast Peloponnese: Topography and History from Prehistoric Times until the End of Antiquity* (Munich: Hirmer), 323–32.

Matthaiou, A. P. (1990–1), 'Συνθήκη Λυσιμάχου καὶ Μεσσηνίων', Ὅρος 8–9: 269–70.

—— (2001), 'Δύο ἱστορικές ἐπιγραφές της Μεσσήνης', in V. Mitsopoulou-Leon (ed.), *Forschungen in der Peloponnes: Akten des Symposions anläßlich der Feier '100 Jahre Österreichisches Archäologisches Institut Athen', Athen 5.3–7.3.1998* (Athens: Österreichisches Archäologisches Institut), 221–32/1.

—— (ed.) (2006), *Καττάδε ἔδοξε τοῖς Λακεδαιμονίοις: ἐπιγραφὲς δημοσίου χαρακτῆρα ἀπὸ τὴν Σπάρτη τοῦ 5ου αἰῶνα π.Χ. (ἔκθεση στὸ Ἐπιγραφικὸ Μουσεῖο 30 Ὀκτωβρίου–23 Νοεμβρίου 2006)*. Athens: Ypourgeio Politismou/Epigraphiko Mouseio/Elliniki Epigraphiki Etaireia.

Mattingly, D. J., and Salmon, J. B. (eds) (2001), *Economies beyond Agriculture in the Classical World*. London and New York: Routledge.

Meadows, A. R. (2001), 'Money, freedom, and empire in the hellenistic world', in A. Meadows and K. Shipton (eds), *Money and its Uses in the Ancient Greek World* (Oxford University Press), 53–63.

(2013), 'Polybius, Aratus and the history of the 140th Olympiad', in B. Gibson and T. Harrison (eds), *Polybius and his World: Essays in Memory of F. W. Walbank* (Oxford and New York: Oxford University Press), 91–116.

Mee, C. B., and Forbes, H. A. (eds) (1997), *A Rough and Rocky Place: The Landscape and Settlement History of the Methana Peninsula, Greece (Results of the Methana Survey Project Sponsored by the British School at Athens and the University of Liverpool)*. Liverpool University Press.

Meiggs, R. (1982), *Trees and Timber in the Ancient Mediterranean World*. Oxford: Clarendon Press.

Melfi, M., and Bobou, O. (eds) (2016), *Hellenistic Sanctuaries: Between Greece and Rome*. Oxford University Press.

Meritt, B. D. (ed.) (1931), *Greek Inscriptions: 1896–1927*. Cambridge, MA: Harvard University Press.

Mertens, N. (2002), 'Οὐκ ὁμοῖοι, ἀγαθοὶ δέ: the perioikoi in the classical Lakedaimonian polis', in C. A. Powell and S. J. Hodkinson (eds), *Sparta: Beyond the Mirage* (London: Classical Press of Wales/Duckworth), 285–303.

Meyer, E. (1967), 'Elis 1', *KP* ii. 249–51.

(1969a), 'Lykosoura', *KP* iii. 820–1.

(1969b), 'Messenien', *KP* iii. 1250–4.

(1972a), 'Nauplia', *KP* iv. 13–14.

(1972b), 'Nemea 2', *KP* iv. 45–6.

(1972c), 'Pellene', *KP* iv. 601–2.

(1975a), 'Sikyon', *KP* v. 186–8.

(1975b), 'Troizen', *KP* v. 984–5.

Migeotte, L. (2001), 'Les concours d'Aktion en Acarnanie: organisation financière et fiscale', *Ancient World* 32. 2: 164–70.

Mikalson, J. D. (1998), *Religion in Hellenistic Athens*. Berkeley–Los Angeles and London: University of California Press.

Miller, S. G. (1994), 'Sosikles and the fourth-century building program of Zeus at Nemea', in N. Winter (ed.), *Proceedings of the International Conference on Greek Architectural Terracottas of the Classical and Hellenistic Periods* (Princeton: American School of Classical Studies at Athens), 85–98.

Millis, B. W. (2006), '"Miserable huts" in post-146 BC Corinth', *Hesperia* 75. 3: 397–404.

Minon, S. (2008), 'Le déclin du dialecte éléen (IVᵉ–IIᵉ siècle a.C.)', in C. Grandjean (ed.), *Le Péloponnèse d'Épaminondas à Hadrien* (Bordeaux and Paris: Ausonius and De Boccard), 247–61.

(ed.) (2014a), *Diffusion de l'attique et expansion des koinai dans le Péloponnèse et en Grèce centrale: actes de la journée internationale de dialectologie grecque du 18 mars 2011, Université Paris-Ouest Nanterre*. Geneva: Droz.

(2014b), 'Les mutations des alphabets péloponnésiens au contact de l'alphabet attique ionisé (ca 450–350 av. J.-C.)', in S. Minon (ed.), *Diffusion de l'attique et expansion des koinai dans le Péloponnèse et en Grèce centrale* (Geneva: Droz), 29–55.

Mitchison, N. (1931), *The Corn King and the Spring Queen*. London: Cape.

Mitsopoulou-Leon, V. (1990), 'Σκύφοι με ανάγλυφο διάκοσμο από τους Λουσούς (βόρεια Αρκαδία)', in *2nd Hellenistic Pottery Meeting*, 120.

(2000), 'Κεραμική από τους Λουσούς', in *1st Hellenistic Pottery Meeting*, 2nd edn, 21–31.

(2005), 'Clay figurines from Lousoi: some thoughts on local production', in E. Østby (ed.), *Ancient Arcadia* (Athens and Sävedalen, Sweden: Norwegian Institute at Athens and Åström), 445–58.

Moggi, M. (1974), 'Il sinecismo di Megalopoli', *ASNP* 3. 4: 71–107.

Möller, A. (2004), 'Elis, Olympia und das Jahr 580 v. Chr.: zur Frage der Eroberung der Pisatis', in R. Rollinger and C. Ulf (eds), *Griechische Archaik: interne Entwicklungen – externe Impulse* (Innsbruck: Akademie-Verlag), 249–70.

(2011), 'Der Preis der Dinge: Fischkauf auf der Athener Agora', in D. Rohde and B. Onken (eds), *In omni historia curiosus: Studien zur Geschichte von der Antike bis zur Neuzeit. Festschrift für Helmuth Schneider zum 65. Geburtstag* (Wiesbaden: Harrassowitz), 13–22.

Morgan, C. A. (2007–8), 'Archaeology in Greece 2007–2008', *AR* 54: 1–113.

(2008–9), 'Archaeology in Greece 2008–2009', *AR* 55: 1–101.

(2009–10), 'Archaeology in Greece 2009–2010', *AR* 56: 1–201.

and Hall, J. (2000), 'Αχαϊκές πόλεις και αχαϊκός αποικισμός', in A. D. Rizakis (ed.), *Δύμη και Δυμαία χώρα – Dymé et son territoire* (Athens: Kentron Ellinikis kai Romaïkis Archaiotitos, Ethniko Idryma Erevnon), 105–12.

and Hall, J. (2004), 'Achaia', in M. H. Hansen and T. H. Nielsen (eds), *An Inventory of Archaic and Classical Poleis* (Oxford University Press), 472–88.

Morris, I. (2007), 'Introduction', in W. Scheidel, I. Morris, and R. Saller (eds), *The Cambridge Economic History of the Greco-Roman World* (Cambridge University Press), 1–12.

and Manning, J. G. (2005), 'Introduction', in J. G. Manning and I. Morris (eds), *The Ancient Economy: Evidence and Models* (Stanford, CA: Stanford University Press), 1–46.

Moschou, L. (1975), 'Τοπογραφικὰ Μάνης: ἡ πόλις Ταίναρον', *AAA* 8. 2: 160–77.

Müller, C. (2002), 'Les Italiens en Béotie du IIe siècle av. J.-C. au Ier siècle ap. J.-C.', in C. Müller and C. Hasenohr (eds), *Les Italiens dans le monde grec: IIème siècle av. J.-C.–Ier siècle ap. J.-C. Circulation, activités, intégration* (Athens: École française d'Athènes), 89–100.

(2013), 'The rise and fall of the Boeotians: Polybius 20.4–7 as a literary topos', in B. Gibson and T. Harrison (eds), *Polybius and his World: Essays in Memory of F. W. Walbank* (Oxford and New York: Oxford University Press), 267–78.

Murray, W. M. (1985), 'The weight of trireme rams and the price of bronze in fourth-century Athens', *GRBS* 26. 2: 141–50.

Nielsen, T. H. (1995), 'Mainalierne: en arkadisk stammestat', in T. H. Nielsen and C. G. Tortzen (eds), *Gammel Dansk: studier et al. til ære for Mogens Herman Hansen* (Copenhagen: Hetaireion), 60–6.

(1996), 'Arkadia: city-ethnics and tribalism', in M. H. Hansen (ed.), *Introduction to an Inventory of Poleis* (Copenhagen: Kongelige Danske Videnskabernes Selskab/Munksgaard), 117–63.

(1997), 'Triphylia: an experiment in ethnic construction and political organisation', in T. H. Nielsen (ed.), *Yet More Studies in the Ancient Greek Polis* (Stuttgart: Steiner), 129–62.

(2002), *Arkadia and its Poleis in the Archaic and Classical Periods*. Göttingen: Vandenhoeck & Ruprecht.

(2004a), 'Arkadia', in M. H. Hansen and T. H. Nielsen (eds), *An Inventory of Archaic and Classical Poleis* (Oxford University Press), 505–39.

(2004b), 'Triphylia', in M. H. Hansen and T. H. Nielsen (eds), *An Inventory of Archaic and Classical Poleis* (Oxford University Press), 540–6.

(2005), 'A polis as a part of a larger identity group: glimpses from the history of Lepreon', *C&M* 56: 57–89.

(2015), 'The Arkadian confederacy', in H. Beck and P. Funke (eds), *Federalism in Greek Antiquity* (Cambridge University Press), 250–68.

and Roy, J. (eds) (1999), *Defining Ancient Arkadia (Symposium, April, 1–4 1998)*. Copenhagen: Kongelige Danske Videnskabernes Selskab.

Nieto Izquierdo, E. (2014), 'La diffusion de la koiné en Argolide au IVe siècle: les premières étapes', in S. Minon (ed.), *Diffusion de l'attique et expansion des koinai dans le Péloponnèse et en Grèce centrale* (Geneva: Droz), 69–86.

Nilsson, M. P. (1951), *Cults, Myths, Oracles, and Politics in Ancient Greece*. Lund: Gleerup.

Noack, F. (1894), 'Arne', *MDAI(A)* 19: 405–85.

Numismatik Lanz (2001), *Münzen von Korinth: Sammlung BCD*. Munich: Numismatik Lanz.

O'Neil, J. L. (1984–6), 'The political elites of the Achaian and Aitolian leagues', *AncSoc* 15–17: 33–61.

(1995), *The Origins and Development of Ancient Greek Democracy*. Lanham, MD.: Rowman & Littlefield.

(2008), 'A re-examination of the Chremonidean war', in P. McKechnie and P. Guillaume (eds), *Ptolemy II Philadelphus and his World* (Leiden and Boston: Brill), 65–89.

Ødegard, K. (2005), 'The topography of ancient Tegea: new discoveries and old problems', in E. Østby (ed.), *Ancient Arcadia* (Athens and Sävedalen, Sweden: Norwegian Institute at Athens and Åström), 209–21.

Okada, T. (2003), 'Livestock trade in classical Arkadia: a study of IG.V.2.3 (Tegea) [in Japanese]', *JCS* 51: 69–77 (Engl. summ., 180–1).

Oliver, G. J. (2003), 'Oligarchy at Athens after the Lamian war: epigraphic evidence for the boule and the ekklesia', in O. Palagia and S. V. Tracy (eds), *The Macedonians in Athens 322–229 BC* (Oxford: Oxbow), 40–51.

Osborne, R. G. (1987), *Classical Landscape with Figures: The Ancient Greek City and its Countryside*. London: George Philip.

(ed.) (2007), *Debating the Athenian Cultural Revolution: Art, Literature, Philosophy, and Politics, 430–380 BC*. Cambridge and New York: Cambridge University Press.

Ostwald, M. (2000a), *Oligarchia: The Development of a Constitutional Form in Ancient Greece*. Stuttgart: Steiner.

(2000b), 'Oligarchy and oligarchs in ancient Greece', in P. Flensted-Jensen, T. H. Nielsen, and L. Rubinstein (eds), *Polis and Politics: Studies in Ancient Greek History Presented to Mogens Herman Hansen* (Copenhagen: Museum Tusculanum Press, University of Copenhagen), 385–96.

Pakkanen, J. (1998), *The Temple of Athena Alea at Tegea: A Reconstruction of the Peristyle Column*. University of Helsinki Department of Art History/Finnish Institute at Athens.

Palagia, O. (2006), 'Art and royalty in Sparta of the 3rd century BC', *Hesperia* 75. 2: 205–17.

(2010), 'Philip's Eurydice in the Philippeum at Olympia', in E. D. Carney and D. Ogden (eds), *Philip II and Alexander the Great: Father and Son, Lives and Afterlives* (Oxford University Press), 33–41.

Palm, J. (1955), *Über Sprache und Stil des Diodoros von Sizilien: ein Beitrag zur Beleuchtung der hellenistischen Prosa*. Lund: Gleerup.

Panagopoulou, K. (2000), 'Antigonos Gonatas: coinage, money and the economy', PhD thesis. University of London.

Papaefthymiou, V. (1993), 'Ἐπιτύμβιες στῆλες τῶν ἑλληνιστικῶν καὶ ῥωμαϊκῶν χρόνων τοῦ Μουσείου Σπάρτης', in O. Palagia and W. Coulson (eds), *Sculpture from Arcadia and Laconia* (Oxford: Oxbow), 237–44.

Papagiannopoulos, K. V., and Zachos, G. A. (2000), 'Ἐντατικὴ ἐπιφανειακὴ ἔρευνα στη δυτικὴ Ἀχαΐα: μια ἄλλη προσέγγιση', in A. D. Rizakis (ed.), *Δύμη καὶ Δυμαία χώρα – Dymé et son territoire* (Athens: Kentron Ellinikis kai Romaïkis Archaiotitos, Ethniko Idryma Erevnon), 139–54.

Papakosta, L. (2005), 'Ἑλληνιστικὴ κεραμικὴ ἀπὸ τὸ Αἴγιο', in L. Kypraiou, *Ἑλληνιστικὴ κεραμικὴ ἀπὸ τὴν Πελοπόννησο* (Athens: Ypourgeio Politismou), 73–82.

(2011), 'Τὸ ἑλληνιστικὸ νεκροταφείο τοῦ συνοικισμοῦ τῆς Ἁγίας Κυριακῆς Αἰγίου', in *7th Hellenistic Pottery Meeting*, 37–46, pls 3–6.

Parlama, L. (1972), 'Νεκροταφεῖον τοῦ IV. αἰ. π. Χ. παρὰ τὸ Μάζι Ὀλυμπίας', *AAA* 5: 206–23.

Pébarthe, C. (2007), review of R. Descat, *Approches de l'économie hellénistique*, in *Annales ESC*, 62. 6: 1437–9.

Peek, W. (1974), 'Artemis Eulakia', in *Mélanges helléniques offerts à Georges Daux* (Paris: de Boccard), 295–302.

Penttinen, A. (1996a), 'The Berbati–Limnes Archaeological Survey: the classical and hellenistic periods', in B. Wells and C. Runnels (eds), *The Berbati–Limnes Archaeological Survey 1988–1990* (Stockholm and Jonsered: Svenska Institutet i Athen and Åström), 229–83.

(1996b), 'Excavations on the acropolis of Asine in 1990', *OAth* 21: 149–67.

(2005), 'From the Early Iron Age to the early Roman times', in J. Hjohlman, A. Penttinen, and B. Wells, *Pyrgouthi: A Rural Site in the Berbati Valley from the Early Iron Age to Late Antiquity* (Stockholm: Paul Åström), 11–125.

Peppa-Papaïoannou, P. (1992), 'Νέα ἀρχαιολογικὰ στοιχεῖα σχετικὰ μὲ τὴν οἰκοδομικὴ δραστηριότητα στὸ Ἀσκληπεῖο Ἐπιδαύρου κατὰ τὴ ρωμαϊκὴ ἐποχή', in *4th Peloponnesian Congress*, ii, 257–71.

Perrin, B. (ed.) (1921), *Plutarch, Agis and Cleomenes, Tiberius and Caius Gracchus; Philopoemen and Flamininus*. Cambridge, MA, and London: Harvard University Press and Heinemann.

Petritaki, M. (2005), 'Κλείτωρ: η πόλη υπό το φως των ανασκαφών. Γενική θεώρηση ανασκαφικών δεδομένων', in E. Østby (ed.), *Ancient Arcadia* (Athens and Sävedalen, Sweden: Norwegian Institute at Athens and Åström), 351–62.

Petropoulos, M. (1994), 'Ἀγροικίες Πατραϊκῆς', in P. Doukellis and L. Mendoni (eds), *Structures rurales et sociétés antiques* (Paris: Les Belles Lettres), 405–24.

(2005a), 'Η ελληνιστική κεραμική της Πελοποννήσου', in L. Kypraiou (ed.), *Ελληνιστική κεραμική από την Πελοπόννησο* (Athens: Ypourgeio Politismou), 23–31.

(2005b), 'Η Πελοπόννησος κατά την ελληνιστική εποχή', in L. Kypraiou (ed.), *Ελληνιστική κεραμική από την Πελοπόννησο* (Athens: Ypourgeio Politismou), 9–22.

and Rizakis, A. D. (1994), 'Settlement patterns and landscape in the coastal area of Patras: preliminary report', *JRA* 7: 183–207.

Pettegrew, D. K. (2016), *The Isthmus of Corinth: Crossroads of the Mediterranean World*. Ann Arbor MI: University of Michigan Press.

Picard, O. (1987), 'L'administration de l'atelier monétaire à Thasos au IVe siècle', *RN* 29: 7–14.

(1989), 'Innovations monétaires dans la Grèce du IVe siècle', *CRAI* 1989: 673–87.

(1990), 'Philippe II et le monnayage des cités grecques', *REG* 103: 1–15.

(2001), 'Thasos et sa monnaie au IIe siècle: catastrophe ou mutation?', in R. Frei-Stolba and K. Gex Bern (eds), *Recherches récentes sur le monde hellénistique* (Bern: Lang), 281–92.

(2006), 'Monétarisation et économie des cités grecques à la basse période hellénistique: la fortune d'Archippè de Kymè', in R. Descat (ed.), *Approches de l'économie hellénistique: 4mes rencontres sur l'économie antique, Saint-Bertrand-de-Comminges, 2004* (Saint-Bertrand-de-Comminges: Musée archéologique départemental de Saint-Bertrand-de-Comminges), 85–119.

(2007), 'Les innovations monétaires du IVe siècle', in P. Brulé, J. Oulhen, and F. Prost (eds), *Économie et société en Grèce antique: 478–88 av. J.-C.* (Presses Universitaires de Rennes), 393–403.

(2010), 'Rome et la Grèce à la basse époque impériale: monnaies et impérialisme', *JS* 2010. 2: 161–92.

(2013), 'La valeur du bronze: du métal à la monnaie', in C. Grandjean and A. Moustaka (eds), *Aux origines de la monnaie fiduciaire: traditions métallurgiques et innovations numismatiques* (Bordeaux: Ausonius), 71–7.

Piérart, M. (2004), 'Argolis', in M. H. Hansen and T. H. Nielsen (eds), *An Inventory of Archaic and Classical Poleis* (Oxford University Press), 599–619.

Pikoulas, G. A. (1986), Ὁ ἀρχαῖος οἰκισμὸς τῆς Δημητσάνας', *Ὅρος* 4: 99–123.

(1988a), Ἡ ἀνατολικὴ ἀκτὴ τοῦ Μαλέα: κόλπος Μονεμβασίας', *ΛΣ* 9: 277–85.

(1988b), *Ἡ νότια μεγαλοπολίτικη χώρα: ἀπό τόν 8ο π.Χ. ὥς τόν 4ο μ.Χ. αἰώνα. Συμβολή στήν τοπογραφία της (διδακτορική διατριβή)*. Athens: Horos.

(1990), 'The Spartan defense network of hellenistic times', in *Akten des XIII. internationalen Kongresses für klassische Archäologie (Berlin 24–30/7/1988)* (Mainz am Rhein: von Zabern), 478.

(1995), *Ὁδικὸ δίκτυο καὶ ἄμυνα: ἀπὸ τὴν Κόρινθο στὸ Ἄργος καὶ τὴν Ἀρκαδία*. Athens: Horos.

(1996–7), Οἱ "πυράμιδες" τῆς Ἀργολίδος', in *5th Peloponnesian Congress*, ii. 43–50.

(1999a), 'The road-network of Arkadia', in T. H. Nielsen and J. Roy (eds), *Defining Ancient Arkadia* (Copenhagen: Kongelige Danske Videnskabernes Selskab), 248–319 (with map 3 at end of vol.).

(1999b), Ἀλειτορία: διαβάσεις καὶ ἄμυνα', *Ὅρος* 13: 137–54.

(2000–3), 'Λακεδαιμονίων συνθῆκαι Αἰτολοῖς', *Ὅρος* 14–16: 455–67, pls 100–1.

(2001a), *Λεξικὸ τῶν οἰκισμῶν τῆς Πελοποννήσου: παλαιὰ καὶ νέα τοπωνύμια*. Athens: Horos.

(2001b), 'Το οδικό δίκτυο της Λακωνίας: χρονολόγηση, απαρχές και εξέλιξη', in V. Mitsopoulos-Leon (ed.), *Forschungen in der Peloponnes* (Athens: Österreichisches Archäologisches Institut), 325–30.

(2002), Ὁ ἀρχαῖος οἰκισμὸς τῆς Δημητσάνας', in *Ἀρκαδία: συλλογὴ μελετῶν* (Athens: Horos), 181–216.

(2008), 'Το αμυντικό δίκτυο της Θεισόας Λυκαίου: ανατρέποντας στερεότυπα', in G. A. Pikoulas (ed.), *Ἱστορίες γιὰ τὴν ἀρχαία Ἀρκαδία* (Stemnitsa: Dimos Trikolonon/Panepistimio Thessalias, Tmima Istorias, Archaiologias kai Koinonikis Anthropologias), 251–60.

with Oikonomos, G. (2012), *Τὸ ὁδικὸ δίκτυο τῆς Λακωνικῆς*. Athens: Horos.

Piper, L. J. (1984–6), 'Spartan helots in the hellenistic age', *AncSoc* 15–17: 75–88.

Piteros, C. I. (1996–7a), Οἱ "πυράμιδες" τῆς Ἀργολίδας', in *5th Peloponnesian Congress*, iii, 344–94.

(1996–7b), '"Πυράμιδες" τῆς Ἀργολίδος (περίληψις ἀνακοινώσεως)', in *5th Peloponnesian Congress*, i. 489–90.

Pleket, H. W. (1964), *Epigraphica*, i. Leiden.

Pomeroy, S. B. (1994), *Xenophon, Oeconomicus: A Social and Historical Commentary (with a New English Translation)*. Oxford: Clarendon Press.

Potter, D. S. (2003), 'Hellenistic religion', in A. Erskine (ed.), *A Companion to the Hellenistic World* (Malden, MA: Blackwell), 407–30.

Powell, A. (1975), *Hearing Secret Harmonies*. London: Heinemann.

Prent, M. (2002), 'Notes on the stratigraphy and phasing of the Hellenistic–early Roman buildings', in J. H. Crouwel, M. Prent, S. M. Thorne, R. T. J. Cappers, S. A. Mulder, T. Carter, E. Langridge-Noti, and L. van Dijk-Schram, 'Geraki', *Pharos*, 10: 1–81, at 42–52.

Pretzler, M. (2005), 'Comparing Strabo with Pausanias: Greece in context vs. Greece in depth', in D. Dueck, H. Lindsay, and S. Pothecary (eds), *Strabo's Cultural Geography: The Making of a Kolossourgia* (Cambridge University Press), 144–60.

—— (n.d. [2008]), 'Making Peloponnesians: Sparta's allies and their regional identities', in W. G. Cavanagh and J. Roy (eds), *Being Peloponnesian* (Nottingham: Centre for Spartan & Peloponnesian Studies, University of Nottingham), ch. 3.

—— and Barley, N. D. (eds) (2017), *Brill's Companion to Aeneas Tacticus: Aineias the Tactician and his World*. Leiden: Brill.

Pritchett, W. K. (1980), 'Ancient Greek roads', in *Studies in Ancient Greek Topography*, iii (Berkeley, CA: University of California Press), 143–96.

Proskynitopoulou, R. (2000), Ἑλληνιστική κεραμική από την αρχαία Επίδαυρο', in *5th Hellenistic Pottery Meeting*, 393–402, pls 207–10.

Psoma, S. E. (1998), 'Le nombre de chalques dans l'obole dans le monde grec', *RN* 153: 19–29.

—— (2009), 'Tas sitarchias kai tous misthous ([Arist.], Oec. 1351b): bronze currencies and cash-allowances in mainland Greece, Thrace and the kingdom of Macedonia', *RBN* 155: 3–38.

—— (2013), 'La monnaie de bronze: les débuts d'une institution', in C. Grandjean and A. Moustaka (eds), *Aux origines de la monnaie fiduciaire: traditions métallurgiques et innovations numismatiques* (Bordeaux: Ausonius), 57–70.

Purcell, N. (2012), 'Peloponnesus', *OCD*[4] 1101.

Quiller-Couch, A. (1900), *The Oxford Book of English Verse, 1250–1900*. Oxford University Press.

Rackham, O. (1996), 'Ecology and pseudo-ecology: the example of ancient Greece', in G. Shipley and J. B. Salmon (eds), *Human Landscapes in Classical Antiquity: Environment and Culture* (London and New York: Routledge), 16–43.

—— (2002), 'Observations on the historical ecology of Laconia', in W. Cavanagh, J. Crouwel, R. W. V. Catling, and G. Shipley, *Continuity and Change in a Greek Rural Landscape: The Laconia Survey*, i: *Methodology and Interpretation* (London: British School at Athens), 73–119.

Raftopoulou, S. (1998), 'New finds from Sparta', in W. G. Cavanagh and S. E. C. Walker (eds), *Sparta in Laconia: The Archaeology of a City and its Countryside* (London: British School at Athens), 125–40.

—— (2000), 'Ταφικό σύνολο από την Σπάρτη', in *5th Hellenistic Pottery Meeting*, 417–26, pls 215–18.

Randall, R. H. (1953), 'The Erechtheum workmen', *AJA* 57. 3: 199–210.

Rathosi, C. (2005), 'Αρχαιολογικά κεραμικά ΒΔ Πελοποννήσου και προέλευση των πρώτων υλών τους: πετρογραφική, ορυκτολογική, γεωχημική και αρχαιομετρική προσέγγιση', PhD thesis. Patra: Paneptistimio Patron.

Reger, G. (1994), *Regionalism and Change in the Economy of Independent Delos: 314–167 BC*. Berkeley-Los Angeles and Oxford: University of California Press.

(1998), review of J. J. Gabbert, *Antigonus II Gonatas*, in *BMCR* 1998.10.17.

(2003), 'The economy', in A. Erskine (ed.), *A Companion to the Hellenistic World* (Malden, MA: Blackwell), 331–53.

Reinholdt, C. (2009), *Das Brunnenhaus der Arsinoe in Messene: Nutzarchitektur, Repräsentationsbaukunst und Hydrotechnologie im Rahmen hellenistisch-römischer Wasserversorgung*. Vienna: Phoibos.

Reinmuth, O. W. (1967), 'Isthmien', *KP* ii. 1474–5.

Rhodes, P. J. (1981), *A Commentary on the Aristotelian Athenaion Politeia*. Oxford: Clarendon Press.

(1997), with D. M. Lewis, *The Decrees of the Greek States*. Oxford: Clarendon Press.

(2005), *Euthynai (Accounting): A Valedictory Lecture (delivered before the University of Durham ... on 9 May 2005)*. [Durham, UK]: privately printed.

(2009), 'Ancient Athens: democracy and empire', *ERH* 16. 2: 201–15.

Riedel, S. (2013), 'Hellenistic pottery in a wider perspective: on the use and misuse of the application of network theory to material culture', in N. Fenn and C. Römer-Strehl (eds), *Networks in the Hellenistic World: According to the Pottery in the Eastern Mediterranean and Beyond* (Oxford: BAR International Series), 371–6.

Rizakis, A. D. (1990a), 'Cadastres et espace rural dans le nord-ouest du Péloponnèse', *DHA* 16. 1: 259–80.

(1990b), 'La politeia dans les cités de la confédération achéenne', *Tyche* 5: 109–34, pl. 15.

(1991), 'Αχαϊκή ιστοριογραφία: απολογισμός και προοπτικές', in A. D. Rizakis (ed.), Ἀρχαία Ἀχαῖα καὶ Ἠλεία/*Achaia und Elis in der Antike* (Athens: Kentron Ellinikis kai Romaïkis Archaiotitos, Ethniko Idryma Erevnon), 51–60.

(1995a), 'Grands domaines et petites propriétés dans le Péloponnèse sous l'empire', in *Du latifundium au latifondo: un héritage de Rome, une création médiévale ou moderne?* (Talence and Paris: Centre Pierre Paris and De Boccard), 219–38.

(1995b), *Sources textuelles et histoire régionale*. Athens: Kentron Ellinikis kai Romaïkis Archaiotitos, Ethniko Idryma Erevnon.

(1997), 'Roman colonies in the province of Achaia: territories, land and population', in S. E. Alcock (ed.), *The Early Roman Empire in the East* (Oxford: Oxbow), 15–36. Trans. L. Hall.

(1998), *La Cité de Patras: épigraphie et histoire*. Athens: Kentron Ellinikis kai Romaïkis Archaiotitos, Ethniko Idryma Erevnon.

(ed.) (2000), Δύμη και Δυμαία χώρα – *Dymé et son territoire* (Πρακτικά του διεθνούς συνεδρίου 'Δυμαία-Βουπρασίου', Κάτω Αχαΐα, 6–8 Οκτωβρίου 1995/

Actes du colloque international 'Dymaia et Bouprasia', Katô Achaïa, 6–8 octobre 1995). Athens and Paris: Kentron Ellinikis kai Romaïkis Archaiotitos, Ethniko Idryma Erevnon, Dimos Kato Achaïas, and de Boccard.

(2001a), 'Les cités péloponnésiennes entre l'époque hellénistique et l'empire: le paysage économique et social', in R. Frei-Stolba and K. Gex Bern (eds), *Recherches récentes sur le monde hellénistique* (Bern: Lang), 75–96.

(2001b), 'La constitution des élites municipales dans le colonies romaines de la province d'Achaïe', in O. Salomies (ed.), *The Greek East in the Roman Context* (Helsinki: Suomen Ateenan-Instituutin Säätiö), 37–49.

(2002), 'L'émigration romaine en Macédoine et la communauté marchande de Thessalonique: perspectives économiques et sociales', in C. Müller and C. Hasenohr (eds), *Les Italiens dans le monde grec: IIème siècle av. J.-C.–Ier siècle ap. J.-C. Circulation, activités, intégration* (Athens: École française d'Athènes), 109–32.

(2004), 'Οικονομία και οικονομικές δραστηριότητες των ελληνικών πόλεων από την Πύδνα έως το Άκτιον', in *6th Hellenistic Pottery Meeting*, 17–28.

(2014), 'Town and country in early imperial Greece', in J. L. Bintliff (ed.), *Recent Developments in the Long-term Archaeology of Greece = Pharos*, 20. 1: 241–67.

(2015), 'The Achaian league', in H. Beck and P. Funke (eds), *Federalism in Greek Antiquity* (Cambridge University Press), 118–31.

and Lakakis, M. (1988), 'Polis et chora: l'organisation de l'espace urbain et rural en Achaïe occidentale', in *12th Classical Archaeology Congress*, 551–2, map.

and Touratsoglou, I. P. (2011), 'Η οικονομία της Πελοποννήσου κατά την ελληνιστική περίοδο', in *7th Hellenistic Pottery Meeting*, 17–34, foldout chart preceding 17.

Robert, J., and Robert, L. (1976), 'Bulletin épigraphique', *REG* 89. 426–7: 415–595.

Robinson, E. W. (2009), 'Ethnicity and democracy in the Peloponnese, 401–362 BCE', in P. Funke and N. Luraghi (eds), *The Politics of Ethnicity and the Crisis of the Peloponnesian League* (Washington, DC: Center for Hellenic Studies and Harvard University Press), 135–47.

(2011), *Democracy beyond Athens: Popular Government in the Greek Classical Age.* Cambridge and New York: Cambridge University Press.

Robinson, H. S. (1968), 'Salvage archaeology in Elis, 1967', *AAA* 1: 46–8.

Roebuck, C. A. (1941), 'A history of Messenia from 369 to 146 BC', PhD thesis (private edition, distributed by University of Chicago Libraries). University of Chicago.

(1948), 'The settlements of Philip II with the Greek states in 338 BC', *CPh* 43: 73–92.

(1984), 'The settlements of Philip II with the Greek states in 338 BC', in *Economy and Society in Early Greece: Collected Essays* (Chicago: Ares), 129–50.

Rogl, C. (1997), 'Homerische Becher aus der Stadt Elis', in *4th Hellenistic Pottery Meeting*, 317–28, pls 235–8.

(2004), 'Hellenistische Reliefbecher aus der Stadt Lousoi: die Erzeugnisse der lokalen Werkstätte(n) [poster]', in *6th Hellenistic Pottery Meeting*, 771.

Romano, D. G., and Voyatzis, M. E. (2015), 'Mt. Lykaion Excavation and Survey Project, 2: the lower sanctuary', *Hesperia*, 84. 2: 207–76.

Rossetto, P. C., and Sartorio, G. P. (eds) (1994), *Teatri greci e romani: alle origini del linguaggio rappresentato*. 3 vols. Rome: SEAT.

Rostovtzeff, M. I. with Milne, J. G., Blake, R. P., Robinson, E. S. G., and Waagé, F. O. (1941), *The Social and Economic History of the Hellenistic World*. 3 vols. Oxford: Clarendon Press.

Rotroff, S. I. (2006), 'Material culture', in G. R. Bugh (ed.), *The Cambridge Companion to the Hellenistic World* (New York: Cambridge University Press), 136–57.

—— (2013), 'Bion international: branch pottery workshops in the hellenistic age', in N. Fenn and C. Römer-Strehl (eds), *Networks in the Hellenistic World: According to the Pottery in the Eastern Mediterranean and Beyond* (Oxford: BAR International Series), 15–23.

Routledge, B. (2013), *Archaeology and State Theory: Subjects and Objects of Power*. London and New York: Bloomsbury Academic.

Roy, J. (1973), 'Diodorus Siculus XV 40: the Peloponnesian revolutions of 374 BC', *Klio*, 55: 135–9.

—— (1983), 'Megalopolis field survey', in D. R. Keller and D. W. Rupp (eds), *Archaeological Survey in the Mediterranean Area* (Oxford: British Archaeological Reports), 265–6.

—— (1994), 'Thebes in the 360s BC', in *CAH*, 2nd edn, vi: *The Fourth Century BC*, 187–208.

—— (1997), 'The perioikoi of Elis', in M. H. Hansen (ed.), *The Polis as an Urban Centre and as a Political Community* (Copenhagen: Kongelige Danske Videnskabernes Selskab/Munksgaard), 282–320.

—— (1999), 'The economies of Arkadia', in T. H. Nielsen and J. Roy (eds), *Defining Ancient Arkadia* (Copenhagen: Kongelige Danske Videnskabernes Selskab), 320–81.

—— (2004), 'Elis', in M. H. Hansen and T. H. Nielsen (eds), *An Inventory of Archaic and Classical Poleis* (Oxford University Press), 489–504.

—— (2005), 'Synoikizing Megalopolis: the scope of the synoikism and the interests of local Arkadian communities', in E. Østby (ed.), *Ancient Arcadia* (Athens and Sävedalen, Sweden: Norwegian Institute at Athens and Åström), 261–70.

—— (2009a), 'Anyte of Tegea and the other dead', in H. Cavanagh, W. G. Cavanagh, and J. Roy (eds), *Honouring the Dead in the Peloponnese: Proceedings of the Conference held in Sparta, 23–25 April 2009* (Nottingham: Centre for Spartan and Peloponnesian Studies, University of Nottingham), 643–56.

—— (2009b), 'Elis', in P. Funke and N. Luraghi (eds), *The Politics of Ethnicity and the Crisis of the Peloponnesian League* (Washington, DC: Center for Hellenic Studies and Harvard University Press), 30–48.

—— (2009c), 'Hegemonial structures in late archaic and early classical Elis and Sparta', in S. Hodkinson (ed.), *Sparta: Comparative Approaches* (Swansea: Classical Press of Wales), 69–88.

(2015a), 'Arkadia and the sea', *Historika* 5: 205–14.

(2015b), 'Elis (with Akroria and Pisatis)', in H. Beck and P. Funke (eds), *Federalism in Greek Antiquity* (Cambridge University Press), 269–84.

Lloyd, J. A., and Owens, E. J. (1989), 'Megalopolis under the Roman empire', in S. Walker and A. Cameron (eds), *The Greek Renaissance in the Roman Empire* (London: Institute of Classical Studies), 146–50, pl. 56.

Lloyd, J. A. and Owens, E. J. (1992), 'Two sites in the Megalopolis basin: suggested locations for Haemoniae and Cromnus', in J. M. Sanders (ed.), *Φιλολάκων: Lakonian Studies in Honour of Hector Catling* (London: British School at Athens), 185–94.

Owens, E. J., and Lloyd, J. A. (1988), 'Tribe and polis in the chora at Megalopolis: changes in settlement pattern in relation to synoecism', in *12th Classical Archaeology Congress*, iv (Athens: Ypourgeio Politismou, Tameio Archaiologikon Poron kai Apallotrioseon), 179–82.

Royal Navy (1969), *The Black Sea Pilot: The Dardanelles, Marmara Denizi, The Bosporus, Black Sea, and Sea of Azov*, 11th edn. Place of publication not stated: Hydrographer of the Navy.

Rubinstein, L. (2013), 'Spoken words, written submissions, and diplomatic conventions: the importance and impact of oral performance in hellenistic inter-polis relations', in C. Kremmydas and K. Tempest (eds), *Hellenistic Oratory: Continuity and Change* (Oxford University Press), 165–99.

Ruggeri, C. (2009), 'Triphylia from Elis to Arcadia', in P. Funke and N. Luraghi (eds), *The Politics of Ethnicity and the Crisis of the Peloponnesian League* (Washington, DC: Center for Hellenic Studies and Harvard University Press), 49–64.

Sacks, K. S. (2012), 'Ephorus', *OCD*[4] 510.

Sakellariou, M., and Faraklas, N. (1971), *Corinthia and Cleonaea*. Athens: Athinaïkos Technologikos Omilos, Athinaïko Kentro Oikistikis/Athens Technological Organization, Athens Center of Ekistics.

Sallares, J. R. (1991), *The Ecology of the Ancient Greek World*. London and Ithaca, NY: Duckworth and Cornell University Press.

Salmon, J. B. (1984), *Wealthy Corinth: A History of the City to 338 BC*. Oxford: Clarendon Press.

(2001), 'Temples the measures of men: public building in the Greek economy', in D. J. Mattingly and J. B. Salmon (eds), *Economies beyond Agriculture in the Classical World* (London and New York: Routledge), 195–208.

Salowey, C. A. (1994), 'Herakles and the waterworks: Mycenaean dams, classical fountains, Roman aqueducts', in K. A. Sheedy (ed.), *Archaeology in the Peloponnese: New Excavations and Research* (Oxford: Oxbow), 77–94.

Sanders, G. D. R., and Whitbread, I. K. (1990), 'Central places and major roads in the Peloponnese', *ABSA* 85: 333–62.

Schauer, C. (1997), 'Ein hellenistischer Brunnen in Olympia', in *4th Hellenistic Pottery Meeting*, 24–31, pls 11–16.

Scheidel, W. (2010), 'Human development and quality of life in the long run: the case of Greece', *Princeton/Stanford Working Papers in Classics* 091006: [1–10].

Schneider, C. (1967–9), *Kulturgeschichte des Hellenismus*. 2 vols. Munich: Beck.

Schoene, A., Petermann, J. H., and Roediger, E. (eds) (1866–75), *Eusebi Chronicorum libri duo*. 2 vols. Berlin: Apud Weidmannos.

Scholten, J. B. (2000), *The Politics of Plunder: Aitolians and their Koinon in the Early Hellenistic Era, 279–217 BC*. Berkeley–Los Angeles and London: University of California Press.

Scholz, P. (2007), 'Elementarunterricht und intellektuelle Bildung im hellenistischen Gymnasion', in D. Kah and P. Scholz (eds), *Das hellenistische Gymnasion*, 2nd edn (Berlin: Akademie Verlag), 103–28.

Schwyzer, E. (1923), *Dialectorum Graecorum exempla epigraphica potiora*. Leipzig: Hirzel.

Scott, S. A. (2004), 'Elites, exhibitionism and the society of the late Roman villa', in N. Christie (ed.), *Landscapes of Change: Rural Evolutions in Late Antiquity and the Early Middle Ages* (Aldershot: Ashgate), 39–65.

Scruton, R. (2006), *A Political Philosophy: Arguments for Conservatism*. London and New York: Continuum.

Scullard, H. H., and Derow, P. S. (2012), 'Social wars', *OCD*[4] 1377.

Sheedy, K. A. (ed.) (1994), *Archaeology in the Peloponnese: New Excavations and Research*. Oxford: Oxbow/Australian Institute at Athens.

Sherwin-White, S. M. (1978), *Ancient Cos: An Historical Study from the Dorian Settlement to the Imperial Period*. Göttingen: Vandenhoeck & Ruprecht.

Shipley, D. G. J. (1987), *A History of Samos 800–188 BC*. Oxford: Clarendon Press.

(1992), 'Perioikos: the discovery of classical Lakonia', in J. M. Sanders (ed.), *Φιλολάκων: Lakonian Studies in honour of Hector Catling* (London: British School at Athens), 211–26.

(1996a), 'Archaeological sites in Laconia and the Thyreatis', in W. Cavanagh, J. Crouwel, R. W. V. Catling, and D. G. J. Shipley, *Continuity and Change in a Greek Rural Landscape: The Laconia Survey*, ii: *Archaeological Data* (London: British School at Athens), 263–313.

(1996b), 'Site catalogue of the survey', in W. Cavanagh, J. Crouwel, R. W. V. Catling, and D. G. J. Shipley, *Continuity and Change in a Greek Rural Landscape: The Laconia Survey*, ii: *Archaeological Data* (London: British School at Athens), 315–438.

(1997), '"The other Lakedaimonians": the dependent perioikic poleis of Laconia and Messenia', in M. H. Hansen (ed.), *The Polis as an Urban Centre and as a Political Community* (Copenhagen: Kongelige Danske Videnskabernes Selskab/Munksgaard), 189–281.

(2000a), 'The extent of Spartan territory in the late classical and hellenistic periods', *ABSA* 95: 367–90.

(2000b), *The Greek World after Alexander: 323–30 BC*. London and New York: Routledge.

(2001–2), ʽΚοινωνικὲς μεταβολὲς στὴν Σπάρτη καὶ Λακωνία κατὰ τὴν ἑλληνιστικὴ περίοδο: ἡ συμβολὴ τῶν δεδομένων ἐπιφανειακῆς ἔρευνας', in *6th Peloponnesian Congress*, ii. 433–45. Trans. E. Boutsikas and E. Panagopoulou.

(2002a), ʽHidden landscapes: Greek field survey data and hellenistic history', in D. Ogden (ed.), *The Hellenistic World: New Perspectives* (Swansea and London: Classical Press of Wales and Duckworth), 177–98.

(2002b), ʽPerioecic society', in M. Whitby (ed.), *Sparta* (Edinburgh: Edinburgh University Press), 182–9.

(2002c), ʽRural landscape change in hellenistic Greece', in K. Ascani, V. Gabrielsen, K. Kvist, and A. H. Rasmussen (eds), *Ancient History Matters: Studies Presented to Jens Erik Skydsgaard on his 70th Birthday* (Rome: ʽLʼErmaʼ di Bretschneider), 39–45.

(2002d), ʽThe survey area in the hellenistic and Roman periods', in W. Cavanagh, J. Crouwel, R. W. V. Catling, and D. G. J. Shipley, *Continuity and Change in a Greek Rural Landscape: The Laconia Survey*, i: *Methodology and Interpretation* (London: British School at Athens), 257–337.

(2003), review of M. H. Hansen and others, *Acts and Papers of the Copenhagen Polis Centre; A Comparative Study of Thirty City-state Cultures*, in *JHS* 123: 234–7.

(2004a), ʽLakedaimon', in M. H. Hansen and T. H. Nielsen (eds), *An Inventory of Archaic and Classical Poleis* (Oxford University Press), 569–98.

(2004b), ʽMessenia', in M. H. Hansen and T. H. Nielsen (eds), *An Inventory of Archaic and Classical Poleis* (Oxford University Press), 547–68.

(2005a), ʽ<Agis IV,> Kleomenes III and Laconian landscapes [abstract]', in *American Philological Association 136th Annual Meeting Abstracts* (Philadelphia: American Philological Association), 215.

(2005b), ʽBetween Macedonia and Rome: political landscapes and social change in southern Greece in the early hellenistic period', *ABSA* 100: 315–30.

(2006a), ʽAreus Iʼ, *CDCC* 74.

(2006b), ʽLandscapes of the ancient Peloponnese: a human-geographical approach', *Cultuur en natuur: geschiedenis van de mens en zijn leefomgeving = Leidschrift*, 21. 1: 27–43.

(2008a), ʽApproaching the Macedonian Peloponnese', in C. Grandjean (ed.), *Le Péloponnèse d'Épaminondas à Hadrien* (Bordeaux and Paris: Ausonius and De Boccard), 53–68.

(2008b), review of K. Tausend, *Verkehrswege der Argolis*, in *BMCR* 2008. 03.40.

(2009), ʽEarly hellenistic Sparta: changing modes of interaction with the wider world?', in N. Kaltsas (ed.), *Athens–Sparta: Contributions to the Research on the Archaeology and History of the Two City-states* (New York and Athens: Alexander S. Onassis Foundation and National Museum of Greece), 55–60.

(2011), *Pseudo-Skylax's Periplous: The Circumnavigation of the Inhabited World (Text, Translation, and Commentary)*. Exeter: Bristol Phoenix Press/The Exeter Press.

(2012), 'Pseudo-Skylax and the natural philosophers', *JHS* 132: 121–38.

(2013a), 'Afterword: hellenistic oratory in context', in C. Kremmydas and K. Tempest (eds), *Hellenistic Oratory: Continuity and Change* (Oxford University Press), 361–8.

(2013b), '"Small things remembered": the under-theorized domestic material culture of hellenistic Greece', in N. Fenn and C. Römer-Strehl (eds), *Networks in the Hellenistic World: According to the Pottery in the Eastern Mediterranean and Beyond* (Oxford: Archaeopress), 3–13.

(2014), review of G. A. Pikoulas, Τὸ ὁδικὸ δίκτυο τῆς Λακωνικῆς, in *BMCR* 2014.06.16.

(2017a), 'Agis IV, Kleomenes III, and Spartan landscapes', *Historia* 66. 3: 281–97.

(2017b), 'Aineias Tacticus in his intellectual context', in M. Pretzler and N. D. Barley (eds), *Brill's Companion to Aeneas Tacticus: Aineias the Tactician and his World* (Leiden: Brill), 49–67.

(2018) 'Why innovate? Between politics, the market, and material culture at the dawn of Eastern Sigillata', in *9th Hellenistic Pottery Meeting*, i. 15–27.

Siapkas, J. (2010), review of P. Funke and N. Luraghi, *The Politics of Ethnicity and the Crisis of the Peloponnesian League*, in *AJPh* 103. 3 [523] (2009): 517–20.

Siebert, G. (1978), *Recherches sur les ateliers de bols à reliefs du Péloponnèse à l'époque hellénistique*. Athens and Paris: École française d'Athènes and De Boccard.

Smith, A. D. (1986), *The Ethnic Origin of Nations*. Oxford: Blackwell.

Soter, S., and Katsonopoulou, D. (2011), 'Submergence and uplift of settlements in the area of Helike, Greece, from the early Bronze Age to late antiquity', *Geoarchaeology*, 26. 4: 584–610.

Sourvinou-Inwood, C. (2003), 'Herodotos (and others) on Pelasgians: some perceptions of ethnicity', in P. Derow and R. Parker (eds), *Herodotus and his World: Essays from a Conference in Memory of George Forrest* (Oxford University Press), 103–44.

Spawforth, A. J. S. (1978), 'Balbilla, the Euryclids and memorials for a Greek magnate', *ABSA* 73: 249–60.

Stavrianopoulou, E. (2002), 'Die Familienexedra von Eudamos und Lydiadas in Megalopolis', Τεκμήρια 7: 117–56.

Stewart, D. R. (2005), review of S. E. Alcock and J. F. Cherry, *Side-by-Side Survey*, in *BMCR* 2005.01.17.

(2013), *Reading the Landscapes of the Rural Peloponnese: Landscape Change and Regional Variation in an Early 'Provincial' Setting*. Oxford: Archaeopress.

Stillwell, R. (1952), *The Theatre*. Princeton: American School of Classical Studies at Athens.

Sturgeon, M. (1998), 'Hellenistic sculpture at Corinth: the state of the question', in O. Palagia and W. Coulson (eds), *Regional Schools in Hellenistic Sculpture* (Oxford: Oxbow), 1–13.

Stylianou, P. J. (1998), *A Historical Commentary on Diodorus Siculus Book 15*. Oxford: Clarendon Press.

Taeuber, H. (1981), 'Sikyon statt Aigeira: neue Beobachtungen zur Stele von Stymphalos (IG V/2, 351–357)', *ZPE* 42: 179–92.

— (1986), 'Ehreninschrift aus Megalopolis für Aristopamon, Sohn des Lydiadas', *Tyche*, 1: 221–6.

Talbert, R. J. A. (1988), *Plutarch on Sparta*, 1st edn. London: Penguin.

— (ed.) (2005), *Plutarch on Sparta*, revised edn. London: Penguin.

Tarn, W. W. (1913), *Antigonos Gonatas*. Oxford: Clarendon Press.

— and Griffith, G. T. (1952), *Hellenistic Civilisation*, 3rd edn. London: Arnold.

Tartaron, T. F., Pullen, D. J., Gregory, T. E., Noller, J. S., Rothaus, R. M., Caraher, W. R., Rife, J. L., Pettegrew, D. K., Tzortzopoulou-Gregory, L., Nakassis, D., and Schon, R. (2006), 'The Eastern Korinthia Archaeological Survey: integrated methods for a dynamic landscape', *Hesperia* 75. 4: 453–523.

Tausend, K. (2006), *Verkehrswege der Argolis: Rekonstruktion und historische Bedeutung*. Stuttgart: Steiner.

Themelis, P. G. (1990), Ἀνασκαφὴ Μεσσήνης', *PAE* 145: 56–103, pls 31–74.

— (1991), Ἀνασκαφὴ Μεσσήνης', *PAE* 146: 85–128, pls 50–78.

— (1994), Ὁ τάφος τῆς ἠλείας Φιλημήνας', in *3rd Hellenistic Pottery Meeting*, 146–58, pls 75–88.

— (1997), Ἀνασκαφὴ Μεσσήνης', *PAE* 152: 79–113.

— (2004a), 'Cults on Mount Ithome', *Kernos* 17: 143–54.

— (2004b), 'Πρώιμη ελληνιστική κεραμική από τη Μεσσήνη', in *6th Hellenistic Pottery Meeting*, 409–38, pls 183–94.

— (2005), 'Η ελληνιστική κεραμική της Μεσσήνης', in L. Kypraiou (ed.), *Ελληνιστική κεραμική από την Πελοπόννησο* (Athens: Ypourgeio Politismou), 95–106.

— (2010), Ἀνασκαφὴ Μεσσήνης', *PAE* 165: 53–64, pls 32–42.

Thompson, D. J. (1984), 'Agriculture', in *CAH*, 2nd edn, vii/1: *The Hellenistic World*, 363–70.

— (2005), 'Posidippus, poet of the Ptolemies', in K. J. Gutzwiller (ed.), *The New Posidippus: A Hellenistic Poetry Book* (Oxford University Press), 269–86.

Thür, G., and Taeuber, H. (1994), *Prozeßrechtliche Inschriften der griechischen Poleis: Arkadien*. Vienna: Österreichische Akademie der Wissenschaften.

Tomlinson, R. A. (1972), *Argos and the Argolid: From the End of the Bronze Age to the Roman Occupation*. London: Routledge & Kegan Paul.

— (1994–5), 'Archaeology in Greece 1994–1995', *AR* 41: 1–74.

— (1995–6), 'Archaeology in Greece 1995–96', *AR* 42: 1–47.

Too, Y. L. (2008), review of R. G. Osborne, *Debating the Athenian Cultural Revolution*, in *BMCR* 2008.08.51.

Touchais, G. (1983), 'Chronique des fouilles et découvertes archéologiques en Grèce en 1982', *BCH* 107: 745–838.

Treister, M. Y. (1996), *The Role of Metals in Ancient Greek History*. Leiden: Brill.

Tsaravopoulos, A. N., Phrangou, E., Tsilogianni, P., and Alexandridou, A. (2014), 'Ελληνιστική κεραμική από την αρχαία Αιγιλία και τη Φαλάσαρνα: συγκριτική παρουσίαση', in *8th Hellenistic Pottery Meeting*, 285–90, pls 98–9.

Tsiolis, V. (1995), 'El "Thersilion" de Megalópoli: funciónes y cronología', *Gerion* 13: 47–68.

Tuan, Y.-F. (1974), 'Space and place: humanistic perspective', in C. Board, R. J. Chorley, P. Haggett, and D. R. Stoddart (eds), *Progress in Geography: International Reviews of Current Research*, vi (London: Edward Arnold), 211–52.

—— (1977), *Space and Place: The Perspective of Experience*. London and Minneapolis: Edward Arnold and University of Minnesota Press.

Tully, J. A. N. Z. (2014), *The Island Standard: The Classical, Hellenistic, and Roman Coinages of Paros*. New York, NY: American Numismatic Society.

Ulf, C. (2009), 'The development of Greek ethnē and their ethnicity: an anthropological perspective', in P. Funke and N. Luraghi (eds), *The Politics of Ethnicity and the Crisis of the Peloponnesian League* (Washington, DC: Center for Hellenic Studies and Harvard University Press), 215–49.

Urban, R. (1979), *Wachstum und Krise des achäischen Bundes: Quellenstudien zur Entwicklung des Bundes von 280 bis 222 v.Chr.* Wiesbaden: Steiner.

Valmin, M. N. (1930), 'Études topographiques sur la Messénie ancienne', Diss. Lund: Blom.

van Andel, T. H., and Runnels, C. N. (1987), *Beyond the Acropolis: A Rural Greek Past*. Stanford, CA: Stanford University Press.

Vasdaris, C. (2004), 'Τὸ ζήτημα τῆς παρουσίας πελοποννησιακῆς καταγωγῆς κατοίκων στὴν πτολεμαϊκὴ καὶ ρωμαϊκὴ Αἴγυπτο ἐπὶ τῆ βάσει παπυρικῶν δεδομένων', *Πελ* 27: 33–40.

Vasilakis, N., and Koutsoubeliti, L. (2011), 'Ελληνιστική κεραμική από την αγορά της Ηλίδας [poster]', in *7th Hellenistic Pottery Meeting*, 729–38, pls 295–8.

Vasilogamvrou, A., Nikolakopoulou, A., and Tsaknaki, V. (2011), 'Δύμη: το βορειοδυτικό νεκροταφείο και οι αποθέτες', in *7th Hellenistic Pottery Meeting*, 76.

Vertsetis, A. V. (1996–7), 'Μυκῆναι: ὀνοματολογικὰ καὶ ἐτυμολογικά', in *5th Peloponnesian Congress*, i, 169–76.

Visscher, H. (1996), 'The hellenistic pottery', in W. Cavanagh, J. Crouwel, R. W. V. Catling, and G. Shipley, *Continuity and Change in a Greek Rural Landscape: The Laconia Survey*, ii: *Archaeological Data* (London: British School at Athens), 91–110.

Vlassopoulos, K. (n.d. [2008]), 'Region and regional identity in ancient Greece: the Peloponnese in comparative perspective', in W. G. Cavanagh and J. Roy (eds), *Being Peloponnesian* (Nottingham: Centre for Spartan & Peloponnesian Studies, University of Nottingham), ch. 4.

Volkmann, H. (1964a), 'Aristippos 1', *KP* i. 562.

—— (1964b), 'Aristippos 2', *KP* i. 562.

—— (1964c), 'Aristodemos 6', *KP* i. 566.

—— (1964d), 'Aristomachos 4', *KP* i. 570.

—— (1969a), 'Machanidas', *KP* iii. 852.

—— (1969b), 'Nabis', *KP* iii. 1550–1.

von Pöhlmann, R. (1893–1901), *Geschichte des antiken Kommunismus und Sozialismus*. Munich: Beck.

(1912), *Geschichte der sozialen Frage und des Sozialismus in der antiken Welt*, 2nd edn. 2 vols. Munich: Beck.

von Pöhlmann, R. with Oertel, F. (1925), *Geschichte der sozialen Frage und des Sozialismus in der antiken Welt*, 3rd edn, i. Munich: Beck.

von Reden, S. (2010), *Money in Classical Antiquity*. Cambridge University Press.

Voyatzis, M. (1999), 'The role of temple building in consolidating Arkadian communities', in T. H. Nielsen and J. Roy (eds), *Defining Ancient Arkadia* (Copenhagen: Kongelige Danske Videnskabernes Selskab), 130–68.

Wace, A. J. B., Heurtley, W. A., Lamb, W., Holland, L. B., and Boethius, C. A. (1921–3), 'The report of the School excavations at Mycenae, 1920–1923', *ABSA* 25: 1–434.

Wagstaff, J. M. (1979), 'Settlement pattern evolution in the Helos plain, Lakonia, Greece', in C. Christians and J. Claude (eds), *Recherches de géographie rurale: hommage au Professeur Frans Dussart* (Liège: Seminaire de Géographie de l'Université de Liège), 133–49.

(1982), *The Development of Rural Settlements: A Study of the Helos Plain in Southern Greece*. Amersham: Avebury Publishing Co.

Walbank, F. W. (1933), *Aratos of Sicyon* (Thirlwall Prize Essay 1933). Cambridge University Press.

(1936), 'Aratos' attack on Cynaetha (Polybios IX, 17)', *JHS* 56. 1: 64–70.

(1940), *Philip V of Macedon* (The Hare Prize Essay 1939). Cambridge University Press.

(1957), *A Historical Commentary on Polybius*, i: *Commentary on Books I–VI*. Oxford: Clarendon Press.

(1957–79), *A Historical Commentary on Polybius*. 3 vols. Oxford: Clarendon Press.

(1979), *A Historical Commentary on Polybius*, iii: *Commentary on Books XIX–XL*. Oxford: Clarendon Press.

(1984a), 'Macedonia and Greece', in *CAH*, 2nd edn, vii/1: *The Hellenistic World*, 221–56.

(1984b), 'Macedonia and the Greek leagues', in *CAH*, 2nd edn, vii/1: *The Hellenistic World*, 446–81.

(1988), 'From the battle of Ipsus to the death of Antigonus Doson', in N. G. L. Hammond and F. W. Walbank, *A History of Macedonia*, iii: *336–167 BC* (Oxford: Clarendon Press), 199–364.

(1992), *The Hellenistic World*, 2nd edn. First published 1981, repr. 1986. London: HarperCollins.

Waldstein, C. (1894), 'The circular building of Sparta', *AJAHFA* 9. 4: 545–6.

Walker, A. S. (2004), *Coins of Olympia: The BCD Collection (May 10, 2004, Hotel Savoy-Baur en Ville)*. Zürich: Leu Numismatics.

(2006), *Coins of Peloponnesos: The BCD Collection (May 8–9, 2006, Hotel Savoy-Baur en Ville)*. Zürich: LHS Numismatics.

Wallensten, J., and Pakkanen, J. (2009), 'A new inscribed statue base from the sanctuary of Poseidon at Kalaureia', *Opuscula* 2: 155–65.

Warren, J. A. W. (2007), *The Bronze Coinage of the Achaian Koinon: The Currency of a Federal Ideal*. London: Royal Numismatic Society.

Warren, P. (2012), 'The rediscovery of Greek rosso antico marble and its use in Britain in the nineteenth and twentieth centuries', *ABSA* 107: 341–86, colour section pp. 389–93.

Wartenberg, U., and Amandry, M. (eds) (2015), *Καιρός: Contributions to Numismatics in honor of Basil Demetriadi*. New York, NY: American Numismatic Society.

Waywell, G. B. (1993), 'The Ada, Zeus and Idrieus relief from Tegea in the British Museum', in O. Palagia and W. Coulson (eds), *Sculpture from Arcadia and Laconia* (Oxford: Oxbow), 79–86.

Weil, S. (1957), *Note sur la suppression générale des partis politiques*. Paris: Gallimard.

with Miłosz, C. (2014), *On the Abolition of All Political Parties*. New York, NY: New York Review of Books. Trans. S. Leys.

Weir, R. G. A. (2007), 'The Stymphalos hoard of 1999 and the city's defences', *AJN* 19: 9–32.

Wells, B. (ed.) (1996), *The Berbati–Limnes Archaeological Survey 1988–1990*. Stockholm and Jonsered: Svenska Institutet i Athen and Åström.

Whitehead, D. M. (1990), *Aineias the Tactician, How to Survive under Siege (A Historical Commentary with Translation and Introduction)*, 1st edn. Oxford: Clarendon Press.

(2002), *Aineias the Tactician, How to Survive under Siege (A Historical Commentary with Translation and Introduction)*, 2nd edn. London: Bristol Classical Press/Duckworth.

Whitley, A. J. M. (2002–3), 'Archaeology in Greece 2002–2003', *AR* 49: 1–88.

(2003–4), 'Archaeology in Greece 2003–2004', *AR* 50: 1–92.

(2004–5), 'Archaeology in Greece 2004–2005', *AR* 51: 1–118.

(2005–6), 'Archaeology in Greece 2005–2006', *AR* 52: 1–112.

(2006–7), 'Archaeology in Greece 2006–2007', *AR* 53: 1–121.

Wickert, K. (1961), 'Der peloponnesische Bund: von seiner Entstehung bis zum Ende des archidamischen Krieges', Inaug.-Diss. Erlangen: Friedrich-Alexander-Universität Erlangen-Nuremberg.

(1972), 'Peloponnesischer Bund', *KP* iv. 605–6.

Wilhelm, A. (1921), 'Hellenistisches', *AAHG* 57: 70–3.

Will, É. (1979), *Histoire politique du monde hellénistique: 323–30 av. J.-C.*, 2nd edn, i: *De la mort d'Alexandre aux avènements d'Antiochos III et de Philippe V*. Presses Universitaires de Nancy.

(1979–82), *Histoire politique du monde hellénistique: 323–30 av. J.-C.*, 2nd edn. 2 vols. Nancy: Presses Universitaires de Nancy.

(1984), 'The formation of the hellenistic kingdoms', in *CAH*, 2nd edn, vii/1: *The Hellenistic World*, 101–17.

Williams, E. H. (2005), 'The exploration of ancient Stymphalos, 1982–2002', in E. Østby (ed.), *Ancient Arcadia* (Athens and Sävedalen, Sweden: Norwegian Institute at Athens and Åström), 397–411.

Williams, H. (2012), 'Stymphalos', in *EAH* (Oxford: Blackwell Publishing), 6430–1.

Williams, M. F. (2004), 'Philopoemen's special forces: peltasts and a new kind of Greek light-armed warfare (Livy 35. 27)', *Historia*, 53. 3: 257–77.

Winter, F. E. (1989), 'Arkadian notes II: the walls of Mantinea, Orchomenos and Kleitor', *EMC* 33(n.s. 8): 189–200.

Winter, J. E., and Winter, F. E. (1983), 'The date of the temples near Kourno in Lakonia', *AJA* 87: 3–10.

Wiseman, J. (1978), *The Land of the Ancient Corinthians*. Göteborg: Åström.

Woodard, R. D. (ed.) (2008), *The Ancient Languages of Europe*. Cambridge University Press.

Woodward, A. M., Forrest, W. G., and Spawforth, A. J. S. (2012), 'Taenarum (2)', *OCD*[4] 1428.

Woolf, G. D. (1994), review of S. E. Alcock, *Graecia Capta*, in *JRA* 7: 417–20.

Wright, J. C., Cherry, J. F., Davis, J. L., Mantzourani, E., Sutton, S. B., and Sutton, R. F., Jr. (1990), 'The Nemea Valley Archaeological Project: a preliminary report', *Hesperia* 59. 4: 579–659.

Yardley, J. C., Wheatley, P., and Heckel, W. (2011), *Justin, Epitome of the Philippic History of Pompeius Trogus*, ii: *Books 13–15. The Successors to Alexander the Great*. Oxford and New York: Oxford University Press.

Yates, D. C. (2005), 'The archaic treaties between the Spartans and their allies', *CQ* n.s. 55. 1: 65–76.

Zangger, E. (1998), 'Naturkatastrophen in der ägäischen Bronzezeit: Forschungsgeschichte, Signifikanz und Beurteilungskriterien', in E. Olshausen and H. Sonnabend (eds), *Naturkatastrophen in der antiken Welt: Stuttgarter Kolloquium zur historischen Geographie des Altertums 6, 1996* (Stuttgart: Steiner), 211–41.

Zavvou, E. P. (1996–7), "Η χώρα τῆς Ἐπιδαύρου Λιμηρᾶς", in *5th Peloponnesian Congress*, ii, 497–508.

—— (2005), 'Σπάρτη: εργαστήρια ανάγλυφων σκύφων', in L. Kypraiou (ed.), *Ελληνιστική κεραμική από την Πελοπόννησο* (Athens: Ypourgeio Politismou), 107–25.

Zehbe, I. (1988), 'Ein "megarischer" Reliefbecher von Asine', *OAth* 17: 217–24.

Ziegler, K. (ed.) (1971), *Plutarchi Vitae parallelae*, 2nd edn, iii/1. Leipzig: Teubner.

Index Locorum

General Index

Other than for sub-section IV.6.b on ceramic production, brief and passing mentions of places (especially *poleis*) are not systematically indexed for reasons of space, but can be searched for in the e-book version. Selected Greek words are grouped at the beginning.

Pel. = Peloponnese.

Romans: and Achaean league, after 197 BC, 91;
 and Nabis, 85; economic impact, 193–4, 238;
 impact on the *polis*, 214; sack Dyme, 81; win
 1st Macedonian war, 83
Rostovtzeff, M.: on C4 economy, 160; on Hl
 Greece, 3–4
routes (*see also* communications): and
 connectivity, 271–2; between non-*polis*
 settlements, 273–5; between *poleis*, 275–6;
 between regions, 275–6; between
 sanctuaries, 275; coastal sailing, 276–7;
 extra-Peloponnesian, 277; local, 273, 274–5
ruler-cult, 248
rural settlement (*see also* settlement patterns):
 explanatory factors, 192–5; in C3 and
 later, 190–1; methodological issues, 197;
 regional variation, 191

sacking, of cities, 181
Samos, modern landscape, 198
sanctuaries (*see also* cult buildings):
 importance to *poleis*, 291–2; routes between,
 275, 277–8
scale (*see also* localism; localities; regions;
 sub-regions), 10, 255
sculpture, production, 215–16
Second Macedonian war, 84–6
Second Mantineia (battle), 37–8
second-order centres, 257
security, as Macedonian aim, 248–9
seismic events, 172–3
Seleukos I, and Pel., 49
Sellasia: battle of, 70; results, 71
semi-free groups, 94–6
serf-like groups, 94–6
settlement patterns (*see also* rural settlement):
 hierarchy, within regions, 260–1; of
 Arkadia, 23–4; regional, 185–90
settlements, non-*polis* (*see also* rural
 settlement), routes between, 273–5
sieges, economic effects, 182
Sikyon (*see also* Sikyonia): ceramic record, 218;
 communications, 278; economy, 19–20;
 exiles from, 108, 109; joins Achaean
 league, 62–3; locational factors, 261; and
 Macedonia, 109; and Phleious, 19–20;
 politics, 129–30 (pre-371), 136 (C4e),
 145 (EHl); renamed, 250; resources, 19;
 strategic location, 281; traders, 242; under
 Cassander, 108; 'tyrannies', 108–10
Sikyonia (*see also* Sikyon): construction
 projects, 202–12; epigraphic activity, 200 *bis*;
 geography, 19; settlement pattern, 186
silver coinage, 227–30, 233–6
site size, in survey data, 194–7

skilled labour, 171
skytalismos, 139
'small change' (money), 229
social change, and survey data, 190–1
Social war, 73–9; effects, 79
soldiers, wages of, 227–8, 232
sources, *see* archaeology; epigraphy; literary
 sources
Southern Argolis, rural economy, 195–6
southern Peloponnese: and distance, 252;
 ceramic record, 221; connectivity, 282; trade
 less important (?), 171
sovereignty (*see also* autonomy), in
 federations, 292–3
Sparta (*see also* kingship; Lakedaimonians;
 and names of individuals; *see also under*
 perioikoi): and 1st Macedonian war, 80
 bis, 81; absence of revolution, 152–4;
 and Achaean league, 65 (early), 91; after
 197 BC, 91; and Aitolian league, 74–5, 81;
 and Argos (Cl), 132–3; and Aristodemos, 48;
 attacks Mantineia (?), 62; attacks
 Megalopolis, 62; captured by Doson, 70;
 ceramic record, 221; in Chremonidean
 war, 61; coins, 225; collaborates with
 Messenians, 60; and democracies, 134–5;
 demography, 34–5, 166–7; distance from
 Messenian *poleis*, 271; economy, 26; and Elis,
 34, 133; fear of, 44, 57; and Flamininus, 90;
 geographical situation, 26; hegemony,
 31–2 (early), 33, 54, 72 *bis*, 73, 86 *bis*, 88;
 impact of Sellasia, 71; internal divisions,
 76, 128; under Kleomenes III, 67–8; and
 Lamian war, 45; and Mantinea (Cl), 131;
 and Messenia, 25, 26–7, 62; and Messenian
 exiles, 74; and oligarchies, 136, 142; and
 'Peloponnesian league', 258; and *perioikoi*, 27;
 and Phigaleia (Cl), 130; and Philip
 II, 40–1; and Phleious, 131, 135–6; politics
 (EHl), 146; power, 36–7, 38 (after Leuktra),
 43 (C4l), 39 (C3m); and Pyrrhos, 59; role
 in C4m Pel., 141, 142; social crisis, 64, 65;
 stasis, 75; and Tegea (Ar–Cl), 130; westward
 interests, 89
Spartiates, defined, 32
specialization, economic, 27
stability, as Macedonian aim, 125–6
stasis (*see also* divisions *b*; factionalism):
 in C4, 129–34; in C4m Achaea, 138; in
 C4m Pel., 134–5; in Cl Phleious, 131; at
 Argos, 133, 139; and constitutions, 142;
 defined, 126; between democrats
 and oligarchs, 127; in EHl, 142–6;
 endemic, 157; and exiles, 144, 167;
 externally provoked, 142; frequency,

stasis (cont.)
    151, 157, 161; frequent in C3b–c,
    143; internal causes, 147, 156, 157;
    mentioned, 289; non-ideological, 149;
    not necessarily linked to class, 151–2;
    in sense of 'party', 96–7; at Sparta, 75; at
    Tegea, 139–40
staters (coins), 227
status divisions, within *poleis*, 94
Strabo, on Pel., 5, 6
strategic locations, 175–6, 270–1, 280
sub-regions: Arkadian, 261, 267; defined, 256;
    in survey data, 198; settlement
    densities, 191
Successors (of Alexander): aims in Pel., 245–6;
    coins, 232; wars, 46–56, 174
survey data: interpreted, 190–2;
    methodological issues, 197–9
surveys, *see* field surveys
synoikism: of Megalopolis, 283–4; of
    poleis, 287

Tainaron, mercenaries at, 45 & n.
Tarn, W. W.: on Achaean league, 246–7,
    292; on Gonatas' use of garrisons and
    'tyrants', 118–20
taxation: and coinage, 232; by Macedonia
    (?), 120; of Pel., 57, 177
techniques, ceramic, 222–3
technological advances, 161
Tegea: in Aitolian league, 66; and Sparta
    (Ar–Cl), 130; ceramic record, 220; locational
    factor, 270; politics, 130 (pre-371), 139–40
    (C4m); and Sparta (Ar–Cl), 130
Telesphoros, in Pel., 49–50
temples, *see* cult buildings
terracotta, production, 215
territories (of *poleis*), see *chōrai*
tetartēmoria, 230
tetradrachms, 225, 227
theatres: C4, 203; Cl/EHl, 206; EHl, 209
Thebes, hegemony of, 28 *bis*, 36, 37
third century BC, historical character, 3
Third Mantineia (battle), 55, 82
'three Ms', 36, 38 *bis*, 39
Thucydides, on trade, 242
Tiryns, and Argos, 132
town-planning, 202
towns (*see poleis*; *see also under* construction
    projects; town-planning)
trade routes, and S. Pel., 252–3
trade (*see also* exports; pottery; travel):
    and coinage, 226–7; by land, 272;

extra-Peloponnesian, 277; in EHl, 238, 242;
    regional variation, 171
tradition, local, 253
travel (*see also* roads; routes; trade), within
    polis territories, 274–5
treasury buildings, EHl, 211
tribute, whether levied, 177
trichalkoi, 230
trihemiobols, 228
triobols (hemidrachms), 228
Triphylia (*see also* Lepreon), 22: and
    Arkadian identity, 22; and Arkadian league,
    22, 39–40; confederacy, 34; construction
    projects, 202–12; creation, 130, 133;
    and Elis, 22; epigraphic activity, 200 *bis*;
    identity, 266; in Social war, 77; settlement
    pattern, 186, 187
Tritaia, co-founds Achaean league, 58
tritartēmoria, or *tritetartēmoria*, 230
Trogus Pompeius, *see* Justin
Troizen: captured by Kleonymos, 106;
    governor of, 98; politics pre-371, 132;
    resources, 16
'tyrants': in Achaea, 111; Achaean league's
    opposition to, 113; at Argos, 113–15;
    at Athens, 47, 50; before 338 BC, 97–8;
    C4l, 107–8; under Cassander, 120;
    defined, 97; under Demetrios I, 120–1,
    122; and garrisons, 107, 122–3; under
    Gonatas, 59, 120–1, 125; as governors, 122;
    or governors, under Gonatas, 59; at
    Hermion, 115; internal support, 118,
    123, 124–5; as label, 108–9, 110; and
    Macedonia, 104–5, 110, 111, 115–20,
    123–4; as mediators, 124; at Megalopolis,
    112–13; at Messene, 107; Nabis described
    as, 83; not imposed by Antipater, 105;
    at Orchomenos, 115; patriotic,
    112–13; at Phleious, 115; popular, 151;
    rehabilitated, 125; reputations, 112–13,
    123–4, 136; at Sikyon, 108–10; at Sparta, 115

unity: Peloponnesian, 40, 258; regional, 265

valleys (*see also* Alpheios; Eurotas), as
    routes, 278
variation: in regional economies,
    170, 172; in rural settlement, 191;
    intra-regional, 264–5
velocity, of monetary circulation, 228
vertical divisions, within *poleis*, 94
vexillological speculation, 126
villas, 194